INTER TIMOREM ET SPEM

STUDIES
IN MEDIEVAL AND
REFORMATION THOUGHT

EDITED BY

HEIKO A. OBERMAN, Tucson, Arizona

IN COOPERATION WITH

THOMAS A. BRADY, Jr., Eugene, Oregon
E. JANE DEMPSEY DOUGLASS, Claremont, California
PIERRE FRAENKEL, Geneva
GUILLAUME H. M. POSTHUMUS MEYJES, Leiden
DAVID C. STEINMETZ, Durham, North Carolina
ANTON G. WEILER, Nijmegen

VOLUME XXXVII

G. H. GERRITS

INTER TIMOREM ET SPEM

LEIDEN
E. J. BRILL
1986

INTER TIMOREM ET SPEM

A STUDY OF THE THEOLOGICAL THOUGHT OF
GERARD ZERBOLT OF ZUTPHEN (1367-1398)

BY

G. H. GERRITS

LEIDEN
E. J. BRILL
1986

The publication of this book was made possible through a grant from the Netherlands Organization for the Advancement of Pure Research (Z.W.O.).

ISBN 90 04 07718 9

PRINTED IN THE NETHERLANDS BY E. J. BRILL

Aan de Nagedachtenis van
Mijn Moeder, Johanna Gerrits-Marsman
(1905-1974)

CONTENTS

Preface... XI
List of Abbreviations....................................... XIII

Introduction 1
   i. Existing Literature on Gerard Zerbolt 4
   ii. Life of Gerard Zerbolt................................. 10
   iii. Writings of Gerard Zerbolt........................... 13
      De Reformatione and *De Ascensionibus*: 13
      Manuals for religious.................................. 13
      Sources of *De Reformatione* and *De Ascensionibus* 18
      Dissemination of *De Reformatione* and *De Ascensionibus*... 27
   iv. Zerbolt's Theological Thought 37

I. The Doctrine of God...................................... 39
   i. Knowability of God.................................... 40
   ii. God's Work of Creation 41
   iii. Divine Providence 45
   iv. Divine Attributes.................................... 47
   v. God's Attitude Towards Fallen Man.................... 51
   vi. Assessment 55

II. The Doctrine of Man 56
  A) *Man as Created* 56
   i. *Dona naturae* and *Dona gratiae*...................... 58
   ii. Philosophical Anthropology........................... 59
      Cognitive powers....................................... 60
      Appetitive powers...................................... 64
      God the natural object of the psychological faculties.... 66
      Augustinian elements in Zerbolt's anthropology........ 67
   iii. Theological Anthropology............................ 69
      Tradition on the '*donum superadditum*' 69
      Zerbolt on the '*dona gratiae*' 70
      Original justice 73
      Man as God's image and likeness....................... 73
      "*De statu naturalis*" 74

  B) *Man As Fallen* 75
   i. The Consequences of the Fall for the *dona gratiae* 77
   ii. The Consequences of the Fall for the *dona naturae*........ 79

iii. Original Sin 86
iv. Hyma and Davis on Zerbolt's Doctrine of the Fall 88
 v. The Fruits of Original Sin 91
C) *Assessment* 94

III. The Doctrine of Christ 96
A) *Christology* 97
 i. Christ: God and Man 98
    Christ as Second Person of the Trinity 98
    Christ as man and the union of his two natures 101
    Reason for safeguarding Christ's dual nature 106
 ii. Consequences of the Union of God and Man in Christ 107
    Christ's perfection and holiness 108
    The communication of attributes in Christ 113
    Christ's free will 119
    Christ's capacity for suffering 120
    The intensity of Christ's suffering 121
    Christ's complaint about his abandonment by God 124
    Christ's ability to die at will 124
    The duration of the hypostatic union 125
 iii. Assessment 127
B) *Soteriology* 127
 i. Some Soteriological Theories 128
 ii. Zerbolt's Soteriology 130
    'Classic' theory of the atonement 132
    The Anselmian theory of the atonement 134
    The doctrine of subjective atonement 139
 iii. Christ as Judge of Mankind 153
 iv. Assessment 153

IV. The Process of Justification 159
A) *Faith* 160
 i. *Fides quae creditur* 160
 ii. *Fides qua creditur* 166
B) *The Sacraments* 168
 i. Baptism 169
 ii. Penance 171
    Self-examination aimed at contrition 172
    Contrition 177
    Contrition and grace 182
    Contrition: Its importance in relation to confession
    and satisfaction 183

Confession.. 185
Satisfaction... 192
The effect of penance 194
C) *Good Works Performed in The State Of Grace* 195
D) *Predestination* 198
E) *No Certainty With Regard To Justification And Salvation* 200
F) *Conclusion*... 204

V. The Eucharist 206
i. The Eucharistic Sacrifice 206
ii. The Eucharistic Sacrament 208
iii. The Eucharistic Celebration as a Commemoration..... 210
iv. Requirements for Fruitful Communion 212
Bodily purity... 213
Purity of conscience.................................... 214
Effective devotion: fear and love 216
v. Can Man Prepare Himself Sufficiently for a Valid
Communion? 219
vi. The Nature of Eucharistic Grace......................... 221
vii. Benefits Derived from Communion 223
viii. Frequency of Sacramental Communion 225
ix. Spiritual Communion.................................... 227
x. Conclusion 229

VI. Spiritual Theology and Life 231
A) *Contemplation As The End Of The Spiritual Life*................... 233
i. *De Reformatione* 233
ii. *De Ascensionibus*............................... 237
B) *The Active Life*... 241
i. *De Reformatione* 241
Structure of *De Reformatione*.................................. 241
Self-examination and self-knowledge..................... 243
The reformation of the intellect............................ 248
The reformation of the memory 250
The second reformation of the will........................ 256
ii. *De Ascensionibus*.................................... 264
Structure of *De Ascensionibus* 264
Self-examination and self-knowledge..................... 265
The second ascent.. 266
The third ascent 272
C) *The Vehicles Of The Spiritual Ascent* 273
i. Manual Work.. 274
ii. *Lectio, Meditatio* and *Oratio* 276

D) *Spiritual Perfection Impossible In This Life* 279
E) *Assessment* 281

Conclusion 284

Appendix 302

Bibliography 309

Index of Names 321

Index of Subjects 323

PREFACE

After languishing somewhat for decades, the study of the Modern Devotion has witnessed an appreciable upsurge in recent years. Indicative of the renewed scholarly interest in the Modern Devotion in recent years is the publication of the *Monasticon Windeshemense* and the *Monasticon Fratrum Vitae Communis*. Of a somewhat different, but no less significant, nature than the rejuvenated scholarly interest in the Modern Devotion are the principles guiding the *Centrum voor Moderne Devotie* founded in Deventer, the cradle of the late medieval movement, some years ago. The *Centrum*'s aim is not only to promote the study of the Modern Devotion, but also to spur, in our own day, a renewal of the movement's spiritual ideals. Just last year we commemorated that Gerard Grote, the founder of the Devotionalist movement, died six hundred years before. The commemoration of his death resulted in a flood of publications dealing with various aspects of the Modern Devotion, and I am pleased that this work will be joining the ever growing ranks of publications about that movement. Gerard Zerbolt, the subject of this study, was one of the earliest members of the Modern Devotion, and through his writings he was, to a considerable degree, responsible for shaping the thought and views of the later members of the movement. The present work aims, as a consequence, to contribute not only to a better understanding of Zerbolt's thought, but to a better understanding as well of the thought and spirituality of the Devotionalist movement in its entirety.

It is not stretching the truth too far, I believe, to assert that the foundations for this work were laid some twenty years ago when, as an undergraduate student at Acadia University, my attention was first drawn to the Modern Devotion and its history. Initially I was intrigued by the movement because of its close association with that part of The Netherlands in which I was born and spent the first ten years of my life. After my first, rather parochial, reaction to the Modern Devotion, I found myself to be genuinely interested in the movement, and that led to a year's study at the Catholic University of Nijmegen following the completion of my undergraduate studies at Acadia University. The year in Nijmegen, made possible by means of a scholarship from the Dutch government, enabled me to become acquainted with Devotionalist sources and literature to an extent which would have been difficult this side of the Atlantic Ocean.

Upon my return to Canada, I enrolled in the school of graduate studies, Queen's University, Kingston, Ontario, and in its original form this work was a Ph.D. dissertation, fulfilling one of the requirements set by the Department of History, Queen's University, for its doctoral degree. In that connection expressions of appreciation and thanks are in order for Prof. Dr. C. M. D. Crowder and Prof. Dr. J. M. Stayer, my two thesis supervisors, for patiently directing and bearing with a rather tardy student. Most of the initial research for the dissertation was done during a second sojourn in The Netherlands, and a grant from the *Nuyensfonds*, administered by the Catholic University, Nijmegen, helped to defray some of the research costs.

Following an extensive revision of the original, Prof. Dr. H. A. Ober-man, Tübingen, graciously accepted the present work for publication in the series "Studies in Medieval and Reformation Thought," and he did so partly upon the recommendation of Prof. Dr. A. G. Weiler, Nij-megen. A special expression of gratitude is extended to both of them, as well as to the Netherlands Organization for the Advancement of Pure Research (Z.W.O.) for making available funds for the publication of this book. Thanks are due also to my colleague, Prof. Dr. B. C. Verstraete, Department of Classics, Acadia University, for proof-reading the foot-notes in the manuscript, and words of appreciation are likewise extended to my two typists, Mrs. Carys Reid and Mrs. Hazel Moulton.

Since a work which has taken some years to research and to write does not leave the members of one's family untouched, I must express my gratitude to them as well. In this connection I must first mention our young daughter Jennifer who frequently had to compete with this work for my attention when I was in the process of revising it for publication. Secondly, the degree of indebtedness to my wife Barbara is greater than I can publicly express, for without her unstinting support, both moral and material, this work would not have achieved its present form.

Acadia University   G. H. GERRITS
Wolfville, Nova Scotia
February 5, 1985

LIST OF ABBREVIATIONS

Acquoy, *Windesheim*
    J. G. R. Acquoy. *Het Klooster te Windesheim en Zijn Invloed.* 3 vols. Utrecht, 1875-1880.
AGAU
    Archief voor de Geschiedenis van het Aartsbisdom Utrecht.
ANKG
    Archief voor Nederlandse Kerkgeschiedenis.
Asc.
    Gerard Zerbolt of Zutphen. *De Spiritualibus Ascensionibus.* Published by M. de la
    Bigne in *Maxima Bibliotheca Veterum Patrum et Antiquorum Scriptorum Ecclesiasticorum.* 27
    vols. 8th ed. Lyon, 1677 (Vol. XXVI, pp. 258-289).
Axters, *Vroomheid*, III
    S. Axters. *Geschiedenis van de Vroomheid in de Nederlanden.* Vol. III: *De Moderne Devotie.*
    Antwerp, 1956.
Bonaventure, *Works*
    The Works of Bonaventure. Translated by J. de Vinck. Paterson, New Jersey, 1960-.
Brinckerinck, "Collatiën"
    Johannes Brinckerinck. "Acht collatiën van Johannes Brinckerinck, een bijdrage tot
    de kennis van den kanselarbeid der Broeders van het Gemene Leven, uit hand-
    schriften der 15de en 16de eeuw." Edited by W. Moll. *Kerkhistorisch Archief,* IV
    (1866), 97-167.
Busch, *Chronicon*
    Johannes Busch. *Des Augustinerpropstes Johannes Busch Chronicon Windeshemense und Liber*
    de reformatione monasteriorum. Edited by K. Grube. Geschichtsquellen der Provinz
    Sachsen und angrenzender Gebiete, Vol. XIX. Halle, 1886.
Cassian, *Conferences*
    John Cassian. *The Conferences.* Translated by E. C. S. Gibson. *Nicene and Post-Nicene*
    Fathers, 2d Series, Vol. XI. New York-Oxford-London, 1894 (pp. 295-545).
Cassian, *Institutes*
    John Cassian. *The Institutes of the Coenobia.* Translated by E. C. S. Gibson. *Nicene and*
    Post-Nicene Fathers, 2d Series, Vol. XI. New York-Oxford-London, 1894 (pp.
    201-290).
D. of Augsburg, *De ext. et int. hom. compositione*
    David of Augsburg. *Spiritual Progress and Life.* A translation of *De Exterioris et Interioris*
    Hominis Compositione by Dominic Devas. 2 vols. London, 1937.
De Beer, *Spiritualiteit*
    K. C. L. M. de Beer. *Studie Over de Spiritualiteit van Geert Groote.* Brussels-Nijmegen,
    1938.
Dempsey Douglass, *Geiler*
    E. J. Dempsey Douglass. *Justification in Late Medieval Preaching. A Study of John Geiler of*
    Keisersberg. Studies in Medieval and Reformation Thought, Vol. I. Leiden, 1966.
DSp
    Dictionnaire de Spiritualité, Ascétique et Mystique. 1932-.
Epiney-Burgard, *Grote*
    G. Epiney-Burgard. *Gérard Grote (1340-1384), et les Débuts de la Dévotion Moderne.*
    Wiesbaden, 1970.
Geesink, *Zerbolt*
    G. H. Geesink. *Gerard Zerbolt van Zutphen.* Amsterdam, 1879.
Goossens, *Meditatie*
    L. A. M. Goossens. *De Meditatie in de Eerste Tijd van de Moderne Devotie.* Haarlem,
    1952.

Jacobus de Voecht, *Narratio*
  Jacobus Traiecti de Voecht. *Narratio de Inchoatione Domus Clericorum in Zwollis*, met
  Akten en Bescheiden Betreffende dit Fraterhuis. Edited by M. Schoengen. Werken
  uitgegeven door het Historisch Genootschap te Utrecht, 3rd Series, No. 13. Amster-
  dam, 1908.
JEH
  Journal of Ecclesiastical History.
NAKG
  Nederlands Archief voor Kerkgeschiedenis.
NCE
  New Catholic Encyclopedia. 1967.
Oberman, *Biel*
  H. A. Oberman. *The Harvest of Medieval Theology. Gabriel Biel and Late Medieval
  Nominalism.* 2d ed. Grand Rapids, 1967.
OGE
  Ons Geestelijk Erf.
PG
  J. P. Migne, ed. *Patrologia Graeca.* Paris, 1857-1912.
PL
  J. P. Migne, ed. *Patrologia Latina.* Paris, 1844-1890.
Post, *Kerkgeschiedenis*
  R. R. Post. *Kerkgeschiedenis van Nederland in de Middeleeuwen.* 2 vols. Utrecht-Antwerp,
  1957.
Radewijns, *Omnes, Inquit, Artes*
  Published by M. Th. P. van Woerkum in *Het Libellus "Omnes, Inquit, Artes," Een
  Rapiarium van Florentius Radewijns.* 3 vols. Mimeographed doctoral dissertation,
  Theological Faculty of the Society of Jesus, Louvain. Limited circulation. Nijmegen,
  1950.
Radewijns, *Tractatulus Devotus*
  Published by L. A. M. Goossens in *De Meditatie in de Eerste Tijd van de Moderne Devotie.*
  Haarlem, 1952 (pp. 209-254).
RAM
  Revue d'Ascétique et de Mystique.
Ref.
  Gerard Zerbolt of Zutphen. *De Reformatione Interiori seu Virium Animae.* Published by
  M. de La Bigne in *Maxima Bibliotheca Veterum Patrum et Antiquorum Scriptorum Ec-
  clesiasticorum.* 27 vols. 8th ed. Lyon, 1677 (Vol. XXVI, pp. 234-258).
Richardson, ed., *Dictionary*
  A. Richardson, ed. *A Dictionary of Christian Theology.* London, 1969.
Steinmetz, *Staupitz*
  D. C. Steinmetz. *Misericordia Dei. The Theology of Johannes von Staupitz in Its Late
  Medieval Setting.* Studies in Medieval and Reformation Thought, Vol. IV. Leiden,
  1968.
SM
  Sacramentum Mundi. An Encyclopedia of Theology. Edited by K. Rahner *et al.* Montreal,
  1968-1970.
Théologie
  Théologie de la Vie Monastique. Etudes sur la tradition patristique (Etudes publiées sous la
  direction de la faculté de théologie S. J. de Lyon-Fourvière, No. 49). Lyon-
  Fourvière, 1961.
Thomas Aquinas, *ST*
  Thomas Aquinas. *Summa Theologiae.* The Blackfriars' Latin-English edition. 60 vols.
  New York-London, 1964-.
Th. a Kempis, *Opera Omnia*
  Thomae Hemerken a Kempis. *Opera Omnia.* Edited by M. J. Pohl. 7 vols. Freiburg
  im Breisgau, 1910-1922.

Tleven Ons Heren
> *Tleven Ons Heren Ihesu Christi. Het Pseudo-Bonaventura-Ludolfiaanse Leven van Jesus.* Edited by C. C. de Bruin. Leiden, 1980.

Van Rooy, *Zerbolt*
> J. van Rooy. *Gerard Zerbolt van Zutphen*. Vol. I: *Leven en Geschriften*. Nijmegen-Utrecht-Antwerp, 1936.

van Woerkum, "Het Libellus '*Omnes, inquit, artes*' "
> M. Th. P van Woerkum. "Het Libellus '*Omnes, inquit, artes*,' Een Rapiarium van Florentius Radewijns." *OGE*, XXV (1951), 113-158 and 225-268.

Van Zijl, *Groote*
> T. P. van Zijl. *Gerard Groote, Ascetic and Reformer*. Washington, 1963.

VSp
> *La Vie Spirituelle*.

INTRODUCTION

Johannes Busch, the most important of all the Devotionalist chroniclers, counted Gerard Zerbolt of Zutphen among the *"patres primitivi, promotores, institutores et consumatores veri"* of the Modern Devotion.[1] However, relatively little information about his short life has come down to us, and what is known about it does not deserve a great deal of attention. His thought, found in a handful of writings now generally attributed to him, is, by contrast, of considerable interest. To Zerbolt belongs the honour of being one of the first spiritual writers of note to be spawned by The Netherlands. The distinction of being the very first goes to Gerard Grote (1340-1384), the spiritual father of the Modern Devotion.[2] To the names of Grote and Zerbolt must be added that of Florens

---

[1] Johannes Busch, *Des Augustinerpropstes Johannes Busch Chronicon Windeshemense und Liber de reformatione monasteriorum*, ed. by K. Grube (Geschichtsquellen der Provinz Sachsen und angrenzender Gebiete, Vol. XIX; Halle, 1886), 28 and 266.

For general histories of the Modern Devotion see: A. Hyma, *The Christian Renaissance: A History of the "Devotio Moderna"* (2d ed.; Hamden, Connecticut, 1965); R. R. Post, *De Moderne Devotie: Geert Groote en Zijn Stichtingen* (2d ed.; Amsterdam, 1950); S. Axters, *Geschiedenis van de Vroomheid in de Nederlanden*, Vol. III: *De Moderne Devotie, 1380-1550* (Antwerp, 1956); R. R. Post, *The Modern Devotion: Confrontation with Reformation and Humanism* (Studies in Medieval and Reformation Thought, Vol. III; Leiden, 1968. This is not a translation of *De Moderne Devotie: Geert Groote en Zijn Stichtingen.*); and W. J. Alberts, *De Moderne Devotie* (Fibulareeks, No. XLVIII; Bussum, 1969). For the Brethren and Sisters of the Common Life in particular see: A. Hyma, *The Brethren of the Common Life* (Grand Rapids, 1950); and C. van der Wansem, *Het Ontstaan en de Geschiedenis der Broederschap van het Gemene Leven tot 1400* (Louvain, 1958). For the Congregation of Windesheim see the unsurpassed work of J. G. R. Acquoy, *Het Klooster te Windesheim* (3 vols.; Utrecht, 1875-1880).

Detailed bibliographies of the Modern Devotion may be found in J. M. E. Dols, *Bibliografie der Moderne Devotie* (Nijmegen, 1941); Axters, *op. cit.*, 420-434; and E. Persoons, *Recente Publicaties over de Moderne Devotie: 1959-1972* (stencilled publication of the Institute for Medieval Studies, Univ. of Louvain; Louvain, 1972). Perhaps more useful than any of these is W. J. Alberts' discursive bibliography: "Zur Historiographie der Devotio Moderna und Ihrer Erforschung," *Westfälische Forschungen*, XI (1958), 51-67, and in: F. Petri and W. J. Alberts, *Gemeinsame Probleme Deutsch-Niederländischer Landes- und Volksforschung* (Bijdragen van het Instituut voor Middeleeuwse Geschiedenis der Rijksuniversiteit te Utrecht, Vol. XXXII; Groningen, 1962), 144-171. References to Alberts' article: "Zur Historiographie...," will be to the version found in Petri and Alberts, *op. cit.*

For the origin and meaning of the term *Devotio Moderna* see M. Ditsche, "Zur Herkunft und Bedeutung des Begriffes *devotio moderna*," *Historisches Jahrbuch der Görres-Gesellschaft*, LXXIX (1960), 124-129. Cf. H. M. Klinkenberg, "Die Devotio Moderna unter dem Thema 'Antiqui-Moderni' Betrachtet," in: *Antiqui und Moderni: Traditionsbewusstsein und Fortschrittsbewusstsein im späten Mittelalter*, ed. by A. Zimmermann (Miscellanea Medievalia, Vol. IX; Berlin, 1974), 394-419.

[2] Also written Groote. Cf. A. C. F. Koch, "Geert Groote of Geert Grote?" *Spiegel Historiael*, I (1966), 37.

Radewijns (1350-1400). He would appear to have played an extremely important role in the founding of the Devotionalist movement, like Grote and Zerbolt he was one of the first Devotionalist writers, and like them he must be numbered with the earliest spiritual writers generated by The Netherlands.[3] The Modern Devotion can claim the distinction, then, of being the first religious movement indigenous to The Netherlands, constituting the first 'school' of spiritual writers and spiritual thought native to this country.[4] In addition to Grote, Zerbolt and Radewijns, this same 'school' was to bring forth other writers such as Gerlach Peters (1378-1411), Hendrik Mande (1360-1431), Jan van Schoonhoven (1356-1432), Dirc van Herxen (c. 1381-1457), Thomas a Kempis (1380-1471) who is now almost universally recognized as the author of the still widely read devotional work entitled *De Imitatione Christi*, and Johannes Mombaer (c. 1460-1501), to name but a few.

On Grote's life and activities see J. van Ginneken, *Geert Groote's Levensbeeld Naar de Oudste Gegevens Bewerkt* (Verhandelingen der Nederlandse Akademie van Wetenschappen, Afdeling Letterkunde, N.S., Vol. XLVII, No. 2; Amsterdam, 1942); T. P. van Zijl, *Gerard Groote, Ascetic and Reformer* (Washington, 1963); and G. Epiney-Burgard, *Gérard Grote (1340-1384) et les débuts de la Dévotion Moderne* (Wiesbaden, 1970).

[3] J. H. Gerretsen, *Florentius Radewijns* (Nijmegen, 1891); and M. Th. P. van Woerkum, *Het Libellus "Omnes, Inquit, Artes," Een Rapiarium van Florentius Radewijns* (3 vols.; mimeographed; limited circulation; Nijmegen, 1950). This three-volume work by van Woerkum represents a doctoral dissertation submitted to the Theological Faculty of the Society of Jesus, Louvain. Vol. 1 was also published in *OGE*, XXIV (1950), 337-364 ("Florentius Radewijns: Leven, Geschriften, Persoonlijkheid en Ideeën"), and XXV (1951), 113-158 and 225-268 ("Het Libellus '*Omnes, Inquit, Artes*,' Een Rapiarium van Florentius Radewijns").

[4] Cf. G. H. Geesink, *Gerard Zerbolt van Zutphen* (Amsterdam, 1879), 80-82; R. R. Post, *Kerkgeschiedenis van Nederland in de Middeleeuwen* (2 vols.; Utrecht-Antwerp, 1957), I, 367-370; and A. G. Weiler, *et al.*, *Geschiedenis van de Kerk in Nederland* (Utrecht: Aula-Boeken, No. 100, 1963), 73-74.
Whether Devotionalist spirituality is unique, and whether it must be regarded as a distinct school of spirituality, has been discussed at some length in the past. Dom J. Huijben denies that Devotionalist spirituality is in a class by itself. He is of the opinion that the spirituality of the Modern Devotion is essentially identical with the spirituality of Western Europe in the later middle ages, although he does not deny that it possesses certain characteristics of its own. (Dom J. Huijben, "Y a-t-il une spiritualité flamande?" *VSp*, L [1937], Supplément, 129-147.) However, the spirituality of the Modern Devotion would appear to be sufficiently different from other schools of spirituality that it may be regarded as a spirituality *sui generis*, as is done by S. Axters and L. A. M. Goossens. (S. Axters, *La Spiritualité des Pays-Bas* [Louvain-Paris, 1948], 99-134 in particular and cf. throughout; and L. A. M. Goossens, *De Meditatie in de Eerste Tijd van de Moderne Devotie* [Haarlem, 1952], 30-34.) This does not, of course, alter the fact that the spirituality of the Devotionalists was firmly rooted in tradition. However, the Devotionalists were not indiscriminate in their dependence upon tradition, and that which they carefully selected they adapted to their own situation and needs. The spirituality of the Devotionalists was shaped by a specific genre of spiritual literature, rather than by a group of select writers. (Post, *De Moderne Devotie*, 141-144; E. de Schaepdrijver, "La Dévotion Moderne," *Nouvelle Revue Théologique*, LIV [1927], 754-760; Goossens, *Meditatie*, 32; and K. Kavanaugh, "Spirituality, History of," *NCE*, XIII, 597.)

For more than a century now Zerbolt's thought in particular has been the subject of monographs and articles. Of particular interest to scholars has been Zerbolt's advocacy, in *De Libris Teutonicalibus* and *Super Modo Vivendi*,[5] of the use of the vernacular for religious purposes. However, Zerbolt's spiritual theology,[6] found in *De Reformatione Trium Virium Animae* and *De Spiritualibus Ascensionibus*,[7] would appear to have received more attention from historians than any other aspect of his thought. That should come as no surprise, for Zerbolt was first and foremost a spiritual theologian, and spiritual theology was his principal concern. Nonetheless, a thorough analysis of Zerbolt's spiritual theology has never before been made, and it is the aim of this study to analyze that theology more thoroughly than has been done before. However, the bulk of this inquiry will not be devoted to Zerbolt's spiritual theology, but to the dogmatic theology contained in, and underlying, his spiritual theology.[8] For, as will be seen shortly, concerning the dogmatic foundations of Zerbolt's spiritual theology very little was said in the past. This was, it would appear, the result of the opinion held by many until recently that with respect to the thought of a writer like Zerbolt, whose primary interests were the doctrine and the practice of the spiritual life rather than dogmatics, one cannot correctly speak of a dogmatic theology but only of

---

[5] "The 'De Libris Teutonicalibus' by Gerard Zerbolt of Zutphen," ed. by A. Hyma, *NAKG*, N.S., XVII (1924), 42-70; "Het Traktaat 'Super Modo Vivendi Devotorum Hominum Simul Commorantium,' door Gerard Zerbolt van Zutphen," ed. by A. Hyma, *AGAU*, LII (1926), 1-100.

[6] The term "spiritual theology" as it is employed here, and throughout this study, has a precisely circumscribed and clearly defined meaning. Spiritual theology is that branch of theology which defines the nature of Christian perfection and outlines the route which the Christian must follow in his quest for that perfection. Spiritual theology is a very practical, non-speculative theology, which deals with the practical question of man's spiritual growth and development along well-defined lines towards a clearly-defined goal.

Spiritual theology is the equivalent of what for a number of centuries was known as ascetical and mystical theology. Before the seventeenth century, however, ascetical and mystical theology were regarded, and treated, as a unit, and of late there has been a general tendency to return once more to this practice: to unite ascetical and mystical theology under the one label of "spiritual theology." (T. A. Porter, "Spiritual Theology," *NCE*, XIII, 588-590. Cf. A. Richardson, ed., *Dictionary of Christian Theology* [London, 1969], 328 ["Spirituality"]; and C. Aalders, *Spiritualiteit: Geestelijk Leven Vroeger en Nu* [The Hague, 1969].)

[7] *De Reformatione* and *De Ascensionibus* have both been printed frequently: see J. van Rooy, *Gerard Zerbolt van Zutphen*, Vol. I: *Leven en Geschriften* (Nijmegen-Utrecht-Antwerp, 1936), 358-391, and below, pp. 27-30.

Throughout this study we will make use of *De Reformatione* and *De Ascensionibus* as they are found in M. de la Bigne, ed., *Maxima Bibliotheca veterum Patrum et antiquorum scriptorum ecclesiasticorum* (27 vols.; 8th ed.; Lyon, 1677), XXVI, 234-258 (*De Reformatione*) and 258-289 (*De Ascensionibus*).

[8] The expression "dogmatic theology" is preferable to "systematic theology," for the adjective "systematic" can be applied to spiritual theology as well. Cf. Richardson, ed., *Dictionary*, 331 ("Systematic Theology").

a Christian *Lebensanschauung*.[9] Presently, however, many, and perhaps most, historians of Christian thought subscribe to the view that a thorough knowledge of dogmatic theology underlies the spiritual thought, or theology, of most writers on the spiritual life, and that it is possible to isolate this foundation of dogmatic theological thought from the doctrine regarding the spiritual life.[10] Zerbolt's spiritual theology possesses such a sound basis of dogmatic theology which may be studied separately and on account of its own, intrinsic qualities.[11]

The Modern Devotion was not a monolithic movement,[12] but an investigation of Zerbolt's thought must of necessity throw some light as well on the nature of that entire body of which Zerbolt was a member and which he partially moulded through his writings.[13] However, before we examine Zerbolt's theological thought we will briefly review the most important existing literature on him. In addition to that we shall look at Zerbolt's life and writings; and with respect to the writings we shall pay special attention to their nature, the relative importance of each one of them for our purpose, their sources, dissemination and influence.

i. *Existing Literature on Gerard Zerbolt*

The foundations for the modern historiography of the *Devotio Moderna* were laid in the nineteenth century. This historiography received its first impulse from Protestant historians who were not always interested in the Modern Devotion for its own sake, but whose study of this movement was frequently motivated by the desire to identify the antecedents of the Protestant Reformation.[14] Consequently, the first historians, all of whom were Protestants, to study Zerbolt and his writings generally sought to answer two questions with respect to his views and their subsequent influence. First they asked whether Zerbolt's purely theological and religious beliefs contributed in any way to the Protestant Reformation.

---

[9] Cf. Ernst-Wilhelm Kohls, *Die Theologie des Erasmus* (2 vols.; *Theologische Zeitschrift*, Special Issue, Vol. I, Pts. 1 and 2; Basel, 1966), I, 2-6; and David C. Steinmetz, *Misericordia Dei: The Theology of Johannes von Staupitz in Its Late Medieval Setting* (Studies in Medieval and Reformation Thought, Vol. IV; Leiden, 1968), 1, 16-17 and 19.

[10] Cf. Jean Leclercq, *The Love of Learning and the Desire for God: A Study of Monastic Culture*, trans. by Catherine Misrahi (New York, 1961), 42-44; Steinmetz, *Staupitz*, 1 and 29-30; E. Jane Dempsey Douglass, *Justification in Late Medieval Preaching: A Study of John Geiler of Keisersberg* (Studies in Medieval and Reformation Thought, Vol. I; Leiden, 1966), throughout; and Kohls, *Die Theologie des Erasmus*, I, 1-17 in particular.

[11] Post, *Kerkgeschiedenis*, I, 381.

[12] Cf. H. A. Oberman, *The Harvest of Medieval Theology: Gabriel Biel and Late Medieval Nominalism* (2d ed.; Grand Rapids, 1967), 351, footnote 87.

[13] Cf. Alberts, "Zur Historiographie der Devotio Moderna und Ihrer Erforschung," 165.

[14] Cf. *ibid.*, 149-153.

The second question they posed was whether in his advocacy of the use of the vernacular for religious writings, and in the realm of religion in general, Zerbolt helped to prepare the way for the Reformation of the sixteenth century. Both W. A. Koning and C. M. Vos answered the first question in the negative, for it soon became apparent to them that Zerbolt's theological opinions were traditional and orthodox.[15] The second question, on the other hand, was answered affirmatively, and they supported the position taken with arguments borrowed from C. Ullmann's well-known work entitled *Reformatoren vor der Reformation.* Some years earlier he had written in this study that, through the *De Libris Teutonicalibus* in particular, Zerbolt greatly promoted the use of the vernacular in the religious sphere. The use of the vernacular in the realm of religion, he continued, awakened nationalistic sentiments and made the peoples of Europe inwardly free from Rome, which sooner or later had to be followed by an open and formal break with the papacy.[16] Following in Ullmann's footsteps, both Koning and Vos wrote that nationalism was a major contributing factor in the Protestant Reformation, and that the use of the vernacular languages in the religious sphere which Zerbolt encouraged through his writings contributed to the growth of nationalistic sentiments.[17]

Convinced of his predecessors' error in studying Zerbolt too one-sidedly as a possible forerunner of the Protestant Reformation, G. H. Geesink was the first nineteenth-century historian to examine Zerbolt's thought from a non-Reformational perspective; and of all the existing literature his dissertation contains the most complete, and certainly the most systematic, treatment of Zerbolt's theological thought.[18] He begins by delineating the anthropological and soteriological underpinnings of Zerbolt's spiritual, largely ascetical, theology, and it is to the latter that he devotes most of his attention. He clearly has a good grasp of Zerbolt's theological thought, but his handling of it is descriptive rather than analytical, and he fails to place it in any historical context. However, this is not surprising, because a century ago the study of the history of Christian thought was still very much in its infancy. Finally, Geesink emphasizes in particular that neither in Zerbolt's spiritual theology, nor in

---

[15] W. A. Koning, *Specimen Historico-Theologicum de Gerardi Zutphaniensis vita, scriptis et meritis* (Utrecht, 1858), 66-72; and C. M. Vos, "Gerard Zerbolt," *Kerkhistorisch Jaarboekje,* N.S., I (1864), 102-138.

[16] C. Ullmann, *Reformatoren vor der Reformation, vornehmlich in Deutschland und den Niederlanden* (2 vols.; Hamburg, 1841-1842). English trans. by R. Menzies: *Reformers before the Reformation, principally in Germany and The Netherlands* (2 vols.; Edinburgh, 1885), II, 105-114.

[17] See references given in footnote 15 above.

[18] G. H. Geesink, *Gerard Zerbolt van Zutphen* (Amsterdam, 1879), 80-142.

its anthropological and soteriological foundations, can one detect any unorthodox sentiments which point to the Protestant Reformation of the sixteenth century. Zerbolt's orthodoxy, Geesink explains, is a direct consequence of his extensive reliance on the writings of Bonaventure and Florens Radewijns. However, this dependence on Bonaventure was not nearly as great as Geesink believed it to be.[19]

No nineteenth-century historian, then, found Protestant opinions in Zerbolt's writings. That is somewhat surprising when one takes into account that all of them were Protestants; and it is also remarkable in view of the tendency shown by nineteenth-century Protestant historiography to Protestantize the Modern Devotion. Only A. Hyma, a Protestant historian living in this century, has attempted to demonstrate, in a work entitled *The Christian Renaissance: A History of the "Devotio Moderna,"* that with respect to theology Zerbolt was a leading forerunner of the Protestant Reformation. He not only maintains that the Reformers' theological anthropology was, in essence, anticipated by Zerbolt, but that for his doctrine of man Luther was, in fact, directly indebted to Zerbolt.[20] The fallacy of this theory will become evident from our discussion of Zerbolt's theological anthropology. Hyma is further of the opinion that not only Zerbolt, but most of the Devotionalists embraced doctrines which had more in common with those of Luther and Calvin than with those of traditional Catholicism. However, Hyma does not simply see a similarity, but he asserts that in the realm of theological thought there was a considerable direct influence of the Modern Devotion on the Protestant Reformation.[21] First formulated in the third decade of this century, Hyma's thesis has been shown to be wrong many times by both Protestant and Catholic historians.[22] However, in a number of new chapters added to the second edition of *The Christian Renaissance: A History of the "Devotio Moderna"* Hyma repeats essentially the same views regarding the relationship between the Modern Devotion, of which he not incorrectly regards Zerbolt as a major spokesman, and the Protestant Reformation first formulated by him some forty years before.[23] More recently K. R.

---

[19] Cf. Goossens, *Meditatie*, 69-70, and below, p. 25, footnote 90.

[20] Hyma, *The Christian Renaissance: A History of the "Devotio Moderna,"* (Grand Rapids, 1924), 309-319.

[21] *Ibid.*, 191-349.

[22] Cf. J. de Jong, "Karakter en Invloed der Moderne Devotie," *Historisch Tijdschrift,* IV (1925), 26-58; *idem,* "Een Nederlandsche Godsdienstige Beweging: de Moderne Devotie," *Nederlandsche Katholieke Stemmen,* XXVIII (1928), 99-109 and 138-147; Axters, *Vroomheid,* III, 411-415; Post, *The Modern Devotion: Confrontation with Reformation and Humanism,* 551-680; Alberts, *De Moderne Devotie,* 78-80; and J. Roelink, *De Moderne Devotie* (Kampen, n.d.), 22-26.

[23] A. Hyma, *The Christian Renaissance: A History of the "Devotio Moderna"* (2d ed.;

Davis has used Hyma's highly questionable interpretation of the Modern Devotion to find in the latter antecedents for sixteenth-century Anabaptism. In his reliance on Hyma, Davis was apparently encouraged by the mistaken notion that the former's portrayal of the Modern Devotion as a harbinger of sixteenth-century theological developments has never been successfully challenged.[24]

The third monograph on Zerbolt appeared in 1936, its author being J. van Rooy.[25] The bulk of this work is devoted to a discussion of Zerbolt's authorship of the works traditionally attributed to him; to abridged, translated versions of these same works; and to a catalogue of manuscripts and printed editions of Zerbolt's writings. Van Rooy does include a brief summary of Zerbolt's theological thought arranged under seventeen separate headings and he touches on most of its salient points. However, the presentation is rather chaotic, and consequently no coherent picture of Zerbolt's theological opinions emerges. It would appear that one of the primary reasons why van Rooy offers a synopsis of Zerbolt's theological thought is to demonstrate its orthodoxy, and that is not surprising in view of the fact that a dozen years before Hyma had attributed quasi-Protestant opinions to Zerbolt.

In a work, published in 1952, L. A. M. Goossens examines the theory and practice regarding meditation among the first Devotionalists, and Zerbolt figures very prominently among those studied by Goossens in this connection.[26] Many years before H. Watrigant had come to the conclusion that the earliest Devotionalists already followed a systematic, methodical and formal mode of meditation.[27] After carefully weighing the evidence Goossens rejects Watrigant's thesis as being untenable. The

---

Hamden, Connecticut, 1965), 511-521, 590 and 604. It is the second edition which will be used throughout this study.

In *The Brethren of the Common Life* (Grand Rapids, 1950) and *Renaissance to Reformation: A Critical Review of the Spiritual and Temporal Influence on Medieval Europe* (Grand Rapids, 1951) Hyma repeats pretty much the same views as are found in *The Christian Renaissance*. The *Brethren of the Common Life* covers much the same ground as do the first five chapters of *The Christian Renaissance*, and *Renaissance to Reformation* covers the remainder of the older work. Cf. "Preface" to *Renaissance to Reformation*.

[24] K. R. Davis, *Anabaptism and Asceticism: A Study in Intellectual Origins* (Scottdale-Kitchener, 1974), 243-266.

[25] J. van Rooy, *Gerard Zerbolt van Zutphen*, Vol. I: *Leven en Geschriften* (Nijmegen-Utrecht-Antwerp), 1936.

This was the first of three planned volumes on Zerbolt (Van Rooy, *Zerbolt*, 278), but volumes two and three never materialized.

[26] L. A. M. Goossens, *De Meditatie in de Eerste Tijd van de Moderne Devotie* (Haarlem, 1952).

[27] H. Watrigant, "La méditation méthodique et l'école des Frères de la vie commune," *RAM*, III (1922), 134-155; *idem*, "La méditation méthodique et Jean Mauburnus," *ibid.*, IV (1923), 13-19; and *idem, Quelques promoteurs de la méditation méthodique au XVe siècle* (Paris, 1919).

earliest Devotionalists, he explains, went no further than to arrange their materials for meditation systematically, and he maintains that Zerbolt played a significant role in this development. For in *De Reformatione* and in *De Ascensionibus* Zerbolt collected and organized subject-matter suitable for meditation, and these two works were subsequently to be widely used by the Devotionalists for their meditations. Goossens does not, in contrast with Watrigant, find any evidence that in the act of meditation the first Devotionalists followed a prescribed or formal method. The Devotionalists did not, in fact, develop a formal mode of meditation until late in the fifteenth century.[28] It is, therefore, somewhat surprising that some years after Goossens' work appeared W. Lourdaux wrote in an article devoted to Zerbolt in the *Dictionnaire de Spiritualité* that he *"a joué un role important dans la méditation méthodique."*[29]

R. R. Post, the leading student of the *Devotio Moderna* in this century, devotes a number of pages to Zerbolt in two of his major works: *Kerkgeschiedenis van Nederland in de Middeleeuwen* and *The Modern Devotion: Confrontation with Reformation and Humanism.*[30] He begins the second of these two works by examining a number of older theories regarding various aspects of the Modern Devotion. One of these is the assertion by William Spoelhof, a pupil of Albert Hyma, that, as one of the Brethren of the Common Life, Zerbolt contributed to the development of the concepts of religious nonconformity and religious toleration.[31] According to Spoelhof, Zerbolt's insistence on the need for a personal, inner piety and religiosity, as well as his practical mysticism which is of a piece with the former, undermined institutional conformity which sooner or later had to lead to a call for religious toleration and freedom. It would appear that Post justly disputes Spoelhof's claim to have established a causal connection between Zerbolt's inner piety and practical mysticism on the one hand, and religious nonconformity and religious toleration on the other. However, he admits that it is perhaps equally difficult to prove the opposite of Spoelhof's argument,[32] and it would appear to be an imponderable. Post deals in much the same way with Spoelhof's contention

---

[28] Goossens, *Meditatie*, 203-205.

[29] W. Lourdaux, "Gérard Zerbolt de Zutphen," *DSp*, VI, 284-289.

[30] R. R. Post, *Kerkgeschiedenis van Nederland in de Middeleeuwen* (2 vols.; Utrecht-Antwerp, 1957), I, 378-382; *idem*, *The Modern Devotion: Confrontation with Reformation and Humanism* (Studies in Medieval and Reformation Thought, Vol. III; Leiden, 1968), 36-37, 205-207, 286-287 and 325-330.

[31] W. Spoelhof, "Concepts of religious nonconformity and religious toleration as developed by the Brethren of the Common Life in the Netherlands, 1374-1489" (unpublished Ph.D. dissertation; University of Michigan, Ann Arbor, 1946). Chapter four: "Concepts of nonconformity and toleration in the thought and expression of Florentius Radewijns and Gerard Zerbolt," is of particular relevance in this connection.

[32] Post, *The Modern Devotion: Confrontation with Reformation and Humanism*, 22-23.

that Zerbolt's advocacy of the use of the vernacular in the realm of religion was conducive to the growth of nonconformity and religious freedom.[33] This second thesis of Spoelhof is clearly reminiscent of that offered by Ullmann and others since him, and it does perhaps possess some degree of credibility, but it is, once again, difficult to prove positively.

Due to the encyclopaedic character of the *Kerkgeschiedenis van Nederland in de Middeleeuwen* and *The Modern Devotion: Confrontation with Reformation and Humanism*, Post does not discuss Zerbolt, his writings and his thought in any detail or depth, nor does he add to our knowledge of him. As one of the severest critics of Hyma's portrayal of the Devotionalists as forerunners of the Protestant Reformation, and consistent with his view of the Modern Devotion as a conservative movement rooted in the past, Post emphasizes the traditional, orthodox nature of Zerbolt's theological opinions.

Even a brief review of the existing literature on Zerbolt reveals that it is dominated by two issues: Zerbolt's views on the translation of religious literature into the vernacular languages, and the nature of his theological thought. We will deal only with the second of these two questions and, although this issue is not raised explicitly, it will become evident from the conclusions drawn that, from a purely theological perspective at least, Zerbolt cannot be regarded as a forerunner of the Protestant Reformation.[34]

---

[33] *Ibid.*, 36-37.

[34] Only the most important interpretations of Zerbolt's life, work and thought were examined in the foregoing historiographical survey. Some of the less significant discussions of Zerbolt and his writings are, in chronological order:

Jac. Revius, *Daventria illustrata sive historia urbis Daventriensis libri sex* (Leiden, 1651), 36-60.

Revius' discussion of Zerbolt is of considerable importance, for he once more established Zerbolt's exact identity which the bibliographer Joh. Trithemius (1462-1516) had confused with that of the theologian Gerardus de Zutphania, a contemporary of Zerbolt (Joh. Trithemius, *De scriptoribus ecclesiasticis* [Cologne, 1546], 273). Furthermore, Revius also names Zerbolt as the author of the six works now generally attributed to him (see below, p. 14, footnote 46).

F. H. van Heussen, *Batavia Sacra* (Brussels, 1714), 206 ff.; *idem, Historia Episcopatuum Foederati Belgii* (2 vols.; 2d ed.; Antwerp, 1733), Vol. II, Pt. III, 87-96.

W. Moll, *Kerkgeschiedenis van Nederland voor de Hervorming* (2 vols.; Utrecht, 1864-1871), Vol. II, Pt. III, 34-42.

S. Kettlewell, *Thomas a Kempis and the Brothers of Common Life* (2 vols.; New York, 1882), I, 290-310.

J. C. van Slee, "Gerhard Zerbolt oder Gerhard von Zutphen," *Allgemeine Deutsche Biographie*, XLV (1900), 87-89.

S. D. van Veen, "Zerbolt van Zuetphen, Gerard," *The New Schaff-Herzog Encyclopedia of Religious Knowledge* (12 vols.; 1908-1912), XII, 509-510. The New Schaff-Herzog Encyclopedia is for the most part a translation of the *Realencyklopaedie für protestantische Theologie und Kirche* (21 vols.; 3rd ed., 1896-1908), and the article on Zerbolt by van Veen is found in Vol. XXI, on pp. 735-737.

ii. *Life of Gerard Zerbolt*[35]

Gerard Zerbolt was born in Zutphen in 1367, and like so many Devotionalists he stemmed from an established and wealthy burgher family. It is also more than probable that he was born into one of the magisterial families of Zutphen like Grote, the master of all the Devotionalists, stemmed from a magisterial family of Deventer. Zerbolt received his earliest instruction in his home town, followed by attendance at *"extraneae scholae"* and the Latin school of St. Lebwin's at Deventer, according to Thomas a Kempis.[36] Koning, Geesink, Hyma and van Rooy all equated the *"extraneae scholae"* with one or more foreign universities,[37] and it is not always clear exactly how they arrived at such an interpretation. For it is highly unlikely that Zerbolt would have transferred from a university to a

---

P. Pourrat, *La Spiritualité Chrétienne*, Vol. II: *Le Moyen Age* (2d ed.; Paris, 1951), 386-387.

A. Lansbergen, "Gerard Zerbolt van Zutphen (d. 1398)," *Ons Geestelijk Erf: Registers op Deel I-XXV* (Tielt, 1951-1953), 52.

L. Reypens, "Gerhard Zerbolt van Zutphen," *Lexikon für Theologie und Kirche* (10 vols.; 2d ed.; 1957-1965), IV, 724.

H. Grundmann, "Zerbolt, Gerhard, von Zutphen," *Die Religion in Geschichte und Gegenwart* (6 vols.; 3d ed.; 1957-1965), VI, 1903.

G. A. Benrath, ed., *Wegbereiter der Reformation* (Bremen, 1967), 123-124.

J. Leclercq, Fr. Vandenbroucke, and L. Bouyer, *The Spirituality of the Middle Ages* (Vol. II of *A History of Christian Spirituality*; trans. by the Benedictines of Holme Eden Abbey, Carlisle; London, 1968), 432.

L. J. Richard, *The Spirituality of John Calvin* (Atlanta, 1974), 19-21.

P. Debongnie, "Dévotion Moderne," *DSp*, III, 730-731. In this article Debongnie devotes a paragraph to Zerbolt's doctrine of the spiritual life as it is set forth in *De Reformatione* and *De Ascensionibus*. Cf. *idem*, "Exercices Spirituels (Dans la *Devotio Moderna*)," *DSp*, IV, 1925. Zerbolt is also one of the writers singled out by Fr. Vandenbroucke in his discussion of mystical contemplation in the fourteenth century ("Contemplation au XIVe Siècle," *DSp*, II, 2001).

[35] The earliest, and most important, *vita* of Zerbolt we possess is that written by Thomas a Kempis: *De domino Gerardo Zutphaniae* (Thomas Hemerken a Kempis, *Opera Omnia*, ed. by M. J. Pohl [7 vols.; Freiburg im Breisgau, 1910-1922], VII, 275-282). A second biography of Zerbolt, which dates from the end of the fifteenth century, is largely a Middle-Dutch translation of Thomas a Kempis' *vita* of Zerbolt (D. A. Brinkerink, ed., "Gerard Zerbolt van Zutphen" ["Biographieën van beroemde Mannen uit den Deventer Kring"], *AGAU*, XXVIII [1902], 335-339). Other sources for our knowledge of Zerbolt's life are: Lubbert ten Busch, *Devota exercitia*, ed. by Th. a Kempis, *Opera Omnia*, VII, 262-263 (a brief characterization of Zerbolt by one of his associates); Rudolph Dier de Muden, *Scriptum de Magistro Gerardo Grote, Domini Florencio et aliis devotis Fratribus*, publ. by G. Dumbar in: *Reipublicae Daventriensis ab Actis Analecta, seu vetera aliquot scripta inedita* (3 vols.; Deventer, 1719-1725), I, 1-87 (for Zerbolt see pp. 22, 30 and 47-50); Busch, *Chronicon*, 28, 49, 128 and 266; *Het Frensweger Handschrift betreffende de geschiedenis van de Moderne Devotie*, ed. by W. J. Alberts and A. L. Hulshof (Groningen, 1958), 32, 36, 49, 50 and 71. Cf. van Rooy, *Zerbolt*, 1-16.

[36] Th. a Kempis, *Opera Omnia*, VII, 275-276.

[37] Koning, *Specimen Historico-Theologicum de Gerardi Zutphaniensis vita, scriptis et meritis*, 18; Geesink, *Zerbolt*, 5; Hyma, *The Christian Renaissance: A History of the "Devotio Moderna*," 66; and van Rooy, *Zerbolt*, 25-27.

Latin school.[38] More recently Post has discovered that by "*extraneae scholae*" was meant not only a school or university in a foreign country, but any school or university beyond the confines of one's own city. Having established that much, he drew the conclusion that the "*extraneae scholae*" and the Latin school at Deventer mentioned by Thomas a Kempis refer to one and the same institution.[39] However, such a conclusion is difficult to accept, for Thomas a Kempis states quite explicitly that, after having received his first schooling in Zutphen, Zerbolt went to "foreign schools," which can refer to a school or schools either in the Low Countries or abroad, and that "at length" he came to Deventer to study at its famous school. It would appear, then, that Zerbolt attended one or more Latin schools, other than those in Zutphen and Deventer, before he enrolled at the latter, and his admission to St. Lebwin's school almost certainly took place some time between the first months of 1383 and the final months of 1385.

Shortly after his arrival in Deventer Zerbolt came under the spell of Florens Radewijns, and it was not long before he joined the newly founded, and still amorphous, group of devout men who were soon to become known as the Brethren of the Common Life. As a member of this Brotherhood, Zerbolt settled down to a relatively quiet and uneventful life. Devout, meditative and studious, he could be found in his cell most of the day, devoting almost all of his time to exercises and study. It would appear that he was particularly interested in theology and canon law, for his writings reveal a considerable knowledge of these two subjects. However, he could not dispose of all his time as he wished, for the Brethren in the vicarage of Radewijns appointed him as their librarian, and his love for books made him particularly suitable for this position. Zerbolt expressed the view that spiritual writings are as indispensable to man's upward journey to God as are the sacraments,[40] and consequently he was, in his capacity as librarian, very diligent in collecting, copying and having spiritual books copied for the Brethren's library. He also tried to further the spiritual growth of those around him through example, conversation and admonition. His manner, while doing so, must have been pleasant, unassuming, yet effective; for he won the respect, admiration and confidence of the Brethren, who held the priesthood in high esteem, to the point where they chose him to be one of the four priests among them. In that capacity, and also because of his innate qualities, Zerbolt was compelled to play a greater role in the management of the

---

[38] Cf. Post, *The Modern Devotion: Confrontation with Reformation and Humanism*, 326.

[39] *Ibid.*, 326. Cf. R. R. Post, *Scholen en Onderwijs in Nederland Gedurende de Middeleeuwen* (Utrecht-Antwerp, 1954), 166-174.

[40] Th. a Kempis, *Opera Omnia*, VII, 279.

Brethren community living in the vicarage of Florens Radewijns, and later in the so-called Master Florens' House, than he was inclined to do so by nature. In the absence of Radewijns, the rector of the Brethren community, Zerbolt assumed his responsibilities; and Zerbolt also advised Radewijns in all matters pertaining not only to the Brethren House in Deventer, but to the Devotionalist movement in its entirety, because after Grote's death in 1384 Radewijns had succeeded Grote as the leader of all the Devotionalists.

It was in this fashion that Zerbolt spent his days, filled with study, meditation, prayer, counselling and priestly duties, until June of the year 1398 when the plague drove most of the Brethren from Deventer, Zerbolt among them. They found a refuge in Amersfoort where they remained until November of that year. During these six months much, or perhaps the greater part, of Zerbolt's time was devoted to warding off attacks made on the Brotherhood from various quarters. The orthodoxy and legality of the movement founded by Grote had been called in question from the outset, and it came under periodic attack. After a period of relative quiet the controversy concerning the Brotherhood's legal status broke out once more in 1397. In defending the Brotherhood against these attacks Radewijns relied heavily on Zerbolt, and it would appear that more than any other Devotionalist Zerbolt must be credited with ensuring the continued existence of the Brotherhood at this time.[41] Zerbolt's knowledge of canon law stood the Brotherhood in good stead since many of the attacks launched against it were based on canon law. Zerbolt had perhaps studied canon law for this very eventuality, but his intelligence, learning and insight would, in any case, have made him the appointed defender of the Brotherhood.

In December of 1398 Zerbolt journeyed from Deventer to Dikninge in Drente to confer there with the learned Arnold, abbot of the Benedictine monastery dedicated to St. Mary, about the attacks made against the Brotherhood and how best to deal with them. On his way home from Dikninge, Zerbolt and his companion, Amilius van Buren, stopped in at Windesheim on the evening of December third to spend the night there. That same night Zerbolt fell mortally ill and died some hours later, being thirty-one years of age. On account of his piety and holiness the Canons at Windesheim quickly buried Zerbolt in an honoured spot in their own chapel before the Brethren from Deventer could come and collect the body.

---

[41] For the attacks which the movement begun by Grote had to endure see Post, *The Modern Devotion: Confrontation with Reformation and Humanism*, 273-292; and for the controversy which raged in 1397-1398 see in particular van der Wansem, *Het Ontstaan en de Geschiedenis der Broederschap van het Gemene Leven tot 1400*, 148-155.

iii. *Writings of Gerard Zerbolt*

Although Zerbolt was only thirty-one years of age when he died, he had already shown himself to be a mature writer: ". . . the most fertile and the most successful writer the Brothers ever produced," in the words of Post.[42] The claim that Zerbolt was the most prolific author of all the Brethren of the Common Life may be questioned, for Dirc van Herxen, the rector of the Brethren at Zwolle from 1410 to 1457, has left us at least as large a body of writings as did Zerbolt.[43] However, to call Zerbolt the most successful—or in other words, the most accomplished, profound, scholarly and popular—writer to emerge from the Brotherhood undoubtedly comes very close to the truth. In fact, Zerbolt must be numbered with the foremost writers to emerge from the Devotionalist movement: i.e., the Brethren and Sisters of the Common Life, and the Augustinian Canons and Canonesses Regular of the Congregation of Windesheim.[44]

De Reformatione and *De Ascensionibus*: *Manuals for Religious.* Zerbolt's fame as a writer during the late middle ages and the early modern period rested on two manuals for the religious life he wrote: *De Reformatione Trium Virium Animae* and *De Spiritualibus Ascensionibus*; and his biographers, as well as a number of Devotionalist chroniclers, expressly mention his authorship of these two works.[45] In them Zerbolt expounds

---

[42] Post, *The Modern Devotion: Confrontation with Reformation and Humanism*, 326.

[43] Cf. P. H. J. Knierim, *Dirc van Herxen (1385-1457), rector van het Zwolse fraterhuis* (Leiden, 1926), 105-142.

[44] Cf. Goossens, *Meditatie*, 24, and Hyma, *The Christian Renaissance: A History of the "Devotio Moderna,"* 565-566.

[45] See Th. a Kempis, *Opera Omnia*, VII, 275; Dier, *Scriptum de Magistro Gerardo Grote, Domino Florencio et aliis devotis Fratribus*, 47-48 and 50; Brinkerink, ed., "Gerard Zerbolt van Zutphen" ("Biographieën van beroemde Mannen uit den Deventer Kring"), 337; Busch, *Chronicon*, 49; and *Het Frensweger Handschrift betreffende de geschiedenis van de Moderne Devotie*, 49.

Most manuscripts of *De Reformatione* and *De Ascensionibus* which mention the author of these works ascribe them to Zerbolt (see van Rooy, *Zerbolt*, 287-336), but some manuscripts name Jean Gerson as their author (van Rooy, *Zerbolt*, 305-306 and 331-332). Furthermore, in his *Bibliotheca Britannica Hibernica* Thomas Tanner, the eighteenth-century British bibliographer, makes reference to a manuscript copy of *De Ascensionibus* in which Richard Rolle of Hampole is named as the author, and he makes reference to a second manuscript of this same work in which it is attributed to Walter Hilton (Thomas Tanner, *Bibliotheca Britannica Hibernica* [London, 1748], 395 and 425 respectively; cf. A. G. Little, *Initia Operum Latinorum quae saeculi xiii. xiv. xv. attribuuntur* [Manchester, 1904], 31). No attempt has been made to establish the source of Tanner's information—although it is most likely the *Index Britannicae Scriptorum* of John Bale (1495-1563)—, nor its accuracy. However, in his inventory of extant manuscripts of *De Ascensionibus* van Rooy does not mention any in which this work is attributed to either Rolle or Hilton (van Rooy, *Zerbolt*, 287-322), nor does H. E. Allen mention *De Ascensionibus* among the *spuria* ascribed to

in a very logical and readable manner his theoretical and practical knowledge concerning the life of the religious and their spiritual concerns. It was perhaps his appreciation for spiritual literature as a means to spread spiritual reform, as well as the practical experience gained as a spiritual adviser, which prompted him to write these two works. And it is from *De Reformatione* and *De Ascensionibus* that we cannot only obtain the clearest picture of Zerbolt's spiritual theology, but of his dogmatic theology, which underlies the former, as well. Zerbolt's four other writings were of too topical a nature to command a general and continued interest,[46] and they will also be of only marginal value for our purpose: i.e., an analysis of Zerbolt's theological thought.

Richard Rolle (H. E. Allen, *Writings Ascribed to Richard Rolle, Hermit of Hampole*, N.Y., 1966; reprint of the ed. dated 1927).

In the first decade of this century B. Kruitwagen pointed out in an article devoted to the authorship of *De Ascensionibus* that at least four bibliographies drawn up in the seventeenth and eighteenth centuries attribute *De Ascensionibus* to a Carthusian of Utrecht by the name of Martin van Schiedam (B. Kruitwagen, "De Karthuizer Martinus van Schiedam en zijn ondergeschoven werkje 'De Spiritualibus Ascensionibus'," *Tijdschrift voor Boek- en Bibliotheekwezen*, VI [1908], 276-280). He found that the origin of this ascription is to be found in a bibliography even older than any of the four just referred to, namely the *Bibliothecae Traiectinae Catalogus*, published in Utrecht in the year 1608 (*ibid.*, 281; cf. A. Sanderus, *Bibliotheca Belgica Manuscripta* [2 vols.; Insulis, 1641-1644], II, 87). The bibliographer responsible for drawing up the *Bibliothecae Traiectinae Catalogus* clearly mistook transcription for authorship. For Ms. 313 of the University Library, Utrecht, ends: "*Explicit devotus tractatus de spiritualibus ascensionibus scriptus per fratrum martinum de sciedam ordinis carthusiensis propre traiectum*" (Kruitwagen, "De Karthuizer Martinus van Schiedam en zijn ondergeschoven werkje 'De Spiritualibus Ascensionibus'," 281-282; and van Rooy, *Zerbolt*, 299).

[46] "Scriptum pro quodam inordinate gradus ecclesiasticos et praedicationis officium affectante," ed. by A. Hyma, *NAKG*, N.S., XX (1927), 179-232; *Het Tractaat "De pretiosis vestibus*," ed. by D. J. M. Wüstenhoff (Ghent-The Hague, 1890); "De libris teutonicalibus et precibus vernaculis," ed. by A. Hyma, *NAKG*, N.S., XVII (1924), 42-70; "Super modo vivendi devotorum hominum simul commorantium," ed. by A. Hyma, *AGAU*, LII (1926), 1-100.

The limited appeal of these four writings is reflected in the fact that, unlike *De Reformatione* and *De Ascensionibus*, they have come down to us in few manuscripts (van Rooy, *Zerbolt*, 336-348). The topical nature of these writings, as well as their restricted appeal, is also illustrated by the fact that, although both Thomas a Kempis and Rudolph Dier indicate that Zerbolt wrote other works in addition to *De Reformatione* and *De Ascensionibus*, they give the titles of only the two manuals for the spiritual life (Th. a Kempis, *Opera Omnia*, VII, 275; and Dier, *Scriptum de Magistro Gerardo Grote, Domino Florencio et aliis devotis Fratribus*, 48). This fact has been partly responsible for the difficulties experienced in establishing the exact identity of Zerbolt's writings other than *De Reformatione* and *De Ascensionibus*, a problem made even more difficult by the absence of manuscripts in which Zerbolt is clearly named as the author of the four 'minor' writings now commonly attributed to him (van Rooy, *Zerbolt*, 336-348). The first person to give us the titles of these 'minor' writings was Revius who wrote in his *Historia urbis Daventriensis*, published in 1651, that, in addition to *De Reformatione* and *De Ascensionibus*, Zerbolt wrote *Super Modo Vivendi, De Libris Teutonicalibus, De Vestibus Pretiosis* and *Scriptum Pro Quodam*. He concludes: "*Et hi quidem libelli in membranis nostris integri habentur.*" (Revius, *Daventria illustrata sive historia urbis Daventriensis libri sex*, 60.) In the nineteenth century Koning, Vos and Geesink

As handbooks for the religious life *De Reformatione* and *De Ascensionibus* must be classified with the *Institutes of the Coenobia* and the *Conferences* of John Cassian, the *Scala Paradisi* of John Climacus, the *Epistola ad Fratres de*

---

accepted Revius' testimony about Zerbolt's authorship of the four works just mentioned without giving it a second thought (Koning, *Gerardi Zutphaniensis, vita, scriptis et meritis*, throughout; Vos, "Gerard Zerbolt," 114-134; and Geesink, *Zerbolt*, 21-24). Following 1879, however, the year in which Geesink's dissertation was published, Zerbolt's authorship of some of the 'minor' writings was contested by F. Jostes and D. J. M. Wüstenhoff. Jostes questioned Zerbolt's authorship of *Super Modo Vivendi* and *De Libris Teutonicalibus* in particular, and Wüstenhoff Zerbolt's authorship of *De Vestibus Pretiosis*, although they doubted whether Zerbolt had written any of the four 'minor' writings (F. Jostes, "Die Schriften des G. Zerbolt van Zutphen. *De libris teutonicalibus*," *Historisches Jahrbuch der Görres Gesellschaft*, XI [1890], 1-22 and 709-717; and Wüstenhoff, ed., *Het Tractaat "De pretiosis vestibus*," 1-31). Some time later A. Hyma came to Zerbolt's defense and argued fairly convincingly that he was indeed the author of *Super Modo Vivendi* (A. Hyma, "Is Gerard Zerbolt of Zutphen the author of the 'Super modo vivendi'?" *NAKG*, N.S., XVI [1921], 107-128; and Hyma, *The Christian Renaissance: A History of the "Devotio Moderna*," 568-571). In the space of some forty-four pages van Rooy tries to prove that Zerbolt wrote all four works under discussion, and he advances both external and internal evidence to bolster his case (van Rooy, *Zerbolt*, 47-90). Following van Rooy most historians have accepted his arguments for Zerbolt's authorship of *Super Modo Vivendi, De Libris Teutonicalibus, De Vestibus Pretiosis* and *Scriptum Pro Quodam* as being convincing and sufficient. Some of these historians are M. Ditsche, R. R. Post, W. Lourdaux and C. C. de Bruin, to name but a few (Ditsche, "Zur Herkunft und Bedeutung des Begriffes *devotio moderna*," 132-133; Post, *The Modern Devotion: Confrontation with Reformation and Humanism*, 283, 286-288 and 326; W. Lourdaux, "Gérard Zerbolt de Zutphen," *DSp*, VI, 286-287; and C. C. de Bruin, "Opmerkingen over de inspiratiebronnen van de moderne devotie," in: *Het Land van Cuijk, Kerkelijk en Politiek Verleden* [Verslagboek Historisch Congress Cuijk, 1971; n. pl., n.d.], 80-81). One historian to question van Rooy's verdict is S. Axters. He questions Zerbolt's authorship of the four 'minor' writings, and of *Super Modo Vivendi* in particular. He expresses the view that *Super Modo Vivendi* was probably written by one of the jurists whom the Brethren in Deventer consulted about the legality of the Brotherhood (Axters, *Vroomheid*, III, 82-84). More recently F. M. Bartoš has expressed the opinion that Radewijns is the author of *Super Modo Vivendi* (F. M. Bartoš, "Hus, Lollardism and Devotio Moderna in the fight for a National Bible," *Communio Viatorum*, III [1960], 253, footnote 17). What emerges from the foregoing is that, while Zerbolt's authorship of *Super Modo Vivendi, De Libris Teutonicalibus, De Vestibus Pretiosis* and *Scriptum Pro Quodam* is fairly certain, it has not been established beyond all doubt. This uncertainty must be kept in mind as we occasionally draw on the 'minor' writings throughout the analysis of Zerbolt's thought.

Nine letters written by Zerbolt during the last year of his life have come down to us (eight letters were published by G. Dumbar, ed., *Reipublicae Daventriensi ab Actis Analecta, seu vetera aliquot scripta inedita* [2 vols.; Deventer, 1719-1725], I, 88-113; and one letter may be found in *De Katholiek*, XLI [1862], 120-121 [ed. by V. Becker]). However, they do not contain anything that is of use to us (van Rooy, *Zerbolt*, 91-92). Furthermore, in the past two works have been mistakenly attributed to Zerbolt, namely *Sermones* (Trithemius, *De scriptoribus ecclesiasticis*, 273), and a tract, entitled *De beneficiis Jesu Christi*. However, no *Sermones* by Zerbolt have ever been discovered, and van Rooy is of the opinion that when Trithemius speaks of *Sermones* by Zerbolt, he most likely has Zerbolt's four 'minor' writings in mind (van Rooy, *Zerbolt*, 93). *De beneficiis Jesu Christi* is, in fact, Thomas a Kempis' *De vita et beneficiis salvatoris Jesu Christi devotissimae meditationes* (Th. a Kempis, *Opera Omnia*, V, 1-53; cf. van Rooy, *Zerbolt*, 92-93). Finally, some thirty years ago Hyma advanced the theory that Zerbolt wrote the first book of *De Imitatione Christi*. He based his argument on the so-called Eutin manuscript containing a copy of the first book of *De Imita-*

Monte Dei of William of St. Thierry, *De exterioris et interioris hominis compositione* of David of Augsburg, and *De Triplici Via* of Bonaventure.[47] When
Zerbolt's manuals are set alongside the older handbooks, they do not
compare unfavourably with them. Looked at from the aspect of organization and structure, *De Reformatione* and *De Ascensionibus* are superior to all
of their predecessors, except for Bonaventure's *De Triplici Via*. With
respect to contents *De Reformatione* and *De Ascensionibus* are, with the exception of Cassian's *Institutes* perhaps, 'inferior' to the other manuals
named in that they do not really move beyond the purely ascetical aspect
of the religious life. The *Conferences, Scala Paradisi, Epistola ad Fratres de
Monte Dei, De exterioris et interioris hominis compositione* and *De Triplici Via*, by
contrast, all deal with the mystical phase of the spiritual life to a greater
or lesser degree.

Florens Radewijns, rector of the Brethren in Deventer and Zerbolt's
'superior', also wrote two manuals for the spiritual life, namely *Omnes,
inquit, artes* and *Tractatulus Devotus*.[48] These must be added to the list of
predecessors of Zerbolt's handbooks named in the previous paragraph.
The works of Radewijns exerted some influence on those of Zerbolt with
respect to their structure and organization.[49] Nonetheless, when they are
set side by side it soon becomes evident that the structure and plan of *De
Reformatione* and *De Ascensionibus* are superior to that of *Omnes, inquit,
artes*, and perhaps to that of the *Tractatulus Devotus* as well. Of much
greater significance is that *Omnes, inquit, artes* and the *Tractatulus Devotus*

---

tione Christi which differs considerably from the 'standard' version (A. Hyma, "The
Original Version of *De Imitatione Christi* by Gerard Zerbolt van Zutphen," *AGAU*, LXIX
[1950], 1-42; cf. J. F. Meyer, *Thomas a Kempis Capita quindecim inedita* [Lübeck, 1854]).
However, Hyma has found no support for his thesis, which is not surprising in view of the
fact that the Eutin manuscript dates from around 1450 (J. Huijben and P. Debongnie,
L'Auteur ou les Auteurs de l'Imitation [Louvain, 1957], 312), and no other copy of this version
of Book One of the *Imitatio* has ever been discovered. Dom J. Huijben and P. Debongnie
give many other reasons why Zerbolt could not have been the author of *De Imitatione
Christi*, or parts thereof (*ibid.*, 45, 274-275, 311-318, 369-370 and 382).

[47] Both Thomas and Kempis and the anonymous author of the Middle-Dutch *vita*
characterize Zerbolt's two major works as manuals for the spiritual life (Th. a Kempis,
Opera Omnia, VII, 275; and Brinkerink, ed., "Gerard Zerbolt van Zutphen"
["Biographieën van beroemde Mannen uit den Deventer Kring"], 377).

[48] Florens Radewijns, *Omnes, inquit, artes*, ed. by van Woerkum, *Het Libellus "Omnes,
Inquit, Artes," Een Rapiarium van Florentius Radewijns*, II and III.

Florens Radewijns, *Tractatulus Devotus*, ed. by Goossens, *Meditatie*, 207-254. There are
two older editions of the *Tractatulus Devotus*: H. Nolte, ed., *Magistri et Domini Florencii Tractatulus Devotus* (Freiburg im Breisgau, 1862), and J. F. Vregt, ed., *AGAU*, X (1882),
383-427. Throughout this study Goossens' edition of the *Tractatulus Devotus* will be used.

M. van Woerkum, "Florentius Radewijns: Leven, Geschriften, Persoonlijkheid en
Ideeën," *OGE*, XXIV (1950), 363.

[49] Cf. van Woerkum, "Het Libellus '*Omnes, inquit, artes*'," 129. See below, pp. 241
and 264, where the structure of *De Reformatione* and *De Ascensionibus* is discussed in some
detail.

served Zerbolt as source books,[50] about which more will be said shortly. In contrast with the works of Radewijns, however, and in contrast with *Omnes, inquit, artes* in particular, the writings of Zerbolt are not simply collections of excerpts arranged topically. Both *De Reformatione* and *De Ascensionibus* reveal, in comparison with *Omnes, inquit, artes* and the *Tractatulus Devotus*, a great degree of originality. Although Zerbolt frequently quotes longer or shorter passages from other works, he has fully assimilated that which he has read and has put his own stamp on it.[51] His works are polished literary productions in contrast with the works of Radewijns which are little more than *catena*.[52] As Post observes, *De Reformatione* and *De Ascensionibus* of Zerbolt are well constructed, readable works.[53] Consequently one cannot agree with S. Axters when he characterizes Zerbolt's two manuals for the spiritual life as *rapiaria*.[54]

The twenty-seventh chapter of *De Ascensionibus* contains what both Geesink and van Rooy take to be a reference to *De Reformatione*.[55] In addition to this reference there are other indications that Zerbolt wrote *De Reformatione* before *De Ascensionibus*. Firstly, *De Ascensionibus* is, to a considerable degree, a revision and elaboration of *De Reformatione*, and not a continuation as Post writes in *The Modern Devotion*.[56] Secondly, in *De Ascensionibus* Zerbolt reveals in most instances a greater degree of independence *vis-à-vis* his sources than he does in *De Reformatione*. There is, on the other hand, no indication at what time between Zerbolt's arrival in Deventer about 1384 and his death in 1398 *De Reformatione* and *De Ascensionibus* were written.[57] However, taking into account his youthfulness when he arrived in Deventer, it is fairly safe to assert that they could not have been written much before the last decade of the fourteenth century.

De Reformatione and *De Ascensionibus* are important not only in themselves, but also—and perhaps more so—because they embody the spirit and spirituality of the Modern Devotion. It is perhaps fair to say that Zerbolt systematized and gave shape to the thought of the young movement, and to that of Grote and Radewijns, the two most important founders of the Modern Devotion, in particular.[58] He did not, however,

---

[50] Cf. van Woerkum, "Het Libellus '*Omnes, inquit, artes*'," 128-130 and W. Lourdaux, "Gérard Zerbolt de Zutphen," *DSp*, VI, 287.

[51] Cf. Mak, ed., *De Dietse Vertaling van Gerlach Peters' Soliloquium*, 80 (Introduction).

[52] Cf. van Woerkum, "Het Libellus '*Omnes, inquit, artes*'," 132.

[53] Post, *Kerkgeschiedenis*, I, 381.

[54] Axters, *Vroomheid*, III, 89 and 194.

[55] Geesink, *Zerbolt* 24, and van Rooy, *Zerbolt*, 95.

[56] Post, *The Modern Devotion: Confrontation with Reformation and Humanism*, 327.

[57] Hyma's assertion that "Zerbolt wrote his two mystical works shorly before his death" cannot be substantiated (Hyma, *The Christian Renaissance: A History of the "Devotio Moderna,"* 82).

[58] Cf. Epiney-Burgard, *Grote*, 302.

organize and mould the thought of the recently founded movement without making a contribution of his own, and without leaving his own imprint on it. M. Th. P. van Woerkum goes as far as to assert that through *De Reformatione* and *De Ascensionibus* Zerbolt contributed to the form and content of Devotionalist spirituality more than anyone else did.[59] Since *De Reformatione* and *De Ascensionibus* reflect so accurately and so completely the spirituality of the founders of the Modern Devotion of whom Zerbolt was one in the broad sense of the term, they became the most sought after manuals for the spiritual life in the establishments of the Modern Devotion.[60] It was perhaps Zerbolt's contribution to the movement in the field of spiritual literature which prompted Busch to add his name to the list of *"promotores, institutores et consumatores"* of the Modern Devotion.[61] For through his spiritual writings Zerbolt unquestionably contributed to the survival and success of the Devotionalist movement. Through *De Reformatione* and *De Ascensionibus* Zerbolt continued, even after his death, to determine, to direct, and to shape the spirituality of the Modern Devotion. These two manuals aided the Devotionalists to remain true to the spirit and intention of the founders of the movement. *De Reformatione* and *De Ascensionibus* must, with *De Imitatione Christi*, be counted among the works which most accurately reflect the spirituality of the Modern Devotion.[62] Hyma points to this fact as one of the reasons why *De Imitatione Christi* must be attributed to Zerbolt, and not to Thomas a Kempis.[63] Therefore, anyone wishing to understand the nature and spirituality of the Modern Devotion will be obliged to make a study of *De Reformatione* and *De Ascensionibus*.

Sources of De Reformatione and De Ascensionibus.[64] In view of the degree of indebtedness to other writers and works, it must be said that Zerbolt re-

---

[59] Van Woerkum, "Het Libellus *'Omnes, inquit, artes'*," 132.

[60] As will be seen below, many mss. of *De Reformatione* and *De Ascensionibus* have survived. Of Radewijns' *Tractatulus* and *Omnes, inquit, artes* only one or two mss. have come down to us, which clearly indicates their respective popularity.

[61] Busch, *Chronicon*, 28 and 266.

[62] Cf. van Rooy, *Zerbolt*, 278.

[63] Hyma, *The Christian Renaissance: A History of the "Devotio Moderna,"* 565-566.

[64] The older monographs on Zerbolt say very little concerning the sources used by Zerbolt for *De Reformatione* and *De Ascensionibus*. All Geesink writes in this connection is that Zerbolt made use of Radewijns' *Omnes, inquit, artes* for *De Reformatione* and *De Ascensionibus*, and that Zerbolt incorporated in *De Reformatione* all of what Geesink believed to be Bonaventure's *Fascicularius* (Geesink, *Zerbolt*, 82-83, 132 and 135-138). Concerning the *Fascicularius* more will be said below (p. 25, footnote 90). Van Rooy tells us even less about Zerbolt's sources than Geesink does, and the reason for this is that van Rooy's work was to have been followed by a second volume in which the sources for Zerbolt's writings were to have been investigated (van Rooy, *Zerbolt*, 278). More useful than Geesink's and van Rooy's monographs for our knowledge of Zerbolt's sources are a number of articles:

mains silent about his sources in most instances. To begin with, both *De Reformatione* and *De Ascensionibus* contain numerous texts from the Scriptures. Some of these are given in their original form, while others have been altered. The indebtedness is acknowledged in some instances, but in others it is not.[65] Of all the non-Scriptural authorities, Zerbolt acknowledges Bernard of Clairvaux most frequently, followed by Augustine,[66] Jerome, Gregory the Great and Cassian,[67] and the frequen-

---

M. Viller, "*Le Speculum Monachorum* et la 'Dévotion Moderne'," *RAM*, III (1922), 45-46; C. Smits, "David van Augsburg en de Invloed van zijn *Profectus* op de Moderne Devotie," *Collectanea Franciscana Neerlandica*, I (1927), 171-203; E. Mikkers, "Sint Bernardus en de Moderne Devotie," *Cîteaux in de Nederlanden*, IV (1953), 149-186; and A. Rayez, "Gérard Zerbolt de Zutphen et Saint Bonaventure. Dépendances Littéraires," in: *Dr. L. Reypens-Album*, ed. by A. Ampe (Studiën en Tekstuitgaven van *Ons Geestelijk Erf*, Vol. XVI; Antwerp, 1964), 323-256. However most important of all for our knowledge of the sources used by Zerbolt for *De Reformatione* and *De Ascensionibus* is van Woerkum's study of Radewijns' *Omnes, inquit, artes* (van Woerkum, "Het Libellus '*Omnes, inquit, artes*'," 113-158 and 225-268), and only a little less important is Goossens' edition of Radewijns' *Tractulus Devotus* (Radewijns, *Tractatulus Devotus*, ed. by Goossens, *Meditatie*, 209-254). The significance of van Woerkum's and Goossens' work for our knowledge of Zerbolt's sources will become clear below.

[65] S. van der Woude has identified at least eighty-seven passages from the Scriptures in *De Reformatione* (Gerard Zerbolt van Zutphen, *Over de Hervorming van de Krachten der Ziel*, introduced and translated by S. van der Woude [Amsterdam, 1951]). Of this number fifteen are from the letters of St. Paul—five from the letter to the Romans alone—, twelve from the Gospel of Matthew, and ten from the Psalms. All other books have been cited less than ten times. Canon J. Mahieu, on the other hand, has found some 160 passages from the Bible in *De Ascensionibus*, although many of them are scarcely recognizable as such (Gerard Zerbolt van Zutphen, *De spiritualibus ascensionibus/Van geestelijke opklimmingen*, ed. by Canon J. Mahieu [2d ed.; Bruges, 1941]). Of these 160, forty-one are from the letters of St. Paul—ten from the epistle to the Romans alone—, twenty-nine from the Book of Psalms, eighteen from the Gospel of Matthew and eleven from the Gospel of Luke. All other books have been cited ten times, or less. In both *De Reformatione* and *De Ascensionibus*, then, the Psalms is the most frequently quoted Old Testament book, and St. Paul the most often cited New Testament writer. The same, it might perhaps be pointed out, holds true for *De Imitatione Christi*. It contains more passages from the Psalms and from the letters of St. Paul than from other books in the Bible (B. Spaapen, "Imitation de Jesus-Christ [Livre]," *DSp*, VII, 2359).

[66] The importance of Augustine's writings as a source for Zerbolt is somewhat more difficult to evaluate than is the importance of most other writers, and their works, for Zerbolt. The reason for this is that Augustine's influence was all pervasive throughout the middle ages. Consequently he exerted an indirect, as well as a direct, influence on Zerbolt, and the former most likely outweighed the latter.

[67] Bernard of Clairvaux: *Sermons on the Song of Songs*, 5; *De Consideratione*, 3; no title supplied, 25; total, 33. Where Zerbolt gives only St. Bernard's name as a source and no title, the origin of the excerpt is, in a number of instances, the *Sermones de tempore, de sanctis, de diversis* or the *Sermones super Cantica Canticorum*.

Augustine: *Confessions*, 4; *De Doctrina Christiana*, 2; *De Opere Monachorum*, 2; a letter to Proba, 2; *De Civitate Dei*, 1; *De Continentia*, 1; *De genesi contra Manichaeos*, 1; a letter to Jerome, 1; no title supplied, 16; total, 30. When Zerbolt quotes "*Augustinus super genesim*" (*De Reformatione*, 215G), the reference is, most likely, to Augustine's *De genesi contra Manichaeos*, rather than to Augustine's *De genesi ad litteram imperfectus*; because Grote, who bequeathed his books to the library of Master Florens' House, owned a copy of *De genesi*

cy with which he acknowledges his indebtedness to these five writers puts
them in a class by themselves. However, the fact that Zerbolt more often
expresses his debt to these five authorities than to others does not mean,
as will be seen, that they represent all of his most important sources, nor
that they are necessarily among the most important ones. Named much
less often by Zerbolt as his source than the authors just named are John
Chrysostom, John Climacus, Hugh of St. Victor, Ambrose, Bede,
Anselm of Canterbury, Bonaventure, Aristotle, Seneca, Basil the Great,
the *Vitae Patrum*, Benedict of Nursia, Isidor of Seville and Thomas
Aquinas.[68] However, not all the excerpts attributed by Zerbolt to a par-

---

contra Manichaeos (W. Mulder, ed., *Gerardi Magni Epistolae* [Antwerp-Nijmegen, 1933], No.
7 [p. 16]).

Jerome: a letter to Rusticus, 3; *Commentary on Ecclesiastes*, 1; no title supplied, 18; total,
22.

Gregory the Great: *Dialogues*, 2; *Moralia in Job*, 1; no title supplied, 18; total 21.

Cassian: *Conferences*, 8; *Institutes*, 2; no title given, 8; total 18. In those instances in which
only Cassian's name is given, either the *Conferences* or *Institutes* are implied, for they were
the only two works of Cassian known to the Devotionalists.

[68] John Chrysostom: *Super Matthaeum*, 1; no title supplied, 7; total 8. The excerpt from
Super Matthaeum (*De Reformatione*, 240C) can be either from Chrysostom's *Homiliae in Matthaeum*, or from pseudo-Chrysostom's *Opus imperfectum in Matthaeum*, the work of a fifth-
century Arian. Grote owned a copy of the former, but the latter was known to the early
Devotionalists as well. Indications are, however, that Zerbolt quoted from the *Homiliae in
Matthaeum*, for one of his 'minor' writings, *Scriptum Pro Quodam*, contains four excerpts
from the *Homiliae* (van Woerkum, "Het Libellus '*Omnes, inquit, artes*'," 140-141; Mulder,
ed., *Gerardi Magni Epistolae*, Nos. 7 and 20 [pp. 15 and 77]; and K. C. L. M. de Beer,
Studie Over de Spiritualiteit van Geert Groote [Brussels-Nijmegen, 1938], 256 and 263).

John Climacus: *Scala Paradisi*, 8.

Hugh of St. Victor: *De Amore*, 4; no title supplied, 3; total 7. In one instance (*De Ascensionibus*, 276A) where Zerbolt gives only Hugh's name, the origin of the excerpt is his
Eruditio Didascalia (*PL*, CLXXVI, 797).

Ambrose: *De Officiis Ministrorum*, 2; no title given, 3; total 5.

Bede: no title given, 2. Although he does not give any titles, Zerbolt almost certainly
quotes from Bede's *Commentary on Luke* from which Grote also quoted in one of his works
(de Beer, *Spiritualiteit*, 255).

Anselm of Canterbury: *De Similitudinibus*, 1; no title supplied, 1; total, 2. *De
Similitudinibus* is, in fact, a work by Alexander of Canterbury.

Bonaventure: no title given, 2. In one of these instances (*De Reformatione*, 248A) Zerbolt
quotes from Bonaventure's *Commentary on the Sentences* (cf. Goossens, *Meditatie*, 194, and'
M. Grabmann, "Der Einfluss des hl. Bonaventura auf die Theologie and Frömmigkeit
des deutschen Mittelalters," *Zeitschrift für Aszese und Mystik*, XIX [1944], 26).

Aristotle: no title supplied, 1.

Seneca: no title given, 1. The excerpts from the writings of Aristotle and Seneca are the
only two excerpts from non-Christian writings to be found in *De Ascensionibus* (p. 268A)
and *De Reformatione* (p. 242F). These are also the only two excerpts from non-Christian
writings to be found in Radewijns' *Omnes, inquit, artes*, and there is no doubt about Zerbolt
having obtained them by way of the work of his *confrère*, about which more will be said
below. It is from Aristotle's *Ethica ad Nicomachum* and from Seneca's *Epistulae ad Lucilium*
that the passages in question have been derived (cf. van Woerkum, "Het Libellus '*Omnes,
inquit, artes*'," 240; Mulder, ed., *Gerardi Magni Epistolae*, No. 13 [p. 45]; de Beer,
Spiritualiteit, 251; and P. F. J. Obbema, *Een Deventer Bibliotheekcatalogus van het Einde der
Vijftiende Eeuw* [2 vols.; Brussels, 1973], II, 184).

ticular author can be found in his authentic writings. This applies especially to Augustine and Bernard of Clairvaux, for in the middle ages they were among the writers who had the most works attributed to them of which they were not the authors. For example, in *De Reformatione* Zerbolt attributes a particular excerpt to Augustine which, in reality, is a passage from Prosper of Aquitaine's *Sententiae ex Augustino Debilitatae*.[69] And in at least one place where Zerbolt gives only Bernard of Clairvaux's name as his source the quotation is, in fact, from William of St. Thierry's *Epistola ad Fratres de Monte Dei* which was universally attributed to St. Bernard in the middle ages.

Having given a synopsis of the authors to whom Zerbolt acknowledges his indebtedness, we must next enumerate those works of which we know for certain that they were used by him for *De Reformatione* and *De Ascensionibus*, but to which he does not express his debt. They are, in the order in which they were written, St. Athanasius' *Vita S. Antonii*,[70] Hugh of St. Victor's *De Modo Orandi*, pseudo-Augustine's *De Spiritu et Anima*, Arnulf

---

Basil the Great: no title given, 1. It is fairly certain that Zerbolt obtained this excerpt (*De Reformatione*, 238F) by way of Radewijns' *Tractatulus Devotus* where it is found as well. Radewijns merely writes: "...*sicut dicit Basilius*," but Goossens has found it in his *Regulae Fusius Tractatae* (Radewijns, *Tractatulus Devotus*, 216; cf. Obbema, *Een Deventer Bibliotheekcatalogus van het Einde der Vijftiende Eeuw*, II, 185-186).

Vitae Patrum, 1.

Benedict of Nursia: Rule, 1.

Isidor of Seville: no title given, 1. Zerbolt mentions Isidor of Seville in connection with the number of capital sins (*De Reformatione*, 255D), but does not supply a title in this connection. Isidor discusses the question of capital sins and their number in two different works: *Differentiorum*, Bk. II, ch. 40 (*PL*, LXXXIII, 96) and *Testimonia Divinae Scripturae, et Patrum*, ch. 29 (*PL*, LXXXIII, 1213). Cf. L. Cristiani, *Jean Cassien: La Spiritualité du Désert* (2 vols.; Saint Wandrille, 1946), II, 62.

Thomas Aquinas, *Summa Theologiae*, 1.

On account of the fact that the contents of *De Reformatione* and *De Ascensionibus* are so much alike, many of the excerpts for which Zerbolt acknowledges indebtedness in *De Ascensionibus* he had previously used, and had given the particulars of, in *De Reformatione*. As a result many excerpts are represented twice in the synopsis of authorities given in this footnote and the previous one.

[69] *De Reformatione*, 242E. Zerbolt attributes it to Augustine as was done by Radewijns whose *Tractatulus Devotus* or *Omnes, inquit, artes* is Zerbolt's source for this excerpt. See Radewijns, *Tractatulus Devotus*, 219-220; and Radewijns, *Omnes, Inquit, Artes*, II, 47. Cf. Goossens, *Meditatie*, 89.

[70] In *De Reformatione* Zerbolt quotes once from the *Vita S. Antonii* (*De Reformatione*, 251E), and here too Radewijns' *Omnes, inquit, artes* served as the intermedium. See Radewijns, *Omnes, Inquit, Artes*, II, 51-52; and St. Athanasius, *Vita S. Antonii*, in: J. P. Migne, ed., *Patrologia Graeca* (Paris, 1857-1912), XXVI, 924-925.

Grote quotes a number of times from the *Vita S. Antonii* (de Beer, *Spiritualiteit*, 255, 258 and 266), and he owned a copy of this work. For in the middle ages the *Vita S. Antonii* constituted a part of the *Vitae Patrum* of which Grote had a copy (M. E. Kronenberg and A. Hulshof, "De Bibliotheek van het Heer-Florenshuis te Deventer," *NAKG*, N.S., IX [1912], 155). Grote bequeathed his books to Master Florens' House, and consequently a copy of the *Vitae Patrum* could be found in its library.

de Boeriis' *Speculum Monachorum*,[71] David of Augsburg's *De exterioris et interioris hominis compositione*,[72] and Bonaventure's *De Triplici Via*,[73] *Lignum Vitae*,[74] and *De Praeparatione ad Missam*.[75] In addition to these eight works from which Zerbolt unquestionably borrowed without mentioning them, there are others which he most probably made use of as well, although there is no conclusive evidence that he did so. These works are pseudo-Bernard's *Meditationes piisimae*,[76] Bonaventure's *Soliloquium*, pseudo-Bonaventure's *Meditationes Vitae Christi*,[77] and Henry Suso's *Horologium Sapientiae*. Radewijns quoted from these four works in *Omnes, inquit, artes*, which adds to the likelihood that Zerbolt knew them and also borrowed from them for his writings.

We know for certain that Zerbolt was familiar with Bonaventure's *Commentary on the Sentences* and Aquinas' *Summa Theologiae*, for *De Reformatione* contains at least one excerpt from each of these two works. However, one might perhaps ask whether for his views and opinions on questions of dogma Zerbolt was not indebted to Bonaventure's *Breviloquium* and Hugh

---

[71] In the middle ages the *Speculum monachorum* was attributed to Bernard of Clairvaux, and consequently was known as *Speculum Bernardi* as well. However, like the work by Arnulf de Boeriis, the first book of David of Augsburg's *De ext. et int. hom. compositione* was also known as the *Speculum monachorum*, and the second and third books of *De ext. et int. hom. compositione* as the *Profectus religiosorum*. Consequently, when Devotionalist sources speak simply of *Speculum monachorum* it is not always clear whether they are referring to the work of Arnulf de Boeriis, or to the work of David of Augsburg. However, M. Viller is of the opinion that the first book of *De ext. et int. hom. compositione* is meant in most instances (Viller, "Le *Speculum Monachorum* et la 'Dévotion Moderne'," 45-56 and 49-51 in particular). And when in his *vita* of Zerbolt, Thomas a Kempis writes that *"ante finem suae quasi noviter conversus Speculum monachorum et Profectus religiosorum iterum legere coepit: ..."* (*Opera Omnia*, VII, 281), it would appear that the entire work of David of Augsburg: i.e. *De ext. et int. hom. compositione*, is being referred to.

It would appear that the more usual title for the first book of *De ext. et int. hom. compositione* was *Formula novitiorum*. (Van Woerkum, "Het Libellus, '*Omnes, inquit, artes*'," 229-231 and P. S. Jolliffe, "Middle English Translations of *De Exterioris et Interioris Hominis Compositione*," *Medieval Studies*, XXVI [1974], 259-277.)

[72] Cf. M. Hedlund, ed., *Epistola de Vita et Passione Domini Nostri* (Kerkhistorische Bijdragen, Vol. V; Leiden, 1975), 20-22; Viller, "Le *Speculum Monachorum* et la 'Devotion Moderne'," 45-56; Smits, "David van Augsburg en de Invloed van zijn *Profectus* op de Moderne Devotie," 171-203; and Rayez, "Gérard Zerbolt de Zutphen et Saint Bonaventure. Dépendances Littéraires," 350-356.

[73] Cf. Rayez, *op. cit.*, 323-350.

[74] Cf. Hedlund, ed., *Epistola de Vita et Passione Domini Nostri*, 12-14.

[75] Cf. Rayez, "Gérard Zerbolt de Zutphen et Saint Bonaventure. Dépendances Littéraires," 323-356.

[76] Cf. Obbema, *Een Deventer Bibliotheekcatalogus van het Einde der Vijftiende Eeuw*, II, 178.

[77] Cf. C. C. de Bruin, "Het Bonaventura-Ludolphiaanse Leven van Jesus," in: *Dr. L. Reypens-Album*, ed. by A. Ampe (Studiën en Tekstuitgaven van *Ons Geestelijk Erf*, Vol. XVI; Antwerp, 1964), 115-130. In recent years the *Meditationes Vitae Christi* have been attributed to John de Caulibus, but that he is, in fact, the author of this work has not been established beyond all doubt.

Ripelin's *Compendium Theologiae Veritatis* as well.[78] There is no positive evidence that the Brethren House at Deventer possessed copies of the *Breviloquium* and the *Compendium Theologiae Veritatis* in the fourteenth century, but that they were present in the library of Master Florens' House at that time is not impossible. In later years a printed copy of the *Breviloquium* could be found in the library of Master Florens' House,[79] and in his *Rosetum* Johannes Mombaer, the Augustinian Canon Regular of Mount St. Agnes, recommended it to his readers.[80] The *Compendium Theologiae Veritatis* of Hugh Ripelin of Strasbourg has been called the most widely read theological work in the late middle ages,[81] and Dirc van Herxen included a number of excerpts from the *Compendium Theologiae Veritatis* in his *Instructio Religiosorum*,[82] a work similar to Radewijns' *Omnes, inquit, artes*. These are, then, a few indications that Zerbolt was, in all probability, familiar with Bonaventure's *Breviloquium* and Hugh Ripelin's *Compendium Theologiae Veritatis*.

Zerbolt's immediate source for most of the authorities quoted by him are Radewijns' *Omnes, inquit, artes* and *Tractatulus Devotus*. Both works are essentially collections of excerpts, or *catena*, although the *Tractatulus Devotus* possesses a greater deal of originality than does *Omnes, inquit, artes*. Except for one or two, van Woerkum was able to identify all the excerpts in *Omnes, inquit, artes*,[83] while Goossens was able to identify all but a few of the excerpts in the *Tractatulus Devotus*.[84] Zerbolt's indebtedness to Radewijns, which is nowhere acknowledged, was not first established by modern historians, because in his *Scriptum*, the 'chronicle' of Master Florens' House, Rudolph Dier of Muden already calls attention to the relationship that exists between the works of Radewijns and those of Zer-

---

[78] On Hugh's authorship of the *Compendium* see M. Grabmann, *Mittelalterliches Geistesleben* (3 vols.; München, 1926), I, 168-185. See also H. Fischer, "Hughes Ripelin de Strasbourg," *DSp*, VII, 894-896.

The works of Aquinas are the most important sources of the *Compendium* which is perhaps not surprising in view of the fact that Hugh Ripelin was a Dominican.

[79] Kronenberg and Hulshof, "De Bibliotheek van het Heer-Florenshuis te Deventer," 269.

[80] P. Debongnie, *Jean Mombaer de Bruxelles* (Louvain-Toulouse, 1927), 238-239 and 329.

[81] F. A. M. Daniëls, *Meester Dirc van Delf, Zijn Persoon en Zijn Werk* (Nijmegen-Utrecht, 1932), 37.

[82] Knierim, *Dirc van Herxen, rector van het Zwolse fraterhuis*, 134. Cf. H. Fischer, "Hughes Ripelin de Strasbourg," *DSp*, VII, 894-895.

In the fifteenth century Hugh's *Compendium* was widely read by the Devotionalists, it would appear, especially by the Augustinian Canons Regular of the Congregation of Windesheim. See G. Steer, *Hugo Ripelin von Strassburg. Zur Rezeptions- und Wirkungsgeschichte des "Compendium theologicae veritatis" im deutschen Spätmittelalter* (Tübingen, 1981), 51 (No. 12), 53 (no. 15), 54 (No. 19), 55 (No. 25), 58 (No. 33), 66 (No. 69), 68 (No. 79), 130 (No. 396), 132 (No. 402) and 159 (No. B107).

[83] Van Woerkum, "Het Libellus '*Omnes, inquit, artes*'," 113-158 and 225-268.

[84] Radewijns, *Tractatulus Devotus*, 209-254.

bolt.[85] It does not, however, appear that Zerbolt was compelled to rely upon the works of Radewijns for source material. For such sources as were available to Radewijns were also available to Zerbolt. What would appear to have happened, then, is that in his choice of sources Zerbolt allowed himself to be led to a great degree by Radewijns and his works, and to a lesser extent by Gerard Grote.[86] In doing so he remained true to their spirit and the spiritual course on which they set the new movement. It is true, of course, that the nature of *De Reformatione* and *De Ascensionibus* as manuals for the religious life determined Zerbolt's choice of sources to a considerable degree like it had earlier determined Radewijns' choice of sources for *Omnes, inquit, artes* and the *Tractatulus Devotus*. Finally, Zerbolt's indebtedness to Radewijns can be properly demonstrated only by placing the relevant passages from Radewijns' and Zerbolt's works in parallel columns. However, that would require a great deal of space, and consequently Zerbolt's dependence on Radewijns can be sketched here in general terms only.

In *Omnes, inquit, artes* Radewijns quotes most extensively from the Scriptures, *Vitae Patrum*, Cassian's *Institutes* and *Conferences*, Climacus' *Scala Paradisi*, St. Bernhard's *Sermones*, pseudo-Bernard's *Meditationes Piisimae*, William of St. Thierry's *Epistola ad Fratres de Monte Dei*, Arnulf de Boeriis' *Speculum Monachorum*, David of Augsburg's *De exterioris et interioris hominis compositione*, Bonaventure's *De Triplici Via* and *Lignum Vitae*, Jacobus de Voragine's *Legenda Aurea*, Suso's *Horologium Sapientiae*, and the Breviary and Missal of the bishopric of Utrecht.[87] The most important sources for the *Tractatulus Devotus* were, it would appear, Cassian's *Institutes* and *Conferences*, Climacus' *Scala Paradisi*, St. Bernard's *Sermones*, William of St. Thierry's *Epistola ad Fratres de Monte Dei*, David of Augsburg's *De exterioris et interioris hominis compositione*, and Bonaventure's *De Triplici Via* and *Lignum Vitae*.[88] Since Radewijns' writings served Zerbolt as source books and also posed as models for his works to some extent, it is not surprising that Radewijns' most important sources emerge as Zerbolt's most important sources as well, and they are: Cassian's *Institutes* and *Conferences*, Climacus' *Scala Paradisi*, William of St. Thierry's *Epistola ad Fratres de Monte Dei*, David of Augsburg's *De exterioris et interioris hominis compositione* and Bonaventure's *De Triplici Via*. To this group one

---

[85] Dier, *Scriptum de Magistro Gerardo Grote, Domino Florencio et aliis devotis Fratribus*, 50-51. Cf. Geesink, *Zerbolt*, 132; Gerretsen, *Florentius Radewijns*, 93; van Rooy, *Zerbolt*, 45; van Woerkum, "Florentius Radewijns: Leven, Geschriften, Persoonlijkheid en Ideeën," 349-350; and *idem*, "Het Libellus '*Omnes, inquit, artes*'," 128-130.

[86] Cf. Klinkenberg, "Die Devotio Moderna unter dem Thema 'antiqui-moderni' betrachtet," 410.

[87] Van Woerkum, "Het Libellus '*Omnes, inquit, artes*'," 258-259.

[88] See Radewijns, *Tractatulus Devotus*, 209-254.

ought perhaps also to add Bernard's *Sermones*.[89] A good deal less important are Gregory the Great's *Moralia in Job* and *Dialogues*, pseudo-Augustine's *De Spiritu et Anima*, Bonaventure's *Lignum Vitae* and *De Praeparatione ad Missam*,[90] and Arnulf de Boeriis' *Speculum Monachorum*.

[89] Cf. Mikkers, "Sint Bernardus en de Moderne Devotie," 157-169.

[90] Van Woerkum wrote almost thirty years ago now that he found little or no trace of Bonaventure's writings in those of Grote and Zerbolt, nor in any other writings of the first Devotionalists, except in Radewijns' *Omnes, inquit, artes* (van Woerkum, *Het Libellus "Omnes, Inquit, Artes,"* Een Rapiarium van Florentius Radewijns, I, 163-164 and 167-168). The truth is that Bonaventure's *De Triplici Via* must be numbered with Zerbolt's major sources, while *Lignum Vitae* and *De Praeparatione ad Missam* also supplied Zerbolt with a considerable amount of source material for *De Reformatione* and *De Ascensionibus*. Furthermore, Radewijns' writings are in most instances, it would appear, the immediate source of the excerpts from Bonaventure's works found in those of Zerbolt. Those excerpts from Bonaventure's work which were transmitted to Zerbolt by Radewijns' writings are in most instances identified in the latter, on account of which Zerbolt was aware of their origin. It is, therefore, striking that Zerbolt acknowledges his indebtedness to Bonaventure in only two instances, and one can only guess at the reason for his reticence in naming Bonaventure as his source. Zerbolt's reserve in this respect indicates perhaps that as an *auctoritas* Bonaventure was not, in Zerbolt's eyes at least, on a par with Augustine, Jerome and Bernard of Clairvaux. And yet, his indebtedness to Bonaventure is greater than it is to the three authorities just named.

In connection with the question of Zerbolt's indebtedness to Bonaventure attention ought to be drawn to the fact that for some four centuries approximately one half of Zerbolt's *De Reformatione*, as well as three chapters from *De Ascensionibus* were included in most editions of Bonaventure's *opera omnia* as well as in many anthologies of his writings. The first time that these parts from *De Reformatione* and *De Ascensionibus*—known collectively as the *Fascicularius*—were attributed to Bonaventure was in an anthology of his works published in Strasbourg in 1495, and in 1868 A.-C. Peltier still included them in the *opera omnia* of the Seraphic Doctor which he edited. However, the editors of the Quaracchi edition of Bonaventure's *opera omnia* (1882-1902) did not include them. (Bonaventure, *Opera Omnia* [10 vols.; Quaracchi, 1882-1902]. See Vol. VIII, pp. CXII-CXIII for their reasons for not doing so.) It must be added that before the publication of the Quaracchi edition of Bonaventure's *opera omnia*, Bonaventure's authorship of the so-called *Fascicularius* had been questioned on a number of occasions, and in some editions of the *opera omnia* it was classified with the *spuria* or *dubia*. As early as 1806 J. H. Sbaralea, a Franciscan bibliographer, mentioned Zerbolt's name in connection with the *Fascicularius* (Rayez, "Gérard Zerbolt de Zutphen et Saint Bonaventure. Dépendances Littéraires," 329-332; Goossens, *Meditatie*, 69-70; and C. Fischer, "Apocryphes attribués à Saint Bonaventure," *DSp*, I, 1843-1856). However, when Geesink was writing his dissertation on Zerbolt in the 1870's he was not aware of the fact that there was some doubt concerning Bonaventure's authorship of the *Fascicularius*. In fact, he points to the *Fascicularius* found in the *opera omnia* of Bonaventura published in Rome in 1588-1596 and the corresponding passages in *De Reformatione* in support of his argument that Zerbolt's writings possess very little originality (Geesink, *Zerbolt*, 136-137). In addition to attributing the *Fascicularius* to Bonaventure, Geesink ascribed David of Augsburg's *De exterioris et interioris hominis compositione*, a major source for *De Reformatione* and *De Ascensionibus*, to him as well. Consequently, Geesink understood Zerbolt's indebtedness to Bonaventure to be paramount.

It is not terribly surprising that in 1495 the editor of an anthology of Bonaventure's writings was able to pass the *Fascicularius* off as an authentic work of the Seraphic Doctor. For in *De Reformatione* Zerbolt ends each of the six *fasciculi* on the passion of Christ with a *consideratio* from Bonaventure's *De Triplici Via* (Bonaventure, *De Triplici Via*, ch. 1, par. 2

The significance of *De Spiritu et Anima* lies primarily in the fact that it would appear to have provided Zerbolt with the plan for *De Ascensionibus* in much the same way that David of Augsburg's *De exterioris et interioris hominis compositione* supplied the plan for *De Reformatione*.[91]

What emerges from a ranking of Zerbolt's sources is that he owes his greatest debt to manuals for the spiritual life, which is not surprising in view of the fact that *De Reformatione* and *De Ascensionibus* are handbooks for the religious. Consequently, it is especially in the analysis of Zerbolt's spiritual theology that his considerable indebtedness to the older guidebooks for the religious life just named will become evident. It is, by contrast, difficult in most instances to pinpoint the origin of Zerbolt's dogmatic views. It can be said, nonetheless, that his opinions on questions of dogma must, in general terms at least, be labelled Augustinian-Thomistic, which then indicates their ultimate origin.

Finally, those works which constituted the most important sources for Radewijns' and Zerbolt's writings continued to dominate the reading lists of the Brethren of the Common Life throughout the fifteenth century and into the sixteenth.[92] Van Woerkum is of the opinion that this conservatism contributed to the decline in religious depth and fervour among the Devotionalists.[93]

[*Works*, I, 82-83]; cf. Rayez, "Gérard Zerbolt de Zutphen et Saint Bonaventure. Dépendances Littéraires," 343-347), and there are many other instances of a similar indebtedness (cf. Rayez, *op. cit.*, 323-356). It would appear, furthermore, that Zerbolt's indebtedness to Bonaventure was one of the main reasons why for some four centuries the *Fascicularius* continued to be regarded as a work of the famous Franciscan.

The *Fascicularius* consists of three separate sections. The first section, called *Fascicularius de exerciciis spiritualibus*, is made up of chs. 19-25 and 27-28 of *De Reformatione*. Chs. 19-25 are meditations on man's sinfulness, the four last things and God's goodness to man. Ch. 27 deals with the Last Supper and the eucharist, and ch. 28 contains instructions how to meditate on Christ's passion. The second part of the *Fascicularius*, the title of which is *Passio Christi breviter collecta ad modum fasciculorum*, consists of seven *fasciculi*. The first six are, in fact, the six *fasciculi* from *De Reformatione* devoted to the passion of Christ, and in that work they constitute chs. 29-34. The seventh *fasciculus* is made up of three chs. (39-41) from *De Ascensionibus: De Resurrectione, De Ascensione* and *De Missione Spiritus Sancti*. The third part of the *Fascicularius*, called *De pugna spirituali contra septem vitia capitalia* is made up of passages drawn from *De Reformatione*, chs. 42-58. In these chapters Zerbolt outlines how the believer must eradicate the vices and cultivate the opposite virtues.

[91] See below, pp. 241-242 and 264.

In most of the older printed editions of *De Ascensionibus*, and perhaps in some manuscripts as well, this work counts 71 chs. The 71st ch., which is identical to Bk. II, ch. 1, of David of Augsburg's *De exterioris et interioris hominis compositione*, cannot be found in the oldest manuscripts of *De Ascensionibus*, and does not properly belong to it. Geesink still assumed that this chapter from the work of David of Augsburg constitutes part of *De Ascensionibus* (Geesink, *Zerbolt*, 95 and C. Smits, "David van Augsburg en de Invloed van zijn *Profectus* op de Moderne Devotie," 197-198).

[92] Van Woerkum, "Het Libellus '*Omnes, inquit, artes*'," 261-268.

[93] *Ibid.*, 267-268.

Dissemination of De Reformatione and De Ascensionibus. The dissemination of *De Reformatione* and *De Ascensionibus* will be briefly indicated. Their impact is, of course, much more difficult to establish, and very little will be said concerning it. However, the investigation into the extent of the dissemination of Zerbolt's manuals for the spiritual life will give us some idea concerning their influence in the late middle ages and early modern period.

De Reformatione and *De Ascensionibus* were widely read in the fifteenth and sixteenth centuries, and the most obvious and convincing evidence for this is the number of manuscripts of *De Reformatione* and *De Ascensionibus* that have come down to us. Van Rooy counts a total of eighty-three manuscripts which contain *De Ascensionibus* in its entirety or partially, and this includes the translations.[94] The corresponding number for *De Reformatione* is thirty-seven.[95] Not only were Zerbolt's two major works copied many times, they were frequently printed as well, according to van Rooy, either in their entirety or in part: *De Ascensionibus* thirty-two times, and *De Reformatione* fourteen times.[96] These figures once again incorporate the translations. Of the thirty-two printed editions of *De Ascensionibus* named by van Rooy, nineteen date from the fifteenth and sixteenth centuries, which clearly illustrates the popularity of this work in the late medieval and early modern period. Furthermore, in the seventeenth century *De Ascensionibus* was included in the six last editions of the *Magna Bibliotheca Veterum Patrum et Antiquorum Scriptorum Ecclesiasticorum* collected by M. de la Bigne.[97] Of the fourteen printed editions of *De Reformatione* enumerated by van Rooy, five were published in the fifteenth and sixteenth centuries. Furthermore, like *De Ascensionibus*, *De Reformatione* was included in the six last editions of de la Bigne's *Magna Bibliotheca*.[98]

Since the publication of van Rooy's dissertation in 1936 more manuscripts of *De Reformatione* and *De Ascensionibus* have been brought to light, as well as two printed editions of *De Reformatione* and one of *De Ascensionibus* dating from before 1936. Furthermore, new editions of both works have been published since that date. A brief review of these, which does not claim to be exhaustive, will help to bring up-to-date the list of manuscripts and printed editions of *De Reformatione* and *De Ascensionibus* drawn up by van Rooy.

---

[94] Van Rooy, *Zerbolt*, 281-283.

[95] *Ibid.*, 283-285. Van Rooy mentions a number of manuscripts containing *De Ascensionibus* and *De Reformatione*, the existence of which he could not positively establish (van Rooy, *Zerbolt*, 350-356).

[96] Van Rooy, *Zerbolt*, 358-360.

[97] *Ibid.*, 359 and 376-379.

[98] *Ibid.*, 360 and 388-390.

At least twenty-five manuscripts containing *De Ascensionibus*, or part thereof, can be added to the catalogue of manuscripts compiled by van Rooy. Of these twenty-five, fourteen are in Latin, eight in Middle-Dutch, one in Middle-Low German and two in Middle-High German.[99]

[99] *Latin Mss.*

1) Liège, Seminary, Ms. 6 M 22. Provenance: monastery of the Crosier Fathers at Huy. Cf. P. van den Bosch, "De Bibliotheken van de Kruisherenkloosters in de Nederlanden voor 1550," in: *Contributions à l'Histoire des Bibliothèques et de la Lecture aux Pays-Bas avant 1600/Studies over het Boekenbezit en Boekengebruik in de Nederlanden voor 1600* (Archives et Bibliothèques de Belgique, Special Issue, No. 11; Brussels, 1974), 609.

2) Liège, University Library, Ms. 3258 (fol. 3r°—92r°). Provenance: monastery of the Crosier Fathers at Huy. Cf. van den Bosch, "De bibliotheken van de Kruisherenkloosters in de Nederlanden voor 1550," 609.

3) Liège, Seminary, Ms. 6 M 10. Provenance: monastery of the Crosier Fathers at Liège. Cf. van den Bosch, "De bibliotheken van de Kruisherenkloosters in de Nederlanden voor 1550," 616.

4) Düsseldorf, Landes- und Stadtbibliothek, Ms. B 129. Provenance: monastery of the Crosier Fathers at Marienfrede (near Emmerich). Cf. P. van den Bosch, *Studiën Over de Observantie der Kruisbroeders in de Vijftiende Eeuw* (Diest, 1968), 146.

5) Bristol, Library of All Saints' Church. Cf. N. R. Ker, *Medieval Manuscripts in British Libraries*, Vol. II: *Abbotsford-Keele* (Oxford, 1977), 185-186; R. Lovatt, "The Imitation of Christ in Late Medieval England," *Transactions of the Royal Historical Society*, 5th Series, XVIII (1968), 109.

6) Liège, University Library, Ms. 3258 (fol. 110r°—116r°) contains *Opus devotum circa Passione Domini*, attributed to Zerbolt. Provenance: monastery of the Crosier Fathers at Huy. Cf. van den Bosch, "De bibliotheken van de Kruisherenkloosters in de Nederlanden voor 1550," 609. We are dealing here, no doubt, with the meditations on the passions of Christ drawn either from *De Ascensionibus* or *De Reformatione*.

7) Charleville-Mézieres, Municipal Library, Ms. 148. Provenance: Charterhouse of Mont-Dieu (Ardennes). Cf. S. Collin-Roset, "Les Manuscrits de l'Ancienne Chartreuse du Mont Dieu (Ardennes)," *Bibliothèque de l'Ecole des Chartes*, CXXXII (1974), 30, 37, 50 and 58.

8) Bruges, Great Seminary (Section Mss.), Ms. not numbered. Cf. Gerard Zerbolt van Zutphen, *De spiritualibus ascensionibus/Van geestelijke opklimmingen*, ed. by Canon J. Mahieu (2d ed.; Bruges, 1941), XIV-XV.

9) Hannover, City Library (formerly Royal and Provincial Library), Ms. I 84². Cf. S. van der Woude, *Johannes Busch, Windesheimer Kloosterreformator en Kroniekschrijver* (Edam, 1947), 140.

10) The Hague, Royal Library, Ms. 135 J 3 (purchased April 19, 1972, at the auction of Dr. Helmut Tenner's library, Heidelberg).

11) Hamburg, Municipal Library, Ms. Theol. 12°, 2174.

12) Utrecht, University Library, Ms. 358, fol. 25v° -27v° and 29v° -31v° (excerpts).

13) Ms. van der Merckt (chs. 1-32). Purchased by bookdealer van der Merckt at Sotheby's public auction, London, December 16, 1970, lot number 20.

14) Ms. Alan G. Thomas, London. Purchased by bookdealer Alan G. Thomas, London, at Sotheby's public auction, London, July 10, 1972, lot number 60. *Middle-Dutch Mss.*

15) Liège, Seminary, Ms. 6 K 29. Provenance: monastery of the Crosier Fathers at Huy. Cf. van den Bosch, "De bibliotheken van de Kruisherenkloosters in de Nederlanden voor 1550," 606.

16) Haarlem, Municipal Library, Ms. 187 D 15. Cf. Kurt Ruh, *Bonaventura Deutsch* (Bern, 1956), 150.

17) Leiden, University Library, Ms. Ltk. 1341.

18) Münster, Paulinische Bibliothek, Ms. 509.

Shortly after van Rooy completed his dissertation on Zerbolt a Latin-Dutch edition of *De Ascensionibus* was published by Canon J. Mahieu.[100] In a study devoted to the libraries of the Crosier Fathers in the Low Countries, P. van den Bosch mentions two manuscripts containing the Latin version of *De Reformatione* not found in van Rooy's list of manuscripts, nor do we find in van Rooy's catalogue the manuscript copy of *De Reformatione* present in the University Library, Leiden.[101] To

---

19) Amsterdam, University Library, Ms. L G 5, fol. 20r°-23r° (excerpts).
20) Berlin, Staatsbibliothek Preussischer Kulturbesitz, Ms. germ. oct. 141, fol. 4v°-72r° (excerpts).
21) Brussels, Royal Library, Ms. IV 817, fragments of chs. 27, 30 and 31.
22) Leiden, University Library, Ms. Ltk. 317, fol. 182-191 (excerpt).
Middle-Low German Mss.
23) Wolfenbüttel, Duke August Library, Ms. Helmstedt 721, 2. Cf. W. Stammler "Studien zur Geschichte der Mystik in Norddeutschland," in: Kurt Ruh, ed., *Altdeutsche und Altniederländische Mystik* (Darmstadt, 1964), 427-428.
Middle-High German Mss.
24) Paris, National Library, Ms. allem. 125 (Suppl. franc. 3175), fol. 131r°-155r°. Title: *Von der uf stigung werdent hie etliche capittel beschrieben.* As the title indicates, we are dealing here with only part of *De Ascensionibus.* Cf. Kurt Ruh, "Altniederländische Mystik in Deutschsprachiger Überlieferung," in: *Dr. L. Reypens-Album,* ed. by A. Ampe (Studiën en Tekstuitgaven van *Ons Geestelijk Erf,* Vol. XVI; Antwerp, 1964), 376.
25) Innsbruck, University Library, Ms. 641, fol. 69r°-116r°. Provenance: monastery Engelberg in Schnals (Tirol). Cf. Ruh, "Altniederländische Mystik in Deutschsprachiger Überlieferung," 376.
   Subiaco, Biblioteca dell' Abbazia, Ms. 297, which contains a Latin edition of *De Ascensionibus,* is, most likely, the same ms. which van Rooy gives as Subiaco, Biblioteca dell' Abbazia, Ms. 290 (van Rooy, *Zerbolt,* 297, No. 31).

[100] Gerard Zerbolt van Zutphen, *De spiritualibus ascensionibus/Van geestelijke opklimmingen,* ed. by Canon J. Mahieu (2d ed.; Bruges, 1941).
In the introduction to this Latin-Dutch edition of *De Ascensionibus* Mahieu mentions a printed Latin edition of *De Ascensionibus,* bound with a printed Latin edition of *De Reformatione,* giving neither date, nor place, of publication. He found this volume, which he describes as a *post-incunabulum,* in the library of the Great Seminary, Bruges, Belgium (*ibid.,* XIII). In response to an inquiry regarding this volume, I was informed that it is no longer present in the library of the Great Seminary at Bruges.
[101] *Latin Mss.*
1) Liège, Seminary, Ms. 6 G 13. Provenance: monastery of the Crosier Fathers at Huy. Cf. van den Bosch, "De bibliotheken van de Kruisherenkloosters in de Nederlanden voor 1550," 609.
2) Liège, Seminary, Ms. 6 L 17. Provenance: monastery of the Crosier Fathers at Huy. Cf. van den Bosch, "De bibliotheken van de Kruisherenkloosters in de Nederlanden voor 1550," 609.
3) Leiden, University Library, Ms. d'Ablaing 38, fol. 147r°-178v°.
   Nijmegen, University Library, Ms. 60, which contains a Latin edition of *De Reformatione,* is, most likely, the same ms. which van Rooy gives as Nijmegen, University Library, Ms. 58 (van Rooy, *Zerbolt,* 329, No. 103).
For manuscripts containing Zerbolt's minor works, or parts thereof, not known to van Rooy see: van den Bosch, "De bibliotheken van de Kruisherenkloosters in de Nederlanden voor 1550," 609; van den Bosch, *Studiën Over de Observantie der Kruisbroeders in de Vijftiende Eeuw,* 146; J. Deschamps, "Middelnederlandse verta-

the early printed editions of *De Reformatione* named by van Rooy we must add that published by Josse Badius Ascensius in the early sixteenth century.[102] Furthermore, in 1951 S. van der Woude published a modern Dutch translation of this same work.[103] The extant manuscripts and early printed editions clearly indicate, then, that of Zerbolt's two manuals for the religious life *De Ascensionibus* was much more in demand than was *De Reformatione*. For the total number of extant manuscripts containing *De Ascensionibus*, or parts thereof, is one hundred and eight, while the corresponding number for *De Reformatione* is only forty. Furthermore, *De Ascensionibus* was printed a total of thirty-four times which contrasts sharply with *De Reformatione* which saw no more than a total of seventeen impressions.

De Reformatione and *De Ascensionibus* must be numbered, like the *Institutes* and *Conferences* of Cassian, the *Scala Paradisi* of Climacus, *De exterioris et interioris hominis compositione* of David of Augsburg, etc. with the standard works read by the Devotionalists;[104] and this is substantiated by the fact that more than one list of recommended readings drawn up for convents of Augustinian Canons Regular belonging to the Congregation of Windesheim names Zerbolt's two manuals for the spiritual life.[105] Furthermore, to his translation of the anonymous *Epistola de Vita et Passione Domini Nostri Jesu Christi*, which was widely read in Devotionalist circles, Johannes Busch added a postscript on meditation in which he gives a list of topics for meditation for every day of the week. In this connection he

---

lingen van *Super modo vivendi* (7e hoofdstuk) en *De libris teutonicalibus* van Gerard Zerbolt van Zutphen," *Handelingen van de Koninklijke Zuidnederlandse Maatschappij voor Taal- en Letterkunde en Geschiedenis*, XIV (1960-1961), 67-108 and XV (1961-1962), 175-220; and Rotterdam, Municipal Library, Ms. 14 C 6, which contains excerpts, in Middle-Dutch translation, from *Super Modo Vivendi*.

[102] *De reformatione virium animae, Domini Gerardi a Zutphania*. Venundatur Ioanni paruo et Iodoco Badio [= Josse Badius Ascensius]. Date: beginning of the sixteenth century. Cf. Ph. Renouard, *Bibliographie des Impressions et des Oeuvres de Josse Badius Ascensius Imprimeure et Humaniste, 1462-1535* (3 vols.; Paris, 1908), II, 470-471; and Rayez, "Gérard Zerbolt de Zutphen et Saint Bonaventure. Dépendances Littéraires," 330, footnote 27.

See footnote 100 above for another printed Latin edition of *De Reformatione* at one time in the library of the Great Seminary, Bruges, Belgium, but now no longer there.

[103] Gerard Zerbolt van Zutphen, *Over de Hervorming van de Krachten der Ziel*. Introduced and translated by S. van der Woude (Amsterdam, 1951).

It has been noted that since 1495 a large part of *De Reformatione* has often been published in the opera omnia of *Bonaventure*, as well as in anthologies of his works.

In up-dating the catalogue of mss. and printed editions of Zerbolt's works I received the assistance of a number of individuals and institutions, and I owe the greatest debt to J. A. A. M. Biemans of the University Library, Leiden; Claudine Lemaire of the Royal Library, Brussels; and Mrs. H. F. Peeters of the Royal Library, The Hague.

[104] Cf. van Woerkum, "Het Libellus '*Omnes, inquit, artes*'," 132.

[105] J. Mombaer, *Tabula Librorum Praecipue Legendorum*, ed. by Debongnie, *Jean Mombaer*, 323; and E. Persoons, "Het intellectuele leven in het klooster Bethlehem in de 15de eeuw," *Archief- en Bibliotheekwezen in België*, XLIII (1972), 59-60 and 57.

refers the readers to *De Ascensionibus* where these topics for meditation are discussed in detail.[106] It was the prominent place occupied by *De Reformatione* and *De Ascensionibus* on the Devotionalists' reading list which, most likely, explains why Zerbolt's biographers and a number of Devotionalist chroniclers paid special attention to Zerbolt's authorship of these two works.[107]

We have seen earlier that the extant manuscripts and early editions of Zerbolt's two manuals for the spiritual life indicate that *De Ascensionibus* was everywhere in greater demand than was *De Reformatione*. This was also the case among the Devotionalists, it would appear, for, apart from specific references to Zerbolt and his literary activities, there are more scattered references to *De Ascensionibus* in Devotionalist chronicles than there are to *De Reformatione*.[108] Furthermore, other Devotionalist writers also quoted more frequently from *De Ascensionibus* than from *De Reformatione*.[109] One cannot, therefore, agree with Goossens who asserts that,

---

[106] Busch, *Chronicon*, 243-244. Cf. Hedlund, ed., *Epistola de Vita et Passione Domini Nostri*, 57 and 156-157; van Rooy, *Zerbolt*, 308-309 and 334-335; Goossens, *Meditatie*, 168; and below pp. 266-268.

These meditations from *De Ascensionibus* were apparently sufficiently popular that they circulated independently, although in a somewhat altered form (cf. V. Becker, ed., "Eenige meditaties uit den Windesheimer kring," *De Katholiek*, LXXXV [1884], 29-47 and 101-116; van Rooy, *Zerbolt*, 380; and Goossens, *Meditatie*, 199).

[107] See footnote 45 above.

[108] Jacobus Traiecti alias de Voecht, *Narratio de Inchoatione Domus Clericorum in Zwollis*, met Akten en Bescheiden Betreffende dit Fraterhuis, ed. by M. Schoengen (Werken uitgegeven door het Historisch Genootschap te Utrecht, 3rd Series, No. 13; Amsterdam, 1908), 159-160; and Busch, *Chronicon*, 195-196. Cf. M. Dusch, ed., *De Veer Utersten. Das Cordiale de quatuor novissimus von Gerhard von Vliederhoven in mittelniederdeutscher Überlieferung* (Cologne-Vienna, 1975), 35*.

[109] See "Parvum et simplex exercitium ex consuetudine humilis patris domini Florencii et aliorum devotorum," ed. D. J. M. Wüstenhoff, *ANKG*, V (1895), 95 and 103-105; A. Deblaere, "Jean Mombaer," *DSp*, X, 1519; Debongnie, *Jean Mombaer*, 137, 141, 157, 165, 192, 218, 244 and 256; and Hyma, *The Christian Renaissance: A History of the "Devotio Moderna,"* 255. Cf. van Rooy, *Zerbolt*, 308-309 and 334-335.

Radewijns' *Omnes, inquit, artes* as we know it contains one long passage from *De Ascensionibus*. How this came about is not altogether clear, and various theories have been advanced to explain it. The explanation provided by Post is perhaps the most plausible of all. See Post, *The Modern Devotion: Confrontation with Reformation and Humanism*, 325-326 and van Woerkum, "Het Libellus 'Omnes, inquit, artes'," 130-33.

Many parallels can be found between Zerbolt's two manuals for the spiritual life and *De Imitatione Christi* of Thomas a Kempis (cf. P. Debongnie, "Les Thèmes de l'Imitation," *Revue d'Histoire Ecclésiastique*, XXXVI [1940], 312, footnote 1; and Gerard Zerbolt van Zutphen, *De spiritualibus ascensionibus/Van geestelijke opklimmingen*, ed. by Mahieu, XXVII), but it is difficult to establish any direct indebtedness. In fact, it is difficult to identify any of the sources of *De Imitatione Christi* because Thomas a Kempis has totally assimilated them, and he does not acknowledge his sources.

John Mombaer's direct indebtedness to Zerbolt would appear to be greater than that of any other Devotionalist writer. For his *Rosetum* Mombaer borrowed from the works of Zerbolt, and from *De Ascensionibus* in particular, as well as from Radewijns' *Tractatulus Devotus*. The indebtedness can be established with respect to both structure and content (see references given above in this same footnote).

although *De Ascensionibus* was generally more popular than *De Reformatione*, the Devotionalists preferred the latter work to the former.[110]

Although one must be careful in drawing conclusions from the chance survival of manuscripts, the provenance of those manuscripts of *De Reformatione* and *De Ascensionibus* which have survived largely confirms what had previously been established about the relationship of the Modern Devotion to other religious orders. The manuscripts of which the provenance is known reveal, not surprisingly, that *De Reformatione* and *De Ascensionibus* were most widely read by the Devotionalists, followed by the Crosier Fathers, the Benedictines and the Carthusians.[111] The reasons why Zerbolt's two manuals for the spiritual life were popular with the Crosier Fathers, the Benedictines and the Carthusians vary somewhat. One of Zerbolt's brothers, Helmicus Amoris, was prior-general of the Crosier Fathers from 1415 to 1433, and a second brother, Johannes Amoris, was also a member of this same order. It would appear that Helmicus and Johannes contributed to an early dissemination of their brother's writings among the Crosier Fathers. For the oldest extant manuscripts of *De Reformatione* and *De Ascensionibus*, both of them copied in the year 1400, or thereabouts, originally belonged to the Crosier Fathers at Huy and Cologne respectively.[112] The fact that Zerbolt's works were well represented in the libraries of the Carthusians would appear to have been the result of a special relationship between the Brethren of the Common Life and the Carthusians which had begun with Grote. Following his 'conversion', Grote lived for a number of years with the Carthusians at Monnikhuizen where he was imbued with their spirit. Consequently, the Brethren movement, of which Grote was the spiritual father, modelled its spirituality and way of life after that of the Carthusians to a considerable degree.[113] It is, therefore, not surprising that *De*

---

[110] Goossens, *Meditatie*, 66-67.

[111] The discussion regarding the provenance of the manuscripts containing *De Reformatione* and *De Ascensionibus* is based on van Rooy, *Zerbolt*, 287-336; van den Bosch, "De bibliotheken van de Kruisherenkloosters in de Nederlanden voor 1550," 563-636; van den Bosch, *Studiën Over de Observantie der Kruisbroeders in de Vijftiende Eeuw*, throughout; and Ruh, "Altniederländische Mystik in Deutschsprachiger Überlieferung," 357-382.

[112] Van den Bosch, *Studiën Over de Observantie der Kruisbroeders in de Vijftiende Eeuw*, 23, 71, 73-75, 100, 107, 155-160, and van Rooy, *Zerbolt*, 277, 292 and 335.

In the 15th century the Crosier Fathers in Cologne had a copy of Th. a Kempis' *Dialogus noviciorum*, which includes biographical sketches of the first Devotionalists, including Zerbolt. To the biography of Zerbolt a Crosier Father at Cologne added the following notice: *Frater fuit iste M. Gerardus junior Venerabilis Patris nostri Helmici Amoris, prior Hoyensis* (van den Bosch, *Studiën Over de Observantie der Kruisbroeders in de Vijftiende Eeuw*, 73-74).

[113] Van den Bosch, *Studiën Over de Observantie der Kruisbroeders in de Vijftiende Eeuw*, 159 and W. Lourdaux, "Karthuizers-Moderne Devoten. Een probleem van afhankelijkheid," *OGE*, XXXVII (1963), 416 and article throughout.

Reformatione and *De Ascensionibus*, which are so representative of Devotionalist spirituality, should have been in vogue among the Carthusians. The dissemination of *De Reformatione* and *De Ascensionibus* among the Benedictines must be attributed, it would appear, to the important role played by the Augustinian Canons Regular of Windesheim in the reformation of the Benedictine monasteries and convents of north-western Europe, and particularly to the part they played in the formation and reformation of the Benedictine Congregation of Bursfeld.[114] Furthermore, wherever possible the Brethren of the Common Life took it upon themselves to provide Latin-school students with room and board in so-called *bursae*. In addition to providing these students with room and board, the Brethren of the Common Life tried to instil in them the desire to adopt the religious life, and in many cases succeeded in doing so. Not only did some of these students join the Brethren of the Common Life, but many more entered the monasteries of the Canons Regular belonging to the Congregations of Windesheim, Sion and Venlo.[115] Other beneficiaries in this connection were the monasteries of the Crosier Fathers and the Carthusians, as well as the monasteries of the Benedictines and the Cistercians which had been reformed through the efforts of the Canons Regular of Windesheim.[116] The Brethren deliberately directed the students in their *bursae* to the monasteries of these particular orders, and it was also through them, it would appear, that the works of Zerbolt found their way to the libraries of the Crosier Fathers, Carthusians and Benedictines in fairly large numbers.

Geographically speaking the distribution of *De Reformatione* and *De Ascensionibus* was, before the last quarter of the fifteenth century at least, pretty well restricted to the Low Countries, Westphalia, the northern Rhineland and central Saxony. It was here, of course, that the Brethren and Sister Houses, as well as the Congregation of Augustinian Canons and Canonesses Regular of Windesheim, were concentrated.[117] The diffusion of *De Reformatione* and *De Ascensionibus* within the other orders discussed in the previous paragraph was largely restricted to the same geographical areas,[118] which indicates that the dissemination of Zerbolt's

---

[114] Post, *Kerkgeschiedenis*, II, 116-144; *idem, The Modern Devotion: Confrontation with Reformation and Humanism*, 515-520; and Acquoy, *Windesheim*, II, 346-349.

[115] Those of Sion and Venlo were offshoots from that of Windesheim. See Post, *Kerkgeschiedenis*, II, 97-114.

[116] Van den Bosch, *Studiën Over de Observantie der Kruisbroeders in de Vijftiende Eeuw*, 153-154. Cf. Post, *Kerkgeschiedenis*, II, 116-149, and Thomas a Kempis, *The Chronicle of the Canons Regular of Mount St. Agnes*, trans. by J. P. Arthur (London, 1906), 191-192.

[117] See two maps at the end of Post, *The Modern Devotion: Confrontation with Reformation and Humanism*.

[118] See references given in footnote 111 above.

writings was clearly tied to the fortunes of the Modern Devotion. The concentration of Zerbolt's works in the Low Countries, Westphalia, the northern Rhineland and central Saxony agrees pretty much with what Kurt Ruh has found concerning the spiritual literature read in Germany and the Low Countries in the fifteenth century. Whatever found acceptance in the Low Countries, he writes, found acceptance as well in lower Germany and middle Franconia. The spiritual literature written in the last mentioned areas in the fifteenth century, he continues, was influenced quite considerably by spiritual literature from the Low Countries, and to a much lesser degree by the writings of Tauler and Suso, for example. The two Devotionalist writings from the Low Countries which would seem to have had the greatest impact on the spiritual literature written in lower Germany and middle Franconia in the fifteenth century were *De Ascensionibus* and the anonymous *Epistola de Vita et Passione Domini Nostri Jesu Christi*, for Ruh numbers them with the most widely read spiritual works in those parts of Germany at that time.[119] It would appear, then, that with respect to religious literature the Modern Devotion set the tone to a considerable degree in those areas of north-western Europe in which the movement was most prominent. Why it was able to do so has been indicated. Consequently it was possible for the Modern Devotion to promote the works of its most accomplished writers of whom Zerbolt was one.

Not only was Zerbolt read by non-Devotionalists, but they also quoted from *De Reformatione* and *De Ascensionibus* in sermons and tracts. Among these were Jan Brugman (c. 1400-1473), the famous late-medieval Franciscan preacher and friend of the Brethren of the Common Life in Deventer;[120] Hendrik Herp (d. 1477), a Brother of the Common Life before he joined the First Order of St. Francis in 1450;[121] Jacobus Philippi (d.c. 1510), pastor of St. Peter's in Basle whose brother was rector of the Brethren of the Common Life at Zwolle from 1487 to 1490;[122] and Johann Geiler of Keisersberg (1445-1510), 'the German Savonarola'.[123]

---

[119] K. Ruh, "Altniederländische Mystik in Deutschsprachiger Überlieferung," 358, 361 and 375; and *idem, Bonaventura Deutsch,* 71.

[120] F. A. H. van den Hombergh, *Leven en Werk van Jan Brugman O.F. M. (c. 1400-1473), met een Uitgave van Twee van Zijn Tractaten* (Groningen, 1967), 91, footnote 5, 121-122 and cf. 115.

[121] Hendrik Herp, O.F.M., *Spiegel der Volkomenheit,* ed. by Lucidius Verschueren (2 vols.; Antwerp, 1931), I, 13-18 and 152.

[122] M. Viller, "Le *Praecordiale Sacerdotum* de Jacques Philippi," *RAM,* XI (1930), 375-395; Post, *The Modern Devotion: Confrontation with Reformation and Humanism,* 516; Jacobus de Voecht, *Narratio,* CXXVII, CXXX, CXLV, 171 and 469; and van Woerkum, "Het Libellus '*Omnes, inquit, artes*'," 132-133.

[123] See Johann Geiler, *Navicula sive speculum fatuorum,* XXIII y-z (E. J. Dempsey Douglass, *Justification in Late Medieval Preaching. A Study of John Geiler of Keisersberg* [Studies in Medieval and Reformation Thought, Vol. I; Leiden, 1966], 106-107) and *De Reformatione,* 237H-238B.

Contrary to Dom J. Huyben's belief, Johannes von Kastl does not appear to have borrowed from Zerbolt's writings for some of his own tracts.[124]

Towards the end of the fifteenth century Devotionalist writings, including *De Reformatione* and *De Ascensionibus*, found their way to Paris where they became popular among those who were interested in the inner life and in the spiritual reformation of the church.[125] This development would appear to have been at least partly due to the influence of Jan Standonck (d. 1504), rector of the Collège Montaigu. As a student he had lived with the Brethren of the Common Life at Gouda, was imbued with the spirit of the Modern Devotion, and made every attempt to further the spirit of the Modern Devotion in Paris and its surroundings.[126] The expansion of the Brethren of the Common Life and the Augustinian Canons Regular of Windesheim into southern Germany and Switzerland in the last quarter of the fifteenth century may perhaps have made itself felt in Paris as well.[127] By the 1490's there was such a demand for Zerbolt's works in Paris that during the last decade of the fifteenth century *De Ascensionibus* was printed three times in that city, and *De Reformatione* once, and perhaps even twice.[128] Furthermore, due largely to the efforts and influence of Standonck, Augustinian Canons Regular from Windesheim were invited to France in 1496 to reform a number of monasteries of the Augustinian Canons Regular in that country.[129] The

---

[124] J. Huijben, "Le *De Adhaerendo Deo*," *La Vie Spirituelle*, VII (1922), Supplément, 89-93; *idem*, "De verspreiding der Nederlandse spiritualiteit in het buitenland in de XIVe en XVe eeuw," *OGE*, IV (1930), 180; and J. Sudbrack, *Die Geistliche Theologie des Johannes von Kastl* (2 vols.; Münster, 1967), I, 159-161.

[125] A. Renaudet, *Préréforme et Humanisme à Paris Pendant les Premieres Guerres d'Italie (1494-1517)* (2d ed.; Paris, 1953), 111-114, 118-121 and 158-159; and Richard, *The Spirituality of John Calvin*, 49. It must be pointed out that *De Imitatione Christi*, frequently attributed to Gerson, was well known in France before the end of the 15th century.

[126] See Hyma, *The Christian Renaissance: A History of the "Devotio Moderna,"* 236-250.

[127] Post, *The Modern Devotion: Confrontation with Reformation and Humanism*, 440-448 and 510-511. Cf. B. M. von Scarpatetti, *Die Kirche und das Augustiner-Chorherrenstift St. Leonhard in Basel (11./12. Jh. -1525). Ein Beitrag zur Geschichte der Stadt Basel und der späten Devotio Moderna* (Basler Beiträge zur Geschichtswissenschaft, Vol. 131; Basel-Stuttgart, 1974), 193-348.

[128] Van Rooy, *Zerbolt*, 358 and 360. See above, footnote 102, where the particulars concerning a printed edition of *De Reformatione* published by Josse Badius, but not mentioned by van Rooy, are given. Renaudet (*Préréforme et Humanisme à Paris Pendant les Premieres Guerres d'Italie [1494-1517]*, 112) writes that *De Reformatione* was published twice in Paris in the year 1493, but van Rooy has found no evidence of this. Claudia Salley repeats what Renaudet wrote in this respect: that *De Reformatione* was printed twice at Paris in 1493 (C. Salley, "The Ideals of the Devotio Moderna as Reflected in the Life and Writings of Jacques Lefèvre d'Etaples," [unpublished Ph. D. Dissertation, University of Michigan, 1953], 53).

[129] Post, *The Modern Devotion: Confrontation with Reformation and Humanism*, 511, 543 and 632-635; *idem*, *De Moderne Devotie*, 121; and Hyma, *The Christian Renaissance: A History of the "Devotio Moderna,"* 250-259.

presence of these Devotionalists in France would appear to have further
stimulated the demand for Zerbolt's manuals for the spiritual life in Paris
and its environs.

At about this same time Garcia Ximenes de Cisneros, abbot of Montserrat near Barcelona, visited Paris and carried back to Montserrat with
him a number of spiritual writings, including *De Ascensionibus* by Gerard
Zerbolt. He himself had *De Ascensionibus* printed at Montserrat,[130] and he
also copied many chapters from this work into his own *Exercitatorio de la
Vida Spiritual.*[131] The Devotionalist influences found in Ignatius of
Loyola's *Spiritual Exercises*, which, it ought to be pointed out, are not as
great as Hyma believes them to be,[132] were probably for the most part
transmitted by Ximenes' *Exercitatorio*, one of the first spiritual tracts read
by Loyola.[133]

It would appear that other leading personalities of the Reformation era
read *De Reformatione* and *De Ascensionibus*. Jacques Lefèvre d' Etaples was
sympathetic towards Standonck's efforts to reform the religion and
morals of the Parisians, and he himself visited the Brethren in Cologne.
John Calvin spent four years at the Collège Montaigu where spiritual
writings like those of Zerbolt were standard fare.[134] However, that
Lefèvre and Calvin were influenced by the views of Zerbolt, and those of
the Devotionalists in general, to the extent that Hyma believes to have
been the case,[135] has not been sufficiently substantiated. Lastly, in his
lectures on St. Paul's letter to the Romans Luther makes a reference to
De Ascensionibus, although he mistakenly attributes it to Grote.[136] That
Luther should have been familiar with *De Ascensionibus* is, of course, not
surprising, for it is fairly certain that he lived for a short span with the
Brethren of the Common Life at Magdeburg.[137] All the evidence suggests, then, that the impact of *De Reformatione* and *De Ascensionibus* in the

---

[130] For this edition see van Rooy, *Zerbolt*, 371-372.

[131] M. Alamo, "Cisneros (Garcia de)," *DSp*, II, 910-917; Hyma, *The Christian
Renaissance: A History of the "Devotio Moderna,"* 267-268, idem, *Renaissance to Reformation: A
Critical Review of the Spiritual and Temporal Influence on Medieval Europe*, 362-363.

[132] Hyma, *The Christian Renaissance: A History of the "Devotio Moderna,"* 268-275; and
idem, *Renaissance to Reformation: A Critical Review of the Spiritual and Temporal Influence on
Medieval Europe*, 128-129, 371 and 365-368.

[133] Post, *The Modern Devotion: Confrontation with Reformation and Humanism*, 548-549; G.
Cusson, "Les 'Exercices Spirituels'," *DSp*, VII, 1309-1310 and M. Alamo. "Cisneros
(Garcia de)," *DSp*, II, 917-919.

One aspect of the question about the influence of the Devotionalists on Ignatius Loyola
is the extent to which Loyola adopted the system of meditation developed by the later
Devotionalists. See below, p. 278, footnote 223.

[134] Hyma, *The Christian Renaissance: A History of the "Devotio Moderna,"* 277-284.

[135] *Ibid.*, 236-349.

[136] *Ibid.*, 309-311.

[137] Post, *The Modern Devotion: Confrontation with Reformation and Humanism*, 628-630.

fifteenth and sixteenth centuries was far from negligible, although it would be an exaggeration if one were to assert that Zerbolt's two manuals for the spiritual life significantly influenced religious developments in the century and a half following his death.

iv. *Zerbolt's Theological Thought*

We begin the examination of Zerbolt's thought with an inquiry into his dogmatic theology. For dogma is commonly regarded as the foundation of spirituality, and the truths of the faith are considered to be the basis of the interior life. The inquiry into Zerbolt's dogmatic views, which begins with an examination of his doctrine of God, will follow fairly conventional lines. The investigation into Zerbolt's spiritual theology does not, by contrast, follow any conventional pattern, and the reason for this is twofold. In the first place, no well-defined and generally accepted pattern for the study of spiritual theology exists. Secondly, in our analysis of Zerbolt's spiritual theology it will be necessary to follow his lead if we are to arrive at an accurate picture of this important part of his religious thought.

CHAPTER ONE

THE DOCTRINE OF GOD[1]

In keeping with his role as spiritual adviser and spiritual theologian, Zerbolt's interest in God is determined by the needs of the spiritual life in general, and by the exigencies of spiritual meditation in particular. He writes that, although the Scriptures and the universe speak of God and instruct man regarding him, not everything found in them is equally suitable for meditation.[2] The purpose of meditation, according to Zerbolt, is to instil in the believer fear of God on the one hand, and love for him on the other. Quoting Gregory the Great, he explains that constant fear and reverence tempered with hope and love is the most salutary, and even indispensable, state for the believer to be in if he wants to ascend in the spiritual life.[3] Fear will prevent the believer from becoming complacent and negligent with respect to his spiritual condition, while hope and love will ban despair. For that reason Zerbolt advocates that in the Scriptures and in creation one must concentrate one's attention exclusively on those things which will most effectively instil either fear of God or love for him, explaining that not all do this equally well and that not all are therefore equally suitable for spiritual meditation.[4]

---

[1] Zerbolt's views regarding God are for the most part dispersed throughout his two major works. However, both works contain a chapter in which Zerbolt describes the blessings bestowed by God on man: *De Reformatione*, ch. 25 (p. 245C-G) and *De Ascensionibus*, ch. 25 (p. 267D-H). The discussion of these blessings provides Zerbolt with an opportunity to comment on a number of issues like God's providential governance of creation, his power and wisdom. In *De Reformatione* ch. 25 constitutes part of a larger section dealing with the reformation of the memory (see below p. 250); and in *De Ascensionibus* ch. 25 constitutes part of the section dealing with the development of *compunctio amoris* (see below, pp. 266-272).

[2] *Ref.*, 243D: Scire etiam debes, quod quamvis omnia quae in divina scriptura reperiuntur, imo coelum et terra, et omnia quae in eius sunt, de Deo loquantur et instruant, non tamen omnia aeque conveniunt ad utiliter meditandum. Sed ea debes potius ad meditandum assumere, unde amplius timore concuteris, vel accenderis ad amorem. *Asc.*, 268G: Ad hoc enim praecipue Christus carnem assumpsit, ut qui Deum spiritualiter intelligere non potuimus, per Christum verbum caro factum ascenderemus ad notitiam et amorem spiritualem. Cf. *Asc.*, 269D-F.

[3] *Asc.*, 271G: Ait enim beatus Gregorius: Nihil enim nobis securius quam sub spe semper timere; *ibid.*, 285F: Quamvis, inquit [Gregorius], securitati timor semper longe videatur abesse, nobis tamen nihil est securius, quam sub spe semper timere,...

[4] See footnote 2 above, and cf. Goossens, *Meditatie*, 181.

i. *Knowability of God*

Since, in Zerbolt's view, heaven and earth, and all that is in them, speak of God and instruct man regarding him,[5] it follows that Zerbolt accepts the possibility and validity of extra-Scriptural knowledge about God. This brings us to the question how, in his opinion, man arrives at an extra-Scriptural knowledge of God from an observation of nature.[6] For Zerbolt's answer to this question we have to go to one of his 'minor' writings, namely to *Scriptum Pro Quodam*. Here he writes that there are two kinds of knowledge: knowledge which does not surpass human understanding and can be grasped by the natural, unaided light of the intellect; and knowledge which does lie beyond the grasp of the human intellect and cannot be understood by the natural light of reason. To this second type of knowledge belong the articles of faith.[7] Clearly a Thomist epistemologically speaking, it follows that in Zerbolt's opinion man can learn about God and his attributes from an observation of nature by means of the natural light of his own intellect unassisted by divine illumination.[8]

---

[5] Christ is, according to Zerbolt, the third avenue to the knowledge of God, which will be discussed when the purpose of the incarnation is examined.

[6] According to Augustine and his 'school' man can abstract the existence of God and his attributes from an observation of the universe only with the aid of divine illumination. Aquinas, on the other hand, held that man can do this by means of the natural light of the intellect unassisted by divine illumination. See: C. C. J. Webb, *Studies in the History of Natural Theology* (Oxford, 1915), 84-136 and 233-291; F. Copleston, *A History of Philosophy* (8 vols.; Garden City, N.Y.: Image Books, 1962-1967), Vol. II, Pt. I, 66-88 and 269-279, and Vol. II, Pt. II, 30-42, 55-65 and 108-117; E. Gilson, *History of Christian Philosophy in the Middle Ages* (New York, 1955), 75-77, 334, 366-372 and 375-379; D. Knowles, *The Evolution of Medieval Thought* (New York: Vintage Books, 1964), 34-43, 45-46 and 261-262; A. Richardson, ed., *A Dictionary of Christian Theology* (London, 1969), 25-27 ("Augustinianism"), 138-142 ("God"), 226 ("Natural Theology; Revealed Theology") and 336-339 ("Thomism"); E. Simons, "God (Knowability of God)," *SM*, II, 391-392; B. M. Bonansea, "God (Existence of God in Philosophy)," *NCE*, VI, 551; R. J. Buschmiller, "God (Existence of God in Theology)," *NCE*, VI, 553-554; and G. Smith, "Theology, Natural," *NCE*, XIV, 61-62.

[7] *Scriptum Pro Quodam*, 231: Est enim secundum doctores duplex doctrina: una, que facultatem mentis humane non transcendit et hec docetur per raciones demonstrativas et principia naturaliter cognita. Quare ut quis sit huis doctrine doctor ydoneus, necesse est, ut habeat scienciam demonstrandi. Alia est doctrina, que excedit facultatem humanam et que non potest per principia naturalia demonstrari, sicut articuli (232) fidei ... *Asc.*, 267E: ..., et magnam claritatem luminis naturalis dedit. Cf. *Super Modo Vivendi*, 38.

[8] This assessment of Zerbolt's epistemological views agrees with van Rooy's brief observation that Zerbolt's epistemology was Aristotelian-Thomistic. From Zerbolt's works it becomes clear, van Rooy adds, that he based the development and perfection of the intellect on sensory experience and that he did not believe this to be possible apart from sensory experience (van Rooy, *Zerbolt*, 275-276). Unfortunately van Rooy does not support his last statements with any particular passage or excerpt from Zerbolt's works. For although Zerbolt was undoubtedly of the opinion that sensory experience is the source of natural knowledge, it does not appear that he asserts this in so many words anywhere.

While Zerbolt believes that the entire Scriptures and everything in the material universe speak of God, they do not, in his opinion, reveal the same things regarding him. He holds the Scriptures and the universe to be complementary instruments of revelation. Zerbolt's understanding of God is dominated by two themes: God the good and loving creator and sustainer of the universe, and God the judge of fallen man whose wrath is tempered with mercy. The former can be learned from creation as well as from the Scriptures, but the latter from the Scriptures only. Zerbolt claims, in fact, that the total contents of the Scriptures illustrate, on the one hand, God's justice and wrath *vis-à-vis* fallen man and, on the other hand, his love and mercy.[9] Contemplation of the former leads to fear of God, while reflection on the latter results in love for him, and without a salutary amalgam of fear and love there can be no spiritual progress and redemption. For that reason Zerbolt can write that all of the Scriptures, because they elucidate God's justice and mercy, are concerned with man's redemption and salvation,[10] which is reminiscent of Bonaventure's statement that the Scriptures are "mainly concerned with the work of redemption."[11]

Having looked at the means available to man by which he may arrive at a knowledge of God, Zerbolt's views regarding God's creative and providential work, as well as his understanding of God's attributes and attitude towards fallen man, remain to be analyzed.

ii. *God's Work of Creation*

That God is the creator of all things constitutes the subject-matter of the opening chapter of the Bible, and it is a presupposition which underlies all of Christian thought as it does Zerbolt's.[12] However, the Scriptures do little more than to assert that God made heaven and earth. Consequently, from a relatively early date onwards Christian thinkers looked to philosophy to provide them with a more extensive and profound

---

[9] *Asc.*, 285F: Ad hos duos ascensus et descensus, omnia quae in scripturis sunt, referuntur, secundum Augustinum: ut videlicet misericordiam ames, timeas potestatem. Unde Propheta sanctus in divina locutione, haec duo se narrat solummodo audivisse: Semel, inquit, locutus est Deus duo haec audivi, quia tibi Domine est misericordia, et tu reddis unicuique iuxta opera sua; propter haec duo, Prophetae, propter haec duo omnes sunt scripturae. Cf. Mulder, ed., *Gerardi Magni Epistolae*, No. 56 (p. 213).

[10] *Asc.*, 269F-G: Circa opus nostrae redemptionis versatur materia totius divinae scripturae, et omnia in Scriptura ad ipsum referuntur.

[11] Bonaventure, *Breviloquium*, Pt. II, ch. 5 (*Works*, II, 81).

[12] Cf. Richardson, ed., *Dictionary*, 78 ("Creation"); and D. J. Ehr, "Creation (Theology of)," *NCE*, IV, 419-420.

Asc., 267G-H: Ecce propter me totum mundum creavit,...ut potes videre in rerum creatione. *Ref.*, 245E: ...; propter te solum creasset coelum et terram. Et hoc docet nos Chrysostomus.

knowledge of God's creative activity than could be derived from the Scriptures. It is not surprising, then, that Zerbolt's understanding of God's creative work owes at least as much to philosophical thought as it does to the Bible, and it is to the philosophical aspect of Zerbolt's doctrine of creation that we now turn our attention.

Zerbolt describes God variously as the *"principium omnium"* or as the *"prima causa omnium,"*[13] and these are concepts which he borrowed from scholastic thought. Furthermore, it is fairly certain that he employs these phrases synonymously, although it is possible that when he calls God *principium omnium* he is thinking of God as the cause of everything in a general and undifferentiated sense: i.e., without distinction as to first or exemplary cause.[14] The concept *prima causa omnium* is not explained any further by Zerbolt. Nonetheless, the very fact that he speaks of God in such terms suggests that he accepted the validity of the Aristotelian-Thomistic theory of causality, and of the philosophical argument advanced by Augustine and Aquinas, to name but a few, that God is the first, and efficient, cause of all things.[15] Hence, it may be concluded as well that Zerbolt was not a nominalist, at least not with respect to this particular question. For the nominalists rejected the idea that it can be proven philosophically that there is a first cause, namely God, responsible for all sensible, finite things.[16]

Not only is God the first, or efficient, cause of all things, Zerbolt writes, but he is also their exemplary cause.[17] The doctrine of exemplary causality is one which had already had a long history. It began with Plato, given a Christian garb by Augustine, and was accepted by Aquinas, albeit with certain Aristotelian modifications. Briefly, the proponents of the doctrine of divine exemplary causality held that God created everything in accordance with eternal models, ideas or exemplars. These divine exemplars were thought to be models for the various species of concrete being, rather than models for concrete particulars. The divine exemplars were, in other words, held to be univer-

---

[13] *Asc.*, 281H, and see footnote 17 below.

[14] See J. Splett, "Principle," *SM*, V, 101-102; W. H. Kane, "Principle," *NCE*, XI, 787; and J. H. Hoffmeister, *Wörterbuch der philosophischen Begriffe* (2d ed.; Hamburg, 1955), 486-487.

[15] Cf. Copleston, *A History of Philosophy*, Vol. I, Pt. I, 195-196, 203-205 and 215-218, Vol. I, Pt. II, 31 and 48-61, Vol. II, Pt. I, 84-87 and 281-283, and Vol. II, Pt. II, 55-65; Bonaventure, *Breviloquium*, Pt. II, ch. 1 and ch. 5 (*Works*, II, 69-71 and 81); T. C. O'Brien, "Causality, Divine," *NCE*, III, 348-349; G. F. Kreyche, "Causality," *NCE*, III, 342-343; M. R. E. Masterman, "Cause, First," *NCE*, III, 352; and Richardson, ed., *Dictionary*, 77-79 ("Creation").

[16] Copleston, *A History of Philosophy*, Vol. III, Pt. I, 104 and 151-156.

[17] *Asc.*, 262C-D: Sic Deus prima causa omnium, non nisi ad essentiale omnium rerum exemplar et ideas res ipsas in congrua dispositione et forma produxit in esse.

sals. Influenced by Plato, Augustine believed the divine exemplars to be objective, subsistent essences of the many classes of concrete being, and consequently he has been labelled an extreme realist. Also Platonic was Augustine's view that man can abstract the existence of universals from an observation of concrete particulars only with the aid of divine illumination. Aquinas, by contrast, did not regard the divine ideas as objectively existing essences, but as objects of divine knowledge: the divine ideas constitute the knowledge God has of that part of his own essence which is imitable in created things external to himself. According to Aquinas, then, essences or universals are not found in God as divine ideas or exemplars; but with Aristotle he argued that essences can be found only in concrete particulars from which man abstracts them naturally, without the aid of divine illumination, and so arrives at a concept of universal essences.[18] For Aquinas, then, universals have an objective existence only *in re* and not *ante rem*, on account of which he has been called a moderate realist. William of Occam rejected the doctrine of divine exemplary causality, and he did so for he felt that it restricts God's creative activity and so destroys his free will. Repudiating the theory of divine ideas or exemplars, he also denied the objective existence of universals *in re* as well as *ante rem*. He held that such universals as man abstracts from particulars are purely mental constructions.[19]

Consequently, when Zerbolt writes that God, the first cause of all things, made everything, or disposed and formed all things, in accordance with the essential example and idea of all things,[20] he was clearly employing, in agreement with virtually all of his predecessors with the important exception of Occam, very traditional philosophical language to describe God's creative activity.[21] It is true that Zerbolt does not say in so many words that the examples and ideas of all things reside in the divine mind, but that is undoubtedly how he understood it. Furthermore, Zerbolt does not indicate whether he regarded the divine ideas, in accordance with which God created all things, as objectively subsistent essences

---

[18] See Copleston, *A History of Philosophy*, Vol. I, Pt. I, 190-191 and 195-196, Vol. I, Pt. II, 35-38, 43-44 and 48-50, and Vol. II, Pt. I, 75 and 87-88; Gilson, *History of Christian Philosophy in the Middle Ages*, 70-74; T. J. Kondoleon, "Exemplarism," *NCE*, V, 713-714; B. J. F. Peiper, "Idea," *NCE*, VII, 338-339; J. B. Lotz, "Essence," *SM*, II, 248; J. Splett, "Idea," *SM*, III, 85; A. Keller, "Universals," *SM*, VI, 325-326; F. D. Wilhelmsen, "Realism," *NCE*, XII, 110-111; E. A. Synan, "Universals," *NCE*, XIV, 452-454; M. Corvez, "Essence," *NCE*, V, 546; and A. D. Woozley, "Universals," in: *The Encyclopedia of Philosophy*, ed. by Paul Edwards (New York and London, 1967), VIII, 194-198.

[19] Copleston, *A History of Philosophy*, Vol. III, Pt. I, 61-63 and 100-103; and Knowles, *The Evolution of Medieval Thought*, 323-324.

[20] See footnote 17 above.

[21] Cf. Gilson, *History of Christian Philosophy in the Middle Ages*, 71-72.

ante rem,[22] but presumably he did not. For we have seen that his epistemology was Aristotelian-Thomistic, and it does not combine well with the ultra-realistic metaphysics of Plato and Augustine. Zerbolt's epistemological views indicate that he was a moderate realist with respect to the question of universals. The divine ideas which served God as models when he created the world have a real, objective existence only *in re*. However, it would not appear that Zerbolt was greatly interested in the perennial debate regarding the status of universals. Writing some years later Thomas a Kempis criticized in *De Imitatione Christi* the ongoing controversy regarding universals, genera and species.[23] Nonetheless, from his reading of scholastic writers Zerbolt was undoubtedly familiar with the debate regarding the status of universals and almost certainly had some definite opinions on the matter along the lines indicated.

Zerbolt's acceptance of the theory of divine exemplary causality contributes considerably to the intelligibility of his argument that the entire creation speaks of, and instructs man regarding, God.[24] God is the first cause of the universe and consequently it proclaims his existence. However, God is also the exemplary cause of creation, on account of which it cannot but tell us something about the divine nature and essence as well. For God made everything in accordance with the divine ideas and there must, therefore, be some positive resemblance between the creator and his creatures. It would appear, then, that, in order to obtain a knowledge and understanding of God, Zerbolt favours the way of analogy as employed by Bonaventure and Aquinas, and that he rejects the way of negation typical of the pseudo-Dionysius and Nicholas of Cusa, for example.[25] Finally, in view of his epistemology it is clear that Zerbolt was of the opinion that man can naturally arrive at some insight into God's nature and essence from an observation of created being.

Before we turn to Zerbolt's understanding of divine providence it is necessary to look briefly at his use of the concept *rationes seminales*. Faced with an exegetical difficulty, Augustine formulated the theory of 'seminal reasons' for his doctrine of creation. According to Ecclesiasticus 18, 1, God created all things at once, while Genesis portrays God's creative work as having been carried out in successive stages. Augustine solved these contradictory statements regarding God's work of creation with the theory that God embedded immaterial seeds or potencies (*rationes seminales*) in matter, one for each species including man, which were to

---

[22] See footnote 17 above.

[23] Th. a Kempis, *De Imitatione Christi*, Bk. I, ch. 3.

[24] See footnote 2 above, first excerpt.

[25] Copleston, *A History of Philosophy*, Vol. III, Pt. II, 51; Richardson, ed., *Dictionary*, 5-6 ("Analogy ofBeing, *Analogia entis*") and 188-189 ("Language, Religious").

unfold to the full in time. The doctrine of the seminal reasons is one
which Augustine would appear to have borrowed from Plotinus.[26]
Aquinas jettisoned Augustine's theory of the *rationes seminales*, although
he does employ the term to describe Adam as the father of all mankind.[27]
Zerbolt uses the phrase *rationes seminales* three times: twice as it had been
employed by Aquinas to describe Adam as the seminal reason or cause of
the entire human race,[28] but in the third instance he gives it a more comprehensive meaning than in the other two passages.[29] The meaning given
by Zerbolt to the term *rationes seminales* in the third passage approaches
that given it by Augustine, it would appear.

iii. *Divine Providence*

From a discussion of God's creative activity as understood by Zerbolt
we must proceed to investigate his views regarding God's providential
care and governance of the universe.

Zerbolt expresses the traditional opinion that creation's dependence
upon God does not end with the act of creation.[30] God, the first cause of
all things, is not only responsible for giving all things their initial existence, but he also maintains and sustains them, we read in *De Ascensionibus*.[31] Divine providence implies two things: an eternal plan for all
things based on foresight, and the execution of this plan in time.[32] Zerbolt
too emphasizes the eternal and fixed nature of God's providential plan.
God predestined from all eternity that which he was going to do in time.[33]
In view of the whole intent and purpose of his writings it is not surprising
that Zerbolt discusses divine providence almost solely in connection with

---

[26] Copleston, *A History of Philosophy*, Vol. II, Pt. I, 91-92; and Gilson, *History of Christian Philosophy in the Middle Ages*, 73.

[27] Copleston, *A History of Philosophy*, Vol. II, Pt. I, 91; and Thomas Aquinas, *ST*, 1a 2ae, 81, 4.

[28] *Asc.*, 259G: Ideoque graviter cecidit et nos omnes in eo. Nam omnes in eo fuimus vi quadam productiva vel seminali ratione. *Ref.*, 237G: Siquidem homo iste, Adam pro-toplastus recte intelligitur, in quo totum genus humanum quod per seminalem rationem in eo fuit et ex eo prodiit, non incongrue subauditur.

[29] *Asc.*, 258H-259A: Sicut etenim res naturalis vi quadam productiva vel seminali ra-tione in se continet ut sit effectus alicuius productiva:...

[30] Cf. M. R. E. Masterman, "Providence of God (In the Bible)," *NCE*, XI, 916-917; E. J. Carney, "Providence of God (Theology of)," *NCE*, XI, 917-918; Richardson, ed., *Dictionary*, 280-281 ("Providence"); and A. C. McGiffert, *A History of Christian Thought* (2 vols.; N.Y.-London, 1932-1933), II, 271.

[31] *Asc.*, 261A: ...patremque dulcem et benignum, qui pro te tanta fecit et sustinuit,...

[32] Cf. Thomas Aquinas, *ST*, 1a, 22, 1-2; and Richardson, ed., *Dictionary*, 280 ("Prov-idence").

[33] *Asc.*, 267G: Secundo debes advertere et cogitare quanta sollicitudine, et quanto desiderio haec tibi beneficia tribuit. Ab aeterno haec tibi dare disposuit, ab aeterno praedisposuit, ab aeterno de te actualissime sine cessatione cogitavit, et tibi benefacere ab aeterno praeordinavit. Cf. *Ref.*, 245E.

God's providential care of man. By drawing attention to this divine care of man Zerbolt aims to instil compunction of hope and love in the reader,[34] sentiments essential to those who wish to progress in the spiritual life.[35] With that purpose in mind he asserts, for example, that God is as busy on behalf of the individual as he is on behalf of a whole city or even the entire world, and that God watches over the individual as anxiously as if he had no other care besides.[36] Zerbolt leaves one with the impression that the end and purpose of God's creative work and his providential care of creation is man's happiness rather than a manifestation of God's goodness and glory. He presents, in other words, an anthropocentric, rather than a theocentric, interpretation of God's creative work and his governance of the universe.[37] That God created and governs all things to proclaim his own goodness and glory is an idea which is not found in Zerbolt's writings.

Zerbolt specifically singles out, in addition to God's providential care of the individual in all things, what in more recent times has come to be known as *Heilsgeschichte*.[38] From divine providence in general Zerbolt separates God's providential plan for the destiny of the entire human race, namely salvation through Jesus Christ. He explains that in order to save mankind God performed many marvellous things from the very beginning of the world: he spoke with the patriarchs and the prophets; he revealed himself *"in figura"* at various times; and he brought the Israelites to the promised land.[39] Zerbolt draws particular attention, then, to the supernatural aspect of God's divine plan which has only the rational being for its object. He adds that contemplation of this divine salvific plan for mankind ought also to instil compunction of hope and love in the individual.[40] The divine salvific plan is, of course, God's prov-

---

[34] *Asc.*, ch. 25 (267D-H) and *Ref.*, ch. 25 (245C-G).

[35] See footnote 3 above.

[36] *Asc.*, 267G-H: Sic fuit semper et est circa te sollicitus, sicut erga integram urbem vel totum orbem, sic intendit tibi sollicitus pro te ac si vacaret ab caeteris. *Ref.*, 245E: Ita enim hic magnus rex tibi et circa te intendit ac si vacaret ab singulis.

[37] Grote's spirituality was also anthropocentric (de Beer, *Spiritualiteit*, 290-291).

[38] Cf. K. Rahner, "Salvation (Universal Salvific Will)," *SM*, V, 405-409; E. L. Peterman, "Salvation History (*Heilsgeschichte*)," *NCE*, XII, 999-1001.
Zerbolt says nothing further regarding the relationship between the natural and supernatural aspects of God's providential plan for the destiny of the universe. Cf. Richardson, ed., *Dictionary*, 153 ("*Heilsgeschichte*").

[39] *Asc.*, 267F-G: ..., cogita quam multa propter salutem tuam Dominus ille magnus peregit. Siquidem locutus est cum patribus, apparuit in figuris, loquebatur in prophetis, eduxit de Aegypto, induxit in terram promissionis, et infinita miracula et mirabilia fecit. *Ref.*, 245G: Cogita quam multa egit ab initio mirifica cum genere humano. Propter genus humanum locutus est cum patribus, apparuit in figuris, [etc.] Cf. Hebrews 1, 1-3.

[40] *Asc.*, 267G: Haec omnia spem tuam et affectum sursum debent erigere in amorem Dei tui.

idential plan for the entire human race, while divine predestination refers to the providentially predetermined destiny of the individual.[41]

It is in connection with Zerbolt's views on divine providence that we must briefly look at his understanding of miracles; and at this point we will concentrate our attention on the nature of miracles while their purpose will be discussed below. Underlying Zerbolt's conception of miracles is the belief that in his providential governance of the universe God works through, and within the bounds of, fixed laws of his own making which are efficacious secondary causes. However, because God remains the first cause at all times, and because he is the author of the laws of nature, he may set the latter aside if he so pleases and act directly in order to effect an extraordinary or supernatural event: a miracle, in other words.[42] His view of miracles being what it is, it is not surprising that Zerbolt should express the opinion, in agreement with Aquinas,[43] that only God can perform supernatural acts.[44] Man can be no more than a secondary, or instrumental, cause, and consequently he cannot perform miracles.[45]

iv. *Divine Attributes*

God's nature and attributes, as well as his attitude towards fallen man, are the aspects of Zerbolt's doctrine of God which remain to be discussed. These two issues are obviously related, for God's nature has, understandably, some bearing on his attitude towards sinful man.[46] The former is, for Zerbolt, the subject-matter of both natural and revealed theology, while the latter is solely a matter of divine revelation.

---

[41] See below, pp. 198-200.

[42] *Asc.*, 269A-B: Quidam sequebantur eum propter miracula eius. Et tu mirare potentiam eius in miraculis. Naturam mutat, elementa commutat,... Ex his disce eum esse Deum, qui naturae suos effectus primo indidit naturales, salva sibi semper obedientia, in omnibus etiam ad effectus supernaturales producendos. Cf. *Scriptum Pro Quodam*, 229; McGiffert, *A History of Christian Thought*, II, 271; and Richardson, ed., *Dictionary*, 280 ("Providence").

[43] Thomas Aquinas, *Summa Contra Gentiles*, Bk. III, ch. 102. Cf. J. G. Pater, "Miracles (Theology of)," *NCE*, IX, 891.

[44] *Scriptum Pro Quodam*, 231-232: Est enim secundum doctores duplex doctrina: una, que facultatem mentis humane non transcendit... Alia est doctrina, que excedit facultatem humanum et que non potest per principia naturalia demonstrari, sicut articuli fidei quia, cum Deus non possit esse testis falsitatis, necesse fuit per confirmacionem talis doctrine inducere opera miraculosa, que a sola virtute divina fieri possunt.

[45] Cf. J. G. Pater, "Miracles (Theology of)," *NCE*, IX, 891.

[46] According to Johannes von Staupitz, Luther's confessor, God's mercy (*misericordia*) with respect to fallen man flows from his goodness (*bonitas*) (Steinmetz, *Staupitz*, 48, footnote 1). We will see that Zerbolt also regards goodness to be a fundamental attribute of God, of which his mercy towards fallen man constitutes a particular, and important, facet.

Zerbolt writes that God granted man the power of desire in order that he might strive after that which he perceives to be good.[47] God, he continues, is the highest good, the *Summum Bonum*, and consequently man will seek God, for man naturally seeks the highest good at all times.[48] If man's vision of God as the highest good is obscured, he may temporarily find rest in a created good, but he will not find permanent rest until he has found rest in God, the highest good.[49] Zerbolt borrowed this characterization of God as the *Summum Bonum*, who will always remain the final object of man's restless search for the good, from Augustine, and he did so either directly or by way of some other writer such as David of Augsburg, for example.[50]

God, the *Summum Bonum*, is also eternal, true and supreme love who loves man with an eternal and unremitting love. It was this love for man, according to Zerbolt, which prompted God, the supreme good, to diffuse his goodness for man's benefit.[51] And the diffusion by God of his own goodness is, in Zerbolt's opinion, seen clearly in his providential care of man. For God, he explains, is a caring and bountiful Father who communicates his goodness to all of creation, but to man in particular, because all created good apart from man was made to serve mankind. God has, in fact, arranged everything with an eye to man's happiness and has bestowed untold benefits on him which are not granted carelessly or indifferently, but in a fashion best suited to the individual.[52] The

---

[47] See below, pp. 64-67.

[48] *Asc.*, 259C: Dedit vim concupiscibilem, ut omne bonum appeteres et summum bonum Deum super omnia desiderares.

[49] *Asc.*, 275F-G: Sed nec est ibi quiescendum, sed adhuc ascendendum. Paululum, inquit, cum pertransissem eos, id est, ad tertium gradum ascendissem, inveni quem diligit anima mea. Itaque in primo, mundi concupiscentia deseritur. In secundo mens superius sublevatur. In tertio quiescit in Deo quieta. Nec tamen putes quod aliquem istorum graduum usque ad summum vel perfectum in hac vita possumus ascendere. Nec enim in hac vita possumus omnes concupiscentias expurgare, cum neque ipse Paulus perficere invenit, id est, perfectionem, quae est in non concupiscere secundum Augustinum.

[50] Augustine, *De Doctrina Christiana*, I, 22, 20; and D. of Augsburg, *De ext. et int. hom. compositione*, II, 174. Cf. Steinmetz, *Staupitz*, 35-37.

[51] *Ref.*, 245F: Perpetua inquit, charitate dilexi te. Et ex perpetua et maxima charitate donat sua beneficia. *Asc.*, 269F: O aeterna veritas, et vera charitas, et chara aeternitas, tu es Deus meus, tibi suspiro die ac nocte. This last passage Zerbolt borrowed from Augustine's *Confessiones*, Bk. VII, ch. 10.

That God is Truth is mentioned only once by Zerbolt, and it will not be dealt with here. It will receive some attention in connection with the discussion of the *fides quae creditur* (see below, pp. 160-161).

[52] *Asc.*, 267G-H: ..., ut diligenter inquiras magnitudinem et potentiam benefactoris qui tibi haec omnia contulit. ...Secundo debes advertere et cogitare quanta sollicitudine, et quanto desiderio haec tibi beneficia tribuit. ...Tertio omnia beneficia divina generaliter humano generi collata, ita tibi debes assumere et attrahere ac si tibi soli forent collata; ut cogites; Ecce propter me totum mundum creavit, et omnia in eo, ... See also footnote 31 above and cf. *Asc.*, 267D. *Ref.*, 245D-E: Attende igitur, quantae sit bonitatis, quod hic

goodness bestowed by God on man must fill him with compunction of hope and love, sentiments necessary for those who desire to make spiritual progress.[53] This would seem to explain why Zerbolt attributes some importance to the fact that God's goodness towards man can be known naturally from an observation of his providential care of mankind, for it is a natural way to compunction of hope and love, or at least it can be.

Is divine goodness good in an ontological sense because it conforms to an objective standard of right reason, or is it good because God arbitrarily wills it so? The question, in other words, is whether it is intellect or will which determines God's actions, and whether his omnipotence is in any way limited by the commands of right reason.[54] Zerbolt does not deal specifically with this issue, but one or two statements do indicate his thinking on this matter. He writes, for example, that God is an intelligent and equitable being, and that, therefore, he cannot judge man otherwise than his works deserve.[55] The implication here is that God, because he is an intelligent and equitable being, does not judge man wilfully and arbitrarily, but in the light of an objective standard of good and evil: i.e., that in judging man God's intellect, which is guided by the dictates of right reason, has the upper hand. The fact that God's judgements are inscrutable to man, as Zerbolt writes elsewhere,[56] does not necessarily mean that God judges arbitrarily, and that in his judgements he is in the first place guided by his will. According to J. H. Gerretsen Grote's understanding of God was Thomistic,[57] which adds to the probability that Zerbolt also regarded God as a being whose will is governed by his intellect. In summary, such clues as we have suggest that Zerbolt con-

---

talis, tantusque Dominus modicum enceniolum tibi tribuit, imo quantae bonitatis, quod tantus de tantillo dignetur cogitare. Considera quam solicita sit tanta maiestas circa te in tribuendo beneficia, modo quo tibi maxime expedit. Cf. *Ref.*, 245D, and footnotes 33 and 36 above.

[53] *Asc.*, 267D: Verum ut maiorem habeas fiduciam sperandi, et futuram gloriam obtinendi, debes nonnumquam signa dilectionis quae tibi Dominus tuus exhibuit studiose revolvere, et eius beneficia diligentius considerare, et tali consideratione accendi, quasi quibusdam stimulis ad reamandum. Cf. *Asc.*, 267H, 283H and 285F. See also *Ref.*, 245C-E.

[54] Cf. Copleston, *A History of Philosophy*, Vol. II, Pt. II, 87-90, 252-256; and Steinmetz, *Staupitz*, 48-50.

[55] *Asc.*, 260H-261A: ..., quod divina iustitia aliter iudicare non potest quam opera tua merentur. Est enim Deus intelligibilis quaedam aequitas, ... *Ref.*, 243F: Cogita secundo quod Deus aliter iudicare non poterit quam opera nostra merentur. Cf. *Ref.*, 243G.

[56] *Ref.*, 243G: Demum cogita, quod iudicia Dei sunt inscrutabilia,... Cf. *Ref.*, 241E and *Asc.*, 264E. The question of God's inscrutability will receive further attention in connection with our discussion of man's uncertainty with respect to his salvation. See below, pp. 200-204.

[57] See Gerretsen, *Florentius Radewijns*, 1-11.

sidered divine goodness to be good ontologically and not merely because
God willed it to be good.[58]

In addition to the attributes of love and goodness, Zerbolt mentions
God's attributes of power and wisdom. Clearly indebted to David of
Augsburg, he writes that the universe and the variety of creatures found
in it constitute witnesses to God's immeasurable power. God's incomparable wisdom, on the other hand, is displayed by the beauty of creation
and its order.[59] Zerbolt sees further proof of God's wisdom in the plan of
salvation he devised for fallen man. He writes that in, and through,
Christ's life, passion and death God prudently deceived the devil and so
rescued mankind from eternal damnation.[60] The interpretation of
Christ's work of redemption as a deception of the devil by either God or
Christ, or by both, was the dominant view of Christ's salvific work from
the days of Origen to those of Anselm; and G. Aulén has therefore labelled it the classic idea of atonement.[61] It is one of three interpretations of
the atonement found in Zerbolt's writings, and it will be discussed in
greater detail in connection with the work of Christ.

It would appear from what has been said that Zerbolt relies more on
the universe, and its operation, as a means to the knowledge of God's attributes than he does on the Scriptures. Furthermore, his epistemology
indicates that he was of the opinion that man can arrive at this knowledge
of God's attributes from an observation of nature without the co-
operation of divine illumination. The notion that creation is a 'book' in
which God reveals himself, as he does in the Scriptures, was widely prop-
agated by the Franciscans in particular,[62] and Franciscan thought

---

[58] Cf. Steinmetz, Staupitz, 48-50.

[59] Ref., 245D: Considera quod sit infinitae potentiae, cuius potentiam declarat univer-
sitas et multitudo creaturarum suarum. Considera quod sit immensae sapientiae. Et hoc
attende ex pulchritudine et ordine totius universitatis. Asc., 267G: Nam est potentissimus,
ut potes videre in rerum creatione. Est sapientissimus, ut apparet in earum gubernatione,
et providentissima dispositione,... See D. of Augsburg, De ext. et int. hom. compositione, II,
145-146. In Omnes, inquit, artes Florens Radewijns uses this same passage from De ext. et int.
hom. compositione in connection with some comments he makes regarding God's power and
wisdom (Omnes, Inquit, Artes, II, 160). Cf. Copleston, A History of Philosophy, Vol. II, Pt. I,
187.

In De Ascensionibus Zerbolt draws attention to God's omnipotence in another connection: it is God's might which enables him to be the supreme benefactor of mankind (Asc.,
267G).

[60] Asc., 274F: Est autem signaculum hoc, Deus admirabilis. De quo in passione ostensum est, quod ipse sit summa sapientia, qui tam prudenter diabolum decepit, ... Cf. Ref.,
249F. Dirc van Herxen expresses much the same view. See Knierim, Dirc van Herxen
(1385-1457), rector van het Zwolse fraterhuis, 121.

[61] Gustaf Aulén, Christus Victor, An historical study of the three main types of the idea of the
atonement (London: S.P.C.K., 1970), 4-7.

[62] Gilson, History of Christian Philosophy, 352-353.

dominated late medieval thought, including that of the Devotionalists, to a considerable degree.[63]

v. *God's Attitude Towards Fallen Man*

According to Zerbolt all of Scripture deals with nothing but God's attitude towards sinful man: his justice and wrath on the one hand, and his mercy and love on the other.[64] It was, and is, commonly held that the primary purpose underlying this revelation of divine justice and mercy is to reveal to man that a just God has justly condemned fallen man to an eternal death, but that this same God, who is also merciful, has devised a plan for man's salvation through the death of his own Son. However, when Zerbolt draws attention to God's justice and mercy, evident from his condemnation of man and his salvific plan respectively, Zerbolt's main purpose is not simply to inform the reader concerning man's fallen condition and the salvation offered him. His primary objective is to instil in the reader that amalgam of fear and hope which he holds to be so indispensable to man's spiritual progress and salvation. The nature of this dual sentiment, how it may best be achieved and its exact function, will be examined in a later chapter. At this point we must restrict ourselves to Zerbolt's understanding of the two divine attributes of justice and mercy.

To Zerbolt, divine justice was obviously an important topic, for it is one to which he returns frequently, and it would appear that he comments on it more often than on God's mercy. Furthermore, he gives three different, but nonetheless related, meanings to the expression "divine justice." In the first place he understands God's justice to be his moral perfection or, in other words, his holiness. It was against God's justice or holiness that man sinned, and it was only in and through the death of his own Son that God's justice or holiness could find satisfaction. The degree of satisfaction required not only illustrates the seriousness of man's sins, but it also illustrates the supreme and incomparable justice and holiness of God.[65]

---

[63] H. A. Oberman, "The Shape of Late Medieval Thought: The Birthpangs of the Modern Era," in: *The Pursuit of Holiness in Late Medieval and Renaissance Religion*, ed. by C. Trinkaus and H. A. Oberman (Leiden, 1974), 7; and Post, *De Moderne Devotie*, 141.

[64] See footnote 9 above. See *Asc.*, 285F further.

[65] *Asc.*, 274F-G: Secundo ostensum est in passione quod ipse sit summa iustitia, in quantum quaesivit redemptionis pretium. ... Si ergo vis te exercere ad timorem, quid magis timendum quam quod Deus est summa iustitia, qui eligit subire mortem potius quam iustitia sua relinqueret peccatum originale inultum. *Ref.*, 243F: Christus pro peccato sustinuit mortem amarissimam, ne peccatum inultum remaneret et suae iustitiae non satisfieret. *Ref.*, 249F: Primum signaculum fuit Deus admirabilis, qui per crucem manifestatus est esse ... summa iustitia in quantum quaesivit redemptionis pretium, ... Cf. Knierim, *Dirc van Herxen (1385-1457), rector van het Zwolse fraterhuis*, 122; and P. de Letter, "Justice of God," *NCE*, VIII, 74-75.

Zerbolt also applies the term "divine justice" to God's function as judge, a capacity in which he renders to every man according to his works. This idea is a biblical one, for St. Paul writes that God "will render to every man according to his deeds."[66] This, or a similar, formulation is found at least six times throughout *De Reformatione* and *De Ascensionibus*.[67] To recompense every man according to his works means that God awards eternal punishment to the wicked, but eternal glory to the good,[68] which is preceded by a strict examination into, and exposure of, every thought, word and deed.[69] And Zerbolt stresses in particular that God is an unchangeable, inflexible and most just judge who cannot but judge man as his works deserve.[70] The implication is that God is not arbitrary in his judgement, but that he is bound by his own plan of redemption for man. Man can be assured of salvation, provided he fulfils the conditions set by God. Inasmuch as God cannot judge otherwise than man's works deserve, it also means that the sentence is irrevocable.[71]

Although Zerbolt writes that divine justice refers to the bestowal of eternal bliss on the good and condemnation of the wicked to eternal perdition, the emphasis is on the latter. However, he was not the first to regard divine justice as punishing justice first and foremost. Augustine already emphasized God's punishing justice, and this was to remain a characteristic of medieval spirituality.[72]

Zerbolt sees evidence of God's punishing justice in the passion. Christ's death was the punishment on man's sins, and it was the only way that God's justice could be satisfied.[73] However, those who do not wish to have a share in Christ's vicarious suffering and death will bear the full punishment for their own sins. For God will leave no evil unpunished, and he requires that satisfaction be made for all sins, either

---

[66] Romans 6, 2.

[67] *Ref.*, 243G: Igitur tibi reddet iuxta opera tua. *Asc.*, 264F: ... quo iudex unicuique iuxta opera sua redditurus adveniet, ... Also *Ref.*, 243F; *Asc.*, 260H-261A; and *Asc.*, 285F. Cf. P. de Letter, "Justice of God," *NCE*, VIII, 74-75.

[68] *Asc.*, 261A: Est enim Deus intelligibilis quaedam aequitas, ... non minus poena malorum quam gloria bonorum. Also *Ref.*, 243G.

[69] See footnote 70 below and also *Asc.*, 265F: Cogita quam districte fiet ibi examinatio operum, locutionum et meditationum, et malarum affectionum, omnia ibi nuda erunt, aperta etiam quae hic fuerunt palliata. Also *Asc.*, 264F and *Ref.*, 241E-F.

[70] *Ref.*, 243G: Est enim Deus ..., inconvertibilis atque indeclinabilis, ...; *Asc.*, 265F: ...Aequissime iudex, ...; and footnote 55 above. Also *Asc.*, 261A.

[71] *Asc.*, 265F: Deinde proferet iudex sententiam diffinitivam, ab qua nullus appellare potest, ...

[72] Cf. P. de Letter, "Justice of God," *NCE*, VIII, 74-75; and D. of Augsburg, *De ext. et int. hom. compositione*, II, 148.

[73] *Asc.*, 260H: Cogita quod tantum Deo peccatum displicuit quod potius ipse voluit moriens satisfacere pro peccato Adae, quam ipsum secundum suam iustitiam dimittere impunitum. And see footnote 65 above.

here or hereafter.[74] Zerbolt's reason for placing so much emphasis on God's punishing justice is, of course, to incite the reader to compunction and repentance.

Thirdly, Zerbolt understands divine justice in terms of wrath.[75] This must be understood in the light of God's justice defined as holiness. Sin is a defilement of God's holiness to which he responds in anger. This ire, Zerbolt writes, underlies God's punishment of sin through the death of Christ, as well as his punishment of individuals.[76] To Zerbolt God is not an impartial, modern-day judge who judges individuals *ex-officio* without becoming personally or emotionally involved.[77]

In conclusion it may be observed that Zerbolt reserves the role of judge primarily for God the Father. He does not very often speak of Christ as the judge of mankind,[78] although it was not an uncommon practice to do so in the late middle ages.[79] Grote frequently refers to Christ as judge, according to G. Epiney-Burgard.[80] She continues that the final judgement played a prominent role in the thought of the Devotionalists, which lent a somber air to their spirituality.[81] This description of the Devotionalists' spirituality applies to that of Zerbolt, and his emphasis on the final judgement had, of course, a very specific purpose, namely to imbue the reader with *compunctio timoris*.

In *De Reformatione* Zerbolt writes that God loved man from the very beginning of time, and that this love, which counterbalances his wrath, is

---

[74] *Asc.*, 261A: Certus igitur esto quod reddet tibi secundum opera tua, nec relinquet aliquod malum in te impunitum. *Asc.*, 261B: ..., et in his peccatis quae post conversionem commisisti, forsitan gravius puniet te Deus tanquam magis ingratum. ...; sciens certissime quod vel hic vel in futuro [thou shalt pay all, yea, to the uttermost farthing. But hereafter,] secundum Bernardum, centuplum reddes quod hic simplo solvere posses. Comparison of the edition of *De Ascensionibus* used by us with J. P. Arthur's translation of this same work reveals that the type-setter of the former accidentally omitted that which has been enclosed in square brackets (*The Spiritual Ascent. A Devotional Treatise by Gerard of Zutphen*, trans. by J. P. Arthur [London, 1908], 15). The confusion would appear to stem from the fact that Zerbolt twice employed "*in futuro*" in the short space of two sentences. *Asc.*, 264C: ...quamque severe et terribiliter adveniet iustus iudex, super his te puniturus. *Ref.*, 243G: Nullum enim malum impunitum erit,...

[75] *Ref.*, 244G: Cogita si potes magnitudinem irae iusti iudicis venientis contra eos, qui eum offenderunt et quantum mali terrebuntur. Cf. Bonaventure, *Soliloquium*, ch. 3, par. 5 (*Works*, III, 98).

[76] See footnotes 65 and 75 above.

[77] Cf. Richardson, ed., *Dictionary*, 362-363 ("Wrath of God").

[78] *Ref.*, 245A: Cogita quam magna sint opera misericordia et pietatis, cum ea solum Christus ad iudicium suum adducere videatur. Cf. *Ref.*, ch. 23 (pp. 244G-245A) and *Asc.*, ch. 20 (p. 265D-F).

[79] Cf. Dempsey Douglass, *Geiler*, 172.

[80] Epiney-Burgard, *Grote*, 277.

[81] *Ibid.*

the driving force behind God's merciful treatment of man.[82] Although
man was disobedient, God did not cease to love him. It was this unflag-
ging love which prompted God to devise a plan for man's salvation: his
work of mercy. Zerbolt elaborates that in order to save man, God, who
was motivated by love, tenderness and mercy for humanity, revealed
himself to the patriarchs and prophets, led his people to the promised
land, and performed numerous marvellous wonders.[83] The greatest
evidence of God's mercy he discerns in the fact that, in order to save
fallen man, God allowed his Son to die on the cross, the central and
culminating part of God's redemptive plan.[84] On the one hand, then,
Zerbolt sees in Christ's passion proof of God's punishing justice,[85] but,
on the other hand, the passion is also proof of God's unlimited mercy *vis-
à-vis* man. Next to the passion as the greatest proof of God's mercy Zerbolt names the sacrament of the eucharist and the descent of the Holy
Spirit.[86] In the passion Christ suffered the punishment on man's sins and
satisfied divine justice. Consequently God can be merciful to the individual and grant him the various graces necessary to achieve justification and sanctification.[87]

Concerning divine mercy and its relationship to divine justice Zerbolt
does not say anything. However, he must have regarded divine mercy as
outweighing divine justice in the final analysis, in spite of the greater em-

---

[82] *Ref.*, 245F: Perpetua, inquit, charitate dilexi te. Et ex perpetua et maxima charitate
donat sua beneficia. ...Circa beneficia dupliciter forma meditationes. Primo, circa hoc
quod mala tua tibi benignissime dimisit. Secundo, quod innumerabilia tibi contulit dona
et munera. Dimisit enim tibi tot mala quod fecisti, de quibus supra dictum est, imo
dimisit tibi tot quot facere potuisti, ab quibus te praeservavit. *Asc.*, 267D: Cogita igitur
primum quam sit magnum signum dilectionis Dei tui, quod te qui toties eum offendisti,
toties ad eum terga vertisti, toties ab eo recessisti, toties gravissime peccasti, quoties reverti volebas ipse te suscepit, dolenti peccata indulsit, emendantem et corrigentem adiuvit.

[83] See footnote 39 above.

[84] *Ref.*, 249F: Primum signaculum fuit Deus admirabilis, qui per crucem manifestatus
est esse ... summa misericordia, quia tradidit pro nobis filium [suum]. Also *Asc.*, 247F-G.
Cf. *Ref.*, 245G and *Asc.*, 267F. The excerpts on p. 245G of *De Reformatione* and on p. 267F
of *De Ascensionibus*, which are identical, were borrowed from Bonaventure's *De Triplici Via*,
ch. 1, par. 2 (*Works*, I, 70).

[85] See footnote 65 above, second excerpt.

[86] *Asc.*, 267F: Cogita de donis superexcellentiae, quae tibi contulit, videlicet quod dedit
tibi dilectissimum suum filium. Primo in incarnatione: ..., deinde in altaris sacramento in
cibum et in potum. Misit tibi Spiritum sanctum in signaculum acceptationis,... Also *Ref.*,
245G. These two, identical excerpts were also borrowed from Bonaventure's *De Triplici
Via*, ch. 1, par. 2 (*Works*, I, 70).

[87] *Asc.*, 267F: Deinde cogita de donis gratiae tibi collatis. Dedit enim tibi contritionem
et dolorem de peccatis, et ab iniustitia revocavit, et iustitiam infudit, quod est solius
Dei,... Dedit et inspiravit voluntatem quod te velles emendare,... Also *Ref.*, 245G. These
two, identical excerpts were borrowed from, or inspired by, Bonaventure's *De Triplici Via*,
ch. 1, par. 2 (*Works*, I, 69-70).

For the process of justification as understood by Zerbolt see below, ch. 4.

phasis he puts on the latter. His reason for stressing divine justice—and punishing justice at that—at the expense of divine mercy was a very practical one, namely to make the reader sufficiently aware of the seriousness of his sins, and so instil in him a salutary dose of compunction of fear.

vi. *Assessment*

Neither Zerbolt's doctrine of God, nor his way to the knowledge of God, reveals anything novel or unexpected. He holds that there are two avenues to the knowledge of God: nature and the Scriptures. His reliance on nature as a means to establish the divine attributes in particular indicates a specifically Franciscan influence, it would seem. Being an Aristotelian—Thomist in his epistemology, Zerbolt held that man can naturally deduce the existence of God, and certain of his attributes, from an observation of nature. Attributes which can thus be ascertained are those of goodness and love on the one hand, and those of wisdom and power on the other. Divine goodness and love are peculiarly Augustinian themes,[88] while those of wisdom and power are more than reminiscent of the Franciscan, David of Augsburg.[89] Zerbolt's natural theology is, in part at least, founded on the doctrine of divine exemplary causality according to which God fashioned everything after the exemplary models or ideas contained in the divine intellect. As in most of his philosophical and theological opinions, so in his doctrine of divine, creative exemplarism Zerbolt follows, in contrast with the *via moderna* for example, in the footsteps of Augustine and Aquinas.

While natural theology may be able to tell man a great many things about God, only the Scriptures reveal that man is sinful and that God's response to man's sinfulness is one of justice tempered with mercy. Zerbolt's understanding of divine justice is altogether traditional, and there is nothing in it that points to Luther's definition of *iustitia dei*: unmerited justification granted in response to a peculiar definition of faith.[90] Zerbolt regards it as essential that man be apprized of divine justice and mercy, for in his view they are the best suited to instil in the believer the fear and hope which, he maintains, are indispensable to spiritual progress. Since only the Scriptures can inform man regarding divine justice and mercy, Zerbolt's advocacy in *De Libris Teutonicalibus*, as well as in *Super Modo Vivendi*,[91] of translating the Bible into the vernacular languages in order that it may be widely read becomes altogether understandable.

---

[88] See footnote 50 above.
[89] See footnote 59 above.
[90] Cf. Oberman, *Biel*, 181-184.
[91] *De Libris Teutonicalibus*, 45-70; and *Super Modo Vivendi*, 56-71.

CHAPTER TWO

THE DOCTRINE OF MAN

A) *Man as Created*

For Zerbolt the goal of the spiritual life is, in very general terms, man's original perfection as it existed prior to the fall.[1] Consequently he writes in the opening chapter of *De Ascensionibus* that when the believer prepares himself for the spiritual ascent he must do three things: acquaint himself with man's condition before the fall; determine the extent of man's fall from his original state; and prepare a plan for his ascend in order that it may follow a logical course and be brought to a successful completion.[2] Zerbolt's description of man's condition both before and after the fall deals exclusively with his psychological and spiritual state: his psychological and spiritual perfection before the fall, and the ruinous effect of Adam's disobedience on this faultless state. The first practical step of the spiritual life has to be, therefore, the reformation of the powers of the soul which were deformed in the fall. For unless the faculties of the soul are restored to their original state, charity, which constitutes perfection and therefore the ultimate goal of the spiritual life,[3] will not be possible.

In view of what Zerbolt regards to be the end of the spiritual life, and the means to that end, it is not surprising that he begins both *De Reformatione* and *De Ascensionibus* with relatively detailed descriptions of man's original condition and the effects of the fall on that state.[4] His interest in philosophical and theological anthropology was considerably greater than that of Radewijns, for example, even though the objective of the spiritual life was essentially the same for both men.[5] However, Zerbolt was not the

---

[1] Zerbolt would agree, as will be seen, that man's prefall perfection cannot be regained in its entirety. Original justice, as defined by him, cannot be recovered. See below in this chapter.

[2] *Asc.*, 258G-H: Haec tibi...amissam dignitatem. Cf. *Ref.*, 238B: In his ... redeas.

When dealing with a long passage which is not of prime importance, only its first and last words will be given. And they will be given merely to facilitate identification of the passage.

[3] See below, pp. 233-41, for a detailed discussion of Zerbolt's views on the goal of the spiritual life.

[4] For Zerbolt's description of man's psychological condition before and after the fall see *Ref.*, chs. 1-2 and 25 (pp. 237G-238B and 245C-G), and *Asc.*, chs. 2-5 and 25 (pp. 259B-260F and 267D-H).

[5] *Ref.*, ch. 3 (p. 238C-H); *Asc.*, chs. 26-27 (pp. 268A-269F); Radewijns, *Tractatulus Devotus*, 213-215; and *idem*, *Omnes, Inquit, Artes*, II, 1-4.

first spiritual writer to include an anthropological analysis in his spiritual theology. Influenced by Bernard of Clairvaux, most of the leading Cistercians of the twelfth century wrote treatises *de anima*, and their spiritual teaching was held to be incomplete without such a discourse dealing with the human psyche from the philosophical, as well as the theological, perspective.[6] "For the twelfth-century Cistercians their teaching *de anima* was the keystone of their doctrine on the sanctification of man," writes L. Savary.[7] However, their anthropological interests, like those of Zerbolt, were never ends in themselves, but they were always subservient to the peculiar needs of the spiritual life.[8] In addition to Bernard of Clairvaux it is necessary to name in particular William of St. Thierry,[9] whose *Epistola ad Fratres de Monte Dei* was a beloved writing among the Devotionalists, and an anonymous Cistercian who compiled a treatise entitled *De Spiritu et Anima*,[10] a work which influenced Zerbolt not a little. If Zerbolt's pronounced anthropological interests would seem to betray a certain indebtedness to Cistercian writers, the contents of his philosophical and theological anthropology reveal a number of influences. The resemblance between Zerbolt's anthropology and that of Aquinas, whose philosophical anthropology is essentially Aristotelian,[11] is considerable, as will be seen. However, Zerbolt's anthropology does not lack some distinctive Augustinian elements either, but then virtually all of medieval anthropological thought was indebted to Augustine to a greater or lesser degree.[12]

---

[6] See B. McGinn, ed., *Three Treatises on Man: A Cistercian Anthropology* (Cistercian Fathers Series, No. XXIV; Kalamazoo, 1977), 1-93 (Introduction).

[7] L. M. Savary, *Psychological Themes in the Golden Epistle of William of Saint-Thierry to the Carthusians of Mont-Dieu* (Analecta Cartusiana, Vol. VIII; Salzburg, 1973), 40.

[8] Cf. McGinn, ed., *Three Treatises on Man: A Cistercian Anthropology*, 78-79 (Introduction).

[9] *Ibid.*, 27-47 (Introduction); Savary, *Psychological Themes in the Golden Epistle of William of Saint-Thierry to the Carthusians of Mont-Dieu*, 32-33, 40 and 54-57; L. Bouyer, *The Cistercian Heritage*, trans. by E. Livingstone (London, 1958), 94-100; and I. C. Brady, "Soul, Human," *NCE*, XIII, 455.

[10] In the middle ages *De Spiritu et Anima* was generally attributed to Augustine. Earlier in the present century Alcher of Clairvaux was widely held to be its compiler (cf. van Woerkum, "Het Libellus 'Omnes, inquit, artes'," 149), but that has more recently been questioned as well (McGinn, ed., *Three Treatises on Man: A Cistercian Anthropology*, 63-74 [Introduction]). For the sources of *De Spiritu et Anima* see *PL*, XL, 779-780.

[11] Thomas Aquinas, *ST*, 1a, 78-80. Cf. H. J. Störig, *Geschiedenis van de filosofie*, trans. by P. Brommer (2 vols.; Utrecht-Antwerp: Prisma Books, 1972), I, 248.

[12] See McGinn, ed., *Three Treatises on Man: A Cistercian Anthropology*, 1-93 (Introduction). Rayez' statement that Zerbolt's description of man's original condition may have been inspired by Bonaventure's *Commentary on the Sentences* is difficult to verify (Rayez, "Gérard Zerbolt de Zutphen et Saint Bonaventure. Dépendances Littéraires," 335, footnote 38). One of the difficulties in this connection is that Bonaventure's anthropology cannot be said to be in any way distinctive. In theological works like the *Sentences* and the *Breviloquium*

i. *Dona naturae* and *Dona gratiae*

The schoolmen distinguished between man's natural gifts or endowments on the one hand, and his supernatural and preternatural endowments on the other; and to the latter they gave the name '*donum
superadditum*'. It was held that man retained the natural gifts after the fall,
in essence at least, but that he lost the *donum superadditum*. The distinction
between natural and supernatural gifts is one which is already found in
the writings of the church fathers,[13] but it received its fullest treatment
from Thomas Aquinas. By the natural endowments Aquinas understood
two different, but very closely related, things. In the first place he
understood by man's natural endowments man *per se*: i.e., that part of
man which remained completely unaffected by the fall and which is
presently considered to be the subject matter of philosophical anthropology. Aquinas also held that man is by nature a moral being with a
natural inclination towards the good, and he maintained that man's
naturally moral nature is inherent in his psychological make-up as such.
This natural morality was not destroyed by the fall, but it was weakened
and partially impaired by it. The *donum superadditum* consisted, according
to St. Thomas, of sanctifying grace, a supernatural knowledge of
spiritual things in particular, immunity from rebellious concupiscence
and bodily immortality,[14] all of which were lost as a result of Adam's
disobedience in paradise.[15]

Zerbolt was obviously familiar with the scholastic practice of
distinguishing between Adam's natural gifts on the one hand, and his
supernatural and preternatural endowments on the other. For in *De*

Bonaventure's anthropological views are essentially Aristotelian, while in a spiritual
writing like the *Soliloquium*, for example, they are clearly Augustinian. See *Soliloquium*, ch.
1, par. 3 (*Works*, III, 43); and *Breviloquium*, Bk. II, ch. 9 (*Works*, II, 93-97). Cf. Copleston,
A History of Philosophy, Vol. II, Pt. I, 308-322.

[13] See J. N. D. Kelly, *Early Christian Doctrines* (4th ed.; London, 1968), 346-347; J.
Pelikan, *The Christian Tradition, A History of the Development of Doctrine*, Vol. I: *The Emergence
of the Catholic Tradition (100-600)* (Chicago-London, 1971), 318-331; F. H. Dudden,
Gregory the Great: His Place in History and Thought (2 vols.; London, 1905), II, 376-378;
Richardson, ed., *Dictionary*, 99 ("Donum Superadditum"); and F. J. Corley, "Man,"
NCE, IX, 128.

[14] Thomas Aquinas, *ST*, 1a 2ae, 85, 1 and Oberman, *Biel*, 58-59. Cf. E. M. Burke,
"Pure Nature, State of," *NCE*, XI, 1033.

[15] For this introductory paragraph on the *dona naturae* and the *dona gratiae* see, in addition to the references given in footnotes 13 and 14: Thomas Aquinas, *ST*, 1a, 90-102; T.
R. Heath, "Adam," *NCE*, I, 114; V. A. Harvey, *A Handbook of Theological Terms* (New
York, 1964), 73 ("Donum Superadditum") and 125 ("Image of God"); K. Rahner and H.
Vorgrimler, *Theological Dictionary*, trans. by R. Strachan (New York, 1965), 231 ("Integri-
ty") and 328-329 ("Original Justice"); M. M. Schanen, "Integrity, Gift of," *NCE*, VII,
554; C. J. Peter, "Original Justice," *NCE*, X, 775; J. P. Kenny, "Concupiscence,"
NCE, IV, 122-123; and L. Scheffczyk, "Concupiscence," *SM*, I, 404.

Ascensionibus he writes that God placed Adam *"in alto monte donorum naturalium et gratiarum,"*[16] the gifts of grace corresponding to what was known in scholastic theology as the *donum superadditum*,[17] a term not found in Zerbolt's writings even though he was familiar with the concept. That Zerbolt had a good grasp of the distinction between man's natural gifts and the *donum superadditum* is also evident from the fact that when he discusses man's natural gifts, the *dona naturae* as he refers to them specifically, he restricts himself to the subject matter of philosophical anthropology and man's natural inclination towards the good.[18] However, he does not, as will be seen, draw a clear-cut distinction between man's nature *per se*, the subject matter of philosophical anthropology, and his natural inclination towards the good. Not only is Zerbolt familiar with the distinction made between man's natural and supernatural gifts, but he describes both of them in some detail. He was obviously cognizant of the fact that the *donum superadditum* cannot be fully understood without some understanding of the natural, psychological endowments. We will, then, discuss Zerbolt's philosophical anthropology first, followed by an analysis of his theological anthropology.

ii. *Philosophical Anthropology*

Repeating what Aristotle had written, Aquinas wrote that all the powers of the soul must be classified as being vegetative, sensitive, appetitive, locomotive or intellective.[19] The vegetative and locomotive powers or faculties are not mentioned anywhere by Zerbolt, and in *De Ascensionibus* he arranges all the remaining psychological faculties under two headings: the *vires intellectuales sives cognoscitivae* and the *vires*

---

[16] *Asc.*, 259C. Cf. *Asc.*, 267E: beneficia naturalia; and *Ref.*, 245F: dona naturae.

[17] Cf. F. J. Corley, "Man," *NCE*, IX, 128.

[18] *Ref.*, 245F-G and *Asc.*, 267D-F.

It is only in ch. 25 of *De Reformatione* and in ch. 25 of *De Ascensionibus* that Zerbolt discusses the natural gifts separately. In the opening chs. of *De Reformatione* and *De Ascensionibus* he does not maintain a clear-cut distinction between the *dona naturae* and the *dona gratiae* in his discussion of them.

In ch. 25 of *De Reformatione*, as well as in ch. 25 of *De Ascensionibus*, the discussion of the *dona naturae* is followed by a discussion of what Zerbolt once again refers to as the *dona gratiae*, and thirdly he discusses what he terms the *dona superexcellentiae*. In this instance the *dona gratiae* are not the equivalent of the *donum superadditum*, but graces bestowed on man necessary for his justification and sanctification. The gifts of supreme excellence, on the other hand, are the incarnation, the sacraments, etc. This particular concept of a triad of graces, as well as their sequence, is clearly inspired by Bonaventure's *De Triplici Via*, ch. 1, par. 2 (*Works*, I, 69-70). However, Zerbolt's description of the graces themselves, and of the *dona naturae* in particular, has very little in common with Bonaventure's definition of them.

[19] Thomas Aquinas, *ST*, 1a, 78, 1. Cf. Copleston, *A History of Philosophy*, Vol. II, Pt. II, 96-97 and Störig, *Geschiedenis van de filosofie*, I, 248.

appetitivae.[20] In view of the fact that under the first heading he mentions
the intellect, reason and the senses,[21] this category is more correctly
described by the term *vires cognoscitivae* than by the expression *vires intellectuales.* In *De Reformatione* he employs a somewhat different terminology.
There he speaks of the *vires apprehensivae* and the *vires appetitivae* respectively.[22] Zerbolt divides the powers of the soul, then, into cognitive and appetitive. As the cognitive powers he names, we have just noted, the intellect, reason and the senses.[23] To lump all the cognitive powers together
in this fashion would appear to have been unusual. It was more common
to separate them into two sub-groups: the sensitive and intellective
powers.[24] As appetitive powers or faculties he mentions the will, concupiscence and irascibility.[25] We must now examine Zerbolt's understanding of the psychological faculties and the functions he assigns to each
one of them.

Cognitive Powers. Zerbolt divides the senses into outward and inward, or
exterior and interior,[26] and in doing so he was following in the footsteps
of scholastic thought.[27] However, his doctrine of the senses is not well
developed. He simply writes that God made man a sensible being and
that he granted him five senses,[28] meaning the exterior senses, for the
scholastics attributed only four interior senses to man.[29] The object of the

---

[20] *Asc.*, 259C: Dederat enim tibi Dominus liberalissimus vires intellectuales sive
cognoscitivas, intellectum, rationem et sensum, ut videlicet Deum per intellectum
cognosceres et immaterialia intelligeres: ... Dedit etiam vires appetitivas, ...

[21] See previous footnote.

[22] *Ref.*, 237G-H: ...vires apprehensivas ... vires etiam appetitivas...

[23] Cf. *Ref.*, 237G and footnote 20 above.

[24] Cf. Bonaventure, *Breviloquium*, Pt. II, ch. 9 (*Works*, II, 95), and Thomas Aquinas,
ST, 1a, 78, 1.

[25] *Asc.*, 259C-D: Dedit etiam vires appetitivas, voluntatem scilicet ... Dedit vim concupiscibilem, ... Dederat item vim irascibilem ... *Ref.*, 237H: Per vires etiam appetitivas,
scilicet voluntatem, irascibilitatem et concupiscibilitatem, ...

[26] *Asc.*, 259C: Per sensum exteriorem rerum materialium particularia et praesentia.
Per interiorem vero et horum etiam absentium imagines et simulacra attraheres pro
adiutorio rationis.

[27] Cf. Bonaventure, *Breviloquium*, Pt. II, ch. 9 (*Works*, II, 96); Thomas Aquinas, *ST*,
1a, 78, 3 and 4; cf. A. M. Perreault, "Senses," *NCE*, XIII, 90-92.

[28] *Asc.*, 267E: Creavit te, et esse dedit tibi ex nihilo, sed esse pulchrum et speciosum,
sensibile, et vivum, quinque sensibus decoratum. This passage would appear to have
been inspired by one in Bonaventure's *Soliloquium*, which the Seraphic Doctor in turn had
copied from Augustine's *De Trinitate* (*Soliloquium*, ch. 1, par. 4 [Works, III, 44]). *Ref.*,
245F-G; Dedit tibi visum, auditum et caetera: ...

[29] See Thomas Aquinas, *ST*, 1a, 78, 3-4 and cf. Copleston, *A History of Philosophy*, Vol.
II, Pt. II, 96-99; F. Copleston, *Aquinas* (Harmondsworth: Penquin Books, 1955),
173-175; and A. M. Perreault, "Senses," *NCE*, XIII, 90-92.
Aquinas distinguished four interior senses and rejected Avicenna's opinion that there
are five. The *sensus communis* sorts and collates the information collected by the exterior
senses. The *phantasia* stores and conserves the purely sensible impressions. The faculty of a
dog, for example, to apprehend whether a man is friendly or unfriendly is the *vis
aestimativa*. It is the *vis memorativa* which conserves such discernments.

five exterior senses, Zerbolt continues, is the material world.[30] Man's
knowledge of the material world as such depends, therefore, upon the
senses, and is obtained through them.[31] Zerbolt does not name any of the
interior senses by their scholastic name, but he is, nonetheless, familiar
with the scholastic theories regarding the interior senses. He writes that
on account of the interior sense one may recall at will the image and
similitude of the objects of the exterior senses in the absence of these same
material entities.[32] Recall of previous sensory experience is possible
because the interior sense stores the impressions passed on to it by the exterior senses. He does not do so here, but Zerbolt usually refers to this
storehouse of the sensory impressions as the memory. However, for Zerbolt the memory is the storehouse of not only sensitive impressions, but of
intellectual impressions as well.[33] In ascribing this comprehensive function to the memory Zerbolt would appear to be standing closer to Plato
and Augustine than to Aristotle and Aquinas.[34] The memory is an important faculty for Zerbolt, for it makes recall possible, and meditation is
none other but a controlled form of recall. Consequently Zerbolt lays
great stress on the reformation of the memory understood as the
storehouse of the mind, for such a reformed memory is necessary for
meditation,[35] an important facet of Zerbolt's spirituality. Finally, Zerbolt
also makes a reference, it would seem, to that interior sense which
Aquinas calls the *vis aestimativa*. For he writes that in each one of the five
exterior senses God created corresponding or fitting delights.[36] What he

---

[30] See footnote 26 above.

[31] Cf. Copleston, *A History of Philosophy*, Vol. II, Pt. II, 80 and 313-314; and Copleston,
Aquinas, 173-174.

The dictum that *nihil est in intellectu quod prius non fuerit in sensu* all of the writers just mentioned were willing to apply to sensible objects. However, beyond one's knowledge of sensible objects Aristotle and Aquinas were willing to apply this dictum to other areas of
knowledge as well, which Augustine and Bonaventure refused to do. They relied on illumination, essentially a Platonic concept.

[32] See footnote 26 above. Cf. *Asc.*, 267E: Dedit tibi memoriam qua similium rerum
simulacra reponeres, donec alicuius tibi placeret reminisci.

[33] See *Ref.*, chs. 18-35 (pp. 243A-250C). See *Ref.*, p. 243B in particular. Cf. below, p.
250; Goossens, *Meditatie*, 88; and P. Siwek, "Memory," *NCE*, IX, 640.

It must be pointed out that for Zerbolt the memory is not only the storehouse of sensible
and intellectual impressions, but that it is also the faculty of remembering. See first four
references just given.

[34] For Plato's view regarding the memory see P. Siwek, "Memory," *NCE*, IX, 640;
for Augustine's views see *De Trinitate* 12.15, and cf. E. A. Synan, "Knowledge, Theories
of," *NCE*, VIII, 235; for Aristotle's and Aquinas' views see the references given in footnote 29 above. In the *Soliloquium* Bonaventure's description of the memory and its function would appear to be Augustinian, but in the *Breviloquium* it is Aristotelian-Thomistic
(Bonaventure, *Soliloquium*, ch. 1, par. 3 [*Works*, III, 43], and *Breviloquium*, Pt. II, ch. 9
[*Works*, II, 95-96]).

[35] See footnote 33 above.

[36] *Ref.*, 245F-G: Dedit tibi visum, auditum, et caetera: et singulis creavit sensibus ea
quae sibi congruunt oblectamenta.

appears to be saying here is that the material world is not delightful in itself, but that God so constructed the exterior senses that they experience the material world as being delightful. This involves a value judgement which the external senses cannot make by themselves, but for which they are dependent on the interior sense labelled *vis aestimativa* by Aquinas.[37]

From the lower cognitive powers we must turn to the superior cognitive powers: the *vires intellectuales*, which set man apart from, and above, the animals with whom he shares the sensitive faculties.[38] Zerbolt mentions two intellective powers or *vires intellectuales*, as he calls them, and they are the intellect (*intellectus*) and reason (*ratio*).[39] There is also a third intellective faculty which Zerbolt variously refers to as the *synderesis*, natural reason, or right reason.[40] He explains that, generally speaking, the function of the superior cognitive faculties is understanding (*intelligere*),[41] a concept which has always been difficult to describe philosophically.[42] However, he also assigns peculiar functions to each of the intellective faculties. It is through reason (*ratio*) that one arrives at an understanding (*intelligere*) of material and inferior things, he writes.[43] What he apparently means is that the *ratio* abstracts intelligible knowledge, which must be contrasted with sensible knowledge and surpasses it, from material and inferior objects. In *De Reformatione* Zerbolt mentions the *ingenium* along with the *ratio* as having the material world for its object.[44] It is through the intellect on the other hand, which Zerbolt

---

[37] See Copleston, *A History of Philosophy*, Vol. II, Pt. II, 98-99; Copleston, *Aquinas*, 174-175; and A. J. Perreault, "Senses," *NCE*, XIII, 90-92. Cf. J. F. Donceel, "Sensation," *NCE*, XIII, 84.

[38] *Asc.*, 267E: Dedit tibi prae caeteris creaturis inferioribus intellectum, quo caeteris animantibus praeemineres et Deum tuum cognoscere posses, et veritatem ipsam intelligere: ...

[39] See first excerpt in footnote 20 above. *Ref.*, 245G: ..., cui dedit rationem, ingenium et industriam, qua omnia materialia posset intelligere. Dedit tibi mentem vel intellectum, qua immateriales spiritus, scilicet Deum et Angelos intelligeres. Cf. *Ref.*, 237G, 241H and 242F.

[40] *Super modo vivendi*, 30: Exponunt autem doctores omnia fuisse communia de iure nature, id est, ex instinctu recte racionis, que quodammodo natura dicitur. *Ibid.*, 29: Sed secundum naturalem racionem et ius naturale, quod hic pro eodem sumitur, omnia erant communia,... *De Libris Teutonicalibus*, 52: ..., quibus oculus eorum interior, sindieresis et racio, sive lex naturalis tamquam pulveribus obfuscatur, ... Cf. van Rooy, *Zerbolt*, 174.

It would appear that Zerbolt established a bond between natural law and divine law, a traditional practice. (*Super modo vivendi*, 94: Haec enim sunt de iure naturali et lege divina, que omnibus est communis.) However, there was a tendency among the nominalists to dissolve this bond between natural law and divine law (Oberman, *Biel*, 100).

[41] See footnotes 20 and 39 above. Cf. *Asc.*, 267E.

[42] Cf. F. E. Crowe, "Understanding (*Intellectus*)," *NCE*, XIV, 389. Aquinas wrote that understanding (*intelligere*) is the fitting act of man's soul (*ibid.*, 391).

[43] *Asc.*, 259C: ...: per rationem de inferioribus recte discerneres, omnia in laudem Dei referres. Also see footnote 39 above, second excerpt.

[44] See footnote 39 above, second excerpt.

also refers to as *mens*,[45] that one obtains an understanding (*intelligere*) of immaterial and spiritual entities such as God and angels.[46] It is, in fact, for the very purpose of knowing God that he granted man the intellect,[47] and virtually the same statement can be found in Radewijns' *Tractatulus Devotus*.[48] Furthermore, Zerbolt is familiar with the Aristotelian-Thomistic practice of attributing two separate parts or functions to the intellect: active and passive. According to this theory the active intellect possesses the capacity to abstract intelligible knowledge which is then impressed upon the possible or passive intellect, an essentially receptive faculty.[49] In other words, the active intellect reduces reality to intelligible proportions so that it can be absorbed by the possible intellect. Zerbolt briefly mentions this possible intellect. It is, he writes, the faculty which receives and collates the *species intelligibilium* or intelligible information.[50] Concerning the relationship between the possible intellect and the memory one can only speculate. All that can be said is that Zerbolt would appear to assign a very specific and limited function to the possible intellect in comparison with the role given by him to the memory. Finally, Zerbolt does not, in contrast with Augustine, Bonaventure and Aquinas,[51] stress the essential unity of the intellective faculties. Zerbolt speaks of *ratio* and *intellectus* as *vires intellectuales*,[52] and nowhere does he indicate that they are, in the final analysis, merely different functions of the one intellective faculty.

Reason and intellect are speculative faculties, but right reason is not. Zerbolt equates right reason with natural reason, which he in turn equates with, or grounds in, natural law.[53] It is by means of right reason that man possesses a natural and innate knowledge of natural law, and consequently knows naturally what is right and wrong.[54] Like Johannes

---

[45] *Ibid.*; and cf. *Asc.*, 259E.

[46] See footnotes 20 and 39 above. Cf. *Asc.*, 267E.

[47] See footnotes 20 and 39 above. Cf. *Asc.*, 267E.

[48] *Tractatulus Devotus*, 215: Nam erant sibi primo dati intellectus ... ut videlicet deum per intellectum cognosceret,...

Radewijns would appear to rely on David of Augsburg for this particular idea (D. of Augsburg, *De ext. et int. hom. compositione*, I, 84; cf. Goossens, *Meditatie*, 215), and Zerbolt on Radewijns.

[49] See Copleston, *A History of Philosophy*, Vol. II, Pt. I, 313-314; Knowles, *The Evolution of Medieval Thought*, 44 and 198-201; Copleston, *Aquinas*, 175-176; J. F. Donceel, "Intellect," *NCE*, VII, 555-556; and E. D. Simmons, "Abstraction," *NCE*, I, 57-58.

[50] *Asc.*, 267E: Similiter dedit intellectum possibilem, ubi intelligibilium species iterum occurrendas collocares.

[51] See Thomas Aquinas, *ST*, 1a, 79, 8-9; Copleston, *A History of Philosophy*, Vol. II, Pt. I, 320; and *ibid.*, Vol. II, Pt. II, 97-98.

[52] See footnote 20 above.

[53] See footnote 40 above.

[54] Cf. M. W. Hollenbach, "Synderesis," *NCE*, XIII, 881-883 and B. F. Brown, "Natural Law," *NCE*, X, 252-256.

Brinckerinck, another of his *confrères*, Zerbolt restricts the operation of right reason, also known as the *synderesis* or *scintilla conscientiae*, to cognition.[55] Zerbolt and Brinckerinck do not, in contrast with Alexander of Hales and Thomas a Kempis for example, regard right reason or the *scintilla conscientiae* as a faculty which not only informs man what is right, but also disposes him to choose that which he knows to be right.[56]

Appetitive Powers. From the cognitive powers (*vires cognoscitivae*) we proceed to the *vires appetitivae.* This is the sequence also followed by Zerbolt, which indicates that, like Aquinas, he regards an appetite as an inclination towards a good following upon a cognitive act.[57] If an appetite is the result of a cognitive act, it follows that there should be as many different types of appetition as there are distinct kinds of cognition, and such indeed, was the view held by Aquinas in particular. He detected two types of appetition in man: sensitive and intellective. The sensitive appetite he subdivided into concupiscible and irascible, and he called the will the intellective appetite.[58] Consistent with his views regarding man's cognitive powers, and in total agreement with Aquinas, Zerbolt also discovers two,

---

[55] See footnote 40 above; and W. Moll, ed., "Acht collatiën van Johannes Brinckerinck, een bijdrage tot de kennis van den kanselarbeid der Broeders van het Gemene Leven, uit hss. der 15e en 16e eeuw," *Kerkhistorisch Archief*, IV (1866), 115. Cf. G. C. Zieleman, *Middelnederlandse Epistel- en Evangeliepreken* (Kerkhistorische Bijdragen, Vol. VIII; Leiden, 1978), 292.

Zieleman is of the opinion that the collection of sermons which constitutes the subject of his study originated in Flanders some time before the emergence of the Modern Devotion in the northern Netherlands. He continues that, although there are similarities between the spirituality found in the sermons and that of the Modern Devotion, the differences perhaps outweigh the resemblances. For the spirituality of the sermons is characterized by strong, mystical overtones, while that of the Devotionalists was essentially ascetical (Zieleman, *op. cit.*, 307-309).

[56] Cf. M. W. Hollenbach, "Synderesis," *NCE*, XIII, 882; and *De Imitatione Christi*, Bk. III, ch. 55.

Zerbolt's use of the terms "natural reason" and "right reason" to describe the faculty under discussion is, in itself, an indication that he restricts its operation to cognition.

In his monograph on Zerbolt, Geesink devotes one paragraph to Zerbolt's views regarding the *vires cognoscitivae* or the *vires apprehensivae:* namely *ratio* and *intellectus* (Geesink, *Zerbolt*, 111). Zerbolt's views on right reason or natural reason which are found in *Super Modo Vivendi* are not examined by Geesink. Geesink's presentation of Zerbolt's views regarding *ratio* and *intellectus* agrees in essence with the analysis just presented. The major shortcoming of Geesink's account is that it does not tell us anything regarding the relationship of Zerbolt's anthropology to that of his predecessors.

[57] See E. M. Stock, "Appetite," *NCE*, I, 703-704. Cf. Geesink, *Zerbolt*, 111-112.

As he did with the cognitive powers, Geesink more or less repeats Zerbolt's description of the appetitive powers. In this instance too Geesink makes no attempt to put Zerbolt's views regarding the appetitive powers into their historical context (Geesink, *Zerbolt*, 111-112).

[58] See Thomas Aquinas, *ST*, 1a, 80. Cf. Copleston, *A History of Philosophy*, Vol. II, Pt. II, 97 and 99; and E. M. Stock, "Appetite," *NCE*, I, 704-705.

basically distinct, appetitive powers in man: the sensitive and the intellective or rational. As the sensitive appetites he names the concupiscent and
irascible powers, and he identifies the will as the one rational appetite.[59]
However, in spite of calling the concupiscent and irascible appetites sensitive appetites, Zerbolt assigns to them sensitive as well as intellective
objects; for he makes God an object of both sensitive appetites,[60] which
indicates an influence exerted upon him by the Franciscan David of
Augsburg whose views regarding the objects of the sensitive appetites
reflect those of Bonaventure.[61] The concupiscent appetite, he writes,
draws man to all that is good, but above all to God, the Supreme Good,[62]
while the irascible appetite enables the believer to repel with indignation
anything which might separate him from God.[63] Aquinas further subdivided the concupiscent and irascible appetites into six and five passions
or emotions respectively.[64] Zerbolt also writes that in the concupiscent
appetite God placed a variety of affections, but names only two of the six
given by Aquinas, namely love and joy.[65] In agreement with Aquinas he
defines love as a movement and inclination towards the good.[66] Joy en-
sues when one attains to the good perceived and desired,[67] and this applies in particular to God, the Supreme Good, in whom man will experience his greatest delight.[68] Of the five irascible affections named by
Aquinas, Zerbolt mentions only hope and courage; and they are
necessary to overcome obstacles which block one's path to the attainment

---

[59] Asc., 259E: Appetitus sensitivus scilicet vis concupiscibilis et irascibilis voluntati et
appetitui rationali promptissime obediebat. Cf. Ref., 237H.

[60] Asc., 259C: Dedit vim concupiscibilem, ut omne bonum appeteres et summum
bonum super omnia desiderares. Asc., 259D: Dederat item vim irascibilem qua firmiter
Deo adhaereres, et si quid ab hoc te posset separare, repelleres indignanter. In qua etiam
affectiones suas delectabiles posuit, spem, audaciam, ut esses virilis ad bonum aggredien-
dum et sperans adipiscendum. Cf. D. of Augsburg, De ext. et int. hom. compositione, I, 100.

[61] See Bonaventure, Breviloquium, Pt. II, ch. 9 (Works, II, 96); and D. of Augsburg, De
ext. et int. hom. compositione, I, 88-89.

[62] See footnote 60 above, first excerpt.

[63] See footnote 60 above, second excerpt.

[64] See Thomas Aquinas, ST, 1a, 80. Cf. E. M. Stock, "Appetite," NCE, I, 703-704.

[65] Asc., 259C-D: In qua vi concupiscibili varias posuit et delectabiles affectiones,
videlicet affectionem amoris, ut ipse te amor per se moveret et inclinaret ad bonum, affectionem gaudii, ut in Deo summe delectareris et iucundareris in intuitu beneficiorum Dei
et in consideratione operum et mirabilium, eius etc.

[66] See previous footnote. Cf. footnote 64 above.

[67] See footnote 65 above. Cf. Thomas Aquinas, ST, 1a, 80 and P. Curran, "Joy,"
NCE, VII, 1113.

[68] See footnote 65 above. Cf. D. of Augsburg, De ext. et int. hom. compositione, I, 101:
"Beyond question man is meant to be happy in God—the aptitude for joy is given him for
this end—and in the hope of winning a joy that is eternal, and in the present relish of
God's goodness to him."

of the good.[69] The will, the appetite of reason, was granted to man in order that he might love God, and all else for his sake.[70] The other acts of the will such as hate, desire, fear, etc. are not mentioned by Zerbolt.[71] To concentrate on love as *the* act of the will, and virtually to equate the faculty of the will with the act of love as Zerbolt would appear to be doing, is a particularly Augustinian characteristic.[72] To regard God as the prime object of the will is in harmony with Zerbolt's Thomistic definition of the will as the intellective appetite, for God is the supreme intellective or spiritual good. However, when Zerbolt continues that God granted man the will in order that he might love all things apart from God for his sake,[73] it would appear that he makes everything else, including sensible things, the object of the will. One cannot but conclude that, although Zerbolt postulates the existence of two distinct kinds of appetites: the sensitive and the rational, he would, nonetheless, appear to assign virtually the same classes of objects to both types of appetites. Summing up, it can be said that Zerbolt's analysis of man's psychological make-up as such has a great deal in common with Aquinas' philosophical anthropology, but his explanations why God granted this or that faculty to man appears to have been inspired by David of Augsburg for the most part. In some instances David's influence on Zerbolt was transmitted by Radewijns.

God the Natural Object of the Psychological Faculties. It is evident from the preceding paragraphs that Zerbolt explicitly makes God the foremost object of virtually all of the psychological faculties. Does this permit one to say that God gave man a natural, innate inclination towards himself, the Supreme Good, an inclination inherent in his psychological make-up? Such an interpretation would appear to be valid, for in the opening paragraph of *De Ascensionibus* Zerbolt writes that man possesses a natural appetite and desire for spiritual improvement: i.e., a natural appetite for God, the highest spiritual good. Further on in the same work he asserts that God made man's soul of such great dignity and nobility that nothing

---

[69] See footnote 60 above, second excerpt.

Perhaps Zerbolt also has anger in mind when he writes: "Dederat..., repelleres indignanter."

Although Zerbolt does not specifically make God the object of hope and courage, that is nonetheless understood.

[70] *Asc.*, 259C: Dedit etiam vires appetitivas, voluntatem scilicet ut Deum super omnia amares, caetera vero propter ipsum et in ordine ad ipsum amando referres. Cf. Copleston, *A History of Philosophy*, Vol. II. Pt. I, 96-99.

[71] See *Asc.*, 259C. Cf. E. M. Stock, "Appetite," *NCE*, I, 705 and V. J. Bourke, "Will," *NCE*, XIV, 910.

[72] See V. J. Bourke, "Will," *NCE*, XIV, 912. Cf. Radewijns, *Tractatulus Devotus*, 215; and D. of Augsburg, *De ext. et int. hom. compositione*, I, 84 and 105.

[73] See footnote 70 above.

can fill it, or surpass its understanding, except the one God, the holy and most glorious Trinity;[74] which suggests once again that man will naturally desire and seek God, for only he can satisfy all human cravings.[75]

Augustinian Elements in Zerbolt's Anthropology. Zerbolt's philosophical anthropology, the examination of which has up to this point been based largely on the first chapters of *De Reformatione* and *De Ascensionibus*, was strongly influenced by scholastic anthropology in general, and by Aristotelian-Thomistic anthropology in particular. However, when he comes to the spiritual reformation of the soul, Zerbolt abandons the Aristotelian-Thomistic anthropology and reverts to the older, and more traditional, Augustinian anthropology.[76] Augustine discerned three main operations of the soul: knowing, remembering and willing, and consequently distinguished three chief psychological potencies, namely *mens* or *intellectus*, *memoria* and *voluntas*.[77] This view of the soul was to be an influential one throughout the middle ages. It carried so much weight, in fact, that Aquinas tried to harmonize Augustinian anthropology with his own. He writes in the *Summa Theologiae* that although Augustine may distinguish between memory, intellect and will in the human psyche, the great church father does not regard memory and the cognitive-intellective faculties to be really distinct powers.[78] Beginning in the thirteenth century, then, one can detect a conflict between the older Augustinian philosophical anthropology and the newer Aristotelian-Thomistic

---

[74] *Asc.*, 258F: Rationalis enim ac nobilis creatura es et magni cuiusdam animi, ideoque altitudinem et ascensum naturali appetis desiderio. *Asc.* 267E: Fecit animam tuam tantae dignitatis, tantaeque nobilitatis, ut nihil eam replere, nihilve posset ipsi illabi, nisi sancta et gloriosissima Trinitas, unus Deus, ad cuius imaginem et similitudinem te creavit. Cf. *Asc.*, 278A-B; D. of Augsburg, *De ext. et int. hom. compositione*, I, 81; and below, pp. 233-241.

[75] See *Asc.*, 275F-G. Cf. Augustine, *Confessions*, I, 1.

[76] *Ref.*, ch. 12 (p. 241G-H). The title of this chapter reads: *De reformatione trium virium animae, scilicet intellectus, memoriae, et voluntatis.* See below, pp. 241-243.
Cf. Geesink, *Zerbolt*, 115-121. As Geesink tells it, Zerbolt first discusses the reformation of the *vires apprehensivae*, and follows with a discussion of the *vires appetitivae*. However, this is terminology which Zerbolt does not employ in connection with his discussion of the reformation of the soul, and for Geesink to use it in this connection leaves one with the wrong impression. For by the *vires apprehensivae* Zerbolt understands the sensitive and intellective faculties as well as the memory, but under the heading of the *vires apprehensivae* Geesink discusses only the reformation of the memory as it is outlined by Zerbolt in *De Reformatione*.

[77] See Copleston, *A History of Philosophy*, Vol. I, Pt. I, 233-236, for the origin of Augustine's view of the soul as a triad consisting of intellect, memory and will.

[78] Thomas Aquinas, *ST*, 1a, 79, 7. While Aquinas regards memory to be part of the cognitive power generally, he does, of course, distinguish between sensitive cognition and sensitive memory on the one hand, and intellective cognition and intellective memory on the other (*ibid.*).

philosophical anthropology. Generally speaking, the former would appear to have been favoured by spiritual writers and the latter by scholastic authors, although in the writings of Bonaventure and Zerbolt, for example,[79] both systems are represented and no attempt is made to reconcile them.[80] That the Aristotelian-Thomistic philosophical anthropology is found in Zerbolt's writings betrays, on the one hand, his interest in, and knowledge of, scholastic philosophy. On the other hand, the reversion to Augustinian philosophical anthropology in his discussion of the reformation of the soul is consistent—from a traditional perspective at least—with his role as a spiritual writer and certainly marks him out to be such.

Like Augustine, Zerbolt writes that there are three powers upon which all others depend in one way or another, and these three are memory, intellect and will. He continues that when these three have been reformed all other faculties can also be regarded as reformed.[81] Zerbolt does not, however, say very much about the intellect, memory, will and their respective operations understood in Augustinian terms.[82] Firstly, we have seen that his description of the memory in the opening chapters of his two manuals is not strictly an Aristotelian-Thomistic one, but that it perhaps comes closer to being Augustinian. Secondly, when he discusses the spiritual reformation of the will Zerbolt, in typical Augustinian fashion,[83] collects together all the affections or appetites under the label 'will',[84] while earlier he had drawn a clear-cut distinction between the sensitive appetites on the one hand, and the will as the rational appetite on the other.

Having looked at Zerbolt's Augustinian anthropology, and at his philosophical anthropology in its entirety, we turn now to his views regarding the *donum superadditum* possessed by Adam before the fall.

---

[79] For example, Bonaventure uses Augustinian psychology in his *Soliloquium*, ch. 1, par. 3 (*Works*, III, 43), and scholastic psychology in his *Breviloquium*, Pt. II, ch. 9 (*Works*, II, 93).

[80] Cf. Vos, "Gerard Zerbolt," 136.

[81] *Ref.*, 241G-H: Scias igitur quod licet anima multas habeat vires, potentias et affectiones, tres tamen in ea praecipue sunt vires, unde omnes aliae quodammodo dependent, quibus reformatis caeterae quoque reformari videbuntur. Sunt autem hae tres: Memoria, intellectus et affectus seu voluntas,... Cf. D. of Augsburg, *De ext, et int. hom. compositione*, I, 81-87.

[82] Goossens is correct when he writes that in ch. 12 of *De Reformatione* Zerbolt does give a "scholastic" description of intellect, memory and will (Goossens, *Meditatie*, 90). However, Goossens neglects to mention that Zerbolt gives an essentially scholastic description of the human psyche in the first chapters of *De Reformatione* and *De Ascensionibus*.

[83] See Augustine, *De Civitate Dei*, XIV, 6; and cf. V. J. Bourke, "Will," *NCE*, XIV, 912.

[84] *Ref.*, ch. 12 (p. 241G-H).

iii. *Theological Anthropology*

Tradition on the 'donum superadditum'. That Adam possessed a *donum super-additum* which did not belong to his nature is already found in the writings of the church fathers,[85] and the idea was developed further by the scholastic theologians of the twelfth and thirteenth centuries.[86] They divided the *donum superadditum* into two categories: the supernatural and the preternatural gifts. Sanctifying grace was held to be the supernatural gift *par excellence*, for it made Adam a sharer in the divine nature. There was also the supernatural gift of extraordinary knowledge: a clear perception of spiritual things and of God in particular, although it did not include a knowledge of God in his essence. Bodily immortality and integrity were considered to be the most important preternatural gifts, and the second of these two will need to be examined briefly.

Scholastic theologians in general believed that man suffers from a natural disability which they called rebellious, or negative, concupiscence. According to this theory the sensitive appetites, and the concupiscent appetite in particular, naturally rebel against the dictates of deliberating reason and right reason, the two intellective faculties which inform the rational appetite: the will. The resistance of the lower powers against the higher ones was regarded as a natural consequence of the fact that man has a body as well as a soul. Since rebellious concupiscence was seen as part of man's natural condition, it was not considered to be culpable. Rebellious concupiscence was held to be innocent as long as the will does not succumb to it. However, as soon as the will surrenders to the concupiscent desires, innocent concupiscence becomes sinful concupiscence, it was asserted, and culpable. However, man was considered to have been free from natural, rebellious concupiscence before the fall. At that time the lower powers were held in check through a gratuitous gift of grace: the gift of integrity. The most important consequence of the gift of integrity was the perfect submission of the concupiscent appetite to reason. The gift of integrity was termed preternatural and not supernatural because, unlike sanctifying grace, it did not make Adam a sharer in the divine nature. On the other hand, it was not understood to have been purely natural either, for if it had been natural, its loss on account of Adam's disobedience would have impaired human nature in a very real sense.[87]

---

[85] See Kelly, *Early Christian Doctrines*, 346-347.

[86] See Dudden, *Gregory the Great: His Place in History and Thought*, II, 376-378; Thomas Aquinas, *ST*, 1a, 90-102; Richardson, ed., *Dictionary*, 99 ("Donum Superadditum"); T. R. Heath, "Adam," *NCE*, I, 114; and F. J. Corley, "Man," *NCE*, IX, 128.

[87] See A. Harnack, *History of Dogma*, trans. from the 3rd German edition by N. Buchanan (7 vols.; London-Edinburgh-Oxford, 1897-1899), VI, 228; M. M. Schanen,

Zerbolt on the 'dona gratiae'. When Zerbolt speaks of the *dona gratiae*[88] which God granted to Adam he has in mind first and foremost, almost exclusively it would seem, the gift of integrity. He does not mention the supernatural gift of sanctifying grace, although it is perhaps included by implication in the *dona gratiae* of which he speaks. Furthermore, in *De Reformatione* Zerbolt writes that pre-fall man possessed a perfectly pure heart and perfect charity,[89] and the latter implies the presence of sanctifying grace.[90] With respect to supernatural knowledge Zerbolt observes that, before the fall, the intellect and reason possessed, as a consequence of the gratuitous divine illumination, an extraordinary keenness, perspicacity, understanding and fulness of knowledge.[91] The supernatural illumination of the intellect also enabled man to have a perfect knowledge and vision of God before the fall, but this knowledge stopped short of the vision of God in his very essence.[92] However, in his account

---

"Integrity, Gift of," *NCE*, VII, 554; J. P. Kenny, "Concupiscence," *NCE*, IV, 123; L. M. Scheffczyk, "Concupiscence," *SM*, I, 404; Rahner and Vorgrimler, *Theological Dictionary*, 328-329 ("Original Justice"); and Harvey, *A Handbook of Theological Terms*, 125-126 ("Image of God") and 55 ("Concupiscence"). Cf. Thomas Aquinas, *ST*, 1a, 95, 1; and Bonaventure, *Breviloquium*, Pt. III, chs. 1 and 3 (*Works*, II, 110 and 123-124).

If the rebellion of the lower powers against the higher is regarded as a natural consequence of man's constitution, then it should logically be regarded as constituting part of man's nature as such, and be treated as a part of philosophical anthropology. However, because this natural strife of the lower powers against the higher was held in check before the fall, and so cannot be predicated of man before the fall but only of man after the fall, it has been ranged under theological anthropology (cf. Oberman, *Biel*, 58-59).

Dempsey Douglass and Steinmetz, as well as Oberman, are in error when they present the view that only Duns Scotus defended the doctrine that rebellious concupiscence is natural to man, and that this concupiscence was rendered inert before the fall through a gratuitous gift of grace. See Dempsey Douglass, *Geiler*, 106; Steinmetz, *Staupitz*, 65; and Oberman, *Biel*, 125.

[88] *Asc.*, 259C: ..., tam alto monte donorum naturalium et gratiarum collocavit,...

[89] *Ref.*, 238E: Sed ne cogites quod hi duo fines ab eo differant quem supra diximus finem esse debere exercitiorum tuorum, ut videlicet illi interiori statui nostro unde sumus prolapsi, redeuntes propinquemus, quia idem est cor purgare, ad puritatem cordis vel ad charitatem tendere, et illi statui propinquare.

On purity of heart and charity as the end of the spiritual life see below, pp. 233-241.

[90] Although perfect charity in pre-fall man was generally considered to be the result of sanctifying grace, purity of heart remained a necessary prerequisite. Purity of heart itself was aided by the "gift of integrity." Cf. Bonaventure, *Breviloquium*, Pt. II, ch. 11 (*Works*, II, 103).

[91] *Ref.*, 237G: ...cum per vires apprehensivas, intellectum videlicet et rationem caeterasque vires, clare ac perspicaciter discerneret,... *Ref.*, 238A-B: Fuisti intellectuali lumine plene illustratus,... *Asc.*, 259E: Intellectus autem signato super se lumine vultus Domini, naturali scilicet et gratuita illustratione plene novit quid fuerat agendum vel dimmittendum. *Ref.*, 237H: ..., cum breviter omne quod debuit, clare intellexit,... Cf. *Asc.*, 259C: Intus vero plenus rerum notitia et affectuum,...

[92] *Asc.*, 259D: Intellectus fuit illuminatus, ita ut noster primus parens, quamvis ut credimus Deum per essentiam non vidit, ipsum tamen puro mentis intuitu et contemplationis excessu speculabatur. *Ref.*, 237G-H: Tunc autem homo iste recte in Ierusalem fuisse dicitur, cum per vires apprehensivas, intellectum videlicet et rationem caeterasque

of the *donum superadditum*, or *dona gratiae*, Zerbolt concentrates on the harmony of the psychological powers, capacities and affections which were so arranged by God, he writes, that the one was not contrary to the other. As a consequence Adam enjoyed inner peace, concord and tranquillity.[93] The inferior powers of the soul, namely the sensitive-bodily faculties, obeyed the superior powers, i.e. the intellective-mental faculties, without contradiction, and the former had no desire to go contrary to the latter.[94] He continues, in language reminiscent of Aquinas, that with respect to the cognitive powers the senses obeyed reason, and reason obeyed the intellect. The intellect, in turn, was subject to God himself.[95] The sensitive appetites, on the other hand, namely the concupiscent and irascible affections, rendered prompt obedience to the appetite of reason: the will.[96] Thus all the inferior, sensitive faculties were subordinate to the superior, rational-intellective powers. Consequently Zerbolt can write that before the fall the law of the flesh, namely the sensitive-bodily faculties, did not war against the law of the mind or the intellective-mental powers.[97]

---

vires, clare ac perspicaciter discerneret, ac etiam ipsum Deum mundis et intellectualibus oculis ac mentalibus extasibus, etsi non per essentiam, intueretur:... Cf. van Rooy, *Zerbolt*, 267; Dudden, *Gregory the Great: His Place in History and Thought*, II, 377; and Thomas Aquinas, *ST*, 1a, 94, 1.

The divine illumination discussed here must be distinguished from the divine illumination which, according to Augustine and Bonaventure for example, is necessary for all knowledge except primary sensory knowledge.

In ch. twenty-five of *De Ascensionibus* Zerbolt makes a reference to infused knowledge in a list of otherwise purely natural endowments specifically labelled by him as such. (*Asc.*, 267E: ...: et huic intellectui tuo lumen vultus sui infudit,...) The inclusion of infused knowledge is an obvious error, since infused knowledge is "produced directly in a created mind by some angelic or divine illumination." (A. B. Wetter, "Knowledge, Infused," *NCE*, VIII, 230.) Such a stray statement regarding infused knowledge would not be sufficient to question whether Zerbolt's epistemology was in fact Aristotelian-Thomistic. His psychology generally would point to his epistemology having been Aristotelian-Thomistic.

[93] See footnote 150 below. *Asc.*, 259C: Intus vero plenus rerum notitia et affectuum, quieta et pacifica concordia. *Ref.*, 238A: Amisisti pacem, tranquillitatem et gaudium, laetitiam et quietem:...

Zerbolt's description of man's condition in heaven also throws some light on his understanding of man's state in paradise, although he also adds that in many ways the former state is superior to the latter. *Asc.*, 267C: Cogita de dotibus...non habebis. Cf. *Ref.*, 245C.

[94] *Asc.* 259E: Sed istas vires optimo modo in te ordinaverat, ut inferiores superioribus sine contradictione, sine quovis appetitu contrario obedirent.

[95] *Asc.*, 259E: Sensus enim obediebat rationi, ratio menti. Mens autem ipsa soli Deo fuisset subiecta. Zerbolt, we have seen, equated *mens* and *intellectus*. Cf. Thomas Aquinas, *ST*, 1a, 95, 1: Deus fecit *hominem rectum*. Erat enim haec rectitudo secundum hoc quod ratio subdebatur Deo, rationi vero inferiores vires, et animae corpus.

It is perhaps of right reason that Zerbolt is thinking in particular here.

[96] *Asc.*, 259E: Appetitus sensitivus scilicet vis concupiscibilis et irascibilis voluntati et appetitui rationali promptissime obediebat. *Ref.*, 237H:..., atque sine appetitu contrario seu quamvis contradictione,...

[97] *Asc.*, 259D-E: Nec erant tunc istae vires, potentiae vel affectiones sibi invicem contrariae, ut lex carnis legi mentis repugnaret. Nondum enim erat corpus quod corrumpitur, ideoque nec animam aggravabat.

There was, therefore, perfect concord in the inner man,[98] and this harmony stemmed above all from the fact that the dominant sensitive appetite, the concupiscent power, did not rebel against the will but was
perfectly obedient to it.[99] Consequently Adam was free from all concupiscent desire,[100] and it is to rebellious concupiscence in particular that Zerbolt applies the term *lex carnalis*,[101] a traditional practice. Although the
will held undisputed sway over all the inferior appetites, it was not a law
unto itself. It carried out everything in accordance with the counsels of
the intellect and the dictates of reason:[102] the dictates of right reason in
particular. The intellect, furthermore, was full of knowledge, for it was il-
lumined by God.[103] God freely granted pre-fall man immunity from
rebellious concupiscence in order that all his faculties, and so his entire
being, might effortlessly serve the supernatural purpose for which they
were created, namely the glory and worship of God.[104] Zerbolt does
describe, as we have seen, man's purely natural faculties, but we may be
certain that he did not believe for one moment that man had ever existed
in a state of pure nature.[105] He held that from the outset man had a
supernatural vocation,[106] and the gift of integrity—a term not used by
Zerbolt himself—was a gratuitous gift designed to further and to perfect

---

[98] *Asc.*, 259E: Et ita in interiori homine summa erat concordia,...

[99] *Asc.*, 259E: ..., et quodcunque volebat ipsa voluntas in hoc parebant reliquae vires et
affectiones inferiores:... In view of the fact that for Zerbolt the objects of the concupiscent
appetite were not exclusively sensible, rebellious concupiscence could have been a desire,
contrary to the dictates of reason, for an inferior good other than a purely sensible one.
Cf. J. P. Kenny, "Concupiscence," *NCE*, IV, 121-124.

[100] *Ref.*, 238B: ..., ab omni fece concupiscentiarum depuratus.

[101] Cf. *Asc.*, 259E and 260A.

[102] *Asc.*, 259E: Voluntas autem omnia agere debuit ad intellectus consilium vel dic-
tamen rationis. *Ref.*, 237H: ..., immo cum delectatione voluit et appetiit, sicut se debere
appetere rationis iudicio intellexit. The "dictate of reason" refers, most likely, to the dictate of right reason in particular.
These two passages indicate that Zerbolt was an intellectualist, which is not surprising
when one considers that his over-all anthropology was very much influenced by Aquinas'
doctrine of man. A voluntarist like Duns Scotus, for example, maintained that the will
leads and commands the intellect (Copleston, *A History of Philosophy*, Vol. II, Pt. II,
263-264). Furthermore, Zerbolt is of the opinion, as will be seen in greater detail in the
final chapter of this essay, that the highest union man can achieve with God in this life is
the beatific vision, rather than charity. That further labels Zerbolt as an intellectualist (cf.
ibid.). Gerretsen concludes that Grote was an intellectualist as well (Gerretsen, *Florentius
Radewijns*, 12-13).

[103] See footnote 91 above.

[104] *Asc.*, 259H: Unde contigit ut nunc istae vires et effectus longe aliter movent quam
ab Deo fuerunt instituae,... Cf. *Asc.*, 259C-D in a number of places: a) intellect was given
to man so that he might know God; b) will was given so that he might love God; c) concupiscent appetite was given so that man might seek God; d) irascible appetite was given
so that man might cleave to God. See above where this has been discussed in detail.

[105] Cf. Rahner and Vorgrimler, *Theological Dictionary*, 328 ("Original Justice").

[106] See footnote 104 above.

this vocation. This gift enabled man to love God without any effort or internal strife.

Original Justice. It is to the gift of integrity that Zerbolt attaches the label
"iustitia originalis."[107] This state of original justice or rectitude, he explains, is still symbolized in man's erect posture.[108] The other preternatural and supernatural graces possessed by pre-fall man remain
unmentioned in his definition of original justice. To equate only part of
the *donum superadditum* with original justice had not been uncommon
throughout the history of Christian thought. Augustine, for example,
singled out sanctifying grace as being the equivalent, or substance, of
original justice.[109] The schoolmen, by contrast, generally equated the
preternatural gift of integrity with original justice and regarded the immunity from rebellious concupiscence to be its substance.[110] Perhaps influenced by Augustine, Dionysius van Rijkel, the Carthusian
(1402-1471), added sanctifying grace to the scholastic definition of
original justice.[111] It is patently obvious, then, that in restricting his
definition of original justice to the harmony between the psychological
faculties enjoyed by pre-fall man, Zerbolt's understanding of original
justice agreed with that of the leading schoolmen like Bonaventure,
Aquinas and Duns Scotus, to name but a few.[112] Inasmuch as Zerbolt
identifies the gift of integrity with original justice, if follows that for him
original justice was a *donum superadditum*, and a century ago Geesink came
to the same conclusion.[113] The concept of original justice or righteousness
as a *donum superadditum* joined to man's constitution is an idea to be found
as far back as Athanasius: in rudimentary form at least.[114]

Man as God's Image and Likeness. That God created man in his image and
likeness is found in Genesis,[115] and from a fairly early date onwards there

---

[107] *Asc.*, 259F: Et istiusmodi virium et affectionum concordia, pacifica ac concors obedientia dicebatur et nominabatur ab sanctis iustitia originalis. Cf. C. J. Peter, "Original
Justice," *NCE*, X, 775.

[108] *Asc.*, 259F: Vide hunc statum rectitudinis quem adhuc erectione corporis figuras,...
Cf. Richardson, ed., *Dictionary*, 202 ("Man, Doctrine of").

[109] See T. R. Heath, "Adam," *NCE*, I, 114.

[110] See Thomas Aquinas, *ST*, 1a 2ae, 82, 3; Harnack, *History of Dogma*, VI, 297, footnote 1; Julius Gross, *Geschichte des Erbsündendogmas*, Vol. III: *Entwicklungsgeschichte des
Erbsündendogmas im Zeitalter der Scholastik* (Munich-Basel, 1971), 204, 265, 383-384, 385,
387, and 389; Oberman, *Biel*, 125; and Dempsey Douglass, *Geiler*, 106.

[111] See previous footnote, the third reference.
In view of Gross' findings K. Rahner would appear to place the tendency to make sanc-
tifying grace a component of original justice much too early. See K. Rahner, "Original
Sin," *SM*, IV, 329.

[112] See footnote 110 above.

[113] Geesink, *Zerbolt*, 112.

[114] See Kelly, *Early Christian Doctrines*, 346.

[115] Genesis 1, 26.

was a tendency to distinguish between the two. We can already detect in
Irenaeus what was to become a general, although perhaps not a universal, tendency to equate God's image in man with his purely natural endowments, and God's likeness in man with the *donum superadditum*.[116]
However, the likeness was rarely equated with the *donum superadditum* in
its entirety; usually it was equated with only one or other component of
the *donum superadditum*.[117] The three concepts *donum superadditum, iustitia
originalis* and *similitudo Dei* were rarely regarded as being synonymous,
but they are, nonetheless, closely related, for all three refer to gifts added
to man's pure nature. Zerbolt too writes that God created man *suam imaginem et similitudinem*,[118] but he does not draw a distinction between image
and similitude. He writes that God created man in his image and likeness
not only when he discusses pre-fall man in his entirety, but also when he
discusses the purely natural endowments of man.[119] Furthermore, he
writes in an Augustinian vein that the image and likeness is Trinitarian:
i.e., man was made in the image and likeness of the Trinity through intellect, memory and will.[120] This, of course, is also consistent with the
Augustinian element in his philosophical anthropology. Johannes Brinckerinck, a *confrère* of Zerbolt, does, by contrast, draw a clear distinction
between image and likeness. The image, he writes, was retained by man
after the fall, but the likeness was greatly corrupted.[121] Obviously he
equated the image with man's natural endowments and the likeness with
the *donum superadditum* as had traditionally been done.

"*De statu naturalis.*" Zerbolt employs the adjective *naturalis* not only to
describe those endowments possessed by man which are the subject matter of philosophical anthropology and man's innate inclination to the
good, but he also speaks of man's total state before the fall as being

---

[116] Kelly, *Early Christian Doctrines*, 171.

[117] See Augustine, *De Trinitate*, 12. 15; Dudden, *Gregory the Great: His Place in History and
Thought*, II, 376; Gilson, *History of Christian Philosophy in the Middle Ages*, 166-167; Bouyer,
The Cistercian Heritage, 98-99; Bonaventure, *Breviloquium*, Pt. II, chs. 9 and 12 (*Works*, II,
93, 94-95, 104 and 105) and *Soliloquium*, ch. 1, pars. 3-4 and 19 (*Works*, III, 43-44 and
56-57); D. of Augsburg, *De ext. et int. hom. compositione*, I, 83-84; Thomas Aquinas, *ST*, 1a,
93, 9; Harnack, *History of Dogma*, VI, 297, footnote, 1; L. Bouyer, *Dictionary of Theology*,
trans. by C. U. Quinn (New York, 1965), 160-161 ("Fall"); Harvey, *A Handbook of
Theological Terms*, 125-126 ("Image of God") and 220 ("Similitudo Dei"); and Rahner
and Vorgrimler, *Theological Dictionary*, 328-329 ("Original Justice").

[118] *Asc.*, 259B: ..., Dominus Deus qui te ad suam imaginem et similitudinem creavit...
Asc., 267E: ...gloriosissima Trinitas, unus Deus, ad cuius imaginem et similitudinem te
creavit.

[119] See *Asc.*, 259B and 267E respectively.

[120] See footnote 117 above. Andries Yserens, a later Devotionalist, also asserted that
man was created in the image of the Trinity (Axters, *Vroomheid*, III, 109).

[121] Brinckerinck, "Collatiën," 156.

naturalis.[122] Augustine also understood man's state before the fall to be a 'natural' one, although he did not deny its partly supernatural nature. By 'natural' he understood in particular that it was man's original condition, the state in which God created him.[123] Like Augustine, Zerbolt does not appear to have looked upon man's condition before the fall as a natural one in the strictest sense of the word. For he did not view the *donum superadditum* as being part of man's natural condition. William of St. Thierry, whose *Epistola ad Fratres de Monte Dei* was read by Zerbolt, frequently expressed the opinion that the aim of the religious life must be man's 'natural' condition. What he meant by this was that man must return to his original state as it existed before the fall. However, as Louis Bouyer comments, even for William of St. Thierry man's return to this 'natural' condition is more particularly a restoration of God's image in man: i.e., his natural endowments and their natural inclination to the good, rather than a restoration of the *donum superadditum* which man cannot regain in its entirety in this life.[124]

In originally granting to man all those gifts of nature and grace which have just been described, God made man of a very sublime dignity indeed, Zerbolt concludes. Man's perfection was such that he could scarcely have been more perfect unless he had gone forward to the vision of God in his very essence.[125]

B) *Man as Fallen*

In *De Ascensionibus* Zerbolt portrays original sin, venial sin and mortal sin as three consecutive descents from man's state of original justice. He devotes a separate chapter to each of these three descents,[126] but the first is discussed in greatest detail and it will also receive by far the most attention from us. To overcome this threefold fall Zerbolt outlines three ascents in *De Ascensionibus* and it is to these three ascents, which also give *De Ascensionibus* its title, that this work is primarily devoted.[127]

---

[122] *Asc.*, 259B: ...statu naturalis...; and *Asc.*, 258G: ...statum naturalis...

Besides referring to man's condition before the fall as his "*status naturalis,*" he also describes it as his "*naturalis dignitas,*" as his "*originalis dignitas,*" as his "*primordialis dignitas,*" and as a "*status rectitudinis* (*Asc.*, 258F and G, 259A, B and F, and 260A and B; *Ref.*, 237F-G and 238A).

[123] See M. J. Dorenkemper, "Nature (in Theology)," *NCE*, X, 278-279.

[124] Bouyer, *The Cistercian Heritage*, 97. Cf. Savary, *Psychological Themes in the Golden Epistle of William of St. Thierry*, 61-62.

[125] *Asc.*, 259B-C: ..., Dominus Deus qui te ad suam imaginem et similitudinem creavit, quondam in tam sublimi dignitate te posuit, tam alto monte donorum naturalium et gratiarum collocavit, ut nisi ad essentialem Dei visionem proficeres, vix altius ascendere posses.

[126] *Asc.*, chs. 3, 4 and 5 (259F-260F). In the *Summa Theologiae* Aquinas follows the same sequence in his discussion of original, venial and mortal sin (*ST*, 1a 2ae, 88-89).

[127] See below, pp. 264-265.

Before the fall the will followed the counsel of the intellect and the dictates of reason, but it was not bound by them. It was this freedom of the will which enabled man to sin. God placed man upon a lofty mountain, Zerbolt writes, from which he descended voluntarily into a deep valley.[128] In eating from the forbidden fruit Adam followed the dictates of his own will rather than those of natural reason or right reason, wherefore sin is contrary to natural reason, Zerbolt explains.[129] He does not describe in any detail the psychological process of the first act of sin. He was primarily interested in its effect on man. Zerbolt merely observes that the formal reason (formalis ratio), cause and essence of all sins is pride which causes one to turn away from God.[130] Consequently the cause of the first sin was pride, although Zerbolt does not state specifically that the pride of the first man consisted of his desire to be like God. With pride sown into man's heart, the devil, who was motivated by envy, played on man's concupiscible power, on gluttony in particular, to lure him into eating from the forbidden tree, and so into disobedience and a rejection of God

---

[128] Asc., 259A: Quondam eras in alto monte naturalis tuae et primordialis dignitatis constitutus, sed inde voluntarie es prolapsus in vallem quandam bassam. Cf. D. of Augsburg, De ext. et int. hom. compositione, I, 89.

Zerbolt opens De Reformatione with Luke 10, 30: "Homo quidam descendit de Ierusalem in Iericho" (Ref., 237G). This text, he writes, is a figurative representation of man's fall from original justice: from the state of uprightness, innocence and inner harmony to a state of misery, mutability and abandonment. For Jerusalem conveys the image of peace and stability, he explains, while Jericho is translated as the 'moon' which indicates mutability and change (Ref., 237G). That Jericho is Hebrew for moon, and symbolizes man's mutability and mortality, is an idea already found in Augustine's writings (cf. F. van der Meer, Augustine the Bishop, trans. by B. Battershaw and G. R. Lamb [New York-Evanston: Harper-Torchbooks, 1965], 66).

The interpretation of Luke 10, 30 as a figurative representation of man's fall is also found in Thomas Aquinas' Summa Theologiae, and he names Bede as his source for this particular exposition of the text in question (Thomas Aquinas, ST, 1a 2ae, 85, 1). The truth is, however, that such an exposition of Luke 10, 30 cannot be found in Bede's commentary on the Gospel of Luke (Venerabilis Bedae Opera Quae Supersunt Omnia, ed. J. A. Giles [12 vols.; London, 1843-1844], Vols. X and XI). Nonetheless, this interpretation of Luke 10, 30, usually attributed to Bede, carried considerable weight with medieval theologians. It can be found not only in Aquinas' Summa Theologiae, but also in Bonaventure's first sermon for the twelfth Sunday after Pentecost (Opera Omnia, IX, 398-401), and there are indications that Zerbolt may have relied on this sermon by Bonaventure for his own interpretation of Luke 10, 30 (cf. Rayez, "Gérard Zerbolt et Saint Bonaventure. Dépendances Littéraires," 335).

[129] Super modo vivendi, 29: Secundo constat, quod homo secundum naturalem racionem inclinatur ad iusticiam, et peccatum est contra naturalem racionem. Cf. Epiney-Burgard, Grote, XV and 288; and Oberman, Biel, 107 and 110.

[130] Asc., 263A: Nam aversus es ab creatore tuo per superbiam, in qua est formalis ratio peccati,... Asc., 263B: Quia vero in peccatis tuis Deum per superbiam contempsisti, ideo necesse est ut te homini Dei vicario claves habenti humiliter subdas vice Dei,... and cf. Asc., 278D.

and his commandments.[131] As a consequence of his disobedience Adam was expelled from paradise, and he and all humanity were deprived of original justice.[132] This brings us, then, to the question how Zerbolt viewed the effects of the fall on man.

i. *The Consequences of the Fall for the* dona gratiae

In his account of the *dona gratiae* possessed by pre-fall man Zerbolt gave most of his attention to the gift of integrity which he equated with original justice, and in his discussion of the effects of the fall on the *donum superadditum* he again concentrates his attention on the gift of integrity or original justice. That man lost sanctifying grace on account of the fall Zerbolt does not state in so many words. However, he does express the view that through actual sin man daily forfeits the grace of God,[133] and since Adam's disobedience was an actual sin committed by him personally, it may be presumed that he lost divine sanctifying grace on account of it. The loss of the supernatural knowledge of God possessed by Adam before the fall is not mentioned either by Zerbolt. He regarded the loss of original justice, on the other hand, as one of the major effects of Adam's disobedience, and consequently it receives a good deal of attention from him.

Zerbolt writes that it was by the just judgement of God that man lost his original justice,[134] which, in effect, meant the loss of integrity. It means, in practical terms, the loss of the inner concord and tranquillity enjoyed by Adam before his disobedience. The faculties now war against one another, striving in opposite directions in their motions and impulses: the lower against the higher.[135] Like Grote, Zerbolt establishes

---

[131] *Asc.*, 281A-B: Primum autem certamen est contra vitium gulae. Inde primo diabolus primum hominem tentavit et superavit; inde secundum hominem primo tentavit et succubuit. *Asc.*, 259G: ..., sed se ab creatoris sui imperio avertit transgrediens praeceptum divinum. *Asc.*, 283A: Invidia enim diaboli intravit mors in orbem terrarum, sequuntur eum qui sunt ex parte eius. Cf. Rahner and Vorgrimler, *Theological Dictionary*, 170 ("Fall of Man"); also Dudden, *Gregory the Great: His Place in History and Thought*, II, 379; and Bonaventure, *Breviloquium*, Pt. III, ch. 3 (*Works*, II, 115).

[132] *Asc.*, 260H: Cogita quod Adam propter inobedientiam expulit de paradiso, et totum genus humanum originali iustitia spoliavit.

[133] *Ref.*, 250D: ...sed quia, heu, multi per actuale peccatum spoliati sunt gratia Dei et culpa propria deformati:...

[134] *Asc.*, 259G-H: Amissa etenim iustitia originali ipso casu et iusto Dei iudicio,... Siquidem ut quotidie ne dicam continue, experiris, nisi totus insensibilis sis, ipsa sensualitas, vis scilicet concupiscibilis et irascibilis voluntari sunt rebelles, et contrariae, sed et ipsa voluntas quamvis non semper, frequenter tamen agit contra rationem. Unde contigit ut nunc istae vires et effectus longe aliter movent quam ab Deo fuerunt institutae, pronae ad malum et proclives semper ad illicitum concupiscendum. Cf. Bonaventure, *Breviloquium*. Pt. III, ch. 5 (*Works*, II, 118-119).

[135] *Asc.*, 259G: ...ipsae vires et affectiones ab suo statu prolapsae,..., sibi invicem motibus suis et impulsibus contrariantes et repugnantes.

what would appear to be an organic connection between man's disobedience to God on the one hand, and the revolt of man's inferior faculties against his superior powers on the other.[136] It is especially to the revolt of the sensible appetites against the rational appetite that Zerbolt draws attention. The concupiscent and irascible appetites rebel against, and are contrary to, the will.[137] Zerbolt views this assertion of rebellious concupiscence, namely concupiscence understood as the desire for an inferior good contrary to the dictates of right reason and the rational appetite, as the most serious consequence of the loss of original justice.[138] Furthermore, Zerbolt continues, the will itself very often acts against the dictates of reason,[139] and by disregarding the commands of reason may lead man into sin. For after the fall the will remained free *vis-à-vis* the intellective faculties as it had been before. With all the faculties thus striving against one another, the gift of integrity, which Zerbolt equated with original justice, has been completely destroyed. Since the gift of integrity was a *donum gratiae*, it follows that its absence after the fall and the consequent presence of the law of the flesh, namely negative concupiscence, are natural conditions which man cannot escape. The loss of integrity is permanent, Zerbolt adds, for the loss of original justice is a lifelong punishment for Adam's disobedience inflicted upon all of humanity. Original justice cannot be regained even by those who are in Christ, although the guilt attached to its loss has been removed by Christ through his death, and about it more will be said below. The natural endowments (*dona naturae*), partially destroyed as a result of the fall, can be reformed and healed in this life, and it is the aim of the spiritual life to do so.[140]

---

[136] *Ref.*, 237H: Sed homo iste dum Deo subesse noluit, cui soli subesse debuit, etiam suum inferius, vires videlicet inferiores, sibi rebelle factum est,..., atque ita homo factus est sibi ipsi gravis, et propria eius vita facta est ei tentatio; ... De Beer, *Spiritualiteit*, 237.

Consistent with the idea that man's inferior faculties rebelled against his superior ones because he himself rebelled against God, is the theory that in Adam his inferior powers obeyed his superior faculties because he himself obeyed God (T. R. Heath, "Adam," *NCE*, I, 114). However, to postulate an organic connection between man's obedience to God on the one hand, and the obedience of man's inferior faculties to his superior powers on the other, would seem to be contrary to the concept of integrity or original justice as a gratuitous gift and the idea that rebellious concupiscence is a natural condition of man.

[137] *Asc.*, 259H: ..., ipsa sensualitas, vis scilicet concupiscibilis et irascibilis voluntati sunt rebelles, et contrariae,...

[138] We saw that for Zerbolt rebellious concupiscence was a desire for a sensible, or other inferior, good contrary to the dictates of reason and the will. For in his opinion, it will be remembered, the objects of the concupiscent appetite are not exclusively sensible.

[139] *Asc.*, 259H: ..., sed et ipsa voluntas quamvis non semper, frequenter tamen agit contra rationem.

[140] *Asc.*, 272D-E: Sed quia Christus passionem suam assumpsit pro satisfactione originalis criminis, quod tantum fuit, ut totum genus humanum iustitia originali spoliaret,... *Asc.*, 260A: ...; ut huiusmodi virium destitutio vel lex carnis iam non sit culpa, cum ad eam non habendam non obligamur ne sit damnatio aliqua his qui sunt in

Since rebellious concupiscence or the *fomes peccati*, which resides in the sensitive appetites, is a natural condition, perfect love for God is impossible in this life. Even holy men, Zerbolt writes, so long as they are sojourners here below and weighed down by the body, cannot ascend without faltering. And if they do reach the summit of the spiritual mount, rebellious concupiscence will soon force them to descend once more. In view of the fact that rebellious concupiscence resides in the bodily appetites, Zerbolt speaks of the body as being corrupt, and he also describes it as "the weight of corruption" which prevents man from ascending spiritually.[141] However, it may be questioned that he understood the body to be corrupt and evil in itself.

Having seen how Zerbolt viewed the impact of the fall on the *donum superadditum*, we must next examine how he understood the impact of the fall on man's natural endowments.

ii. *The Consequences of the Fall for the* dona naturae

Zerbolt writes that in the fall nature itself was infected,[142] and what he means is that man's natural inclination to the good has weakened. The natural operation of the psychological faculties as such was not, by contrast, modified or diminished by the fall.[143] Zerbolt would appear to at-

---

Christo Iesu: Sed in pristinum statum rectitudinis nequaquam nos restituit, nec vires animae reformavit, sed ad nostrum exercitium et meritum nobis eas reliquit per sancta exercitia reformandas. Cf. Thomas Aquinas, *ST*, 1a 2ae, 85, 1; and D. of Augsburg, *De ext. et int. hom. compositione*, II, 85.

[141] *Asc.*, 275G: Corpus quod corrumpitur aggravat animam, et deprimit terrena inhabitatio sensum multa cogitantem. Sed multo minus possumus tam parati et idonei fieri, ut possimus iugiter Deo adhaerere. Quoniam quamdiu sumus in corpore, peregrinamur ab Deo. *Asc.*, 285B-C: Quamvis autem hoc non absurde possit intelligi, quod etiam ipsi sancti viri quamdiu peregrinantur, quamdiu praegravantur in corpore quod corrumpitur, non ita possunt continue et indesinenter ascendere, quin aliquando corruptibilitatis pondere gravati deficiant in ascensu, et descendant ad tempus relaxando exercitium spirituale:...

[142] *Asc.*, 272D-E: ...ut totum genus humanum iustitia originali spoliaret, et ipsam naturam inficeret...

[143] This distinction between the natural operation of the soul as such which remained unaffected by the fall, and the natural inclination of the soul towards the good which was wounded as a result of Adam's disobedience, is an extremely important one for a correct understanding of medieval philosophical and theological anthropology. As Dempsey Douglass points out, Oberman's failure to grasp this distinction in Duns Scotus' thought leads him to write without any further qualification that according to Scotus human nature remained intact after the fall. Dempsey Douglass continues that in actual fact Scotus presents the view that man's faculties as such remained untouched by the fall, but that their natural inclination to the good was 'wounded' or weakened. We may be confident that Dempsey Douglass correctly interprets Scotus' views regarding man's natural make-up and the effect of the fall on it, but she does not make it sufficiently clear that this was a generally held opinion. Aquinas had already put it quite succinctly. He detected three aspects in prefall man: a) his nature *per se*; b) a connatural inclination to virtue or the good inherent in man's natural make-up as such; c) and the gift of original justice. The

tribute the weakening of the faculties' natural inclination towards the
good to the loss of original justice,[144] and to regard the former as a direct
and immediate result of the latter was not uncommon.[145] The weakening
of man's natural inclination towards the good had traditionally been
referred to as the 'wounding of nature';[146] and Zerbolt also speaks of a
'wounding' of man's psychological faculties, and of the 'wounding' of
their natural disposition to the good in particular.[147] He further describes
the impact of the fall on the powers of the soul generally, all of which were
at one time most excellently disposed by nature, in a variety of terms. He
writes that, once excellently disposed towards God, the faculties are now
deformed, disordered and indisposed. They are inclined in a direction far
removed from that to which God ordained them: the desire for the good
or God himself. They are prone to evil, and always inclined and disposed
to the desire of unlawful and inferior things. Their efficacy—efficacy for
the good, that is—has diminished, and they have been crushed, broken
and grievously wounded, as was observed. Although greatly wounded,
the original, natural inclination of the powers and affections to the good
has not been totally destroyed by the fall and the loss of original justice.
There remains some good in man, and a certain inclination to the
good.[148]

Having described the impact of the fall upon the psychological faculties
in general, Zerbolt then goes on to elaborate how the fall affected the

---

first, he held, remained totally unaffected by the fall; the second was weakened or lessened
through sin; and the third was totally lost or destroyed (Oberman, *Biel*, 125; Dempsey
Douglass, *Geiler*, 108-109; and Thomas Aquinas, *ST*, 1a 2ae, 85, 1; cf. Steinmetz,
Staupitz, 65).

[144] See footnote 134 above.

[145] Richardson, ed., *Dictionary*, 99 ("*Donum Superadditum*").

[146] Thomas Aquinas, *ST*, 1a 2ae, 85, 1. Cf. Dempsey Douglass, *Geiler*, 108.

[147] *Asc.*, 259G: Unde et coinquinati fuimus originali culpa, sed et collisi et confracti, et
in omnibus viribus et potentiis animae optime, ut praemissum est, dispositis, graviter
vulnerati.

[148] *Ref.*, 239A: ..., quam sint vires et affectiones animae tuae deformatae, indispositae
et deordinatae, ... vires potentiae et affectiones animae tuae deformatae sunt, ... *Ref.*,
241H: Intellectus hominis et ratio deformati sunt ... *Ref.*, 250D: ... vires animae sunt
destitutae in lapsu primi hominis, ... et culpa propria deformati ... see previous footnote
and *Asc.*, 259G-H: ..., ipsae vires et affectiones ab suo statu prolapsae, diminutae, sunt
pariter et deordinatae, non autem omnino destructae, sed contrario modo se habentes
quam prius habuerunt, ... istae vires et effectus longe aliter movent quam ab Deo fuerunt
institutae, pronae ad malum et proclives semper ad illicitum concupiscendum. *Asc.*, 260C:
Siquidem in casu primi hominis, ut praemissum est, pronitatem concupiscentiarum ad infima contraximus: ... *Asc.*, 278D: In casu autem primi hominis ipsae vires destitutae ...
Asc., 279H: ..., quae maxime surgunt ex virium animae destitutione per primum tuum
descendum ab iustitia originali. Also see *Asc.*, 260D-E.

Cf. Radewijns, *Tractatulus Devotus*, 215-216; van Rooy, *Zerbolt*, 254; and D. of
Augsburg, *De ext. et int. hom. compositione*, I, 89.

various faculties individually,[149] and we shall begin by looking at what he writes about the sensitive appetites in this respect. We have seen that, according to Zerbolt, God granted man the concupiscent appetite in order that through it man might desire to seek God either through sensible things or directly.[150] However, the concupiscent appetite, because it is a sensible and inferior appetite, naturally inclines man towards inferior things which are detrimental to his spiritual well-being. Through the gift of integrity man enjoyed immunity from this negative concupiscence before the fall, but lost the immunity on account of his disobedience in paradise. However, not only did man forfeit the immunity from rebellious concupiscence, but the natural, rebellious concupiscence was greatly aggravated and increased by man's fall from original justice. With respect to the concupiscent power man did not merely regress from a state of original justice to one of 'pure nature' following his disobedience, but his nature was also positively infected. It is to the positive infection of the concupiscent power that Zerbolt refers when he writes in one of the first chapters of De Ascensionibus that it has become disordered, and that it "has fallen through some impulse or other to the lusts of the flesh, the desire of the eyes and carnal pleasures: i.e., gluttony, fornication and avarice."[151] The natural operation of the concupiscent power as such has not been in any way affected by the fall, but it is only with respect to its natural purpose that the concupiscent power has been grievously wounded and corrupted.[152] If before the fall man had not enjoyed the gift of integrity he might have experienced some difficulty in directing the concupiscent power to the service and worship of God; as a result of its positive infection it has fallen almost totally "to the lusts of the flesh, etc."[153] Hence it has departed almost completely from its natural and intended purpose.

Like the concupiscent power, the irascible appetite has become maladjusted as a result of the fall. Rather than repelling and overcoming obstacles in man's ascent to God, the purpose for which it was granted, it has embraced them, for it has fallen victim to the pride of life and worldly

---

[149] Cf. Thomas Aquinas, ST, 1a 2ae, 85, 3; Bonaventure, Breviloquium, Pt. III, ch. 5 (Works, II, 120-121); and D. of Augsburg, De ext. et int. hom. compositione, I, 97.

[150] See footnote 60 above.

[151] Asc., 259H: Vis autem concupiscibilis destituta est et quodammodo prolapsa in concupiscentiam carnis, concupiscentiam oculorum, et carnales voluptates, id est, gulam, luxuriam et avaritiam. Cf. Asc., 278E: Itaque sicut ex superius dictis apparuit, quoniam via graduum directa est per castra concupiscibilis et irascibilis, etc. quae sunt ab inimicis propter lapsum primi hominis quodammodo possessa, videlicet gula, luxuria, etc. Cf. 1 John 2, 16; Thomas Aquinas, ST, 1a 2ae, 85, 3; and Bonaventure, Breviloquium, Pt. III, ch. 5 (Works, II, 120-121).

[152] Cf. Dempsey Douglass, Geiler, 109.

[153] See footnote 151 above, first excerpt.

glory.[154] As in the case of the concupiscent power, then, the purely natural process of the irascible appetite has not suffered as a consequence of the fall; but that the irascible power was, nonetheless, wounded in the fall is evident from the fact that it now acts altogether contrary to its intended purpose.

Towards the end of *De Ascensionibus* Zerbolt asserts that there is no good in man, that is, in his flesh, and he goes on to say that by 'the flesh' he means the concupiscent and irascible appetites.[155] Thus, in contrast with what he has said before, Zerbolt now describes the concupiscent, as well as the irascible, appetite as having been totally corrupted. On account of the fall they have lost all natural inclination to the good. In only this instance, and only with respect to the concupiscent and irascible powers, does Zerbolt write that the result of the fall was total corruption. Even if he regarded the concupiscent and irascible powers as having been totally corrupted, and this must remain an open question in view of his contradictory statements, Zerbolt is far from maintaining that all the faculties have been completely perverted. As will be seen, to the will he attributes a considerable appetite for the good, even after the fall. Zerbolt does not come anywhere near to the Protestant doctrine of total depravity attributed to him by Albert Hyma, but this will be discussed at greater length below.

Zerbolt makes God the proper object of hope which he calls an irascible affection.[156] However, as a result of the fall, he explains, hope no longer puts its trust in God, but in riches and in its own merits to a greater or lesser degree than is justified.[157] On account of the fall, then, the faculty of hope has not lost its capacity for hoping as such, but it has turned away from its natural object, namely God.

God granted man the intellect in order that he might know and understand God and all things spiritual, and he endowed him with reason in order that he might understand intellectual matters of an inferior nature

---

[154] *Asc.*, 259H: Irascibilis vero deordinata est et prolapsa in superbiam vitae, et gloriam mundanam. Cf. *Asc.*, 278E and 1 John 2, 16.

[155] *Asc.*, 279D: Quia autem non invenis in te bonum, id est, in carne tua, sed ipsa vitia in te castra metata sunt contra te in concupiscibili et irascibili, et sola voluntas tua tecum est, nam velle adiacet tibi, ideo ipsam voluntatem necesse est armari contra omnia huiusmodi genera vitiorum.

[156] See footnote 60 above. Cf. E. M. Stock, "Appetite," *NCE*, 704-705; and S. M. Ramirez, "Hope," *NCE*, VII, 138.

[157] *Asc.*, 259H-260A: Spes non sperat de Deo, sed vel in divitiis vel in propriis meritis, vel sperat plus vel minus iusto.
Radewijns writes much the same thing in his *Tractatulus Devotus*, 216: Sic eciam spes deformata est, quia aut homo minus sperat quam debet, aut plus quam justum est, ... Both he and Zerbolt are most likely indebted to D. of Augsburg's *De ext. et int. hom. compositione*, I, 106.

and ascribe all to God.[158] As a result of the fall, however, the intellect and reason have been deformed, have become obtuse, have been blinded by a cloud of ignorance, and their natural understanding has diminished.[159] Reason has not lost its capacity for rational, speculative, discursive reflection as such, nor has the intellect *per se* lost its capacity for understanding. What Zerbolt tries to convey is that as a result of the fall the intellect and reason have lost a good deal of their natural capacity to understand, and to concern themselves with, the truth: God, the Supreme Truth, in particular. For, as Zerbolt explains further, reason and intellect have wandered away from the truth, namely spiritual things and God. They have fallen into error, often taking falsehood for truth, and they frequently concern themselves with useless and curious matters.[160]

Since man's intellective powers have been deformed, dulled and blinded with regard to their natural capacity to understand spiritual matters and God, he can arrive at a knowledge of the invisible and spiritual only by means of the visible and sensible.[161] Consequently, Zerbolt explains, the Son of God became man in order that through God become flesh man might arrive at a spiritual knowledge, and love, of the Godhead. That, Zerbolt adds, was in fact the primary reason why the Word became flesh.[162]

Natural reason did not remain untouched by the fall either, for man's understanding and knowledge of natural law has been imperfect since the fall, Zerbolt writes. His innate ability to distinguish between good and evil has been partially destroyed, an opinion which was later to be

---

[158] See footnotes 20, 39 and 43 above.

[159] *Ref.*, 241H: Intellectus hominis et ratio deformati sunt et quodammodo caecati per ignorantiam. *Ref.*, 238B: Nunc autem es ignorantiae nubilo excaecatus,... *Asc.* 259H: Siquidem ratio ipsa caeca facta, ... et obtusa ... Radewijns talks about reason having been blinded in much the same terms. See *Tractatulus Devotus*, 216. Both he and Zerbolt may have relied on David of Augsburg in this instance (*De ext. et int. hom. compositione*, I, 84 and cf. 89-90). Cf. Geiler who also talks about reason having been blinded and who may have borrowed from Zerbolt in this instance (Dempsey Douglass, *Geiler*, 108).

[160] *Asc.*, 259H: Siquidem ratio ipsa ... erronea et ... saepe falsa pro veris receipit, frequenter inutilibus et curiosis se involuit. This excerpt has very much in common with a similar one by Radewijns. See *Tractatulus Devotus*, 216. Both Radewijns and Zerbolt rely on David of Augsburg in this instance, it would appear (*De ext. et int. hom. compositione*, I, 84).

Cf. Dudden, *Gregory the Great: His Place in History and Thought*, II, 381-382; D. of Augsburg, *De ext. et int. hom. compositione*, I, 89-90; and Thomas Aquinas, *ST*, 1a 2ae, 85, 3.

[161] *Asc.*, 265G: Quia autem mens nostra caeca melius per visibilia et sensibilia ducitur ad notitiam invisibilium ...

[162] *Asc.*, 268G-H: Ad hoc enim praecipue Christus carnem assumpsit, ut qui Deum spiritualiter intelligere non potuimus, per Christum verbum caro factum ascenderemus ad notitiam et amorem spiritualem.

repeated by Thomas a Kempis. And it was to remedy his defective innate knowledge of natural law that God gave man the Scriptures.[163] Zerbolt adds that, because the fall partially destroyed natural reason, man was not held accountable for sins committed before his impaired knowledge of natural law was rectified by means of the Bible.[164]

According to Zerbolt the will is, in the first place, an instrument of love, and it was granted to man in order that he might love God above all, and everything else for his sake.[165] However, as a result of man's first disobedience the will was wounded in its natural inclination towards the good, its natural purpose and function. As Zerbolt explains, the will has become crooked. It often, though not always, chooses inferior things: i.e., things other than it ought to. It has a tendency to incline to carnal things or, in other words, to give in to the sensible appetites. Spiritual and heavenly things, its natural objects, it deprecates.[166]

While Zerbolt believes, then, that the will has lost much of its natural inclination towards the good, his view of the will after the fall is not near-ly as negative as was Augustine's, for example. Augustine denied that as a result of the fall the will is compelled to do evil in any metaphysical sense, but he believed that psychologically it is inexorably inclined to do wrong and 'bound' by evil. This is particularly the case with the unregenerate.[167] Zerbolt believes that the will has become crooked and inclined to evil, but we find in him none of the Augustinian sentiment that on account of the fall the will is 'compelled' to choose evil. To the contrary: throughout both of his manuals he emphasizes time and again the will's complete and perfect freedom to choose the good rather than evil,[168] and he does so in spite of his earlier statement that because of the fall the will has become warped and inclined towards evil.

---

[163] De libris teutonicalibus, 52: Sacra scriptura data est homini ab Deo in adiutorium et adminiculum legis naturalis, ut videlicet, quod homo per legem naturalem iam ob-fuscatam seu minus illuminatam interius videre non potuit, divina scriptura foris adiutus disceret et videret, ut discerneret bonum et ipsum apprehenderet, et malum ut vitaret. Thomas a Kempis, De Imitatione Christi, Bk. III, ch. 55. Cf. below, pp. 160-166.

[164] De libris teutonicalibus, 52: Unde propter hoc dicit apostolus ad Romanos V. capitulo: "Peccatum non imputabatur, cum non esset," id est, non reputabatur. Cum enim lex divina nondum erat data nec Scriptura divina divinitus promulgata, peccatum non im-putabatur seu reputabatur, quia propter obfuscacionem legis naturalis homines peccatum non curabant, et peccatum esse peccatum non reputabant. Cf. Romans 5, 13.

[165] See footnote 70 above.

[166] Asc., 259H: Voluntas facta curva, saepe deteriora eligit, carnalia diligit, spiritualia et coelestia vilipendit. Cf. Radewijns, Tractatulus Devotus, 216. Both Zerbolt and Radewijns may have borrowed from David of Augsburg in this instance (De ext. et int. hom. compositione, I, 84).

That the will is crooked is also said by Geiler, and he may have relied on Zerbolt for this particular idea (see Dempsey Douglass, Geiler, 108).

[167] Kelly, Early Christian Doctrines, 365-366.

[168] Dempsey Douglass has found that throughout his works Johann Geiler, who quoted

This relatively positive portrayal of the will's ability to combat evil must perhaps be seen against the background of Zerbolt's role as a spiritual adviser and director. In such a capacity he would, of course, not have wanted to discourage his readers unduly by portraying to them a greatly weakened will: i.e., a will weakened in its ability and determination to fight against evil. He depicts the will as being perfectly free and capable of fighting rebellious concupiscence which has been unloosened on account of the fall. The will, in others words, has remained psychologically free with regard to sin, and it remains free to combat concupiscence and the vices lodged in the sensible appetites.[169] In fallen man himself it is only the will, and its freedom to go against concupiscence and the dictates of the sensible appetites, which assists him in the fight against sin and evil.[170] It is man's will alone which chooses the good, while his sensible affections fight against it.[171] Finally, it must be remarked that Zerbolt does believe that in turning against evil the will must be assisted by grace,[172] but this will be discussed in more detail below.

Summarizing the foregoing it can be said that according to Zerbolt the natural operations of the faculties as such have not suffered on account of the fall. What has suffered is their natural inclination to the good: their

---

from Zerbolt's works, also emphasizes frequently the will's "freedom to turn away from sin" (Dempsey Douglass, *Geiler*, 113).

Gregory the Great also held a relatively positive view with regard to the will's freedom and its capacity to choose between good and evil (Dudden, *Gregory the Great: His Place in History and Thought*, II, 382). Cf. Oberman, *Biel*, 129 and Steinmetz, *Staupitz*, 70.

[169] See footnote 155 above.

[170] *Ref.*, 239F: Invenies quod solum tibi velle adiaceat, et in nullo alio in te perficere invenias. Igitur velle tuo et voluntati tuae districte praecipias, ut omne quod per istam discussionem invenisti in te et in regno tuo neglectum, dirutum vel male actum, ipsa voluntas disponat, reaedificet et emendet. Cf. Romans 7, 18.

[171] *Asc.*, 281H: In hoc ascensu est homo adhuc in labore pugnae, et non multum distat ab inimicis cum sola voluntas castitatem eligit affectu repugnante. Cf. *Asc.*, 267D: Cogita igitur primum quam sit magnum signum dilectionis Dei tui, quod te qui toties eum offendisti, toties ad eum terga vertisti, toties ab eo recessisti, toties gravissime peccasti, quoties reverti volebas ipse te suscepit, ... *Asc.*, 281E: Istis igitur et similibus remediis, oportet te pugnare contra gulam, ut tandem ascendas ad superiorem gradum, qui est ut ita proficias, ut iam prompta voluntate velis, et sine magno appetitu contrario possis abstinere ab illis cibis delectabilibus qui possunt haberi, ... *Asc.*, 282H: ..., ut nulli faciat vel cupiat malum cum voluntatis consensu, ... *Ref.*, 240B: ..., hinc tu velut alter Phinees zelo ignitus fervida voluntate incipis omnia agere quae huiusmodi concupiscentiis etiam iam quiescentibus sint contraria et eorum expulsiva, omnia scilicet vilia et despecta agere, loqui, etc. Cf. D. of Augsburg, *De ext. et int. hom. compositione*, I, 87.

[172] *Asc.*, 258H: Verum quia ascensus iste non est in currente vel ascendente, sed ex dono Dei miserentis, ideo quarto tibi consulitur ab Domino adiutorium et auxilium postulandum, quia nulla est industria tua, nisi te in omnibus divina gratia comitetur. *Asc.*, 284G-H: Non ego, sed gratia Dei mecum, et gratia Dei sum id quod sum, et Deus est qui operatur velle et perficere pro bona voluntate. This last excerpt is a combination of 1 Corinthians 15, 10 and Philippians 2, 13, although Zerbolt does not identify it in any way.

raison d'être. This wounding of the natural inclination to the good Zerbolt
would appear to have viewed as a direct result of the loss of original
justice.[173] It would appear, furthermore, that he regards the wounding of
the lower powers, especially of the concupiscent and irascible appetites,
to have gone very far, and he thinks that the superior powers such as
reason, natural reason, the intellect and will have been damaged less
severely.[174] While man cannot regain the state of original justice in this
life, he can undo the wound sustained by nature.[175] To recast the powers
of the soul is the aim of the spiritual life and the major theme of Zerbolt's
two manuals. Evidence of progress in the spiritual life is the subjection of
vice to the rule of reason or, in other words, the subjection of rebellious
concupiscence, the source of vice, to the dictates of reason: deliberating
reason as well as right reason. Further proof of spiritual growth is the
restoration of man's natural affection for what is good.[176]

   The total effect of the fall, then, was the loss of the *donum superadditum*,
namely sanctifying grace, original justice, etc., and the wounding of the
natural endowments. Aquinas had written in the previous century that as
a result of man's first sin he was *expoliatus gratuitus, et vulneratus in
naturalibus.*[177] This combined effect makes the supernatural vocation a
difficult one.

iii. *Original Sin*

   Having seen how Zerbolt views the effects of the fall, we next come to
his definition of original sin. He defines original sin as the law of the
flesh: i.e., as concupiscence which inclines man to act contrary to the dictates of reason, and as the deformation of the powers of the soul and their
natural inclination towards the good.[178] In defining original sin in these
terms Zerbolt would appear to be standing closer to the Augustinian position regarding the understanding of original sin than to the schools

---

[173] See footnote 134 above.

[174] Cf. Geesink, *Zerbolt*, 112.

[175] *Asc.*, 260A: Sed in pristinum statum rectitudinis nequaquam nos restituit, nec vires
animae reformavit, sed ad nostrum exercitium et meritum nobis eas reliquit per sancta
exercitia reformandas.

[176] *Asc.*, 279C: ..., iam ipsa vitia imperio rationis subegit, indutus quodammodo
naturali affectu boni, ... *Asc.*, 280E: Cum autem illud unum vitium de quo superius fuit
dictum, adeo per devotum exercitium, per virile praelium debilitaveris, ut rationi obe-
diens contradicere non praesumat, ... Cf. *Ref.*, 252E-F and 255B.

[177] Thomas Aquinas, *ST*, 1a 2ae, 85, 1.

[178] *Asc.*, 260A: Sane Christus morte sua preciosissima ab culpa originali nos redemit;
ut huiusmodi virium destitutio vel lex carnis iam non sit culpa, cum ad eam non habendam non obligamur ne sit damnatio aliqua his qui sunt in Christo Iesu:... *Asc.*, 272D-E:
Sed quia Christus passionem suam assumpsit pro satisfactione originalis criminis, quod
tantum fuit, ut totum genus humanum iustitia originali spoliaret, et ipsam naturam inficeret,...

represented by Anselm of Canterbury and Thomas Aquinas respectively.[179] The presence of rebellious concupiscence and the wounding of the natural endowments implies, of course, the loss of original justice, but Zerbolt does not formally include its absence in his definition of original sin.[180]

Like Bonaventure and Aquinas, for example, Zerbolt did not make sanctifying grace a constituent of original justice,[181] and, like them once again, Zerbolt does not make the absence of sanctifying grace a component of original sin. Julius Gross has found that the first time that the absence of sanctifying grace is made a component of the scholastic definition of original sin is in the later writings of Dionysius van Rijkel, the Carthusian.[182]

Zerbolt continues that Adam did not fall alone, but that as a consequence of his disobedience the entire human race fell with, and through, him, was despoiled of original justice, and was defiled with original guilt.[183] That all men have fallen in Adam is because they are all in him by virtue of *"vi quadam productiva vel seminali ratione."*[184] If all have fallen in Adam the question arises how original sin is transmitted, and this issue is tied to that of the origin of the soul. The prevalent medieval view was that the soul is not 'passed on' by the parents, but that God creates each particular soul at the moment of an individual's conception.[185] The difficulty with the doctrine of creationism is how individually created souls can become tainted with original sin. The common answer given was that the soul is tainted with original sin—original sin defined in terms of rebellious concupiscence—by the body (flesh) which itself is the result of concupiscence, namely sexual desire.[186] Zerbolt writes in much the same vein that the soul incurs the tinder of sin (*fomes peccati*): i.e., inveterate

---

[179] Cf. Oberman, *Biel*, 122; Steinmetz, *Staupitz*, 64; Thomas Aquinas, *ST*, 1a 2ae, 82, 1 and 3; Harnack, *History of Dogma*, VI, 297, footnote 1; and Gross, *Geschichte des Erbsündendogmas*, III, 207 and 265-266.

[180] Cf. Geesink, *Zerbolt*, 112.

[181] Cf. Gross, *Geschichte des Erbsündendogmas*, III, 204, 265 and 385.

[182] *Ibid.*, 384-385.

[183] *Asc.*, 259G: ..., sed se ab creatoris sui imperio avertit transgrediens praeceptum divinum. Ideoque graviter cecidit et nos omnes in eo. See footnote 132 above. Cf. *Asc.*, 272D-E.

[184] *Asc.*, 259G; and *Ref.*, 237G: Siquidem homo iste, Adam protoplastus recte intelligitur, in quo totum genus humanum quod per seminalem rationem in eo fuit et ex eo prodiit, non incongrue subauditur. See above, pp. 44-45.

Aquinas expressed the opinion that if a human being should be created miraculously by God, such a person would be free from original sin (*ST*, 1a 2ae, 81, 4).

[185] Richardson, ed., *Dictionary*, 79-80 ("Creationism"); and Copleston, *A History of Philosophy*, Vol. II, Pt. I, 94-95.

[186] Cf. Dudden, *Gregory the Great: His Place in History and Thought*, II, 335-336 and 390-391; and Bonaventure, *Breviloquium*, Pt. III, ch. 6 (*Works*, II, 123).

concupiscence which is the same as original sin, from the body which
itself is born of concupiscence.[187]

Zerbolt concludes with the observation that through his death Christ
has redeemed man from the guilt attached to original sin, so that those
who are in Christ no longer stand condemned on account of it. If the guilt
attached to original sin is removed through baptism, original sin remains
as a punishment,[188] for Christ has not, through his death, restored man
to his original state of uprightness or justice: i.e., immunity from concupiscence or the gift of integrity. Neither has Christ, by means of his
death, healed the wound sustained by man's natural endowments. It is
man's duty to heal this wound through spiritual exercises,[189] but he cannot regain original justice, a preternatural gift, by such means.

Furthermore, rebellious concupiscence is not in itself sin, nor is there
any guilt attached to it after baptism, because it is man's natural condition which had been gratuitously held in abeyance by God before the fall;
and after the fall he cannot avoid it, Zerbolt writes.[190] It becomes sin only
after the consent of the will.

iv. *Hyma and Davis on Zerbolt's Doctrine of the Fall*

Having analyzed Zerbolt's views regarding the fall and original sin, we
must now briefly evaluate the older interpretation of these same issues by
Albert Hyma, as well as Kenneth R. Davis' recent interpretation which
rests largely on that by Hyma.

Writing some fifty years ago Hyma's point of departure was Luther's
statement in his lecture on Romans that he had "not found so clear a
discussion of the subject of original sin as in Gerard Groote's treatise
Blessed is the Man, in which he speaks not as an arrogant philosopher but
as a sound theologian."[191] The work Luther referred to was not Grote's,
but Zerbolt's *De Spiritualibus Ascensionibus*, which Luther identified by giving its *incipit*: *Beatus vir*. Encouraged by Luther's statement, and influ-

---

[187] *Asc.*, 260A: Nam ipsa anima ex carne concupiscibiliter concepta contrahit fomitem
et concupiscentiarum inclinationem ad malum. To refer to original sin defined as
rebellious concupiscence as the *fomes peccati* was traditional (cf. Dempsey Douglass, *Geiler*,
110).

[188] This presentation of original sin as guilt and punishment, of which the former is
removed through the death of Christ in which man shares through baptism, is quite traditional (cf. Dempsey Douglass, *Geiler*, 110-111).

[189] See footnote 175 above.

[190] See footnote 178 above, first passage. Cf. Th. a Kempis, *De Imitatione Christi*, Bk. I,
ch. 13 and Bk. III, ch. 55.

[191] See Hyma, *The Christian Renaissance: A History of the "Devotio Moderna,"* 309-310 and
Luther's Works, trans. by J. Pelikan and H. T. Lehmann (55 vols.; St. Louis and
Philadelphia, 1955-), XXV, 300.

enced by a nineteenth-century Protestant tendency to regard the Devotionalists as 'reformers before the Reformation', Hyma set out to demonstrate that if the Devotionalists—and in this he assigned an important role to Zerbolt—had not exactly formulated the Protestant doctrine of total depravity in its entirety, they had at least contributed greatly to its development. Consequently he draws attention only to Zerbolt's description of man's corruption and leaves unmentioned Zerbolt's statement that the destruction of man's innate tendency towards the good was not total.[192] Through this omission Hyma creates the impression that, if Zerbolt's views regarding the effects of the fall are not altogether like those of Luther, they nonetheless approximate his. Hyma singles out the will in particular, and asserts that "Groote's followers held that man possesses a very small remnant of free will; . . ."[193] We have seen, however, that Zerbolt attributed a considerable capacity to the will to turn to the good and to do good. Hyma continues that, in the last analysis, the small remnant of free will which Grote's followers still allowed to man "amounted to nothing of any value in itself, since man could do nothing without God's aid."[194] He is, however, mistaken in his notion when he implies that, because the Devotionalists argued for the need of grace in all things, they, as a result, rejected the doctrine of man's ability to cooperate with grace and the necessity to do so. We will see that Zerbolt, who attributed a considerable capacity to the will to choose the good, also held that man can do nothing without grace. This opinion was also that of Wessel Gansfort who, when he was a student at the city school of Zwolle, spent a number of years in a hostel operated by the Brethren of the Common Life in that same city. He writes that the contribution made by the faithful in their spiritual ascent is their own contribution in the real sense of the word as well as God's who enables them, through his grace, to make this contribution.[195]

Davis has taken Hyma's views regarding the contribution of the Devotionalists to the development of the Protestant doctrine of total depravity and has applied them to his own thesis: namely, that, if the Anabaptists are not directly dependent upon the Devotionalists, there is, nonetheless, a striking similarity between their views regarding the effects of the fall on man.[196] First, Davis' comparison is a highly dubious one in view of the

---

[192] Hyma, *The Christian Renaissance: A History of the "Devotio Moderna,"* 319.

[193] *Ibid.*, 519-520.

[194] *Ibid.*, 520.

[195] Wessel Gansfort, *De benignissima Dei providentia*, in: *Opera Omnia* (Groningen, 1614), 713. Cf. Axters, *Vroomheid*, III, 415. Cf. Hyma, *The Christian Renaissance: A History of the "Devotio Moderna,"* 319.

[196] K. R. Davis, *Anabaptism and Asceticism* (Scottdale and Kitchener, 1974), 251-252 and 260.

fact that he himself has not consulted the Devotionalist sources but has relied entirely on what Hyma has said regarding the Devotionalists' doctrine of original sin. Furthermore, his assertion that Hyma's interpretation of the Devotionalists' "concepts of grace, free will, repentance and the powers of man, remains relatively unchallenged"[197] is just not true. As early as 1925 the Dutch scholar Johannes de Jong devoted a lengthy review article in the *Historisch Tijdschrift* to Hyma's *The Christian Renaissance*.[198] In this article he convincingly refuted Hyma's Protestantizing of the Modern Devotion, as well as the greatly exaggerated influence attributed by Hyma to the Modern Devotion with regard to the theological and ecclesiastical developments in Europe during the sixteenth century. In spite of this refutation, as well as other confutations,[199] of Hyma's interpretation of the Modern Devotion, and of his interpretation of Devotionalist anthropology in particular, Davis speaks of a "distinctiveness of much of the Devotio Moderna's anthropology."[200] And he adds that Hyma made extensive use of Zerbolt's writings in particular in order to prove this 'distinctiveness' of Devotionalist anthropology. However, that Zerbolt, who unquestionably helped to mould Devotionalist anthropology by means of his influential manuals for the spiritual life, had a distinctive anthropology is not borne out by the sources. Zerbolt's anthropology was in every way conventional, we have seen, shaped by the Aristotelian-Thomistic tradition as well as by the Platonic-Augustinian one. The distinctiveness of Devotionalist anthropology, Davis explains—and here he once more relies totally on what Hyma has written regarding this matter—is "the retention of a very limited free activity of the will in salvation in conjunction with a strong stress on the effects of the 'fall'; the 'fall' produced a universal situation of bondage to sin and a state of depravity which can be described as 'total', but which is still not identical to Luther's absolute use of the term."[201] Thus Davis attributes to the Devotionalists a doctrine of original sin which comes very close to Augustine's view that, although the will remains ontologically free, psychologically it is 'bound' by evil.[202] We have seen, however, that the Devotionalists, and Zerbolt in particular, were very far from holding such a view of the will after the fall. What Davis believes to be the Devotionalists' views regarding original

---

[197] *Ibid.*, 252.

[198] J. de Jong, "Karakter en Invloed der Moderne Devotie," *Historisch Tijdschrift*, IV (1925), 26-58.

[199] Van Rooy, *Zerbolt*, 253-254 and Axters, *Vroomheid*, 414-415.

[200] Davis, *Anabaptism and Asceticism*, 251.

[201] *Ibid.*, 252.

[202] Kelly, *Early Christian Doctrines*, 365-366.

sin he also detects in the Anabaptists,[203] but in reality no such parallel between their beliefs regarding the effects of the fall on man exists; because, led by Hyma, Davis has misread and misrepresented the Devotionalists' views regarding the fall and its impact on man.

v. *The Fruits of Original Sin*

Finally, we must look at how Zerbolt views the practical consequences of the loss of integrity and the wounding of nature, or, in other words, at how he views the consequences of original sin for man's daily existence.

With the loss of integrity, he writes, and the resultant strife between the higher and lower powers, man has lost the spiritual peace, tranquillity, joy, happiness and rest which he formerly possessed, and he has fallen into a permanent state of spiritual grief, unrest, weariness, suffering and mutability.[204] The primary cause of man's spiritual distress is rebellious concupiscence, a function of the concupiscent appetite, which at all times resists the law of the intellect and the will. Rebellious concupiscence was, of course, unleashed as a result of the fall and now assails man incessantly. The struggle against this indomitable concupiscence is an exhausting one in which man is hampered by the partial destruction of his faculties' knowledge of, and inclination towards, the good. Due to the difficulty experienced in combating rebellious concupiscence man will be compelled to call out with Paul: "Who shall deliver me from the body of this death."[205] This proneness to evil which stems from the loss of integrity is with man from his conception onwards,[206] for this condition is natural to him. As a consequence of the fall, then, life has become a continuous and endless temptation.[207]

It is because of the loss of integrity and the resultant rebellious concupiscence that man falls into actual sin, and Zerbolt compares the descent into actual sin to the prodigal son's journey into a far country where he led a riotous life. Rebellious concupiscence he likens to harlots who entice man into wilfully giving in to his lusts, thereby committing actual,

---

[203] Davis, *Anabaptism and Asceticism*, 252.

[204] *Ref.*, 238A: Amisisti pacem, tranquillitatem et gaudium, laetitiam et quietem: Invenisti inquietudinem, tristitiam, labores et dolores, et continuam mutabilitatem. Cf. footnote 128 above; and Savary, *Psychological Themes in the Golden Epistle of William of Saint-Thierry*, 73-74.

[205] *Ref.*, 240B: ..., atque multoties fatigatus cum videris legem carnis tuae tam fortem et tam importune legi mentis et voluntati tuae resistentem, clamare necesse habeas ex sententia cum Apostolo: Quis me liberabit de corpore mortis huius? (Romans 7, 24.) Cf. Oberman, *Biel*, 126-128.

[206] *Asc.*, 260A: Breviter, ex amissione originalis justitiae omnes affectiones pronae sunt in malum ab adolescentia, imo ab conceptione sua.

[207] See footnote 136 above.

personal sins. The final surrender to rebellious concupiscence and lusts he equates with fornication.[208] The consequence of this surrender to rebellious concupiscence is an impure heart which Zerbolt describes variously as polluted, sordid, defiled and unclean.[209] The impurity and sordidness of the heart consist in the vices of which pride is the queen, all sorts of evil passions and desires, an inordinate affection for created good, and the "defilement of concupiscence."[210] All inordinate affections, then, Zerbolt reiterates, spring from the loss of integrity and the disorder of the powers of the soul, and they in turn stem from man's fall and the loss of original justice.[211] And he defines an inordinate affection as an

---

[208] *Asc.*, 260B-C: Sed utinam hic permansisses, utinam hic quievisses, et non longius discessisses, sed heu tu fili prodige quarundam meretricum, id est, concupiscentiarum abstractus illecebris inisti ad partes adhuc multo remotiores, imo ut ait sanctum Evangelium, in longissimam regionem abiens post concupiscentias tuas, et fornicans cum meretricibus, id est, cum concupiscentiis. Nam quoties concupiscimus, toties, ut ait Hieronymus, fornicamur.

[209] *Asc.*, 260C: ..., et haec dicitur propria impuritas cordis. *Ref.*, 239A: ... cor tuum sit pollutum .. cor tuum est sordidum,... *Asc.*, 260D: Ita homo, anima tua..., immunda fit et impura. *Asc.*, 260D-E: Ecce cernis quid sit impuritas cordis de qua in scriptura legis,... Cf. Footnote 211 below, second excerpt.

[210] *Asc.*, 279D: ..., sed ipsa vitia in te castra metata sunt ... *Asc.*, 278D: Superbia etenim vitiorum regina...; *Ref.*, 238H ..., cor tuum ab cupiditatibus et affectionibus inordinatis [239A] et noxiis concupiscentiis purges. ..., quamque multis et variis cupiditatibus cor tuum sit pollutum. ...Si ignoras quibus cupiditatibus cor tuum est sordidum,... et quibus cupiditatibus pollutus fueris edoceri. *Asc.*, 279H: ...contra omnes inordinatas affectiones ... *Ref.*, 238B: ..., omniaque ossa tua concupiscentiarum faecibus medullitus sunt infusa. *Asc.*, 260E: Certa ipsa est illa affectio qua inordinate ad infirma inclinaris et adhaeres, ... *Asc.*, 260D: Ita, homo anima tua rationalis quae est dignior omnibus temporalibus creaturis, impuritatem et immunditiam contrahit ex hoc quod rebus temporalibus subiicitur per amorem; et ex hoc quod huiusmodi adhaeret per affectionem et per desideria ipsis affixa, assueta et conglutinata, immunda fit et impura.

By the "defilement of concupiscence" Zerbolt does not mean rebellious concupiscence which is natural to man, but concupiscence consequent on the consent of the will which is sinful. Zerbolt, it would appear, was familiar with the careful distinction first made by scholastic theologians between innocent and sinful concupiscence (see Harnack, *History of Dogma*, VI, 228; and cf. D. of Augsburg, *De ext. et int. hom. compositione*, II, 151). Grote also distinguished between innocent and sinful concupiscence. Concupiscence, he wrote, is not sinful as long as the will does not succumb to, and cooperate with, it (de Beer, *Spiritualiteit*, 237-238).

Furthermore, in reference to both rebellious concupiscence and actual sin Zerbolt speaks of "impurity of heart." (See passages in this footnote and those in footnote 209 above, as well as those in footnotes 212 and 213 below.) However, it may be questioned whether Zerbolt is not contradicting himself when he describes rebellious concupiscence in such terms. For he regards rebellious concupiscence to be part of man's natural condition, and in itself non-culpable. Rebellious concupiscence becomes sinful and culpable only when the will yields to it.

[211] *Asc.*, 279H: Itaque pugnandum tibi est, contra omnes inordinatas affectiones, quae maxime surgunt ex virium animae destitutione per primum tuum descensum ab iustitia originali. *Asc.*, 260B: Quod homo non solum progressus est ab statu rectitudinis in lapsum primi hominis, sed etiam illectus concupiscentiis longius abiit ad impuritatem cordis,...

excessive inclination to, and love for, an inferior thing;[212] and such an inordinate affection for created good was held to be sinful because man must love God above all else. Finally, Zerbolt warns that if man does not resist rebellious concupiscence, a natural condition, he may suffocate all disposition to the good which remained after the fall.[213] Once all inclination to the good is destroyed as a result of willful surrender to rebellious concupiscence, man will find it increasingly difficult to extricate himself from his impure and sinful state. He then runs the risk that sinful concupiscence, which must be distinguished from rebellious concupiscence,[214] will become second nature to him.[215]

Zerbolt divides actual sin, which has thus far been discussed in general terms only, into venial sin and mortal sin.[216] However, he does not draw any real distinction between the two, nor does he indicate in any way that their consequences for man may vary. His description of them is essentially identical, except that he regards mortal sin to be of a greater magnitude than venial sin.[217] He does not see the difference between venial sin and mortal sin to be one of kind but of degree. He further diminishes the difference between venial sin and mortal sin when he writes that on account of actual sins man is despoiled of grace, and what he presumably has in mind is sanctifying grace.[218] The traditional view was, of course, that man loses sanctifying grace only as a result of mortal sin. However, it had always been maintained as well that it is difficult to draw an accurate and reliable distinction between venial sin and mortal sin.[219] It is possible that this difficulty caused Zerbolt to write, as a

---

[212] *Asc.*, 260E: Certe ipsa est illa affectio qua inordinate ad infirma inclinaris et adhaeres. ..., quam impuritatem in casu primi hominis contraxisti, sed ex tua assuefactione, affectione et adhaesione multo amplius addidisti, ut qui sordebat prius, sordescat iam amplius.

[213] *Asc.*, 260C: Tu vero non solum eis non restitisti, sed te eis inclinans cum ipsis descendisti, et desideriis et affectionibus carnalibus, et rebus mundanis adhaesisti, atque proinde si qua in te remanserat ad bonum inclinatio, vel donorum naturalium vel spiritualium amisisti. *Asc.*, 260C: Itaque omnia bona et portionem bonorum naturalium et gratuitorum quae tibi contigerat, consumpsisti. *Asc.*, 260C: Siquidem in casu primi hominis, ut praemissum est, pronitatem concupiscentiarum ad infima contraximus: ut nisi eis continuo resistamus, ipsarum impetu cogimur descendere ad inferiora. Cf. footnote 212.

[214] See footnote 210 above.

[215] *Asc.*, 260C: Insuper huiusmodi rebus vilibus desiderio et affectu inhaerens, quodammodo ipsis connaturalis et conformis factus es, et ita contraxisti quandam quasi limositatem et viscositatem in concupiscentiis et viribus, qua quasi glutinosa lubricitate inferius ligatus quodammodo retineris,...

[216] *Asc.*, chs. 4 and 5 (260B-F).

[217] *Ibid.*

[218] *Ref.*, 250D: ..., sed quia, heu, multi per actuale peccatum spoliati sunt gratia Dei et culpa propria deformati: ...

[219] De Beer, *Spiritualiteit*, 62; and Dempsey Douglass, *Geiler*, 111.

precaution, that actual sin in general results in the loss of sanctifying grace, and some years earlier Grote had expressed similar views.[220] With respect to the question of actual sin, then, both Zerbolt and Grote showed themselves to be rigorists, and this rigorism was, no doubt, intended to maintain the greatest possible distance between the believer and authentic mortal sins.

While, as a consequence of original sin, all people fall into actual sin sooner or later, Zerbolt writes that the Virgin Mary never committed even venial sin.[221] He does not explain why Mary should have remained free from all actual sin. However, this had traditionally been attributed to her freedom from original sin, and while some held that Mary had been freed from original sin some time between conception and birth, others held that Mary was conceived without the blemish of original sin.[222] Whether or not Zerbolt accepted the doctrine of the immaculate conception of Mary is not clear, nor can we draw conclusions regarding this question on the basis of what other Devotionalists' views on this subject were. For on the whole the Devotionalists said very little about the Virgin Mary.[223]

C) Assessment

Zerbolt's considerable interest in anthropology betrays a Cistercian influence, but it also sprang naturally from his role as a director of souls. In that capacity he was particularly interested in the consequences of the fall for man's ability to contribute to his own salvation. He adopts a moderate position with respect to this issue as had Thomas Aquinas, thereby rejecting the extremism of both Augustine and the *via moderna*.[224] Zerbolt's doctrine of post-fall man is consistent with his view that nothing so assures man's ready cooperation in the process of salvation as constant fear tempered with hope.[225] Man must fear presumptuousness with respect to his ability to further his own salvation, for as a result of the fall his ability to do so has been severely curtailed. However, man has not been altogether corrupted as a consequence of the fall, and he may be confident that with the aid of grace he can promote his own salvation to

---

[220] See Grote's letter to William Vroede ed. by Mulder, *Gerardi Magni Epistolae*, 19. Cf. De Beer, *Spiritualiteit*, 291; Post, *The Modern Devotion: Confrontation with Reformation and Humanism*, 315; and Axters, *Vroomheid*, III, 53.

[221] *Asc.*, 273A: ..., maxime Dei genitrix, quae nec unquam venialiter peccavit per aliquam deordinationem.

[222] Richardson, ed., *Dictionary*, 166 ("Immaculate Conception of the Blessed Virgin Mary").

[223] Van Rooy, *Zerbolt*, 270-271.

[224] See Kelly, *Early Christian Doctrines*, 365-366; and Oberman, *Biel*, 146-160.

[225] *Asc.*, 285F: ..., nobis tamen nihil est securius, quam sub spe semper timere,...

the extent that that is required of him. There is, therefore, no need for
him to despair. Zerbolt is of the opinion, we have seen, that after the fall
man's will in particular remains a positive element in the human psyche.
The will is not 'bound' by evil, but it has retained a considerable capacity
for willing and doing the good, albeit with the help of grace. Consequently man can, when supported by divine grace, contribute to his own
justification and sanctification. However, his contribution possesses efficacy only in the context of Christ's salvific life and death. And, as Zerbolt writes, in spite of man's sinful condition he remains a being of great
dignity for whose salvation Christ was willing to die.[226] It is to Zerbolt's
doctrine of Christ's person and work that we must now turn our attention.

---

[226] *Ref.*, 249F: ..., quantae dignitatis quo ad homines: nam propter eos Christus
crucifixus est,...

CHAPTER THREE

THE DOCTRINE OF CHRIST

Zerbolt manifestly regards history in terms of *Heilsgeschichte*. History is an unfolding of God's plan for man's salvation.[1] The central event of this divine design for man's felicity was the incarnation of God's own Son who, through his life and death, has made salvation possible for all those who wish to share in his salvific work. The doctrine of Christ divides, then, into two parts: the nature of God's Son who became man, and the nature of his salvific work. The terms 'Christology' and 'soteriology' were coined to describe the doctrines of Christ's person and work respectively.[2]

De Reformatione and *De Ascensionibus* each contains a *vita Christi* in which Zerbolt's views regarding Christ's person and work are found for the most part.[3] The context in which each of the two *vitae* occurs is, however,

---

[1] See above, pp. 45-47.

[2] Properly speaking, Christology refers only to the examination into Christ's person and attributes: i.e., the nature of the incarnated Son of God whom the New Testament refers to as Christ, and above all the union in him of the human and divine natures. However, Christology may be expanded to include the investigation into Christ's pre-existence as Son of God, or Logos, and also deal, therefore, with the question of his position within the Trinity. That Christ's divine pre-existence can logically be discussed under the heading of Christology is due to the fact that it is held to be identical with the divine nature to which Christ's humanity was joined in the incarnation. In the investigation into Zerbolt's Christology which follows his views concerning Christ and his previous divine existence will be discussed together.

Some would call soteriology any part of Christian theology that studies and deals with the subject of salvation. However, in view of the fact that all of revelation and its systematic study centers around the question of salvation, all facets of Christian theology could be arranged under the heading soteriology, thus making soteriology as wide-ranging as Christian theology itself. For that reason many theologians have considered it advisable to reserve the term soteriology for the study of the central and culminating part of God's salvific plan: the saving work of Christ. Whenever used below, the term soteriology will also stand for the inquiry into, and the doctrine of, Christ's saving activity (J. J. Walsh, "Christology," *NCE*, III, 662; A. Grillmeier, "Jesus Christ," *SM*, III, 186-188; E. L. Peterson, "Soteriology," *NCE*, XIII, 444; Richardson, ed., *Dictionary*, 316 ["Soteriology"]; and K. Rahner, "Salvation," *SM*, V, 435-436).

[3] Christ's life is discussed in *Asc.*, chs. 27-40 (268G-275D) and *Ref.*, chs. 26-34 (245H-249G) in particular.

The sources of Zerbolt's works have been discussed in an earlier chapter. However, in addition to the *vitae Christi* mentioned there, a number of other "lives of Christ" may have contributed to Zerbolt's *vitae Christi*, namely Ludolph of Saxony's *Vita Iesu Christi*, Henry Suso's *One-Hundred Articles*, and Jordan of Quedlinburg's *Meditationes de passione Christi*. These three works were read in Devotionalist circles, and were almost certainly known to, and read by, Zerbolt (H. Meyboom, ed., "De hondert Artikelen," *Archief voor Nederlandse Kerkgeschiedenis*, I [1885], 173-207; D. de Man, "Heinrich Suso en de Moderne

not identical. Zerbolt writes in *De Ascensionibus* that the aim of the spiritual life is charity and the vision of God, and the prerequisite for this twofold goal, he continues, is purity of heart.[4] He then outlines two means by which purity of heart may be achieved, one of which consists of imitation of Christ. Through an imitation of Christ in his humanity the believer eradicates vices and cultivates virtues.[5] Indeed, it is for the purpose of achieving a pure heart by this means, from whence one may then ascend to charity and the vision of God, that Zerbolt inserts the *vita Christi* in *De Ascensionibus*. The *vita Christi* is included in *De Reformatione* for essentially the same purpose, although in this work Zerbolt inserts the life of Christ in the section which deals with the reformation of the memory. The memory, viewed as storehouse, is reformed by filling it with material suitable for spiritual meditation.[6] The life of Christ constitutes excellent subject-matter for meditation, because reflection on Christ's life and death may result in the desire to imitate him, one of the means named by Zerbolt to achieve purity of heart. That meditation is the foundation of imitation is an idea which underlies all of Zerbolt's thought on imitation of Christ,[7] as it does that of all Devotionalists.

A) *Christology*

In *De Reformatione* we read that it is necessary to form a concept of Christ as "*personae unius quae simul est Deus et homo, et in qua deitas et humanitas sine essentiarum permixtione in uno supposito coegerunt.*"[8] In this one

---

Devoten," *NAKG*, N. S., XIX [1926], 279-283; Axters, *Vroomheid*, III, 71, 112, 359 and 452; K. Lievens, *Jordanus van Quedlinburg in de Nederlanden* [Ghent, 1958]; and Goossens, *Meditatie*, 190, 195, 200-201). Zerbolt could not, it would appear, have been familiar with the pseudo-Bonaventuran-Ludolphian *Vita Ihesu Christi* which was to be widely read in the Low Countries during the fifteenth century (cf. *Tleven Ons Heren Ihesu Christi. Het Pseudo-Bonaventura-Ludolfiaanse Leven van Jesus*, ed. by C. C. de Bruin [Leiden, 1980], VII-XXV; and C. C. de Bruin, "Middeleeuwse Levens van Jesus als Leidraad voor Meditatie en Contemplatie," *NAKG*, N.S., LVIII [1978], 129-155, and LX [1980], 161-181 [to be continued]).

Zerbolt's source for the strictly doctrinal part of his views regarding the person and work of Christ may have been Bonaventure's *Commentary on the Sentences* or the *Breviloquium*, Aquinas' *Summa Theologiae*, and Hugh Ripelin's *Compendium Theologiae* (see above, p. 22). The Devotionalists did not have their 'own' theologian, and consequently Zerbolt was pretty much at liberty to read those theologians whom he desired to read. This being the case he probably turned his attention in the first place to the great *doctores communis* of the middle ages, namely Bonaventure and Aquinas, whose works were on account of their general acceptability also plentiful and easily accessible.

[4] On charity and the vision of God as the aim of the spiritual life, and on purity of heart as its prerequisite, see below, pp. 233-241.

[5] See below, pp. 139-153.

[6] See below, pp. 250-256.

[7] See the chs. of *De Ascensionibus* and *De Reformatione* mentioned in footnote 3 above.

[8] *Ref.*, 247E. Cf. *Asc.*, 269C-D: ..., et hoc propter personae unitatem, in qua divinitas

sentence Zerbolt expresses succinctly, but clearly, his understanding regarding the person of Christ, and it will serve as a useful guide throughout the analysis of his Christology which follows. For this single statement contains Zerbolt's Christology in a nutshell: Christ is both God and man, and his two natures, the divine and the human, are carried by one person without a confusion of their essences.

i. *Christ: God and Man*

Christ as Second Person of the Trinity. Turning first to Zerbolt's understanding of Christ as God—and he frequently refers to Christ as God, true God and very God without any equivocation—,[9] we find that he speaks of Christ as the incarnation of the pre-existent Son of God and as the second person of the Trinity, or at least as being a member of the Trinity.[10] That Christ is the incarnation of God's Son was disclosed at the time of his baptism by John, Zerbolt informs us, and the entire Trinity was revealed at that time, he adds.[11] However, in his account of Christ's baptism Zerbolt does not mention the Holy Spirit by name, but he must have viewed the dove descending upon Christ as a symbol of the third person of the Trinity because of his statement that the existence of the Trinity was made public at Christ's baptism.[12]

In *De Libris Teutonicalibus* Zerbolt writes that it is not safe for laymen to read books which deal with God's nature, his oneness of essence and Trinity of persons.[13] By oneness of essence Zerbolt clearly means that Father, Son and Holy Spirit constitute one substance, and so he safeguards not only the oneness of God, but also proclaims the true divinity of Christ and the Holy Spirit. Furthermore, Zerbolt also calls the

---

et humanitas sine naturarum permixtione substiterunt, et hoc credit quilibet verus Christianus; ... The passage found on p. 247E of *De Reformatione* is reminiscent of a similar passage in Bernard's *De Consideratione*, Bk. V, ch. 9 (20). Cf. M. C. Slotemaker de Bruine, *Het Ideaal der Navolging van Christus ten Tijde van Bernard van Clairvaux* (Wageningen, 1926), 27-28.

[9] *Ref.*, 245B: ..., ibi sublimis erit Deus et homo. *Ref.*, 247D-248F: Circa passionem...opus quod fecit. *Asc.*, ch. 28 (268G-269F). *Asc.*, 272B-H: Ut autem melius...pie protulit. *Asc.*, ch. 33 (273D-F).

[10] *Ref.*, 245G: ..., quod propter te misit filium suum incarnari, ... *Ref.*, 246A: Cogita quod Dei filius, ..., factus est infantulus, ... *Asc.*, 270C: Tricesimo vero anno ab Ioanne baptizatur. Cogita Ioannis reverentiam, qualiter ad Christi tactum tremuit. Cogita Christi humilitatem, qui se Ioanni subiecit, et omnem iustitiam, id est, perfectam humilitatem implevit. Nota qualiter hic se tota Trinitas personarum ostendit, qualiter pater Christum ad praedicandum misit, dicens: Ipsum audite, etc.

[11] See footnote 10, second excerpt. Cf. Matt. 3, 13-17.

[12] J. Kurzinger, "Zur Deutung der Johannestaufe in den Mittelalterlichen Theologie," in: *Aus der Geisteswelt des Mittelalters*, Festschrift für Martin Grabmann (Munich, 1935), 954-973.

[13] *De libris teutonicalibus*, 60: ...tractantes ac declarantes de divina essencia, de personarum trinitate, et de essencia unitate, ...

Trinity indivisible.[14] If the Trinity is indivisible, the implication is that it constitutes one being and hence one substance. The emphasis on the oneness and indivisibility of the Trinity serves further to protect the true divinity of Christ. Notwithstanding the fact that Father, Son and Holy Spirit are one because they constitute one substance or essence, they remain three distinct persons: a Trinity of Persons.[15] Zerbolt's belief in the continued individuality of the persons of the Trinity was important on account of the fact that he understood only the person of God the Son to have assumed humanity at the incarnation.[16] Finally, from his oneness with God it follows that Christ is eternal, that his pre-existence has been from before all time and that there was not a time that he was not. Christ's eternity follows not only from his oneness with God, but it is specifically emphasized by Zerbolt.[17]

With respect to the origin of the second person of the Trinity Zerbolt indicates a twofold source. On the one hand he holds that Christ owes his existence to himself. For he writes that Christ is the beginning and origin of all things,[18] which implies that he considers Christ to be the source of his own being in the same manner as God is held to owe his existence to himself.[19] And it is, of course, as true God that Christ is the source of his own being as he is of everything else. However, his status as Son of God, to which Zerbolt refers a number of times,[20] implies an altogether different origin. Sonship signifies generacy and, consequently, that for his existence Christ, the Son of God, is dependent upon God the Father and begotten of him.[21] Aseity and generacy are, strictly speaking, incompatible concepts. However, Zerbolt's position reflects the stand taken by the church at the Council of Nicea in 325 A.D., where it was asserted that Christ is not only the Son of God who finds the source of his being in God, but that he is also true God, consubstantial with the Father, and that he therefore owes his existence to himself.[22]

---

[14] *Asc.*, 267B: ...individuam Trinitatem...

[15] See footnote 10 above, second excerpt, and footnote 13 as well.

[16] See footnote 10 above, and cf. *Ref.*, 247E.

[17] *Asc.*, 274B: Est enim immensus potestate, ..., aeternitate. Admirare igitur maiestatem annihilari, ..., aeternitatem mori.

[18] *Ref.*, 248G and *Asc.*, 273F: ..., cogita ipsum veraciter esse Dei filium, omnium principium, ... See above, pp. 41-42.

[19] Cf. W. N. Clarke, "Aseity (Aseitas)," *NCE*, I, 945-946.

[20] See footnote 10 above; *Ref.*, 246A and 248G; and *Asc.*, 269H and 273F.

[21] Cf. Steinmetz, *Staupitz*, 134-135.

[22] E. R. Hardy, ed., *The Christology of the Later Fathers* (London, 1954), 343-345 and 373; Kelly, *Early Christian Doctrines*, 83-162 and 223-343; J. N. D. Kelly, *Early Christian Creeds* (3rd ed.; London, 1972), 205-295; H. Chadwick, *The Early Church* (The Pelican History of the Church, Vol. I; Harmondsworth, 1967), 123-151; Harnack, *History of Dogma*, IV, 1-137; and Pelikan, *The Christian Tradition, A History of the Development of Doctrine*, I, 172-277.

Zerbolt evidently understands the three persons of the Trinity to be one not only with respect to substance and being, but also with regard to will, operation and activity. It has been observed that he calls Christ the "*omnium principium*,"[23] from which it follows that Christ shares in the divine act of creation, and Christ is specifically referred to as the almighty creator, as well as the ruler, of heaven and earth.[24] Furthermore, as creator Christ devised the laws of nature, but as their author he remains in control of them and can dispense with them at will in order to perform supernatural acts.[25] This is clearly an allusion to Christ's miracles which he was able to perform on account of his divinity: i.e., the power to override the laws of nature, a divine power in which Christ shares as a member of the Trinity.[26] Finally, Zerbolt also assigns to Christ the office or function of judge of rebellious and disobedient mankind.[27] All this is evidence enough that Zerbolt understood God the Father and God the Son to possess one will and activity, and it is consistent with his view of the Trinity as one, indivisible being. It is also in agreement with the traditional and orthodox teaching that the activities of the three persons of the Trinity are inseparable and that the entire Godhead is operative in each of the three persons.[28]

In harmony with the teaching of the church, then, and at the same time bolstering his own views regarding the oneness of God, Zerbolt attributed unity of will and activity to God the Father and God the Son. In spite of the unity, however, the church also held that a certain distinction between the operation and activity of God the Father and God the Son must not be overlooked. The church maintained, for example, that it cannot be said that God the Father became incarnate and died on the cross, but that this can be said only of God and Son. However, Zerbolt tends to blur the distinction. He tells us in one breath—and he adds that for this particular passage he is indebted to John Chrysostom—that

---

[23] See footnote 18 above.

[24] *Asc.*, 272C: ...Deum omnipotentem,... creatorem et iudicem tuum, .. *Asc.*, 274A: Considera autem hic, quantus et quam gloriosus rex coeli et terrae, et Dominus sabaoth sit iste, qui sic illuditur regis schemate,...

[25] *Asc.*, 269A-B: Quidam sequebantur eum propter miracula eius. Et tu mirare potentiam eius in miraculis. Naturam mutat, elementa commutat, daemones fugat, omnemque infirmitatem sanat. Ex his disce eum esse Deum, qui naturae suos effectus primo indidit naturales, salva sibi semper obedientia, in omnibus etiam ad effectus supernaturales producendos.

[26] *Asc.*, 270D: Siquidem inter homines ambulans, et ubique verbum Dei seminans multa miracula, quae nisi ab Deo fieri non potuerunt, fecit; ... See above, pp. 46-47. Cf. Thomas Aquinas, *ST*, 3a, 43, 2-3 and 1a, 110, 4.

[27] See footnote 24, first excerpt; *Asc.*, 271C: Ipse iste quem sumis, erit iudex tuus, et eius tribunali iudicandus astabis. Cf. *Ref.*, 246H-247A. See above, pp. 51-53.

[28] Cf. Dudden, *Gregory the Great: His Place in History and Thought*, II, 320-321.

God's benefits are manifold, for he created heaven and earth, became incarnate and was crucified,[29] without any reference to God the Father or God the Son. Elsewhere he writes that God chose rather to die than that his justice should remain unsatisfied and original sin unpunished,[30] without specifying that it was God the Son who died on the cross. In addition to that, he continues, man daily crucifies God anew on account of his own, personal sins.[31] Such occasional obliteration by Zerbolt of the distinction between the activity of God the Father and that of God the Son must be attributed to the West's interpretation of the Trinity;[32] and it provides us with an example of the widespread difficulty experienced in the West in maintaining the distinction between the persons of the Trinity. For Zerbolt does not stand alone in blurring the distinction between God the Father and God the Son. This may be observed in the writings of David of Augsburg,[33] but it is particularly evident in the writings of many of the Devotionalists, and not only in those of Zerbolt. Among those Devotionalists who tend to disregard and obscure the distinction between God the Father and God the Son are Gerlach Peters, Dirc van Herxen and Thomas a Kempis.[34]

Christ as Man and the Union of His Two Natures. Zerbolt writes that Christ is the Son of God who was sent by the Father in order to save mankind,[35] which recalls the words spoken by Christ himself that he was sent by

---

[29] *Ref.*, 245E: Et hoc affectum tuum non modicum ad gratitudinem et amorem accenderet, si singula divina beneficia toti generi humano collata, ita tibi attraheres, et ita ex eis te ad gratitudinem intelligeres obnoxium, ac si tibi soli fuissent collata. Verbi gratia; Ac si pro te solo crucifixus esset, et homo factus, propter te solum creasset coelum et terram. Et hoc docet nos Chrysostomos.

[30] *Asc.*, 260H: Cogita quod tantum Deo peccatum displicuit quod potius ipse voluit moriens satisfacere pro peccato Adae, quam ipsum secundum suam iustitiam dimittere impunitum. *Asc.*, 274G: Si ergo vis te exercere ad timorem, quid magis timendum quam quod Deus est summa iustitia, qui elegit subire mortem potius quam iustitia sua relinqueret peccatum originale inultum. Cf. *Ref.*, 249F.

[31] *Asc.*, 261A: Quis numerabit quot peccata commisisti corde, ore, et opere. Deinde percurre singula, et vide quam gravia sunt quibus Deum omnipotentem et terribilem iudicem patremque dulcem et benignum, qui pro te tanta fecit et sustinuit, offendisti, et quodammodo iterum crucifixisti.

[32] See references given in footnote 22 above.

[33] D. of Augsburg, *De ext. et int. hom. compositione*, I, 4 and II, 52. Without drawing any distinction between God the Father and God the Son, David of Augsburg writes that it was God who created the world, became man, died on the cross and gave his body as food in the Eucharist.

[34] Mak, *De Dietse Vertaling van Gerlach Peters' Soliloquium*, 94-95; Knierim, *Dirc van Herxen (1385-1457), rector van het Zwolse fraterhuis*, 122; and J. Sudbrack, "Existentielles Christentum. Gedanken über die Frömmigkeit der 'Nachfolge Christi'," *Geist und Leben*, XXXVII (1964), 38-63.

[35] *Ref.*, 245G: ...quod propter te misit filium suum incarnari, ut esset amicus et frater tuus, qui propter te mortuus est,...

God.[36] However, it does not appear that Zerbolt believed God the Son to
have become man against his own will. For he asserts that, prompted by
his love for fallen mankind, God freely gave his own Son in order that
man might be redeemed.[37] And in view of the fact that God the Father
and God the Son share one will and operation, it is permissible to assert
that God the Son voluntarily assumed human flesh out of compassion for
fallen man and the desire to redeem him. For as Zerbolt writes, Christ so
esteemed and loved man that he was willing to be crucified for man's
redemption,[38] and the redemptive death of Christ had, of course, to be
preceded by the incarnation of God's eternal Son or Logos.[39]

The Council of Chalcedon (451 A.D.) asserted that Christ is true man,
because in his humanity Christ is consubstantial with man.[40] In *De Reformatione* and *De Ascensionibus* there are many references to Christ's
manhood and the human form which he adopted in the incarnation,[41] but
Zerbolt never explains or defends the authenticity of Christ's humanity
in terms of consubstantiality. The nearest he comes to the doctrine of
consubstantiality is in his statement that in Christ God was made flesh.[42]
Nonetheless, throughout *De Reformatione* and *De Ascensionibus* Christ's true
humanity is an all-pervasive assumption, although it is nowhere spelled
out either philosophically or theologically. This implicit acceptance of,
and belief in, the true humanity of Christ is perhaps not surprising when
one takes into consideration that with respect to their spirituality the
Devotionalists stood very much in the Bernardine and Franciscan traditions.[43] Since about 1200 A.D. there had been an ever-growing interest

---

[36] John 6, 38-39. Elsewhere Zerbolt expresses a similar sentiment when he writes that
Christ was chosen to redeem man through his death (*Ref.*, 246C).

[37] *Ref.*, 249F: Primum signaculum fuit Deus admirabilis, qui per crucem manifestatus
est esse summa sapientia,..., summa misericordia, quia tradidit pro nobis filium. See
footnote 35 above; and cf. *Ref.*, 245F and Steinmetz, *Staupitz*, 135.

[38] *Asc.*, 274H: Si vis ad amorem inflammari, cogita quod Christus tanti te reputavit,
tantumque amavit, ut pro te redimendo voluit crucifigi.

[39] Quoting St. Paul, Zerbolt calls Christ the "firstborn of creatures." (*Ref.*, 246A:
...primogenitus creaturae...; cf. Col. 1, 15.) The appellation "firstborn of every
creature" has been interpreted variously (M. D. Meilach, "Firstborn of Every
Creature," *NCE*, V, 941), but Zerbolt does not indicate what he understood by this expression.

[40] See the references given in footnote 22 above and R. Seeberg, *Text-Book of the History
of Doctrines*, trans. by C. E. Hay (2 vols.; Philadelphia, 1905), I, 112-115, 124-128,
142-143, 148-151, 152-153, 162-174 and 201-288; Chadwick, *The Early Church*, 192-212;
F. X. Murphy, "Christological Controversy," *NCE*, III, 660-662; and K. Rahner,
"Jesus Christ," *SM*, III, 200-202.

[41] *Ref.*, 245B, G and H; 247E-H; 248B and F. *Asc.*, 268G; 269C-D; 270H; 272B-D
and G; 273D and F.

[42] *Asc.*, 269H: ..., missus est Angelus Gabriel, qui Virgini nunciaret Dominum incar-
nandum.

[43] Post, *De Moderne Devotie*, 141.

in Christ's human existence, and St. Bernard and St. Francis had been among the chief promotors of this trend.[44]

We may be certain, then, that Zerbolt holds Christ to be true God and true man; and he emphasizes time and again that the appellations Jesus and Christ designate at all times one being who is both God and man or, in other words, a single individual who is both divine and human.[45] This brings us to the christological issue in its restricted sense: i.e., to the question regarding the relationship existing between Christ as God and Christ as man as understood by Zerbolt. He writes that Christ is one person, not two, who is at one and the same time both God and man: Christ as God and Christ as man are united in one person.[46] And this one person, Christ, is both God and man to the same degree.[47] However, there is no confusion of the two natures in the one person Christ.[48] While on the one hand, then, Zerbolt stresses the union of the divine and human natures in one person, and so safeguards the unity of Christ's person,[49] on the other hand he is also concerned to maintain the integrity of each of Christ's two natures. That in the one person Christ the divine and human natures are united without confusion Zerbolt regards as a necessary belief for all Christians, and as a doctrine which must not be called in question.[50] It would appear, then, that Zerbolt's views accurately reflect the doctrine concerning the dual nature of Christ which was first adopted by the church at the Council of Chalcedon.

The Decree of Chalcedon merely asserts that in Christ the divine and human natures are united without confusion, but it does not explain how such a union of two natures in one person is possible. In the Latin West three different theories which were meant to elucidate the hypostatic union gradually emerged, but by the end of the thirteenth century only the so-called subsistence theory was still held to explain adequately how the divine and human natures were united in the one person of Christ. The exponents of this doctrine maintained that in the incarnation the eternal and divine Son of God became the carrier of Christ's human nature in the way that it had always been the carrier of its own divine

---

[44] Cf. J. Thornhill, "Christocentrism," *NCE*, III, 660; Goossens, *Meditatie*, 196; Oberman, "The Shape of Late Medieval Thought: the Birthpangs of the Modern Era," 7.

[45] See footnotes 46 and 52 below.

[46] *Ref.*, 247E: and *Asc.*, 269C: ...quae simul est Deus et homo, ... *Asc.*, 272B: ...Christum...unam personam concipias, quem Deum et hominem esse ...; *Asc.*, 273D: ... Christi Deum simul est hominem... *Asc.*, 272D: ...Iesu Christo homini et Deo...

[47] See footnote 52, second excerpt.

[48] See footnote 52.

[49] See footnote 52, second excerpt.

[50] *Ref.*, 247F: Et quidem omnibus fidelibus Iesus vel Christus, Deum hominem repraesentat. And see footnote 52, second excerpt.

nature. Under normal circumstances every nature was held to have its own peculiar carrier, but the uniqueness of the incarnation was seen to lie in the fact that the divine Son of God, who had always subsisted in the divine nature, now came to subsist in human nature as well.[51] It does, therefore, not come as a surprise that when Zerbolt explains how two natures can be united in one person, and how one person can be both God and man, he does so in terms of the subsistence theory of the hypostatic union. The one person (*persona*) Christ, he writes, is the one and only carrier (*suppositum*) of Christ's divinity as well as of his humanity without a confusion of their natures or essences. Or to put it differently, in the one person of Christ the divine and human natures are united and subsist without a confusion of their essences or beings.[52] For Zerbolt the terms *persona* and *suppositum* obviously refer to the same entity. *Suppositum* describes the function of *persona*: the latter is the carrier of Christ's two natures, and the relationship existing between the person of Christ and his two natures is that of carrier and that which is carried. Zerbolt does not explicitly identify the *suppositum* with the eternal Son of God or the Logos, but his assertion that in the incarnation the Son of God became man[53] suggests that he too thought the Son of God to have become the carrier of human nature at that time just as he had always been the carrier of the divine nature. St. Thomas called it a mystery that one person can subsist in two natures,[54] and Zerbolt also refers to Christ's incarnation as a mystery.[55] It is not certain that Zerbolt regarded the incarnation as a mystery for the same reason that St. Thomas thought of it as a mystery, but it is not unlikely that he did so.

The subsistence theory regarding the hypostatic union was almost from the beginning seen to constitute a threat to Christ's humanity. However, in the late middle ages it was Christ's divinity, rather than his humanity, which stood in danger of being compromised especially in the spheres of piety and devotion. Due to the influence of St. Bernard on late

---

[51] Seeberg, *Text-Book of the History of Doctrines*, II, 17-18, 27-29, 30, 64-66, 108-110 and 154-155; and M. E. Williams, "Assumptus-Homo Theology," *NCE*, II, 976; and Oberman, *Biel*, 251-255.

[52] *Ref.*, 247E: ... per nomen Iesus...in mente formabis conceptum personae unius quae simul est Deus et homo, et in qua deitas et humanitas sine essentiarum permixtione in uno supposito coegerunt. *Asc.*, 269C-D: ..., sed Christum Deum pariter et hominem comprehendere,..., talem tibi conceptum de Christo Iesu poteris formare, ut tibi lucide Deum et hominem repraesentet, id est, unam personam significet, quae simul est Deus et homo...et hoc propter personae unitatem, in qua divinitas et humanitas sine naturarum permixtione substiterunt, et hoc credit quilibet verus Christianus,...

[53] See footnote 10 above.

[54] Cf. Steinmetz, *Staupitz*, 134.

[55] *Ref.*, 245H: Nihil apparet utilius quo salubrius occupes memoriam tuam, quam mysterium incarnationis Iesu Christi.

medieval spirituality, and even more so as a result of the influence of St. Francis and the Franciscans, there was a deep and intense interest in Christ's humanity which tended to overshadow Christ's divinity and on occasion caused it to be called in question.[56] The Devotionalist movement did not escape the perils attached to displaying too great an interest in Christ's humanity and in his sojourn on earth.[57] Grote's Christology was restricted almost totally to Christ's humanity,[58] and Johannes Busch, the great Devotionalist chronicler, found it difficult to believe that Christ, who was so obviously human while on earth, is also true God.[59] In contrast with Grote and Busch, Zerbolt does not neglect Christ's divinity, but he does not gloss over Christ's humanity either. His presentation of Christ's two natures is well balanced. He makes a determined effort to safeguard the authenticity of Christ's dual nature and is far from undermining or compromising either his divinity or humanity. He asserts more than once that the divine and human natures were united in the one person, the Logos, without a confusion or diminution of their essences.[60] Furthermore, Zerbolt frequently reminds the reader that the name Jesus or Christ must always call to mind a being who is at one and the same time true God and true man, and for this injunction he calls on support from St. Bernard in at least one instance.[61] It is an injunction which he himself would appear to have obeyed, for a number of times a

---

[56] J. Thornhill, "Christocentrism," *NCE*, III, 660; Oberman, "The Shape of Late Medieval Thought: The Birthpangs of the Modern Era," 7; F. Welter, "Franciscan Theology," *SM*, II, 348; A. Rayez, "Dévotion à l'humanité du Christ," *DSp*, VII, 1063; *idem*, "Gérard Zerbolt de Zutphen et Saint Bonaventure. Dépendances Littéraires," 342; and G. Clamens, *La dévotion à l'humanité du Christ dans la spiritualité de Thomas a Kempis* (Lyon, 1931), vi and 120.

[57] Goossens, *Meditatie*, 30.

[58] Epiney-Burgard, *Grote*, 276 and H. Gall, "De Christus-gedachte bij Geert Grote," *Ons Geestelijk Leven*, XX (1941), 237.

[59] Mak, "Christus bij de Moderne Devoten," 112-113 and 127-128.

[60] See footnote 8. While Zerbolt's belief in the true humanity of Christ is beyond all doubt, it will be seen below that in specific and concrete instances he does not always protect this humanity sufficiently.

[61] *Ref.*, 247E: ...ut quoties audis Christum vel Iesum hoc fecisse vel sustinuisse, per nomen Iesus, in mente tua repraesentetur, non homo solum, nec solum Deus, nec sola deitas vel humanitas, sed in mente formabis conceptum personae unius quae simul est Deus et homo, ... *Ref.*, 247E-F: ..., cum legis Christum flevisse super Lazarum vel Ierusalem, in mente tua concipies, non nudum hominem... Sic cum audis Christum in cruce perpendisse, non hominem solum in mente cogita, sed hominem Deum; ... *Ref.*, 247H: Siquidem, inquit [Bernardus], cum nomino Iesum, hominem mihi propono..., eundem ipsum Deum omnipotentem. *Asc.*, 272B: ..., ut semper Christum quo lucidius poteris unam personam concipias, quem Deum et hominem esse et fuisse non dubites ..., ut nomen Iesus tibi Deum et hominem repraesentet, ... *Ref.*, 247E: Itaque Christus vel Iesus cum dicitur, Deus et homo, id est, persona deitatis et humanitatis designatur,... See footnote 50, and footnote 52, second excerpt. Cf. Rayez, "Gérard Zerbolt de Zutphen et Saint Bonaventure. Dépendances Littéraires," 342; and Goossens, *Meditatie*, 193.

reference to Jesus or Christ is followed by the observation that he is both God and man.[62]

A. Rayez' opinion that *De Reformatione* and *De Ascensionibus* of Zerbolt contributed notably to the development of the devotion to Christ's humanity is undoubtedly valid.[63] However, if one is to obtain a true picture of Zerbolt's devotion to Christ, then Rayez' assertion must be complemented by an equally valid statement that in his devotion to Christ Zerbolt did not neglect Christ's divinity. Furthermore, in view of the balance maintained by Zerbolt between Christ's divinity and his humanity, R. Garcia-Villoslada's statement that the "disciples of Groote and Radewijns did not meditate upon the divine nature and attributes but rather upon Christ's humanity the virtues of which they sought to imitate,"[64] is misleading, at least with respect to Zerbolt. For it is patently obvious from what has been said that for Zerbolt Christ's divinity was as important as his humanity, and he instructs the reader more than once to reflect and to meditate on both of Christ's natures.[65]

Reason for Safeguarding Christ's Dual Nature. The considerable effort made by Zerbolt to safeguard Christ's divinity as well as his humanity is motivated not only by the desire to maintain doctrinal purity, but also, and perhaps primarily, by somewhat more practical considerations, namely by the conviction that in the spiritual life nothing is safer for man than constant fear tempered with hope and love.[66] Fear, dread and awe ensue when the believer meditates on Christ's divinity, the authenticity of which was firmly established by Zerbolt, for in his divinity Christ is,

---

[62] *Ref.*, 248F: ..., Christus Deus et homo, videns appropinquare tempus suum, surrexit ut iret ad mortem,... *Asc.*, 268G: ..., quod Christus Iesus Deus et homo, Dei et hominum mediator,... *Asc.*, 273D: ..., Christus Deus et homo surrexit...

[63] A. Rayez, "Dévotion a l'humanité du Christ," *DSp*, VII, 1095.

[64] R. Garcia-Villoslada, "Devotio Moderna," *NCE*, IV, 831.

[65] See footnote 61 above, first two excerpts (*Ref.*, 247E and *Ref.*, 247E-F). *Ref.*, 247F-G: Si hominem cogitas,... Si Deum cogitas,... Si hominem Iesum imaginaris,... Si Deum hominem attendis, ... Hunc nos modum de Christo vel de Iesu meditandi, sacra Evangelia docent, quae fere nullum factum vel miraculum referunt in quo Christi simul humanitatem et divinitatem non manifestent. *Ref.*, 247G-H: Item hunc modum habuit in suis meditationibus devotissimus doctor Bernardus, ait enim super Cantica: Siquidem, inquit cum nomino Iesum, hominem mihi propono.., eundem ipsum Deum omnipotentem. *Asc.*, 269C: Secundus ascensus per vitam et passionem Christi est, iam aliquantulum altius ascendere, et non solum circa Christi humanitatem se exercere,... *Asc.*, 273D: ...et devotam meditationem trahens, ante omnia cum reverentia et pia dulcedine, recole personam Christi Deum simul et hominem,...

[66] *Asc.*, 285F: Audi beatum Gregorium hunc tibi ascensum et descensum recommendantem. Quamvis, inquit, securitati timor semper longe videatur abesse, nobis tamen nihil est securius, quam sub spe semper timere, ne incauta mens aut desperando se in vitiis deiiciat, aut extollendo de donis ruat.

after all, true God, the almighty creator and judge of mankind.[67] Fear of Christ the judge serves to prevent the believer from falling into spiritual complacency. Love and adoration on the other hand, are the result of meditating on Christ's humanity,[68] although Zerbolt frequently expresses the view that a correct and profound understanding of Christ's dual nature can also be a stimulus to love and devotion.[69] Love for Christ and devotion to him are preconditions for imitation, although fear of Christ will also induce the believer to take imitation of Christ, without which he cannot be saved, seriously; and concerning the prominent role which imitation of Christ plays in Zerbolt's spirituality more will be said below. Furthermore, meditation on Christ's humanity imbues the believer with a sense of trust, confidence and hope, and these sentiments serve to prevent the development of the despair and despondency that might result from the remembrance of Christ's role as implacable judge.[70] By pointing, then, to Christ's humanity and divinity, and by emphasizing them to an equal degree, Zerbolt aims to instil in the believer a salutary balance between fear and love which will compel him to follow and to imitate Christ.[71]

ii. *Consequences of the Union of God and Man in Christ*

Now that we have seen that Zerbolt regards the incarnation as a union of divinity and humanity in the person of the Logos, we turn to his views

---

[67] *Ref.*, 247F: Si hominem cogitas, inde fiducialius adorabis, securiusque accedes...Si Deum cogitas, inde omnia quae fecit et patitur, vel loquitur, vel respondet, magis videbuntur cordi tuo admiranda, reverenda, terrifica, et metuanda. *Asc.*, 269D: Si Christum hominem cogitas, inde tibi dulcis affectio et magna fiducia ... Sed si Christum Deum cogitas, inde tibi omnia verba, facta miracula, gustui magis apparent metuenda, terrenda, horrenda, et admiranda. Et sic si utrumque in Christo intelligis et concipis, magna tibi nascetur devotio, amor et fiducia, et rursum timor, et reverentia. *Asc.*, 272B-C: Si enim humano affectu bruto animali compateris intense afflicto, quanto magis compatereris Christo, si eum non solum ut hominem piissimum, dulcissimum, mitissimum, nobilissimum, amantissimum, gratiosum et decorum in conceptu assumeres, verum insuper ut Deum omnipotentem, metuendum, reverendum, adorandum creatorem et iudicem tuum, mentis tuae oculis repraesentares? Cf. Goossens, *Meditatie*, 193-194.

[68] See previous footnote.

[69] *Ref.*, 247F: Sic cum audis Christum in cruce perpendisse, non hominem solum in mente cogita, sed hominem Deum; et amplius miraberis, et multo plus ad devotionem accenderis, et moveberis ad compassionem. Et quidem omnibus fidelibus Iesus vel Christus, Deum hominem repraesentat. Sed quanto id lucidius et clarius attendere poteris, tanto eris devotior in Christi vita, morte, miraculis et factis. *Asc.*, 272B: Cum igitur legis Christum talem poenam sustinuisse, vel sic et sic respondisse, vel tacuisse, cogita semper et in conceptu sic forma, ut nomen Iesus tibi Deum et hominem repraesentet, et sic Christum devotius et maiori reverentia aspicis, multoque amplius compatieris. *Asc.*, 269C: ..., sed Christum Deum pariter et hominem comprehendere, Christumque ut Deum pariter et hominem diligere, diligere et adorare.

[70] See footnote 67 above.

[71] Sudbrack, ''Existentielles Christentum. Gedanken über die Frömmigkeit der 'Nachfolge Christi','' 51.

concerning the practical consequences of this union. What sort of person was this concrete, historical Christ who was at one and the same time both God and man? The answer to this question is a complex one and can best be answered under a number of headings.

Christ's Perfection and Holiness. Zerbolt holds Christ to be free from the taint of original sin, because he writes that Christ, who was without sin, accepted the mark of the forgiveness of sins.[72] The reference is to Christ's circumcision and Zerbolt clearly equates circumcision with baptism as the 'sacrament' which removes the guilt attached to original sin. Christ was not only born without sin, but he remained sinless throughout his whole life: *"purissimus," "mundissimus," "innocentissimus,"* according to Zerbolt.[73] Why Christ was born free from all sin and blemish, and why he remained that way, Zerbolt does not explain. However, the hypostatic union was generally held to have been responsible for Christ's freedom from all sins. It was on account of that union that Christ was free from original sin, and therefore free from the effects of original sin which sooner or later lead all men into committing personal sins. In addition to being free from original sin and its power to force men into committing personal sins, Aquinas, for example, argued that because of the hypostatic union Christ possessed the beatific vision from the very beginning, and that this vision in itself made it altogether impossible for Christ to commit personal sins.[74]

However, sinlessness is merely the negative side of holiness, and the great scholastic theologians of the middle ages held that as a positive consequence of the hypostatic union Christ possessed, in his humanity, more graces and a greater degree of sanctity from his conception onwards than any human even before the fall could have hoped to acquire.[75] Zerbolt likewise assigns a degree of perfection and holiness to Christ in his

---

[72] *Asc.*, 270A: Octavo die circumciditur, et Iesus vocatur. Attende quod sine peccato assumpsit peccati remedium.

[73] *Ref.*, 246B and 249A; *Asc.*, 273H.
In addition to these general references to Christ's purity Zerbolt draws particular attention to Christ's chastity, and to the fact that he was free from rancour, envy and impatience (*Ref.*, 247H and *Asc.*, 273A).

[74] Thomas Aquinas, *ST*, 3a, 41, 1. Bonaventure writes as well that Christ could not have sinned (*Breviloquium*, Pt. IV, ch. 5 [*Works*, II, 157]). Cf. E. A. Weis, "Impeccability of Christ," *NCE*, VII, 395.
Scotus, in contrast with Bonaventure and Aquinas, was not of the opinion that Christ lacked the freedom to sin. For him Christ was ontologically free to sin, but God the Father 'prevented' him from doing so (*NCE*, VII, 395).

[75] Thomas Aquinas, *ST*, 3a, 10, 1-4 and 3a, 12, 2; Bonaventure, *Breviloquium*, Pt. IV, ch. 5 (*Works*, II, 157); cf. J. J. Walsh, "Jesus Christ," *NCE*, VII, 922-24; P. de Letter, "Jesus Christ (Beatific Vision)," *NCE*, VII, 930; J. B. Endres, "Jesus Christ (Sanctifying Grace)," *NCE*, VII, 946-947; and E. A. Weis, "Incarnation," *NCE*, VII, 414.

humanity which exceeds that to be found in any other human being.[76] For he writes that Christ's sanctity was complete,[77] or, in other words, that he possessed fulness of grace, but he does not specifically ascribe Christ's matchless sanctity to a positive influence of the hypostatic union. However, his assertion that the Trinity, of which Christ in his divinity constitutes the second person, is the essence and source of all good and holiness[78] perhaps indicates that he did, nonetheless, regard Christ's human perfection and sanctity as direct and positive results of the hypostatic union. Furthermore, Zerbolt is clearly of the opinion that Christ was aware of his divine ego and divine mission from his birth on,[79] and it was widely held that Christ owed this knowledge to the beatific vision,[80] itself a consequence of the hypostatic union. It might perhaps be concluded, then, that Zerbolt also considered Christ to have possessed the beatific vision from the outset, and perfect holiness and fulness of grace as a consequence of that vision.

Aquinas and Bonaventure, to name but two, expressed the view that the fulness of grace enjoyed by Christ was responsible for the incomparable degree of virtuousness displayed by him at all times.[81] Zerbolt likewise draws attention to Christ's virtuousness. He writes that Christ is the sum of all virtues, and, consequently, an abundant store of virtue.[82] No Christian, he adds, is ignorant of the fact that Christ possessed all virtues and that he conducted himself most excellently in all situations,[83] which suggests that he regarded this knowledge to be an intuitive one. And although Zerbolt discovered incomparable virtuousness and most edifying behaviour in all of Christ's life, he found it pre-eminently in Christ's passion.[84] Christ's virtuousness is defined by Zerbolt as a most

---

[76] Perfection, Zerbolt writes, lies in achieving one's end and the purpose for which one was created. (Ref., 238H: Tanto enim unumquodque est perfectius, quanto plus appropinquaverit sua fini.) Man was created to love God above all, and this goal was realized by Christ, largely because he was free from original sin. As a consequence of his perfection Christ also enjoyed an immeasurable felicity (Ref., 249B and Asc., 274B).

[77] Ref., 247H: ...omni denique sanctitate... This statement is found in a longer excerpt borrowed by Zerbolt from one of St. Bernard's sermons on the Song of Songs (Ref., 247G-H). Cf. Thomas Aquinas, ST., 3a, 7, 11-12; and Bonaventure, Breviloquium, Pt. IV, ch. 5 (Works, II, 157-159).

[78] Asc., 267B: ...Trinitatem...omnisque bonitatis exemplar essentiale...

[79] Asc., 269H-270B. See below for a fuller analysis of this knowledge enjoyed by the infant Christ.

[80] P. de Letter, "Jesus Christ (Beatific Vision)", NCE, VII, 930.

[81] Thomas Aquinas, ST, 3a, 7, 2; and Bonaventure, Breviloquium, Pt. IV, ch. 7 (Works, II, 164-166).

[82] Asc., 273A-B: ...Christo omnium virtutum summam... Asc., 272H: Et sic invenies in Christo...omnium virtutum copiam,... Dirc van Herxen expresses much the same view (Knierim, Dirc van Herxen [1385-1457], rector van het Zwolse fraterhuis, 122).

[83] Ref., 248C: Nam nullus Christianus ignorat, quin in omnibus optimo modo se habuit.

[84] See below, pp. 147-150.

excellent disposition of character which found expression in his outward manner and conduct;[85] and this definition of Christ's virtuousness agrees with the definition of virtue Zerbolt offers in *De Vestibus Pretiosis*. He writes there that although virtue resides in the heart, the exercise of virtue cannot take place in the heart but must be expressed overtly. Consequently, virtuousness is determined by one's conduct,[86] and Zerbolt gives voice here to the typically Devotionalist view that *"exteriora interiora trahunt."*[87]

In addition to describing and defining Christ's virtuousness in general, Zerbolt mentions a number of specific virtues, all of which Christ possessed to an incomparable degree, by name.[88] Of all the virtues it is Christ's perfect humility in particular which attracts his attention.[89] Following in the footsteps of St. Paul, Augustine made a great deal of Christ's humility, and, as a result of Augustine's influence, humility became the focal point of all of Christ's virtues as can be seen in the writings of St. Bernard and Bonaventure, for example. The interest in Christ's humility, and the stress placed on the importance of humility in general, stemmed to a considerable extent from the fact that humility stands diametrically opposed to pride, the cause of man's fall and all sins.[90] Like Augustine, Zerbolt regards the incarnation itself as an act of humility.[91] However, humility is the term which Zerbolt employs more frequently than any other to describe and to characterize Christ's disposi-

---

[85] *Asc.*, 269A: ..., optimam morum dispositionem in exteriori compositione.

[86] *De Vestibus Pretiosis*, 45: ..., quod virtus in corde consistat et non in vestitu, etc. Ut huius racionis error evidencius appareat, tria declaranda sunt, primo quod circa exteriorem vestitum virtutes consistant, nam licet omnes virtutes essentialiter sunt in anima veluti habitus in subtero, attamen circa exteriores actus exercentur, unde et virtutes per actus determinantur; ... Cf. *Asc.*, 285G.

Zerbolt's definition of virtue approximates that definition of virtue which had found widespread acceptance, namely, that virtue is a morally well-directed disposition which governs conduct (T. C. O'Brien, "Virtue," *NCE*, XIV, 104-107).

[87] Cf. van Woerkum, "Florentius Radewijns: Leven, Geschriften, Persoonlijkheid en Ideeën," 363.

[88] *Asc.*, 269D, 272C, 273F and H, and 274D; and *Ref.*, 249D. Also see footnote 92 below.

[89] *Asc.*, 270C. Zerbolt writes that through his perfect humility Christ fulfilled all righteousness or, in other words, satisfied divine justice (*Ref.*, 248C). Only the realization that perfect humility renders a perfect act of obedience possible makes Zerbolt's statement, that God's demand for justice was satisfied through Christ's perfect humility, intelligible. However, this matter will receive further attention in the discussion of Christ's works.

[90] Harnack, *History of Dogma*, II, 106; Kelly, *Early Christian Doctrines*, 393-395; Slotemaker de Bruine, *Het Ideaal der Navolging van Christus ten Tijde van Bernard van Clairvaux*, 54-58; P. Zerbi, "Bernard of Clairvaux," *NCE*, II, 337; and Bonaventure, *Lignum Vitae*, chs. 5-8 (*Works*, I, 107-109).

[91] *Asc.*, 269H: Attende Angeli reverentiam ad Mariam. Mirare Dei humiliationem. Considera virginis exaltationem: ...

tion in general, as well as his conduct in all situations.[92] And, influenced by St. Paul, later Devotionalist writers referred to humility as "the virtue of Christ."[93] It is, therefore, not surprising that the Devotionalists considered humility to be the most important of all virtues and the foundation of all virtue. Humility was considered to be an altogether indispensable requirement for progress in the spiritual life,[94] and the purpose behind all of Christ's humility was to instruct man through the example of his humility.[95]

Zerbolt's intense interest in Christ's sanctity and virtuous conduct is prompted by the fact that imitation of Christ's virtues plays an important role in his soteriology as well as in his doctrine regarding the spiritual life.[96] Imitation of Christ had always played an important role in soteriological thought, but it was only with St. Bernard and St. Francis that imitation of Christ began to play a major role in the spiritual life. The aim of the spiritual life being for them, as for Zerbolt, a return, as far as possible, to man's spiritual condition as it had existed before the fall, they saw in Christ an example of man as he had been at that time, or of one even holier than that.[97]

---

[92] Although it cannot be claimed that the list which follows is totally complete, it nonetheless gives some indication as to the terms used by Zerbolt to describe Christ's inner disposition and outward conduct and bearing. The number following each word indicates the frequency with which it occurs, and it clearly shows that Zerbolt favoured the term "humility" to describe Christ's character and conduct: *humilitas-humilis* (24); *mitis* (12); *dulcis* (11); *benignus* (7); *pius-pietas* (5); *compassio* (5); *patiens* (5); *nobilis* (4); *amandus-amans* (3); *suavis* (3); *decorus* (3); *mansuetus* (2); *caritas* (2); *lenis* (2); *zelus* (2); *gratiosus* (2); *misericordia* (1); *largus* (1); *munificentia* (1); *sobrius* (1); *liberalis* (1); *venustus* (1); and *devotus* (1). These descriptions of Christ are found on the following pages: *Ref.*, 246C-D, 247E-H, 248B-E, 249A and D; and *Asc.*, 269A and D, 270A-C, E and G, 272C and H, 273A, D-F and H. For his description of Christ on p. 247H of *De Reformatione* Zerbolt is indebted to St. Bernard; and for the description on p. 249A of *De Reformatione* and p. 273H of *De Ascensionibus* he is indebted to Bonaventure (*De Triplici Via*, ch. 3, par. 2 [*Works*, I, 82-83]). For Christ's sanctity and perfection cf. D. of Augsburg, *De ext. et int. hom. compositione*, I, 21-23.

[93] J. F. Vregt, ed., "Sommige vermaninge tot eenen doechliken leven," *AGAU*, X (1882), 331 and 365. Cf. Mak, "Christus bij de Moderne Devoten," 119-120.

[94] Cf. Post, *De Moderne Devotie*, 145-146. In assigning such a great degree of importance to the virtue of humility the Devotionalists were following the Bernardine and Franciscan traditions on this point. St. Bernard called humility the basis of all virtues (Post, *De Moderne Devotie*, 146), and St. Bonaventure referred to humility as "the root and guardian of all virtues" (Bonaventure, *Lignum Vitae*, ch. 5 [*Works*, I, 107]).

[95] *Ref.*, 246C: Quodque pedes eorum humilitatis volens exemplum altius imprimere, prostratus humiliter abluebat. Cf. *Asc.*, 270G.

[96] See below, pp. 139-153, 262-263 and 273.

[97] Slotemaker de Bruine, *Het Ideaal der Navolging van Christus ten Tijde van Bernard van Clairvaux*, 25-27, 29-31, 58-67 and 100-104; Mak, "Christus bij de Moderne Devoten," 105-166; Etienne Ledeur, "Imitation de Christ," *DSp*, VII, 1571-1577; F. Wetter, "Franciscan Theology," *SM*, II, 348; A. McDevitt, "Franciscan Spirituality," *NCE*, VI, 37-38; P. Zerbit, "Bernard of Clairvaux," *NCE*, II, 337; and W. M. Davish, "Jesus Christ (Example)," *NCE*, VII, 535. Cf. below, pp. 139-153.

Also Bernardine, but even more typically Franciscan,[98] is the attention given by Zerbolt to Christ's physical appearance. He writes that Christ possessed a bodily elegance, beauty and fairness of form the likeness of which has never been seen among "the sons of men."[99] It would appear, moreover, that he attributed Christ's physical beauty directly to the hypostatic union. For he observes that the Trinity is the essence and fount of all beauty,[100] which suggests that Christ, the second person of the Trinity, owes his matchless beauty to the hypostatic union. Dionysius the Carthusian, who was subjected to much the same influences as Zerbolt had been,[101] wrote many years later that Christ constitutes the link with the eternal beauty of the Trinity.[102]

Cf. David of Augsburg who writes: "His [Christ's] example sets for us a rule of life, He Himself instructs us that—created as we are to His image—we may by following His footsteps, renew in ourselves that likeness to Him which sin has defaced" (De ext. et int. hom. compositione, I, 22).

[98] Oberman, "The Shape of Late Medieval Thought: The Birthpangs of the Modern Era," 7; A. Rayez, "La Dévotion à l'Humanité du Christ," DSp, VII, 1095; J. Thornhill, "Christocentrism," NCE, III, 660; and Post, De Moderne Devotie, 141.

[99] Asc., 268H-269A: Cogita quam fuerit eius praesentia dulcis. Cogita corporis elegantiam et speciositatem. Nam speciosus forma prae filiis hominum. When Zerbolt calls Christ "the fairest among the children of men" he is most likely quoting a scriptural text: Psalm 44, 3 (45, 2 in the AV). Asc., 270A: Nota faciem et dispositionem pulcherrimi pueri. Cf. Asc., 269D, 272C, and 274B; and Ref., 249B. On p. 274B of De Ascensionibus and p. 249B of De Reformatione Zerbolt refers to Christ's "immeasurable beauty" ("immensus speciositate"), and this description of Christ's physical appearance occurs in a longer excerpt taken from Bonaventure's De Triplici Via, ch. 3, par. 2 (Works, I, 82-83).

The anonymous Epistola de Vita et Passione Domini, an important devotional work read by all the Devotionalists, also refers to Christ as the fairest of all men (de Bruin, ed., "De Dietse oertekst van de anonieme 'Epistola de vita et passione domini nostri Jesu Christ et aliis devotis exerciciis'," 15). The same thing is done by Dirc van Herxen (Knierim, Dirc van Herxen [1385-1457], rector van het Zwolse fraterhuis, 121).

Cf. Bonaventure, Lignum Vitae, chs. 8 and 35 (Works, I, 109 and 133-134); and J. Moellerfeld, "Die schönheit des Menschen nach Dionys dem Kartäuser," in: Dr. L. Reypens-Album, ed. by A. Ampe (Antwerp, 1964), 238.

[100] Asc., 267B: ...Trinitatem..., in qua relucet omnis pulchritudinis,...

Gregory of Nyssa also regarded God to be the essence, archetype and fount of all beauty. He, as well as Augustine and Pseudo-Dionysius, applied the Greek and Neoplatonic theories regarding beauty to God and the Trinity. It was the Neoplatonists who first applied the older Greek theories regarding beauty to the metaphysical (C. Putnam, "Beauty," NCE, II, 202-203). Bonaventure also refers to the Trinity as "supreme beauty" (Breviloquium, "Prologue" [Works, II, 13]).

[101] The Carthusian Order lacked its own 'school' of spirituality as well as theology because the individual members of the order were allowed, and encouraged, to devise their own brand of spirituality provided it remained within the bounds of orthodoxy (B. du Moustier, "Carthusian Spirituality," NCE, III, 161). There was, however, a fair degree of similarity between the spirituality of the Devotionalists and that of the Carthusians of North Western Europe in the late middle ages. This similarity must be attributed, in part at least, to a common source, namely Franciscan spirituality (cf. I. C. Brady, "Bonaventure," NCE, II, 664). Furthermore, it was while living with the Carthusians at Monnikhuizen that Grote's spirituality took shape. And Grote's spirituality, which betrays Carthusian characteristics, set the tone for Devotionalist spirituality (van Zijl, Groote, 104-105 and 112-116).

[102] Moellerfeld, "Die schönheit des Menschen nach Dionys dem Kartäuser," 238.

The Communication of Attributes in Christ. Inasmuch as the various attributes of Christ, both divine and human, cannot be logically separated from his two natures, the relationship which is seen to exist between Christ's two natures determines the relationship which is seen to exist between his divine and human attributes.[103]

The orthodox position regarding the relationship between the two natures of Christ was, it has been observed, that they are united in the one person of Jesus without confusion. Consistent with this view the church stated as early as the fifth century that, because the two natures of Christ retain their integrity after the incarnation, there is no communication of attributes or qualities between them. However, because the two natures are united in one person, it can be said that a communication of attributes takes place in the one, concrete, historical person of Jesus. On account of the hypostatic union all the qualities of Christ's two natures must at all times be assigned to the one person of Jesus. But human properties may not, however, be assigned to Christ's divine nature or *vice versa*, because the separate natures in Christ retain their own identities. There is no transfer of attributes or qualities between them. By thus denying a communication of idioms between Christ's two natures their integrity was preserved. On the other hand, the doctrine that a communication of attributes takes place in the one person of Christ safeguarded Christ's unity of person.[104]

It is clearly at the level of the historical Christ, then, that Zerbolt's fidelity to the formula "two natures in one person without confusion" may be tested most accurately.[105] One looks in vain in Zerbolt's writings for the term *communicatio idiomatum* but the issue is, nonetheless, broached a number of times in his discussion of the historical Christ, and he is obviously familiar with this problem area regarding the person of Christ. It is evident too that he understands the *communicatio idiomatum* question to be of a piece with that regarding the union of two natures in one person, for he considers the communication of attributes to be a natural consequence of the hypostatic union. Consequently he explains that whatever act or quality is attributed to Christ must be assigned, in accordance with

---

[103] The question regarding the relationship existing between Christ's divine and human attributes does not only follow logically from the question regarding the relationship existing between the two natures of Christ, but the two issues are basically identical. The one deals with the problem of Christ's two natures and their relationship to one another in general and abstract terms, the other in specific and concrete ones (cf. J. F. Rigney, "Communication of Idioms," *NCE*, IV, 37).

[104] *Ibid.*, 35-37; Seeberg, *Text-Book of the History of Doctrines*, I, 250-255 and 270; Richardson, ed., *Dictionary*, 56-58 ("Christology") and 68 ("*Communicatio Idiomatum*"); Chadwick, *The Early Church*, 195-196; and Thomas Aquinas, *ST*, 3a, 16, 4-5. Cf. Seeberg, *Text-Book of the History of Doctrines*, I, 110.

[105] Cf. Oberman, *Biel*, 263.

the Catholic Faith, to Christ the God as well as to Christ the man because of his unity of person, or, in other words, because Christ the God and Christ the man constitute a single, unified entity.[106] Zerbolt maintains, then, that because of the hypostatic union a communication of idioms takes place in the one person (*hypostasis*) of Christ, and thus he adequately preserves and protects, in theory at least, the oneness of Christ's person. Having formulated this general principle regarding the communication of attributes in the one person of Christ, Zerbolt goes on to illustrate his point with a number of examples. He explains that the miracles performed by Christ such as the raising of the dead, and similar feats generally held to be acts of God, must be attributed not only to Christ the God but also to Christ the man, and that this is so because of the hypostatic union.[107] For the same reason, Zerbolt elaborates, when one reads that Christ wept, that he suffered and that he died, all attributes typical of humans, one must believe that it was not only Christ the man who wept, suffered and died but that it was also Christ the God who did so.[108] Likewise one must believe that in Christ the Son of God became a

---

[106] *Asc.*, 269C-D: Multum quidem fructum in exercitio confert circa vitam et passionem Christi Domini, si quoties legis vel cogitas Christum hoc vel illud fecisse vel sustinuisse, talem tibi conceptum de Christo Iesu poteris formare, ut tibi lucide Deum et hominem repraesentet, id est, unam personam significet, quae simul est Deus et homo et quicquid legis vel cogitas Christum fecisse, sive in mortuis suscitandis, sive in miraculis faciendis hominem fecisse Christum non dubites; quicquid Christum legis sustinuisse, sive in manuum perforatione et pedum conclavatione, Deum credas indubitanter sustinuisse, et hoc propter personae unitatem,..., et hoc credit quilibet verus Christianus; ... *Ref.*, 247E-F: Cum autem sacramenti Dominicae passionis historiam in mente tua revolvis, ut ad literam opus nostrae redemptionis contempleris, diligenter debes ad hoc niti, ut quoties audis Christum vel Iesum hoc fecisse vel sustinuisse, per nomen Iesus, in mente tua repraesentetur, non homo solum, nec solum Deus, nec sola deitas vel humanitas, sed in mente formabis conceptum personae unius quae simul est Deus et homo,... Itaque Christus vel Iesus cum dicitur, Deus et homo, id est, persona deitatis et humanitatis designatur, ita ut quicquid Deus fecisse firmiter fide Catholica retineamus, quicquid homo sustinuit Deum credamus et cogitemus sustinuisse. Verbi gratia, cum legis Christum flevisse super Lazarum vel Ierusalem, in mente tua concipies, non nudum hominem, quoniam tunc minus mirabile est hominem flevisse. Sic cum audis Christum in cruce perpendisse, non hominem solum in mente cogita, sed hominem Deum; ... See footnote 116 below as well. Cf. Steinmetz, *Staupitz*, 135.

[107] See previous footnote.

[108] That in Christ God wept see *Ref.*, 247E-F (see footnote 106 above).

That in Christ God suffered see *Ref.*, 247E (see footnote 106 above); *Ref.*, 248B: Noli solum cogitare de poena exteriore, sed ita Dominum Iesum respice in talibus poenis quasi hominem Deum exterius summa poenalitate afflictum, et etiam ultra quam humana mens comprehendere potest, interius tribulatum et dolorosum. *Asc.*, 269C; and *Asc.*, 272B: Cum igitur legis Christum talem poenam sustinuisse,..., cogita semper et in conceptu sic forma, ut nomen Iesus tibi Deum et hominem repraesentet,...

That in Christ God died see *Ref.*, 247G: Si Deum hominem attendis, id est, ita Iesum concipis quasi personam deitatis et humanitatis, statim cum dicitur, surrexit Iesus, etiam si nil audis, aliquid mirificum menti tuae repraesentatur, scilicet, quod Deus surrexit et

little child and that in Christ God lay in a manger.[109] The examples provided reveal that Zerbolt does not regard the hypostatic union to be an
abstract notion, but that he understands the unity of Christ's person to be
real and concrete. The examples also show clearly that in concrete situations Zerbolt remains faithful to his general statements regarding the
oneness of Christ's person, and that he protects it adequately in such instances. Finally, because of the doctrine regarding the communication of
idioms in the one, historical person of Christ, it had been a generally accepted tenet since patristic times that not only was Christ the man born of
Mary, but Christ the God as well,[110] and Zerbolt too refers to Mary as
the Mother of God.[111]

The doctrine regarding the unity of Christ's person obliged Zerbolt to
avow that a communication of properties takes place in the one, historical
person of Christ. His acceptance of the doctrine that the two natures of
Christ are united in him without confusion forced him to assert as well
that there is no communication of attributes between Christ's divinity
and humanity.[112] However, in concrete situations he does not, it would

---

ad mortem ivit. *Ref.*, 248F: ..., Christus Deus et homo, videns appropinquare tempus
suum, surrexit ut iret ad mortem,... *Ref.*, 249B and *Asc.*, 274B: ...aeternitatem mori.
   In his discussion of the communication of idioms Zerbolt draws on the story of Lazarus
to illustrate two concrete points regarding this matter. He writes that the hypostatic union
requires one to say that at the grave of Lazarus God wept and that it was a man who
raised him from the dead (see footnote 106 above). In drawing on this particular episode
from sacred history to explain his views regarding the communication of idioms Zerbolt
was following what would appear to have been an old tradition. For Gregory of Nyssa also
drew on the story of Lazarus to explain his doctrine regarding the *communicatio idiomatum*,
as did Pope Leo I (Seeberg, *Text-Book of the History of Doctrines*, I, 251 and 270).
   [109] *Asc.*, 269H-270A: Dehinc Dei filius, cuius magnitudinis non est finis, factus est parvulus infantulus. Cogita quod Deus parvulus vagiit, et lachrymatus est in praesepio. Cf.
Chadwick, *The Early Church*, 194-198.
   [110] Pelikan, *The Christian Tradition, A History of the Development of Doctrine*, I, 241-242 and
P. C. Hoelle, "Mother of God," *NCE*, X, 21.
   Athanasius was, however, not the first to call Mary the Mother of God, for since the
third century it had been a devotional practice to do so (Pelikan, *op. cit.*, I, 241-242 and
Chadwick, *The Early Church*, 192).
   [111] *Asc.*, 267B-C: Cogita quantum sit gaudium interesse societati coelestis curiae,
quanta laetitia reginam coeli matrem Dei cum caeteris virginibus intueri,...
   [112] *Ref.*, 249C: Designans tandem quanta sua esset poena, et quod humanitas quodammodo fuit deserta, eo quod non fuit redundantia virium supernarum quibus fruebatur, ad
inferiores quibus patiebatur, clamabat: Eli, Eli, etc.
   Asc., 274C: Clamans proinde eli, eli, quanta sua foret poena, et quod humanitas ab
divinitate quodammodo fuit deserta, designavit. Et hoc propterea, quod nulla fuit redundantia virium superiorum, quibus fruebatur ad vires inferiores, quibus patiebatur.
   Zerbolt writes that in Christ "there was no overflow from the higher powers which he
enjoyed to the lower powers," but the context indicates that the "higher powers" must be
equated with Christ's divinity and the "lower powers" with Christ's humanity. Zerbolt is
saying, in effect, that there was no movement of divine attributes and qualities to Christ's
humanity which would have destroyed the latter's authenticity.

appear, remain true at all times to his principle regarding the non-communication of attributes between Christ's humanity and divinity. The Latin Church had always maintained that God is impassible, and that Christ did not, therefore, suffer in his divinity. The Eastern Church, on the other hand, had always held the opposite view with respect to the question of divine passibility.[113] It may be said, then, that Zerbolt accurately reflects the West's position on this point when he writes that Christ did not suffer in his divinity, but that he suffered everything in his humanity.[114] To attribute to Christ's divine nature the capacity to suffer would, in view of the West's doctrine regarding the impassibility of God, have constituted a confusion of natures in Christ.[115] Zerbolt also observes briefly that it was through his divine power that Christ prostrated his enemies in the garden of Gethsemane and dimmed the sun while on the cross.[116] These are acts which no man can perform, and in order to safeguard Christ's humanity Zerbolt points out that they were the work of Christ in his divinity. That he singles out these two acts does not appear to carry with it any particular significance. What he clearly aims at

---

The statement that in Christ there was no overflow from his superior powers to his inferior ones is reminiscent of Aquinas. He twice employs the exact same statement in his discussion of Christ's suffering (Thomas Aquinas, *ST*, 3a, 46, 6), and it is also in connection with Christ's suffering that Zerbolt uses it. However, by the statement that in Christ there was no overflow from his superior powers to his inferior ones Aquinas meant something rather different from the interpretation given it by Zerbolt. All that Aquinas had in mind was that there was no overflow from Christ's beatific vision, a superior human endowment, to his inferior human powers, which allowed him to suffer in the latter. (The question of Christ's suffering will be examined in greater detail below.) Zerbolt, on the other hand, means that there was no overflow from Christ's divinity to his humanity or, in other words, no movement of attributes between them. Since there was no commingling of the natures it was possible for Christ's humanity to be deserted by his divinity causing Christ to suffer to an extreme degree in his humanity, and causing him to cry out: "My God, My God, etc."

[113] See Thomas Aquinas, *ST*, 3a, 16, 5; Bonaventure, *Breviloquium*, Pt. IV, ch. 9 (*Works*, II, 170 and 173) and Richardson, ed., *Dictionary*, 58 ("Christology"). Cf. Steinmetz, *Staupitz*, 135-136.

[114] *Ref.*, 247G: Ex humanitate autem omnia passus est. Cf. above footnote 112.

Van den Hombergh writes that according to Jan Brugman Christ suffered in his divinity as well as in his humanity (*Leven en Werk van Jan Brugman, O.F.M.*, 87). However, it may be questioned whether van den Hombergh's interpretation of Brugman's position on this issue is correct (*ibid.*, 256).

[115] See footnote 113 above.

[116] *Ref.*, 247G: Hunc nos modum de Christo vel de Iesu meditandi, sacra Evangelia docent, quae fere nullum factum vel miraculum referunt in quo Christi simul humanitatem et divinitatem non manifestent. Ita invenies in Christi baptismo, tentatione, miraculis, et maxime in pluribus locis in passione. Nam adversarios prostravit deitate, sol obscuratus est, clamans voce magna, emisit spiritum, ita ut etiam ex hoc Centurio gentilis Deum intelligeret.

Bonaventure too writes that it was Christ the God who prostrated his enemies in the garden of Gethsemane (*Lignum Vitae*, ch. 19 [*Works*, I, 118]).

is to indicate to the reader that while some acts are acts of Christ the God, other acts are acts of Christ the man, and that there must not be a confusion of Christ's two natures in this respect. However, Christ's human knowledge, especially in his infancy, childhood and youth, is one of the best areas in which Zerbolt's fidelity to his general statement regarding the non-communication of attributes between Christ's two natures may best be tested. Of special concern to us will be Christ's Messianic consciousness or self-awareness, because that is the only aspect of Christ's knowledge concerning which Zerbolt really says anything.

From his account of Christ's infancy and childhood it quickly becomes evident that Zerbolt detected no development in Christ with respect to his Messianic consciousness, nor any growth in self-awareness with regard to his divine ego and power. The Christ-child, he begins, may have cried outwardly, but inwardly he was showing compassion to man in his role as Saviour.[117] The infant Christ, in other words, was fully aware of his Messianic mission, and by implication of his divinity as well. Zerbolt also leaves one with the impression that he viewed the crying of the infant Jesus to be in some sense feigned: that Christ cried to prove his humanity but that somehow it was not truly natural to him. Then when the wisemen came to pay their respects Christ did not install himself in surroundings worthy of his 'royal' status,[118] although he possessed the power to do so, Zerbolt implies. Again, when Christ was persecuted by Herod he bore it patiently, the purpose of which was to set an example for man.[119] In other words, this too was a conscious and deliberate act by Christ carried out in accordance with his Messianic calling. Altogether, Zerbolt assigns a masked, and still to be revealed, degree of knowledge, wisdom and greatness to the infant Jesus[120] which leaves one with the impression that he regarded all of Christ's human limitations and weaknesses in evidence at this time to have been feigned and hence unauthentic.

Turning to Christ's youth, Zerbolt writes that when Christ 'hid' himself from his twelfth to his thirtieth year he did this with a specific purpose in mind, namely, to teach man that he must be humble and not

---

[117] *Asc.*, 270A: Considera quomodo lachrymatur exterius, interius homini compatiebatur.

That Christ was aware of his divine sonship from the outset is also expressed by the anonymous author of the *Epistola de Vita et Passione Domini Nostri* (de Bruin, ed., "De Dietse oertekst van de anonieme 'Epistola de vita et passione domini nostri Jesu Christi et aliis devotis exerciciis'," 15).

[118] *Asc.*, 270B: Considera quantam vilitatem et paupertatem magi invenerunt, nec Christus aliter se disposuit propter magorum adventum.

[119] *Asc.*, 270B: Christus adhuc parvulus fugatur ab Herode. Attende Christi patientiam et disce pati.

[120] *Asc.*, 270A: Mirare sapientiam,... Sed et attende parvuli magnitudinem interiorem.

come forward too hastily and assume the role of teacher.[121] In other words, Christ's conduct was governed by a Messianic consciousness during this period as well. It was also a time when he did not perform any miracles,[122] although he was not incapable of doing so, the implication would seem to be. Finally, Zerbolt observes that after his forty days in the wilderness, and after having chosen his disciples, Christ went out "to make all the world subject to the sword of his preaching."[123] This statement shows that he considers Christ to have been fully aware of his Messianic calling at least by the time that he began his teaching. However, all the indications are that Zerbolt deemed Christ to have been aware of his Messianic mission from his birth onwards, and conscious of his divinity and his divine might as well.

To hold, as Zerbolt does, that Christ was conscious of his divine ego and Messianic mission from his birth onwards implies, according to presently-held views, a certain transmission of properties from Christ's divinity to his humanity. However, most medieval theologians held that, because of the beatific vision enjoyed by Christ from the moment of the incarnation onwards, he had always been conscious of his own divine ego and status as Son of God, as well as of his Messianic mission.[124] With respect to these questions, then, Zerbolt's position reflected the generally accepted opinion of his day, and his views on these matters can be judged

---

[121] *Ref.*, 246B: Cogita deinde, quod ab duodecimo anno usque ad tricesimum, tanquam unus de populo incognitus, et ignotus, omnium Dominus latitabat, ut te doceret, ut non surgas ad agenda publice in quibus laus et honor conquiri poterit nisi prius sederis diutius te humiliando. This same passage is also found in *Asc.*, 270B-C, but with some variations (see footnote 122).

That one ought not to become a priest too hastily is the topic of one of Zerbolt's minor tracts, and it reflects the Devotionalists' generally cautious approach to the priestly office.

[122] *Asc.*, 270B-C: A duodecimo autem anno usque ad tricesimum, ipse rex gloriae in populo absconditus latitabat, non docebat, nec mirabilia faciebat, sed dum tam diu tacuit, tacendo maxime docuit, et nihil faciendo maximum quid egit, docens te non cito ad docendum surgere, nisi sedendo prius et humiliando. Cf. Zieleman, *Middelnederlandse Epistel- en Evangeliepreken*, 283-284.

[123] *Ref.*, 246B: Tunc deinde paucos de mundo abiectos homines et humiles elegit, cum quibus paucis, totum mundum incepit gladio praedicationis debellare. *Asc.*, 270C: Extunc quosdam abiectos eligens piscatores, cum eisdem, praedicationis gladio, coepit totum mundum debellare.

[124] Thomas Aquinas, *ST*, 3a, 10-12; Bonaventure, *Breviloquium*, Pt. IV, ch. 6 (*Works*, II, 160-163); J. J. Walsh, "Jesus Christ," *NCE*, VII, 924-926; *idem*, "Christology," *NCE*, III, 662; P. de Letter, "Jesus Christ (Beatific Vision)," *NCE*, VII, 930-931; *idem*, "Jesus Christ (Knowledge)," *NCE*, VII, 937-939; C. J. Peter, "Jesus Christ (Messianic Consciousness)," *NCE*, VII, 939-940. Cf. Dudden, *Gregory the Great: His Place in History and Thought*, II, 326-332.

In the middle ages there was a tendency to deny that there was any development in Christ with respect to his human knowledge. Duns Scotus, however, suggested that the knowledge which Jesus derived from his vision of God was potential knowledge (*NCE*, VII, 926 and 938).

historically only in that light.[125] However, not only does Zerbolt assign no limitations to the infant Jesus with respect to his divine and Messianic consciousness, but he would seem to deny all human limitations to the Christ-child. Reading through Zerbolt's biography of Christ, and his account of the infant Jesus in particular, one is left with the impression that he allows Christ's divinity to compromise his humanity: that there is, in fact, a wide ranging transfer of attributes from Christ's divinity to his humanity, and not solely in the area of Christ's knowledge regarding his own divine status and mission. Zerbolt's writings would appear to exemplify, then, the difficulty experienced in safeguarding the oneness of Christ's person without at the same time confusing his two natures.

Christ's Free Will. Christ's plea in the garden of Gethsemane: "If it be possible, let this cup pass from me,"[126] had always interested theologians. They asked the question whether this prayer indicates that Christ did not possess freedom of will, and that he, therefore, suffered and died involuntarily. According to Aquinas, for example, this prayer does not signify that Christ suffered and died against his own will. He believes that it was prompted by an "instinctive dread of death; sorrow at the disloyalty of friends; sadness over the rejection by His own people; and loathing at His sense of solidarity with a guilt-laden human race, ..."[127] Much like Aquinas, Zerbolt writes that Christ's anguish was greatly increased because it was at the hands of his own people, upon whom he had bestowed so many benefits, that he suffered. For that reason, and also because Christ had compassion for the Jews, he prayed: "'If it be possible, let this cup pass from me,' that is: 'Let not this people administer it to me,' for so some of the saints would have us interpret."[128] Who these saints are Zerbolt does not indicate, although Aquinas may have been one of the ones he had in mind.

---

[125] In view of the fact that Zerbolt attributed a Messianic consciousness to the infant Christ, and because he held that the infant Christ acted accordingly, it follows that he did not attribute any moral growth to Christ either. Presently it is generally held that Christ's Messianic awareness grew step by step, and that his obedience to God the Father increased accordingly until it led him to his death on the cross. This, however, was certainly not the position of Zerbolt, who detected in the Christ-child a fully developed Messianic consciousness and a corresponding degree of obedience to God's will.

While Zerbolt does not detect any moral growth in Christ, he does see Christ's obedience best exemplified in the passion, but that is due to its nature. For that reason Zerbolt devotes more space to Christ's passion than to his life up to that point.

[126] Matthew 26, 39.

[127] A. P. Hennessy, "Passion of Christ," *NCE*, X, 1057 (based on Thomas Aquinas, *ST*, 3a, 46, 6; cf. *ibid.*, 3a, 18, 5-6); and Bonaventure, *Breviloquium*, Pt. IV, ch. 8 (*Works*, II, 169).

[128] *Asc.*, 272E: Praeterea tertio non modicum auxit Christi dolorem, quod hanc passionem ab tali populo sustinuit, cui tot beneficia contulit, cui merito dicere potuit: Popule

It would appear, then, that Zerbolt did not view Christ's prayer in the garden as an indication that Christ suffered and died involuntarily; and this interpretation is supported by some of his own statements. Influenced by Augustine, Zerbolt writes that Christ willingly subjected himself to all suffering, that he freely took the passion upon himself, and that it was his own decision to offer himself as a sacrifice.[129] Exactly how Zerbolt viewed Christ's freedom of will is not certain. We do not know whether he subscribed to the commonly held theory that Christ's freedom of will did not consist in the ability either to conform to God's will or to reject it, but in the inability to go against the divine will.[130]

Christ's Capacity for Suffering. Consistent with Western thought Zerbolt wrote that Christ suffered only in his humanity.[131] However, even the issue of Christ's human suffering had always posed a problem. The difficulty was how Christ, who possessed the beatific vision from the very beginning and thus enjoyed perfect felicity, could experience deep mental agony or even great physical pain. For it was generally held in the middle ages, and Aquinas reflects this trend of thought, that the strength of spirit which flows from the beatific vision precludes mental distress and even dulls physical pain. That, notwithstanding his perfect vision of God, Christ was capable of suffering extreme mental and physical agony was attributed to his ability to prevent his spiritual vitality and strength from dominating his inferior faculties, mental as well as physical. Not only did Christ have the power to neutralize the effects of the vision of God, but he was also able to neutralize its effects to the extent that he wished, and consequently he possessed the power to limit his suffering to the degree that he desired.[132]

---

meus, quia ego Deus tuus, quid pro te facere potui et non feci: tu vero quid mihi peius rependere posses, quam quod acerrimam mortem inflixisti? Unde propterea compatiens huic populo orabat. Si possibile est, transeat ab me calix iste, id est, ab hoc populo infligendus, ut quidam sancti voluerunt. Cf. *Ref.*, 252H.

[129] *Ref.*, 248A: Item secundum Augustinum, Christus non patiebatur nisi volens. Ipse enim passiones voluntarie sibi assumpsit,... *Asc.*, 270D: Volens autem hostiam offerre, propter quam venerat,... *Asc.*, 272D: Item oblatus est, quia voluit.

[130] Cf. Augustine, quoted by Zerbolt, *Ref.*, 248A; Dudden, *Gregory the Great: His Place in History and Thought*, II, 126; Bonaventure, *Lignum Vitae*, ch. 18 (*Works*, I, 117); idem, *Vitis Mystica seu Tractatus de Passione Domini*, ch. 5, par. 5 (*Works*, I, 166); idem, *Breviloquium*, Pt. IV, ch. 5 (*Works*, II, 157); Thomas Aquinas, *ST*, 3a, 18, 4-6; J. J. Walsh, "Jesus Christ," *NCE*, VII, 924 and 928; R. J. Gillis, "Mandate, Problem of," *NCE*, IX, 146; and McGiffert, *A History of Christian Thought*, II, 97.

According to Bonaventure the hypostatic union made it impossible for Christ to go contrary to the will of God (*Breviloquium*, Pt. IV, ch. 8 [*Works*, II, 169]).

[131] Only Christ's suffering as such will be discussed here. Why he suffered and died will be discussed in the part on Christ's work.

[132] Thomas Aquinas, *ST*, 3a, 46, 6 and 3a, 47, 1. Cf. *ibid.*, 3a, 14, 1 and 3a, 15, 5;

Zerbolt would appear to have viewed Christ's suffering in much the same light as Aquinas had done before him. He writes that Christ suffered to the extent that he wished or accepted of his own volition, adding that it was not the suffering and punishment (*passio*) that distressed him, but that he distressed himself.[133] By this Zerbolt may have meant nothing more than that Christ, who was God and had power over those inflicting suffering upon him, allowed his persecutors to punish him to the extent that he desired to suffer. However, taking into account what has been said about the commonly held views regarding Christ's suffering, it is more than likely that Zerbolt had in mind Christ's ability to control the effects of the punishment inflicted upon him, rather than Christ's power to control the instruments of this punishment: i.e., the Jews and the Roman soldiers.

The Intensity of Christ's Suffering. The ability to neutralize the effects of the beatific vision not only made it possible for Christ to experience authentic suffering, but according to the leading medieval theologians it also resulted in greater suffering, both mental and physical, than ever experienced by any other person.[134] Zerbolt writes much the same thing about the intensity of Christ's physical and mental suffering as do Aquinas and Bonaventure, for example. The similarity is, in fact, so great that an influence, direct or indirect, of the latter two on the former seems likely. Zerbolt begins with the observation that Christ suffered more acutely, both physically and mentally, than any other person ever

---

footnote 112 above; and A. P. Hennessy, "Passion of Christ," *NCE*, X, 1057. Bonaventure, *Breviloquium*, Pt. IV, ch. 8 (*Works*, II, 167).

Gregory the Great held that Christ's mental agony and suffering had been feigned for the purpose of human instruction, and that it had not been authentic. As a result Gregory compromised Christ's true humanity, although he did accept that Christ's bodily suffering had been genuine (Dudden, *Gregory the Great: His Place in History and Thought*, II, 332-333 and 335). Why Gregory regarded Christ's mental suffering to have been feigned is not clear, but it may be assumed that he held Christ to have been incapable of true mental distress on account of the hypostatic union and the beatific vision flowing therefrom. Bonaventure, on the other hand, emphasizes more than once that the suffering which Christ took upon himself was authentic (*Breviloquium*, Pt. IV, ch. 8 [*Works*, II, 168] and *Lignum Vitae*, ch. 18 [*Works*, I, 117]), but he does not explain why Christ could suffer in an authentic manner. Aquinas does not draw special attention to the reality of Christ's suffering. However, when he writes that Christ's ability to suffer at all was a consequence of his ability to neutralize the effects of the beatific vision, he would appear to be defending the authentic human quality of Christ's distress, pain and agony.

[133] *Ref.*, 248A: Ipse enim passiones voluntarie sibi assumpsit, et tantum patiebatur, quantum noluit seu sponte assumpsit,... *Asc.*, 272D: Nam secundum Evangelistam Iesus turbavit seipsum non passio, sed ipse seipsum.

[134] Thomas Aquinas, *ST*, 3a, 14, 1; 3a, 15, 5 and 3a, 46, 6. Bonaventure, *Breviloquium*, Pt. IV, chs. 8 and 9 (*Works*, II, 167-173); and Bonaventure, *De Perfectione Vitae ad Sorores*, ch. 6, pars. 5-6 (*Works*, I, 242-243).

endured or will endure, and like Aquinas he quotes Jeremiah to this effect.[135] He continues that the *doctores* are agreed that the sum of Christ's
sorrow and suffering surpassed the combined anguish and suffering endured by mankind throughout its entire history.[136] Finally, Zerbolt
observes regarding Christ's suffering in general that he endured every
kind of pain and sorrow possible, both physical and mental,[137] a point
also made by Aquinas and Bonaventure.[138]

Like Aquinas,[139] Zerbolt bases the argument that Christ's physical suffering exceeded that of any other human being on the premise that Christ
was by nature more sensitive to physical stimulation, and so to physical
pain, than was any other human being. This incomparable sensitivity,
Zerbolt explains, stemmed from the fact that Christ's physical senses
were more tenderly, nobly and delicately wrought than were those of any
other person.[140] Why Christ's bodily senses possessed these qualities Zer-

---

[135] *Ref.*, 247H: ...Christum in sua passione ultra omnem hominem fuisse afflictum.
Quod ex multis causis poteris considerare,.. *Asc.*, 272C: Primo igitur quoties legis aliquam poenalitatem, vel aliquod opprobrium Christo illatum, non per illud ita accipias
Christum passum et sustinuisse, sicut si alius aliquis homo per eandem poenam
sustinuisset, sed indicibiliter aliter et amplius ultra omnem hominem. *Asc.*, 272D: ...ideo
maximam sustinuit poenalitatem ultra quemvis alium hominem. Vide ergo, si est aliquis
dolor similis sicut dolor eius. *Asc.*, 272E: ..., et quia Dei perfecta sunt opera, videtur omnino quod Christus assumpsit mortem amarissimam. Unde Ieremias: O vos omnes qui
transitis per viam, videte si est dolor similis sicut dolor meus, ac si diceret, nequaquam:
...(see Lamentations 1, 12). Cf. Goossens, *Meditatie*, 194.

[136] *Asc.*, 272E: ...: imo dicunt doctores, quod dolor eius et passio fuit adeo acerbissimus
et afflictivus, quod excederet dolores omnium hominum, quos ab initio saeculi passi sunt
vel passuri.
Zerbolt does not identify these *doctores*, but it is conceivable that he is thinking, among
others, and perhaps in the first place, of Aquinas and Bonaventure, two of the foremost
doctores communes of the middle ages. However, it must be added that this opinion is not
readily found in the *Summa Theologiae* of Aquinas, nor in Bonaventure's *Breviloquium*.

[137] *Ref.*, 248B: Item poena Christi erat in omni sensu, in omni membro,... *Asc.*, 272C:
..., debes Christum in quavis poena constitutum, non solum respicere, quasi exterius
summo dolore afflictum, sed etiam summopere eum diligentissime interius cernere omni
dolore repletum,... See also *Asc.*, 272F, where the statement regarding Christ's suffering
in all senses and members, also found on p. 248B of *De Reformatione*, is repeated.

[138] Thomas Aquinas, *ST*, 3a, 46, 5 and Bonaventure, *Breviloquium*, Pt. IV, ch. 9
(*Works*, II, 170 and 172).
Zerbolt writes that one would feel pity for a wild animal should it be tormented and tor-
tured like Christ was (*Asc.*, 272B). Henry Suso expresses the same idea in the *Little Book of
Eternal Wisdom* (*The Exemplar. Life and Writings of Blessed Henry Suso*, trans. by M. Ann Ed-
wards [2 vols.; Dubuque, Iowa, 1962], II, 9).

[139] Thomas Aquinas, *ST*, 3a, 14, 1; 3a, 15, 5 and 3a, 46, 6.

[140] *Ref.*, 248A: Unusquisque enim homo in eodem gradu poenalitatis plus, minusve
patitur, quanto poenam plus senserit sicut notum est. Tanto autem quisque poenam
facilius et acrius sentit, natura vivacior, et sensus ejus facilius percipit, sed Christus erat
natura vivacissimus, ideo quaelibet poena sibi inflicta erat ei gravissima. Cogita ergo si illa crucifixio et illa elevatio manuum et pedum de qua Propheta ait: Foderunt manus meas
et pedes meos, alteri cuivis hominum fuisset intolerabilis, quanto gravior et acerbior
Christo in sui natura delicatissima, nobilissima et vivacissima? *Asc.*, 272D: Igitur notum

bolt does not explain, but it may be presumed that he attributed them to the hypostatic union as had been done by Aquinas in the previous century.[141] The extreme degree of Christ's mental anguish Zerbolt attributes, like Aquinas once again,[142] to a number of causes, and he is of the opinion that the spiritual anguish endured by Christ almost certainly surpassed the bodily suffering.[143] The mental anguish stemmed from his love for mankind which had fallen so deeply; from the realization that for many his suffering would have no efficacy on account of their unbelief and wickedness; from the love and compassion for his mother; from his compassion and pity for the Jews, his own people, who crucified him; from the sorrow experienced on account of his disciples' sins and the sin of Judas in particular; and from man's blindness and ingratitude.[144] However, the greatest mental suffering endured by Christ, according to Zerbolt, was the abandonment of Christ's humanity—and Christ suffered in his humanity only, as has been seen—by his divinity, which was possible, he explains, because there was no confusion of the two natures or, in other words, no communication of idioms between them.[145] In the incarnation the two natures remained distinct, for otherwise no abandonment of Christ's humanity by his divinity could have taken place. The desertion of Christ's humanity by his divinity implies the loss of the beatific vision, and it is undoubtedly for that reason that Zerbolt regards the separation of Christ's two natures as the cause of the greatest mental anguish suffered by the Son of God.

---

est, tantum praecise unumquemque aliqua poena sensibili torqueri et affligi, quanto plus aliquis sensuum illam poenam tanquam sibi inconvenientem sentit. Sed et iterum non est dubium sensus alicuius hominis tanto plus et citius poenam sentire, et ex eadem torqueri, quanto sensus illius hominis fuerint vivaciores. Christus autem natura vivacissimus, et complexionis dignitate nobilissimus extitit,... Cogita ergo si tibi vel alteri tenero homini intolerabilis esset poena, caput spinis perforari, totum corpus acerrime flagellari, etc. quanto magis Iesu Christo homini et Deo fuit illa poena gravissima in natura sua nobili et delicata. Cf. A. P. Hennessy, "Satisfaction of Christ," NCE, XII, 1097. Cf. Goossens, Meditatie, 194.

[141] In contrast with Aquinas and Bonaventure, Zerbolt does not in any way ascribe Christ's physical sensitivity to the total absence in him of sin and its destructive and brutalizing effect on the body (see references given in footnote 134 above).

[142] See the references given in footnote 139 above.

[143] Asc., 272F-G: Adverte nunc etiam et diligenter in corde colloca causas afflictionum et dolorum internorum Christi, quae forsitan sensibilem poenam praecellabant. Ref., 248B: Item devote imaginare interiorem Christi poenalitatem, quae forte exteriore poena non erat minor imo forsitan multo major.

[144] Ref., 248B: Quae interior poena causabatur in eo ex nimio zeli fervore pro humano genere, in quo tamen ad majorem partem videbat passionem suam fore inutilem propter propriam malitiam. Item haec interior poena surrexit ex maxima compassione suae dilectissimae matris. Item ex miseratione Iudaeorum. Item ex dolore discipulorum et peccatorum eorum, et maxime Iudae. Item ex nostra coecitate [caecitate] et ingratitudine. See Asc., 272G-H as well. Cf. Goossens, Meditatie, 194.

[145] See footnote 112 above for relevant passages.

Christ's Complaint about His Abandonment by God. It was the desertion of
Christ's humanity by his divinity, Zerbolt writes, which caused Christ to
cry out in his humanity that he had been abandoned by God.[146] This
complaint of Christ had always interested theologians and Christian
writers. However, Zerbolt's explanation of it must be called untradi-
tional, if not heterodox, when viewed in the light of Aquinas' and
Bonaventure's interpretations of Christ's plaint about his abandonment
by God. They interpret it variously, but both strongly and categorically
reject the idea that Christ's cry of abandonment indicated a desertion of
Christ's humanity by his divinity.[147] For to assert, as Zerbolt does, that
Christ's divinity deserted his humanity is to say, in effect, that the
hypostatic union had been dissolved, and Bonaventure hurls anathemas
at those who suggest that the divine Son of God ever relinquished, either
in its entirety or in part, the human nature he assumed in the incarnation.[148] The suggestion that there was a break in the hypostatic union,
even though Zerbolt considered it to have been a short-lived one as will
be seen, clearly throws up many problems with respect to the person of
Christ. That may have been one of the considerations why Aquinas and
Bonaventure dismissed any suggestion that the two natures of Christ
were ever separated after they were united in the incarnation. A more important consideration may have been that the suffering of Christ who is
merely a man lacks salvific and reconciliatory efficacy. Zerbolt's interpretation of Christ's cry of despair about his abandonment was,
however, not altogether unique (*sui generis*), because it is essentially the
same explanation given it by Ambrose. According to Ambrose the man
Christ cried out in despair and agony when about to be severed from God
in his death, and he adds that the death of the man stemmed, in fact,
from this desertion.[149]

Christ's Ability to Die at Will. According to Aquinas the suffering inflicted
upon Christ did not gradually sap his strength until he died. He asserts
that Christ freely, and deliberately, gave up his spirit when he had com-

---

[146] *Ibid.*

[147] Thomas Aquinas, *ST*, 3a, 50, 2; Bonaventure, *Breviloquium*, Pt. IV, ch. 9 (*Works*,
II, 170 and 173); and Bonaventure, *Vitis Mystica seu Tractatus de Passione Domini*, ch. 10
(*Works*, I, 177-178).

[148] See second reference in previous footnote.

[149] Thomas Aquinas, *ST*, 3a, 50, 2. Ambrose was a writer with whom Zerbolt was well
acquainted and whom he quoted frequently. While there is a similarity between their
thought on this point, then, the sources do not allow one to speak of a direct influence.

[150] See Thomas Aquinas, *ST*, 3a, 47, 1 regarding Christ's death, and 3a, 43, 2 regarding Christ's miracles. Bonaventure too writes that Christ's loud voice with which he surrendered his spirit betrayed the might of his divinity (*Lignum Vitae*, ch. 29 [*Works*, I, 127]).

pleted his mission of suffering, and that the loud voice in which he surrendered his spirit constitutes proof that the crucifixion had not sapped his strength. That Christ could thus die at will was due to the fact that he was able to control the effects of the violence inflicted upon him. And when he was ready to die, he wilfully allowed that violence to have its full effect, which then resulted in his instant death. Consequently Aquinas calls Christ's death a miracle, a miracle performed by Christ in his divinity. For it was only because of his divinity that Christ could control the consequences of the punishment he had to endure, on account of which he could die, or surrender his spirit, at will.[150]

Zerbolt writes, we have seen, that Christ suffered to the extent that he freely desired, from which it was concluded that Zerbolt too attributed to Christ the power to control the effects of the punishment inflicted upon him. The correctness of this interpretation is bolstered by Zerbolt's understanding of Christ's death. He writes that when Christ had accomplished everything he called out with a loud voice and surrendered his spirit. This signifies, he continues, that Christ could have lived longer had he wished, that he retained his powers until the very end, and that no one could take his life from him but that he surrendered it freely in his own time.[151] Why Christ could freely lay down his life at the exact point in time he desired to do so Zerbolt does not explain, but the implication is that Christ could do so because he was able to control the effects of the punishment he had to endure. Zerbolt concludes that Christ surrendered his spirit in his divinity only.[152] The ability to control the consequences of suffering imposed upon him was, therefore, solely a divine power not shared by Christ's humanity. In specifically assigning this power to Christ's divinity Zerbolt showed some concern to safeguard the integrity of Christ's two natures.

The Duration of the Hypostatic Union. Both Aquinas and Bonaventure strongly rejected any suggestion that the hypostatic union was dissolved at any time following the incarnation.[153] Zerbolt, on the other hand, interpreted Christ's complaint on the cross about his abandonment by God

---

[151] *Ref.*, 249C-D: Accepto aceto consummatis jam omnibus, cum nihil restabat agendum, clamans alta voce, emisit spiritum: Innuens quod si vellet, quamdiu vellet, viveret, et quod nullus animam suam ab se tolleret, sed quod ipse eam sponte poneret. Cf. *Ref.*, 247G: ..., clamans voce magna, emisit spiritum,... *Asc.*, 274C: Igitur accepto aceto, cum iam nil restaret agendum vel implendum, clamans voce magna, spiritum misit, innuens quod quam diu voluit vires sibi retinuit, et quod nullus animam suam ab se tolleret, nisi ipse eam poneret.

[152] See footnotes 116 and 151 above.

[153] Thomas Aquinas, *ST*, 3a, 50, 2 and Bonaventure, *Breviloquium*, Pt. IV, ch. 9 (*Works*, II, 170 and 173).

as a real desertion of Christ's humanity by his divinity or, in other words, as some sort of break in the hypostatic union. However, Zerbolt also regarded Christ to have surrendered his spirit in his divinity, and on that account he must have understood the disruption of the hypostatic union to have been of very short duration. He does not say anything regarding the hypostatic union during the three days of Christ's interment, but a number of times he refers to Christ's humanity in heaven, thereby implying that he considers the hypostatic union to be essentially eternal.[154]

Furthermore, Zerbolt apparently regards Christ's resurrection body to be the same as that possessed by him before his death, for he writes that in heaven Christ's body will forever carry the signs of his suffering and death.[155] However, he does not clearly indicate to what extent he holds Christ's heavenly humanity to be identical with Christ's humanity prior to the crucifixion, nor what the differences are between these two states of Christ's humanity. When he speaks of Christ's glorious humanity in heaven he may have in mind a glorified body which lacks the imperfections of Christ's body before the crucifixion such as passibility and mortality, for example,[156] but that can be no more than a surmise. Similarly, when Zerbolt draws attention to Christ's most holy humanity in heaven he may mean that in heaven Christ's sanctity is even greater than it was on earth, or he may mean that in heaven Christ's human sanctity is matchless and exceeds that of all beatified souls.[157] Altogether, then, Zerbolt pays little attention to the differences between Christ's humanity before his death and following his resurrection, and in doing so he would appear to have been following the accepted practice. Throughout the history of the church Christian writers and theologians had been primarily concerned with the two natures of Christ and their relationship to one another. They did not ask, nor answer, the question whether their conclusions applied equally to the Christ who walked the earth prior to his crucifixion and the Christ who sits on the right hand of God. The statements they made concerning the person of Christ are, presumably, applicable to Christ in both states, and this would seem to be largely, and

---

[154] *Ref.*, 245B: ..., quomodo qui hic fuit propter nos pauper et vilis homo, ibi [i.e. heaven] sublimis erit Deus et homo. *Asc.*, 272B: ...ut semper Christum quo lucidius poteris unam personam concipias, quem Deum et hominem esse et fuisse non dubites.

[155] *Ref.*, 245A: Cogita quomodo ibi Christus exhibebit passionis suae insignia,... Cf. Bonaventure, *Lignum Vitae*, ch. 38 (*Works*, I, 135).

[156] *Asc.*, 267B: Cogita quantum sit gaudium Domino Iesu semper assistere, et eius sanctissimam et gloriosissimam humanitatem semper aspicere,... Cf. Bonaventure, *Breviloquium*, Pt. IV, ch. 10 (*Works*, II, 174). He writes here: "Then, on the third day, He rose from the dead, assuming the same body He had quickened before, but a body no longer in the same state: for what had been subject to pain and death had risen impassible and immortal, to live forever."

[157] See previous footnote.

fundamentally, true for Zerbolt's observations regarding the person of Christ.[158]

The assertion that Christ retained his human body even after his ascension into heaven is dictated, partly at least, by Zerbolt's eucharistic doctrine as will be seen. For Zerbolt Christ is bodily present in the eucharist, and the eucharistic body and blood of Christ are one with Christ's historical body which suffered on the cross, died, arose from the grave and ascended into heaven. If Christ had discarded this body at his ascension the doctrine that he is bodily present in the eucharist would, presumably, be difficult to uphold.

iii. *Assessment*

For a spiritual writer Zerbolt pays a good deal of attention to the person of Christ, and much more so than do many other spiritual writers.[159] However, it is for very practical reasons that Zerbolt devotes as much space to the incarnation of the Son of God as he does. Zerbolt's Christology is governed by the conviction that a confrontation with Christ's divinity and humanity will be conducive to imitation of him. And, as will be seen, it is Christ's work of subjective atonement, i.e., his exemplary life which the believer must imitate if he is to be saved, which dominates Zerbolt's thought regarding the work of Christ.

It is frequently argued that in the late middle ages theology and piety drifted ever further apart.[160] However, in view of the fact that Zerbolt sees the doctrine regarding Christ's two natures as a strong inducement to imitate him, it cannot be said that there is, in this particular instance at least, a deep rift between Zerbolt's theological opinions on the one hand, and his piety and devotion on the other.

B) *Soteriology*

It had always been maintained that, when described in very general terms, the end of the incarnation and Christ's work is man's salvation and reconciliation with God. How Christ was seen to effect this was largely determined by an individual's conception of Christianity as a code of conduct or as a cult. To those for whom Christianity was essentially a code of conduct, Christ's salvific work consisted in the first place of instruction and enlightenment which he provided by means of his teaching and exemplary life. For them Christ's redemptive work was first and foremost of a didactic nature. Christ shows man the way in the

---

[158] Cf. Richardson, ed., *Dictionary*, 59-60 ("Christology").
[159] Cf. Steinmetz, *Staupitz*, 136.
[160] Axters, *Vroomheid*, III, 19-27.

spiritual life and in his upward journey to God. On the other hand, those who regarded Christianity as a cult rather than as a code of conduct held that the central, and most important, feature of Christ's salvific work was a vicariously redemptive act in which the believer must secure participation if he is to be saved. Consequently, two basic types of soteriological theories, or theories of atonement, emerged. On the one hand there was the subjective type according to which man is saved in the first place by following the example set by Christ, and on the other hand there was the objective type which held that man is saved above all through a vicariously redemptive act of Christ.[161]

i. Some Soteriological Theories

The immediate heirs of the New Testament writers, namely the Apostolic Fathers and following them the Apologists, held a very moralistic and legalistic view of Christianity; and consequently they understood Christ's mission as having been one of instructor and lawgiver above all else. He is the revealer of a new doctrine and law without which man cannot be saved. However, Christ makes his teaching known not only by word of mouth, but also through his exemplary life, suffering and death. In contrast with the Apostolic Fathers and the Apologists, Irenaeus' (c. 130-c. 200) understanding of the atonement was essentially an objective one. Central to his soteriology is the theory of recapitulation. He calls Christ the second Adam and draws a number of parallels between Adam's life and that of Christ to show how Christ reversed the fall. "Going step by step up the ladder down which Adam descended when he fell Christ accomplished a work of recapitulation, ..."[162] Inasmuch as Adam's fall was essentially a question of disobedience, Irenaeus emphasizes the obedience displayed by Christ in the various steps of recapitulation, and he regards obedience to be their essence. It was through Adam's disobedience that man became subject to sin, death and Satan, and it is only through Christ's vicarious obedience

---

[161] The brief survey of the most important developments in the history of soteriological thought which follows is based on V. Taylor, *The Atonement in New Testament Teaching* (3rd ed.; London, 1958), 191-197 and throughout; Pelikan, *The Christian Tradition, A History of the Development of Doctrines*, I, 163-177, 232-234, 375 and 381-395; McGiffert, *A History of Christian Thought*, I, 92-95, 116-121, 134-137 and 282-283, II, 19, 55, 105-106, 195-200 and 213; Aulén, *Christus Victor*, 1-100 and 143-159; Krijn Strijd, *Structuur en Inhoud van Anselmus' "Cur Deus Homo"* (Assen, 1958), 301-310 (English Summary); Richardson, ed., *Dictionary*, 18-24 ("Atonement") and 285 ("Recapitulation"); Rahner and Vorgrimler, *Theological Dictionary*, 309-310 ("Necessity for Salvation"), 414-417 ("Sacraments"), 419-420 ("Salvation") and 423 ("Satisfaction"); J. Jensen and E. L. Peterman, "Redemption," *NCE*, XII, 136-160; E. L. Peterman, "Soteriology," *NCE*, XIII, 444-445; and W. G. Topmöller, "Salvation," *NCE*, XII, 994-995.

[162] McGiffert, *A History of Christian Thought*, I, 135.

that he can be freed from them. Gustaf Aulén calls Irenaeus' interpretation of Christ's salvific work the 'classic' theory of the atonement, because he is of the opinion that it is the prevailing soteriological theory in the New Testament and that it dominated soteriological thought in the Eastern Church from Irenaeus in the second century to John of Damascus in the eighth. Gregory of Nyssa, a fourth century theologian, set forth his own version of the 'classic' theory of the atonement. It was fitting, he held, that on account of the fall man became a subject of Satan who could, therefore, justly claim compensation if he were to surrender what was rightfully his, namely man. God could, of course, have snatched man away from Satan through a show of force, Gregory explains, but God is a God of justice who does not treat even Satan unfairly. Consequently God offered Christ the man as a ransom to Satan in return for man's freedom, an offer which was accepted by Satan. However, Satan could not maintain his hold on Christ for he was also God, and so Satan's hold over man was destroyed through what was, in part at least, a deception. In spite of the popularity of the 'classic' doctrine of the atonement, and notwithstanding Aulén's argument to the contrary, it is generally maintained that the dominant soteriological theory in the Eastern, as in the Western, Church in the fourth century was the interpretation of Christ's death as a vicarious sacrifice. Christ's death was presented as being either an expiatory or a propitiatory sacrifice, and even as being both at one and the same time, with 'satisfaction' being an important component in both instances. Hilary of Poitiers (c. 315-c. 367), for example, seems to have been of the opinion that through his death as an expiatory sacrifice Christ made satisfaction for man's sins, while Ambrose (c. 330-397) defended the view that through his death as a propitiatory sacrifice Christ satisfied divine honour and justice. Augustine summed up the soteriological thought of the Western Church, and it would appear, according to J. N. D. Kelly, that of a number of soteriological doctrines found in his writings Augustine attached the greatest importance to the theory according to which Christ's sacrifice expiates man's sins on the one hand, and propitiates God on the other. However, Kelly writes as well that ''Augustine's teaching stresses the exemplary aspect of Christ's work in a way that is without precedent.''[163] In spite of the many soteriological theories in circulation, the question of Christ's salvific work did not give rise to a major theological dispute before the early scholastic period. The protagonists in the controversy were Anselm (1033-1109)

---

[163] Kelly, *Early Christian Doctrines*, 393. Kelly must be speaking in absolute terms here, for Clement of Alexandria and Origen, for example, had held Christ's didactic and exemplary work to be much more important than his vicarious atonement.

and Abelard (1079-1142). Anselm's theory, which was essentially that through his sacrificial death Christ expiated man's sins and so satisfied divine justice, was to become the dominant theory of atonement in the West, and it remained so after the Protestant Reformation. Abelard's theory of atonement, on the other hand, is of the subjective type, and it was to find favour with liberal Protestant theologians in the nineteenth and twentieth centuries.

It would appear that at no time throughout the history of the Church was the emphasis placed exclusively on this or that soteriological theory and were the other theories considered superfluous. It was recognized by practically everyone at all times that the various soteriological theories must join forces to explain the salvific work of Christ. At the same time, however, there has been the tendency from the very beginning of the Christian era to emphasize this or that soteriological motif or theory at the expense of the others, although the latter were seldom relegated to the dustbin altogether. This did not happen since all these different theories found at least some support in the Scriptures.[164]

ii. *Zerbolt's Soteriology*

Zerbolt writes that the literal meaning of the name Jesus is "saviour,"[165] and that Christ's work was above all one of salvation around which his entire earthly sojourn was centered.[166] If Christ is the saviour, whom is it that he saves, and what is it that he saves them from? To the first question Zerbolt gives two answers which, at first sight at least, are difficult to reconcile with one another. For on the one hand he writes that at his circumcision the Son of Joseph and Mary was given the name Jesus to indicate that he was to save only his own, and not strangers,[167] but elsewhere he voices the opinion that Christ came to save

---

[164] See the references given in footnote 161 above.

[165] *Asc.*, 271E: ...Dominum Iesum, cuius nomen dicitur Iesus, id est, salvator. Cf. *Asc.*, 270F and 288B; and *Ref.*, 246E.

[166] *Asc.*, 272G: Haec autem interior afflictio surgebat primo ex fervido Christi zelo pro humano genere salvando. *Ref.*, 246A: Et nomen accepit ut Iesus vocaretur, ut intelligeres quia suos, non autem alienos esset salvaturus. *Ref.*, 241B: ..., sciens quod non est preciosius munus ab Deo in hac vita quam zelus animarum, pro quarum salute Christus de coelo descendit, et mortem amarissimam toleravit.

[167] *Ref.*, 246A (see footnote 166 above, the second passage).
When Zerbolt speaks of Christ having come to save "his own" and not "strangers," the terminology has, quite obviously, been borrowed from the angel's message to Joseph and the prophecy of Zacharias, two instances in the New Testament in which Christ's salvific work is clearly reserved for the Jews (Matthew 1, 21; Luke 1, 68-77 and cf. J. Jensen, "Redemption," *NCE*, XII, 137-139). However, it does not appear likely that by "his own" and the "strangers" Zerbolt meant the Jews and the gentiles respectively. For in spite of the angel's message to Joseph and the prophecy of Zacharias, the New Testament emphasizes time and again that Christ came to save the non-Jew as well as the Jew (cf. Rahner and Vorgrimler, *Theological Dictionary*, 420-421 ["Salvific Will of God"]).

all men: i.e., the entire human race.[168] What Zerbolt would appear to be saying with his two apparently contradictory statements is that although the Son of God became man to save the entire human race, in reality he saved only those who received him, or were to receive him.[169] In other words, Christ's sacrifice on the cross sufficed for all, but it is efficacious only for those who wish to share in Christ's atoning death.[170]

If the Son of God became man to save all men, what is it that he saves them from? By means of his life and death, Zerbolt writes, Christ does not restore to man during this life all the perfections possessed by him before the fall, even though the purpose of Christ's coming is, in essence at least, to undo the effects of the fall. For example, in this life man will not, in spite of Christ's salvific work, regain original justice as defined by Zerbolt: i.e., immunity from rebellious concupiscence.[171] Redemption or salvation through Christ, Zerbolt writes briefly, is a question of enlightenment or illumination, justification and glorification.[172] In this description of salvation as illumination, justification and glorification one can detect the three major strands which make up Zerbolt's soteriological thought: a) it is by means of his role as teacher and example that Christ enlightens man and shows him the way in the religious life; b) it is through his death that Christ makes amends for man's sins, on account of which he is then justified before God; c) and it is as a consequence of Christ's victory over Satan, death and hell that man can share in his everlasting glory.[173] The three components of Zerbolt's soteriological thought correspond to the subjective, Anselmian and 'classic' or

---

[168] *Asc.*, 272G (see footnote 166 above, the first passage); *Ref.*, 248G: ..., salvatorem omnium,... *Ref.*, 248B: Quae interior poena causabatur in eo ex nimio zeli fervore pro humano genere,... and *Ref.*, 248G, which is identical to the passage found on p. 273F of *De Ascensionibus*. This last passage, found in both *De Reformatione* and *De Ascensionibus*, is drawn from Bonaventure's *De Triplici Via*, ch. 3, par. 2 (*Works*, 1, 82-83).

[169] Cf. John 1, 11-12.

[170] See below, p. 138.

[171] *Asc.*, 260A: Sane Christus morte sua preciosissima ab culpa originali nos redemit; ...: Sed in pristinum statum rectitudinis nequaquam nos restituit, nec vires animae reformavit, sed ad nostrum exercitium et meritum nobis eas reliquit per sancta exercitia reformandas.

[172] *Asc.*, 273B: Nam passus est propter tuam illuminationem, redemptionem, iustificationem et glorificationem. The same passage is found in *De Reformatione*, 248E, and it is derived from Bonaventure's *De Triplici Via*, ch. 3, par. 2 (*Works*, I, 82-83).

[173] *Asc.*, 273B-C: ...: Propter tuam redemptionem, quia propter peccatum originale eras perpetue damnatus. Cogita ergo quam grave est peccatum tuum propter quod expiandum tantum exigitur medicamentum, tantum pretium; et inde tibi nascitur timor et horror peccandi, et sic de aliis propter tuam iustificationem. Inde gratitudo oritur, quod tantum voluit pati, ut tu dignus possis haberi iustificatione Dei. Propter tuam glorificationem, et inde maxime tibi exurget amor quod ille qui te non indiguit, nec bonorum tuorum eget, propter tuam gloriam tanta voluit sustinere.

dramatic theories of the atonement respectively.[174] With regard to their respective importance in Zerbolt's soteriological thought they are listed here in descending order. However, in our discussion of them we will begin with the least important of the three, namely with the 'classic' theory of the atonement, which will then be followed by an examination of the Anselmian and subjective doctrines of the atonement as they are understood by Zerbolt.

'Classic' Theory of the Atonement. Zerbolt's 'classic' theory of the atonement is a blend of the two versions of this particular theory: the recapitulation theory which is associated with Irenaeus in particular; and the theory, often linked to Gregory of Nyssa, that in Christ's death and resurrection Satan was deceived either by God or Christ, or by both. Dealing with the recapitulation theory first, Zerbolt writes that in paradise Satan tempted, and overcame, the first Adam by playing on his natural appetite for a desirable food. As a consequence of this act of disobedience the entire human race was to be blemished with original sin. In the wilderness Satan tempted Christ, the second Adam, in a similar fashion by offering him nourishment when hungry. Christ withstood the temptation. He remained obedient to God and so nullified Adam's disobedience,[175] and by implication its effects for those who are one with Christ.[176] On the cross Christ continued, and completed, his work of 'recapitulation', because in the crucifixion he totally reversed and swept away the disobedience of Adam through one act of perfect and supreme virtue, namely his obedience to the death.[177] However, Zerbolt depicts Christ's victory over

---

[174] Of these three soteriological theories found in Zerbolt's writings Geesink analyses only the Anselmian one, and makes a brief reference to the subjective theory of the atonement (Geesink, *Zerbolt*, 113-115 and 121).

[175] *Asc.*, 281A-B: Primum autem certamen est contra vitium gulae. Inde primo diabolus primum hominum tentavit et superavit; inde secundum hominem primo tentavit et succubuit.

[176] The similarity between Zerbolt's argument and Irenaeus's recapitulation theory is obvious, to say the least (cf. Aulén, *Christus Victor*, 48-49 and 51-53). However, Zerbolt's immediate source for the argument that in the wilderness Christ reversed Adam's act of disobedience was, most likely, the *Moralia in Job* of Gregory the Great (Dudden, *Gregory the Great*, II, 339-340).

[177] *Asc.*, 275A-B: ..., et invenies in morte Christi quam sit virtus pretiosa, speciosa et fructuosa. ...Fructuosa, quia unus perfectus actus virtutis infernum spoliavit, coelum aperuit, perditum restauravit. This same passage is found in *De Reformatione*, 249G. Its source is Bonaventure's *De Triplici Via*, ch. 3, par. 2 (*Works*, I, 84-86). *Asc.*, 275B: Tertia autem die Christus victor mortis resurrexit, et nos resurrecturos monstravit. ...Cogita devote qualiter anima Christi ad infernum descendit, quid ibi egit, de gaudio sanctorum patrum, et tristitia daemoniorum. *Asc.*, 275D: Post quadraginta dies resurrectionis ascendens Christus in altum, captivam duxit captivitatem sanctorum patrum. Meditare de gloriosa processione ascendentium cum Christo. Nam sancti sequebantur, Angeli venientes obviabant,... Cf. *Asc.*, 275A: ..., lege signaculum sextum apertum, id est, paradisum desiderabilem, qui ex passione aperitur, et monstratus est esse locus plenus gloriae, laetitiae et opulentiae, in eo quod Christus propter eius restitutionem factus est

Satan not only as a victory achieved through an act of obedience nullifying Adam's disobedience, but also as a victory gained through deception in which Christ was aided by God.[178] In the passion, he writes, Christ displayed great prudence and wisdom *vis-à-vis* his adversary, Satan,[179] and consequently he was able to deceive him. The same degree of wisdom and prudence, Zerbolt points out, had been employed by Christ to resist Satan's temptations in the desert.[180] He continues that God possessed the power to wrest man away from Satan, but rather than doing so he prudently outwitted, or deceived, the devil, because he did not want to use his supreme power against the devil or oppress him in a violent manner.[181] Underlying this statement is the traditional idea, first clearly formulated by Gregory of Nyssa, that God is a God of justice who recognizes Satan's rights over man, and therefore offers him Christ as a ransom in return for man's freedom.[182] Zerbolt himself, it must be added, does not explain how God and Christ outwitted the devil in the passion, but neither does his source, Bonaventure's *De Triplici Via*.[183] Nonetheless, the 'classic' theory of the atonement, which portrays Christ's salvific work as being a dramatic struggle between Christ and

---

vilis, pauper et miser. This same passage is found in *De Reformatione*, 249G. Its source is Bonaventure's *De Triplici Via* and it may have come to Zerbolt by way of Radewijns' *Omnes, inquit, artes*. See Bonaventure, *De Triplici Via*, ch. 3, par. 2 (*Works*, I, 84-86), and Radewijns, *Omnes, Inquit, Artes*, II, 113-114.

For his account of Christ's descent into hell and ascent to heaven Zerbolt may have borrowed from Bonaventure's *Lignum Vitae*, ch. 37 (*Works*, I, 135), and perhaps from his *Breviloquium*, Pt. IV, ch. 10 (*Works*, II, 175), as well. Radewijns' account of Christ's descent into hell and ascent to heaven is based on Bonaventure's *Lignum Vitae* (*Omnes, Inquit, Artes*, II, 119), which makes Zerbolt's indebtedness to *Lignum Vitae* in this instance a near certainty. However, Goossens is of the opinion that for his description of Christ's ascent into heaven Zerbolt relied on the *Meditationes Vitae Christi* (Goossens, *Meditatie*, 191), attributed to Bonaventure in the middle ages.

In *De Ascensionibus* Zerbolt speaks of Christ having "led captivity captive," as does Bonaventure in *Lignum Vitae* and the *Breviloquium*. This idea is based on Psalm 68, 18 (A.V.).

[178] Cf. Kelly, *Early Christian Doctrines*, 381-382; and Aulén, *Christus Victor*, 48-49 and 51-53.

[179] *Asc.*, 274C-D: Et hic considera quali forma Christus passus est,... Passus est enim sicut verus agnus..., prudentissime respectu adversarii. The same passage may be found in *De Reformatione*, 249D, and it is derived from Bonaventure's *De Triplici Via*, ch. 3, par. 2 (*Works*, I, 82-83).

[180] *Asc.*, 270C: Dehinc quadraginta diebus et quadraginta noctibus in eremo ieiunans, postea tentatur ab satana. ...Cogita quam sapienter satanae restitit,...

[181] *Asc.*, 274F: Est autem signaculum hoc, Deus admirabilis. De quo in passione ostensum est, quod ipse sit summa sapientia, qui tam prudenter diabolum decepit, non autem per infinitam potentiam suam violenter oppressit. This same passage is found in *De Reformatione*, 249F. Its source is Bonaventure's *De Triplici Via*, ch. 3, par. 2 (*Works*, I, 84-86).

[182] Kelly, *Early Christian Doctrines*, 381-382; and Aulén, *Christus Victor*, 48-49 and 51-55.

[183] See footnotes 179 and 181 above.

Especially the idea that God used deception rather than brute force to free man from Satan's clutches is one which Zerbolt may have borrowed from Gregory the Great's *Moralia in Job* (cf. Dudden, *Gregory the Great*, II, 337-340; and Aulén, *Christus Victor*, 47-55).

Satan,[184] is not an altogether negligible strand in Zerbolt's soteriological thought.

As a consequence of his victory over Satan, death and hell Christ opened heaven for man, and at his ascension Christ led the procession of all those souls whom he had freed while in hell. These were the souls of all those believers who had died before his crucifixion. At his ascension Christ demonstrated that the gates of heaven had truly been opened.[185] In short, through his costly victory over Satan, death and hell Christ restored to man all that had been lost through the disobedience of Adam: he restored to man his lost inheritance of an eternal life in glory.[186]

The Anselmian Theory of the Atonement. A more important component in Zerbolt's soteriological thought than the 'classic' theory of the atonement is the Anselmian doctrine regarding Christ's salvific work. The core of this doctrine is that man's sin constitutes an outrage committed against God's honour and sanctity for which satisfaction must be made in accordance with the requirements of divine justice. The outrage was, in fact, so great that only the death of Christ was sufficient to satisfy divine justice.[187] Zerbolt likewise proceeds from the argument that sin constitutes an offence against God,[188] against his holiness and honour presumably, and that divine justice demands that satisfaction be made for this offence. For he writes that sin was so displeasing to God that he—that is to say, God the Son—was willing to die in order to make satisfaction for the outrage committed against divine justice and holiness.[189] By taking the passion upon himself, then, Christ made vicarious satisfaction for the sins of mankind.[190]

---

[184] Cf. *Ref.*, 249F: ..., quantae crudelitatis quo ad daemones, qui Dominum Deum suum fecerunt crucifigi. This same passage is found in *De Ascensionibus*, 274G. It is derived from Bonaventure's *De Triplici Via* and may have come to Zerbolt by way of Radewijns' *Omnes, inquit, artes*. See Bonaventure, *De Triplici Via*, ch. 3, par. 2 (*Works*, I, 84-86), and Radewijns, *Omnes, Inquit, Artes*, II, 113-114.

[185] See footnote 177. Zerbolt does not explain in any detail why Christ descended into hell. According to Gregory the Great's *Moralia in Job*, one of Zerbolt's sources, Christ descended into hell to free the saints of the Old Dispensation who had been sent there on account of original sin (Dudden, *Gregory the Great*, II, 347). This interpretation of Christ's descent into hell adds further weight to the view that Christ died for original sin only.

[186] See footnote 173. Cf. Aulén, *Christus Victor*, 21-22 and 29-30; and E. R. Carroll, "Recapitulation in Christ," *NCE*, XII, 126-127.

[187] Strijd, *Anselmus' "Cur Deus Homo,"* 301-310 (English Summary).

[188] *Ref.*, 243G: Cogita quam gravia, quibus Deum offendisti,...

[189] *Asc.*, 260H: Cogita quod tantum Deo peccatum displicuit quod potius ipse voluit moriens satisfacere pro peccato Adae, quam ipsum secundum suam iustitiam dimittere impunitum.

Here is further evidence of Zerbolt's tendency to blur the distinction between God the Father and God the Son.

[190] *Asc.*, 272D: Sed quia Christus passionem suam assumpsit pro satisfactione originalis criminis,... *Ref.*, 248A: ..., Christus autem patiebatur ut satisfaceret pro pec-

It is necessary to draw attention to the fact that in the three instances in which Zerbolt speaks of Christ as having made satisfaction for man's sins he singles out original sin,[191] and there are three other places where he restricts the application of the benefits issuing from Christ's vicarious death to original sin.[192] Consequently, one cannot but be struck by the fact that there are only three instances in which Zerbolt holds Christ's vicarious death to be efficacious for the remission of man's sins in general: i.e., original sin as well as actual sin.[193] That Christ died for all the sins of man, original as well as actual, presumably reflects Zerbolt's authentic views. When he singles out original sin, as he so frequently does, as being the only sin deleted by Christ's death, he most likely wants to impress upon the reader that with respect to the remission of actual sin Christ's vicarious death has not made human co-operation unnecessary.[194] With respect to actual sin man must add his own works of satisfaction to Christ's vicarious work of satisfaction offered in, and through, his death.[195] However, it ought to be added that Zerbolt did not stand alone in portraying Christ's vicarious death as being efficacious for the forgiveness of original sin only. John Cassian, one of Zerbolt's favourite authors as he was to be of the Devotionalists in general, was of the opinion that Christ's death has wiped out original sin only,[196] and he established no connection between Christ's vicarious, sacrificial death and actual sins committed by man. Furthermore, according to J. H. Srawley it was a commonly held opinion in the later middle ages that the sacrifice of the cross availed for the remission of original sin only, and the sacrifice of the mass for the forgiveness of actual sins, both mortal and venial.[197] The sacrifice of the mass was, of course, generally understood to derive its efficacy from Christ's sacrificial death on the cross.

---

cato nostro. Credendum est quod ipse perfectissimi satisfecit, et igitur amarissimam etiam poenam assumpsit. Peccatum enim primi hominis poena infinita indiguit ad satisfaciendum. Et haec ratio est Bonaventurae.

A. Rayez ("Gérard Zerbolt de Zutphen et Saint Bonaventure. Dépendances Littéraires," 342) writes that Zerbolt borrows here from Bonaventure's *Commentary on the Sentences*, Lib. 3, dist. 16, art. 1, quaest. 2-3 (*Opera Omnia*, III, 348-352), and Lib. 3, dist. 20, art. 1, quaest. 3 (*Opera Omnia, III*, 422-423). Goossens (*Meditatie*, 194, footnote 58) comes to the same conclusion. Cf. M. Grabmann, "Der Einfluss des hl. Bonaventura auf die Theologie und Frömmigkeit des Mittelalters," 26.

[191] See footnotes 189 and 190.

[192] *Asc.*, 260A, 273B, and 274G.

[193] *Ref.*, 243F; and *Asc.*, 271H and 273B.

[194] Cf. Steinmetz, *Staupitz*, 145; Dempsey-Douglass, *Geiler*, 182-183; and Oberman, *Biel*, 268.

[195] See below, pp. 193-194.

[196] John Cassian, *Conferences*, No. 23, ch. 12. Cf. M. Olphe-Galliard, "Jean Cassien," *DSp*, II, 227; and P. Munz, "John Cassian," *JEH*, XI (1960), 15.

[197] J. H. Srawley, "Eucharist," *Encyclopedia of Religion and Ethics*, ed. by J. Hastings (13 vols.; N. Y.—Edinburgh, 1912-1927), V, 562.

Zerbolt was of the opinion, it would appear, that Christ's work of satisfaction on the cross contained a large element of punishment endured vicariously for man's sins; and it is not altogether impossible that his understanding of Christ's work of satisfaction was totally in terms of punishment. For in the centuries following St. Anselm of Canterbury Christ's work of satisfaction came increasingly to be regarded in terms of punishment,[198] and Zerbolt does not appear to have escaped the influence of this trend. He writes that divine justice demands not only that satisfaction be made for man's sins, but also that sins be punished, for sins are too great an offence against God's honour and glory than that divine justice could, or can, leave them unpunished.[199] He continues that God is supreme justice who chose rather to see his own Son die on the cross than that his justice should leave (original) sin unavenged.[200] On Calvary, then, Christ bore the measureless burden of punishment for man's sins. He died there a most bitter death in order that sins should not go unpunished, and to the end that God's justice should not remain unsatisfied.[201] Original sin required an infinite punishment to satisfy divine justice and honour, and it was for that reason that Christ took upon himself the most bitter punishment, thus rendering a most perfect satisfaction.[202] This emphasis on Christ's passion and death as punishment endured vicariously for man's sins is consistent with his view of divine justice as being punishing justice in particular.

Zerbolt's interpretation of Christ's death as punishment which constitutes satisfaction for the outrage committed against divine justice and honour perhaps indicates a view of Christ's death as punishment motivated by divine wrath and anger. Consequently it is not out of the question that Zerbolt regarded the passion as a propitiatory sacrifice: i.e., as a sacrifice designed to appease God's wrath and anger,[203] even though the term propitiation cannot be found in Zerbolt's writings. The idea of Christ's death as a propitiatory sacrifice occurs fairly frequently, for example, in the writings of Gregory the Great[204] which were well known to Zerbolt.

---

[198] Cf. Aulén, *Christus Victor*, 93.

[199] See footnote 189 above.

[200] *Asc.*, 274G: Si ergo vis te exercere ad timorem, quid magis timendum quam quod Deus est summa iustitia, qui elegit subire mortem potius quam iustitia sua relinqueret peccatum originale inultum. Here we have another example of Zerbolt's practice to blur the distinction between God the Father and God the Son.

[201] *Asc.*, 271H: ..., dum vides Dominum tuum ascendisse montem mirrhae, id est, montem Calvariae vel magnitudinem poenae, propter peccata tua sustinuisse. *Ref.*, 243F: Christus pro peccato sustinuit mortem amarissimam, ne peccatum inultum remaneret et suae iustitiae non satisfieret.

[202] See previous footnote, second excerpt, and footnote 166 above.

[203] Cf. Aulén, *Christus Victor*, 90.

[204] Dudden, *Gregory the Great*, II, 337.

Vicarious satisfaction constitutes the core of Zerbolt's Anselmian doctrine of the atonement, but the sacrificial-expiatory theme is not absent from his thought, for he makes a brief reference to Christ's death as a piacular, or expiatory, sacrifice. The enormity of man's sin, he writes, is best illustrated by the fact that for its forgiveness or remission so great a piacular sacrifice was needed, namely the sacrifice on the cross of God's own Son.[205] Christ, the true Paschal Lamb, Zerbolt elaborates, undertook to suffer and to die that he might be a sacrifice sufficient for all men.[206] Through Christ's expiatory sacrifice, then, man's sins have been erased, washed away, blotted out.[207] Consequently, he is justified in God's eyes.[208]

A number of times Zerbolt refers to Christ as "the redeemer," and he describes Christ's work of atonement in the passion as a work of "redemption."[209] However, it would appear that he does not, in contrast with many writers, use the terms 'redeemer' and 'redemption' as synonyms for the terms 'saviour' and 'salvation' respectively.[210] For he employs the terms 'redeemer' and 'redemption' only in connection with Christ's salvific death and never uses them to describe Christ's salvific office and work in general. Closely associated with the concept redemption is that of ransom; and in the 'classic' doctrine of the atonement, for example, Christ's life was the ransom paid to Satan in return for the release

---

[205] *Asc.*, 275A: ..., lege signaculum quintum in passione reseratum, id est, reatum culpabilem, qui ex hoc mirabiliter probatur Deo detestabilis quod ad sui remissionem indigeat tam magno pretio, tam grandi piaculo, tam difficili medicamento. The same passage is found in *De Reformatione*, 249G-H. It is derived from Bonaventure's *De Triplici Via*, possibly by way of Radewijns' *Omnes, inquit, artes*. See Bonaventure, *De Triplici Via*, ch. 3, par. 2 (*Works*, I, 84-86), and Radewijns, *Omnes, Inquit, Artes*, II, 113-114.

[206] *Asc.*, 273B: Cogita ergo quam grave est peccatum tuum propter quod expiandum tantum exigitur medicamentum, tantum pretium;... *Asc.*, 270D-E: Volens autem hostiam offerre, propter quam venerat, ut se agnum verum paschalem ostenderet, quinta die ante Pascha per allatum ab discipulis asellum, coeli terraeque Dominus ascendit,... *Asc.*, 272E: Et item assumpsit passionem et mortem, ut ipse esset hostia sufficiens pro omnibus hominibus,... *Asc.*, 273E: ..., et pro te immolari,... The first part of the second excerpt is also found on page 246C of *De Reformatione*.

[207] *Asc.*, 275A: ...Christus passus est propter peccati deletionem,... The same passage is found on page 249G of *De Reformatione*.

[208] *Asc.*, 273C: Inde gratitudo oritur, quod tantum voluit pati, ut tu dignus possis haberi iustificatione Dei.

[209] *Asc.*, 273B: Nam passus est propter tuam...redemptionem,... The same statement is found on page 248E of *De Reformatione*, and it is derived from Bonaventure's *De Triplici Via*, ch. 3, par. 2 (*Works*, I, 82-83). *Asc.*, 273E: Deinde cogita tertio quod pro tua redemptio iam incepit ire ad mortem,... Also *Asc.*, 274A and 274H. *Ref.*, 247E: Cum autem sacramenti Dominicae passionis historiam in mente tua revolvis, ut ad literam opus nostrae redemptionis contempleris,... *Ref.*, 248E: ...ita lege et cogita de passione Redemptoris tui,...

[210] Richardson, ed., *Dictionary*, 21-22 ("Atonement") and 285-286 ("Redemption").

of sinful mankind, an idea Anselm found highly objectionable. He wrote that Christ's life was a ransom paid to an offended God of righteousness in order to satisfy divine justice, honour and sanctity which suffered as a result of man's sins,[211] and Zerbolt expresses a similar view. For he writes that God, the supreme justice, demanded the price of redemption.[212] This price—better known as 'ransom' in soteriological thought, although Zerbolt does not use this term—was Christ's life which satisfied divine justice and so effected man's redemption.[213] However, the Scriptures do not, in spite of the 'classic' and Anselmian doctrines of the atonement, speak of Christ's life as a ransom paid to either God or Satan, but according to the New Testament Christ, through his death, redeemed man from sin, the powers of evil, death, etc.[214] Consistent with this biblical description of Christ's redemptive work Zerbolt writes, in at least one instance, that through his death Christ has redeemed man from sin: from original sin, to be exact.[215]

Zerbolt observes that Christ rendered a most perfect satisfaction, and that his sacrificial death was sufficient for the sins of all men.[216] He continues that although the passion of Christ was sufficient and superabundant for all, i.e. for their reconciliation with God, because of the maliciousness of many it could not be all-efficient.[217] In other words, Christ's passion and death remain ineffective for those unwilling to take advantage of it. In fact, writes Zerbolt, most of Christ's suffering was in

---

[211] Richardson, ed., *Dictionary*, 285-286 ("Redemption"), and Aulén, *Christus Victor*, 84-92.

[212] *Asc.*, 274F-G: Secundo ostensum est in passione quod ipse sit summa iustitia, inquantum quaesivit redemptionis pretium. The same passage is found in *De Reformatione*, 249F. It is derived from Bonaventure's *De Triplici Via*, possibly by way of Radewijns' *Omnes, inquit, artes*. See Bonaventure, *De Triplici Via*, ch. 3, par. 2 (*Works*, I, 84-86), and Radewijns, *Omnes, Inquit, Artes*, II, 113-114.

[213] Cf. Richardson, ed., *Dictionary*, 23 ("Atonement") and 286 ("Redemption").
That the ransom was paid to the devil because men's souls were legally in his possession is implicitly suggested by Zerbolt in his classic interpretation of the atonement.

[214] Richardson, ed., *Dictionary*, 286 ("Redemption").

[215] *Asc.*, 260A: Sane Christus morte sua preciosissima ab culpa originali nos redemit; ...

[216] *Ref.*, 248A: Credendum est quod ipse perfectissime satisfecit,... *Asc.*, 272E: Et item assumpsit passionem et mortem, ut ipse esset hostia sufficiens pro omnibus hominibus,... See footnotes 190 and 206 as well.
Zerbolt speaks of the perfection and sufficiency of Christ's vicarious death with respect to original sin only, but this issue has been discussed above.

[217] *Asc.*, 272G: Haec autem interior afflictio surgebat primo ex fervido Christi zelo pro humano genere salvando. Pro quo tamen ad maiorem partem passionem suam videbat infructuosam et inutilem, licet pro omnibus esset sufficiens et superabundans, non autem efficiens propter malitiam multorum.
Cf. Aquinas who writes: Et ideo Passio Christi non solum sufficiens, sed etiam superabundans satisfactio fuit pro peccatis humani generis,... (*ST*, 3a, 48, 2.)

vain because people, on account of their wickedness, refuse to make it their own.[218]

All indications are that Zerbolt had a good grasp of the Anselmian doctrine of the atonement,[219] which should come as no surprise in view of the fact that this was one of the more important doctrines regarding the atonement in circulation during the middle ages.

The Doctrine of Subjective Atonement. Christ may have vanquished Satan, death and hell, and he may have made vicarious satisfaction for man's sins and have endured punishment for them, but that does not free man from making his own contribution if he wishes to be saved.[220] It is in the context of man's own contribution to his salvation that Zerbolt discusses Christ's didactic and exemplary work. This soteriological theme, the so-called doctrine of subjective atonement which dominates Zerbolt's understanding of Christ's work, takes us to the very heart of Zerbolt's spirituality, and to the very core of Devotionalist spirituality in general.

For Zerbolt the immediate goal of the spiritual or religious life is purity of heart which constitutes the indispensable basis for the ultimate aim of the spiritual life, namely the contemplative state of charity followed by that of the vision of God.[221] Relying on Augustine, as he himself acknowledges, Zerbolt writes that it is only through Christ Jesus, who is God and man, that man can ascend to a knowledge of God, to charity and the vision of God. Since Christ is the way to God for man, he can be said to be the mediator between them.[222] Influenced by Bernard of Clairvaux, Zerbolt explains further that the most important reason, in fact, why the Son of God assumed flesh is that, whereas man was unable to arrive at a spiritual knowledge of God, through Christ, the Word made flesh, he might ascend to such a knowledge of God and to charity.[223] It is

---

[218] *Ref.*, 248B: Quae interior poena causabatur in eo ex nimio zeli fervore pro humano genere, in quo tamen ad majorem partem videbat passionem suam fore inutilem propter propriam malitiam. Cf. W. G. Topmoeller, "Salvation," *NCE*, XII, 994-995.

[219] Cf. Mak, "Christus bij de Moderne Devoten," 135-141.

[220] Cf. van Rooy, *Zerbolt*, 255.

[221] Zerbolt discusses the goals of the religious life in *De Reformatione*, ch. 3, and in *De Ascensionibus*, ch. 26. See below, pp. 233-241.

[222] *Asc.*, 268G: Pro quibus ascensionibus disponendis scire debes, quod Christus Iesus Deus et homo, Dei et hominum mediator, ipse est via per quam ad divinitatis notitiam simul et amorem debes ascendere secundum Augustinum 7. confessionum. This passage is inspired by Augustine's *Confessions*, Bk. VII, ch. 18.

[223] *Asc.*, 268G-H: Ad hoc enim praecipue Christus carnem assumpsit, ut qui Deum spiritualiter intelligere non potuimus, per Christum verbum caro factum ascenderemus ad notitiam et amorem spiritualem. Although Zerbolt does not acknowledge any indebtedness to St. Bernard for this passage, it is clearly influenced by the *Sermons on the Song of Songs*, XX, 6. Cf. E. Ledeur, "Imitation du Christ," *DSp*, VII, 1571-1572; Harnack, *History of Dogma*, VI, 10 ff; Goossens, *Meditatie*, 151 and 195; and Slotemaker de Bruine, *Het Ideaal der Navolging van Christus ten Tijde van Bernard van Clairvaux*, 24-27.

indeed striking that in Zerbolt's view Christ's most important function is to serve as a stepping-stone to a spiritual knowledge of God and love for him. To render vicarious satisfaction for man's sins, or to free man from the dominion of Satan and death does not, in Zerbolt's eyes, constitute Christ's most important work. Inasmuch as it is only through Christ that man can reach his ultimate spiritual goals, namely a knowledge of God, charity and the vision of God, it follows that Zerbolt's entire spirituality must be characterized as being essentially Christocentric.[224]

Zerbolt briefly outlines how, in three consecutive ascents, man may arrive at a knowledge of God, charity and the vision of God through Christ. This program for the spiritual ascent owes a great deal to Bernard of Clairvaux, as Zerbolt indicates.[225] In the first ascent the believer must acquire all the knowledge he can regarding Christ's exemplary life and passion, following which he must meditate on the same. Meditation on Christ's exemplary humanity generates devotion, and devotion must be followed by imitation of Christ who can, of course, be imitated in his humanity only. Imitation of Christ is extremely important, because through imitation of Christ's perfect humanity man can hope to conquer vice and acquire virtue, the conditions for union with Christ's human nature which is the goal of the first ascent;[226] and such a union is in-

---

The spiritual knowledge of God of which Zerbolt speaks here must perhaps be contrasted with an intellectual or natural knowledge of God, which, according to Zerbolt, man can obtain from nature by rational means (see above, pp. 40-41). Cf. Geesink, *Zerbolt*, 121; Hyma, *The Christian Renaissance*, 80; Goossens, *Meditatie*, 150-152; Mikkers, "Sint Bernardus en de Moderne Devotie," 178; and Steinmetz, *Staupitz*, 139.

[224] Cf. van Rooy, *Zerbolt*, 269.

[225] See following footnote. Zerbolt does not accurately identify his source in this instance, but it would appear to have been the *Sermons on the Song of Songs*, XX, 6-9.

[226] *Asc.*, 268H: In Christi ergo vita et morte, constitue tibi triplicem ascensionem per devota exercitia. Prima ascensio sit, ut affectu quodam dulci et desiderio cordiali, licet quodammodo carnali adhaereas Christo, comiteris Christum, iugiter circa Christi vitam et mortem affectatus, et eius praesentia et recordatione in tuis exercitiis delectatus. *Asc.*, 269B-C: Sed scias, quod licet haec exercitatio in re spirituali satis utilis sit, scilicet occupare se circa mores et gestus Iesu Christi Domini nostri, tamen quantum ad ascensum ad Christi amorem non sufficit, imo per se parum prodest. Quid profuit inde Pilato, Herodi, vel Pharisaeis, quod Christi mores vel gestus, aut praesentiam corporalem viderunt, qui eum imitari noluerunt? Igitur terminus huius primae ascensionis secundum Bernardum super Cantica, erit tibi, ut sicut Apostoli hoc affectu tracti omnia, mundi divitias, et caet. reliquerunt: ita et tu in isto gradu perseverabis; ut cor tuum illa suavitas occupat, et totum sibi ab amore universae carnis ac carnalis illecebrae vendicet, id est, breviter, homo cor suum in tali exercitio debet extendere in affectum et amorem humanitatis Christi, ut omnis affectus suus et appetitus ad dulcedinem humanitatis Christi transferatur. Also see passages quoted in footnote 245 below. Cf. van Rooy, *Zerbolt*, 255-256 and Goossens, *Meditatie*, 151-152 and 195-196.

Grote, like Zerbolt, wrote that meditation on Christ's exemplary conduct is worthless if it does not lead to imitation (Mak, "Christus bij de Moderne Devoten," 125 and 126). For Grote held, as did Zerbolt, that imitation of Christ constitutes the basis of man's ascent to the contemplation of God (Goossens, *Meditatie*, 144).

dispensable for it constitutes the basis for union with the God-man from whence the believer can then ascend to a union with the Godhead, the ultimate aim of the spiritual life. It is, therefore, not surprising that the fight against vice and the struggle for virtue are among Zerbolt's primary concerns in both *De Reformatione* and *De Ascensionibus*, for together they constitute the foundation of the three stages of the spiritual life. In the second of these three ascents man adds an understanding and love of Christ the God to his knowledge and love of Christ the man.[227] And finally, in the third ascent the believer goes beyond the knowledge and love of Christ the God-man and proceeds to an understanding and love of Christ in his divinity only in which he is one with the Godhead. In this third, and final, ascent man must attain to a spiritual knowledge of God, cleave to him, and be united with him in love.[228] Charity may be followed by the vision of God. However, while man can, and must, contribute to charity by means of spiritual exercises, the vision of God remains, in the final analysis, a gratuitous gift of God.[229]

Zerbolt explains in some detail why in his ascent to charity and the vision of God the believer must begin with Christ's humanity.[230] It is

---

The passage on p. 269B-C of *De Ascensionibus* about Pilate, Herod and the Pharisees not imitating Christ is clearly inspired by a similar passage in Grote's *De quattuor generibus meditationum*, ed. by A. Hyma, *AGAU*, XLIX (1924), 305: Quid profuit vel Herodi vel Pylato vel Iudeis vidisse Christum oculo cuius non sequebantur precepta? And both passages are reminiscent of one found in Jordan of Quedlinburg's (d. 1380) *Meditationes de passione Christi* (*De LXV artikulen vander passien Ons Heren Jhesu Christi*) quoted by Epiney-Burgard, *Grote*, 256, footnote 65.

The Middle-Dutch versions of Jordan of Quedlinburg's *Meditationes de passione Christi*, as well as of his sermons, were widely read throughout the Netherlands in the fifteenth century and were also well known to the Devotionalists (see Axters, *Vroomheid*, III, 71, 112, 359 and 452; cf. Lievens, *Jordanus van Quedlinburg in de Nederlanden*).

When Goossens writes that the Devotionalists' interest in God is limited to Christ the God, and then to Christ the God as example rather than as redeemer (*Meditatie*, 30), he is mistaken. For Zerbolt states quite plainly that Christ can be imitated in his humanity only. (*Ref.*, 247F and H: Si hominem cogitas, magis movebit te ejus exemplum,... Sumo mihi itaque exemplum de homine, auxilium de omnipotente.)

[227] *Asc.*, 269C: Secundus ascensus per vitam et passionem Christi est, iam aliquantulum altius ascendere, et non solum circa Christi humanitatem se exercere, sed ut Bernardus dicit, in homine Christo Deum invenire licet, non Deum nudum, neque nudum hominem, sed Christum Deum pariter et hominem comprehendere, ... See St. Bernard, *Sermons on the Song of Songs*, XX, 6-9. Cf. *The Golden Epistle of Abbot William of St. Thierry*, a trans. of William of St. Thierry's *Epistola ad Fratres de Monte Dei* by W. Shewring (London, 1973), 76 and 77-78.

[228] *Asc.*, 269D-E: Tertius ascensus est iam per humanitatem Christi ad spiritualem affectum assurgere, et iam ipsum Deum per speculum in aenigmate mentalibus oculis intueri, et sic ex humanitate ad notitiam et amorem divinitatis pervenire. Et hic maxime abiicitur tertia mentis impuritas per adhaesionem et transformationem, incipit quodammodo homo unus spiritus cum Deo fieri, et extra seipsum transgredi, et ipsam veritatem intueri, et ad unionem et adhaesionem habilitari.

[229] See below, pp. 233-241.

[230] Cf. Goossens, *Meditatie*, 193-194.

relatively easy for humans, he writes, to understand Christ's humanity, but it is more difficult for them to form a concept of Christ's divinity.[231] Consequently the believer will approach Christ with greater confidence if he 'studies' his humanity before his divinity. Christ's humanity will instil in the believer confidence and love.[232] This will encourage him to inquire also into Christ's divinity, and to gain some insight into Christ's entire person. On the other hand, if man first approaches Christ in his divinity he will find it difficult to form a concept of Christ, to approach him with confidence, and to love him. If the believer begins his study of Christ with his divinity, Christ's role as divine judge, for example, may fill him with debilitating fear,[233] and there was a widespread tendency in the late middle ages to stand in awe of Christ the God as judge of mankind.[234]

Zerbolt's outline of man's ascent to God through Christ the God-man draws attention to two points in particular. In the first place, Zerbolt, like Grote before him,[235] solidly bases man's ascent to charity and the vision of God on imitation of Christ's humanity, thus making imitation of Christ fundamental to the spiritual life.[236] Zerbolt mentions only the

---

[231] *Ref.*, 247F: Si hominem cogitas, inde tibi facilior cogitatio, quia humanitatis conceptus est menti tuae propinquior et facilior... Si hominem cogitas, magis movebit te ejus exemplum, mititas scilicet, humilitas, mansuetudo, quia melis intelligis quid sit homo mitis et humilis quam de Deo. *Asc.*, 269D: ...: nam facilior est nobis humanitatis notitia, ut puta menti impressa, quam Dei ab mente remotissima.

[232] *Asc.*, 269D: Si Christum hominem cogitas, inde tibi dulcis affectio et magna fiducia, quia homo mitissimus, benignissimus, nobilissimus, suavissimus, totus decorus, gratiosus, et formosus. Inde tibi fiducia accedendi, adorandi, et facilior conceptus: ... *Ref.*, 247F: Si hominem cogitas, inde fiducialius adorabis, securiusque accedes. Si hominem cogitas, magis... (see footnote 231 further).

John Busch, the chronicler *par excellence* among the Devotionalists, was of the opinion that the infant Christ may be approached with greater confidence than the adult Christ (Mak, ''Christus bij de Moderne Devoten,'' 114).

[233] *Ref.*, 246H-247A and *Asc.*, 271C. Christ in his role as judge will be examined below.

[234] It was this fearsome aspect of Christ which contributed greatly to giving Mary the prominence she gained in the late middle ages (cf. Brinckerinck, ''Collatiën,'' 167).

We have seen that Zerbolt deliberately cultivated fear of Christ's divinity, for he saw in it a salutary means, in conjunction with love for Christ's humanity, to draw man to Christ. What is clear, then, is that he does not want one to begin with Christ's divinity, for this may so instil fear of Christ's divinity in the believer as to prevent him from approaching Christ altogether. However, if one begins with Christ as man, whom one can understand, it will lead to love for him, and from there one can move on to a study of Christ's divinity which ought then to infuse a salutary fear as a counterbalance to hope and love which, when left unchecked by reverence and fear, may lead to complacency.

[235] Cf. de Beer, *Spiritualiteit*, 184 and 188.

[236] Like Zerbolt, Radewijns understands the ultimate aim of the spiritual life to be purity of heart and love for God (Radewijns, *Tractatulus Devotus*, 213-215), but he does not explain anywhere that Christ is the way to love for God. For Radewijns, as for Zerbolt, Christ is the perfect example of all virtues (Radewijns, *Omnes, Inquit, Artes*, II, 56), but he does not make imitation of Christ's human virtues the first step on the way towards love for God. The anonymous author of the *Epistola de Vita et Passione Domini Nostri Jesu Christi*,

names of Augustine and Bernard of Clairvaux in connection with the view that the way to God proceeds by way of Christ. However, for this theory, and above all for the idea that the ascent to God is based on imitation of Christ in his humanity, he, like Grote, would appear to have been indebted to Gregory the Great, a beloved writer among the Devotionalists.[237] Secondly, the considerable attention which Zerbolt devotes to the dual nature of Christ, a peculiarity which would appear to set him apart from other Devotionalists, becomes quite intelligible in light of his Augustinian-Bernardine argument that it is only through Christ, who is both God and man, that man can ascend to a knowledge of God and to charity. And it is only in the doctrine of subjective atonement that Zerbolt establishes an organic connection between the person of Christ and his work.[238]

After having briefly indicated how man may ascend to God through Christ the God-man, Zerbolt gives a relatively detailed account of Christ's life, and of the passion in particular, to assist the reader in his ascent to a knowledge of God and to charity by way of Christ.[239] However, in this narrative of Christ's life and passion the emphasis falls on Christ the exemplar who shows man the way in his fight against sin, as well as in his pursuit of virtues.[240] That Christ is also the way to charity and to the vision of God as Zerbolt explains in his preliminary outline of man's spiritual ascent is barely mentioned by him in his detailed account of Christ's life, although it may have been a guiding principle at all times. The concentration on Christ's didactic and exemplary conduct is consistent with Zerbolt's, and most of the Devotionalists', essentially ethical and moralistic spirituality in which the emphasis is on life and conduct.[241]

---

on the other hand, expresses views similar to those of Zerbolt. He writes that the exercise of virtue in imitation of Christ leads to knowledge, and knowledge to love, the ultimate aim of the spiritual life (Hedlund, ed., *Epistola de Vita et Passione Domini Nostri*, 91-92). And some years later Thomas a Kempis was to write that only the humanity of Christ provides one with an access to the divine being who is God (cf. A. Rayez, "Humanité du Christ," *DSp*, VII, 1095).

[237] Goossens, *Meditatie*, 40-42; and McGiffert, *A History of Christian Thought*, II, 155.

[238] Cf. Aulén, *Christus Victor*, 143-159, and throughout.

[239] *Asc.*, 269F: Ut etiam circa has ascensiones modum habeas te exercitandi, etiam hic sicut in praecedentibus generalem modum meditandi de vita et passione Christi Iesu curavimus annotare. Cf. Goossens, *Meditatie*, 151-152 and Hyma, *The Christian Renaissance*, 80.

The life of Christ by Radewijns in *Omnes, inquit, artes* is considerably longer. His rationale for giving an account of Christ's life is that Christ is the mirror of all virtues and that he is the way to all sanctity (*Omnes, Inquit, Artes*, II, 56). In contrast with Zerbolt he does not give an account of Christ's life because Christ is the way to a knowledge of God and love for him.

[240] *Ref.*, chs. 26-34 (pp. 245H-249H) and *Asc.*, chs. 28-40 (pp. 269F-275D).

[241] *Asc.*, 286A: Ergo ut ait Hugo: Si cum aliis fueris, et mutua delectat verborum collatio; fiat sermo de moribus,... (Hugo is Hugh of St. Victor.)

Zerbolt's, and most of the Devotionalists', first aim was to acquire a pure heart, beyond which charity and union with God lay as an ultimate, but distant, goal. K. C. L. M. de Beer writes that Grote's spirituality, which largely determined Devotionalist spirituality, aims in the first place at a morally upright life and only secondly at union with God.[242] Zerbolt, too, is content to remain for the most part at the lower levels of the spiritual life: i.e., the ascetical stage, in spite of his assertion that the ultimate aim of the spiritual ascent is charity and the vision of God.[243]

It is primarily to reveal the exemplary nature of Christ's entire life, then, that Zerbolt includes a 'life of Jesus' in his two manuals.[244] Quoting what he believes to be a passage from one of Augustine's writings, Zerbolt explains that all that Christ did, he did for man's instruction and benefit.[245] Zerbolt portrays the young Christ as being above all an exemplar of patience, poverty and humility,[246] and he places particular emphasis on the latter. Earlier we saw that humility is the term employed most frequently by Zerbolt to describe Christ's disposition and conduct in all situations, and Christ's exemplary humility claimed the Devotionalists' attention to a greater degree than any other aspect of his disposition.[247] This is consistent with Christ's view of himself because, as Zerbolt points out, later in life he pointed to himself as the example of

---

[242] De Beer, *Spiritualiteit*, 146 and cf. 96.

[243] See below, pp. 233-241.

[244] Cf. Mak, "Christus bij de Moderne Devoten," 115.

[245] *Super modo vivendi*, 32: Sexto omnis Christi accio nostra est instructio secundum Augustinum. *De vestibus pretiosis*, 43: Quinto inquiunt: Christus cuius omnis actio est instructio, preciosias et conpetentes vestes habuit... et nos eum debemus imitari.

Zerbolt attributes the statement "that everything Christ did for us, he did for our instruction" to Augustine, but it cannot be found in any of Augustine's authentic writings (Bartoš, "Hus, Lollardism and Devotio Moderna in the Fight for a National Bible," 251-252). John Geiler quotes this passage as well, but he attributes it to Gregory the Great rather than to Augustine: Et beatus Gregorius omnis cristi actio est nostra instructio... (quoted by Dempsey-Douglass, *Geiler*, 181, footnote 1).

[246] *Asc.*, 269H-270A: Cogita quod Deus parvulus vagiit, et lachrymatus est in praesepio. Attende hic paupertatem. Nota humilitatem.

Grote also draws attention to Christ's humility and lowliness in the manger and the exemplary value it has for man. Through imitation of this humility and lowliness man shares in Christ's birth, and through his conformity with Christ man achieves a certain spiritual identity with him (de Beer, *Spiritualiteit*, 85). *Asc.*, 270B: Christus adhuc parvulus fugatur ab Herode. Attende Christi patientiam et disce pati. Sequere peregrinantes, attende colloquentes, in omnibus disce paupertatem et humilitatem. Cf. Bonaventure, *Lignum Vitae*, ch. 8 (*Works*, I, 108-109), and Radewijns, *Omnes, Inquit, Artes*, II, 73-74. *Asc.*, 270A: Cogita de dulce nomine Iesus. Sume exemplum teipsum circuncidendi [circumcicendi].

Zerbolt does not explain in what way Christ's circumcision was exemplary. However, in *Omnes, inquit, artes* Radewijns quotes both Bernard of Clairvaux and Bonaventure to the effect that Christ's circumcision was an act of humility in that Christ, in allowing himself to be circumcised, submitted himself to the law (Radewijns, *Omnes, Inquit, Artes*, II, 71-72).

[247] Cf. Mak, "Christus bij de Moderne Devoten," 119.

humility and lowliness from whom people must learn.[248] Zerbolt further
notes that from his twelfth to his thirtieth year Christ chose to remain
unknown, neither teaching nor performing miracles.[249] Christ's purpose
in maintaining such a low profile during this period, he explains, was to
show man that he must not rashly come forward as a teacher and a
spiritual leader. He must first humbly submit himself to others.[250] Thus
Zerbolt finds support in Christ's exemplary life for an issue to which he
devoted a separate treatise and to which he returns a number of times in
De Reformatione and *De Ascensionibus*, namely the question of assuming ecclesiastical office.[251] He was of the opinion that ecclesiastical office leads
to pride, vanity and vainglory, that it destroys humility and, as a consequence, true piety.[252]

Zerbolt discovers further evidence of Christ's exemplary humility in
his baptism by John[253] which marked the beginning of his public life. He
explains, like Grote before him,[254] that, in his baptism by John, Christ
subjected himself to an inferior, and that in doing so he performed an act
of humility.[255] Furthermore, Zerbolt claims that it was through his hum-

---

[248] Matthew 11, 29. Quoted by Zerbolt, *Asc.*, 284H.

[249] *Asc.*, 270B: A duodecimo autem anno usque ad tricesimum, ipse rex gloriae in
populo absconditus latitabat, non docebat, nec mirabilia faciebat,...
Zerbolt's "Life of Christ" is consistent with the Christ who emerges from the Gospels,
in essence at least. (Cf. van Rooy, *Zerbolt*, 270.) Christ's dispositions such as humility, patience, etc. which Zerbolt detects in various situations are not, of course, described in so
many words in the Scriptures. Nor is Christ's outward bearing described in all situations.
Nonetheless, Zerbolt asserts, one can easily enough form a mental picture of Christ's inner disposition and outward deportment in all situations, for he conducted himself most
excellently in all things. (*Ref.*, 248C [see footnote 266 below, first passage].) Zerbolt also
attributes utterings to Christ not found in the Gospels. (See *Asc.*, 272E for an example of
this. Also *Asc.*, 273B: Igitur omnia quae legis Christum fecisse, attrahe tibi quasi propter
te solum facta, et cogita semper quasi Christus dicat tibi: hoc feci, ut sequaris me: ... This
last statement, which he attributes to Christ, Zerbolt would appear to have borrowed from
Grote. Cf. de Beer, *Spiritualiteit*, 98.) Like Zerbolt, Grote was also of the opinion that one
can profitably use one's imagination when meditating on Christ's life and passion. (Cf. de
Beer, *Spiritualiteit*, 99.)

[250] *Ref.*, 246B: Cogita deinde, quod ab duodecimo anno usque ad tricesimum, tanquam unus de populo incognitus, et ignotus, omnium Dominus latitabat, ut te doceret, ut
non surgas ad agenda publice in quibus laus et honor conquiri poterit nisi prius sederis
diutius te humiliando. See *Asc.*, 270B for a similar passage, as well as *Scriptum Pro Quodam*,
224.

[251] The treatise is *Scriptum Pro Quodam*. See also *Ref.*, 251A and 257A; and *Asc.*,
280G-H and 284C.

[252] Cf. de Beer, *Spiritualiteit*, 230-234 and van Zijl, *Groote*, 243-253.

[253] *Asc.*, 270C: Tricesimo vero anno ab Ioanne baptizatur... Cogita Christi
humilitatem, qui se Ioanni subiecit, et omnem iustitiam, id est, perfectam humilitatem
implevit. Cf. *Ref.*, 246B: Cogita deinde,..., ut omnem iustitiam impleret, ab Ioanne baptizatus est,...

[254] Epiney-Burgard, *Grote*, 276-277; and Mak, "Christus bij de Moderne Devoten,"
117.

[255] See footnote 253 above; and cf. Epiney-Burgard, *Grote*, 276-277.

ble submission to John that Christ "fulfilled all righteousness" of which St. Matthew speaks in his Gospel.[256] The idea that Christ fulfilled all righteousness by humbly submitting himself to John's baptism is one which Zerbolt borrowed from Bernard of Clairvaux, and he did so either directly or by way of Radewijns' *Omnes, inquit, artes*.[257] Christ's temptation by Satan in the desert, which took place shortly after his baptism by John, also receives special attention from Zerbolt. We saw earlier that, according to Zerbolt, Christ's victory over temptations by Satan freed mankind from Satan's dominion just as it had succumbed to him as a consequence of his victory over Adam in a similar situation. However, Zerbolt places a great deal more emphasis on Christ's victory over Satan as an example to be imitated than as a substitutional act. The vicarious value of Christ's triumph over Satan is mentioned just once by Zerbolt, but to its exemplary usefulness he returns a number of times. Christ went to the desert to be tempted by Satan in order to teach the believer that Satan and temptations must be resisted, as well as to show him how to do this. By going to the desert Christ taught his followers to thwart and to oppose the forces of evil at all times, for without such a struggle there can be no spiritual improvement, Zerbolt explains.[258] This interpretation of Christ's temptation by Satan is very similar to that given by Aquinas who acknowledged some indebtedness to Augustine.[259]

The period falling between Christ's temptation in the desert and the Last Supper is treated very briefly and cursorily by Zerbolt. Furthermore, he does not isolate any one specific incident from this period as being particularly exemplary or imitable. He does, nonetheless, believe that throughout all this time Christ conducted himself more as a servant than as a master,[260] thereby teaching all his followers to be humble through the example he gave them. In concentrating his attention on Christ's infancy and passion—and of these two the latter receives considerably more attention than the former—Zerbolt was following a common medieval

---

[256] Matthew 3, 13-15.

[257] Bernard of Clairvaux, *Sermo in Oct. Epiph.*, No. 5 (*PL.*, CLXXXIII, 154); and Radewijns, *Omnes, Inquit, Artes*, II, 74-75.

[258] *Ref.*, 246B. Cogita qualiter ut nobis exemplum tribueret tentationibus resistendi, ipse ab diabolo tentatus est, vicitque, atque nobis dedit exemplum legitime contra inimicos praeliandi. *Ref.*, 252H-253A: Sic Christus exivit in desertum ad hoc ut tentaretur; ut videlicet doceret ligitimos bellatores, quod semper ipsi debeant aliquid arripere pro emendatione, quamvis difficile videatur,... *Asc.*, 270C: Cogita Christi in eremo conversationem,... Cogita quam sapienter satanae restitit, et tibi exemplum contulit resistendi.

[259] Thomas Aquinas, *ST*, 3a, 49, 1.
It would appear that Zerbolt's understanding of Christ's temptation and its purpose is to some extent influenced by Bonaventure's *Lignum Vitae*, ch. 10 (*Works*, I, 110).

[260] *Asc.*, 270C-D: Nota eius communem vitam cum Apostolis...Vide quomodo ipse inter eos est, sicut qui ministrat, cum eis comedit una mensa et scutella, non habet privilegium, etc.

practice, one which was adopted by the Devotionalists in general.[261] Apart from Christ's infancy and passion only his baptism by John and his temptation in the desert are singled out, we have seen, as being of considerable importance.[262]

Zerbolt himself devotes more attention to Christ's passion than to any other aspect of his life and urges the believers to devote most of their attention to the same theme, because he believes that for their spiritual improvement they can benefit from Christ's passion in particular.[263] He regards Christ's passion to be supremely exemplary, instructive and inspirational for the eradication of vice and the advancement of virtue, his major concern.[264] Diligent and devout meditation on the passion, he elaborates, will reveal that at that time Christ conducted himself most excellently and correctly in all situations and vis-à-vis all people.[265] In Christ, and in the suffering Christ in particular, the believer will find the perfect model and example for all the virtues which he needs to cultivate in his quest for a pure heart.[266] Therefore, if the individual is to derive

---

[261] De Bruin, "Het Bonaventura-Ludolphiaanse Leven van Jesus," 119-120; Mak, "Christus bij de Moderne Devoten," 117 and 124; cf. Axters, Vroomheid, III, 188; J. Tiecke, "Gérard Groote,"DSp, VI, 273 and de Beer, Spiritualiteit, 85-87.

[262] Cf. Epistola de vita et passione domini nostri Iesu Christi, for it also concentrates on Christ's infancy, baptism and passion.

[263] Ref., 247D-E: Circa passionem Dominicam in qua te prae caeteris exercitiis ardentius et devotius exercebis, ut ea quae in sacris Evangeliis legeris, ad tuam utilitatem melius scias reflectere ac diligere ad propriam utilitatem:... Cf. Ref., 249H and Asc., 271H.

[264] Asc., 272A: Secundo debes ad Christi passionem tanquam mirrham ire, et inde aliqua ad tuam utilitatem trahere, sive medicinam contra vulnera passionum, sive exempla virtutum. Tertio debes ad ipsum ire, et ex illa mirrha prima mentem tuam ad devotionem perungere, et amorem inflammare, et teipsum promptum efficere ad omnium tolerantiam tribulationum.

[265] Zerbolt stipulates that meditation on the various aspects of Christ's passion must follow three consecutive steps: opus, modus and causa (Ref., 247E). Zerbolt borrowed this approach to the meditation of Christ's passion from Bernard of Clairvaux (cf. Goossens, Meditatie, 193 and 196).

[266] Ref., 248C: Circa modum autem patiendi si diligens fueris et devote rimaveris, invenies praecipue humilitatem, mititatem, et generaliter omnium virtutum perfectum exemplar imitandum. Ut autem modum patiendi in Christo in te melius sentias, debes in omnibus quae de Christi passione legis vel cogitas, semper in mente tua revolvere, quomodo Christus se habuit in verbis, in responsionibus, in factis, in poenis, quomodo se habuit tam interius quam exterius, et quomodo illa prout loco et personis congruebant, optimo modo formabat; et hoc poteris in Evangelio invenire, vel certe si ibi non est expressum, ex teipso formare. Nam nullus Christianus ignorat, quin in omnibus optimo modo se habuit. Ref., 248D-E: Et sic omnia pertracta, imitans modum Christi se habendi secundum loca et tempora, et invenies omnem virtutem in Christo et optimum modum in quo se habere potuit. Ref., 247G-H: Item hunc modum habuit in suis meditationibus devotissimus doctor Bernardus, ait enim super Cantica: Siquidem, inquit, cum nomino Iesum, hominem mihi propono mitem et humilem, corde benignum, sobrium, castum, misericordem et omni denique sanctitate et honestate perspicuum, eundem ipsum Deum omnipotentem. Sumo mihi itaque exemplum de homine, auxilium de omnipotente. Asc., 274C-D: Et hic considera quali forma Christus passus est, ut eum studeas imitari. And see footnote 231 above.

maximum benefit from Christ's passion, he must first familiarize himself thoroughly with, and attempt to comprehend, Christ's conduct during his passion, both inwardly and outwardly.[267] For it is only after the believer has gained a profound understanding of Christ's exemplary conduct during his passion that he can benefit to the fullest extent from the passion through his imitation of the incomparable virtues exhibited by Christ in his suffering. In brief, then, the believer will find in Christ, by means of devout meditation, a store of all virtues which, when he actively imitates them, will prove to be very effective medicine to heal all vices.[268] Christ is the great physician whose exemplary, virtuous behaviour possesses the efficacy to heal man's vices, provided, of course, man follows the example set by Christ. It is for man's own benefit, then, and his moral instruction or education that he must ponder, and meditate on, Christ's instructive and exemplary behaviour as exhibited in the passion in particular.[269] Finally, Zerbolt briefly observes that Christ suffered in order that through imitation of his suffering man might have his understanding enlightened in the knowledge of the truth.[270] This, it would appear, is a reminder that imitation of Christ's humanity is the basis for man's ascent to a spiritual knowledge and love of Christ, the God-man, from whence one can then ascend to an understanding and love of the Godhead himself. Imitation of Christ's humanity as a means to eradicate vice and to acquire virtue is not an end in itself, although Zerbolt would, for all practical purposes, appear to make it the end of the spiritual life.

In view of what has been said one might reasonably expect Zerbolt to describe Christ's exemplary behaviour during the passion in some detail. The truth is, however, that he does not do so, because he would appear to have been interested in the first place in the tenor of Christ's life and con-

---

[267] *Asc.*, 272A: Et hoc fit dum Christi passionem circumspecte, morose, et devote ruminas, diligenter ad literam seu secundum sensum verborum speculando.

[268] *Asc.*, 272A (see footnote 264 above). *Asc.*, 272H: De secundo autem, quomodo tibi utiliter passionem Christi assumere debes ad fructum et utilitatem, ad imitationem scilicet virtutum, vel fugam vitiorum, debes summo conamine ad hoc affectum et intellectum tuum dirigere, ut in omnibus gestis, verbis et responsionibus Christi quae in historia legis passionis Dominicae, ... Et sic invenies in Christo passo omnium virtutum copiam, et contra omnia vitia summa medicamina. *Asc.*, 273A-B: Et si ista bene tractaveris, invenies in Christo omnium virtutum summam et compatiendi materiam, et debita medicamina vitiorum.

[269] *Asc.*, 273D: Deinde ad tuam utilitatem et morum informationem diligenter considera, quam dulciter verba protulit, quam benigne se habuit, quam dulci colloquio admonuit,...

[270] *Asc.*, 273B: Nam passus est propter tuam illuminationem,... Propter tuam illuminationem ut sequereris exemplum eius, et intellectus tuus illuminaretur in cognitione veritatis. A shorter version of this same passage is found in *De Reformatione*, 248E. It is inspired by Bonaventure's *De Triplici Via*, ch. 3, par. 3 (*Works*, I, 82-83).

duct, rather than in the fine details of his life and passion.[271] Starting with the Last Supper, Zerbolt writes that at that time Christ washed the feet of his disciples in order to impress upon them a very superior example of humility, and this act was, as it were, a summary of Christ's life of exemplary lowliness.[272] With regard to the events following the Last Supper Zerbolt calls attention to Christ's patience, lowliness, meekness and amiableness as exhibited by him in a number of specific situations, but he also uses these same terms, and similar ones, to describe Christ's behaviour and bearing during the passion in its entirety.[273] These qualities of kindness, humility, lowliness, etc. must be cultivated by the believer in his own life. He must attempt to conform his conduct to the pattern of the imitation of Christ,[274] and in that way fight vice and ac-

---

[271] St. Bernard's and St. Francis' imitation ideals, although essentially the same, did, nonetheless, reveal some differences. St. Bernard was primarily concerned to act in the spirit of Christ's conduct. St. Francis, on the other hand, put considerable emphasis on a literal imitation of Christ in all situations (Slotemaker de Bruine, *Het Ideaal der Navolging van Christus ten Tijde van Bernard van Clairvaux*, 25-27, 29-31, 58-67 and 100-104; Mak, "Christus bij de Moderne Devoten," 105-166; Etienne Ledeur, "Imitation du Christ," *DSp*, VII, 1571-1577; A. McDevitt, "Franciscan Spirituality," *NCE*, VI, 37-38; and P. Zerbit, "Bernard of Clairvaux," *NCE*, II, 337). The Devotionalist movement, of which Zerbolt was a leading spokesman, represents a renewal of the Bernardine and Franciscan imitation ideals, as well as a renewal of the profound interest in Christ's humanity which follows logically from the imitation ideal. Some Devotionalists, and Zerbolt was one of them, allowed themselves to be led in the first place by the tenor of Christ's life and conduct, while others sought above all to imitate Christ in concrete ways.

[272] *Ref.*, 246C: Cogita igitur quantae fuerit humilitatis, quod Dominus Christus cum illis pauperculis discipulis suis, praecipue cum Iuda proditore, eadem mensa et scutella coenauerit. Quodque pedes eorum humilitatis volens exemplum altius imprimere, prostratus humiliter abluebat. *Asc.*, 270F: In qua coena multa mirabilia fecit, imo mirabilium omnium suorum quoddam memoriale et compendium instituit,... *Asc.*, 270G: Meditare igitur, quomodo in hac coena ipse Dominus magnus et laudabilis nimis, pedes discipulorum et sui traditoris lavit, inclinans se usque ad terram, et praecingens se linteo, ut nos instrueret suae humilitatis exemplo. Cf. Bonaventure, *Lignum Vitae*, ch. 16 (*Works*, I, 114).

[273] See *Ref.*, 247F-249A and *Asc.*, 273D-274C. Cf. Bonaventure, *Lignum Vitae*, chs. 21-28 (*Works*, I, 119-126) and Radewijns, *Omnes, Inquit, Artes*, II, 96-118.

[274] *Asc.*, 274D: Stude igitur ad habendum habitum secundum effigiem imitationis Christi, scilicet benignitatis, severitatis, humilitatis, et perspicuitatis. The same passage is found in *De Reformatione*, 249D. Cf. Mak, "Christus bij de Moderne Devoten," 119 and 121.

It is not exactly clear what Zerbolt means when he writes that man must "conform his conduct to the pattern of the imitation of Christ." This statement is, however, reminiscent of the doctrine of recapitulation as it was first formulated by Irenaeus. Pelikan writes in this connection: "Irenaeus' doctrine of the recapitulation can be read as the most profound theological vindication in the second and third centuries of the universal Christian ideal of the imitation of Christ. For Irenaeus, the imitation of Christ by the Christian was part of God's cosmic plan of salvation which began with Christ's imitation of the Christian or, more precisely, with Christ's imitation of Adam." (Pelikan, *The Christian Tradition, A History of the Development of Doctrine*, I, 144.)

quire virtue. In the fight against evil and the struggle for holiness Zerbolt does not very frequently hold the saints up as examples to be imitated.[275] For him the saints are primarily the teachers who through their writings initiate man in the spiritual life. While the saints provide theoretical instruction in the fight against sin and the quest for virtue, it is Christ who gives the practical example.[276] In adopting this attitude towards the saints, Zerbolt would appear to have acted in the spirit of Grote, and according to van Rooy most Devotionalists adopted a critical attitude towards the hagiographical literature in circulation in the middle ages.[277]

Christ's passion can serve to eradicate vice and contribute to the development of virtue in another way, Zerbolt writes. Reflection on the bitter punishment suffered by Christ for man's sins will serve to instil compunction of fear, he believes, and the fear will drive out vice and corruption. On the other hand, reflection on the fact that Christ died for man's sins will also serve to instil compunction of hope,[278] as well as love and thankfulness. The hope will incite man to purify his heart and to live virtuously in anticipation of eternal salvation.[279]

---

[275] *De vestibus pretiosis*, 43: ..., ad Cristi et aliorum sanctorum exemplum.

[276] Van Rooy, *Zerbolt*, 269-270 and W. Lourdaux, "Gérard de Zutphen," *DSp*, VI, 285.

[277] Van Rooy, *Zerbolt*, 269-270.

[278] On the function of compunction of fear and compunction of hope in Zerbolt's religious though see below, pp. 250-256 and 266-272.

[279] *Asc.*, 271H-272A: Vadam ad...tuo imprimendo. And see footnote 264 as well.

We see that Zerbolt speaks here (*Asc.*, 271H-272A) of the "bitter myrrh of fear" which results from a reflection on Christ's death and the bitter punishment suffered by him for man's sins. Consequently, he writes, one may refer to Christ as the "mountain of myrrh," for it is through reflection on Christ's death that one obtains the "bitter myrrh of fear" which serves to eradicate vice and to nurture virtue. Zerbolt did not stand alone in his characterization of Christ, and his passion in particular, as a "mountain of myrrh." W. Stammler mentions a nun from Engeltal who compared Christ's passion to a "mountain of myrrh" (Stammler, "Studien zur Geschichte der Mystik in Norddeutschland," 114). The expression "mountain of myrrh" itself may be found in the Song of Songs (4, 6), and that myrrh signifies bitterness is and idea already expressed by Bernard of Clairvaux in his *Sermons on the Song of Songs* (XLIII, 1).

Not only does Zerbolt refer to Christ as the "mountain of myrrh" since his passion is the source of the "bitter myrrh of fear," but Zerbolt divides the meditation on Christ's passion into "bundles of myrrh": six in *De Reformatione* and five in *De Ascensionibus* (*Ref.*, 248F: Ut autem etiam tu quicunque memoriam tuam per meditationem mortis reformare desideras, qui in promptu habeas fasciculos qui in memoria tui commorentur, passionem Christi hic tactam solummodo ordine Evangelistarum inseruimus compendiose,...). Each "bundle" is the equivalent of a chapter devoted to a particular aspect of Christ's passion (*Ref.*, chs. 29-34 and *Asc.*, chs. 33-37). The practice of referring to meditations on Christ's passion as one or more "bundles of myrrh" can be traced back to St. Bernard of Clairvaux. The theme of his 43rd sermon on the Song of Songs is: *Fasciculus myrrhae dilectus meus mihi, inter ubera mea commorabitur.* (Cf. Song of Songs, 1, 12.) The remembrance of Christ's suffering and passion, he writes, must be carried like a bundle of myrrh between one's breasts in order that one may derive benefit from the bitterness of Christ's passion at all times (*Sermons on the Song of Songs*, XLIII, 2-3). Therefore, when Zerbolt writes:

Finally, Zerbolt mentions a third manner in which the passion can contribute to the eradication of vice and to the cultivation of virtue. The passion, he quotes from Bonaventure's *De Triplici Via*, revealed seven things previously unknown, and the notion that the number of revelations totals seven is inspired by the 'seven seals' of the Apocalypse.[280] These revelations,[281] he explains in *De Ascensionibus* in particular, will, depending upon their nature, cultivate compunction of fear and compunction of hope and love in the believer; and this twofold compunction will then instigate him to fight against vice, to cultivate virtue, and so lead him to charity.[282] The purpose of these seven revelations is, then, to aid man in his quest for spiritual perfection through the compunction of fear and the compunction of hope which they are meant to arouse in the believer.

Imitation of Christ's virtuous conduct is a most effective way to acquire a pure heart, the basis for man's ascent to God. However, in addition to imitating Christ's virtues, the believer must also imitate the suffering endured by Christ during the passion, Zerbolt writes. Like Christ, and in imitation of him, the believer must willingly accept injury, injustice, evil treatment, mockery and abuse.[283] To imitate Christ in his

---

"*Fasciculus myrrhae dilectus meus mihi, inter ubera mea commorabitur. Loquitur anima devota, designans se Christi amaritudinem simul collectam jugitur in suo pectore circumferre*" (*Ref.*, 248E-F), the origin of this exegesis is obvious.

The influence of St. Bernard in the middle ages made it inevitable that many writers fashioned the meditations on Christ's suffering and passion into a *fasciculus*, or *fasciculi, myrrhae*. (G. Eis, "Fasciculus Myrrhae," *Leuvense Bijdragen*, XLIX [1960], 90-96.) Bonaventure writes in the introduction to *Lignum Vitae*: "I have attempted to gather this bundle of myrrh from the groves of the Gospels,..." (*Lignum Vitae*, Prologue [*Works*, I, 97].) The meditation on Christ's passion with which Radewijns concludes the *Tractatulus Devotus* is divided into *fasciculi* (*Tractatulus Devotus*, 250-254), and these *fasciculi* are among the most important sources for Zerbolt's own *fasciculi* on the passion of Christ (cf. above, p. 25 f). Goossens suggests that the *fasciculi* found in the *Tractatulus Devotus* were not compiled by Radewijns himself, but that he borrowed them from Grote, and that they are, in fact, the *Concordia Evangelistarum de Passione Domini*, generally believed to be one of Grote's lost works (Goossens, *Meditatie*, 70-72 and 190-191; cf. Post, *Kerkgeschiedenis*, I, 409).

[280] *Ref.*, 249E-F: Passio Christi non solum memoriam reformat..., et ducit ad cognitionem veritatis. Siquidem in universitatis cognitione maxime 7. erant clausa ante Christi passionem, quae sunt in ejus passione reserata. De quibus intelligi potest illud Apocalypsis: Aperta sunt signacula ejus 7. Essentially the same passage is found in *De Ascensionibus*, 274F. It is inspired by Bonaventure's *De Triplici Via*, ch. 3, par. 2 (*Works*, I, 84-86), possibly by way of Radewijns' *Omnes, Inquit, Artes*, II, 113-114.

[281] Most of these revelations have been discussed earlier in a variety of contexts.

[282] *De Ref.*, 249E-H: Passio Christi ... fasciculus sextus. *De Asc.*, 274F-275B: Si vero ... perditum restauravit. These passages are inspired by Bonaventure's *De Triplici Via*, ch. 3, par. 3 (*Works*, I, 84-86), possibly by way of Radewijns' *Omnes, Inquit, Artes*, II, 113-114.

[283] *Ref.*, 249E: Hic considera quanta pro te passus sit, et crucem amplectere per passionis desiderium, ut sicut ipse passus est injuriam, convitia, ludibria, supplicia, sic et tu passionem Christi imitando amplectere pro eo omnem passionem plenam injuriis, convitiis,... The same passage is found in *De Ascensionibus*, 274E. It is derived from *De Triplici Via* by Bonaventure, ch. 3, par. 2 (*Works*, I, 82-83), perhaps via Radewijns' *Tractatulus Devotus*, 251-254.

suffering requires preparation just as imitation of his virtuous conduct is based on meditation, devotion and love. One must go to Christ and meditate on his suffering, meditation must instil devotion and love, and they in turn must rouse the believer to imitate Christ and to bear all tribulations with him.[284] Why man must suffer in imitation of Christ Zerbolt does not explain in any detail. He merely writes that man must suffer on account of Christ,[285] and what he presumably means is that, because Christ suffered on account of man, man must be willing to become one with Christ through suffering. Suffering is the lot of the Christian, the imitator of Christ. Consequently, when the believer meditates on Christ's suffering he must imagine that Christ is saying to him: I did this in order that you might follow in my footsteps and humbly and patiently take up your cross and follow me, for the servant is not above the master.[286] In contrast with Zerbolt his *confrère* Radewijns says very little regarding Christ's suffering which must be imitated;[287] but the idea that the believer must suffer in imitation of Christ is an important theme in Grote's spirituality, in fact, more prominent than is imitation of Christ's virtues as a means of cultivating one's own virtues.[288] With respect to this particular issue, then, Zerbolt stood closer to Grote than to Radewijns.

In the foregoing discussion of the doctrine of subjective atonement as understood by Zerbolt imitation of Christ by the believer has received a

---

[284] *Asc.*, 272A: Tertio debes ad ipsum [= Christ] ire, et ex illa mirrha prima mentem tuam ad devotionem perungere, et amorem inflammare, et teipsum promptum efficere ad omnium tolerantiam tribulationum. *Asc.*, 274C-D: Et hic considera quali forma Christus passus est, ut eum studeas imitari. Cf. Pourrat, *La Spiritualité Chrétienne*, Vol. II: *Le Moyen Age*, 389.

[285] See footnote 283 above.

[286] *Ref.*, 248E: Item cogita semper quicquid legeris vel cogitaveris, quasi dicat tibi Christus: Hoc feci ut tu sequaris vestigia mea, te humilies, patiens sis, tollas crucem tuam et sequaris me, quia non est servus supra Dominum suum. *Asc.*, 273B: Nam passus est propter tuam..., redemptionem,... Igitur omnia quae legis Christum fecisse, attrahe tibi quasi propter te solum facta, et cogita semper quasi Christus dicat tibi: hoc feci, ut sequaris me: ... Cf. Matthew 10, 24; 1 Peter 2, 21; Mak, "Christus bij Moderne Devoten," 124-131; and Goossens, *Meditatie*, 195.

[287] *Omnes, Inquit, Artes*, II, 56; and Goossens, *Meditatie*, 192.

[288] Mulder, ed., *Gerardi Magni Epistolae*, 238: Unde in qualibet meditacione quarumcunque parcium passionis Christi, vocem Christi quasi desuper audire debemus: Sic fac et vives; vel ideo passus sum pro te et propter te, ut sequaris vestigia mea. Cf. de Beer, *Spiritualiteit*, 86-87, 96 and 98.

Letter No. 62 (Mulder, ed., *Gerardi Magni Epistolae*, 232-243), the complete title of which reads: "*Notabilis epistola est et valem ad pacienciam et eciam ad imitacionem Christi*," is important for an understanding of Grote's views regarding imitation of Christ. Cf. Goossens, *Meditatie*, 191-192; J. Huyben and P. Debongnie, "Geert Groote's Brief over de Navolging van Christus," *OGE*, XXI (1951), 271-272; de Beer, *Spiritualiteit*, 86-87, 96 and 98; Epiney-Burgard, *Grote*, 248-258; and B. Spaapen, "Middeleeuwse Passiemystiek, I," *OGE*, XXX (1961), 169.

good deal of attention. That it did so stems from the fact that it is difficult to discuss Christ's role as example in isolation from man's imitation of him, although the latter ought, by rights, to be discussed in the chapter dealing with the spiritual life. However, having been dealt with in detail here, imitation of Christ will be mentioned in a general way only in the chapter devoted to the spiritual life.

iii. *Christ as Judge of Mankind*

Before some general conclusions are drawn from the foregoing analysis of Zerbolt's soteriology it is necessary to point out that for him Christ is not only the Saviour, but also the wrathful judge who will return at the end of time to bestow on all their just deserts.[289] The two functions are not incompatible. In fact, Christ's task as judge is implied in his role as saviour. For, as Zerbolt explains, in the final judgement Christ will show the signs of the passion, and they will constitute an accusation against those who refused to share in the passion. Christ will then take away the benefits of his incarnation and passion from those who have despised him and his salvific work.[290] According to Epiney-Burgard, Grote, and most of his followers as well, put considerable emphasis on the last judgement and Christ's role as judge which lent their spirituality a somber note.[291] Of course, in the later middle ages the emphasis on Christ's role as terrible judge at the last judgement was generally more pronounced than it had been some centuries earlier.

iv. *Assessment*

Summing up it may be said that Zerbolt's soteriology, which according to E. Mikkers is more elaborate than that of any other Devotionalist,[292] is traditional in that it consists of a number of essentially different, yet complementary, theories of which one stands out from all the others. The soteriological theory which demands most of Zerbolt's attention is the so-

---

[289] *Asc.*, 263B-C: Quia vero in peccatis tuis Deum per superbiam contempsisti, ideo necesse est ut te homini Dei vicario claves habenti humiliter subdas vice Dei, et ei tanquam Christo Domino iudici tuo assistens humiliter et contrite et dolorose peccata tua confitearis. *Asc.* 271C: Ipse [Christ who is also found in the eucharist] iste quem sumis, erit iudex tuus, et eius tribunali iudicandus astabis. Ipse est in cuius manus anima tua hinc egressa deveniet ab eo prout meruit receptura. A similar passage is found in *De Reformatione*, 246H-247A. *Ref.*, 248G: Crede igitur et cogita ipsum esse veraciter Dei filium,... et retributorem omnium. The same passage is found in *De Ascensionibus*, 273F. It is borrowed from Bonaventure, *De Triplici Via*, ch. 3, par. 2 (*Works*, I, 82-83), perhaps via Radewijns' *Tractatulus Devotus*, 251-254.

[290] *Ref.*, 245A: Cogita quomodo ibi Christus exhibebit passionis suae insignia, et quomodo per signa illa exprobrabit nobis quod ea contempsimus. For a similar passage see *Asc.*, 265F.

[291] Epiney-Burgard, *Grote*, 277; and cf. Mak, "Christus bij de Moderne Devoten," 140-141.

[292] Mikkers, "Bernardus en de Moderne Devotie," 170.

called doctrine of subjective atonement, the core of which is, according to Zerbolt, that the Son of God became man primarily to enable man to ascend to a knowledge of the Godhead and to charity. This ascent begins with imitation of the example set by Christ in his humanity, and attention was drawn to the fact that Zerbolt does not really go beyond that point.

In spite of Zerbolt's overriding concern with Christ the man as the example for the Christian to imitate, it cannot be said of him, notwithstanding what some have claimed,[293] that he put so much emphasis on Christ's humanity that Christ's divinity was endangered. For in the first part of this chapter it was found that Zerbolt made considerable efforts to safeguard Christ's dual nature: i.e., his divinity as well as his humanity. One of his reasons for doing so is that Christ's twofold nature plays an important role in his doctrine of subjective atonement, for he holds that only through Christ the God-man can man ascend to a knowledge of the Godhead and to charity, the end of the religious life. And it is in his doctrine of subjective atonement, and in this soteriological theory only, that Zerbolt establishes an organic link between Christ's person and work. Furthermore, Zerbolt's doctrine of subjective atonement is not Abelardian, but it is, in essence at least, as old as Christianity itself, for it was already set forth by the Apostolic Fathers and the Apologists.[294]

Zerbolt clearly regards Christ's passion and death to be the focal, and high, point of his salvific work. This holds true not only for his classic and Anselmian theories of the atonement both of which, by reason of their very nature, put Christ's death centrally, but also for his subjective doctrine of the atonement. It was in his passion and death, then, that Christ performed his greatest exemplary, as well as vicarious, work of salvation. However, one must not overlook the fact that for Zerbolt Christ's entire life was salvific, for all Christ did he did for man's instruction and enlightenment.

Inasmuch as Zerbolt's views regarding man's imitation of Christ have been discussed in conjunction with his doctrine of subjective atonement, it is not out of place to observe here that in van Rooy's view Zerbolt was the first Devotionalist to discuss imitation of Christ in detail,[295] and Zerbolt's earlier biographer would appear to have been correct on this point. Grote, we have seen, was concerned with imitation of Christ's suffering in particular, and less with imitation of Christ in general. Furthermore, he did not, in contrast with Zerbolt, leave us a 'life of Christ', and it is particularly in the account of Christ's life found in *De Reformatione* and *De*

---

[293] R. Garcia-Villoslada, "Devotio Moderna," *NCE*, IV, 831.

[294] See references given in footnote 161 above.

[295] Van Rooy, *Zerbolt*, 256-257.

Ascensionibus that Zerbolt dwells on imitation of him. Radewijns, on the other hand, did include a fairly detailed 'life of Christ' in *Omnes, inquit, artes*, but throughout the biography he says relatively little regarding Christ's role as exemplar and man's imitation of him.[296] One can also agree with van Rooy's assertion that Zerbolt's views regarding the imitation of Christ have a great deal in common with those of the writer of *De Imitatione Christi*.[297] For both authors imitation of Christ helps to lay the foundation on which the spiritual life is built; but how Christ may be imitated in specific, concrete situations for the benefit of one's spiritual well-being and growth receives virtually no attention from them.[298]

It was observed earlier that the salvation brought by Christ consisted, according to Zerbolt, of illumination, justification and glorification. However, in view of the fact that for Zerbolt Christ was above all the teacher and example, it follows that Christ provides man in the first place with the knowledge and enlightenment without which he cannot ascend to God and be united with him. The justification and glorification which Christ has earned vicariously for man by making satisfaction for his sins and by means of his victory over Satan, etc. are no less necessary for man's salvation than is the enlightenment provided by Christ's teaching and exemplary conduct. That Zerbolt's overriding concern is, nonetheless, with the latter is consistent with his understanding of Christianity as an essentially ethical religion. This conception of Christianity as a code of conduct, rather than as a cult, goes hand in hand with a preference for the doctrine of subjective atonement, and both found extensive support in the late middle ages.[299] Their popularity in the fourteenth and fifteenth centuries would seem to have stemmed to a considerable degree from the fact that at that time piety, spirituality and

---

[296] It is only in the "Prologue" to this biography of Christ that Radewijns describes Christ as the exemplar whose virtues man must imitate for his own spiritual improvement (Radewijns, *Omnes, Inquit, Artes*, II, 56, and the passage is borrowed from D. of Augsburg, *De ext. et int. hom. compositione*, I, 21-22).

[297] Van Rooy, *Zerbolt*, 257.

[298] See below, p. 262 f; and cf. Leclercq, Vandenbroucke and Bouyer, *The Spirituality of the Middle Ages*, 437; and A. Rayez, "Humanité du Christ," *DSp*, VII, 1095.

[299] Cf. Seeberg, *Text-Book of the History of Doctrines*, II, 197-198; H. A. Oberman, "'Iustitia Christi' and 'Iustitia Dei': Luther and the Scholastic Doctrines of Justification," *Harvard Theological Review*, LIX (1966), 22; van Woerkum, "Het Libellus 'Omnes, inquit, artes'," 255; McGiffert, *A History of Christian Thought*, II, 229-230; and Slotemaker de Bruine, *Het Ideaal der Navolging van Christus ten Tijde van Bernard van Clairvaux*, 101.

In the thirteenth century the Anselmian doctrine of the atonement gained preeminence over the subjective interpretations (Harnack, *History of Dogma*, VI, 190 and cf. 191), but this preeminence of the objective Anselmian doctrine over the subjective theories of the atonement does not appear to have lasted very long.

theology were dominated by the Franciscan 'school' of thought,[300] although it ought to be added that Franciscan spirituality owed a great deal to Bernard of Clairvaux.[301] However, that Zerbolt favoured the theory of subjective atonement must not be attributed solely to the strength and influence of Franciscan thought in the later middle ages. For the theory of subjective atonement was the dominant interpretation of Christ's salvific work not only in the *Sermones Super Cantica Canticorum* of St. Bernard,[302] in *De Triplici Via* and *Lignum Vitae* of the Franciscan Bonaventure,[303] as well as in *De exterioris et interioris hominis compositione* of the Franciscan David of Augsburg,[304] but also in the *Conferences* and *In-*

---

[300] Oberman, "The Shape of Late Medieval Thought: The Birthpangs of the Modern Era," 7.

[301] Seeberg, *Text-Book of the History of Doctrines*, II, 72-73 and Mikkers, "Bernardus en de Moderne Devotie," 170.

[302] Seeberg, *Text-Book of the History of Doctrines*, II, 72-73; McGiffert, *A History of Christian Thought*, II, 229-230; Harnack, *History of Dogma*, VI, 9-14; and Mikkers, "Bernardus en de Moderne Devotie," 170.

We have seen that according to Bernard's *Sermons on the Song of Songs*, XX, 6-9, Christ became man in order that through him man might ascend to a knowledge of God and love for him. Not only in this particular sermon, but in Bernard's works generally, Zerbolt could find an emphasis on Christ's exemplary humility and lowliness which the believer must imitate, as well as an emphasis on Christ's suffering which the believer must imitate and share. The need to imitate Christ in his suffering focuses upon the passion, and from about the time of St. Bernard onwards there was an ever-increasing tendency to extol the exemplary conduct of Christ during his passion, and to give it more attention than Christ's conduct up to that time.

Cf. *The Golden Epistle of Abbot William of St. Thierry*, 76 and 77-78.

[303] Cf. Pourrat, *La Spiritualité Chrétienne*, II: *Le Moyen Age*, 275-277; I. C. Brady, "St. Bonaventure," *NCE*, II, 661-664; and E. Longpré, "Bonaventure," *DSp*, I, 1806-1809.

[304] D. of Augsburg, *De ext. et int. hom. compositione*, I, 21-23. Cf. A. Rayez, "David d'Augsbourg," *DSp*, II, 42-44.

It is David of Augsburg in particular who holds Christ up as the perfect model and example of all virtues, and he does this in *De ext. et int. hom. compositione*, one of Zerbolt's favourite works as we have seen above, pp. 23-26, more so than anywhere else.

Additional works unquestionably known to Zerbolt, and perhaps used by him, which also emphasize Christ's didactic and exemplary work at the expense of his vicarious work are:

a) Pseudo-Bonaventura's *Meditationes Vitae Christi* now commonly attributed to John de Caulibus. See Pourrat, *La Spiritualité Chrétienne*, II: *Le Moyen Age*, 278-283; and M. Grabmann, *Die Geschichte der Katholischen Theologie Seit demAusgang der Väterzeit* (Freiburg im Breisgau, 1933), 126 and 131.

b) Ludolph of Saxony's *Vita Iesu Christi*. See Pourrat, *La Spiritualité Chrétienne*, II: *Le Moyen Age*, 485-488.

In his account of Christ's life in *Omnes, inquit, artes*, Radewijns makes use of the two works just listed, and they must be counted among the favourite works of the Devotionalists in general. Cf. de Bruin, "Het Bonaventura-Ludolphiaanse Leven van Jezus," 115-117.

c) Suso's *Horologium Sapientiae* and *One-Hundred Articles*. Cf. Meyboom, ed., "De hondert Artikelen," 173-207; and de Man, "Heinrich Suso en de Moderne Devoten," 279-283.

It would appear that Zerbolt made use of the *Horologium* in at least one instance (see footnote 138 above). The *Horologium* is a Latin translation of the *Little Book of Eternal Wisdom*, originally written in German. Suso himself was the translator, and he introduced some changes in the translation.

stitutes of John Cassian[305] and in John Climacus' *Scala Paradisi*.[306] Furthermore, the doctrine of subjective atonement figures prominently in the soteriological thought of Augustine and Gregory the Great,[307] and the writings of Augustine and Gregory the Great were, together with the writings of Cassian, Climacus, St. Bernard, Bonaventure and David of Augsburg just mentioned, Zerbolt's most important sources. Zerbolt's preference for these works is explained by the fact that, save for those by Augustine and Gregory the Great, they, like Zerbolt himself, portray Christianity as being a code of conduct first and foremost, and consequently they invariably concentrate on Christ's didactic, exemplary and inspirational work while they pay relatively little attention to the other aspects of his salvific work.[308] Clearly, Zerbolt allowed himself to be guided by a specific genre of religious literature rather than by some select authors, and this was to be a trait of the Devotionalists in general.[309]

In holding such views of Christ's work and the purpose of the incarnation as he did, it may be assumed that Zerbolt was also influenced by Grote, Radewijns and Brinckerinck. The first two, we saw earlier, regarded Christ primarily as the teacher and example for the Christian to follow and to imitate,[310] while Brinckerinck may have regarded Christ

d) Jordan of Quedlinburg, *Meditationes de passione Christi*. There are indications that Zerbolt borrowed from this work as well (see footnote 226 above).

[305] Munz, "John Cassian," 2 and 14-19; M. Olphe-Galliard, "Jean Cassien," *DSp*, II, 228 (cf. 233 and 235); and L. Cristiani, *Jean Cassien* (2 vols.; Abbaye Saint Wandrille, 1946), I, 141 and II, 204, 233-239.

To Cassian, who was greatly influenced by Origen, "Christianity was an educational ideal—not the forgiveness of sins through Christ's Passion" (Munz, *op. cit.*, 16). However, it would appear that Cassian did not altogether deny the objective value of Christ's death.

[306] Cursory reading of the *Scala Paradisi* reveals that Climacus frequently holds Christ up as the example to be imitated (St. John Climacus, *The Ladder of Divine Ascent*, trans. by Archimandrite Lazarus Moore [London, 1959], 50, 57, 73, 95, 109, 187, 189, 197 and 247), and that for him Christ's vicarious atonement is of relatively little importance (*ibid.*, 90).

[307] For some interpretations of Augustine's soteriology see Kelly, *Early Christian Doctrines*, 393 and also 390-395; McGiffert, *A History of Christian Thought*, II, 105-106; Seeberg, *Text-Book of the History of Doctrines*, I, 360-361; and Harnack, *History of Dogma*, VI, 191. For Gregory the Great see Dudden, *Gregory the Great*, II, 336-337; Seeberg, *Text-Book of the History of Doctrines*, II, 20-21; McGiffert, *A History of Christian Thought*, II, 153-155. Gregory's works may also have been a source for Zerbolt's classic theory of the atonement, because Gregory understands Christ's salvific work above all in terms of Christ's victory over Satan and all forces of evil.

[308] Cf. Peterman, "Redemption," *NCE*, XII, 149.

[309] Post, *De Moderne Devotie*, 138-141.

[310] See Grote's letter *"De paciencia,"* ed. by Mulder, *Gerardi Magni Epistolae*, 232-243; and Radewijns, *Omnes, Inquit, Artes*, II, 56. Cf. Huyben en Debongnie, "Geert Groote's Brief over de Navolging van Christus," 269-278; Goossens, *Meditatie*, 156 and 191-192; de Beer, *Spiritualiteit*, 85-87, 96-98, 294-295; Gall, "De Christus-gedachte by Geert Groote," 229-240; Epiney-Burgard, *Grote*, 276-277; van Zijl, *Groote*, 87-92, 112-116, 163-165 and 317-318; and van Woerkum, "Het Libellus *'Omnes, inquit, artes'*," 255.

exclusively as the model for all Christians to imitate in their quest for spiritual perfection.[311] With these three men Zerbolt largely determined the direction which Devotionalist spirituality and thought was to take. It is, therefore, not surprising that the movement, taken as a whole, expressed views similar to theirs regarding Christ's work and the purpose of the incarnation,[312] and it continued to do so throughout its entire pre-Reformation history. Illustrative of the continued importance attributed by the Devotionalists to Christ's didactic and exemplary work is Claus of Euskirchen's (d. 1520) statement that if man had stood in need of vicarious redemption only, then there is no reason why Christ could not have come to earth a full-grown man, and have allowed himself to be crucified the very next day.[313] Finally, Mak is of the opinion that for the Devotionalists Christ is more important as the teacher and example of virtues who must be imitated than as the man of sorrows whose sufferings the believer must share.[314] If this be true, then with respect to this particular question the Devotionalist movement stood closer to Radewijns and to Zerbolt than to Grote.

---

[311] Mak, "Christus bij de Moderne Devoten," 119.

[312] *Ibid.*, 105-166.

[313] D. A. Brinkerink, ed., "Dit sijn goede punten, vergadert uytten collatiën ons eersamen paters here Claus van Euskerken," *NAKG*, N.S., III (1905), 364: Hadde wi allene verloesinge behoeft, soe mochte hij wel een groet man gecomen hebben ende hebben hem voert des anderen dages laten crucen.

Claus of Euskirchen (from Euskirchen in the German Rhineland) was a member of Master Florens' House and a priest of Master Gerard's House.

[314] Mak, "Christus bij de Moderne Devoten," 125.

CHAPTER FOUR

THE PROCESS OF JUSTIFICATION

Discussion in the previous chapter of Christ's vicarious death on the cross leads naturally to the question how man is made a participant in that death through which he is saved from eternal damnation. According to the theologians of the twelfth and thirteenth centuries, who were the first to develop a coherent and satisfactory sacramental theology, the benefits of Christ's vicarious death are transmitted to the believer chiefly by way of the sacraments. They elaborated that for his justification, the prerequisite for his sanctification and salvation, man is particularly dependent upon the sacraments of baptism and penance, and much more so upon the latter than upon the former. It is through baptism that man is first justified, for baptism removes the guilt attached to original sin, but its punishment, namely rebellious concupiscence, remains, as a consequence of which he frequently commits personal sins. If such sins are mortal, the believer falls from the state of grace, and it is only by means of the sacrament of penance that he can recover justifying grace, for the sacrament of baptism cannot be repeated.[1] Consequently, the sacrament of penance came to play a much greater role in the doctrine of justification than did the sacrament of baptism,[2] and Zerbolt likewise describes the process of justification in the context of the sacrament of penance rather than within the framework of the sacrament of baptism. However, man's quest for justification through the sacraments presupposes faith: i.e., faith in, and acceptance of, God's revelation which informs man that he is sinful and, therefore, damned, but which tells him as well how he may be saved.[3] Zerbolt's understanding of faith is, then, the logical point from which to launch our investigation into his doctrine of justification.

---

[1] Bonaventure, *Lignum Vitae*, ch. 28 (*Works*, I, 128); *idem*, *Breviloquium*, Pt. VI, chs. 2 and 5 (*Works*, II, 229 and 238-239); Thomas Aquinas, *Summa Contra Gentiles*, Bk. IV, ch. 56; and Thomas Aquinas, ST, 3a, 60-65 and 3a, 84, 7. Cf. Harnack, *History of Dogma*, VI, 200-219; McGiffert, *A History of Christian Thought*, II, 313-318; J. R. Quinn, "Sacraments, Theology of," *NCE*, XII, 806-812; and Rahner and Vorgrimler, *Theological Dictionary*, 415-416 ("Sacrament") and 481 ("Vienne").

[2] Cf. Steinmetz, *Staupitz*, 97.

[3] Cf. Rahner and Vorgrimler, *Theological Dictionary*, 310 ("Necessity for Salvation"); and P. K. Meagher, "Faith (Theology of)," *NCE*, V, 798-804; and *The Teaching of the Catholic Church as Contained in Her Documents*, originally prepared by J. Neuner and H. Roos, ed. by K. Rahner, and trans. by G. Stevens (Staten Island, N.Y., 1967), 19-20.

A) *Faith*

Zerbolt's writings, like Grote's[4] say relatively little on the topic faith, but it is possible, nonetheless, to extract from them a rudimentary outline of his views on this subject. The common practice of distinguishing between *fides qua creditur* and *fides quae creditur* is found in Zerbolt's writings, although he himself speaks simply of the "*habitus fidei*" and the "*articuli fidei*" respectively,[5] and we will look at these separately, beginning with the latter.

i. *Fides quae creditur*

The analysis of Zerbolt's epistemology has shown that, on the authority of the *doctores*, he divides all knowledge into two categories: a) that which can be known naturally; b) and that which lies beyond the grasp of man's purely natural intellectual capacities and cannot be arrived at by rational means, such as the articles of faith.[6] This second class of knowledge is, of course, identical with the *fides quae creditur*. Since the articles of faith, and revelation in general, transcend natural reason and man's natural faculty of understanding, it follows that with respect to them man is faced with an epistemological dilemma: how does he know that they are true? Zerbolt proceeds to deal with this problem in a very traditional way. He starts with the premise that revelation, including the articles of faith, is God's own word, and that God, who is Truth,[7] cannot deceive or testify falsely.[8] The veracity of revelation, he continues, is further substantiated by God himself through miracles which only his divine

---

[4] See Epiney-Burgard, *Grote*, 129.

[5] *De Vestibus Pretiosis*, 45, and *Scriptum Pro Quodam*, 231-232. Cf. F. L. Cross, ed., *The Oxford Dictionary of the Christian Church* (2d ed.; London-New York-Toronto, 1974), 499-500 ("Faith"); Oberman, *Biel*, 69; and Steinmetz, *Staupitz*, 116-117.

[6] *Scriptum Pro Quodam*, 231-232: Est enim secundum doctores duplex doctrina: una, que facultatem mentis humane non transcendit et hec docetur per raciones demonstrativas et principia naturaliter cognita. Quare ut quis sit huius doctrine doctor ydoneus, necesse est, ut habeat scienciam demonstrandi. Alia est doctrina, que excedit facultatem humanam et que non potest per principia naturalia demonstrari, sicut articuli fidei... See above, pp. 40-41.

[7] *Asc.*, 269F: O aeterna veritas,..., tu es Deus meus,... It was generally held that it can be known naturally that God is "Truth," and that for that knowledge man is not dependent upon revelation. Cf. Gilson, *History of Christian Philosophy in the Middle Ages*, 72 and 372; Copleston, *A History of Philosophy*, Vol. II, Pt. I, 78, 86-87, 185-186, 217 and 285-287.

[8] See footnote 9 below. Cf. Bonaventure, *Breviloquium*, Pt. V, ch. 7 (*Works*, II, 207-210); Thomas Aquinas, *Summa Contra Gentiles*, Bk. I, chs. 7 and 8, Bk. III, chs. 40 and 152; and Steinmetz, *Staupitz*, 117.

THE PROCESS OF JUSTIFICATION

power is capable of performing;[9] and the theory that revelation, the truth of which cannot be demonstrated by natural means, must be authenticated by divine miracles if man is to be expected to give his assent to it, is one which was widely upheld in the middle ages.[10] Influenced by Augustine, Zerbolt also makes the observation that the apostles, because of their simplicity and lack of formal education, were particularly suited to proclaim a doctrine which lies beyond the grasp of man's purely natural intellectual capacities. For it was not eloquence and learning which persuaded the world to accept the doctrine preached by the apostles; rather, it was the miracles performed by God through the apostles, authenticating this new doctrine, which convinced the world regarding its veracity.[11] The *fides quae creditur* is, then, a body of extrarational knowledge, and it is accepted on the authority of a creditable witness rather than as a consequence of a rational demonstration or proof. The credibility of the *fides quae creditur* does not stem from any inherent quality but leans on a superior, trustworthy authority.[12] Having looked at Zerbolt's understanding of the nature of revealed, extrarational knowledge, it is necessary to look at what he writes regarding the contents of the *fides quae creditur*.

In an earlier chapter it was established that, according to Zerbolt, man's natural, inborn knowledge of good and evil was partly obscured

---

[9] *Scriptum Pro Quodam*, 232: ..., cum Deus non possit esse testis falsitatis, necesse fuit per confirmacionem talis doctrine inducere opera miraculosa, que a sola virtute divina fieri possunt.
The nature of miracles, as understood by Zerbolt, has been discussed before. Therefore, only their purpose is discussed here.

[10] Thomas Aquinas, *Summa Contra Gentiles*, Bk. I, ch. 6; Dempsey Douglas, *Geiler*, 55; Richardson, ed., *Dictionary*, 216-217 ("Miracle"); J. G. Pater, "Miracles (Theology of)," *NCE*, IV, 891; McGiffert, *A History of Christian Thought*, II, 120 and 272; and Rahner and Vorgrimler, *Theological Dictionary*, 287-289 ("Miracle").

[11] *Scriptum Pro Quodam*, 232: Apostoli autem assumpti erant ad predicandum doctrinam, facultatem humanam execendentem, quam non confirmasset scienciam acquisita: ymmo si bene respiciatur inydoneitas maxime ista simplicitatis [sic] fecit apostolos ydonea et aptissima instrumenta. Et est maxime argumentum fidei christiane, secundum Augustinum; aut enim apostoli mundum converterunt per miracula sermonem confirmantes signis et prodigiis, ut dicitur Marci ultimo et eciam doctrina eorum falsa esse non potest, ad cuius probacionem Deus qui mentiri non potest, signa adhibuit miraculosa. Si autem fecerunt sine miraculis, hoc esset miraculum quod tot sapientes, tot prudentes, tot philosophi, tot principes, tot potentes nudis verbis simplicium crediderunt in tam ardua doctrina, omnem humanam intellectum transcendente.
Although Zerbolt does not accurately identify the passage from the writings of St. Augustine, it is virtually certain that he obtained it from *De Civitate Dei*, Bk. XXII, ch. 5. Cf. *The Golden Epistle of Abbot William of St. Thierry*, 60.

[12] Cf. Bonaventure, *Breviloquium*, Prologue, ch. 5 (On how Holy Scripture proceeds) and Pt. V, ch. 7 (*Works*, II, 17 and 207-210); Thomas Aquinas, *Summa Contra Gentiles*, Bk. III, chs. 40 and 152; D. of Augsburg, *De ext. et int. hom. compositione*, II, 14; Steinmetz, *Staupitz*, 117; Dempsey Douglas, *Geiler*, 53; and Oberman, *Biel*, 68-82.

and diminished as a result of Adam's disobedience in paradise. Influenced by John Chrysostom and Augustine, Zerbolt writes that, in order to remedy this defective innate knowledge of natural law, God gave man the Scriptures. The Scriptures serve as an aid, addition and extension to man's imperfect knowledge of natural law, greatly adding to his knowledge of that law and consequently to his ability to discern the good and to avoid evil.[13] In view of the fact that Zerbolt regards the Scriptures as a means to correct man's weakened and faulty knowledge of natural law, it follows that for him there is no disparity between the two, but rather a continuity. To postulate such a continuity between natural law, which is known innately, and divine law, which is revealed in the Scriptures in order to remedy man's defective native knowledge of natural law, was traditional among the members of the *via antiqua*. The *moderni*, on the other hand, have frequently been charged with the destruction of the organic unity between natural and divinely revealed law. That they actually did so has recently been disputed.[14]

Influenced by St. Paul, Zerbolt continues that before man was in possession of the Scriptures his knowledge of natural law was so faulty that at that time he was altogether unaware of any trespasses committed against it. Consequently he had no way of knowing what constituted sin, and for that reason he was not held accountable for sins committed before he was in possession of the Scriptures, nor were these sins imputed to him.[15] However, having been instructed by the Scriptures regarding God's law, and thus having had his faulty knowledge of natural law corrected, man learned about his sinful, and therefore condemned, state.[16] Having learned that he is sinful, it was then possible for man to experience compunction for sins committed, and to refrain from commit-

---

[13] *De Libris Teutonicalibus*, 52; Sacra scriptura data est homini a Deo in adiutorium et adminiculum legis naturalis, ut videlicet, quod homo per legem naturalem iam obfuscatam seu minus illuminatam interius videre non potuit, divina scriptura foris adiutus disceret et videret, ut discerneret bonum et ipsum apprehenderet, et malum ut vitaret. Sicut pulchre declarat beatus Iohannes Crisostomus in prohemio "Operis Perfecti" super Matheum. Et sanctus Augustinus ostendit supra psalmum LVII.

The "*Operis Perfecti*" *super Matheum* is, most likely, Chrysostom's *Homiliae in Matthaeum*, rather than pseudo-Chrysostom's *Opus imperfectum in Matthaeum*, the work of a fifth-century Arian. Grote owned a copy of the former, although the latter was not unknown to the early Devotionalists (Mulder, ed., *Gerardi Magni Epistolae*, 15 and 77).

The *supra psalmum LVII* points to Augustine's widely read *Enarrationes in Psalmos*.

[14] Oberman, *Biel*, 90-119 and Dempsey Douglass, *Geiler*, 48-57 and 69.

[15] *De Libris Teutonicalibus*, 52: Unde propter hoc dicit apostolus ad Romanos V. capitulo: "Peccatum non imputabatur, cum non esset," id est, non reputabatur. Cum enim lex divina nondum erat data nec scriptura divina divinitus promulgata, peccatum non imputabatur seu reputabatur, quia propter obfuscacionem legis naturalis homines peccatum non curabant, et peccatum esse peccatum non reputabant. Cf. Romans 5, 13.

[16] *De Libris Teutonicalibus*, 59: Unde dicit apostolus: "Per legem autem cognovi peccatum." Cf. Romans, 7, 7.

ting more sins. For that reason, Zerbolt concludes, it is essential that all people, including laymen, read the Scriptures.[17] For he is of the opinion that laymen in particular have lost the natural ability to distinguish between good and evil, and he attributes this to the fact that they are daily immersed in secular activities. Therefore, he writes in *De Libris Teutonicalibus*, it is of the greatest importance that laymen read the Scriptures and devotional books in order that their particularly defective natural knowledge concerning good and evil may be rectified.[18] In fact, Zerbolt continues, the study of God's law as it is found in the Scriptures is commanded many times in the Old Testament, and even more frequently in the New Testament. Nowhere, he points out, does it say there that only the clergy have an obligation to read the Scriptures and that the laity is exempted from doing so.[19] That everyone must read the Bible is confirmed by the doctors of theology and jurists, he adds, for they maintain that laymen too are under obligation to know exactly what is prescribed and proscribed in the divine law as it is revealed by God in the Scriptures.[20] For it is only through revealed law, which comes to the aid of man's defective natural ability to distinguish between good and evil, that man can learn that he is sinful and stands condemned; and that he, therefore, stands in need of salvation. Zerbolt concludes that, in order for

---

[17] *De Libris Teutonicalibus*, 48: Quis igitur sane mentis dicat quod layci peccant, si ad hoc divina utantur scriptura, propter quod a Deo ipsis est data, et a spiritu sancto conscripta? ut videlicet peccata sua cognoscant, et de eis compungantur ut melius ea possent devitare? See *Super Modo Vivendi*, 58, as well. Cf. Dempsey Douglass, *Geiler*, 49.

[18] *De Libris Teutonicalibus*, 52: Cum enim layci continue occupentur negociis secularibus et sollicitudinibus et occupacionibus terrenis, quibus oculus eorum interior, sindieresis et racio, sive lex naturalis tamquam pulveribus obfuscatur, non utique videtur esse illicitum, ymmo vero valde necessarium quod huiusmodi adminiculo devotorum librorum per illustracionem et adiutorio legis naturalis utantur et ceteris temporibus ad se redeuntes de occupacionibus, legant, et in quibus excesserunt in speculo scripturarum videant. Cf. *ibid.*, 59: Ymmo legere divinam scripturam et scire eam est precipuum instrumentum ut homo possit fieri bonus et vitare malum.

[19] *De Libris Teutonicalibus*, 48-49: Sciencia legis...instanter adhortatur. *Super Modo Vivendi*, 63-64: Item sicut dicit Thomas "Secunda Secunde," qu. XVII, art. I: Sciencia legis divine magis precipitur in Novo Testamento quam in Veteri Testamento. Sed in Veteri Testamento multa vel precepta dabantur exhortaciones populo de lectione et studio scripturarum, ut patet Deut. VI°, et Deut. XI°, et in multis aliis locis. Unde dicitur Deut. XI: "Ponite hec verba in cordibus vestris et suspendite ea pro signis in manibus vestris et inter oculos vestros collocate. Docete filios vestros ut illa meditentur, quando sederis in domo tua et ambulaveris in via et accubueris atque surrexeris, scribesque ea super postes et ianuas domus tue, ut multiplicentur anni tui et filiorum tuorum." [Deut. 11, 18-21.] Idem pene habetur Deut. VI°. Hec autem non loquitur clericis solum, sicut planum est et sicut dicit Thomas ubi supra. Ex quibus omnibus et multis aliis, que poni possent, satis patet quod non est prohibitum laycis sacram scripturam legere, eo quod laycis non conveniat vel prohibitum sit studium scripturarum.

[20] *De Libris Teutonicalibus*, 53: Layci tenentur scire ea que expresse omnibus in divina lege precipiuntur vel expresse prohibentur, secundum doctores theologie, et eciam secundum iuristas.

man to be apprised of his sinfulness, knowledge of the decalogue and the seven deadly sins is a minimal requirement, and that cognizance of these will make it impossible to plead ignorance.[21] Here the influence on Zerbolt of contemporary catechetical literature is quite obvious, for the catechetical manuals invariably contained the ten commandments and a summary of the seven deadly sins, confronting the reader with his sinful and condemned state.[22]

It is particularly in *De Libris Teutonicalibus*, then, that Zerbolt portrays the Scriptures, the object of the act of faith, as an aid to man's natural understanding of good and evil, and as a mirror which reflects his depravity. That man is sinful, on account of which he merits eternal damnation, is, of course, only the negative aspect of the divinely revealed plan of salvation advanced in the Scriptures. For the Scriptures not only inform man that he must be saved, but they tell him as well how he may be saved, Zerbolt elaborates in *De Ascensionibus*. In fact, everything contained in the Scriptures deals either directly or indirectly with man's salvation,[23] and, more specifically, they deal exclusively with two matters: namely with God's wrath and eternal punishment of man's sins, and with God's mercy which underlies the divine salvific plan designed to save man from eternal damnation.[24] Confrontation, through the Bible, with God's wrath and mercy *vis-à-vis* fallen man will instil in him a salutary balance between compunction of fear and compunction of hope without which he cannot progress in the spiritual life.[25] Consequently, Zerbolt draws the conclusion, in *De Ascensionibus*, that everything contained in the Scriptures refers to man's salvation.

---

[21] *De Libris Teutonicalibus*, 53-54: Unde tenetur ad minus scire decem precepta, et septem peccata mortalia in genere, que expresse in lege divina ponuntur prohibita, ita quod in talibus nemo ex ignorancia poterit excusari, ... Zerbolt then quotes a few writers to support his statement: apostolum ad Corinthios; Cesarius episcopus in admonicionibus suis; beatum Ieronymum in epistola ad Paulinum; beatus Gregorius in prohemio "Moralium".

[22] Post, *Kerkgeschiedenis*, II, 224-226 and 312; Moll, *Kerkgeschiedenis van Nederland voor de Hervorming*, Vol. II, Pt. III, 11-21.

[23] *Asc.*, 269F-G: Circa opus nostrae redemptionis versatur materia totius divinae scripturae, et omnia in scriptura ad ipsum referuntur.

The Scriptures, according to David of Augsburg, "adequately and truthfully set out all that is necessary for our salvation" (*De ext. et int. hom. compositione*, I, 85).

[24] *Asc.*, 285F: Ad hos duos ascensus et descensus, omnia quae in scripturis sunt, referuntur, secundum Augustinum: ut videlicet misericordiam ames, timeas potestatem. Unde Propheta sanctus in divina locutione, haec duo se narrat solummodo audivisse: Semel, inquit, locutus est Deus duo haec audivi, quia tibi Domine est misericordia, et tu reddis unicuique iuxta opera sua; propter haec duo, Prophetae, propter haec duo omnes sunt scripturae. Cf. above, pp. 51-55.

[25] *Asc.*, ch. 65 (pp. 285C-G). The role played by fear and hope in man's spiritual ascent will be discussed in more detail below.

In *De Reformatione*, on the other hand, he throws a somewhat different light on what is contained in the Scriptures, although his comments in his two manuals regarding the contents of the Bible are not contradictory. Quoting from the third book of Augustine's *De Doctrina Christiana*, Zerbolt writes in *De Reformatione* that everything contained in the sacred Scriptures serves, on the one hand, to feed and to strengthen love, and, on the other hand, to overcome cupidity and lust.[26] In other words, then, Zerbolt holds that the total contents of the Scriptures serve the aim and purpose of the spiritual life, namely charity which is founded upon a pure heart from which all sin has been purged.[27] For contemplation of God's mercy revealed in the Scriptures increases man's love for him, while reflection on God's wrath and punishment of sinful man instils fear which induces the believer to overcome cupidity and lust.[28] In his two manuals, then, Zerbolt presents a harmonious view with respect to the contents of the Scriptures, as well as with respect to their purpose.

Finally, a few words about Zerbolt's views regarding the relationship between the Old and New Testaments. When he asserts that the total contents of the Scriptures deal with man's redemption, he goes on to explain that the Old Testament foretells that, and how, this salvation is to come, while the New Testament shows that, and the manner in which, it is wholly accomplished and fulfilled.[29] For Zerbolt, then, the Old and New Testaments are clearly in agreement with one another and form an authentic unity. He does not, however, gloss over the difference between them, but detects a progression in their contents. Zerbolt's views regarding the harmony and uniformity between the Old and New Testaments were, of course, in no way unique. Similar views had been asserted many times throughout the history of Christian thought,[30] and they can also be

---

[26] *Ref.*, 238D: ..., dicit Augustinus in tertio libro de doctrina Christiana: Omnia in sacra scriptura valent ad charitatem nutriendam et corroborandam, et cupiditatem vincendam.

Zerbolt does not identify his source more accurately than this, but it is virtually certain that he is quoting, perhaps from memory, from Bk. III, ch. 10: "But Scripture teaches nothing but charity, nor condemns anything except cupidity, and in this way shapes the minds of men" (Saint Augustine, *On Christian Doctrine*, trans. by D. W. Robertson [Indianapolis-New York, 1958], 88). Cf. *De Doctrina Christiana*, Bk. I, ch. 35 and Bk. II, ch. 7.

[27] *Ref.*, 238D: Et secundum Apostolum: Finis praecepti est charitas, de corde puro, etc. The text quoted here by Zerbolt is I Timothy 1, 5.

[28] Cf. Augustine, *De Doctrina Christiana*, Bk. II, ch. 7, and Bk. III, ch. 11.

[29] *Asc.*, 269F-G: Circa opus nostrae redemptionis versatur materia totius divinae scripturae, et omnia in scriptura ad ipsum referuntur. Ipsum futurum, testamentum vetus pronunciat, ipsum factum et impletum, novum clarius demonstrat.

[30] Henri de Lubac, *Exégèse Médiévale. Les Quatre Sens de L'Ecriture* (2 vols.; études publiées sous la direction de la faculté de théologie S. J. de Lyon-Fourvière, 1959), Vol. I, Pt. I, pp. 328-355.

found in the writings of Grote,[31] the founder of the Devotionalist movement.

ii. *Fides qua creditur*

Regardless of the fact that God is Truth and that he vouches for the truth of revelation through miracles which only he can perform, the *fides quae creditur* remains beyond the grasp of man's natural understanding, and its acceptance remains an act of faith regarding which Zerbolt makes a number of observations. Nevertheless, like most other spiritual writers he would appear to be more interested in the object, than in the act, of faith.[32]

The theological virtue of faith, Zerbolt writes, is an infused habit of the mind.[33] Thereby he testifies to its supernatural nature and implicitly denies that man can acquire it by means of his own efforts, unassisted by divine grace.[34] Furthermore, the description of faith as a divinely infused habit places Zerbolt solidly within the mainstream of the Christian tradition. Augustine strongly emphasized that faith is a gift of grace, and the Augustinian doctrine regarding the divinely infused nature of the act of faith was almost universally accepted in the middle ages,[35] as it was by Grote.[36] Only among the exponents of the *via moderna* was there a tendency to reject the teaching that faith is an infused habit,[37] and this tendency is clearly evident in the writings of Gabriel Biel, the leading fifteenth-century theologian of the *via moderna*. He was afraid that, if faith were

---

[31] G. Grote, *Tractatulus de quatuor generibus meditationum*, *AGAU*, XLIX (1924), 306 and 308. Cf. Goossens, *Meditatie*, 177.

According to Albert Paep of Calcar, rector of the Brethren House at Zwolle from 1457 to 1482, everything found in the N.T. is prefigured in the O.T. The N.T. resolves all the obscurities of the O.T., and fulfils all that has been foretold there. (Jacobus de Voecht, *Narratio*, 144. Also see footnote 46 below.)

[32] Cf. A. R. Jonsen, "Faith (Patristic Tradition and Teaching of the Church)," *NCE*, V, 796-798. Cf. J. Alfaro, "Faith (Faith as a gift of God)," *SM*, II, 317; and Dempsey Douglass, *Geiler*, 45-69, 91, 117 and 148.

[33] *De Vestibus Pretiosis*, 45: Sic fides prout virtus theologycalis est habitus menti infusus circa actus cum exteriores exercetur [exercentur] scilicet per confessionem, oracionem etc. For the argument leading up to this statement see p. 45.

[34] Cf. Richardson, ed., *Dictionary*, 169-170 ("Infusion"); Rahner and Vorgrimler, *Theological Dictionary*, 169 ("Faith"); P. K. Meagher, "Faith (Theology of)," *NCE*, V, 798-804; and Harvey, *A Handbook of Theological Terms*, 98 ("Faith, Infused").

[35] Augustine, *The Enchiridion on Faith, Hope and Love*, ch. 31. Cf. Thomas Aquinas, *ST*, 1a 2ae, 62, 113 and 2a 2ae, 1-16; *idem*, *Summa Contra Gentiles*, Bk. I, ch. 6 and Bk. III, chs. 40 and 152.

[36] De Beer, *Spiritualiteit*, 147. Cf. D. of Augsburg, *De ext. et int. hom. compositione*, I, 111.

[37] In patristic times the Pelagians and semi-Pelagians had, of course, also denied that the act of faith is a gift of grace (P. K. Meagher, "Faith [Theology of]," *NCE*, V, 798-804).

treated as a gift of grace, the independence and the freedom of the human will would be in jeopardy.[38]

Aquinas gave voice to the commonly held view that, although the intellect plays a role in it, the act of faith is primarily an act of the will.[39] That faith is primarily an act of the will Zerbolt does not assert in so many words, but a number of times he draws attention to the role played by man's will in his spiritual ascent taken as a whole. The point Zerbolt is particularly anxious to make is that man's will must be informed by divine grace if he is to make a beginning with the spiritual life and if he is to bring it to a successful conclusion,[40] which, of course, reinforces his assertion that the act of faith is an infused habit. If Zerbolt regards the entire spiritual ascent as an act of the will informed by grace, it automatically follows that he looks upon faith as being primarily an act of the will as well. However, that does not mean that Zerbolt was simply a fideist: i.e., that he saw the act of faith as being solely an act of the will in which the intellect plays no role. For we have seen that, according to him, it can be known naturally that God is Truth, that he cannot deceive, and that only he can perform miracles by means of which he vouches for the veracity of revelation. Consequently, it follows that in the act of faith the will is moved at least partially by the intellect.[41]

Finally, Zerbolt makes faith the basis and beginning of human salvation. It has been noted a few times that, in Zerbolt's view, the believer can progress in the spiritual life only when he is being propelled by the sentiments of fear and hope.[42] Through fear the heart is purged and purified of sin and vice, and only then can man attain to charity which is the end of the spiritual life.[43] However, fear itself, Zerbolt explains, is the

---

[38] Oberman, *Biel*, 71-74.

[39] Thomas Aquinas, *Summa Contra Gentiles*, Bk. III, ch. 40. Cf. P. K. Meagher, "Faith (Theology of)," *NCE*, V, 798-804; and L. Bouyer, *Dictionary of Theology*, 158-159 ("Faith").

[40] *Ref.*, 245G: Dedit dona gratiae. Primo quod voluntatem tuam ab eo aversam ad se revocavit,... Dedit voluntatem ut te velles emendare,... *Ref.*, 257D: Qui autem huius nequissimi spiritus laqueos vult evadere, debet in singulis virtutibus, in quibus se senserit profecisse dicere ex sententia: Gratia Dei sum id quod sum, et cogitare Deum esse qui operatur in nobis velle et perficere, pro bona voluntate. (The texts from the Bible quoted here are 1 Cor. 15, 10 and Phil. 2, 13.)
The same two passages are found in *De Ascensionibus*, 267F and 284G-H respectively. Cf. Augustine, *The Enchiridion on Faith, Hope and Love*, ch. 32, and below, pp. 195-198.

[41] Cf. Thomas Aquinas, *Summa Contra Gentiles*, Bk. III, ch. 40; Oberman, *Biel*, 68-69; and P. K. Meagher, "Faith (Theology of)," *NCE*, V, 798-804.

[42] See below, p. 250, where this issue will be discussed in detail.

[43] *Asc.*, 266C: Ergo ab timore Domini secundum prophetam [Ps. 111, 10 (AV)] debemus parturire spiritum salutis. Est enim initium sapientiae timor Domini, et in ipso debemus nos studiose exercere, et cor nostrum purgare, ut ad charitatem possimus pervenire. Unde sapiens: initiandi sunt ab timore, ut ad charitatem perveniant. *Asc.*, 276A: Nam lectio secundum Hugonem ad incipientes pertinet, qui utique in primo gradu ab timore concipiunt, et parturiunt spiritum salutis. (See Hugh of St. Victor, *Eruditio didascalia*, *PL*, CLXXVI, 797.)

result of faith, and it is, in fact, its first effect.[44] For that reason, he continues, it is fitting that in the Scriptures faith and purity of heart should be mentioned together, and that Saint Peter should affirm that through faith the heart is purified;[45] because it is through fear, the first fruit of faith, that the heart is purged of all sins. Faith, then, because it leads to fear of eternal judgement and punishment, induces man to combat vice and sin, the prerequisite for charity.[46] Consequently it may be concluded that, because Zerbolt calls fear the first fruit of faith, he in effect makes faith the foundation of man's salvation.[47] For fear, the first effect of faith, purges the heart of vice and sin, and it is from a pure heart that the believer ascends to charity and hence to salvation. Clearly, in Zerbolt's understanding of the act of faith as the beginning of salvation there is nothing which points to the definition of faith which was to be espoused by the Protestants.[48]

B) *The Sacraments*

The theologians of the high middle ages were the first to formulate a detailed, and comprehensive, sacramental theology, and some of the questions they had to answer pertained to the number of sacraments,

---

[44] *Asc.*, 266C: ..., eo quod timor qui est in primis effectus fidei, evellit et extrahit cor ab immundis affectionibus et vitiosis inquinamentis. Est igitur primus gradus secundae ascensionis, qua tenditur ad puritatem cordis, fides vel timor, qui est eius effectus.

[45] *Asc.*, 266C: Vides ergo quam congrue divina scriptura puritatem cordis fidei ascribit, iuxta illud: Fide purificans corda eorum, ... (Acts 15, 9.)

[46] *Asc.*, 266D: Sicut fides timore futuri iudicii ac suppliciorum metu, facit vitiorum contagia declinare, concutiens quodammodo medullitus omnia interiora et extrahens ab inferiorum vitiosa affectione et inhaesione: Ita consequenter spes mentem nostram de huiuscemodi affectionibus avulsam, sed non elevatam, imo timoris pondere depressam de praesentibus avocat, et ad superiora elevat,...

[47] Cf. P. K. Meagher, "Faith (Theology of)," *NCE*, V, 798-804; and Rahner and Vorgrimler, *Theological Dictionary*, 166 ("Faith").

[48] According to Zerbolt man's intellect and understanding suffered as a result of the fall, and his knowledge of God, and of spiritual matters generally, was impaired in particular (see above, pp. 77-86). Now it was commonly held that the act of faith, a cognitive act because its object is knowledge, represented an important step in the reformation of the intellect and the understanding which had lost a good deal of their original potency as a result of the fall (cf. D. of Augsburg, *De ext. et int. hom. compositione*, I, 84-85). Zerbolt does not explicitly characterize the acceptance of the articles of the Christian faith as the beginning of the reformation of the intellect. However, it will be seen in a later chapter that he, like David of Augsburg, views the reformation of the intellect as a gradual development, and that he regards the act of faith as a part of this development is virtually certain.

[49] Cf. Bonaventure, *Breviloquium*, Pt. VI, ch. 2 (*Works*, II, 229) and Pt. VI, ch. 4 (*Works*, II, 233, 235 and 236); idem, *Lignum Vitae*, ch. 30 (*Works*, I, 127-128); Thomas Aquinas, *Summa Contra Gentiles*, Bk. IV, ch. 56; idem, *ST*, 3a, 62, 5, 3a, 84, 7 and 3a, 66, 3; Harnack, *History of Dogma*, VI, 201-206, 216 and 219-220; and McGiffert, *A History of Christian Thought*, II, 313-316.

their origin, and the source of their efficacy.[49] About the number of sacraments there is nothing in Zerbolt's writings. Their origin, on the other hand, does receive some attention from him, for he gives an account of the institution of the sacraments of baptism and the eucharist by Christ, but that will be dealt with in our discussion of those two sacraments. It is in connection with Christ's death on the cross that Zerbolt briefly touches on the reason for the sacraments' efficacy in general. When Christ's side was pierced, he writes in *De Reformatione*, the sacraments of the church flowed therefrom.[50] What he undoubtedly means to say here is that, because the sacraments derive their efficacy from Christ's death of which the water and blood flowing from his side were a clear proof, it can be said that the sacraments flowed from Christ's side. Consistent with this line of thought, and in keeping with what had traditionally been said about the relationship between Christ's passion and the sacraments, Zerbolt writes in *De Ascensionibus* that the water and blood flowing from Christ's pierced side consecrated the sacraments of the church.[51] In other words, the efficacy of the sacraments derives from Christ's passion, and it is transmitted to the sacraments by way of the water and blood flowing from Christ's side. The water and blood, evidence of Christ's redemptive death, consecrate the sacraments and bestow on them their efficacy.

The significance of the sacraments lies, of course, in their capacity as vehicles of grace and this grace emanates, in the final analysis, from Christ's redemptive death. However, about sacramental grace in general, and its nature, Zerbolt does not say anything. Sacramental grace is mentioned by him only in connection with specific sacraments, and his views on sacramental grace will be discussed there.

i. *Baptism*

According to Aquinas, Christ instituted the sacrament of baptism at the time of his own baptism by John and that, as John baptized Jesus with the water from the Jordan, water as a species was consecrated as the fitting material for the sacrament of baptism.[52] Bonaventure observes in the *Breviloquium* that this eliminated the danger that anyone should ever go unbaptized for lack of the necessary material element.[53] Zerbolt writes

---

[50] *Ref.*, 249E: Latus ejus aperitur, unde profluunt Ecclesiae sacramenta,...

[51] *Asc.*, 274D: Latus eius unus militum aperuit, unde sanguis et aqua exivit, et sacramenta Ecclesiae consecravit.

[52] Thomas Aquinas, *ST*, 3a, 38, 4 and 3a, 66, 3. Cf. T. M. de Ferrari, "Baptism (Theology of)," *NCE*, II, 63.

[53] Bonaventure, *Lignum Vitae*, ch. 9 (*Works*, I, 110); *idem, Breviloquium*, Pt. VI, ch. 7 (*Works*, II, 247). Cf. Harnack, *History of Dogma*, VI, 227.

that Christ, who was free from all sin and blemish, was baptized by John for two reasons: to fulfil all righteousness or justice;[54] and to consecrate or sanctify the water of baptism.[55] This statement clearly echoes what had by then become two commonly held views with respect to the sacrament of baptism, namely that Christ instituted the sacrament of baptism when he was baptized by John, and that at that time he also consecrated water as a species to be used as the material element in the sacrament of baptism. Regarding the impact of the sacrament of baptism on the believer Zerbolt does not say anything explicitly. However, to write, as he does, that Christ was baptized even though he was free from all sin and corruption implies that baptism cleanses the recipient from all sins: original sin in the case of infants, and original sin as well as actual sins in the case of adults.[56] Furthermore, Zerbolt observes that when Christ was circumcized he took upon him the mark of the forgiveness of sins,[57] from which it would appear that, in his opinion, circumcision served the same purpose as does baptism, and that baptism replaced circumcision as the sacrament which removes the guilt attached to original sin. Finally, it is permissible to conclude as well that for Zerbolt baptism removes the guilt associated with original sin, but not the punishment. He defines original sin, we have seen, as the post-fall state of natural, rebellious concupiscence: the state marked by the absence of the pre-fall gratuitous exemption from rebellious concupiscence.[58] But through his death, Zerbolt writes, Christ has redeemed man from the guilt attached to original sin.[59] The punishment, on the other hand, remains, namely the loss of the gratuitous gift of integrity, on account of which man is burdened by rebellious concupiscence from which he cannot escape because it is, as Zerbolt explains, a natural condition. Since rebellious concupiscence is a

---

For his argument that water as a species was consecrated as the material element for baptism when John baptized Christ with water, Bonaventure makes use of Aristotle's *Topica*, I, ch. 6. Aquinas would appear to be doing the same.

[54] See above, p. 146.

[55] *Ref.*, 246B: Cogita deinde, quod ipse purissimus et mundissimus ab omni macula, ut omnem iustitiam impleret, ab Ioanne baptizatus est, et ut aquas baptismatis sanctificaret. Cf. *Asc.*, 270C.

In the *Lignum Vitae* Bonaventure gives the same two reasons for Christ's baptism, and in the same sequence, as does Radewijns in *Omnes, inquit, artes* (*Lignum Vitae*, ch. 9 [*Works*, I, 110]; *Omnes, Inquit, Artes*, II, 74-75). The usual indebtedness of Radewijns to Bonaventure, and of Zerbolt to Radewijns, would appear to apply here as well.

[56] Cf. Radewijns, *Tractatulus Devotus*, 249.

[57] *Asc.*, 270A: Octavo die circumciditur, et Iesus vocatur. Attende quod sine peccato assumpsit peccati remedium.

[58] See above, pp. 86-88.

[59] *Asc.*, 260A: Sane Christus morte sua preciosissima ab culpa originali nos redemit; ut huiusmodi virium destitutio vel lex carnis iam non sit culpa, cum ad eam non habendam non obligamur ne sit damnatio aliqua his qui sunt in Christo Iesu:...

natural condition, it is no longer culpable for those who are in Christ:
i.e., for those whose guilt has been removed through baptism. However,
the loss of the gift of integrity does, nonetheless, remain a severe punishment.[60]

Having looked at what Zerbolt writes regarding the sacrament of baptism we are ready to investigate his views on the sacrament of penance,
and about this sacrament he says a good deal more than about baptism.
Following faith he regards the sacrament of penance as the first step in
man's spiritual ascent, and consequently makes it an integral part of the
spiritual life.

ii. *Penance*

We have already seen that in *De Ascensionibus* Zerbolt divides man's fall
from his original impeccable condition into three stages. Over against
these three spiritual descents Zerbolt places, in this same work, three
spiritual ascents which, apart from the first few chapters, take up the entire treatise. Understandably the purpose of the three ascents is to nullify
the three descents,[61] although Zerbolt is well aware that in this life man
will never reach the perfection enjoyed by Adam before the fall. This is
because in this life man will always be saddled with the burden of
rebellious concupiscence which will prevent him from loving God as he
ought to. Nonetheless, it is man's duty to ascend spiritually as far as he
can.[62]

The purpose of the first ascent described by Zerbolt in *De Ascensionibus*
is to undo the third fall and its effects: that is, the fall into mortal sin and
the loss of justifying grace.[63] Consequently the first ascent is a discussion
of the sacrament of penance as it was understood by Zerbolt, and at this
point only the first ascent will be dealt with. The second and third
ascents, which aim at reversing the second and first descents, and their
effects, respectively, are of particular concern to the religious, and they
will be discussed in the final chapter of this essay.[64]

---

[60] See previous footnote. Cf. D. of Augsburg, *De ext. et int. hom. compositione*, II, 85.

[61] *Asc.*, ch. 11 (p. 262G-H).

[62] *Asc.*, 275G: Nec tamen putes quod aliquem istorum graduum usque ad summum vel
perfectum in hac vita possumus ascendere. Nec enim in hac vita possumus omnes concupiscentias expurgare, cum neque ipse Paulus perficere invenit, id est, perfectionem,
quae est in non concupiscere secundum Augustinum.

Regarding man's duty to seek perfection, even though perfection in this life is impossible, see all of ch. 42 of *De Ascensionibus* (pp. 275E-G). These questions will receive more attention below.

[63] *Asc.*, ch. 11 (p. 262G-H).

[64] In *De Ascensionibus* chs. 12-14 are devoted to the first ascent; chs. 15-46 to the second
ascent; and chs. 47-63 to the third ascent.

The second and third ascents deal with issues which are of particular concern to the
religious. Consequently, Zerbolt devotes a good deal more space to them than to the first
ascent.

While the contents of *De Reformatione* and *De Ascensionibus* are essentially the same, the arrangement of the material, and its exposition, is rather
dissimilar in the two works. In *De Reformatione* Zerbolt does not speak of a
threefold fall, but of a single fall in which man's descent into actual sin is
portrayed as a logical outgrowth of original sin. The powers of the soul
are deformed as a result of original sin, and it is because of this deformation that man commits personal sins.[65] Consequently, in *De Reformatione*
Zerbolt outlines in detail how the fall and its effects may be undone
through a reformation of the powers of the soul, namely the intellect,
memory and will.[66] And it is in connection with the reformation of the
will that Zerbolt discusses the sacrament of penance. Repentance and
sorrow for sin, which leads to confession and absolution, is understood by
Zerbolt to be the first reformation of the will, followed by a second reformation of the will in which the will asserts its control over rebellious concupiscence.[67] The second reformation of the will concerns the religious in
particular.[68] Such, then, is the manner in which Zerbolt integrates the
doctrine of penance into his over-all teaching on the spiritual life found in
De Reformatione and *De Ascensionibus*, and we are now ready to examine it
in some detail.

Self-examination aimed at contrition. In *De Reformatione* Zerbolt states pointed-
ly that *"cognitia propria initium sit salutis,"*[69] for unless the believer first
becomes thoroughly acquainted with his fall, and its extent, he cannot
take the necessary steps to raise himself, with God's help, out of his
miserable and damned state.[70] Knowledge of self is acquired through
self-examination, and Zerbolt's practical hints for the penitent regarding
self-examination are much like those found in the many manuals for

---

[65] See above, pp. 91-94.

[66] Chs. 13-17 deal with the reformation of the intellect; chs. 18-34 with the reformation
of the memory; and chs. 36-58 with the reformation of the will. In ch. 35 Zerbolt discusses
prayer. As in *De Ascensionibus*, the first chapters deal with man's condition before the fall,
the fall itself, and self-examination into one's fallen state.

[67] *Ref.*, 250D: Dicto de reformatione intellectus et memoriae, consequenter agendum
est de reformatione voluntatis. Sed quia non solum vires animae sunt destitutae in lapsu
primi hominis, sed quia, heu, multi per actuale peccatum spoliati sunt gratia Dei et culpa
propria deformate: Idcirco duplici indigent voluntatis reformatione. Prima, qua eis infundatur gratia et justificatio. Secunda, qua pronitas voluntatis et inclinatio appetituum
refrenetur. Prima reformatio, de qua non nisi modicum dicemus, quia non est tantum ad
propositum sicut secunda. Secunda [From the context it is clear that he means "prima".]
sit quae per poenitentiam, quae tribus partibus constat, contritione, confessione, satisfactione, integratur.

[68] Being primarily concerned with providing a manual for the religious or spiritual life,
Zerbolt devotes far more attention to the second reformation of the will than to the first
reformation of the will. The first reformation of the will receives one chapter; the second
reformation twenty-two.

[69] *Ref.*, 239A. Cf. Goossens, *Meditatie*, 129-130 and de Beer, *Spiritualitit*, 131.

[70] See *Asc.*, ch. 1 (pp. 258A-259B), and below, pp. 243-248 and 265-266.

penitents in circulation during the later middle ages.[71] In *De Ascensionibus* Zerbolt divides the indispensable self-examination into three stages corresponding to the three spiritual descents and ascents to which the work is devoted.[72] The first self-examination is set aside for the third fall, namely the descent into mortal sin,[73] and the purpose of this examination is to cultivate compunction and contrition in the believer.[74] The same self-examination is dealt with by Zerbolt in *De Reformatione*, but in a different context,[75] for there it constitutes part of the discussion dealing with the reformation of the memory: memory understood as a store-house of sensible and intellective impressions, as well as act. As act it is the equivalent of meditation,[76] and the purpose of meditating on one's sins and their enormity is, once more, to foster compunction and contrition.[77] The self-examination into mortal sin, it must be said, deals less with the technique involved in self-examination than with its objective.

Those who have fallen into mortal sin, Zerbolt observes, are commonly blind and insensible to sin and its seriousness, on account of which they no longer fear God and his punishment.[78] The first step which they must undertake, therefore, is to recover their sensibility with respect to sin in order that they may appreciate the gravity of their state.[79] The most

---

[71] Thomas N. Tentler, *Sin and Confession on the Eve of the Reformation* (Princeton, New Jersey, 1977), 109-120.

[72] *Asc.*, chs. 6, 7 and 8 (pp. 260F-262A).

[73] The title of *De Ascensionibus*, ch. 6 (p. 260F) reads: De tribus examinationibus, et qualiter homo per memoriam peccatorum recuperat sensum, maxime ut sentiat ultimum descensum, scilicet per peccatum mortale. *Asc.*, 260G: Postquam descensus tuos vidisti, congruum esset ascensiones disponere; ...Igitur ut noveris quantum per ultimum descensum videlicet per peccatum actuale mortale graviter sis prolapsus, et de loco in quo fueras cum haberes naturam integram et non viciatam, positus discessisti, debes teipsum diligenter discutere et districte examinare, ut tandem oculos aperias et videre posses quo iaceas prolapsus.

[74] *Asc.*, 271B: Ideoque ante reverendi huius Sacramenti sumptionem [i.e., the Eucharist], maxime debes teipsum secundum primam et secundam examinationem discutere modo superius posito, et sic ad contritionem exercere et ad compunctionem inflammare, ut scilicet doleas de peccatis commissis, corde, ore, et opere, et insuper de his quae facere omisisti.

[75] Cf. Goossens, *Meditatie*, 182-183.

[76] See above, pp. 60-62, and Goossens, *Meditatie*, 88-92.

[77] The title of *De Reformatione*, ch. 20 (p. 243F) reads: Qualiter fiat memoria peccatorum. And the chapter itself begins: Ut tibi de memoria tuorum criminum nascatur compunctio,...

Regarding the role played by *examinatio* in Zerbolt's spiritual program see below, p. 243 f, and cf. Goossens, *Meditatie*, 121-131.

[78] *Asc.*, 260G: ...; sed quoniam peccatum frequenter comitatur caecitas et insensibilitas ut qui peccato premitur, non tamen sese sentiat peccatorem, sed sit stupidus et nascitur ei frons meretricis et duritia cordis ut nec Deum iam timeat, nec homines vereatur.

[79] *Asc.*, 260G: Igitur antequam ascendas studiose teipsum debes discutere, et omnibus modis quibus possis niti, ut sensum recuperes quo descensum agnoscas et peccata tua deplores.

effective method to become sensitive once more to sin and its seriousness is to meditate on the extent to which God detests sin and has punished it throughout all of history. It was because of pride that Lucifer was banned from heaven, and on account of disobedience that Adam was driven from paradise. Self-indulgence was the reason that God destroyed practically the whole world in the flood and overturned Sodom and Gomorrah. Many similar examples, Zerbolt adds, can be gleaned from the Scriptures.[80] However, that sin is displeasing to God and that he cannot leave it unpunished is best illustrated by the fact that he allowed his Son to suffer a bitter death rather than leave sin unpunished and his divine justice unsatisfied.[81] Zerbolt is confident that meditation on these and similar truths will instil fear and compunction in the believer.[82] Fear and compunction are not incompatible sentiments, because like Gregory, his teacher on the 'doctrine' of compunction, Zerbolt writes that all compunction stems either from fear or love.[83]

Having first offered some suggestions how the reader may best develop an awareness regarding the seriousness of sin in general, Zerbolt then proceeds with the question of making an inventory of specific personal sins committed in the past, especially of the most serious ones.[84] He divides this inquest and self-examination into sin into two stages. First, he explains, the reader must recall, and make note of, the most serious sins perpetrated before his conversion, and having accomplished this he

---

[80] *Asc.*, 260G-H: Districte igitur etsi non semper, saepe tamen teipsum iudica, formans in te primo et pertractans quantum Deo unumquodque peccatum displiceat, quantumque horreat, et detestetur. Ut autem hoc melius sentire valeas, diligenter rumina, et donec ex affectu sentias studiose pertracta, quod adeo displicuit Deo superbia, ut nobilissimae quondam creaturae suae non parceret, sed Luciferum de coelo proiecit. Cogita an tibi parcet, quia forsitan melior aut nobilior es. Cogita quod Adam propter inobedientiam expulit de paradiso, et totum genus humanum originali iustitia spoliavit. Propter luxuriam subvertit Sodomam et Gomorrham et in diluvio pene totum mundum submersit. Et plura talia his similia recitat tibi divina scriptura. The same passage is found in *De Reformatione*, on p. 243F. Cf. Cassian, *Institutes*, Bk. XII, ch. 4; and Goossens, *Meditatie*, 183.

[81] *Asc.*, 260H: Cogita quod tantum Deo peccatum displicuit quod potius ipse voluit moriens satisfacere pro peccato Adae, quam ipsum secundum suam iustitiam dimittere impunitum. *Ref.*, 243F: Christus pro peccato sustinuit mortem amarissimam, ne peccatum inultum remaneret et suae iustitiae non satisfieret.

[82] *Asc.*, 261A: Si igitur hoc modo intus revolveris, non credo quin timore concuteris horrore obstupescis. *Ref.*, 243F: Ut tibi de memoria tuorum criminum nascatur compunctio, talibus stimulis te concute meditando. And then follow the points just listed which must instil this compunction (see footnote 80 above).

[83] *Ref.*, 241F: Potes autem haec et si qua alia genera compunctionis ad duo reducere; quia omnis compunctio, vel ex amore surgit vel ex timore. Cf. Gregory the Great, *Dialogues*, Bk. III, ch. 34 (*PL*, LXXVII, 300-301).

[84] It too takes on the form of a meditation, because in connection with the construction of this inventory of sins Zerbolt consistently speaks of *memorare* and *cogitare* (see *Asc.*, 261A-B and *Ref.*, 243G), both of which he equates with *meditare* (cf. Goossens, *Meditatie*, 88-94, 122-124 and 182-183).

must then do the same with those sins committed after his conversion.[85] Whether in this instance Zerbolt is thinking of *conversio mentis* or *conversio ab saeculo ad vitam religiosam* is not altogether clear, and he may even have both in mind, regarding the latter as a logical, although not inevitable, consequence of the former.[86]

Only mortal sins are supposed to be the object of the first self-examination, which Zerbolt divides into two stages, but it is clear that in reality he makes this a fairly wide ranging inquest into actual sins.[87] This stems undoubtedly in part from the fact that Zerbolt, like Grote, did not draw too clear a distinction between mortal and venial sins, and there was a tendency amongst the Devotionalists to magnify the gravity of all sins.[88] Furthermore, the first examination is carried out in preparation for the sacrament of penance, and for centuries it had been the practice to confess not only mortal sins, but venial sins as well.

Zerbolt obviously believes that there is a marked difference between the sins committed before conversion and those committed thereafter. The former are sins of commission: they are sins of thought, word and deed, and many of them definitely are mortal sins.[89] Since they are so

[85] *Asc.*, 261A: Cogita quam multa peccata commisisti. Pene enim omni die, omni hora ante conversionem tuam graviter deliquisti. *Asc.*, 261B: Quamvis etiam iam ad Dominum sis conversus, non tamen hanc vilipendas memoriam peccatorum, sed et tunc adde ut etiam summa diligentia pertractes peccata tua quae post conversionem commisisti. *Ref.*, 243G: Cogita de peccatis tuis praeteritis ante conversionem. Cogita quam multa sint in locutione, opere, consensu et in cogitatione: Tot enim sunt ut nequeas numerare. Cogita quam turpia, praecipue quantum ad carnalia, in quibus tamen minus immoreris, ne delectatio surrepat. Cogita quam gravia, quibus Deum offendisti, et rursum Christum quodammodo crucifixisti. Cogita de peccatis tuis post tuam conversionem, quod semper tam negligens, tam tepidus et tot annis sine profectu fuisti, et vide de singularibus tuis criminibus, numera ea si potes in conspectu Domini, et pete veniam de praeteritis, adiutorium de praesentibus, et cautelam contra futura.

[86] To understand *conversio* either in terms of *conversio mentis* or *conversio ab saeculo ad vitam religiosam* was traditional (Dudden, *Gregory the Great*, II, 420-424; John Baillie, *Baptism and Conversion* [New York, 1963], 67-68; and B. Poschmann, *Penance and the Anointing of the Sick*, trans. by F. Courtney [New York, 1964], 113-116). And it is evident from a number of passages in *De Reformatione* and *De Ascensionibus* that Zerbolt now invests the term *conversio* with the first meaning (*Asc.*, 261B: Quamvis etiam iam ad Dominum sis conversus, ... *Ref.*, 243G: ..., nescis si vere conversus fueris, ...), then with the second one (*Asc.*, 261B: Cogita quam tepide, quam infructuose tot annos in divino servitio expendisti, vix scis invenire profectum, et in his peccatis quae post conversionem commisisti, ...) and, as would appear from the passage in *De Ascensionibus* just adduced, even combines them.

[87] *Asc.*, 261A: Tunc igitur tertio veniat memoria, et in medium producat omnia peccata tua praeterita, gravia maximeque maxima. The first self-examination deals, of course, with the third fall: i.e., the fall into mortal sin.

[88] See above, pp. 91-94.

[89] *Asc.*, 261A-B: Cogita quam multa peccata commisisti. Pene enim omni die, omni hora ante conversionem tuam graviter deliquisti. Quis numerabit quot peccata commisisti corde, ore, et opere. Deinde percurre singula, et vide quam gravia sunt quibus Deum omnipotentem et terribilem iudicem patremque dulcem et benignum, qui pro te tanta fecit et sustinuit, offendisti,... Deinde revolve quam sint quaedam eorum turpia, maxima quantum ad carnalia,... See footnote 85 above for the corresponding passage in *De Reformatione* (243G).

foul, Zerbolt warns not to dwell on them too long, lest they be the cause of more sin.[90] The sins committed after conversion are, by contrast, sins of omission and they consist, most commonly, in the absence of desirable and required attitudes and dispositions such as humility and spiritual fervour, and in the failure to make spiritual progress.[91] These sins, Zerbolt adds, will be punished even more severely than the grosser sins perpetrated before conversion, because sins committed after conversion are in a sense more heinous than those committed before.[92] And, concludes Zerbolt, if this first examination, consisting of two parts, should reveal numerous sins, mortal as well as venial, the appropriate attitude is, of course, one of humility, sorrow and grief.[93] In addition to that the believer must, following this first self-examination, ponder how slight has been his contrition, and how little satisfaction he has offered for all the sins committed before and after his conversion.[94] The objective again is that reflection on these matters result in fear, grief and sorrow.[95] However, Zerbolt adds a final warning that meditation on past sins must not be conducted in such a way that it results in despair, excessive sorrow and dejection, but that it must be carried out in such a manner that it creates the desire to improve spiritually and to make satisfaction for past sins.[96] Man need not despair because, as a consequence of his divine

---

[90] *Asc.*, 261B: (Deinde revolve quam sint quaedam eorum turpia, maxime quantum ad carnalia), quae tamen magis succincte debes transcurrere, ne immunda subrepat delectatio immoranti. See footnote 85 above for the corresponding passage in *De Reformatione* (243G).

[91] *Asc.*, 261B: Cogita singula vitia quibus adhuc sordes. Cogita in singulari de superbia tua quanta est, quantum concupiscis honorem, laudes desideras, ad altum statum aspiras. Cogita quam tepide, quam infructuose tot annos in divino servitio expendisti, vix scis invenire profectum,... See footnote 85 above for the corresponding passage in *De Reformatione* (243G).

[92] *Asc.*, 261B: ..., et in his peccatis quae post conversionem commisisti, forsitan gravius puniet te Deus tanquam magis ingratum.

[93] *Asc.*, 277D: Si te in prima examinatione discusseris et inveneris peccata tua multiplicata super numerum arenae maris, forma in te affectum humilitatis vel moeroris, et assume personam servi qui Dominum suum offendit,...

[94] *Asc.*, 261B: Deinde cum haec ita in cogitatu tuo examinaveris, diligenter pertracta quam modicam pro his omnibus fecisti satisfactionem, quam modica fuit tua contritio, quam parva opera in nullo satisfactoria;... *Ref.*, 243G: Deinde cogita in quanto pro istis [i.e., sins committed before and after conversion] satisfecisti,... Cf. Goossens, *Meditatie*, 183.

[95] *Asc.*, 261B-C: Haec igitur et his similia cum peccator in cogitatione revolverit, et se timore percussum, et dolore interno perfusum senserit: tunc cor suum humillime et dolore plenum immediate dirigat ad Deum suum orationem faciendo,...

[96] *Asc.*, 261C: Hanc tamen formulam meditandi aut similem ita debes dirigere, ut non incidas in desperationem, sed inflammaris ad satisfactionem et emendationem,... *Ref.*, 243H: Cave tamen desperationem si profundius huiusmodi meditationibus te immerseris, atque ita huiusmodi meditationes dirige non ut absorbearis ab nimia tristitia et deiectione, sed ut instigeris ad vitae emendationem et tolerantiam omnium tribulationum. Cf. Goossens, *Meditatie*, 183; and Tentler, *Sin and Confession on the Eve of the Reformation*, 113-116.

goodness and mercy, God grants man the grace which enables him to change his life and to improve himself spiritually.[97]

Zerbolt's teaching that the beginning of salvation lies in self-knowledge, and in the perception of one's sinfulness in particular, is found as well in Gregory the Great's *Moralia*, one of Zerbolt's major sources. Gregory writes here that the first step in the sacrament of penance is *conversio mentis*, and that this is "a process which begins in the perception of sin, passes on to sorrow for sin springing from fear of God's judgements, and ends in the sorrow which springs from love of God."[98] The same sequence is to be found in Zerbolt's doctrine: the cognitive act, namely the perception of sin, is followed by the volitional act, which is compunction of fear succeeded by compunction of love and contrition. It is the volitional act as understood by Zerbolt which must now be considered.

Contrition. Zerbolt writes, in both *De Reformatione* and *De Ascensionibus*, that those who have fallen into mortal sin can regain justifying grace only by means of the sacrament of penance consisting of contrition, confession and satisfaction,[99] from which it may be deduced that he subscribed to the Thomistic teaching regarding the constituent parts of this sacrament.[100] In order to convey what is meant by contrition, Zerbolt has

---

[97] *Asc.*, 261C:...,et ipsius [God's] bonitatem et misericordiam cum summo desiderio implorando:... *Asc.*, 261C: ...mutationem vitae et emendationem morum promittendo et promissionem Dei adiutorio adimplendo.

[98] Dudden, *Gregory the Great*, II, 420.

[99] See footnote 67 above.
The title of ch. 12 of *De Ascensionibus* reads: De prima ascensione contra peccatum mortale, et de tribus gradibus huius ascensionis et de contritione (p. 262H). Chs. 13 and 14 deal with confession and satisfaction respectively.

[100] Satisfaction, consisting of some form of public penance, was granted the most prominent place in the patristic sacrament of penance. By the eleventh century, however, contrition, the subjective state of the penitent, had replaced the satisfaction offered by the penitent as the dominant element in the sacrament of penance. Priestly absolution, on the other hand, was held to be no more than a formal confirmation of the forgiveness of sins already conferred by God in response to contrition. Such was the doctrine regarding the sacrament of penance defended by Peter Lombard, but it was not long before its validity was challenged by William of Auvergne (d. 1249). The latter admitted that while there can be no forgiveness without contrition, the divine forgiveness does not, however, take effect until the penitent has been formally absolved by the priest. He argued that Lombard's teaching regarding the sacrament of penance undermines the objective efficacy of all the sacraments, and so the position of the church. Building on William of Auvergne and others, Thomas Aquinas adduced his own doctrine of the sacrament of penance. He asserted that the acts of the penitent, namely contrition, confession and satisfaction, constitute the matter of penance, and that the priestly absolution is its form. However, this definition of the sacrament of penance did not immediately receive universal recognition. It was challenged by Duns Scotus. He maintained that the sacrament of penance consists solely of the priestly absolution, and that the acts of the penitent do not constitute part of this sacrament. His aim was, of course, to protect the objective efficacy of the sacrament,

recourse to the etymology of this term. In the world of nature, he writes, there are many hard objects; but they are said to be crushed (*conteri*) when they are broken up and reduced to small pieces. In the same way, Zerbolt continues, man's heart may be called hard when it is turned away from God, when it stubbornly clings to sin, when it is impervious to the influence of divine grace which can extricate the will from sin, and when it rejects the inbreathing of the Holy Spirit and stops its ears so as not to hear. But metaphorically speaking, a hard heart may be said to be crushed when it is broken—broken by the perception of its sinfulness—and softened of its hardness.[101] In order to explain even further exactly what he understands by the term contrition, Zerbolt has recourse to Bernard of Clairvaux's *De Consideratione*. According Bernard, Zerbolt writes, a hard heart is one which is not rent by compunction nor softened by piety, it remains unmoved by prayer, does not yield to threats, but hardens under affliction and in adversity. However, it is contrite when it is melted by compunction and softened by piety.[102]

This passage from *De Consideratione* reveals clearly that Zerbolt understood compunction to contribute substantially to the development

---

although he did not deny that a certain disposition on the part of the penitent is a necessary requirement for an efficacious reception of the sacrament of penance. (Poschmann, *Penance and the Anointing of the Sick*, trans. by. F. Courtney, 1-121 and 133-193; Kelly, *Early Christian Doctrines*, 216-219 and 436-440; Harnack, *History of Dogma*, V, 323-330 and VI, 243-258 and 275-301; McGiffert, *A History of Christian Thought*, II, 100 and 151-153; H. A. Oberman, "Some Notes on the Theology of Nominalism with Attention to its Relation to the Renaissance," *Harvard Theological Review*, LIII [1960], 53-56 and 63-65; Oberman, *Biel*, 131-160; Neuner and Roos, *The Teaching of the Catholic Church*, 309-324; P. Palmer, "Penance, Sacrament of," *NCE*, XI, 73-76; *idem*, "Attrition and Attritionism," *NCE*, I, 1032-1033; P. de Letter, "Contrition," *NCE*, IV, 279-280; K. Rahner, "Penance," *SM*, IV, 390-397; and Rahner and Vorgrimler, *Theological Dictionary*, 347-348 ["Penance, Sacrament of"], 42-43 ["Attrition"] and 100-101 ["Contrition; Contritionism"].)

[101] *Ref.*, 250D-E: In naturalibus dicitur res conteri, quando res dura frangitur vel imminuitur in partes minutas. Ita similitudinarie cor hominis durum dicitur, quamdiu aversum ab Deo moratur in peccatis, non cedens divinae motioni trahenti voluntatem ab peccatis. Tunc conteri dicitur, quia ab illa obstinatia et duritia mollitur et frangitur. *Asc.*, 263A-B: Sicut enim in naturalibus res durae dicuntur conteri, cum in partes minutas franguntur vel minuuntur, ita metaphorice cor dicitur conteri, quando ipsum ab sua duritia emollitur, quod prius aversum ab Deo durum et obstinatum fuit in peccatis, non cedens divinae motioni, non admittens instinctum Spiritus sancti, sed obturans aurem ne audiret. Cf. Goossens, *Meditatie*, 138; and P. de Letter, "Contrition," *NCE*, IV, 278.

In the *Scala Paradisi* John Climacus also alludes to the etymological origin of the term contrition to explain its meaning (*The Ladder of Divine Ascent*, 197). Zerbolt quotes frequently from this work.

[102] *Ref.*, 250E: Est autem cor durum secundum Bernardum de consideratione, quod nec compunctione scinditur, nec pietate mollitur, nec movetur precibus, minis non cedit, flagellis duratur. *Asc.*, 263B: Vel cor durum secundum Bernardum I. de consideratione, dicitur, quod nec compunctione scinditur, nec pietate mollitur nec movetur precibus, etc. Conterit autem quando iam liquesit compunctione, et emollitur pietate (Bernard of Clairvaux, *De consideratione libri V ad Eugeniam papam*, Bk. I, ch. 3).

of contrition, and to be in a sense identical with it.[103] Consequently, he adds, if the believer wants to come to confession contrite and grief

---

[103] *Ref.*, 250E: Nihil autem tantum valet contra cordis duritiam, quantum compunctio,...

In using the expression *contritio cordis*, rather than *compunctio cordis*, to describe the subjective disposition required of the penitent for the forgiveness of his sins in the sacrament of penance Zerbolt was following what had by then become a well established practice.

The author of the Acts of the Apostles writes that those who listened to Peter's sermon on the day of Pentecost *compuncti sunt corde* (Acts 2, 37). However, it was not until the second half of the fourth century that *compunctio cordis* became a favourite expression with Christian writers, and it would appear that it was generally understood to be a broad, complex sentiment. Compunction was commonly described as sorrow, remorse, regret and repentance experienced on account of one's sins. Defined in this way compunction does not differ substantially from the scholastic definition of contrition, and in patristic literature the term contrition, although it does not often appear there, is generally used as a substitute for compunction. However, it was held that compunction must not be just a temporary sentiment necessary for the sacrament of penance, but that it must be an abiding one, an idea which appears for the first time in the writings of Origen. In patristic writings, therefore, the term compunction can refer to a permanent and abiding sorrow and repentance for sin, or to the repentance required for a fruitful reception of the sacrament of penance. Finally, Origen introduced into Christian thought the concept of the desire for union with God experienced as an abiding, heartfelt sorrow and sadness because of man's separation from God in this life. This sentiment too was given the name compunction, and it frequently merged with compunction understood as sorrow and grief experienced on account of one's sins.

Gregory the Great further added to the 'doctrine' of compunction. To begin with, to the two traditional sources of compunction, namely the remembrance of sin and the contemplation of heaven, he added the thought of the last judgement and the consideration of the evils of this life. He then continues that, as the believer progresses from a remembrance of his own sins to a contemplation of the heavenly joys, his compunction changes from one motivated by fear to one inspired by love. That the emotions of fear and love play a role in compunction was not a totally new idea, but Gregory was the firs to spell this out clearly. Like his predecessors he held that compunction must be cultivated at all times, but like them he also used the term compunction to designate the repentance for sin necessary for man's justification through the sacrament of penance. However, Gregory is careful to add that in order to have one's sins forgiven in the sacrament of penance it is necessary to move from compunction motivated by fear to compunction motivated by love.

It was the introduction of frequent sacramental penance which would appear to have been responsible for the more or less clear-cut distinction that came to be drawn between the repentance necessary for the sacrament of penance and the lasting, perpetual sorrow and grief brought on as a result of sin. The term contrition, although used infrequently before the eighth century, had generally been regarded as a synonym for compunction; but now it came to be reserved for the repentance required for the sacrament of penance, while the term compunction continued to be employed pretty much as it had always been, namely, to describe an abiding sorrow and repentance for sin. However, because of their respective natures, the connection between compunction and contrition remained a close one, the former in a sense overlapping the latter. It was for this reason, it would appear, that spiritual writers in particular continued to use the term compunction even when discussing the repentance necessary for the forgiveness of sins in the sacrament of penance, while systematic theologians of the middle ages virtually always resorted to the term contrition in this connection (J. Pegon, "Componction," *DSp*, II, 1312-1321; D. Hurst, "Compunction," *NCE*, IV, 96; J. de Guibert, "La Componction du Coeur," *RAM*, XV [1934], 225-240; P. Régamey, "La 'Componction du Coeur'," *VSp*, XLIV

stricken, he ought first to exercise himself in compunction.[104] In view of the fact that he assigns a major role to compunction in the development of contrition, a few words are in order at this point about Zerbolt's understanding of compunction and what he means by "exercising oneself in compunction."

Very briefly, Zerbolt understood compunction to be a feeling of sorrow, grief, regret and repentance for sins committed, and this sentiment he understood to be motivated by either fear or love, or by the two conjointly. The compunction of fear, he explains, arises from a consideration of one's sinfulness, the final judgement and the horrors of hell, while compunction of love results from meditating on God's mercy and goodness towards fallen man as well as on the glories of heaven. Furthermore, it would appear that Zerbolt was of the opinion that compunction of fear must precede that of love, and that without the former the latter cannot develop.[105] For Zerbolt, then, the only sure way to contrition leads via compunction motivated by fear, followed by compunction motivated by love. And Zerbolt is quite emphatic about the insufficiency of compunction motivated by fear only for the forgiveness of sins in the sacrament of penance. For he writes in De Ascensionibus that it is not sufficient for the penitent to be smitten with fear only, but that he must possess compunction—compunction of love he means quite obviously, or at least compunction motivated primarily by love—and contrition if his sins are to be forgiven in the sacrament of penance.[106]

The term attrition does not appear anywhere in Zerbolt's writings. However, his unequivocal rejection of the idea that repentance motivated by fear is adequate for man's justification clearly implies that he rejects the attritionism of the late middle ages with which he must have been familiar.[107] This supposition about his rejection of attritionism is, of

[1935], Supplément, 1-16 and 65-84, XLV [1935], Supplément, 8-21 and 86-99, XLIX [1936], Supplément, 179-186 and 302-315; Dudden, Gregory the Great, II, 420-421; Goossens, Meditatie, 132-133; Aquinas, Summa Contra Gentiles, Bk. IV, ch. 72; and idem, ST, 3a, 84-90).

Like most spiritual writers, Zerbolt employs both concepts, compunctio cordis and contritio cordis, in his discussion of the sacrament of penance, and the final chapter of this essay will reveal that compunctio cordis plays a major role in Zerbolt's entire spiritual program.

[104] Asc., 263C: ..., exercens te ante confessionem ad compunctionem modo quo postea habebitur, ut ita contritus et dolorosus venias ad confessionem.

[105] Asc., chs. 16-25 (pp. 264B-267H) and Ref., ch. 11 (p. 241C-G); and see below, pp. 268-270. Cf. Goossens, Meditatie, 136-141.

[106] Asc., 264E. ...et licet sciat se poenituisse, nescit tamen an solo timore percussus, an ex gratia infusa compunctus et contritus;... Cf. Dudden, Gregory the Great, II, 420.

[107] Cf. P. F. Palmer, "Attrition and Attritionism," NCE, I, 1032-1033; Rahner and Vorgrimler, Theological Dictionary, 42-43 ("Attritionism"); and Dudden, Gregory the Great, II, 420-421.

Contrition, always understood as repentance for sins motivated by love, could, of course, be either perfect and sufficient or imperfect and insufficient, and among the first

course, corroborated by his insistence on the need for compunction motivated by love, and contrition, if the penitent's sins are to be forgiven in the sacrament of penance.[108] In fact, it does not appear that Zerbolt sees a great deal of difference between compunction of love and contrition. He almost certainly perceives both to consist in repentance, grief and sorrow for sin motivated by love, a spiritual condition which is indispensable for the forgiveness of sins in the sacrament of penance. Consequently, he can on occasion restrict himself to the use of the term compunction when referring to the disposition needed for a fruitful reception of the sacrament of penance.[109] But when he does so, it is clear that he has in mind compunction of love which, admittedly, is preceded by compunction of fear. The term contrition, on the other hand, is never used by Zerbolt except to describe the sorrow and repentance motivated by love which is required of the penitent for a fruitful reception of the sacrament of penance.[110]

In addition to repentance for sin motivated by love, Zerbolt understood contrition to consist of another element as well, namely the resolve not to sin again. This too was commonly understood to be a

---

to distinguish clearly between the two was Alan of Lille (d. 1202). He attached the label attrition to imperfect repentance, and contrition to repentance sufficient for the forgiveness of sins in the sacrament of penance. To differentiate between perfect and imperfect repentance in this fashion became the standard practice. Aquinas adopted it too, and he asserted quite vigorously that contrition is necessary for the forgiveness of sins and justification. Duns Scotus, on the other hand, considered attrition to be sufficient for the forgiveness of sins and justification in the sacrament of penance. This position was, of course, consistent with his aim to magnify the objective efficacy of the sacrament of penance.

The late medieval *moderni* such as William of Occam and Gabriel Biel, for example, invested the terms *attrition* and *contrition* with a new meaning. They defined attrition and contrition in terms of repentance motivated by fear in the case of attrition, and repentance motivated by love in the case of contrition. About the adequacy of attrition for the forgiveness of sins in the sacrament of penance opinions diverged considerably, although it would appear that the *moderni* were for the most part of the opinion that the penitent must be contrite if he is to be justified through the sacrament of penance (see references given in footnote 100 above).

[108] See footnote 106 above.

[109] *Asc.*, 263C: ..., sed si vere spiritum compunctionis concepisti, interdum difficile erit tibi, imo vero lachrymas cohibere nequibis.

[110] In his brief discussion of Zerbolt's thought R. R. Post consistently speaks of contrition, but the context clearly indicates that he ought to be using the term compunction in most instances (*The Modern Devotion*, 327).

In his work *Anabaptism and Asceticism*, p. 254, K. R. Davis deals briefly with some of the Devotionalists' views on repentance and contrition, although Zerbolt is not one of those whom he mentions. Davis leaves one with the impression that the Devotionalists' emphasis on the need for repentance and contrition in order to be forgiven and justified was something new. If that is, in fact, what he means, then the erroneousness of his view needs hardly to be pointed out. In this instance, as in most others, Davis' understanding of the *Devotio Moderna* is based on Albert Hyma's *The Christian Renaissance: A History of the "Devotio Moderna."*

necessary and indispensable component of contrition.[111] On account of rebellious concupiscence, Zerbolt writes in *De Ascensionibus*, man has forsaken God and has turned to the creature which he has come to love inordinately; and it is in this excessive love for created things that man's sin consists. Consequently, if man desires to progress spiritually, one of the first requirements is that he turn away from created objects, turn to God with the intention to serve him, and resolve never again to subject himself to the creature through an unlawful lust or willful concupiscence. Such an aversion to sin, Zerbolt concludes, is termed contrition, and in this manner the hardness of heart is shattered.[112]

Contrition and grace. In harmony with the Augustinian-Thomistic position on this particular question, Zerbolt writes that man needs grace in order to achieve contrition, thereby rejecting the position taken by the late-medieval *moderni* who maintained that man is capable of loving God for God's sake *ex puris naturalibus*. For in a passage in *De Reformatione* Zerbolt observes that if man is to achieve contrition, the first requirement is that he deny himself and submit his own will to the divine will. And that, he concludes, can take place only with the aid of divine grace.[113] In a corresponding passage in *De Ascensionibus* Zerbolt further elaborates on the need for grace if man is to prepare himself adequately for the reception of justifying grace in the sacrament of penance. Sorrow for sin, the rejection of iniquity and contrition are all gifts of grace, he explains,[114] as is compunction motivated by love. Compunction motivated by fear he holds to be possible without the aid of grace.[115] Furthermore, throughout *De*

---

[111] McGiffert, *A History of Christian Thought*, II, 325; P. de Letter, "Contrition," *NCE*, IV, 278; and cf. Neuner and Roos, *The Teaching of the Catholic Church*, 314.

[112] *Asc.*, 263A: Nam aversus es ab creatore tuo per superbiam, in qua est formalis ratio peccati, conversus es ad creaturam per delectationem, ac deinde per operationes contra legem divinam Dei tui transgressus es praeceptum: Ita tribus gradibus oportet te contrario ascendere. Primo ut avertas cor tuum ab creaturis et ab peccatis et habeas quandam cordis firmam aversionem, et firmum quoddam propositum Deo tuo serviendi, et nunquam te creaturis per illicitam delectationem subiiciendi, etiamsi mille mortibus mori te oporteret. Hoc autem in genere debes proponere, non autem super hoc in singulari te examinare, dolebisque multum quod tantum ab Deo tuo recessisti, quod tantum eum offendisti, et quodammodo iterum crucifixisti. Ecce talis aversio ipsa est una ascensio, cuius nomen est contritio, qua cor tuum quodammodo ab sua duritia frangitur.
Cf. *Asc.*, 267F: Dedit et inspiravit voluntatem quod te velles emendare, ... *Ref.*, 245G: Dedit voluntatem ut te velles emendare,... For the last two excerpts Zerbolt is dependent on Radewijns, *Omnes, Inquit, Artes*, II, 159-160. Cf. Tentler, *Sin and Confession on the Eve of the Reformation*, 120-123.

[113] *Ref.*, 245G: Dedit dona gratiae. Primo quod voluntatem tuam ab eo aversam ad se revocavit,...For this passage Zerbolt is dependent on Radewijns, *Omnes, Inquit, Artes*, II, 159-160. Cf. footnote 100 above.

[114] *Asc.*, 267F: Deinde cogita de donis gratiae tibi collatis. Dedit enim tibi contritionem et dolorem de peccatis, et ab iniustitia revocavit,... For this passage Zerbolt is dependent on Radewijns, *Omnes, Inquit, Artes*, II, 159-160.

[115] See footnote 106 above.

Reformatione and *De Ascensionibus* Zerbolt continuously emphasizes the need for grace in the spiritual life generally,[116] and thus we have further evidence of Zerbolt's belief in the need for grace to achieve contrition. For, in *De Ascensionibus* at least, he makes justification, for which contrition is the prerequisite,the first of the three spiritual ascents.

About the nature of grace which enables man to achieve contrition Zerbolt does not say anything specifically, except that it is divinely infused.[117] However, those within the Augustinian-Thomistic tradition with regard to the general question of grace *versus* nature held that all grace is a gift granted and infused directly by God. For they defended the doctrine that, without divine aid, man cannot prepare himself for grace in the true sense of the word and that, consequently, he is unable to merit grace by his own, unassisted powers.[118]

Contrition: Its importance in relation to confession and satisfaction. By making priestly absolution the form of the sacrament of penance, Aquinas tried to safeguard the objective element in this sacrament which was being undermined by Peter Lombard's emphasis on contrition as the only constituent that matters in the sacrament of penance. However, it would appear that, on balance, Aquinas too magnifies the importance of contrition, for he writes that it can achieve perfect remission of sin even before confession and absolution, provided the resolve to confess and to submit to the keys of the church is present.[119] Grote was, like Aquinas, of the opinion that it is contrition which, in the final analysis, achieves forgiveness of sins, and that the priest's absolution plays perhaps no more

---

[116] *Asc.*. 258H: Verum quia ascensus iste non est in currente vel ascendente, sed ex dono Dei miserentis, ideo quarto tibi consulitur ab Domino adiutorium et auxilium postulandum, quia nulla est industria tua, nisi te in omnibus divina gratia comitetur. *Asc.*, 267D: ..., quoties reverti volebas ipse te suscepit, dolenti peccata indulsit, emendantem et corrigentem adiuvit. *Asc.*, 277G: ...multo amplius et saepius debemus orare pro divina gratia,... *Asc.*, 284G-H: Sed ut etiam hunc tumorem interdum deprimas et ad praefatum humilitatis gradum ascendas, debes in omnibus virtutibus in omni profectu, in omnibus bonis operibus, ex toto corde, et ex sententia dicere et sentire: Non ego, sed gratia Dei mecum, et gratia Dei sum id quod sum, et Deus est qui operator velle et perficere pro bona voluntate. *Ref.*, 240H: Ego autem, in me scilicet, ad nihilum redactus sum et nescivi. Nescivi, inquam, priusquam hoc praedicto modo discerem. Indeque in amorem et charitatem Dei, qui te tam fragilem, tam pie protegit, contre tam fortes vitiorum spiritus, accenderis. See also footnote 40 above. Cf. 1 Cor. 15, 10; and Phil. 2, 13; and D. of Augsburg, *De ext. et. int. hom. compositione*, I, 111.

[117] See the passage given in footnote 106 above.

When the Devotionalists speak of grace, it is usually in very general terms, and in this they followed the example of Grote. Cf. Epiney-Burgard, *Grote*, 290, footnote 46.

[118] Bonaventure, *Breviloquium*, Pt. V, chs. 1-3 (*Works*, II, 181-192); Rahner and Vorgrimler, *Theological Dictionary*, 192-196 ("Grace") and Richardson, ed., *Dictionary*, 169-170 ("Infusion").

[119] Aquinas, *Summa Contra Gentiles*, Bk. IV, ch. 72.

than a declaratory role. In a letter to Jan van de Gronde he writes that, without contrition, absolution is granted in vain; for in the absence of contrition God does not forgive sins, and no priest on earth can forgive what has not been forgiven in heaven. He does not deny the need for confession and absolution, but he states emphatically that the subjective condition of the penitent determines the value and efficacy of the priestly absolution.[120]

Zerbolt would appear to follow pretty much in the footsteps of Aquinas and Grote. To begin with, he places as much emphasis on contrition as he does because, as he explains, there can be no forgiveness of sins without contrition; and without contrition justifying grace, which has been lost on account of mortal sin, cannot be regained. Without contrition, therefore, there can be no salvation, and on that account man must be on his guard against a hard and insensible heart which is not contrite. Not only does God not bestow justifying grace on an unrepentant soul, but such a soul would not be receptive to justifying grace in any case.[121] Zerbolt elaborates further that the believer can be assured that his sins are forgiven through confession and absolution in direct proportion to the degree of contrition and humility possessed by him.[122] In other words, it is contrition which in effect determines the forgiveness of sins and the extent to which they are forgiven. Sacramental confession and absolution ratify the forgiveness of sins achieved through contrition, a subjective spiritual condition. Although confession and absolution do not add to the forgiveness of sins as such, there can, however, be no forgiveness of sins without them because they constitute essential parts of the sacrament of penance. And they are necessary parts of the sacrament of penance because God gave the church the power of the keys, to which Zerbolt refers a number of times in his discussion of confession.[123] On the other

---

[120] Mulder, ed., *Gerardi Magni Epistolae*, 101-102. The entire letter to Jan van de Gronde covers pp. 100-106. Its contents are discussed by Post, *The Modern Devotion*, 110-114. Cf. de Beer, *Spiritualiteit*, 64-65 and Epiney-Burgard, *Grote*, 227-228.

[121] *Ref.*, 250E: Sine hac contritione, gratia quae per peccatum mortale amittitur, nunquam recuperatur. Cave ergo homo, cor durum et insensibile, ab quo gratia divina resilit.

[122] *Asc.*, 263C-D: Et certe scire debes quod secundum intentionem contritionis et humilem verecundiam, peccata tibi in confessione remittuntur.

Zerbolt does not explain why man's sins will be forgiven in proportion to his humility. However, the thought underlying this statement is, no doubt, that only humility enables man to see things as they are, and that without humility he will not be able to see that he is sinful, nor experience repentance for his sins (cf. Cassian, *Conferences*, No. 20, chs. 6 and 7; and G. Gilleman, "Humility," *NCE*, VII, 236). Without humility, then, there can be no contrition, and the latter can be no greater than the former; the degree of the latter is determined by that of the former. It is for that reason, it would appear, that Zerbolt writes that forgiveness of sins is in direct proportion to the humility and contrition felt by the penitent.

[123] See the passages given in footnotes 126 and 160 below.

hand, in the absence of contrition, confession and absolution are meaningless. Finally, it might be observed that, although the emphasis on contrition and its importance in the sacrament of penance was obviously not something which was exclusive to the Devotionalists, it was consistent, nonetheless, with their general effort to increase spiritual fervour and the subjective element in religion which they described with the term *innicheit*.

Confession. Even though it was widely taught that the forgiveness of sin in the sacrament of penance is in direct proportion to the degree of contrition possessed by the penitent, the importance of making a good confession is clearly revealed by the voluminous literature which appeared on the subject in the middle ages, and that literature belonged, for the most part, to either of two categories: to *summae* for confessors or to manuals for penitents. However, much of the devotional literature also dealt with the subject of confession in one context or another,[124] as do Zerbolt's two manuals. Much of what Zerbolt writes about confession is drawn from the traditional literature on the subject, although he also raises a number of questions not normally discussed.

Zerbolt's discussion of confession concentrates on four major points: the penitent's bearing before his confessor which must, in some overt way, provide proof of his inner state of repentance and contrition; the frequency with which the believer must confess his sins; the confessor; and, what Zerbolt terms, lay confession. We will now look briefly at these four topics in this order.

The penitent's conduct in the confessional had long been regarded as a fairly reliable indicator of his inner, spiritual condition, and it was, consequently, a topic of interest not only to confessors, but to theologians as well. The conditions for a good confession came, in fact, to be summarized in popular verses which found their way even into the theological writings of Aquinas and other doctors of theology. One of the most popular of such verses named sixteen conditions to be met for a good confession,[125] and though Zerbolt does not mention all sixteen, he touches upon the most important among them.

He begins with the observation that, through his sins motivated by pride, man has shown contempt for God, on account of which it is necessary that he confess those sins to a man who is God's deputy and who has been granted the power of the keys. The penitent must appear before this deputy as if he were standing before the divine judge, the Lord

---

[124] Tentler, *Sin and Confession on the Eve of the Reformation*, 28-53.
[125] *Ibid.*, 106-109.

Christ, and confess his sins in a spirit of humility, contrition and sorrow, as well as in a spirit of simplicity and sincerity.[126] Humility must manifest itself in the penitent's willingness to accuse himself before his judge of having committed sins of word and deed.[127] He must refrain from excusing his sins,[128] for that would be contrary to humility. At the same time the penitent must not, motivated by pride or other worldly consideration, exaggerate his sins in order that he might earn praise from his confessor for his candidness. Academics come in for special criticism, because Zerbolt accuses them of making their confession in a disputatious fashion, and of attempting to steal a march upon their confessor.[129] The penitent, he reiterates, must simply and humbly confess whatever is gnawing at his conscience.[130] And if the penitent is truly humble, this cannot but become evident in the way in which he makes his confession. For he will not then recount his sins as a mere story, or as if he were speaking of some worldly matter, as is done by those who lack the spirit of humility, compunction and contrition. But those who possess this spirit, Zerbolt continues, will frequently not be able to confess without tears,[131] which

---

[126] *Asc.*, 263B-C: Quia vero in peccatis tuis Deum per superbiam contempsisti, ideo necesse est ut te homini Dei vicario claves habenti humiliter subdas vice Dei, et ei tanquam Christo Domino iudici tuo assistens humiliter et contrite et dolorose peccata tua confitearis. *Ref.*, 250E: ..., et tanquam in omnibus assistens judici, loquere et responde. See footnote 131 below.

[127] *Asc.*, 263C: Humiliter videlicet te in omnibus accusans, et propria peccata agnoscens, in moribus, in gestis, in prolatione verborum, in responsionibus, singulisque aliis tanquam iudici tuo assistens te habeas. Cf. Steinmetz, *Staupitz*, 102.

[128] *Asc.*, 263C: Noli etiam peccata tua vel intentionem tuam excusare,... *Ref.*, 250F: ...; ut non excuses intentionem,...

[129] *Asc.*, 263C: Cave ne, ut quidam, magna crimina cofitens, inde quaeras laudari, unde ab Deo mereris reprobari. Sicut nonnulli quod in scholis acute solebant arguere confitentur, etc. *Ref.*, 250E-F: Sit etiam humilis, ut non dicas quaedam, quae licet turpia, tamen propter aliquam secularitatem inde velis laudari, sicut quidam qui acute disputando alium superaverunt, etc.
We may have here some evidence of the anti-intellectualism of which the Devotionalists have been accused (cf. Alberts, *Moderne Devotie*, 46-49).

[130] *Asc.*, 263C: ..., sed dic simpliciter et humiliter quod remordet tuam conscientiam. *Ref.*, 250F: Sit etiam simplex,..., sed simpliciter quicquid conscientiam remordet confitere.

[131] *Ref.*, 250E: Post contritionem sequatur confessio simplex, humilis et fidelis. Humilis, ut cum vera compunctione peccata nostra confiteamur, non recitando sicut fabulam: Sicut quidam faciunt qui spiritum compunctionis non habent. *Ref.*, 250E: Nam qui spiritum compunctionis per sui discussionem eo modo quo supra dictum est, acquisierunt, facile in lachrymas prorumpunt, imo saepe peccata sua sine lachrymis dicere non possunt. *Asc.*, 263C: Debes etiam contrite et dolorose confiteri, exercens te ante confessionem ad compunctionem modo quo postea habebitur,... Et si hoc bene feceris, nequaquam sicut quidam faciunt, peccata tua sicut fabulam proferes, vel ita simpliciter proferes sine dolore quasi de alia seculari materia loquereris, sed si vere spiritum compunctionis concepisti, interdum difficile erit tibi, imo vero lachrymas cohibere nequibis. Cf. footnotes 103 and 104. These three passages are inspired by *The Golden Epistle of Abbot William of St. Thierry*, 48. Cf. Tentler, *Sin and Confession on the Eve of the Reformation*, 107.

serves as further overt evidence of the sincerity and authenticity of the believer's repentance without which his sins cannot be forgiven.

Humility clearly is the word Zerbolt uses more frequently than any other to describe the bearing required of the penitent when he makes his confession. Zerbolt's reason for fastening on humility is understandable in view of the fact that it was held to be the opposite of pride. And just as pride was held to be the cause of sin, so overt humility was held to indicate inner repentance. For the Devotionalists in particular believed that *exteriora interiora trahunt*.[132]

As his second point Zerbolt discusses the frequency of confession. The Fourth Lateran Council, which sat in 1215, decreed that all the faithful should communicate at least once a year, preceded by confession.[133] However, most writers on the subject urged more frequent confession not only to have one's sins forgiven, but also on account of the private spiritual guidance received in the confessional.[134] Zerbolt urges frequent confession only by implication. For he writes that if the believer desires to confess all his sins faithfully and sincerely, it would be well if he were to make note of them in a booklet in accordance with the advice given by Saint Anthony.[135] This advice to record and to confess every last peccadillo entails fairly frequent sacramental penance, and the idea underlying the confession of all sins is that sins are not forgiven unless they are absolved by a priest who has the power of the keys. The necessity to confess sins, if they are to be forgiven, does not diminish the need for repentance. In fact, Zerbolt's belief that sins are forgiven in proportion to the degree of contrition possessed by the penitent would appear to be at least partially responsible for his attempt at completeness in the confessional. This extreme degree of scrupulousness which Zerbolt advocates with regard to confession of sins would appear to have been fairly widespread

---

[132] Van Woerkum, "Florentius Radewijns: Leven, Geschriften, Persoonlijkheid en Ideeën," 363.

[133] McGiffert, *A History of Christian Thought*, II, 322; and N. Halligan, "Confession, Frequency of," *NCE*, IV, 132.

[134] Cf. Municipal Archives, Zwolle: Ms. Emmanuelshuizen, No. 5, fol. 30r°-30v°; de Beer, *Spiritualiteit*, 65; and Tentler, *Sin and Confession on the Eve of the Reformation*, 70-82.

[135] *Ref.*, 250F: Et ut fidelius confitearis, potes tuos defectus quotidianos, secundum Antonium, in scriptis notare.

St. Antony's advice to keep a record of one's sins, and of one's spiritual development and progress in general, is found in the *Vita S. Antonii* by Athanasius, bishop of Alexandria (*Nicene and Post-Nicene Fathers*, IV, 211). The passage from the *Vita S. Antonii* in question may be found in Radewijns' *Omnes, Inquit, Artes*, II, 51-52, and that perhaps explains Zerbolt's knowledge of it. However, if the *Vita S. Antonii* was available to Radewijns, Zerbolt must have had access to it as well.

It was common among the Devotionalists to keep a written record of all spiritual self-examinations, and not only of those carried out before going to confession. See Radewijns, *Tractatulus Devotus*, 222-223, and Goossens, *Meditatie*, 125-126.

during the late middle ages, and it was a form of piety which was to drive Luther to despair.[136]

Thirdly, Zerbolt discusses the confessor who is God's deputy, and who has been granted the power of the keys. For that reason, he writes, it is important that the penitent choose a confessor who knows how to loosen or to bind with discretion and prudence.[137] For if the confessor should absolve sins in the absence of genuine repentance that would not only increase the penitent's punishment, Grote wrote some years before,[138] but also give him a sense of all being well when, in fact, it is not, and so his future spiritual well-being might be endangered. However, a priest who knows how to forgive and to retain sins prudently is one to whom the believer can entrust his soul with confidence, Zerbolt continues, for such a priest will be able to offer sound advice on all spiritual matters. Consequently, the believer must humbly submit himself to all the things he prescribes, including the satisfaction set by him following confession.[139] Zerbolt concludes with the advice that once the believer has found a prudent and wise confessor, he must not change him lightly. Different physicians prescribe different medicines, he explains, and when medicines are changed too often they do not restore health, but make the malady even worse than it was before. However, in the selection of a confessor the canonical stipulations with regard to confessors, as well as obedience to religious superiors, must always be observed, he warns.[140] Being a priest

---

[136] Cf. Steinmetz, *Staupitz*, 103 and H. Boehmer, *Martin Luther, Road to Reformation* (Cleveland and New York: Meridian Books, 1957), 195.

[137] *Asc.*, 263D: Si etiam fieri potest, talem tibi debes confessorem eligere, qui discrete et prudenter sciat absolvere vel ligare,... Cf. Mulder, ed., *Gerardi Magni Epistolae*, 100-106. On the desirable qualities in a confessor see Tentler, *Sin and Confession on the Eve of the Reformation*, 95-104.

[138] Mulder, ed., *Gerardi Magni Epistolae*, 101-102.

[139] *Asc.*, 263D: ..., cui animam tuam poteris fiducialiter committere, cui statum tuum, vitam tuam, et omnia exercitia tua secure poteris exponere, ab eodem super singulis consilia recepturus. *Ref.*, 250F: Item salvo jure debes meliori quem invenire poteris confiteri, et maxime viro spirituali, cui conscientiam tuam possis committere, et consilia ab eo recipere, et cui in omnibus acquiescas. *Ref.*, 250E: Sit etiam humilis; ut humiliter et subjecte te habeas ad confessorem, in omnibus te sibi subjiciens ad satisfaciendum, ... Cf. van Rooy, *Zerbolt*, 261-263; *The Golden Epistle of Abbot William of St. Thierry*, 47-48; and Dempsey Douglass, *Geiler*, 155.

[140] *Asc.*, 263D: Cumque talem confessorem inveneris, noli eum leviter variare. Diversi enim medici, diversis utuntur medicinis. Medicina autem saepe mutata non sanat, sed turbat aegrotum. In his tamen omnibus semper salvo iure et obedientia Ecclesiae et superioris. Also see the second passage in footnote 139 above.
The warning not to change confessors too often in view of the fact that they prescribe different medicines is clearly inspired by *The Golden Epistle of Abbot William of St. Thierry*, 47-48.
It was a common practice to compare confessors to physicians (Tentler, *Sin and Confession on the Eve of the Reformation*, 98 and 100).

himself, Zerbolt was, understandably, well acquainted with the juridical aspects of the sacraments of penance.

The difficulty encountered in determining the sincerity and sufficiency of a penitent's repentance put considerable strain upon the confessors, and particularly upon the most scrupulous among them. It was for that reason that Grote refrained from becoming a priest and assuming a *cura animarum*; and it was on those same grounds that he also advised others against taking on a *cura animarum*.[141] Zerbolt, like Grote, discouraged people from assuming the priestly office, although his reason for doing so differed somewhat from Grote's. In *Scriptum Pro Quodam*, which is devoted entirely to this question, he writes that the cure of souls consists of two kinds. On the one hand there is that carried out by the ordained clergy who preach, dispense the sacraments, excommunicate, and the like. This *cura animarum* must never be sought voluntarily, he cautions; for he is of the opinion that those who do are simply self-seekers motivated primarily by pride and ambition and that, in their desire to become priests, they are jeopardizing their own salvation.[142] These same people, he observes, often use the argument that they want to win souls for God.[143] But what benefit, he asks, will they obtain from converting the entire world while losing their own soul?[144] This does not mean that Zerbolt was unconcerned about the spiritual welfare of others: quite to the contrary. For he writes that there is also the cure of souls motivated

---

[141] Mulder, ed., *Gerardi Magni Epistolae*, 100-106 and Post, *The Modern Devotion*, 110-114.

Johann Geiler also relinquished his *cura* and restricted his activities to preaching, because his scrupulousness as a confessor made the *cura* an intolerable burden for him (Dempsey Douglass, *Geiler*, 153).

[142] See *Scriptum Pro Quodam*, ch. 3 (pp. 187-198), entitled: *De vicioso affectu et inordinato appetitu ad sacerdocium*, and ch. 4 (pp. 199-201), entitled: *Quam periculosa sit multis temptacio affectus inordinatus ad predicandum vel aliis proficiendis*, in particular. Also see footnote 143 below and *Ref.*, 257A.

The idea that the priesthood constitutes a danger to one's soul does not originate with Grote and Zerbolt. Cassian already warned the readers of the *Institutes* to avoid the priestly office for the same reason as that given by Zerbolt. (*Institutes*, Bk. XI, chs. 14, 16 and 18.) Among the Devotionalists only those became priests who were requested to do so by the majority of the members of a given community. In following this practice the Devotionalists may have been influenced by the advice given by Gregory the Great on this particular question (see *Asc.*, 284C).

[143] *Asc.*, 284C: Sed et ipsa vana gloria ut ab hoc ascensu deceptorie trahat, frequenter, non violenter, sed fraudulenter hominem deiicit, id est, aliquando suggerit aliquod magnum arripiendum, non intentione gloria, sed zelo Dei. Verbi gratia: suscipere officium praedicationis, presbyteratus vel diaconatus ordinem, ut possit domino animas lucrari et aliis formam praebere vitae exemplaris, sed est appetitus vanus et repellendus. Nam eo ipso homo ad talia indignus efficitur, si ex appetitu ad talia afficiatur.

[144] *Scriptum Pro Quodam*, 196: ..., quod regimen animarum semper male et nunquam bene appetitur,... *Scriptum Pro Quodam*, 222: Et quid prodest homini si multos convertat, ymno totum lucratur mundum, seipsum vero perdat. Cf. Mark 8, 36.

by love which consists in brotherly admonition and correction, and in offering advice and aid to all.[145] This cure of souls, motivated by love, is incumbent upon all believers, he emphasizes; because no one is allowed to
say that his own salvation keeps him sufficiently occupied, that he will be
concerned about his own salvation only and not with that of others.[146] It
is incumbent upon all who have made some headway in the spiritual life
to offer such spiritual advice, guidance and encouragement to the beginners as is dictated by their individual needs. God has, he asserts, given
man no more precious task in this life than to work zealously for the
salvation of souls, and he calls on Bede in support of this assertion.[147]

Finally, we must look at what Zerbolt writes regarding lay confession
which is of a piece with the cure of souls carried out by those who have
not received holy orders, and to this question he devotes an entire chapter
in *Super Modo Vivendi*.[148] This tract is a defense of the Brethren's way of

---

[145] *Ibid.*, 203: Sciendum tamen, quod secundum Antisidorensem super IV "Sentenciarum", titulo "De correpcione superna", quod dupliciter aliquis potest habere curam
animarum. Uno modo ex officio, ad quam pertinet predicare, corrigere, punire, excom-
municare et sic de aliis. Et hac est prelatorum dumtaxat vel quibus iniungunt, et de hac
loquitur Thomas. Alia est cura animarum ex caritate, ad quam pertinet ammonicio,
fraterna correccio, erranti consulere, neminem scandalizare, consilium et auxilium
prebere. Et hec omnia pertinent ad omnes caritatem habentes. It is fairly certain that the
work by William Antissiodorensis from which Zerbolt quotes here was at one time the
property of Grote (Lourdaux, "Het Boekenbezit en het Boekengebruik bij de Moderne
Devoten," 260).
Also see *Asc.*, ch. 69 (pp. 287C-288A).

[146] *Ref.*, 241C: Nec dicas: Sufficit mihi mea salvatio, pro me volo esse sollicitus, non
pro aliis. Quisquis hoc dixerit, non comeditur zelo Dei. Cf. *Asc.*, 287E and *Super Modo
Vivendi*, ch. 5 (pp. 46-52).

[147] *Ref.*, 241B-C: Non ergo peccatores ab te repelles, sicut false iustus et arrogans
Pharisaeus, sed pie compatiendo, debes totis viribus niti, si quem eorum potueris eripere
de laqueis inimici; sive hoc feceris piis admonitionibus, sive correptionibus tuis, unumquemque prout ratia exigit, et conditio cuiuscunque corripiendo vel admonendo, sciens
quod non est preciosius munus ab Deo in hac vita quam zelus animarum, pro quarum
salute Christus de coelo descendet, et mortem amarissimam toleravit. Hoc est enim
secundum Bedam, excellentissimum genus, vitae, si te ab vitiis purgaveris, et alios ad
bonam conversationem traxeris. Esto igitur animarum zelo fervidus, omnes trahe amore,
nondum conversos, timore terre: Iam incipientes de tentationibus praemuni, et induc ut
crimina confiteantur, omnibus in tentationibus et passionibus consule, conforta, dirige
pro ut tibi visum fuerit uniquique convenire. *Asc.*, 261F: Item an ferveas zelo ad alios
charitative admonendum vel etiam humiliter increpandum. Item, si opus tibi commissum
studeas fideliter adimplere. Cf. *Asc.*, ch. 69 (pp. 287C-288A) and *Super Modo Vivendi*, ch. 5
(pp. 46-52).
This concern for the spiritual welfare of others is echoed in the *Constitutiones* which M.
Schoengen attributes to the Brethren House in Zwolle. In the chapter dealing with the
founding of the House and its purpose, the *Constitutiones* have it that the House was founded "*non solum de sua bona conversatione, sed etiam de aliorum conversione et salute.*" (Jacobus de
Voecht, *Narratio*, 240.)

[148] *Super Modo Vivendi*, ch. 9 (pp. 80-87). Zerbolt begins the chapter by stating the
problem: Queri eciam potest, utrum ad recipiendum consilium vel alia qualibet ex causa
potest aliquis sua peccata revelare ei, qui nec claves habet nec iurisdictionem. He then
states his case for the validity of making one's confession to someone who does not possess
the power of the keys. The arguments are generally too lengthy to be given in full.

life which had come under attack from various quarters,[149] and one of the practices in vogue amongst the Brethren was lay confession, although it cannot be said to have been altogether unique to them. In 1215 the Fourth Lateran Council had decreed that all believers must confess at least once a year to a priest who possesses the power of the keys.[150] But that, Zerbolt argues, does not make it illegal, as some maintain, to confess one's sins, whether they be venial or mortal, to someone who does not possess the power of the keys. He believes, in fact, that in his *Commentary on the Sentences* Aquinas makes the confession of mortal sins to a layman mandatory in an emergency. Nevertheless, Zerbolt takes care to add that those lacking the power of the keys cannot absolve or retain sins, whether they be venial or mortal.[151]

Even though he touches on the confession of mortal sins to a layman—whom he defines as one who does not possess the power of the keys and who cannot, therefore, absolve sins or impose penance—, Zerbolt is primarily interested in the confession of venial sins to such an individual; and he mentions a number of benefits to be derived from such a practice. The first advantage named by him is the forgiveness of the venial sins confessed, although he concedes that sacramental confession is more efficacious for the forgiveness of venial sins than is confession to a layman. Relying on Aquinas' *Commentary on the Sentences*, Zerbolt explains that the forgiveness of venial sins may be accomplished through good works whatever their nature may be, because all good works are, in fact, a form of penance. And to confess one's venial sins to a layman is, when accompanied by a contrite heart, a good work in itself, he asserts, and an act of penance.[152] That confession accomplishes the forgiveness of venial

---

[149] Cf. Post, *The Modern Devotion*, 273-292.

[150] Cf. Harnack, *History of Dogma*, VI, 243-258.

[151] *Super Modo Vivendi*, 81: Et sic potest quivis peccatum suum confiteri cuilibet, sive clerico, sive layco...Item patet Iohannes Andre,... "Quod cuicumque voluero possum confiteri in salutem anime petendo consilium. Sed ille non potest absolvere vel ligare, quia non habet claves."

Super Mode Vivendi, 80-83: Queri eciam...penitencie iniunctio.

Zerbolt does not say anything about the effect the confession of mortal sins to a layman might have on such sins.

[152] *Super Mode Vivendi*, 83-84: Unde hec confessio non sacramentalis, qui fit alicui non ut ministro, est simplex revelacio peccati vel temptacionis pro habendo auxilio vel consilio, nec fit absolucio, nec fit per modum confessionis sacramentalis, nec debet fieri penitencie iniunctio.

Est tamen hec confessio non sacramentalis, que fit alicui non ut ministro, sive revelacio peccatorum, valde utilis et expediens et precipue valet ad quator. Primo autem credendum est quod per hanc humilem revelacionem pene remissio, licet plus in confessione non sacramentali, que fit alicui ut ministro, sed multo amplius in confessione sacramentali, que fit ut ministro proprio sacerdoti. Unde nota secundum Petrum [Lombard] super IV Sentenciarum, distinctio XVI, in exposicione litere quod venialia peccata dupliciter dimittuntur. Uno modo quasi virtute sacramenti, sicut per penitenciam et eukaristie

sins was based on the widely accepted teaching that the act of confession itself constitutes the expiation of the venial sins confessed.[153] It was commonly understood, however, that if confession itself is to expiate sins, it has to be made to a priest who possesses the power of the keys; but Zerbolt asserts that confession of venial sins to a layman achieves the same result. Such a doctrine could easily be construed, of course, as an attempt to undermine the position of the church and its sacraments.

In addition to forgiveness which he clearly regards as being the most important, Zerbolt names three more benefits which may be derived from confessing one's venial sins to a layman. First, it is a means of obtaining spiritual guidance and advice from a layman with insight into the spiritual life from which the penitent can benefit. Secondly, frequent confession of venial sins, even to a layman, is a very useful weapon in the fight against sin and vice. For the penitent, Zerbolt believes, will be ashamed to confess the same sins over and over, thereby revealing that he has made no progress in the spiritual life. Lastly, confession, irrespective of to whom it is made, will destroy the hold which temptations and passions have on the penitent. Zerbolt quotes Cassian to the effect that evil thoughts rule a man only as long as they remain hidden in his heart. Their revelation stimulates the growth of humility and compunction while it destroys pride and vainglory. All of these benefits, Zerbolt concludes, can be derived from non-sacramental confession of venial sins, and it is only for the absolution of mortal sins that it is strictly necessary to confess to a priest who possesses the power of the keys.[154]

Satisfaction. The purpose of sacramental penance was commonly held to be twofold. Its *raison d'être* was, in the first place, to expiate sin; but sacramental penance was imposed on the penitent for a therapeutic reason as well. Its end was to prevent the penitent from committing in the future those same sins for which the penance was being prescribed.[155] Zerbolt likewise assigns these two related roles to sacramental penance, although the former receives most of the attention from him.

---

sumpcionem, et cetera. Alio modo quasi per modum meriti, ut per martirium et per dimissionem iniuriarum, et cetera...Et sicut dicit Thomas plura vel pauciora per hec dimittuntur secundum quod per hec maior vel minor fervor concitatur. Et ita per hanc humilem peccatorum vel defectuum revelacionem per modum meriti venialia dimittuntur, et eo amplius, quo fit devocius, et quo quis ad maiorem per eam accenditur contricionem.

[153] Aquinas, *Summa Contra Gentiles*, Bk. IV, ch. 72; and K. Rahner, "Penance," *SM*, IV, 397.

[154] *Super Modo Vivendi*, 84-87: Et ita per hanc...sociorum suorum.

[155] Thomas Aquinas, *Summa Contra Gentiles*, Bk. IV, ch. 72; P. E. McKeever, "Penance, Sacrament of," *NCE*, XI, 81; and C. I. Litzinger, "Penance, Sacramental," *NCE*, XI, 83-84.

To begin with, Zerbolt makes satisfaction a real and integral part of the sacrament of penance. For without rendering satisfaction for sins, he explains, penance is incomplete and, consequently, does not suffice for justification.[156] He does not spell out why this is so, but the reason is that Christ's death did not totally remove the penalty, or punishment, attached to actual sin. God's justice demands that the penitent should bear part of the penalty himself if he wishes to share in Christ's vicarious and redemptive death. This penalty consists of the penance prescribed by the confessor following confession, and these acts of penance satisfy God's justice and so expiate sin.[157] In view of the importance of penance, Zerbolt emphasizes that God requires total and complete satisfaction for sins committed. Man can rest assured, he observes, that if he does not make satisfaction for them in this life, satisfaction will be exacted from him in the hereafter (in futuro), namely in purgatory, and to the last farthing at that. For God does not leave any sin unpunished and demands that satisfaction be made for all of them.[158] According to Saint Bernard, Zerbolt warns, it is advisable to make satisfaction for one's sins in this life, because satisfaction exacted from the penitent in the hereafter will be a hundred times more rigorous than the satisfaction imposed upon him in this life.[159] As regards the acts of penance which offer the most satisfaction Zerbolt names fasting, vigils, manual tasks, and similar devout exercises. However, he adds that the acts of penance prescribed by the confessor must, irrespective of their nature, be performed before any others. For good works enjoined by the confessor give infinitely more satisfaction, are more efficacious, and are more meritorious than are good works undertaken of one's own accord. This is so, he explains, because of the power of the keys which was granted to the church and is exercised by the clergy, and because of the humble obedience shown by the penitent in

---

[156] *Ref.*, 250F: Satisfactionem ad confessoris arbitrium prompto animo adimplebis, eo quod sine satisfactione poenitentia non sit integra, ideo neque sufficiens. Cf. the passage given in footnote 67 above and Rahner and Vorgrimler, *Theological Dictionary*, 345-346 ("Penance, Sacrament of").

[157] Cf. Harnack, *History of Dogma*, VI, 243-258 and K. Rahner, "Penance," *SM*, IV, 397.

[158] *Ref.*, 243G: ..., et vide de singularibus tuis criminibus, numera ea si potes in conspectu Domini, et pete veniam de praeteritis, adiutorium de praesentibus, et cautelam contra futura. Deinde cogita in quanto pro istis satisfecisti, certus quod quicquid hic non reddideris, in futuro ab te exigetur usque ad minimum quadrantem. *Asc.*, 261B: ...; sciens certissime quod vel hic vel in futuro [ab te exigetur usque ad minimum quadrantem. Sed in futuro,] secundum Bernardum,... Comparison with other editions and translations of *De Ascensionibus* shows that the type-setter of the edition we are using omitted the part enclosed by the square brackets.

[159] *Asc.*, 261B [Sed in futuro,] secundum Bernardum, centuplum reddes quod hic simplo solvere posses. See previous footnote.

performing the penance set by the confessor.[160] Therefore, Zerbolt points out, the penitent must be ready and willing to undertake whatever the priest should impose in the way of penance and works of satisfaction. And if the priest should be prepared to let the penitent off more lightly than he ought to, then the penitent should urge the confessor to prescribe a more arduous penance from which he may derive spiritual benefit and healing,[161] which brings us to the therapeutic reason for doing penance.

Influenced by William of Saint Thierry, Zerbolt writes that those powers and faculties which the penitent previously employed in the service of iniquity ought now to become instruments of righteousness. Instead of putting them at the service of sin and vice he ought now to place them in the service of works of expiation and satisfaction.[162] In thus opposing good works to vices and passions, satisfaction is made for sin, the wounds created by sin are healed, and at the same time man is prevented from committing further sins because his powers and faculties are devoted to works of righteousness and satisfaction.[163]

In view of the foregoing it can hardly be said of Zerbolt that he glossed over the question of doing penance for sins confessed as a means of expiating them. The considerable emphasis placed by him on the need to make satisfaction for sins confessed would appear to reflect the renewed late-medieval concern with this facet of the sacrament of penance.[164]

The effect of penance. As a result of the three parts of the sacrament of penance man's sins are totally remitted, he is reconciled to God and in-

---

[160] *Asc.*, 263F: ..., et maxime illis vitiis et passionibus, quibus frequentius impugnaris, in ieiuniis, in vigiliis, laboribus, aliisque devotus exercitiis, et hoc, ut dictum est, maxime ad iniunctionem tui confessoris, quia sic sunt tibi magis meritoria. *Asc.*, 263D: Scire etiam debes quod multo plus sunt satisfactoria bona opera tua ab sacerdote tibi iniuncta quam sponte ab teipso assumpta, praecipue propter vim clavium Ecclesiae et propter humilem obedientiam confitentis. Cf. Aquinas, *Summa Contra Gentiles*, Bk. IV, ch. 72; McGiffert, *A History of Christian Thought*, II, 325-326.

Underlying the emphasis on manual tasks is the idea that someone who is occupied is not subjected to the same temptations as one who is idle. See below, pp. 274-275.

[161] *Asc.*, 263D-E: Ideo cum vulnera tua sacerdoti tuo exposueris, et ipse sicut merito debet, levioribus uti voluerit medicamentis, insta opportune nonnunquam importune ut tibi non parcat, sed quae sibi pro tuo statu et emendatione expedire videbuntur audacter iniungat, et promptum exhibe ad tolerandum. See the passage in footnote 156 above.

[162] *Asc.*, 263E-F: Tertius autem huius primae ascensionis gradus est, ut sicut exhibuisti membra tua arma iniquitatis peccato per varia peccata et mala opera; ita nunc facias ea arma iustitiae in satisfactionem: ut scilicet contraria contrariis cures, faciens contraria illis criminibus quae commisisti, et maxime illis vitiis et passionibus, quibus frequentius impugnaris,... Cf. *The Golden Epistle of Abbot William of St. Thierry*, 45; and Romans, 6, 19.

The idea that *"contrariis sanare contraria,"* borrowed from Hippocratic medicine, was widely employed by spiritual writers in their expositions on the vices and how to deal with them (A. Cabassut, "Défauts," *DSp*, III, 81-82).

[163] Cf. Dempsey Douglass, *Geiler*, 160.

[164] Cf. Dempsey Douglass, *Geiler*, 158; Dudden, *Gregory the Great*, II, 423; and footnote 103 above.

fused with justifying grace which can come from God only.[165] However, as Zerbolt explains, to be justified and reconciled to God through penance does not mean that man has achieved the state of perfect charity: i.e., a state in which he loves God more than anything else, and in which all of his actions are motivated by love for God.[166] The state of justification is merely the indispensible basis for perfect charity, and it is to the attainment of charity following justification that *De Ascensionibus* as well as *De Reformatione* are chiefly devoted.[167]

C) *Good Works Performed in the State of Grace*

Good works performed in the state of grace do not receive much attention from Zerbolt, and there is very little in his writings which deals directly with this topic. However, some indication of what Zerbolt's views on good works must have been may be gleaned from his discussion of pride and its opposite: i.e., humility, in *De Reformatione* and *De Ascensionibus*.[168] For the purpose of combating pride, Zerbolt writes, man must ever be mindful of the fact that the good that is in him and, consequently, the good works performed by him, are not altogether good but contain many imperfections. Negligence, tepidity, hypocrisy, vainglory, and so forth, often taint the good that is in man and the good that he does, on account of which they possess little merit and are little accepted of God.[169] For the purpose of combating pride Zerbolt even goes so far as to assert that man is incapable of any good whatsoever,[170] but such an extreme statement must be viewed in the context in which it is written.

---

[165] *Ref.*, 245F: Dimisit enim tibi tot mala quod fecisti, de quibus supra dictum est,... *Ref.*, 245G: ..., et ei gratiam suae iustificationis infudit, quae solum ab ipso descendit. *Ref.*, 250D: ...: Idcirco duplici indigent voluntatis reformatione. Prima, qua eis infundatur gratia et justificatio. *Asc.*, 263F: ..., et his tribus partibus poenitentiae redis ad cor, et Deo pariter reconciliaris...Ecce homo sanus factus es et Deo reconciliatus,... *Asc.*, 267F: Deinde cogita de donis gratiae tibi collatis..., et ab iniustitia revocavit, et iustitiam infudit, quod est solius Dei,... *Asc.*, 267D: ..., dolenti peccata indulsit,... Cf. Dempsey Douglass, *Geiler*, 160.
The excerpts from *Ref.*, 245G and *Asc.*, 267F were inspired by Bonaventure's *De Triplici Via*, ch. 1, par. 2, *via* Radewijns' *Omnes, Inquit, Artes*, II, 159-160.
[166] *Asc.*, 263G: ..., nec putes sufficere quod per poenitentiam sis Deo reconciliatus, ut ad eius familiaritatem accepiaris et perfectam charitatem.
[167] See below, pp. 233-241.
[168] *Ref.*, chs. 57-58 (p. 257C-G); and *Asc.*, ch. 63 (pp. 284D-285A).
[169] *Asc.*, 284H: Bona nostra non sunt pure bona, sed multipliciter imperfecta. Negligentia, tepiditas, hypocrisis, vana gloria, etc. adeo saepe bona nostra coinquinant, ut et nobis parum sint meritoria, et Deo minus accepta, Cf. D. of Augsburg, *De ext. et int. hom. compositione*, I, 117-118 and II, 80.
[170] *Ref.*, 257F-G: Humilitas quae contra superbiam pugnat tres gradus habet. Primus gradus est, ut homo seipsum cognoscat infirmum, inopem boni, vitiosum et si quos alios habet defectus, et non elevet se supra se. *Asc.*, 284E: Oportet autem contra eam ascendere per gradus humilitatis. Quorum primus est, quod homo in veritate cognoscat seipsum esse infirmum, inopem boni, vitiosum, et siquos alios habet defectus, et non elevet se super se. Cf. D. of Augsburg, *De ext. et int. hom. compositione*, I, 117-118 and II, 80.

In regarding good works performed in the state of grace as faulty, defective and unsatisfactory, Zerbolt did not, of course, stand alone. It is a prominent theme in the writings of Augustine, Gregory the Great and Bernard of Clairvaux,[171] all of which constituted major sources for Zerbolt's thought. Furthermore, it is also a recurring theme in the sermon literature and spiritual writings of the late middle ages.[172]

Zerbolt continues that, in order to become truly humble, the believer must also acknowledge that such good as there is in him, and such good works as he does perform, are not his own but gifts of the merciful God.[173] Man does not possess true humility unless he can sincerely confess with both heart and voice that all his virtues, spiritual progress and good works are gratuitous gifts of the merciful God who "worketh both to will and to do according to His good pleasure."[174] Consequently, whatever merit there may be in man's good works performed in the state of grace is a gift of God, the result of divine grace and not of his own, unaided efforts. In fact, the emphasis placed by Zerbolt on the need for grace to perform meritorious works is so considerable that it has the appearance of totally neglecting the role played by man's free will in the performance of good works. Once the believer fully recognizes the extent to which meritorious works are dependent upon divine grace, a profound humility follows automatically. And humility is a first requirement in the spiritual life generally; because nothing is so destructive of the believer's righteousness and sanctity as is the evil of pride which causes him not only to slight God's indispensable grace and mercy, but gives rise to negligence as well.[175]

---

[171] A. Zumkeller, "Das Ungenügen der menschlichen Werke bei den deutschen Predigern des Spätmittelalters," *Zeitschrift für katholische Theologie*, LXXXI (1959), 265-268.

[172] *Ibid.*, 176-178 and 268-301, and Dempsy-Douglass, *Geiler*, 167-168 and 177-178.

[173] *Asc.*, 284H: Item diligenter considerare propriam vilitatem, diligenter perpendere, quod bona mentis tuae non sunt tua, sed Dei dona, et de ipsis rationem redditurus sis. *Ref.*, 257D: Item diligenter considerare, quia bona nostra non sunt ab nobis, sed dona Dei, de quibus districte rationem sumus reddituri. *Ref.*, 257G: Tertius est, quando homo etiam in magnis virtutibus et honoribus non extollitur, et nihil ex hoc sibi blanditur, totum in illum refundens ab quo totum accepit, et ei in integrum restituens. Cf. D. of Augsburg, *De ext. et int. hom. compositione*, I, 118 and II, 80; Mulder, ed., *Gerardi Magni Epistolae*, 294-303; and G. Gilleman, "Humility," *NCE*, VII, 235.

[174] See footnotes 40 and 116 above. Cf. D. of Augsburg, *De ext. et int. hom. compositione*, I, 118 and II, 80.
Synergism is clearly rejected by Zerbolt (Rahner and Vorgrimler, *Theological Dictionary*, 452 [Synergism]).

[175] *Ref.*, 257D: Nullum vitium est quod ita omnes virtutes exhauriat, cunctaque iustitia et sanctitate hominem exspoliet quemadmodum huius superbiae malum. *Asc.*, 284G; Et haec est multo periculosior quam vitia carnalia, Nullum est aliud vitium quod ita omnes virtutes exhaurit, cunctaque iustitia ac sanctitate hominem spoliat atque denudat, quemadmodum hoc superbiae malum, quod in virtutem iam fastigio collocatos, gravissima ruina deiicere ac trucidare solet.

That without the aid of grace man cannot perform meritorious works even in the state of grace was a traditional doctrine, as was the teaching that all of man's good works are faulty, and the former finds forceful expression in the writings of Augustine and Bernard of Clairvaux, to name but two writers on whom Zerbolt relied heavily.[176] In the fourteenth century Grote, the spiritual father of the Modern Devotion, likewise warned against thinking that man can perform meritorious works without divine assistance, and he also cautioned against the spiritually destructive pride to which such thinking may lead.[177]

Although man's works performed in the state of grace were held to be faulty and imperfect, and although such goodness and merit as they possessed were held to be the result of grace for the most part, it had been a central doctrine of the church since at least the time of Augustine that there can be no salvation without meritorious works.[178] Not surprisingly Zerbolt touches on the necessity of meritorious works for salvation in connection with his discussion of the final judgement. By then, he writes, time in which the believer might have obtained and "purchased" for himself the oil of meritorious deeds will have slipped away irrevocably.[179] He elaborates that, although no good and meritorious work will go unrewarded,[180] works of mercy and piety are the most meritorious, and they will receive the most consideration from Christ in the last judgement.[181] Clearly, then, Zerbolt does not deny the value and need of

---

[176] Augustine, *The Enchiridion on Faith, Hope and Love*, ch. 107, and Zumkeller, "Das Ungenügen der menschlichen Werke bei den deutschen Predigern des Spätmittelalters," 267.

[177] N. van Wijk, ed., *Het Getijdenboek van Geert Groote, naar het Haagse Handschrift 133 E 21* (Leiden, 1940), 150: Van allen quaden behaeghen ons of onser goeder werke. verloes ons here. Van dunken dat wi yet goets wt ons seluen hebben. verloes ons here. Cf. Epiney-Burgard, *Grote*, 290. Cf. Dempsey Douglass, *Geiler*, 166-167 and cf. 177-178.

[178] Augustine, *The Enchiridion on Faith, Hope and Love*, ch. 107. Cf. W. Molinski, "Merit," *SM*, IV, 13; Richardson, ed., *Dictionary*, 146 ("Good Works") and 211-212 ("Merit"); Dudden, *Gregory the Great*, II, 424; Dempsey Douglass, *Geiler*, 171-176; and Zumkeller, "Das Ungenügen der menschlichen Werke bei den deutschen Predigern des Spätmittelalters," 265-305.

[179] *Asc.*, 265E: ..., tempus enim abiit et recessit, non est quo eant et emant oleum meritorum. Cf. Matthew 15, 1-13.

[180] *Ref.*, 243G: Nullum enim malum impunitum erit, sicut nec aliquod bonum irremuneratum.

[181] *Ref.*, 245A: Cogita quam magna sint opera misericordiae et pietatis, cum ea solum Christus ad iudicium suum adducere videatur. Cf. Radewijns, *Tractatulus Devotus*, 228.
Zerbolt does not indicate whether he regards the merit attached to good works to be condign or congruous. The fact that he does not really spell out what the impact of justifying grace is on man, adds to the difficulty in determining whether Zerbolt understood merit to be condign or congruous. However, if his generally Thomistic outlook applies in this instance, then he would regard the merit attached to good works as being condign. Cf. Molinski, "Merit," *SM*, IV, 11-13; C. S. Sullivan, "Merit," *NCE*, IX, 683-684; Richardson, ed., *Dictionary*, 146 ("Good Works") and 211-212 ("Merit"); Oberman, *Biel*, 160-184; and Oberman, "'Iustitia Christi' and 'Iustitia Dei'. Luther and the Scholastic Doctrines of Justification," 1-26.

meritorious works. His emphasis on humility with regard to good works does not imply that he questions the validity of human works, but it is a means to guard against presumption as well as negligence.[182]

About the insufficiency of man's meritorious works for salvation there is nothing in Zerbolt's writings, although the emphasis placed by him on the faulty nature of man's works most certainly implies such a doctrine. Furthermore, this teaching was not foreign to the Devotionalists. It is found in the writings of Gerard Grote and Hendrik Mande,[183] as well as in those of Dirc van Herxen, for example. Van Herxen wrote towards the end of his life that he was no longer relying on his own merits, but that he was placing all his hope and trust in God's mercy and in the only meritorious work which can satisfy God's justice, namely Christ's death on the cross.[184] However, the Devotionalists were not the only ones to assert that human works are insufficient for salvation. This idea finds vigorous expression in the writings of Augustine and Gregory the Great, both of whom greatly influenced Zerbolt and the Devotionalists in general.[185] Furthermore, the doctrine regarding the insufficiency of good works for salvation, which follows logically from the teaching that they are faulty and imperfect, was an almost universally held doctrine in the fourteenth and fifteenth centuries, the heyday of the Devotionalist movement.[186]

D) *Predestination*

With regard to predestination there were two dominant trends of thought. On the one hand there were those who held that God freely chose a certain number of individuals to be saved from eternal damnation *ante praevisa merita*, as the expression went. They believed that in the matter of predestination God's will was determined by his mercy, and not by his intellect providing his will with information regarding man's future co-operation with divine grace. The opponents of this essentially Augustinian view of predestination held that God does base his election of the predestined on foreknowledge: i.e., on his foreknowledge of

---

[182] Cf. Dempsey Douglass, *Geiler*, 175.

[183] Mulder, ed., *Gerardi Magni Epistolae*, 294-303, and L. Knappert, *Het Ontstaan en de Vestiging van het Protestantisme in de Nederlanden* (Utrecht, 1924), 24. Cf. Richard, *The Spirituality of John Calvin*, 14.

[184] Knierim, *Dirc van Herxen (1385-1457), rector van het Zwolse fraterhuis*, 127. Cf. Post, *The Modern Devotion*, 475-476 and 482-483; and *Hier beginnen sommige stichtige punten van onsen oelden zusteren*, ed. by D. de Man (The Hague, 1899), 240-241.

[185] Dudden, *Gregory the Great*, II, 426.

[186] Zumkeller, "Das Ungenügen der menschlichen Werke bei den deutschen Predigern des Spätmittelalters," throughout; and Dempsey Douglass, *Geiler*, 176-178.

In the *One-Hundred Articles*, which were read by the Devotionalists, Suso writes that Christ's death must complete man's insignificant, and hence insufficient, works. (Meyboom, "Suso's Honderd Artikelen in Nederland," No. 75 [p. 185].)

whether a given individual will co-operate with the grace granted him for the purpose of achieving justification and sanctification.[187] Aquinas' doctrine of predestination was essentially Augustinian, but its uniqueness lies in the fact that he treated predestination as part and parcel of divine providence in general. Just as everything develops and unfolds in accordance with God's eternal plan for the universe and its ultimate purpose, so he directs everything in order that those elected to eternal life will reach their pre-ordained goal of salvation.[188]

The questions of justification and predestination were always discussed in close conjunction with one another,[189] and it is in connection with his discussion of man's justification through the sacrament of penance that Zerbolt briefly alludes to the matter of predestination. Furthermore, the little Zerbolt writes about predestination has a Thomistic ring to it. He maintained, as has been noted, that sorrow for sin, the resolve not to sin again, and contrition, all of which are necessary for the forgiveness of sins and justification, are gifts of grace. It is virtually certain that he was not of the opinion that God grants these gifts of grace to those of whom he knows in advance that they will co-operate with it, or to those who might be worthy of them on account of any desirable qualities possessed naturally. For Zerbolt informs the reader that the gifts of grace which make sorrow for sin and contrition possible, and which are then followed by the grace of justification, are withheld from many who are better than he is.[190] In other words, God grants man the grace necessary for repentance and contrition not from any consideration of such merits as man may possess; but these gifts of grace which enable man to fulfil the requirements necessary for justification are totally the result of God's gratuitous and undetermined mercy and love.[191] Furthermore, Zerbolt

---

[187] A. G. Palladino, "Predestination (In Catholic Theology)," NCE, XI, 714-719; Steinmetz, Staupitz, 75-79; Oberman, Biel, 185-216; and Richardson, ed., Dictionary, 264-268 ("Predestination").

With respect to the doctrine of predestination the more or less standard divisions commonly understood to exist in the history of Christian thought are not reliable, and can actually be misleading. Theologians like Alexander of Hales and Bonaventure, who must be called Augustinians with regard to their thought in general, both maintained that God's election of the predestined is based on foreknowledge: on his foreknowledge of men's free cooperation with the grace granted them to achieve justification and sanctification.

[188] Aquinas, ST, 1a, 23. Cf. A. G. Palladino, "Predestination (In Catholic Theology)," NCE, XI, 714-717; Richardson, ed., Dictionary, 267-268 ("Predestination"); Steinmetz, Staupitz, 76-77; McGiffert, A History of Christian Thought, II, 278-279.

[189] Cf. Oberman, Biel, 185.

[190] See the first passage in footnote 192 below.

[191] With regard to this question, then, the divine intellect does not inform, or determine, the divine will, which would appear to be inconsistent with Zerbolt's concept of God as a being whose will is generally informed and determined by his intellect. However, much the same inconsistency is to be observed in Aquinas' understanding of God on the one hand, and his doctrine of predestination on the other.

continues, God also pre-ordained the time, place and manner in which such individuals might make use of this grace without which repentance is impossible.[192] And Zerbolt would appear to have been influenced here by Radewijns' observation that not only does God grant the grace necessary for repentance, but that he grants it at a time when it is most opportune.[193] However, the views of both men on this issue are reminiscent of Aquinas' teaching that the manner in which God predestines men to eternal life is merely one aspect of his providential design for the entire universe in accordance with which it unfolds and develops.[194]

It might be concluded that, according to Zerbolt, God grants to certain individuals the grace necessary for repentance and contrition without regard to merit, and that he also ordains the time and place in which they may repent of their sins and be contrite. However, there is no indication that Zerbolt considered this to diminish in any way man's freedom either to co-operate or not to co-operate with divine grace at the divinely appointed time and place. Consequently, those who are saved, are saved because of God's gratuitous mercy, and those who perish do so of their own free will and because of their own wickedness.

E) No Certainty with Regard to Justification and Salvation

It was generally held that the number and identity of the predestined remains unknown to man in this life. For most theologians were of the opinion that man can never be certain whether he is in the state of grace, even after he has received the sacrament of penance; and spiritual writers who touched on this issue generally repeated this view. The uncertainty, it was commonly held, stems from the fact that man can never be certain that he has achieved the state of contrition, the condition necessary for the forgiveness of sins and the infusion of justifying grace.[195] Zerbolt too

---

[192] *Asc.*, 267F: Deinde cogita de donis gratiae tibi collatis. Dedit enim tibi contritionem et dolorem de peccatis, et ab iniustitia revocavit, et iustitiam infudit, quod est solius Dei, quod tamen multis negavit. Dedit et inspiravit voluntatem quod te velles emendare, tempus et locum ordinavit, ubi et quando te emendare posses, et haec omnia multis te melioribus non dedit. *Ref.*, 245G: Dedit dona gratiae. Primo quod voluntatem tuam ab eo aversam ad se revocavit, et ei gratiam suae iustificationis infudit, quae solum ab ipso descendit. Dedit voluntatem ut te velles emendare, tempus et locum ordinavit, ut posses. For these two passages Zerbolt is indebted to Bonaventure's *De Triplici Via*, ch. 1, par. 2 (*Works*, I, 69-70), by way of Radewijns' *Omnes, Inquit, Artes*, II, 159-160.

[193] *Ref.*, 245G: Dedit voluntatem ut te velles emendare, tempus et locum ordinavit, ut posses. *Asc.*, 267F: Dedit et inspiravit voluntatem quod te velles emendare, tempus et locum ordinavit, ubi et quando te emendare posses, et haec omnia multis te melioribus non dedit. For these two passages Zerbolt is indebted to Bonaventure's *De Triplici Via*, ch. 1, par. 2 (*Works*, I, 69-70), by way of Radewijns' *Omnes, Inquit, Artes*, II, 159-160.

[194] Zerbolt's understanding of providence has been dealt with above, pp. 45-47.

[195] Experiential knowledge of justifying grace was held to be altogether impossible, or at best unreliable. It was believed that solely by means of special divine revelation can the

expresses the opinion that it is extremely difficult to know whether it is God's love or hatred that a man deserves. And this is so, he explains, in that, although the believer may experience repentance and know himself to be penitent, it is difficult for him to know whether his repentance is motivated by fear only, or whether he possesses compunction and contrition, the *sine qua non* for justification, through the grace that is infused into him.[196] Since man cannot know whether he has been truly converted to God, he cannot know whether he is in the state of grace.[197] Man might consider himself to be sufficiently penitent and contrite for forgiveness, but it is difficult, if not impossible, for him to see himself as he is seen by God. He does not know what lies hidden in his own heart, but which is not hidden from God and might be offensive to him.[198] The penitent must, therefore, not be complacent, but he must fear at all times that there may still be evil hidden in his heart for which he has not done penance, and on account of which he will be condemned by God's strict and unbending justice.[199] However, contemplation of the truth that man cannot know whether he is sufficiently contrite, whether he is converted, or whether there may be something hidden in his heart which is offensive to God, must not paralyze him or give rise to despair and despondency. It must be an incentive to him to exert himself in the spiritual life even

---

believer receive certainty that he possesses a contrite heart and is, on that account, in the state of grace. Only an attritionist like Scotus, for example, could be virtually certain, even without divine revelation, that he was in the state of grace following the reception of the sacrament of penance.

[196] *Asc.*, 264E: ..., et nescit homo an sit dignus odio vel amore, et licet sciat se poenituisse, nescit tamen an solo timore percussus, an ex gratia infusa compunctus et contritus;...

That a man knoweth not whether he be worthy hatred or love (Ecc. 9, 1), was a frequently quoted text in the middle ages. Zerbolt quotes it in connection with the penitent's inability to know whether he is truly contrite, on account of which he does not know whether he is worthy of divine hatred or love. (Cf. Staupitz' use of this text, which would appear to be similar to Zerbolt's use of it [Steinmetz, *Staupitz*, 122]. Geiler also quotes this text a number of times, according to Dempsey Douglass, but she does not indicate in exactly what context he employs it [Dempsey Douglass, *Geiler*, 176].)

In most cases, however, the text would appear to have been quoted in connection with the discussion of man's imperfect and faulty works performed in the state of grace, on account of which he knows not whether he deserves salvation or condemnation. See Zumkeller, "Das Ungenügen der menschlichen Werke bei den deutschen Predigern des Spätmittelalters," 278 and 298; D. of Augsburg, *De ext. et int. hom. compositione*, II, 201; and cf. Oberman, *Biel*, 181-183.

[197] *Ref.*, 243G: ..., nescis si in gratia, nescis si vere conversus fueris..., nescis si eris perseveraturus.

[198] *Ibid.*, ..., nescis quid in te lateat quod Deum non latet, sed offendit,...

[199] *Ref.*, 241E-F: ...et inde timet aliqua in se esse unde possit reprobari ab districta iustitia Dei.

more than before: to strive even harder for compunction and contrition, and to perform even more meritorious works.[200]

Not only is it impossible to know with certainty whether one is in the state of grace, but writers from Gregory the Great to Gabriel Biel considered certainty with regard to the state of grace to be highly dangerous: a liability rather than a benefit or advantage. They were of the opinion that such certainty, if possible, would only lead to presumptuousness and complacency which could be fatal on the final, and most important, day in one's life. Not knowing for certain whether one is in the state of grace was considered to be a desirable condition, for it was seen as an incentive to do penance daily.[201] Zerbolt likewise doubts the wisdom of knowing for certain whether one is justified before God. For, influenced by Gregory the Great, he writes that there is no surer way to salvation than to be guided at all times by fear and hope. Fear will prevent presumptuousness and complacency; hope, on the other hand, will check despair.[202] Fear of not being in the state of grace will be conducive to the development of compunction,[203] without which there can be no contrition, nor true and adequate penance. However, lest fear should cripple the penitent, he may always rely on God's mercy, and hope for forgiveness.[204] But forgiveness can never be a certainty, because the believer cannot know with certainty whether he is contrite, or whether his repentance is merely motivated by fear.

In his uncertainty, then, the believer must ever be goaded forward by this salutary balance between fear and hope; because, even if he should be in the state of grace at the present, he has no assurance that he will persevere in it until the end of his days.[205] Nonetheless, concludes Zer-

---

[200] *Ref.*, 243H: Cave tamen desperationem si profundius huiusmodi meditationibus te immerseris, atque ita huiusmodi meditationes dirige non ut absorbearis ab nimia tristitia et deiectione, sed ut instigeris ad vitae emendationem et tolerantiam omnium tribulationum.

[201] Dudden, *Gregory the Great*, II, 424-426; Oberman, *Biel*, 217-220; and Oberman, "'Iustitia Christi' and 'Iustitia Dei'. Luther and the Scholastic Doctrines of Justification," 22-23.

[202] *Asc.*, 285F: Audi beatum Gregorium hunc tibi ascensum et descensum recommendantem. Quamvis, inquit, securitati timor semper longe videatur abesse, nobis tamen nihil est securius, quam sub spe semper timere, ne incauta mens aut desperando se in vitiis deiiciat, aut extollendo de donis ruat. Cf. *Asc.*, 271G and Dudden, *Gregory the Great*, II, 424-426.

[203] *De Reformatione*, ch. 11, deals with compunction and how it may be achieved. Fear of not being in the state of grace is one way to develop compunction. In *De Ascensionibus* ch. 17 is devoted to the development of compunction of fear, which results from not knowing whether one is in the state of grace, and from not knowing what will happen to one in the final judgement.

[204] *Ref.*, 250F: Sit etiam fidelis, ut in spe veniae confitearis.

[205] See footnote 197 above. *Asc.*, 264E: ...; et ita totus horrore concutitur nesciens et incertus quid de eo fiet in futuro, an sit damnandus vel salvandus. Cf. Richardson, ed., *Dictionary*, 129 ("Final Perseverance").

bolt, the just—and by the just he obviously means those who have done their utmost for their justification and sanctification—can face death with confidence, rejoicing in the testimony of their conscience that they have done whatever they could for their own salvation.[206]

Thus far only the uncertainty of salvation arising from the believer's inability to know whether he is truly contrite has been discussed. The extent to which Zerbolt understands the uncertainty to arise from God's response to the repentant believer is problematic. He asserts a number of times that God's judgements are inscrutable,[207] which leaves one with the impression that, in his opinion, God is not bound, and under no constraint, to grant justifying grace to those who are truly contrite, or to deny it to those who are not contrite. It would appear, then, that Zerbolt understands God's dealings with man to be wilful and arbitrary. However, it is necessary to take into account the context in which Zerbolt speaks of the inscrutability of God, and his reason for doing so. He does so to instil in the reader the fear and compunction without which he cannot achieve contrition.[208] Furthermore, all the indications are that Zerbolt regarded God as a being whose actions are, in the last analysis, governed by his intellect rather than by his will.[209] Finally, inscrutable and incomprehensible judgements do not necessarily imply arbitrary and wilful judgements. Bonaventure, whose writings are among Zerbolt's most important sources, stressed the incomprehensibility of God, but he did not conclude from this that God is arbitrary, or that his dealings with man are unpredictable, on account of which man can never gain any certainty with regard to the state of grace. The emphasis on the inscrutability of God's judgements would, on the whole, appear to have been a recognition of the fact that God, being the wholly other, judges man by a standard of justice which lies beyond the grasp of the human intellect. However, it was widely accepted as well that divine justice, in spite of its incomprehensibility, is not necessarily arbitrary.[210] It can be said with some degree of certainty, then, that in Zerbolt's view man's uncertainty

---

[206] *Ref.*, 244C-D: Poteris autem modum hunc ex contrario assumere de morte iustorum. Nam ipsi videntes se de hoc mundo migraturos, gaudent in testimonio conscientiae, exultant quod liberantur de istis miseriis.

[207] *Ref.*, 241E: Aut certe ex consideratione iudiciorum Dei, cum scilicet homo considerat quod divina iudicia sint inscrutabilia,... (This passage occurs in ch. 11 of *De Reformatione* which deals with the development of compunction.) *Ref.*, 243G: Demum cogita, quod iudicia Dei sunt inscrutabilia, ... *Asc.*, 264E: Quarto cum homo considerat quod iudicia Dei sunt inscrutabilia,... (This passage is found in ch. 17 of *De Ascensionibus* which deals with the development of compunction motivated by fear.)

[208] See the previous footnote.

[209] See above, pp. 49-50.

[210] Cf. Bonaventure, *Breviloquium*, Pt. I, chs. 8 and 9 (*Works*, II, 58-65); Fr. Wetter, "Franciscan Theology," *SM*, II, 348; and cf. Dempsey Douglass, *Geiler*, 163-165.

with regard to his justification and salvation stems primarily from his inability to know with certainty whether he possesses the necessary contrition for the forgiveness of his sins and reconciliation with God.

F) *Conclusion*

Zerbolt makes the sacrament of penance, by means of which the
believer is reconciled to God, the foundation of his entire spiritual program. For unless the believer is first justified before God, he lacks the
basis from which to ascend spiritually. The process of justification begins
with faith, a divinely infused gift, for faith induces repentance and compunction motivated by fear. However, repentance and compunction
motivated by fear only are insufficient for the forgiveness of sins in the
sacrament of penance. If sins are to be forgiven, then repentance and
compunction must be motivated by love. In other words, contrition
rather than attrition is demanded of the penitent. Furthermore, while
repentance and compunction motivated by fear are possible without the
aid of grace, repentance and compunction motivated by love are not.
Like Augustine and Thomas Aquinas, Zerbolt held that contrition cannot be achieved *ex puris naturalibus*. The considerable emphasis placed by
him on the need for grace places him solidly over against the many *moderni* who maintained that contrition is possible without divine assistance.

According to Zerbolt the penitent's degree of contrition determines the
extent to which sins are forgiven in the sacrament of penance. Consequently it can be said that in this particular sacrament he assigns pride of
place to the believer's subjective disposition. That does not, however,
make confession, absolution and satisfaction superfluous. Christ gave the
church the power of the keys, on account of which sins remain unforgiven
until they are formally confessed by the penitent and absolved by the confessor. Furthermore, divine justice demands that the believer bear part of
the penalty for his personal sins. He must offer satisfaction in the form of
good works.

However, human works performed in the state of grace are imperfect,
and whatever good they contain is the consequence of divine grace.
Without the aid of grace man can do no good, not even in the state of
grace. Therefore the merit possessed by such works is the result of grace
as well. The stress on the need of grace with respect to good works is as
great, then, as it is in connection with repentance and contrition. The
emphasis Zerbolt places on the imperfection of good works carries with it
the connotation of insufficiency, although he does not spell this out in so
many words. However, the doctrine of the insufficiency of good works
was a traditional one and was expressed by many other Devotionalists. It
may be assumed then that Zerbolt subscribed to it as well.

Zerbolt's views on predestination are somewhat vague and in-complete, but it would appear that according to him God grants to some individuals the grace needed to achieve justification and sanctification *ante praevisa merita*. God also appoints the time and place in which man might make most effective use of this grace; and so predestination, as understood by Zerbolt, becomes part of God's over-all providential plan for mankind. The individual, however, can never be certain whether he will finally be saved. For he cannot be certain whether his contrition is sufficient for his justification, and consequently he cannot be certain whether he is in the state of grace and capable of performing the necessary meritorious works. Zerbolt in fact doubts the wisdom of total certainty with respect to the state of grace, for the result would, most like-ly, be a complacency dangerous to one's spiritual welfare and ultimate salvation. Uncertainty, on the other hand, is conducive to the develop-ment of both fear and hope which must be the believer's constant com-panions in his spiritual pilgrimage, for without them he is bound to falter.

CHAPTER FIVE

THE EUCHARIST

The discussion of the sacrament of penance in the previous chapter has set the stage for the analysis of Zerbolt's views regarding the eucharist. For Zerbolt mentions three conditions which must be met by the believer if he wants to derive the maximum benefit from communion; and one of these three prerequisites is a pure conscience which, he indicates, can be acquired only by means of the sacrament of penance.[1]

In *De Reformatione* as well as in *De Ascensionibus* Zerbolt devotes a chapter to the eucharist.[2] In both works this chapter is inserted into the "*Vita Christi*," for the account of the Last Supper serves as an opening for the discussion of the eucharist. Zerbolt, like most of his contemporaries, devotes much more attention to the eucharistic sacrament than to the eucharistic sacrifice,[3] and he is particularly interested in the communicant's preparation for a fruitful communion. In fact, in both manuals for the spiritual life the primary purpose of the chapter on the eucharist is, it would appear, to instruct the reader how he may best achieve a fruitful communion.[4] Finally, Zerbolt's eucharistic views owe a great deal to Bonaventure's *Tractatus de praeparatione ad missam*. However, the influence does not appear to have been a direct one, but seems to have been transmitted to Zerbolt by David of Augsburg's *De exterioris et interioris hominis compositione*, and perhaps by Radewijns' *Omnes, inquit, artes* as well.[5]

i. *The Eucharistic Sacrifice*

There are no more than a few oblique references to the eucharistic sacrifice in Zerbolt's writings, but from those it is possible to deduce that

---

[1] See footnotes 35 and 40 below.

[2] *Ref.*, ch. 27 (pp. 246C-247D) and *Asc.*, ch. 31 (pp. 270F-271G).

[3] Cf. van Rooy, *Zerbolt*, 272.

Like Zerbolt, Grote displayed relatively little interest in the eucharistic sacrifice (de Beer, *Spiritualiteit*, 92), and Brinckerinck, who devotes a 'sermon' to the eucharist, does not mention the eucharistic sacrifice at all (Brinckerinck, "Collatiën," 143-147).

[4] Cf. Goossens, *Meditatie*, 188-190, and Mak, "Christus bij de Moderne Devoten," 160-161.

[5] For the origin of much of Zerbolt's eucharistic thought, and its transmission to him, compare Bonaventure's *De Praeparatione ad Missam* (ch. 1, par. 15 [*Works*, III, 231-232]), D. of Augsburg's *De ext. et int. hom. compositione* (II, 210-211) and Radewijns' *Omnes, Inquit, Artes* (II, 89) with Zerbolt's *De Reformatione Virium Animae* (247A-B) and Zerbolt's *De Spiritualibus Ascensionibus* (271D-E). Cf. Smits, "David van Augsburg en de invloed van zijn *Profectus* op de Moderne Devotie," 196; Rayez, "Gérard Zerbolt de Zutphen et Saint Bonaventure. Dépendances Littéraires," 341-342; and Goossens, *Meditatie*, 188-190.

he did, at least, regard the eucharistic celebration as a true sacrifice, and it would have been unusual had he done otherwise. Zerbolt quotes from Gregory the Great's *Dialogues* that, when the eucharist is celebrated, it is necessary for the believer to offer himself to God with a contrite heart; for when the mystery of the Lord's passion is celebrated, it is incumbent upon the believer to imitate that which is being celebrated.[6] The injunction to offer oneself to God during the eucharistic celebration in imitation of that which is being celebrated points to a conception of that rite as being, at least partially, a sacrifice. Furthermore, Zerbolt repeats the traditional view that the eucharistic sacrifice—and here he specifically refers to the eucharistic rite as a sacrifice—benefits both the living and the dead.[7] It is doubtful he would have made this statement had he not regarded the eucharistic celebration as a true sacrifice, but merely as a symbolic and figurative representation of Christ's historical death on the cross. Zerbolt does not, however, specify how the eucharistic sacrifice benefits the living and the dead, but presumably he means that it remits the penalty of those in purgatory and expiates the sins of the living.[8] With respect to the sins of the living Zerbolt may have held, as was common at that time, that the eucharistic sacrifice is an expiatory sacrifice solely for the mortal and venial sins.[9] For in the analysis of his soteriology it has been noted that Zerbolt nearly always connects Christ's death on the cross with original sin only. Some years later Thomas a Kempis was to assert likewise that the eucharist is an expiatory sacrifice which effects the remission of the sins of the living, without specifying which sins, as well as the penalty of those in purgatory.[10] It would appear, then, that Zerbolt, like most of his contemporaries, attributed an extensive *ex opere operato* efficacy to the eucharistic sacrifice. For if the eucharistic sacrifice is held to be efficacious for the remission of mortal sins, that means, in effect, that the

---

[6] *Ref.*, 246G: Gregorius in libro dialogorum: Necesse est ut cum haec divina mysteria agimus, nosmetipsos Deo in cordis contritione mactemus, quia qui passionis Dominicae mysteria celebramus, debemus imitari quod agimus. This passage may be found in the *Dialogues*, No. 4, ch. 59. Cf. Dudden, *Gregory the Great*, II, 417-418.

[7] *Ref.*, 247B: Aliquos trahit amor et compassio proximi, ut succurrant per hanc hostiam vivis simul et defunctis,... Also see *Asc.*, 271E. For the origin, and transmission to Zerbolt, of the passage from *De Reformatione*, 247B, see footnote 5 above.

On the traditional view that the eucharistic sacrifice benefits both the living and the dead see Kelly, *Early Christian Doctrines*, 453-454; Harnack, *History of Dogma*, VI, 234; and J. H. Srawley, "Eucharist (to the end of the Middle Ages)," in: *Encyclopedia of Religion and Ethics*, ed. by J. Hastings, V, 540-563.

[8] See the last three references given in the previous footnote.

[9] J. H. Srawley, "Eucharist (to the end of the Middle Ages)," in: *Encyclopedia of Religion and Ethics*, ed. by J. Hastings, V, 562.

[10] Thomas a Kempis, *De Imitatione Christi*, Bk. IV, chs. 5 and 9.

eucharistic sacrifice avails even for those who are not in the state of grace and are not properly disposed.[11]

ii. *The Eucharistic Sacrament*

We may perhaps begin the investigation into Zerbolt's views regarding the eucharistic sacrament by looking at his understanding of the Last Supper as an eucharistic sacrament. He writes that the sacrament of the body of the Lord was first instituted by Christ himself at the Last Supper. For on that occasion, he elaborates, Christ, after having eaten the Paschal Lamb, a symbolic representation of himself, with his disciples, gave the true Paschal Lamb to his disciples for their consumption. To that end Christ consecrated his own body, gave it to his disciples to eat, and he also gave to them the power to consecrate his body and to distribute it to others.[12] Clearly, then, Zerbolt understood the Last Supper to have been a true eucharistic sacrament identical to those celebrated following Christ's passion and death. In this primordial eucharistic sacrament Christ consecrated his own body and so effected the real presence hidden under the veil of bread and wine. At the point of their consecration by Christ, the bread and wine became his own body and blood.

In *Scriptum Pro Quodam* Zerbolt reiterates that at the time of the Last Supper Christ gave to his disciples the power to consecrate his body, and there he adds the observation that the power to consecrate the elements lends the priestly office an awe-inspiring dignity.[13] However, when in *De*

---

[11] Cf. J. H. Srawley, "Eucharist (to the end of the Middle Ages)," in: *Encyclopedia of Religion and Ethics*, ed. by J. Hastings, V, 562.

[12] *Ref.*, 246D: Sed super omnia quotidie, et maxime Dominici corporis sacramenta sumpturus, memoriam facias devotissimi illius mysterii quod ibi primitius erat institutum. Siquidem postquam agnum paschalem typicum cum discipulis suis comedit more Iudaeorum, ex tunc verum agnum paschalem comedendum dedit. Consecravit enim corpus suum, atque discipulis tradit manducandum, quibus et potestatem tribuit idipsum consecrandi aliisque tribuendi. *Asc.*, 270G-H: Cogita qualiter agnum typicum comedit, et tibi quomodo verum agnum et Eucharistiae sacramentum manducare debeas, figuravit. Sed super haec omnia mentalibus oculis et devotissimis desideriis semper recogitare, et ad cor tuum reducere debes ipsum excellentissimum Sacramentorum quod ibi instituit.

In *De Ascensionibus* Zerbolt calls attention to the 'farewell address' given by Christ at the Last Supper, and to the fact that John records this 'address' in much greater detail than do the other evangelists. This is due to the fact, he explains, that John "saw more clearly than the rest and soared higher than they" (*Asc.*, 270G). Johann Geiler expresses essentially the same idea when he writes that while "the synoptic gospels reveal the humanity of Christ and the outward manner of his life, only the gospel of John, like an eagle, brings the inner core of his divinity" (Dempsey Douglass, *Geiler*, 186-187). Cf. Bonaventure, *Lignum Vitae*, ch. 16 (*Works*, I, 114).

[13] *Scriptum Pro Quodam*, 191: Satis ergo apparet, quod si eciam quis ydoneus esset vocatus ab Deo tamquam Aaron, vel superiorum coactus imperio, attamen deberet cum timore, tremore et reverencia accedere per huiusmodi sacramenti summam excellentiam et officii huius ordinis terribilem dignitatem, quod est illum consecrare, contrectare et in corpus proprium trahicere,...

Reformatione Zerbolt briefly returns to this same question he diminishes the role played by the priest in the consecration of the eucharistic elements. Christ, he writes, consecrates all sacraments; and for that reason, he explains, it is not the priest, a human being, who effects the real presence, but it is the crucified one himself: Christ. It is the priest who utters the words of consecration, but it is God's power and grace which lend them their effectiveness for the consecration of the bread and the wine through which the real presence is effected.[14] These two, clearly contradictory, positions held by Zerbolt with regard to the priest's role in the consecration of the eucharistic elements represent those held by Aquinas and Scotus respectively.[15] Contradictions of this nature, whether real or apparent, are perhaps to be expected from a spiritual writer like Zerbolt, and they are difficult to resolve, partly because his statements and observations on issues pertaining to dogmatic theology tend to be brief. Furthermore, the fact that the sources of Zerbolt's ideas are not always known adds to the difficulty in resolving both real and apparent inconsistencies in his thought.

Zerbolt's belief in the real presence, evident from what has just been said, is further illustrated when he writes that Christ, who is present in the sacrament under the veil of bread and wine, is God's Son whom John the Baptist trembled to touch; whom Peter repelled because of his own sinfulness; before whom powers tremble and whom dominions adore; and who shall be man's judge at his death and at the last judgement.[16] Not only does Zerbolt accept the real presence, but he clearly regards the Christ who is present in the sacrament to be identical with the historical Christ who died on the cross and ascended into heaven. From which it

---

[14] *Ref.*, 246H: Siquidem in hac sacerdotalia mensa, nunc praesens est Christus, et qui ultimam coenam cum Apostolis ornavit, ipse istam quoque consecrat. Non enim homo est qui proposita corpus Christi facit et sanguinem, sed ille qui pro nobis crucifixus est Christus. Sacerdotis ore verba proferuntur, et Dei virtute consecrantur et gratia.

[15] Aquinas had taught that Christ gave to the words (*forma*) of institution an objective, intrinsic power and efficacy to effect the conversion of the sacramental elements; and that at his ordination the power of consecration is bestowed upon the priest himself. Duns Scotus denied that the words of institution possess an objective, intrinsic power of consecration, and that such power is possessed by the priest in the true sense of the word. For him the priest is merely the administrator, or medium, of the divine power which effects the real presence.

Cf. Seeberg, *Text-Book of the History of Doctrines*, II, 131; Harnack, *History of Dogma*, VI, 235; and J. H. Srawley, "Eucharist (to the end of Middle Ages)," in; *Encyclopedia of Religion and Ethics*, ed. by J. Hastings, V, 562.

[16] *Ref.*, 246H-247A: Quomodo igitur tu ad illam mensam, ad praesentiam Christi, ad tactum filii Dei intrepidus audes accedere, quem Ioannes Baptista tangere contremiscit, Petrus Apostolorum princeps se prae formidine repulit dicens: Exi ab me Domine quia homo peccator sum, quem tremunt potestates, et adorant dominationes? Denique cogita, quod iste quem sumis, erit judex tuus. See *Asc.*, 271C and *Scriptum Pro Quodam*, 191, for identical passages.

may be deduced that he would have rejected any suggestion that in the eucharistic sacrament the real presence is a new creation.[17] Furthermore, from his description of the Christ who is present in the eucharist it is patently obvious that Zerbolt considers the whole Christ to be present in each of the individual particles of the consecrated bread.[18] Finally, it must be pointed out that, although Zerbolt believed in the real presence and believed the *Christus Eucharisticus* to be identical with the historical Christ, he does not indicate in any way how the real presence in the eucharistic sacrament comes into existence. The term transubstantiation cannot be found in *De Reformatione* and *De Ascensionibus*, nor is there any mention of the transformation of the eucharistic elements in terms of substances and accidents according to which the substances are transformed into the body and blood of Christ and the accidents of the original substances, namely the bread and wine, remain.[19]

Finally, attention must be drawn to Zerbolt's description of the eucharistic sacrament as being the most exalted, and as possessing the most profound dignity, of all the sacraments.[20] The eucharistic sacrament had traditionally been regarded as the most important of all the sacraments, the reason being that the eucharistic sacrament not only contains grace, but also contains Christ himself who, on account of his passion and death, is the source of all grace.[21] Zerbolt does not explain why of all the seven sacraments the eucharistic sacrament is the most exalted, but Christ's presence in this particular sacrament clearly influenced his description of it as possessing the greatest dignity.

iii. *The Eucharistic Celebration as a Commemoration*

In the early church it was already held that the commemorative aspect of the eucharistic celebration is much more than a subjective act of

---

[17] Cf. Harnack, *History of Dogma*, VI, 235-240; and Seeberg, *Text-Book of the History of Doctrines*, II, 132-133.

[18] Cf. Mak, "Christus bij de Moderne Devoten," 158; Harnack, *History of Dogma*, VI, 236; Bonaventure, *De Praeparatione ad Missam*, ch. 1, par. 1 (*Works*, III, 219-110); and *idem, Breviloquium*, Pt. VI, ch. 9 (Works, II, 255).
This same teaching is also found in Peter Lombard's writings and in those of many other writers. See J. H. Srawley, "Eucharist (to the end of the Middle Ages)," in: *Encyclopedia of Religion and Ethics*, ed. by J. Hastings, V, 558.

[19] In *De Imitatione Christi* Th. a Kempis advises the reader not to delve into the mystery of transubstantiation. Johannes Busch, on the other hand, analyzed the transubstantiation which is held to take place in the eucharist in some detail. (Th. a Kempis, *De Imitatione Christi*, Bk. IV, ch. 18; and Mak, "Christus bij de Moderne Devoten," 154-155.)

[20] *Ref.*, 246E: Hoc sacramentum omnium sacramentorum excellentissimum,... See also the passage from *Scriptum Pro Quodam* given in footnote 13 above; and footnote 24 below.

[21] Cf. Aquinas, *ST*, 3a, 65, 3; Harnack, *History of Dogma*, VI, 234; McGiffert, *A History of Christian Thought*, II, 319; W. F. Dewan, "Eucharist (As Sacrament)," *NCE*, V, 600-602; and J. R. Quinn, "Sacraments, Theology of," *NCE*, XII, 808.

remembrance and symbolic ceremony of commemoration. Thus it was believed that the eucharistic celebration as a memorial or commemorative act brings into the present in an objective and concrete fashion the Last Supper in all its detail, as well as the sacrifice of Christ in a mysterious manner: i.e., under the species of bread and wine. As a commemorative act, then, the eucharistic celebration was not only a subjective remembrance, but it assumed the form of a cult as well. This conception of the commemorative aspect of the eucharistic celebration as both a subjective remembrance and an objective actualization in the present of an historical event received universal endorsement.[22]

On the one hand Zerbolt clearly regards the commemorative or recollective aspect of the eucharistic celebration as a subjective act. In this connection he writes that prior to communion, and when one receives the eucharistic sacrament, it is necessary to call Christ's passion to mind, and to meditate on it with extra diligence. For it was especially for the remembrance of Christ's passion and death that the eucharistic sacrament was instituted; Christ gave the eucharistic sacrament to his disciples in order that they might always remember that he died for them.[23] In addition to that Zerbolt urges the reader to call the eucharistic sacrament itself to mind frequently, and this, he continues, must automatically lead to a mental review of all that Christ did while on earth. For when Christ instituted the eucharistic celebration he issued the command: "So often as ye shall do this, do it in remembrance of me." The remembrance of all Christ did for man while in the flesh, Zerbolt explains, focuses upon the incarnation itself, Christ's suffering, and finally his death on the cross.[24]

---

[22] Kelly, *Early Christian Doctrines*, 440-455; Rahner and Vorgrimler, *Theological Dictionary*, 19-20 ("Anamnesis"); Richardson, ed., *Dictionary*, 7 ("Anamnesis"); C. Bernas, W. F. Dewan and E. J. Kilmartin, "Eucharist," *NCE*, V, 594-615; and J. H. Srawley, "Eucharist (to the end of Middle Ages)," in: *Encyclopedia of Religion and Ethics*, ed. by J. Hastings, V, 560-561.

[23] *Asc.*, 271F: Cum etiam ad huius sacramenti sumptionem disposueris te, debes te in memoria passionis Dominicae diligentius exercere. *Ref.*, 247B: Debes etiam praecipue ante hujus sacramenti susceptionem, devotissime Christi passionem percurrere. Nam specialiter in memoriam passionis hoc sacramentum legitur institutum. *Ref.*, 246E: Ideoque Salvator hoc tradidit sacramentum, ut semper commemoremur quia pro nobis mortuus est. The last passage quoted here is found in *De Ascensionibus* (p. 270F) as well, and is part of a longer passage which Zerbolt ascribes to Jerome (see footnote 26 below).
Ref., 246E: Hoc igitur cum accipimus ab sacerdotibus, commemoremur, quod corpus et sanguis Christi est, ut non simus ingrati tantis beneficiis. See *Asc.*, 270F-G, for an identical passage.

[24] *Asc.*, 270H: Sed super haec omnia mentalibus oculis et devotissimus desideriis semper recogitare et ad cor tuum reducere debes ipsum excellentissimum Sacramentorum quod ibi instituit. Mirare Christi largissimam munificentiam, et huius Sacramenti profundissimam dignitatem. At dum huius dignissimi Sacramenti facis memoriam, in mentem tibi veniant omnia quae Christus pro te gessit in carne. Hoc enim est quod ait: Haec quotiescumque feceritis in mei memoriam facite, eorum scilicet quae pro te gessi in

The subjective aspect of the eucharistic celebration as a memorial does not overshadow Zerbolt's belief in the eucharistic celebration as a concrete actualization in the present of a past event, namely the eucharistic celebration instituted by Christ at the Last Supper. For when Christ instituted the eucharistic celebration at the Last Supper, Zerbolt writes, and commanded his disciples to celebrate the same in remembrance of him, he gave them the power to effect the presence of the Last Supper in all its detail, and with all its primordial efficacy, in their own time.[25] The memorial which Christ instituted at the Last Supper is a tangible and concrete memorial to all that Christ did for man, Zerbolt quotes from one of St. Jerome's writings. For in the eucharist Christ is present bodily as he was in the original eucharistic celebration at the Last Supper. This objective memorial contributes, of course, to the subjective remembrance of Christ's redemptive passion and death, which must lead to thankfulness on the part of man for what Christ has done for him.[26]

iv. *Requirements for Fruitful Communion*

The internal disposition necessary for a fruitful communion is discussed at some length by Zerbolt, as is the means by which it is required, and also the impact of communion on the believer. It is important, he writes, to acquire the proper disposition before one communes, for the effect of the eucharistic sacrament, and of the sacraments generally, is determined by the disposition of the believer. Those properly disposed

---

carne, quod propter te homo sum factus, propter te amarissime et multa passus, propter te tandem crucifixus. *Ref.*, 246D-E: Quid ultra faceret; Omnia quae potuit, pro nobis fecit, omnia quae habuit, dedit. Dedit regnum suum, dedit seipsum. Ideoque in hac coena dicebat: Haec quotiescunque feceritis, in mei memoriam facite. In memoriam scilicet eorum quae propter te in carne gessi. Quia propter te derisus, illusus et crucifixus sum.

[25] See footnote 12, the first passage quoted there.

[26] *Asc.*, 270F-G: In qua coena multa mirabilia fecit, imo mirabilium omnium suorum quoddam memoriale et compendium instituit, dans escam timentibus se in memoriam mirabilium suorum. Hoc, inquiens, facite in meam commemorationem. Hieronymus: Hanc ultimam nobis memoriam reliquit, quemadmodum si quis peregre proficiscens, aliquod pignus ei quem diligit relinquat, ut quotienscumque videri possit eius beneficia et amicitias commemorari, quem si ille perfecte dilexit, sine ingenti desiderio vel fletu illud videre non potest...Hoc igitur cum accipimus ab sacerdotibus, commemoremur quia corpus et sanguis Christi est, ut non simus ingrati tantis beneficiis. See *Ref.*, 246E, for an identical passage.

The passage: "..., imo mirabilium omnium suorum quoddam memoriale et compendium instituit,..." (*Asc.*, 270F) would appear to have been inspired by David of Augusburg's *De ext. et int. hom. compositione*, I, 12. The passage: "Hanc ultimam...tantis beneficiis," which Zerbolt ascribes to Jerome, is found in *Omnes, inquit, artes* as well. Like Zerbolt, Radewijns attributes it to Jerome, but van Woerkum, the editor of *Omnes, inquit, artes*, was unable to find this passage anywhere in the writings of Jerome (*Omnes, Inquit, Artes*, II, 89). It would appear that Zerbolt copied this passage, attributed by Radewijns to Jerome, directly from *Omnes, inquit, artes*.

will benefit from the eucharistic sacrament, but those who have not prepared themselves will be negatively affected.[27] Judas received the eucharistic sacrament at the Last Supper, but he did not receive its benefits, because he lacked the necessary disposition for fruitful communion. Consequently it is necessary for the believer to do his utmost to prepare himself for a worthy communion.[28] Zerbolt then lists the three traditional prerequisites which must be met if the believer wishes to commune not only validly and worthily, but also wishes to derive more than the minimum benefit from communion. The three prerequisites are cleanness of body, purity of conscience and active or effectual devotion.[29] The first two are necessary for the sacrament to be at all valid and efficacious. What degree, or level, of active devotion Zerbolt holds to be necessary for a valid communion as such is not clear. What is fairly obvious, however, is that he establishes a positive correlation between the level of active devotion on the part of the believer, and the degree of fruitfulness experienced in communion.[30] Consequently, it comes as no surprise that the question of effectual devotion receives considerably more attention from Zerbolt than do purity of body and conscience.

Bodily Purity. Zerbolt does not specify what he understands by the bodily purity which he mentions as a prerequisite for valid communion. All he observes in this connection is that bodily purity is, on the one hand, a question of necessity, and, on the other hand, a matter of congruity, decency or propriety[31] The bodily purity which must be achieved of necessity is almost certainly the eucharistic fast without which there can be no valid or worthy communion.[32] The bodily purity which must be attained as a matter of propriety or decency is, most likely, sexual con-

---

[27] *Ref.*, 246F: Adverte tamen quod effectus sacramentorum solet esse secundum dispositionem et praeparationem accipientium. *Asc.*, 271A: Sunt enim frequenter effectus Sacramentorum secundum dispositionem accipientium, ut ad bonum vel ad malum cooperentur. Cf. Axters, *Vroomheid*, III, 74.

[28] *Ref.*, 246F-G: Neque enim Iudas haec praemissa dona accepit qui corpus Domini suscepit, si tamen suscepit. Ideoque summopere studendum est, ut quantum potueris ante eius sumptionem te digne praepares.

[29] *Asc.*, 271A: Ut autem ipsum digne possis suscipere in tribus te debes exercere ad huius Sacramenti dignam susceptionem requisitis, quae sunt corporalis munditia, puritas conscientiae, et devotio actualis. The same passage, with only minor differences, is found in *De Reformatione*, 246G. Cf. Bonaventure, *De praeparatione ad missam*, ch. 1, pars. 2 and 3 (*Works*, III, 222-225); idem, *Breviloquium*, Pt. IV, ch. 9 (*Works*, II, 256) and Harnack, *History of Dogma*, VI, 221-226.

[30] See the first passage in footnote 27, and the passage in footnote 28. Cf. Brinckerinck, "Collatiën," 144.

[31] *Asc.*, 271A-B: Corporalis munditia, interdum est de congruo, interdum vero est necessario requisita secundum quod corporalis immunditia est diversa, et secundum quod habet variam causam et originem. *Ref.*, 246G: Corporalis autem munditia aliquando est ex decenti, aliquando necessario requisita.

[32] Cf. A. M. Carr, "Fast, Eucharistic," *NCE*, V, 847.

tinence, as well as modesty in dress and appearance.[33] They are demanded of the believer because of the exalted nature of the eucharistic sacrament in which Christ is present bodily. They do not, however, affect the
validity of communion, but they do add to its fruitfulness.

Purity of Conscience. Zerbolt writes that purity of conscience is the most important condition to be met if the believer is to communicate validly.
More particularly, he must be free from all guilt arising from sin.[34] This
means, in the first place, that the believer must be free from mortal sin,
and that he must be in the state of grace. Those who are not in the state of
grace cannot communicate validly, and to be in the state of grace is the
chief necessity for a valid communion, outranking in importance purity
of body. However, Zerbolt is not satisfied with an absence of mortal sin
only. While this may be sufficient for a valid communion, the believer's
conscience must be completely pure if he is to benefit maximally from the
eucharistic sacrament. He must be free from guilt stemming from any,
and all, sins. In order to achieve this the believer must first examine his
conscience for the purpose of uncovering all sins: sins of omission as well
as sins of commission. The unveiling of these sins must be followed by
remorse, compunction and contrition, for that is the only way that the
believer can be cleansed of all his sins and his conscience purified.[35] Bor-
rowing from St. Gregory the Great's *Dialogues*, Zerbolt adds the observation that in, and through, the repentance for sins which prepares the
believer for communion he must make an offering of himself in imitation
of Christ who offered himself on the cross, a sacrifice which is commemorated in the eucharistic feast.[36] The idea that before one communicates one must purify one's conscience by offering oneself as a
sacrifice in penitence of heart is found as well in John Brinckerinck's 'sermon' on the eucharist and receives considerable emphasis there.[37]

---

[33] Cf. Bonaventure, *De praeparatione ad missam*, ch. 1, par. 2 (*Works*, III, 223-224).

[34] See footnote 35 below.

[35] *Asc.*, 271B: Puritas autem conscientiae ipsa est tibi praecipue et ante omnia
necessaria. Ideoque ante reverendi huius Sacramenti sumptionem, maxime debes teipsum secundum primam et secundam examinationem discutere modo superius posito, et
sic ad contritionem exercere et ad compunctionem inflammare, ut scilicet doleas de peccatis commissis, corde, ore, et opere, et insuper de his quae facere omisisti. *Ref.*, 246G:
Puritas autem conscientiae, praesertim ab criminibus, ipsa est necessaria. Ideo vide ut
ante susceptionem huius sacramenti contritionem habeas, atque si fieri potest ante con-
spectum Domini humiliter lachrymas fundas, quibus te laves ab peccatis tuis quae fecisti,
et bonis quae omisisti, et quae facere potuisti corde, ore et opere. Cf. Brinckerinck, "Collatiën," 144.

[36] See the passage quoted in footnote 6 above. Cf. Harnack, *History of Dogma*, V,
269-270.

[37] Brinckerinck, "Collatiën," 144. Thomas a Kempis stresses time and again that the
believer must offer himself in penitence of heart, etc. if he wishes to communicate worthily
and fruitfully (*De Imitatione Christi*, Bk. IV, chs. 7, 8 and 9).

In making penitence, compunction and contrition the prerequisite for a worthy reception of the eucharistic sacrament Zerbolt was in full agreement with Peter Lombard, Alexander of Hales, Bonaventure and Thomas Aquinas. He obviously rejected the view, held by many of the late medieval theologians, that the mere absence of a barrier, or impediment, to efficacious communion is sufficient preparation for a worthy communion. By a barrier the late medieval theologians understood

"the presence of a '*motus contrarius malus*,' i.e., contempt for the Sacrament, positive unbelief, or an unforgiven mortal sin. They said that the dignity of the New Testament Sacraments consists just in this, that they presuppose *no* positive disposition, while such disposition is to be presupposed in the case of all other grace."[38]

Also rejected by Zerbolt is the dominant, late medieval doctrine that attrition, rather than contrition, is sufficient for valid communion.[39] With his emphasis on contrition and active devotion he categorically rejects any suggestion that only negative preparation for the eucharistic sacrament is sufficient for valid and efficacious communion.

If the believer wants to communicate validly and worthily, that is to say, with a pure conscience, penitence and contrition must be followed by confession; for repentance and contrition are not, by themselves, sufficient to achieve a pure conscience. The believer must confess not only his mortal sins, but also his venial sins. He must confess as well the guilt of those less notable sins which may have been overlooked and of which he may be totally ignorant. For it is only through contrition and confession that the believer can cleanse his conscience of all impurities,[40] the most basic prerequisite for a valid and worthy communion. To prepare oneself for communion through the sacrament of penance was, of course, the accepted practice and had long been prescribed by the church.[41]

---

[38] Harnack, *History of Dogma*, VI, 224.

[39] Cf. Harnack, *History of Dogma*, VI, 223-226; McGiffert, *A History of Christian Thought*, II, 317 and Seeberg, *Text-Book of the History of Doctrines*, II, 128-129.

[40] *Asc.*, 271B: Ac deinde eo modo, quo dictum est, accede confessorem et confitere peccata tua, praecipue graviora, sed et poteris confiteri peccata tua notabilia, communia et ignorata. *Ref.*, 246G: Sequitur deinde confessio omnium peccatorum te urget conscientia, praesertim notabilia, quae omnia expedit ut confitearis et de ignotis reddas te culpabilem sacerdoti. In his igitur duobus, contritione et confessione, lavas conscientiam ab impuritate. Cf. Brinckerinck, "Collatiën," 144.

Aquinas had written that one must not confess sins of which one is ignorant (Harnack, *History of Dogma*, VI, 253).

[41] Cf. Bonaventure, *De praeparatione ad missam*, ch. 1, par. 2, and ch. 2, par. 1 (*Works*, III, 222-223 and 236); Post, *Kerkgeschiedenis*, I, 140, and II, 313; and Harnack, *History of Dogma*, VI, 253.

In 1215 the Fourth Lateran Council prescribed confession as the prerequisite for communion (see last reference just given).

In *De Imitatione Christi* Thomas a Kempis also points to the sacrament of penance, accompanied by compunction and contrition, as the means to purify one's conscience before one goes to communion (*De Imitatione Christi*, Bk. IV, ch. 7).

Effective Devotion: Fear and Love. Although Zerbolt writes that purity of conscience is the most fundamental and important prerequisite for valid communion, he particularly drives home the significance of what he calls effective or efficacious devotion which consists of two elements. They are, on the one hand, fear and reverence for the eucharistic sacrament, and, on the other hand, a desire for union with Christ through this same rite. The desire for union is motivated by love.[42] We must now examine the significance of these sentiments and how they may best be cultivated.

Fear and reverence are important in that they prevent the believer from approaching the eucharistic sacrament unprepared and stop him from receiving the sacrament unworthily,[43] that is, without the required purity of body and conscience. The believer must fear to commune unworthily, or without reverence, in order that Christ may not be angry with him when after his death he will appear before the Son of God to be judged. For he who receives unworthily eats and drinks judgement to himself, Zerbolt quotes from St. Paul's first letter to the Christians in Corinth.[44] He then lists a number of means how fear and reverence for the eucharistic sacrament may be cultivated. This may be done above all through meditation on the profound worthiness of the eucharistic sacrament in which the historical Christ is present bodily under the species of bread and wine. Fear and reverence are further increased through the realization that in communion one actually partakes of the historical Christ whom even his own disciples feared on account of his exalted majesty and their own sinfulness, before whom nations quake, and who shall decide man's eternal destiny. Comparison of one's own sinfulness with the exalted nature of Christ of whom one partakes in communion will also add to the necessary fear and reverence.[45] But, cautions Zerbolt,

---

[42] *Asc.*, 271B-C: Tertio debes te exercere ad actualem devotionem, quae viditur in duobus consistere, ut ad sumptionem huius Sacramenti, scilicet timorem et reverentiam habeas, atque insuper actuali amore unionis ad Christum, et desiderio movearis. *Ref.*, 246G: Actualem autem devotionem in te faciunt timor et amor, Timor incutit reverentiam, Amor autem desiderium et affectum.

[43] *Asc.*, 271C: Igitur tibi timor inducat reverentiam,... Itaque ut reverentiam huius Sacramenti et dignitatem intelligas, et non insensibilis sine timore accedas, diligenter adverte quis est quem sumis, quis sis qui sumis.

[44] *Asc.*, 271D: Time indigne suscipere, ne iudicium tibi manduces et bibas. Cf. 1 Cor. 11, 29 and following footnote.

[45] *Asc.*, 271C: ..., adducens internis obtutibus huius Sacramenti profundissimam dignitatem, et dignissimam et metuendam profunditatem... 271D: Cogita deinde tu quis es. Certe homo tepidus, negligens, vitiosus. Reduce ad memoriam qualis sis ex tribus examinationibus praemissis. (The three examinations referred to are those which correspond to man's threefold fall and threefold ascent.) *Ref.*, 246G-H: Terribilis enim est haec mensa, ad quam cum debita reverentia et congrua vigilantia necesse est ut accedas. *Ref.*, 247A: Time igitur ne si indigne sumpseris, et sine reverentia, post mortem inventas iratum, cum ad ejus tribunal praesentatus fueris judicandus... Item attende propriam utilitatem [vilitatem], modo superius dicto, et reputabis te indignum, et acquires reverentiam congruam,... Cf. footnote 16 above.

this fear and reverence must not be so great as to suppress all desire for communion. Communion is necessary for the believer, for it stills the hunger of the interior, i.e., the spiritual, man, Zerbolt quotes from one of St. Augustine's writings.[46] Consequently, the believer must cultivate love and desire for the eucharistic sacrament in order that he may be drawn to it, and there are various ways in which the believer may inflame his love for the eucharistic sacrament and the desire to receive it.[47]

Relying on Bonaventure's *De praeparatione ad missam* which was written for priests, Zerbolt writes that meditation on the three benefits which flow from worthy communion will instil in all believers, celebrants as well as communicants, love and desire for the eucharistic sacrament. The benefits, which will be discussed in greater detail below, are union with Christ through the eucharistic sacrament; spiritual health, for the eucharistic sacrament is a spiritual food which strengthens the believer in his fight against sin; and the remission of sin.[48] Love for their fellow men, and remembrance of the benefits which the dead as well as the living derive from the eucharistic sacrifice, instil in priests in particular a love for the eucharist and the desire to celebrate it.[49] For while all believers may receive the benefits of the eucharistic sacrament and be drawn to it on their account, only priests can celebrate the eucharist and so dispense the benefits of the eucharistic sacrifice to the living as well as the dead.[50] Finally, commemoration of all that Christ did for mankind during his entire sojourn on earth, and especially in the passion, cannot but instil love for Christ in the believer and the desire to be united to him through the eucharistic sacrament. Zerbolt believes, in fact, that the remembrance of

---

[46] *Asc.*, 271D: (Time indigne suscipere, ne iudicium tibi manduces et bibas.) Non tamen sit hic timor tantus, ut desiderium penitus excludat et devotionem tollat. Nam panis iste secundum Augustinum, quaerit esuriem hominis interioris. *Ref.*, 247A: Habe etiam desiderium ad huius reverendi sacramenti susceptionem. Panis enim iste, ut dicit beatus Augustinus, esuriem quaerit hominis interioris. The passage attributed to Augustine, is from: *In Evangelium Iohannis tractatus*, 26 (*PL*, XXXV, 1606). Cf. L. de Bazelaire, "Communion Spirituelle," *DSp*, II, 1296.

[47] *Asc.*, 271D: Unde necesse est te etiam habere desiderium et amorem! Multis autem modis poteris desiderium tuum inflammare erga huius reverendi Sacramenti sumptionem. *Ref.*, 247A: Diversi autem diversimode affectum ad susceptionem hujus sacramenti sibi formant.

[48] *Ref.*, 247A-B: Aliqui enim trahuntur amore unionis Christi, ut ipsum in se saepius amplexentur. Aliqui trahuntur desiderio sanationis passionum suarum et desideriorum malorum, ut eum quasi medicum ad se vocent, per quem ab omni infirmitate curentur. Aliquos trahit conscientia delictorum, eo quod hoc sacramentum institutum sit in remissionem peccatorum. For the origin, and transmission to Zerbolt, of this passage see footnote 5 above.

[49] See footnote 7 above.

[50] Cf. Bonaventure, *De Praeparatione ad Missam*, ch. 1, par. 15 (*Works*, III, 231-232); D. of Augsburg, *De ext. et int. hom. compositione*, II, 210-211; and Radewijns, *Omnes, Inquit, Artes*, II, 89.

all that Christ did for man will inflame the believer's love and desire for the eucharistic sacrament, and his devotion to it, to a greater degree than anything else can do.[51]

Zerbolt concludes with some comments regarding the relative merits of fear and love for the believer who prepares himself for a valid and fruitful communion. Some, he writes, long for the eucharistic sacrament and consequently commune frequently, while others regard this same sacrament with dread and reverence on account of which they stay away from it. He then asks rhetorically which of these two sentiments is to be praised. He begins his answer with the observation that both sentiments have been lauded by the saints, but that they, and Augustine in particular, held as well that in the final analysis this matter must be left to the conscience of the individual. Zerbolt himself believes in the advisability of a salutary interaction between fear and reverence on the one hand, and love and desire on the other. He does not believe that it is wise to allow one or other of the sentiments to become predominant. It is without doubt the safest rule of all, he quotes from one of Gregory the Great's writings, not to exclude love and desire on account of fear and reverence, nor to abandon fear and reverence for the sake of love and desire. The mind must unceasingly ebb and flow between the sentiments of fear and love, for a continuous interplay between these two sentiments will prevent unworthy communion, but at the same time ensure that the believer will, none the less, be drawn to the eucharistic sacrament.[52] It

---

[51] *Asc.*, 271E-F: Pro maiori autem desiderio tuo inflammando, et exercitando potes diligenter ex vita Christi revolvere, quomodo ipse dolores et infirmitates omnium desiderantium, adorantium, et in se credentium tulit, et infirmitates omnium ipse portavit... Cum etiam ad huius Sacramenti sumptionem disposueris te, debes te in memoria passionis Dominicae diligentius exercere. *Ref.*, 247B: Ut autem desiderium tuum accendatur, cogita quod Christus omnium dolores ad se accedentium tulit, et ipse infirmitates nostras portavit... Debes etiam praecipue ante hujus sacramenti susceptionem, devotissime Christi passionem percurrere. Nam specialiter in memoriam passionis hoc sacramentum legitur institutum.

[52] *Asc.*, 271F-G: Inter praedictos autem duos affectus, timoris scilicet et amoris fluctuat mens et exercitium devotorum, et aliqui quidem magis ad eius sumptionem ardenti desiderio anhelant et frequentius accedunt. Alii timore et reverentia huius Sacramenti territi, attendentes Sacramenti dignitatem et propriam vilitatem, periculumque indigne sumentium, magis se retrahunt, et prae formidine ab eius sumptione se cupiunt elongari. Verum uterque affectus recommendandus est, et interdum ex desiderio accedere, interdum ex reverentia dimittere laudabile est, pro loco et tempore opportunis. Et secundum Augustinum uniuscuiusque conscientiae relinquendum est quod faciendum videtur. Unum tamen omnibus indubitanter securum est, ut scilicet nec ex reverentia desiderium et spem excludamus, nec rursum ex spe et desiderio relinquamus reverentiam et timorem, sed inter utrumque affectum medij fluctuemus, aliquando plus de uno habentes, aliquando plus de alio. Ait enim beatus Gregorius: Nihil enim nobis securius quam sub spe semper timere. Affectus tamen amoris absolute loquendo excellit. Sed quod absolute est melius, in casu sit et est multis periculosius, magisque timendum. See *Ref.*, 247C-D, for an identical passage.

may be concluded, then, that the interaction between fear and love, which, in Zerbolt's view, guarantees the believer's progress in the spiritual life, also plays an important role in his eucharistic piety and thought.

Notwithstanding the need for bodily purity, a clear conscience and devotion, Zerbolt concludes with the observation that nothing so contributes to worthy communion as to regard oneself as vile and unworthy to communicate.[53] Humility, in other words, is the most valuable disposition for worthy communion. It is important not only because it underlies repentance and contrition without which purity of conscience is impossible, but perhaps even more so because humility is the only acceptable disposition on the part of the communicant vis-à-vis Christ of whom he partakes in the sacrament.[54] Zerbolt did not stand alone in stressing the importance of approaching the eucharistic sacrament in humility. Bonaventure and Jean Gerson expressed a similar view,[55] as did John Geiler of Keisersberg who wrote that "it is humility alone which provides the proper disposition and preparation for the reception of such a guest [i.e., *Christus Eucharisticus*] in the upper room of the soul."[56]

v. *Can Man Prepare Himself Sufficiently for a Valid Communion?*

According to Zerbolt all the preparations for the eucharistic sacrament just outlined do not add up to what one could call a truly satisfactory disposition for the worthy reception of the eucharistic sacrament. He writes that even if the believer prepared himself for a thousand years, or many thousands of years, he would still not be properly disposed to receive the eucharistic sacrament worthily. Such a lengthy preparation would, in fact, contribute nothing to a worthy reception of the sacrament.[57] In the previous century Bonaventure had made a similar

---

With respect to the question whether the believer must allow love and desire to draw him to communion regularly, or whether he must allow fear and reverence to discourage him from communicating frequently, Zerbolt may have been influenced by David of Augsburg as well (*De ext. et int. hom. compositione*, II, 207). He may be one of the "*sancti*" to whom Zerbolt refers in *De Reformatione*, 247C, in addition to Augustine and Gregory the Great.

[53] *Ref.*, 247A: .., et hoc maxime valet pro hujus sacramenti digna susceptione, ut quantum poteris fias vilis in oculis tuis.

[54] Cf. Chapter 4, footnote 122.

[55] Bonaventure, *De praeparatione ad missam*, ch. 2, par. 5 (*Works*, III, 238).

[56] Dempsey Douglass, *Geiler*, 169.

[57] *Ref.*, 247A: Cogita quod licet mille millibus annorum te ad hoc sacramentum per puras orationes, sanctissimas meditationes praeparaveris, nihil esse ad condignam sumptionem... Also see footnote 59 below. Cf. Th. a Kempis, *De Imitatione Christi*, Bk. IV, ch. 1.

observation.[58] Zerbolt continues that even if one possessed all the merits of all the saints and all the purity that may be attained by men and angels, the believer would still not be properly disposed to receive the sacrament worthily. How then, he asks, does the believer dare to approach the sacrament without fear and reverence? Especially in view of the fact that he has made preparations but for a short while and can, therefore, hardly have made a beginning with the required disposition.[59] Must the believer consequently despair of ever being able to communicate worthily? No, writes Zerbolt, if the believer has done all he can, if he has done his utmost to achieve that disposition which is a prerequisite for worthy communion, he may approach the eucharistic sacrament with confidence, and rely on God's goodness and mercy.[60] In other words, if the believer has done his utmost to achieve the disposition required of him for a valid communion, God will be merciful and accept his effort as being sufficient for worthy communion even if the required disposition has not been actually attained. God will grant to man that which is lacking in his disposition in order that he may commune efficaciously and worthily. That Zerbolt did not mean his statement, that God will be gracious to those who have done what is in them for the preparation of worthy communion, to be an invitation to a minimum amount of preparation follows automatically from the considerable emphasis placed by him on the necessity to prepare oneself positively for worthy communion. However, such preparations for a valid and fruitful communion as can be made by the believer can be carried out only with the aid of grace. For Zerbolt was of the opinion that in the spiritual life

---

[58] Bonaventure, *De praeparatione ad missam*, ch. 2, par. 4 (*Works*, III, 237). Cf. Dempsey Douglass, *Geiler*, 170.

[59] *Asc.*, 271D: Cogita deinde quod quamvis mille annis te praeparaveris, nullatenus sufficeres ad condignam Sacramenti huius sumptionem, etiam si omnium Sanctorum meritis gauderes, et Angelorum et hominum puritate floreres. Quomodo igitur audes accedere sine timore, sine reverentia, qui vix ad modicum tempus te in corde disponis praeparare. *Ref.*, 247A: ..., nihil esse ad condignam sumptionem etiam si haberes merita omnium sanctorum, quanto minus tu qui tepide, qui sine devotione et sine praeparatione accedis?

[60] *Ref.*, 247B: Igitur cum feceris quod in te est, accede in fide et fiducia sperans de infinita Dei pietate. *Asc.*, 271F: Igitur cum feceris quod in te est, cum reverentia et timore, cum desiderio pariter et amore accede, sperans de infinita Dei pietate.

That God will be gracious and merciful to those who have done what is in them is a doctrine which was employed frequently in scholastic theology in connection with the doctrine of justification (cf. G. N. Buescher, "Facienti quod est in se," *NCE*, V, 785, and Oberman, *Biel*, 131-139). Whether or not it was customary to employ this same doctrine in connection with man's preparation for communion, as is done by Zerbolt, is not altogether clear, although it would appear to have been a common practice among the Devotionalists. For in *De Imitatione Christi* Thomas a Kempis asserts at least three times that God will be merciful to those who have done their utmost to prepare themselves for communion (Thomas a Kempis, *De Imitatione Christi*, Bk. IV, chs. 7, 10 and 12).

man can do nothing without the aid of grace,[61] and presumably he included preparation for worthy communion in this general statement.

Does Zerbolt believe, then, that even when aided by divine grace man can never prepare himself sufficiently for worthy communion and that, in the end, the disposition necessary for worthy communion is always a gift of God? No, it is virtually certain that this does not reflect Zerbolt's real opinion. What he most likely means is that those who have prepared themselves for the eucharistic sacrament in accordance with the three steps outlined above do indeed possess the required disposition for a worthy, and even fruitful, communion. If the believer cannot at least contribute to a valid reception of the eucharistic sacrament he will, of course, make no effort to prepare himself in any way. But the believer can, and must, so prepare himself, and for that reason Zerbolt devotes a considerable amount of space to the question of preparation. However, the believer should not rely on his own preparations as though they had in fact given him the disposition necessary for a valid and fruitful communion, but always assume that the necessary disposition is a gift of God who, in his goodness and mercy, 'rewards' man's efforts and not the results attained. The supposition that man possesses the capacity to prepare himself—even with the aid of grace—for a worthy and fruitful communion leads to presumption and the destruction of humility which, according to Zerbolt, is the most valuable sentiment and disposition for a worthy communion. On the one hand, then, the believer must prepare himself for communion with such diligence as if the disposition required of him for a worthy reception of the sacrament depended solely on his own efforts. On the other hand, however, humility demands of the believer to ascribe the disposition necessary for a valid communion entirely to divine grace.[62] It is important to remember in this connection that Zerbolt was writing as a spiritual adviser and counsellor, and not as a theologian.[63]

vi. *The Nature of Eucharistic Grace*

It has been noted that Zerbolt establishes a positive correlation between man's disposition and the effects of the eucharistic sacrament on him, and it is necessary to return briefly to this issue. By the late middle ages three distinct views regarding the relationship between the subjec-

---

[61] *Asc.*, 258H: Verum quia ascensus iste non est in currente vel ascendente, sed ex dono Dei miserentis, ideo quarto tibi consulitur ab Domino adiutorium et auxilium postulandum, quia nulla est industria tua, nisi te in omnibus divina gratia comitetur. See above, pp. 182-183 and 196-197, and below, 280-281.

[62] Cf. Thomas a Kempis, *De Imitatione Christi*, Bk. IV, ch. 12.

[63] Cf. Dempsey Douglass, *Geiler*, 169-171.

tive disposition of the communicant and the effect of the eucharistic sacrament on him had been advanced. Some of the earlier scholastic theologians held that the eucharistic sacrament, like every other sacrament, has some degree of positive effect on the communicant irrespective of his subjective spiritual condition. This was held to be possible because of the *ex opere operato* efficacy of the sacraments generally.[64] In the late middle ages, however, there were some theologians who questioned this *ex opere operato* efficacy of the sacraments, and that of the sacrament of penance in particular. They held that sacramental grace is primarily, and perhaps even exclusively, the result of the believer's positive spiritual disposition. However, by far the greatest number of theologians—and their view was later to be adopted by the Council of Trent—defended the *ex opere operato* efficacy of the sacraments, but they added that the believer does not benefit from the sacrament in any way whatsoever unless he is properly disposed. They held sacramental grace to be the result of the sacrament and its *ex opere operato* efficacy, *and* of the believer's positive disposition.[65]

Zerbolt does not mention the *ex opere operato* efficacy of the eucharistic sacrament. That he nonetheless attributed such a potency to this sacrament is fairly certain, for he writes that the eucharistic sacrament confers mighty and abundant grace when it is well and worthily received.[66] Thus the eucharistic sacrament, because of its intrinsic nature, confers grace, but only on those who receive the sacrament worthily and have prepared themselves well for an efficacious reception. Zerbolt continues that the ill effects which flow from communicating unworthily are not the result of any defect in the sacrament itself, but solely the consequence of the ill disposition of the communicant.[67] This statement not only constitutes further evidence that Zerbolt attributes an *ex opere operato* efficacy to the eucharistic sacrament, but it reveals as well that he understands this intrinsic potency to be of a positive nature only. Like the *moderni*, Zerbolt clearly refutes Augustine's doctrine, which was repeated by some of the early scholastic theologians, that the intrinsic beneficial potency of the eucharistic sacrament becomes harmful for those who are negatively disposed.[68] In Zerbolt's opinion the deleterious effects which result from

---

[64] Harnack, *History of Dogma*, VI, 221. Cf. J. R. Quinn, "Sacraments, Theology of," *NCE*, XII, 808.

[65] Harnack, *History of Dogma*, VI, 222-223. Cf. Seeberg, *Text-Book of the History of Doctrines*, II, 128-129; McGiffert, *History of Christian Thought*, II, 317.

[66] *Asc.*, 271A: Nam sicut hic cibus bene et digne susceptus, magnam et multam confert animae gratiam,...

[67] *Asc.*, 271A: ..., ita male dispositis, maiorem infert culpam et mortem, non sui culpa, sed vitio recipientis.

[68] Cf. Harnack, *History of Dogma*, VI, 221; and McGiffert, *A History of Christian Thought*, II, 317. St. Augustine based the doctrine that the sacrament becomes harmful for those who are negatively disposed on 1 Cor. 11, 27-29.

communicating unworthily are not the product of the sacrament (*ex opere operato*), but solely the consequence of the communicant's negative spiritual disposition (*ex opere operantis*).[69]

vii. *Benefits Derived from Communion*

Zerbolt mentions much the same advantages to be derived from the eucharistic sacrament as were enumerated by Bonaventure in the thirteenth century.[70] Zerbolt refers to the eucharistic sacrament as a food which sustains man in his spiritual ascent and which is indispensable to him in this endeavour. However, it is a food and medicine not only for the soul, but for the body as well. Quoting from one of St. Bernard's sermons "*in Coena Domini*," Zerbolt writes that the eucharistic sacrament, when received worthily, is a medicine for those who are bodily ill and that it heals them; that it strengthens the weak, refreshes the healthy and protects them from all diseases; that it helps the believer to accept reproof and correction with greater humility; that it makes him patient in hardship; that it increases his charity; that it grants him wisdom when he must be prudent; that it gives him greater willingness to be obedient; that it helps him to be more thankful in all things; and that it aids him in the fight against sin. Consequently, when after communion the believer does not feel inclined to evil, hatred, unchaste behaviour and other vices to the same degree as he did before, he must be thankful for the body and blood of the Lord. For such spiritual progress indicates that the eucharistic sacrament is having an effect on him, and is healing the wound of sin. It

---

[69] From Peter Lombard onward it was commonly held that the sacraments confer not only grace *ex opere operato* on those who receive them worthily, but that those who have prepared themselves beyond what is necessary for merely an efficacious or valid reception are rewarded with an additional gift of grace *ex opere operantis* (McGiffert, *A History of Christian Thought*, II, 317; Harnack, *History of Dogma*, VI, 224; and Oberman, *Biel*, 358). When Zerbolt writes that the eucharistic sacrament well and worthily received confers mighty and abundant grace upon the communicant (see footnote 66 above), the implication is that the better one is prepared for the reception of the eucharistic sacrament the more benefit one derives from it in the form of grace. That Zerbolt understands at least some of this grace conferred in the eucharistic sacrament to be of an *ex opere operantis* nature is quite conceivable.

Thomas a Kempis writes that he who maintains a devotional disposition immediately after sacramental communion will receive additional grace, and he clearly means sacramental grace. This would then have to be grace *ex opere operantis* (*De Imitatione Christi*, Bk. IV, ch. 12).

[70] Bonaventure, *De praeparatione ad missam*, ch. 1, par. 2 (*Works*, III, 225-226).

For Aquinas the benefits of communion are much the same as those mentioned by Bonaventure (Harnack, *History of Dogma*, VI, 234).

is not surprising, then, that Zerbolt refers to the *Christus Eucharisticus* as the physician: the physician of both soul and body.[71] To the benefits of communion which Zerbolt quotes from one of St. Bernard's sermons he adds a few more for which he is indebted to David of Augsburg's *De exterioris et interioris hominis compositione*. These benefits are: union with Christ; spiritual health, for the eucharistic sacrament helps to combat concupiscence and passions which man cannot overcome by himself; and the remission of venial sins.[72] In his 'sermon' on the eucharist Brinckerinck lists pretty much the same benefits to be obtained from valid

---

[71] *Ref.*, 246E-F: Hoc sacramentum omnium sacramentorum excellentissimum, aegrotis est medicina, peregrinantibus diaeta, debilesque confortat, valentes delectat, languores sanat, sanitatemque servat. Fit homo mansuetior ad correptionem, patientior ad laborem, ardentior ad amorem, sagacior ad cautelam, ad obediendum promptior, ad gratiarum actionem devotior. Item hoc sacramentum sensum munit, et in gravioribus peccatis tollit omnino consensum. Si igitur post sumptionem huius gloriosissimi sacramenti non tam saepe, non tam acerbos motus sentis iracundiae, invidiae, luxuriae, et caeterorum huiusmodi, gratias age corpori et sanguini Domini, quia virtus sacramenti operatur in te, et gaude quod pessimum ulcus accedit ad sanitatem. (From "Si igitur..." on, Zerbolt quotes from St. Bernard's *Sermo in Coena Domini* [*PL*, CLXXXIII, 272-273]. Cf. Radewijns, *Omnes, Inquit, Artes*, II, 90.) *Asc.*, 270H-271A: Verum quia tibi per tot arduas et difficiles ascensiones gradienti adhuc multa restat via et magnus ascensus, hic cibus est summe necessarius in hac via qua gradieris. Unde et nomen sumpsit, ut viaticum appelletur. Bernardus: Corpus Christi aegrotis est medicina, peregrinantibus dieta, debiles confortat, valentes delectat, languorem sanat, sanitatem servat, fit homo mansuetior ad correptionem, patientior ad laborem, ardentior ad amorem, sagacior ad cautelam, ad obediendum promptior, ad gratiarum actionem devotior. (It is not from Bernards's *Sermo in Coena Domini* [*PL*, CLXXXIII, 271-274] that Zerbolt quotes in this instance.) Also see footnotes 46 and 66. Cf. Thomas a Kempis, *De Imitatione Christi*, Bk. IV, chs. 1, 3, 4, 10 and 11; and D. of Augsburg, *De ext. et int. hom. compositione*, II, 208.

In the passage from *De Ascensionibus* quoted in this footnote Zerbolt refers to the eucharistic sacrament as the "*viaticum.*" In the early church this term (the literal meaning of which is provisions for a journey) was given to anything, such as sacraments and prayers for example, which might strengthen and comfort the dying when they were about to depart from this life. Gradually, however, this term came to be reserved for the eucharist in general, but presently it has an even more restricted meaning. Today it is used exclusively for communion given to those in danger of death (M. Burback, "Viaticum," *NCE*, XIV, 637; and A. J. Schulte, "Viaticum," *The Catholic Encyclopedia* [1912], XV, 397). In using the term *viaticum* to describe the eucharist in general Zerbolt obviously belongs to the transitional period before this term had come to be reserved for communion administered to the mortally ill and wounded.

[72] See footnote 48 above, and footnote 5 as well. *Super Modo Vivendi*, 83: Unde nota secundum Petrum super IV Sentenciarium, distinctio XVI, in exposicione litere quod venialia peccata dupliciter dimittuntur. Uno modo quasi virtute sacramenti, sicut per penitenciam et eukaristie sumpcionem, et cetera. (The reference here is, of course, to Peter Lombard's *Sentences.*)

That the eucharistic sacrament deletes venial sins was a standard doctrine. The eucharistic sacrifice was held to delete both mortal and venial sins. Cf. J. H. Srawley, "Eucharist (to the end of the Middle Ages)," in: *Encyclopedia of Religion and Ethics*, ed. by J. Hastings, V, 562.

communion as those enumerated by Zerbolt in *De Reformatione* and *De Ascensionibus.*[73]

viii. *Frequency of Sacramental Communion*

In the late middle ages there was a tendency among the religious to communicate more frequently than they had previously been in the habit of doing.[74] The Devotionalists in particular, and those influenced by them, were in favour of communicating more often than had traditionally been the practice among the religious. Frequent communion by laymen was a fruit of the Counter-Reformation, and was advocated by the Jesuits in particular.[75] With regard to this matter, then, the Counter-Reformation followed the course indicated by the *Devotio Moderna.*

Zerbolt, who as an early and prominent Devotionalist would appear to have had a hand in the general direction taken by the *Devotio Moderna,* makes somewhat contradictory statements regarding the frequency with which he advises his readers to communicate. On the one hand he writes that that which is all important is daily communion, and he clearly means sacramental communion and not merely spiritual communion.[76]

---

[73] Brinckerinck, "Collatiën," 147.

Bonaventure as well as Aquinas mention union with Christ's mystical body: i.e., the church, as a benefit of communion (Harnack, *History of Dogma*, VI, 233). Zerbolt does not mention this as one of the benefits the communicant derives from the eucharistic sacrament, nor does Johannes Brinckerinck, his contemporary in the Brethren House at Deventer. Those who have studied this particular issue have found that union with Christ's mystical body, the church, was commonly emphasized in the high middle ages as an important benefit to be derived from fruitful communion, but that in the late middle ages the interest in the eucharistic sacrament as a means to be united with the mystical body of Christ had virtually disappeared (see Gregory Dix, *The Shape of the Liturgy* [London, 1945], 266ff; Gustaf Aulén, *Eucharist and Sacrifice*, trans. by E. H. Wahlstrom [Philadelphia, 1958], 41-42; and Richard, *The Spirituality of John Calvin*, 34-35). This development was undoubtedly influenced, to some degree at least, by the *via moderna* of the late middle ages. In the fourth book of *De Imitatio Christi*, which deals with the eucharist, one finds as well that the emphasis is placed, for all practical purposes, exclusively on the relationship between the *Christus Eucharisticus* and the individual. That the *Christus Eucharisticus* is the bond which unites the individual with the mystical body of Christ receives little or no attention (Thomas a Kempis, *De Imitatione Christi*, Bk. IV throughout).

[74] The religious had been in the habit of communicating four times a year. Laymen, on the other hand, generally communicated only once a year, namely at Easter, as had been prescribed by the Fourth Lateran Council in 1215. Catechetical manuals for laymen which date from the late middle ages advocate sacramental communion four times a year, in spite of which communion just once a year: i.e., at Easter, would appear to have remained the dominant practice among laymen. (R. R. Post, *Kerkelijke Verhoudingen in Nederland voor de Reformatie* [Utrecht-Antwerp, 1954], 406, 408 and 421; idem, *Kerkgeschiedenis*, II, 224-226, 299-300 and 312; Moll, *Kerkgeschiedenis van Nederland voor de Hervorming*, Vol. II, Pt. III, 11-26; E. Day, "Communion, Frequency of," *NCE*, IV, 38; and W. F. Dewan, "Eucharist [As Sacrament]," *NCE*, V, 608.)

[75] See references given in the previous footnote.

[76] *Ref.*, 246D: Sed super omnia quotidie, et maxime Dominici corporis sacramenta sumpturus, memoriam facias devotissimi illius mysterij quod ibi primitius erat in-

However, he concludes his discussion of the question whether the believer should allow his desire for the eucharistic sacrament to draw him to communion every day, or whether he should allow fear to discourage him from doing so, with the advice given by St. Augustine that with respect to this matter the individual must follow his own conscience.[77] This advice echoes as well David of Augsburg's opinion that no fixed rule can be laid down with regard to this question.[78] What Zerbolt perhaps means to say is that daily sacramental communion is the ideal in view of the benefits which the believer derives from such communion, but that in practice the frequency of sacramental communion must be left up to the individual as his conscience dictates.[79]

It would appear, then, that Zerbolt was, in the final analysis, in favour of frequent sacramental communion, and that he urged the members of the recently established movement to commune more often than had been the practice among the religious up to that time. The constitutions of the Brethren of the Common Life would seem to reflect his promotion of frequent sacramental communion, for they prescribe it at seventeen feast days throughout the year, to which some constitutions add all the Lenten Sundays.[80] The Canons and Canonesses Regular of Windesheim, on the other hand, communicated every two weeks.[81]

stitutum. (For the distinction between sacramental and spiritual communion see below.)

Daily sacramental communion was advocated by only a very small number of people in the middle ages, it would appear, Aquinas and Tauler being among the few to do so (E. Day, "Communion, Frequency of," NCE, IV, 38). Whether Zerbolt was familiar with Aquinas' and Tauler's advocacy of daily sacramental communion is not known, but he must have read about daily communion in the Conferences and Institutes in which John Cassian discusses this practice among the religious of the Egyptian desert. Cf. O. Chadwick, John Cassian (2d ed.; Cambridge, 1968), 69-70.

[77] See the excerpts given in footnote 52 above.

In De Reformatione Zerbolt does not point to Augustine as an authority on this issue, but to the "sancti" in general.

[78] D. of Augsburg, De ext. et int. hom. compositione, II, 207.

[79] In the Conclusa et Proposita Grote expressed a fairly profound appreciation for the eucharist. In this guide for his own personal conduct he resolved to attend mass daily, but it is not clear how frequently he communicated sacramentally. (Thomas a Kempis added the Conclusa et Proposita to his biography of Grote: Th. a Kempis, Opera Omnia, VII, 98-102.)

[80] "The Original Constitution of the Brethren of the Common Life at Deventer," ed. by Hyma, The Christian Renaissance, 471-472; and "Consuetudines domus nostre (= Brethren House at Zwolle)," in: Jacobus de Voecht, Narratio, ed. by Schoengen, 272. Cf. the constitution of the Brethren of the Common Life at Emmerich, ed. by W. J. Alberts and M. Ditsche, Fontes Historiam Domus Fratrum Embricensis Aperientes (Groningen, 1969), 91. It may be observed that the first two constitutions prescribe daily attendance at mass: Hyma, The Christian Renaissance, 445; and Jacobus de Voecht, Narratio, 243-244. Cf. Goossens, Meditatie, 170 and 189, footnote 44; and L. van Miert, "Eene Bijdrage tot de Geschiedenis van de Eucharistie in de Nederlanden," Tijdschrift voor Liturgie, III (1921-1922), 117-119.

[81] Acquoy, Windesheim, I, 154; Post, Kerkelijke Verhoudingen in Nederland voor de Reformatie,

ix. *Spiritual Communion*

Not only was there a trend towards more frequent sacramental communion in the later middle ages, but spiritual communion also received a good deal more attention than it had previously. Daily sacramental communion was, generally speaking, out of the question, even for the religious. Consequently, spiritual writers advocated daily spiritual communion for the religious while attending mass, and for the laymen whenever they happened to be present at the celebration of the eucharist, as a means of union with Christ. It was held, in fact, that spiritual communion can take place at all times if the believer so desires, even outside the mass. Meditation on Christ's passion and death, it was believed, will lead to the desire to be united with him, and that a spiritual communion can, therefore, be effected at any time.[82]

The Modern Devotion did not remain untouched by this growing interest in spiritual communion as is evident from the writings of Grote, Brinckerinck, a Kempis and other Devotionalists. In the *Conclusa et Proposita* Grote resolved to commune spiritually every day during his attendance at mass, and more particularly at the reception of the pax.[83] Johannes Brinckerinck, Zerbolt's contemporary and *confrère* in the Brethren House at Deventer, held spiritual communion to be as efficacious and

---

408; Post, *The Modern Devotion*, 334; and van Miert, "Eene Bijdrage tot de Geschiedenis van de Eucharistie in de Nederlanden," 117-119.

The anonymous author of the *Epistola de Vita et Passione Domini Nostri* advocated "weekly" communion: "...semper ad octo dies communicares,..." (*Epistola de Vita et Passione Domini Nostri*, ed. by Monica Hedlund, 106.) Thomas a Kempis also advised frequent sacramental communion (*De Imitatione Christi*, Bk. IV, ch. 3).

[82] On the concept and practice of spiritual communion, as well as its history, see: Louis de Bazalaire, "Communion Spirituelle," *DSp*, II, 1294-1300; F. Costa, "Communion, Spiritual," *NCE*, IV, 39; J. H. Srawley, "Eucharist (to the end of the Middle Ages)," in: *Encyclopedia of Religion and Ethics*, ed. by J. Hastings, V, 558; M. Smits van Waesberghe, "Iets over leer en praktijk van de geestelijke communie in de Middeleeuwen, voornamelijk in het licht van de vaderlandsche devotie-literatuur," *Studia Catholica*, XIX (1943), 129-140, 172-187; Post, *Kerkgeschiedenis*, II, 299-300; and *idem, Kerkelijke Verhoudingen in Nederland voor de Reformatie*, 405-406.

According to the pseudo-Bonaventuran-Ludolphian *Vita Ihesu Christi* Christ commanded his disciples at the Last Supper to eat his body both sacramentally and spiritually (*Tleven Ons Heren*, 148).

[83] Thomas a Kempis, *Opera Omnia*, VII, 98-102. Peter Horn, one of Grote's biographers, writes that when he attended mass Grote always communed spiritually (W. J. Kühler, ed., "De 'Vita magistri Gerardi Magni' van Petrus Horn," *NAKG*, N.S., VI [1909], 359). Cf. Axters, *Vroomheid*, III, 54; and de Beer, *Spiritualiteit*, 90-91.

The constitutions of the Brethren of the Common Life stipulated that during attendance at the daily mass the Brethren had to meditate on Christ's life and death in preparation for spiritual communion. See "The Original Constitution of the Brethren of the Common Life at Deventer," ed. by Hyma, *The Christian Renaissance*, 445; and "Consuetudines domus nostre* (= Brethren House at Zwolle)," in: Jacobus de Voecht, *Narratio*, ed. by Schoengen, 244. Cf. Goossens, *Meditatie*, 170; and Post, *The Modern Devotion*, 236.

fruitful as sacramental communion. He wrote, in fact, that the believer will not suffer even though he should never again attend church and commune sacramentally, provided he communes spiritually on a daily basis.[84] In *De Imitatione Christi* Thomas a Kempis too urges the reader to communicate spiritually on those days that he is prevented from communicating sacramentally. The believer, he writes, can communicate spiritually every day, every hour, when he recalls Christ's incarnation and death in a spirit of love and devotion.[85] Both Brinckerinck and Thomas a Kempis held, then, that spiritual communion can take place outside the mass as well as during it. Wessel Gansfort (d. 1489), who as a young student spent many years in the Brethren *bursae* in Zwolle but never joined a Devotionalist institution on account of which he cannot be labelled a Devotionalist, went a step further than Brinckerinck had done. He asserted that spiritual communion is superior to sacramental communion.[86] It would appear that only one Devotionalist adopted the extreme position taken by Gansfort, namely Johannes Mombaer (d. 1501), and he may have been directly indebted to Gansfort in this instance.[87]

In view of the importance which many Devotionalists attributed to spiritual communion, it is surprising that Zerbolt does not mention spiritual communion even once. He places, on the other hand, considerable emphasis on sacramental communion, and holds daily sacramental communion to be the ideal, but realizes that in practice this may not always be advisable or possible. Why Zerbolt shows such a marked preference for sacramental communion to the extent that he does not even mention spiritual communion, a fact which sets him apart from other early Devotionalists like Grote and Brinckerinck, is not altogether clear. Presumably he held sacramental communion, for which the believer has prepared himself well, to be of much greater benefit to the believer than mere spiritual communion, on account of which he urges the reader to communicate sacramentally as often as his conscience will allow him to do so. About a century after Zerbolt wrote his two manuals, Gabriel Biel advised frequent sacramental communion on the basis that those who prepare themselves well for sacramental communion receive

---

[84] Brinckerinck, "Collatiën," 146. Cf. Smits van Waesberghe, "Iets over leer en praktijk van de geestelijke communie in de Middeleeuwen, voornamelijk in het licht van de vaderlandsche devotie-literatuur," 181-182 and 184.

[85] Th. a Kempis, *De Imitatione Christi*, Bk. IV, ch. 10. Cf. Smits van Waesberghe, "Iets over leer en praktijk van de geestelijke communie in de Middeleeuwen, voornamelijk in het licht van de vaderlandsche devotie-literatuur," 184.

[86] Post, *Kerkgeschiedenis*, II, 299; and Post, *Kerkelijke Verhoudingen in Nederland voor de Reformatie*, 405.

[87] Debongnie, *Jean Mombaer de Bruxelles, abbé de Livry, ses écrits et ses réformes*, 200-201; and Post, *The Modern Devotion*, 547-548.

grace *ex opere operantis* as well as grace *ex opere operato*.[88] A similar consideration may have played a role in Zerbolt's advocacy of frequent sacramental communion, for those communing only spiritually would receive only grace *ex opere operantis* according to traditional thought regarding sacramental grace.[89] In upholding the importance of sacramental communion Zerbolt was, of course, upholding the importance of the church at the same time,[90] while Brinckerinck's position could lead to a neglect of sacramental communion, and so to a downgrading of the church.

K. R. Davis seems to be in error when he writes that most of the Devotionalists held spiritual reception of the sacraments to be more important than sacramental reception and he makes this assertion in reference to the sacraments of penance and communion in particular. Having said that, Davis is able to provide only two examples to support his argument, namely Wessel Gansfort and Peter of Dieburg (d. 1491).[91] However, whether Gansfort can be called a Devotionalist in the true sense of the word is debatable, and it would seem to be advisable to side with Post on this question.[92] Peter of Dieburg puts considerable emphasis on spiritual communion as was done by many of the Devotionalists, but it is not certain that he actually maintained that spiritual communion is superior to sacramental communion, although the possibility exists that he did.[93] However, even if Davis has correctly represented Dieburg's views on this matter, that still leaves only a maximum of two Devotionalists of whom we know that they regarded spiritual communion as being superior to sacramental communion, namely Dieburg and Mombaer, although Davis does not mention the latter. To hold such an opinion was, then, very much of an exception among the Devotionalists, and not the rule as Davis suggests. Furthermore, Davis overlooks the Devotionalists' practice of frequent sacramental communion, a habit which clearly underlines the esteem in which sacramental communion was held by the Devotionalists.

x. *Conclusion*

Zerbolt's writings betray a profound interest in the eucharist, and in its sacramental aspect in particular. He is concerned above all with the

---

[88] Oberman, *Biel*, 358.

[89] F. Costa, "Communion, Spiritual," *NCE*, IV, 39.

[90] Cf. van Rooy, *Zerbolt*, 273; and Post, *Kerkgeschiedenis*, I, 382.

[91] Davis, *Anabaptism and Asceticism*, 256-257.

[92] Post, *The Modern Devotion*, 476-486.

[93] R. Doebner, ed., *Annalen und Akten der Brüder des gemeinsamen Lebens im Lüchtenhove zu Hildesheim* (Hanover-Leipzig, 1903), 144-150. Cf. Post, *The Modern Devotion*, 463-464 and 467-468.

disposition required of the communicant for a valid and fruitful communion. Such a disposition, he explains, must consist of an amalgam of fear
and love. Fear of Christ the judge who is present bodily in the sacrament
will prevent the believer from communicating unworthily. Love, on the
other hand, will draw him to the *Christus Eucharisticus* without whom he
cannot progress in the spiritual life. The eucharistic sacrament is indispensable because it is, on account of the real presence, the most potent
of all vehicles of grace. The believer can, with the aid of grace, develop
the disposition necessary for communion. However, humility, without
which a valid and fruitful communion is impossible, requires him to attribute all to God. Finally, Zerbolt's implicit advocacy of frequent
sacramental communion, added to the fact that he nowhere mentions
spiritual communion, secures the position of the priesthood, and of the
church, in man's spiritual ascent.

CHAPTER SIX

SPIRITUAL THEOLOGY AND LIFE[1]

Man's return to the state of grace through the sacrament of penance has been looked at in some detail in an earlier chapter. However, man's reconciliation with God in this manner constitutes only the indispensable basis for further progress in the spiritual life. For, as Zerbolt writes in *De Ascensionibus*, to be reconciled to God through the sacrament of penance is not sufficient. Following his justification the believer must progress from virtue to virtue in order that he might finally be accepted into God's friendship and be united with Him in perfect charity.[2] In other words, sanctification does not automatically accompany justification, as Martin Luther was to assert little more than a century later.

In his quest for sanctity man is urged on by a natural appetite and desire to ascend spiritually and to seek spiritual heights; for man, a rational and noble creature, has been furnished with a certain greatness of mind.[3] This loftiness of mind, on account of which man goes in quest of

---

[1] This chapter owes more to the following works than has been indicated in each and every instance: P. Pourrat, *La Spiritualité Chrétienne*, Vol. I: *Des Origines de l'Eglise au Moyen Age*; Vol. II: *Le Moyen Age* (4 vols.; 2d ed.; Paris, 1947-1951); L. Bouyer, *The Spirituality of the New Testament and the Fathers* (*A History of Christian Spirituality*, Vol. I), trans. by M. P. Ryan (London, 1963); J. Leclercq, F. Vandenbroucke and L. Bouyer, *The Spirituality of the Middle Ages* (*A History of Christian Spirituality*, Vol. II), trans. by the Benedictines of Holme Eden Abbey (London, 1968); and *Théologie de la Vie Monastique, Etudes sur la tradition patristique* (Etudes publiées sous la direction de la faculté de théologie S. J. de Lyon-Fourvière, No. 49; Lyon-Fourvière, 1961).

[2] *Asc.*, 263F-G: Ecce homo sanus factus es et Deo reconciliatus, vade et procede ulterius et amplius noli peccare, sed magis stude de virtute in virtutem proficere, nec putes sufficere quod per poenitentiam sis Deo reconciliatus, ut ad eius familiaritatem accipiaris et perfectam charitatem. Cf. *Asc.*, 266C.

The Council of Trent asserted that the just, justified through the sacrament of penance, may already be called friends of God. However, spiritual writers in the centuries before Trent—and Thomas a Kempis may be counted among them—expressed the view that this friendship between God and man is not established as a result of the latter's justification through the sacrament of penance; rather this friendship is established, and grows, as man progresses in virtue following his justification, and as he progresses towards Christian perfection, namely purity and charity. (J. F. Dedek, "Friendship with God," *NCE*, VI, 207-208. Cf. A. Hallier, *The Monastic Theology of Aelred of Rievaulx* [Shannon, 1969], 25-55.) It is patently clear from what has been said that Zerbolt too sees friendship with God as the consequence not of man's justification, but as a result of his gradual sanctification through the spiritual life.

[3] *Asc.*, 258F: Novi, homo, quod ascensionum sis cupidis, quodque exaltationem vehementer concupiscis. Rationalis enim ac nobilis creatura es et magni cuiusdam animi, ideoque altitudinem et ascensum naturali appetis desiderio. Cf. *Asc.*, 278A-B; W. Lourdaux, "Gérard Zerbolt de Zutphen," *DSp*, VI, 285.

spiritual heights, consists of the divine image and likeness in which he was made, and it is the soul as the image and likeness of God which seeks its creator. Therefore, man's soul, on which God has bestowed such great dignity and nobility by making it in his own image and likeness, cannot be satisfied by anything less than the one God, the holy and most glorious Trinity.[4] For that reason man will not find any rest until he finds peace and rest in God,[5] as Augustine had first written many centuries before.[6]

The pursuit of virtue and charity which follows justification is the subject-matter of spiritual theology; and it is with spiritual theology, which divides into ascetical theology and mystical theology,[7] that Zerbolt's two major works, *De Reformatione* and *De Ascensionibus*, are primarily concerned. Of the two disciplines into which spiritual theology divides, ascetical theology receives by far the most attention from Zerbolt.[8] In both manuals he makes the mystical union with God the end of the spiritual life and briefly discusses it in that context. Having done that, he does not return to the question of the mystical experience of God, but concentrates his attention solely on the ascesis which provides the only access to such an experience. In his concentration on ascetical theology and neglect of mystical theology, Zerbolt followed in the footsteps of Grote and also helped to shape the *Devotio Moderna* as a movement concerned primarily with the ascesis and only marginally with mystical contemplation.[9] Having made these introductory remarks we are now ready

[4] See above, pp. 66-67. Cf. *The Golden Epistle of Abbot William of St. Thierry*, 91; and D. of Augsburg, *De ext. de int. hom. compositione*, I, 81.

[5] *Asc.*, 275F-G: Itaque in primo, mundi concupiscentia deseritur. In secundo mens superius sublevatur. In tertio quiescit in Deo quieta.

The statement "that man will remain restless until he finds rest in God" is found in *De Imitatione Christi* as well, but with a variation. Thomas a Kempis writes that man will remain restless until he has been united with Christ (*De Imitatione Christi*, Bk. II, ch. 1).

[6] Augustine, *Confessions*, I, 1. Cf. Copleston, *History of Philosophy*, Vol. II, Pt. II, 96-99. Cf. *The Golden Epistle of Abbot William of St. Thierry*, 91; and D. of Augsburg, *De ext. et int. hom. compositione*, I, 88-89 and cf. 81.

[7] J. de Guibert, "Ascétique," *DSp*, I, 1010-1017; T. A. Porter, "Spiritual Theology," *NCE*, XIII, 588-590; E. E. Larkin, "Ways, The Three Spiritual," *NCE*, XIV, 835-836.

[8] Cf. van Rooy, *Zerbolt*, 265-266; W. Lourdaux, "Gérard Zerbolt de Zutphen," *DSp*, VI, 285; and Post, *The Modern Devotion*, 327.

[9] Cf. Post, *De Moderne Devotie*, 140; Mak, "Christus bij de Moderne Devoten," 141-154; Goossens, *Meditatie*, 28; S. Axters, "Inleiding tot een geschiedenis van de mystiek in de Nederlanden," *Verslagen en Mededeelingen van de Koninklijke Vlaamse Akademie voor Taal en Letterkunde*, 1967, pp. 286-287 and cf. p. 217; Knierim, *Dirc van Herxen*, 131-142; K. Kavanaugh, "Spirituality, History of," *NCE*, IV, 831. See the following as well: J. van Mierlo, "Over het ontstaan der Germaansche mystiek," *OGE*, I (1927), 11-37; L. Reypens, "Le sommet de la contemplation mystique," *RAM*, III (1922), 249-271, IV (1923), 256-271, and V (1924), 33-59 (deals with the mysticism of Jan van Ruusbroec, Jan van Schoonhoven, Th. a Kempis, Gerlach Peters and Hendrik van Herp); and B. Spaapen, "Middeleeuwse Passiemystiek," *OGE*, XXXV (1961), 167-185, and 252-299, XL (1966), 5-64, XLI (1967), 209-301, and 321-367, XLII (1968), 5-32, 225-261 and 374-421 and XLIII (1969), 270-304.

to examine Zerbolt's spiritual theology. We will look first at what he writes concerning the goal of the spiritual life, and then inquire into his ascetical theology.

A. Contemplation As The End Of The Spiritual Life

In *De Reformatione* Zerbolt sets what had traditionally been regarded as a lower goal for the spiritual life than he does in *De Ascensionibus*, and we will look successively at the spiritual goal he erects in each of his two manuals for the religious life.

i. De Reformatione

In *De Reformatione* Zerbolt writes that in all of one's spiritual exercises it is necessary to keep two goals in mind, namely purity of heart and charity.[10] In terms of importance charity outranks a pure heart, but both are indispensable, for charity has a pure heart for its foundation. Purity of heart, the immediate goal, prepares the believer for the ultimate goal of charity.[11] Zerbolt points out that in setting purity of heart and charity as the goals of the spiritual life he is essentially following biblical commandments. For according to St. Paul *"finis praecepti est charitas de corde puro."*[12]

---

[10] Chapter three of *De Reformatione* in which Zerbolt delineates the end of the spiritual life is, to a considerable degree, influenced by John Cassian's first "Conference," and even more by chapters two and three of Radewijns' *Tractatulus Devotus*. However, these two chapters of the *Tractatulus* are themselves largely inspired by Cassian's first "Conference." Therefore, in this instance as in so many others, Zerbolt's indebtedness to Cassian is both direct and indirect. See *De Reformatione*, ch. 3 (p. 238C-H); Cassian, *Conferences*, No. I, chs. 4-7; and Radewijns, *Tractatulus Devotus*, 213-215. Cf. Cassian, *Institutes*, Bk. IV, ch. 43; and Radewijns, *Omnes, Inquit, Artes*, II, 1-4.
On Zerbolt's indebtedness to Cassian with respect to the goal of the spiritual life see Goossens, *Meditatie*, 29; van Woerkum, "Het Libellus 'Omnes, inquit, artes'," 245-247; and Rayez, "Gérard Zerbolt de Zutphen et Saint Bonaventure. Dépendances Littéraires," 333-334.
For a discussion of Cassian's understanding of the purpose of the spiritual life see Christiani, *Jean Cassien*, II, 11-26; and B. Griffiths, "John Cassian," in: J. Walsh, ed., *Spirituality Through the Centuries* (London, n.d.), 34-35.

[11] *Ref.*, 238C: De primo exercitio, et quod homo devotus in omnibus exercitiis suis habebit pro oculis finem suum qui est puritas cordis et charitas. *Ref.*, 238C-D: Hic autem finis tuus, ut dictum est, debet esse ut statui unde corruisti, possis propinquare. Ut autem de hoc fine tuo enucleatius sub aliis vocabulis intelligas, scire debes, quod duo sunt tibi fines in omnibus exercitiis tuis praefigendi. Unus principalis seu ultimatus, et hic est charitas. Alius secundarius, et dispositivus, seu ultima dispositio ad finem principalem, et hic est puritas cordis. Cf. Goossens, *Meditatie*, 154-158; van Woerkum, "Het Libellus 'Omnes, inquit, artes'," 247-248; and R. Masterson, "Perfection, Spiritual," *NCE*, XI, 126-127.

[12] *Ref.*, 238D. The text Zerbolt quotes here is 1 Timothy 1, 5. Cf. P. Salmon, "L'ascèse monastique et la spiritualité," *VSp*, XXIX (1954), Supplément, 195, 196 and 221; Goossens, *Meditatie*, 52; and E. E. Larkin, "Ways, The Three Spiritual," *NCE*, XIV, 836.
It must be pointed out that Zerbolt begins chapter three of *De Reformatione* with the

It is to Augustine's *De Doctrina Christiana* that Zerbolt goes for a definition of charity. Charity, he quotes, is the motion of the soul towards the enjoyment of God for his own sake, while cupidity, by contrast, is the motion of the soul towards the enjoyment of one's self or any corporeal thing for the sake of something other than God.[13] To which Zerbolt adds that cupidity might briefly be defined as an inordinate motion to delight in things created.[14] Cupidity, then, is the equivalent of sinful concupiscence,[15] and it is the very opposite of charity. For while cupidity is the inordinate desire for created things motivated by love of self, charity is the love of one's self and all corporeal things not for their own sake, but because of God who is their origin.

The question arises whether Zerbolt understood the state of charity to be a contemplative one. All indications are that he did, and a number of arguments can be brought forward in support of this position. In the first place, when he writes that the goal of the spiritual life is twofold, namely purity of heart followed by charity, a twofold division of the spiritual life, inspired by the traditional division of the spiritual life into active and contemplative,[16] is implied. For the heart is purified through the eradication of all the vices, the chief of which is cupidity or sinful concupiscence,[17] and the elimination of the vices was universally regarded as a pivotal component of the active phase of the spiritual life. Following the purifica-

---

observation that the end of all spiritual exercises must be man's original condition, on account of which the believer must at all times keep in mind the state from which he has fallen (*Ref.*, 238C). Therefore, when later in this same chapter he makes charity the ultimate goal of the spiritual life, he somewhat adulterates the objective first set by him. For a pure heart and charity, even though they come near to man's first perfection, do not constitute the equivalent of man's original condition (*Asc.*, 238E). Charity falls short of man's primordial state, because in *De Reformatione* Zerbolt portrays the mystical vision of God as the summit of man's condition before the fall (see above, pp. 70-73).

[13] *Ref.*, 238E-F: Quod ut melius intelligas, scire debes quod secundum Augustinum: Charitas est motus animi ad fruendum Deo propter se. E contrario autem: Cupiditas est motus animi ad fruendum se vel quolibet corpore non propter Deum,... Zerbolt quotes from Augustine, *De Doctrina Christiana*, III, 10, 16. Cf. Steinmetz, *Staupitz*, 35-36 and T. Gilby, "Charity," *NCE*, III, 464-470.

[14] *Ref.*, 238E-F: .., id est, breviter quivis appetitus vel motus inordinatus ad delectandum in creaturis.

[15] Zerbolt distinguishes between sinful, culpable concupiscence and natural, nonculpable concupiscence (see above, pp. 91-93).

[16] Cf. R. Petry, ed., *Late Medieval Mysticism* (Philadelphia, 1957), 23-45; Chadwick, *John Cassian*, 82-90; and E. E. Larkin, "Ways, The Three Spiritual," *NCE*, XIV, 835-836.

Some writers labelled both the purgative and illuminative phases active, calling only the unitive phase contemplative. Others, however, asserted that only the purgative stage belongs to the active life, and that both the illuminative and unitive stages are part of the contemplative life. A writer's definition and understanding of the three stages determined his arrangement of them under the label active or contemplative.

[17] *Ref.*, 238F: Cor autem purgare nihil aliud est, quam cupiditates extinguere.

tion of the heart and the growth in virtue which accompanies the extirpation of vice,[18] the believer is capable of charity, the second, and final, stage of the spiritual life in *De Reformatione*, and, by implication, a contemplative one. Secondly, some of the major sources of Zerbolt's spirituality such as Bernard's *Sermons on the Song of Songs* and Bonaventure's *De Triplici Via* are works in which the sentiment of affective contemplation is a pervasive one.[19] Consequently, it would appear likely that Zerbolt absorbed the teaching of Bernard and Bonaventure regarding the affective nature of contemplation, and that as a result he understood the

---

[18] *Ref.*, 238F: Quantum autem secundum Augustinum, regnum cupiditatis destruitur, tantum regnum charitatis augetur. Zerbolt quotes here from Augustine's *De Doctrina Christiana*, Bk. III, ch. 10.

Ref., 238G: Hoc modo cor purgare et vires animae reformare, est virtutes menti inserere. Nihil enim aliud est virtus secundum beatum Basilium, quam bene uti motibus ab Deo naturaliter nobis insitis:... In his *Tractatulus Devotus* Radewijns quotes the same definition of virtue by St. Basil (*Tractatulus Devotus*, 216), which is taken from St. Basil's *Regulae Fusius Tractatae*, *PG*, XXXI, 910. It is possible that Zerbolt quotes St. Basil *via* Radewijns, rather than directly.

The virtues referred to here are moral virtues, rather than theological virtues like hope and charity.

[19] Influenced by Neo-Platonic thought the spiritual writers of the later patristic period held that the supreme, and most perfect, experience of God is an intellectual one. Consequently, contemplation, the final stage of the spiritual life, was defined in terms of intellectual intuition, or vision, of the divine, rather than in terms of a perfect submission of man's will to the divine will expressed in active charity. This conception of contemplation remained essentially unchallenged until the twelfth century. However, with St. Bernard, William of St. Thierry and the first Franciscans one sees the beginning of a reaction against the traditional definition of contemplation as the intellectual intuition of God. They, and many others following them, held that contemplation can be an affective experience of God instead of an intellectual one, but both mystical theologies were frequently espoused by the same person. Nonetheless, many, and perhaps most, continued to regard intellectual contemplation to be a more profound experience of God than the affective, volitional contemplation of him. The next major development in mystical theology came with the *moderni* of the fourteenth and fifteenth centuries who totally denied the possibility of the intellectual intuition of God in this life. They would go no further than accept the possibility of an affective, acquired contemplation of God by mortal man (M. Olphe-Galliard and P. Phillipe, "Contemplation," *DSp*, II, 1911-1921, 1970, 1979-1981, 1983 and 1987-1988; E. Longpré, "Bonaventure [Saint]," *DSp*, I, 1796-1798; J. M. Dechanet, "Guillaume de Saint-Thierry," *DSp*, VI, 1241-1263; Petry, ed., *Late Medieval Mysticism*, 17-48; C. Butler, *Western Mysticism. The Teaching of Augustine, Gregory and Bernard on Contemplation and the Contemplative Life* [New York: Harper Torchbook, 1966], 55-62, 87-92, and 102-120; D. Knowles, *The English Mystical Tradition* [New York: Harper Torchbook, 1965], 21-38; E. R. Elder, "William of St. Thierry: Rational and Affective Spirituality," in: *The Spirituality of Western Christendom*, ed. by E. R. Elder [Kalamazoo, Michigan, 1976], 85-105; T. Corbishley, "Mysticism," *NCE*, X, 175-178; D. Phillips, "The Way to Religious Perfection According to St. Bonaventure's *De Triplici Via*," in: *Essays in Medieval Life and Thought*, presented in honour of Austin P. Evans and ed. by J. H. Mundy, R. W. Emery and B. N. Nelson [New York, 1965], 33 and 51; F. Vandenbroucke, "Le Divorce entre Théologie et Mystique. Ses Origines," *Nouvelle Revue Théologique*, LXXII (1950), 383-388; Axters, "Inleiding tot een geschiedenis van de Mystiek in de Nederlanden," 261-262; and Oberman, *Biel*, 327-340).

union established with God through perfect charity to be a contemplative one. The possibility and likelihood that in *De Reformatione* Zerbolt understood charity to be an act of contemplation becomes even more probable when one takes into consideration that in a letter to a rector of a convent Grote, the founder of the *Devotio Moderna*, equates perfect charity with contemplation. The end of the religious life, he wrote, is *"contemplacio seu perfeccio caritatis."*[20] Thus, if we are correct in assuming that in *De Reformatione* Zerbolt embraces the possibility of an affective contemplation of the divine, it means that he rejected the still widely accepted pseudo-Dionysian definition of contemplation according to which the mystical experience is restricted to the intellectual intuition, or vision, of the divine. For, although Zerbolt accepts the possibility of the intellectual intuition of God as will be seen from the discussion of *De Ascensionibus*, he sets affective contemplation alongside it; or, perhaps more accurately, he regards affective contemplation as the highest level of perfection attainable by man before he proceeds to the vision of God.

In *De Reformatione* there is nothing about charity, or the affective mystical experience, as being the result of an extraordinary gift of grace. It is virtually certain that Zerbolt was of the opinion that affective contemplation can be achieved by all those who are in the state of grace and who possess, therefore, common habitual, or sanctifying, grace directing the activities of the soul towards a union with God.[21] It would appear, then, that Zerbolt regarded affective contemplation as an acquired, rather than as an infused, state.[22] This assumption gains credibility in view of Zerbolt's assertion in *De Ascensionibus* that the intellectual intuition of God is the consequence of a special gift of grace for which man can prepare himself, but which remains, in the end, totally gratuitous.[23] In contrast with the vision of God, then, affective contemplation is the natural outgrowth, apex and end of the spiritual life because it is not dependent on a special gift of grace but is attainable with the aid of habitual grace only. Consequently, all those in the state of grace are in a position actually to ascend to the affective contemplation of the divine provided they will work for it through spiritual exercises. The active life makes the contemplative life possible. Without asceticism there can be no mysticism.

Following chapter three of *De Reformatione* Zerbolt does not again mention charity, the ultimate goal of the spiritual life, but he concentrates his

---

[20] Mulder, ed., *Gerardi Magni Episolae*, 181. Cf. de Beer, *Spiritualiteit*, 56-57 and 188; and Goossens, *Meditatie*, 142-144.

[21] Cf. Richardson, ed., *Dictionary*, 147-149 ("Grace").

[22] Cf. P. Phillipe, "Contemplation," *DSp*, II, 1981 and 1983.

[23] See footnote 36 below.

attention exclusively on the means to obtain a pure heart, the immediate objective of the believer's spiritual exercises.[24] In this connection it is not without some significance that at least two extant constitutions used by the Brethren of the Common Life name purity of heart as the *raison d'être* for the existence of the Brethren Houses in which these constitutions were in use;[25] and it is likely that either Radewijns or Zerbolt, or perhaps both of them, had a hand in drafting these rules of conduct.[26] These constitutions, as well as the manuals for the spiritual life by both Radewijns and Zerbolt, were to a large extent responsible for making the Brotherhood of the Common Life an essentially ascetical movement.

ii. *De Ascensionibus*

Turning to *De Ascensionibus*, we find that Zerbolt writes there that the return to the state of grace through the sacrament of penance was arduous enough, but that the battle for a pure heart, namely the elimination of sinful concupiscence, and charity is infinitely more difficult and demanding. In *De Ascensionibus*, as in *De Reformatione*, the spiritual life is described in terms of a battle between man's natural desire for creaturely things and his innate desire to ascend to God in whose image and likeness he was created. Evidence of success in the battle for purity and charity, which Zerbolt equates with virtue in *De Ascensionibus*,[27] is a love of purity and charity motivated neither by fear of punishment nor by hope of reward, but motivated by a love of purity and charity for their own sake.[28] One who has achieved this state in which purity and charity

---

[24] For Grote a morally upright life, rather than union with God, is the first objective as well (de Beer, *Spiritualiteit*, 146).

[25] "The Original Constitution of the Brethren of the Common Life at Deventer," ed. by Hyma, *The Christian Renaissance*, 442; and "*Consuetudines domus nostre* (= Brethren House at Zwolle)," in: Jacobus de Voecht, *Narratio*, ed. by Schoengen, 241. Cf. Goossens, *Meditatie*, 24-27 and 29; Axters, *Vroomheid*, III, 67-68; and C. van der Wansem, *Het Ontstaan en de Geschiedenis der Broederschap van het Gemene Leven tot 1400* (Louvain, 1958), 25-47.

[26] Cf. van Woerkum, *Het Libellus "Omnes, Inquit, Artes," Een Rapiarium van Florentius Radewijns*, III, 34-35.

[27] Quoting St. Basil, Zerbolt defines virtue in *De Reformatione* as the use of one's faculties in accordance with the purpose for which they were created (see footnote 18 above). For if all the faculties are directed towards their proper object, namely God (see above, pp. 66-67), sinful concupiscence will be eradicated, the heart purified, and charity will have become a possibility. Virtue, then, is the equivalent of an absence of sinful concupiscence and the possession of a pure heart which enable man to ascend to a union with God in love.

[28] How this love for purity and charity for their own sake is arrived at through fear and hope will be looked at below.

In distinguishing between love of purity and charity motivated by fear of punishment and hope of reward, and love of purity and charity for their own sake, Zerbolt would appear to be echoing the Augustinian teaching regarding *uti* and *frui* with which he must

are loved on their own account has, as it were, put on a new nature. He does virtuous deeds not as one striving against his concupiscent desires, but as one who, because of his altered nature, cannot but do virtuous deeds. He is one in whom the will, the rational appetite, has successfully mastered the sensitive appetites and their natural desire for created things. Even the concupiscent power will then take delight in the divine, its proper, and only legitimate, object.[29]

Once rebellious concupiscence has been conquered, and the concupiscent power even desires God, man is governed solely by his natural desire for spiritual improvement and union with God. He is then not only willing to do God's will in all things, but capable as well; and the submersion of man's will into the divine will is central to man's love for God above all else. Being thus disposed, man is ready to ascend even further and be united with God in ardent love. Zerbolt would appear to view this union in love as a mystical contemplation of the divine, and he would even seem to equate it with the intuition (*intueri*) of God,[30] although the term *intueri* is normally reserved for the intellectual contemplation of the divine.[31] But in speaking of what apparently has to be understood as an affective intuition, or vision, of God, Zerbolt links affective contemplation of the divine with the intellectual contemplation of him as was commonly done by those who understood contemplation to be an affective as well as an intellectual act. They tended to hold the view that intellectual contemplation cannot take place without affective contemplation preceding, or at least accompanying, it.[32] In this connection it might be observed that Gerson defined mystical theology as "the knowledge of God by experience, arrived at through the embrace of unifying love."[33] As in *De Reformatione*, Zerbolt obviously regards the affective contemplation of the divine as an acquired, rather than as an infused, state, attainable by all those in the state of grace and who enjoy, therefore, the aid of habitual, or sanctifying, grace.

---

have been familiar through his reading of *De Doctrina Christiana*, a work he quotes a number of times in *De Reformatione* and *De Ascensionibus*. (*De Doctrina Christiana*, I, 4, 4.) Cf. Steinmetz, *Staupitz*, 35-37.

[29] The preceding paragraph is based on *Asc.*, 268B-E: Siquidem non ..., modestiam, etc. Cf. *Asc.*, chs. 9 and 10 (p. 262A-G).

[30] *Asc.*, 268D-E: Secundum est quod sicut affectus virtutum est in eo habituatus modo praedicto, ita affectus sit Deo per ardentem amorem unitus, et ad divinae voluntatis beneplacitum semper ex fervore paratus et in divina speculatione erectus. Siquidem ei adhaeret per fervidum amorem, et ad eius intuitum omne perhorret vitium et peccatum, eius amore et intuitus zelo semper est accensus,... Cf. Goossens, *Meditatie*, 150; and van Rooy, *Zerbolt*, 266.

[31] M. J. Redle, "God, Intuition of," *NCE*, VI, 562-563.

[32] P. Phillipe, "Contemplation," *DSp*, II, 1970, 1979-1981 and 1983.

[33] T. Corbishley, "Mysticism," *NCE*, X, 175-178. Cf. M. J. Reddle, "Beatific Vision," *NCE*, II, 186.

After having reached the affective contemplation of God, Zerbolt continues, man often—and it is somewhat peculiar that Zerbolt believes this to be a frequent happening in view of the fact that he himself most likely never enjoyed the vision of God—ascends even higher, namely to the intellectual vision, or intuition, of God, something which he also enjoyed before the fall. However, our author is quick to add that this intellectual vision falls short of the vision of God in his very essence. On account of his own insufficiency, residual impurity, and the weakness of the mind's eye, man's vision of God will remain dim, and he will see God only as in a glass darkly.[34] Nonetheless, it is fairly certain that Zerbolt regards the vision of God as the crown on the reformation of the intellect following the fall, a reformation of the intellect which begins with the act of faith.[35]

Of some considerable significance is Zerbolt's observation that the intellectual vision of God may be attained by no man, except it be granted to him by the special grace of God. Nonetheless, Zerbolt warns, this grace is not bestowed on sleepers and the negligent, nor on those that will not co-operate with divine grace.[36] In other words, with the aid of grace the believer can prepare himself for the mystical vision of God; and the spiritual life, as it is described by Zerbolt in De Ascensionibus in particular, has the mystical vision of God as its goal. However, the vision itself remains, in the final analysis, a totally gratuitous gift, an infused state; it is the consequence of a special grace granted to certain individuals over and above the ordinary sanctifying grace bestowed on all those who are in the state of grace.[37] But all Christians are, nonetheless, obliged to prepare

---

[34] *Asc.*, 268E-F: Intellectu saepe ultra se ascendit ad intuitum divinae speculationis, licet per speculum in aenigmate. *Asc.*, 278A-B: Bene cor hominis altum Propheta describit, ad cuius summitatem vel summum apicem non nisi tot ascensionibus pervenitur. Nec mirum tamen si altum dicitur ipsum, cum superior eius portio si bene esset ordinata, immediate Deum attingeret et ei soli subesset, ita ut si in superiori parte mentis tuae stares, adeo alte respiceres, ut ipsum Deum cernere posses, quamvis non per essentiam, propter tuam inidoneitatem, vel oculorum adhuc impuritatem et infirmitatem. In another passage Zerbolt leaves one with the impression that it is possible, even in this life, to ascend *"ad Dei essentialem visionem"* (*Asc.*, 269F). Nonetheless, that man's vision of God will always remain imperfect in this life clearly represents Zerbolt's real position. He maintains, as will be seen below, that spiritual perfection is impossible as long as man is burdened with his body and bodily senses. Cf. Goossens, *Meditatie*, 150-151; van Rooy, *Zerbolt*, 266-268; Vandenbroucke, "Contemplation (La Dévotion Moderne)," *DSp*, II, 2001; and Leclercq, Vandenbroucke and Bouyer, *The Spirituality of the Middle Ages*, 432.

The fact that Zerbolt regards the intellectual vision of God, rather than charity, to be man's most profound experience of the divine perhaps indicates that he was an intellectualist. Cf. Copleston, *A History of Philosophy*, Vol. II, Pt. II, 263-264.

[35] See above, pp. 166-168. Cf. D. of Augsburg, *De ext. et int. hom. compositione*, I, 84-85.

[36] *Asc.*, 268F: Quamvis hic status perfectionis, nisi Dei speciali gratia ab nemine acquiritur, gratia tamen dormientibus, negligentibus, et non cooperantibus non datur,... Cf. Goossens, *Meditatie*, 151; and van Rooy, *Zerbolt*, 265 and 268.

[37] Vandenbroucke, "Contemplation (La Dévotion Moderne)," *DSp*, II, 2001; and Post, *Kerkgeschiedenis*, I, 381-382. Cf. Knowles, *The English Mystical Tradition*, 13-14.

themselves, through the eradication of vice and the cultivation of virtue, for this special gift of grace: the ascesis is the only way to the mystical vision of God. Consequently, it is on the ascesis that Zerbolt concentrates his attention in *De Ascensionibus*, as he does in *De Reformatione*; and he does not treat of the vision of God except as a potential summit of the spiritual life over which man has, in the end, no control.[38]

In contrast with some, then, Zerbolt did not regard the intellectual vision of God as the normal crown on the spiritual ascent. For him the intellectual vision was due to a special gift of grace not bestowed by God on all those in the state of grace. Those who held the opposite view did not regard the intellectual vision as an abnormal and special gift of grace, but merely as the logical conclusion to the life of a Christian who enjoys ordinary habitual grace.[39] In holding the view that the mystical vision is a special gift, an infused state, Zerbolt remained true to the founder of the movement. For Grote the mystical vision of God is the reward granted by him to those who have prepared themselves diligently for this gift through the eradication of vice, the acquisition of virtue, and the nurturing of charity. The mystical vision of the divine is God's field of operation where man can contribute nothing. It is only in the realm of the ascesis that he can make his contribution.[40] Furthermore, of those authors to whom Zerbolt was most deeply indebted the majority would appear to have held the mystical vision of God to be a special, infused gift, rather than the natural conclusion to the Christian's spiritual quest. Among these were Cassian, William of St. Thierry and David of Augsburg.[41] Bonaventure, on the other hand, does not appear to have regarded the vision of God as an extraordinary gift of grace.[42]

The fact that in *De Ascensionibus* he makes the intellectual vision of God the ultimate goal of the spiritual life places Zerbolt well within the pseudo-Dionysian mystical tradition. By contrast, the contemplative goal he sets for the spiritual life in *De Reformatione* is of a Bernardine nature in

---

[38] Cf. van Rooy, *Zerbolt*, 266 and 268; Mak, "Christus bij de Moderne Devoten," 148 and 166; and van Woerkum, *Het Libellus "Omnes, Inquit, Artes," een Rapiarium van Florentius Radewijns*, I, 217-218.

Grote too stresses that all must strive for perfect charity and contemplation, even though he holds that this highest state of the spiritual life will not be achieved by all (Mulder, ed., *Gerardi Magni Epistolae*, 181). Cf. Goossens, *Meditatie*, 144.

[39] Butler, *Western Mysticism*, 55-62 and 87-92; Knowles, *The English Mystical Tradition*, 13-14 and 113; T. Corbishley, "Mysticism," *NCE*, X, 176-177; Rahner and Vorgrimler, *Dictionary*, 50-51 ("Beatific Vision"); and van Rooy, *Zerbolt*, 265.

[40] De Beer, *Spiritualiteit*, 191 and 290-291.

[41] M. Olphe-Galliard and P. Phillipe, "Contemplation," *DSp*, II, 1927 and 1970; and Savary, *Psychological Themes in the Golden Epistle of William of St. Thierry to the Carthusians of Mont-Dieu*, 121.

[42] E. Longpré, "Bonaventure (Saint)," *DSp*, I, 1814.

its concentration on the affective mystical experience of God. The two views are, however, not contradictory but complementary. Or, more accurately, the affective contemplation of God was regarded by many, including Bonaventure, as the pre-condition for the intellectual vision of him.[43] Zerbolt too proceeds from perfect love of God to the intellectual vision of him: from the affective contemplation of God in *De Reformatione* to the vision of him in *De Ascensionibus*. However, notwithstanding the fact that Zerbolt's conception of contemplation as such is more or less identical to that of Bernard and Bonaventure,[44] there is in his writings a total absence of the nuptial mysticism of Bernard as well as of the profound intellectual contemplation of Bonaventure. Finally, because Zerbolt accepts the possibility of the vision of God in this life, his understanding of contemplation is clearly unlike that of the *moderni*.[45]

B) *The Active Life*

It is to the active or ascetical phase of the spiritual life, namely the pursuit of a pure heart and moral virtues following man's justification through the sacrament of penance, that both *De Reformatione* and *De Ascensionibus* are primarily devoted. In both manuals Zerbolt deals with the eradication of the vices and the cultivation of the moral virtues in a very systematic fashion. However, in *De Reformatione* he handles the ascetical phase of the spiritual life rather differently than he does in *De Ascensionibus*,[46] and the dissimilar moulds into which he pours the doctrine of the active life in his two manuals reflect two distinct ways of looking at the course of the ascetical life. For that reason it will be necessary to examine Zerbolt's doctrine of the ascetical life as it is found in *De Reformatione* and *De Ascensionibus* separately.

i. *De Reformatione*

Structure of De Reformatione. In *De Reformatione* Zerbolt writes that only through a reformation of the powers of the soul: i.e., the intellect,

---

[43] T. Corbishley, "Mysticism," *NCE*, X, 175-178; and Phillips, "The Way to Religious Perfection According to St. Bonaventure's *De Triplici Via*," 33 and 51.

[44] In thus lumping Bernard and Bonaventure together the purpose is not to diminish the difference between the two. Bernard was essentially an affective mystic, while Bonaventure was much more of an intellectual one, especially in the *Itinerarium Mentis in Deum*. However, their understanding of the fundamental nature of contemplation was pretty much the same.

[45] Cf. Oberman, *Biel*, 327-331.

It must be pointed out that at times Zerbolt employs the term *contemplatio* in a non-mystical sense: that is, in the sense of reflection, consideration, etc. Cf. Goossens, *Meditatie*, 150. On occasion David of Augsburg also employs the term contemplation as a synonym for meditation and reflection (P. Phillipe, "Contemplation," *DSp*, II, 1970).

[46] Cf. Goossens, *Meditatie*, 66-69.

memory and will, can the heart be purged of all cupidity and sinful concupiscence which stand in the way of charity and spiritual perfection.[47]
Consequently it is around the reformation of these three faculties that *De
Reformatione* is constructed, and in taking this approach to the problem of
cleansing the heart of all sins and unrighteousness Zerbolt was quite obviously following the lead of David of Augsburg.[48]

The reformation of the will is somewhat complicated by the fact that
Zerbolt speaks of two such reformations,[49] the first one of which has
already been examined. For the first reformation of the will is none other
than the sacrament of penance through which man is reconciled to God
following the commission of a mortal sin. However, man's return to the
state of grace was not normally considered to be part of the active phase
of the spiritual life, Zerbolt's primary concern, and consequently he
devotes relatively little attention to the first reformation of the will.[50] The
first reformation of the will, by means of which man returns to the state of
grace, constitutes, nonetheless, the indispensable foundation for progress
in the ascetical phase of the spiritual life. Furthermore, the ascetical life is
essentially a continuation of the process of purgation begun in the sacrament of penance. For in the active phase of the spiritual life, as in the
sacrament of penance, the objective is to cleanse the heart of all obstruc-
tions which stand in the way of charity. However, the aim of the ascetical
life is not merely to purge the soul of sins, but also to remove the cause of
sin, namely a wrongly directed will which succumbs to concupiscent
desires.

---

[47] *Ref.*, 238F-G: Cupiditates et inordinatas concupiscentias extinguere, est vires
animae reformare. Vires animae reformare, est statui unde corruimus, propinquare.
Ergo quantum cor purgamus ab cupiditatibus, tantum animae vires reformamus ab
cupiditatibus, tantumque regnum caritatis in nobis aedificamus, et statui unde lapsi
sumus propinquamus. Igitur breviter finis tuus ad quem omnem mentis intentionem,
omnem conatum et laborem debes dirigere et ordinare, est, ut cum Dei adiutorio quantum poteris vires animae tuae deordinates et indispositas ex lapsu tuo in protoplasto, ad id
et secundum id ad quod et sicut tibi fuerunt ab Domino Deo utiliter inditae, studeas reformare. Intellecum scilicet, ut Deum caeteraque, et maxime spiritualia et divina cognoscen-
da, intelligas. Voluntatem et appetitum, ut Deum aliaque diligenda et appetenda diligas
atque ames. Memoriam, ut spiritualibus et coelestibus valeas iugiter inhaerere. Cf. *Ref.*,
238G-H; and *Ref.*, ch, 12 (p. 241G-H).

[48] D. of Augsburg, *De ext. et int. hom. compositione*, I, 81-87 and 99. Cf. Goossens,
Meditatie, 67; and Smits, "David van Augsburg en de invloed van zijn *Profectus* op de
Moderne Devotie," 195. For a schema of the structure of *De Reformatione* see van Rooy,
Zerbolt, 96-97.

[49] *Ref.*, 250D: Id circo duplici indigent voluntatis reformatione.

[50] *Ref.*, 250D: Prima, qua eis infundatur gratia et justificatio. Secunda, qua pronitas
voluntatis et inclinatio appetituum refrenetur. Prima reformatio, de qua non nisi
modicum dicemus, quia non est tantum ad propositum sicut secunda. Consequently Zerbolt devotes only one chapter to the first reformation of the will, and nineteen chapters to
the second reformation of the will.

Regarding the order in which the reformation of the faculties takes place Zerbolt takes two, essentially different, positions. On the one hand he makes it quite clear that man must first be reconciled to God through the sacrament of penance before he can make any progress in the ascetical life since man's reconciliation with God is the foundation for all advancement in the spiritual life. In other words, the first reformation of the will must precede the second reformation of the will, as well as the reformation of the intellect and memory. On the other hand, however, it is not at all unlikely that Zerbolt regards the two reformations of the will and the reformation of the intellect and memory as collateral developments. For he does not discuss the first reformation of the will until after he has dealt with the reformation of the intellect and the memory. Before the thirteenth century man's over-all spiritual development was commonly represented as consisting of a series of successive steps. However, William of St. Thierry and David of Augsburg, whose writings were among Zerbolt's most important sources, portrayed man's entire spiritual progress in terms of concurrent, interrelated and mutually supporting developments, rather than as successive stages of spiritual improvement.[51] Zerbolt's portrayal of the reformation of the three faculties as successive spiritual developments, or as collateral and interdependent progressions, reflects, then, the two, rather dissimilar, ways of looking at man's spiritual progress which had emerged by the end of the fourteenth century.

If, as would appear, Zerbolt was of the opinion that the reformation of the three faculties can take place either consecutively or simultaneously, he leaves no doubt that he regarded the reformation of each of the three faculties as a progressive development. He divides the reformation of the memory, as well as the two reformations of the will, into three consecutive ascents,[52] and in thus dividing the reformation of two out of the three faculties into three successive developments Zerbolt would appear to be following in the footsteps of Bonaventure. For in *De Triplici Via* Bonaventure divides each of the three ways into three consecutive stages.[53]

Self-examination and self-knowledge. Many early Christian writers were aware of the importance of the self-examination of one's conscience in the

---

[51] Phillips, "The Way to Religious Perfection According to St. Bonaventure's *De Triplici via*," 36-44.

[52] *Ref.*, ch. 18 (p. 243A-B); *Ref.*, ch. 36 (p. 250C-F); and *Ref.*, 254B-C; 254F-G; 254H; 255C; 255F-G; 256G; 257B-C; and 257F-G. In connection with the first reformation of the will see above, pp. 171-172.

[53] Cf. Phillips, "The Way to Religious Perfection According to Bonaventure's *De Triplici Via*," 36-40.

quest for spiritual improvement and perfection.[54] However, it was not
until the twelfth century and later that spiritual writers developed a comprehensive 'doctrine' of self-examination with detailed rules, instructions
and guidelines. Self-examination looms large in the anonymous *Meditationes piisimae de cognitione humanae conditionis*, in William of St. Thierry's
Epistola ad Fratres de Monte Dei, in the *Speculum Monachorum* of Arnulf de
Boeriis, and in Bonaventure's *Soliloquium*.[55] All of these writings were
well known to Zerbolt,[56] who likewise devotes considerable space to
spiritual self-examination in his two manuals for the spiritual life. In fact,
the entire Modern Devotion occupies a fairly prominent place in the
history of the examination of conscience,[57] and that role was studied
around the turn of the century by H. Watrigant and more recently by L.
A. M. Goossens.[58]

Self-examination figures prominently in Zerbolt's doctrine of penance,
it will be recalled, and it is not any less essential to his spiritual theology
and his teaching regarding the spiritual life. Zerbolt attaches a great deal
of importance to self-examination, for it leads to self-knowledge which is
the beginning of salvation.[59] Self-knowledge is the beginning of salvation,
for unless man is first confronted with his sinful condition he will do
nothing to extricate himself from that state. However, man has no way of

---

[54] H. Jaeger and J.-C. Guy, "Examen de conscience," *DSp*, IV, 1795-1807; L. de
Bazelaire, "Connaissance de soi," *DSp*, II, 1516-1520; and J. B. Wall, "Conscience, Examination of," *NCE*, IV, 203-204.

[55] *PL*, CLXXXIV, 494-495 and 1175-1178; and Bonaventure, *Soliloquium*, ch. 1, par.
2 (*Works*, III, 41-42). Cf. I. Noye, "Examen de conscience," *DSp*, IV, 1812-1815; and J.
M. Carnivez, "Arnoul de Boheries," *DSp*, I, 894.

In the middle ages the *Meditationes piisimae* were attributed to St. Bernard, and Zerbolt
also attributes the *Epistola ad Fratres de Monte Dei* to St. Bernard, as was then commonly
done.

[56] See above, pp. 13-27; and van Woerkum, "Het Libellus '*Omnes, inquit, artes*',"
226-227.

[57] I. Noye, "Examen de conscience," *DSp*, IV, 1819-1823 and A. Liuima and A. Derville, "Examen particulier," *ibid.*, 1843-1845.

Throughout the 15th century the Devotionalists contributed to the development of the
practice of self-examination. The last Devotionalist to make a considerable contribution in
this field was John Mombaer (d. 1501), an Augustinian Canon at Mount St. Agnes near
Zwolle. In his *Rosetum* he pays a great deal of attention to self-examination which he
handles in a very rational and systematic fashion. With respect to the practice of self-
examination Ignatius Loyola was influenced to a considerable degree by the methods in
vogue among the Devotionalists, and this influence came, in part at least, by way of Garcia de Cisneros (d. 1510), it would appear.

[58] H. Watrigant, "*De Examine Conscientiae*" *juxta Ecclesiae Patres, Sanctum Thomam et
Fratres Vitae Communis* (Enghien, 1909); and Goossens, *Meditatie*, 121-131.

[59] *Ref.*, 239A: ..., quod cognitio propria initium sit salutis. Cf. Geesink, *Zerbolt*, 114.

For St. Bernard knowledge of self and knowledge of God together constitute the "*Somme
du salut*" (R. P. Placide Deseille, "Théologie de la vie monastique selon Saint Bernard,"
in: *Théologie*, 508).

naturally knowing that he is sinful. He can discover that only by examining himself in light of what the Scriptures reveal regarding his sinfulness, and it was for the express purpose of confronting man with his own depravity that God granted him the Bible.[60] It is for that same reason that Zerbolt begins *De Reformatione*, like *De Ascensionibus*, with an account of man's original condition and his descent into sinfulness.[61] In *De Reformatione* Zerbolt discusses the question of self-examination immediately following his account of man's fall but before he embarks upon the discussion of the reformation of the powers of the soul,[62] and this sequence is clearly a logical one. For self-examination enables the believer to learn the truth concerning himself without which he will not, Zerbolt seems to think, reform the faculties of his soul.

Goossens detects three distinct types of spiritual self-examinations in the early history of the *Devotio Moderna*: the general, the daily and the particular examination of conscience, all of which are peculiar to the spiritual life. What these three examinations have in common with the self-examination for the sacrament of penance is that they, like that one, serve purity of heart, Zerbolt's main concern. Furthermore, Goossens finds all three examinations peculiar to the spiritual life represented in *De Reformatione* as well as in *De Ascensionibus*.[63] The purpose of the general self-examination of conscience is to establish the impact of original sin on the believer. Through self-examination he must determine to what degree his faculties have been weakened as a result of original sin and have, as a consequence, been the cause of actual sin. The faculties were given to man for the purpose of knowing, desiring and loving God,[64] and the believer must determine to what extent his psychological powers have strayed from the task for which they were granted to him. He must concentrate in his self-examination on the three major powers of the soul, namely the intellect, the memory and the will. The examination of the psychological faculties: i.e., of the inner man, must be followed by an examination of the outward man. Such an examination is useful, Zerbolt explains, because inordinate desires which find overt expression point to

---

[60] See above, pp. 160-166.

[61] *Ref.*, 238B: In his duobus...proficiendo redeas. *Ref.*, 238H-239A: Vidisti homo...sit pollutum. Cf. Goossens, *Meditatie*, 122, and 129-130; and A. Cabassut, "Défauts," *DSp*, III, 74.

[62] In *De Reformatione* self-examination is discussed in chs. 4-6 (pp. 238H-239F), 20 (p. 243F-H) and 41 (p. 252C-G).

[63] Goossens, *Meditatie*, 124-129. In *De Reformatione* ch. 5 is set aside for the general examination of conscience, ch. 6 for the daily examination, and ch. 41 for the particular examination. It is on these three chapters that the ensuing analysis of Zerbolt's views regarding the self-examination is based. And these same three chapters in *De Reformatione* correspond, respectively, to chs. 7, 8 and 53 of *De Ascensionibus*.

[64] See above, pp. 59-67.

an inner man that is disordered. He is giving voice here to the view widely held among the Devotionalists that *exteriora interiora trahunt*.[65] The
general examination of the inner, as well as of the outward, man must
take place often, he adds, or at least regularly, and at such times that it is
fitting and opportune. Finally, Zerbolt's directions for the general examination of conscience reveal the influence of the anonymous *Meditationes piisimae de cognitione humanae conditionis*, Bonaventure and David of
Augsburg.[66]

Whereas in the general examination of conscience the first aim is to
determine to what extent the fall has weakened the capacity of the
faculties for the good and so has been the cause of actual sin, in the daily
examination of conscience the purpose is to establish to what extent the
weakened faculties have actually led man into committing personal sins.
Furthermore, instead of scrutiny of intellect, memory and will, the self-
examination is now restricted to the will. The believer must examine
whether the rebellious, concupiscent powers have been kept in check by
the will, and if the will has not been successful in doing so the believer
must determine as well the gains made by sinful concupiscence. Such
gains must be attributed to the disinclination of the will to fight rebellious
concupiscence. For Zerbolt is of the opinion that in spite of the fall the
will has retained the capacity to withstand rebellious concupiscence, and
that of all the psychological powers only the will is capable of reversing
man's spiritual descent.[67] For his views on the daily examination of conscience Zerbolt is clearly indebted to Arnulf de Boeriis' *Speculum
Monachorum* and to William of St. Thierry's *Epistola ad Fratres de Monte
Dei*.[68]

Zerbolt discusses the particular examination of conscience in connection with the extirpation of the capital sins, the subject matter of the
second reformation of the will in *De Reformatione* and of the third ascent in
De Ascensionibus. If these sins have gained a foothold in the soul, he writes,
it is because the will succumbed to rebellious concupiscence. However,
he warns that the believer must not try to eradicate all capital sins at the
same time, but that he must single out the dominant vice, subdue it, pro-

---

[65] Cf. van Woerkum, "Florentius Radewijns: Leven, Geschriften, Persoonlijkheid en
Ideeën," 362-363.

[66] *PL*, CLXXXIV, 494; Bonaventure, *De Triplici Via*, ch 1, par. 1 (*Works*, I, 64-68);
and D. of Augsburg, *De ext. et int. hom. compositione*, I, 87.

[67] See above, pp. 84-85; and cf. D. of Augsburg, *De ext. et int. hom. compositione*, I, 87.

[68] Arnulf de Boeriis, *Speculum Monachorum*, *PL*, CLXXXIV, 1176; and *The Golden Epistle of Abbot William of St. Thierry*, 42 and 52-53. Cf. Radewijns, *Tractatulus Devotus*, 223; Th.
a Kempis, *Opera Omnia*, VII, 197; *Frensweger Handschrift*, 143; Goossens, *Meditatie*, 125;
and Savary, *Psychological Themes in the Golden Epistle of William of St. Thierry to the Carthusians
of Mont-Dieu*, 48 and 102-103.

ceed to deal with the one that is next strongest, and so forth. For if all the vices are assaulted at the same time, not one of them will be subdued, and there will be no spiritual progress. Therefore, before he begins the struggle against the vices the believer must scrutinize himself to determine which of them is the strongest just then and dominates him, and this vice he must make the object of his attack.[69] Zerbolt adds that to approach the struggle against the vices in this fashion is consistent with the tradition of the "holy fathers." He does not further identify them, but it was Cassian in particular who advised that in the extirpation of the vices one must deal with them one at a time beginning with the strongest after it has been identified through self-examination.[70]

The three self-examinations peculiar to the spiritual life are closely related. For the particular examination of conscience is aimed at uncovering vices which are the consequence of the will yielding to rebellious concupiscence, and in thus laying the vices bare the weaknesses of the will, which are a consequence of the fall, are revealed as well. The objective of all self-examinations is, then, to ferret out the weaknesses of the powers of the soul, and of the will in particular, as well as the sinful concupiscences, sins and vices which are a consequence of the debilities of the psychological faculties.[71] It is quite clear as well that all the self-examinations serve the first goal of the spiritual life, namely purity of heart.

In addition to the self-examinations Zerbolt mentions two other ways by means of which the believer may learn about his own sinful condition. In the first place there is the testimony of others which constitutes an important and valuable means to self-knowledge,[72] Zerbolt writes, for according to St. Bernard the eye of another sees better and is more impartial than one's own.[73] Consequently it will detect faults which have been overlooked. Also, there is the temptation to find excuses for the defects one has uncovered by means of the self-examinations of conscience and

---

[69] Zerbolt himself does not give it that name, but the inquiry to determine which vice is dominant at any given time fits the description of what was known as the particular examination of conscience. Cf. J. B. Wall, "Conscience, Examination of," *NCE*, IV, 204; A. Liuima and A. Derville, "Examen particulier," *DSp*, IV, 1838 and 1844; and I. Noye, "Examination de conscience," *ibid.*, IV, 1820-1822.

[70] Cassian, *Conferences*, No. V, chs. 14 and 27. Cf. A. Liuima and A. Derville, "Examen particulier," *DSp*, IV, 1841 and 1844; A. Cabassut, "Défauts," *DSp*, III, 82-83; Goossens, *Meditatie*, 128; and Radewijns, *Omnes, Inquit, Artes*, II, 13-14. Radewijns quotes most of Cassian's *Conferences*, No. V, ch. 14, here.

[71] Cf. *Asc.*, 261H.

[72] Ch. 7 (p. 239G-H) of *De Reformatione* is devoted to this question. Cf. *Asc.*, ch. 8 (pp. 261F-262A).

[73] The passage in question is, in reality, from *The Golden Epistle of Abbot William of St. Thierry*, 99. Cf. A. Cabassut, "Défauts," *DSp*, III, 75 and 79.

for that reason it is useful to have them confirmed by others.[74] However, better than any other way to self-knowledge is the struggle against one's weaknesses and sins which have been uncovered through the three self-examinations peculiar to the spiritual life.[75] The attempt to extirpate the inordinate desires and sins laid bare by means of these three self-examinations will disclose to man, better than anything else will, the disordered nature of the powers of the soul, and that he is governed by an inordinate desire for worldly things, both material and non-material, as well as by vice. Zerbolt goes as far as to assert that until such time as one takes up the battle against one's inordinate concupiscent desires and sins, they will remain as good as hidden. It is only when one tries to extirpate them that one will become truly aware of their existence. For when one does not resist inordinate concupiscence and vice, one becomes insensible to them. However, the struggle against them will reveal how strong and deeply rooted they are, and that they have become a part of one's nature. The attempt to eradicate inordinate concupiscence and sin, both of which have their origin in the sensible appetites, will reveal their power of resistance, and a battle will ensue: i.e., between the law of the flesh on the one hand, and the will or the law of the mind on the other. This battle constitutes the subject matter of what Zerbolt refers to in *De Reformatione* as the second reformation of the will.[76]

The reformation of the intellect. It would appear that for Zerbolt the reformation of the intellect is a process which begins with the act of faith and culminates in the vision of God.[77] However, in those chapters of *De Reformatione* set aside specifically for the reformation of the intellect Zerbolt

---

[74] For the argument that there is profit to be derived from having one's faults pointed out by someone else Zerbolt calls on support from Augustine as well (Augustine, *Letters*, No. XXVIII, ch. 4 [*Nicene and Post-Nicene Fathers*, I, 253].)

It may be assumed that Zerbolt understood the identification of faults in others to be part and parcel of the work of spiritual guidance in which, he believed, all those who have progressed in the spiritual life must engage (see above, pp. 189-190).

[75] *Ref.*, 239A-B: Tria autem sunt praecipue quibus tuam deformitatem poteris agnoscere, et quibus cupiditatibus pollutus fueris edoceri. Primum est, ut te ipsum diligenter discutias. Secundum est, ut tuos defectus ab aliis frequenter et libenter audias. Tertium, ut viriliter vitiis resistendo, eorum in te fortitudinem per eorundem contra te resistentiam experiaris. Chs. 8 and 9 (pp. 239H-240F) of *De Reformatione* deal with the third method. Cf. *Asc.*, ch. 8 (pp. 261F-262A).

[76] Zerbolt concludes with the observation that, in addition to self-knowledge, self-examination and the struggle against sin lead to love of God, love and compassion for one's fellow and the desire to assist him in the spiritual life (*Ref.*, 241C). Some centuries before St. Bernard had written in much the same vein that only through self-knowledge can one understand one's fellowman, the precondition for experiencing compassion for him (see L. de Bazelaire, "Connaissance de soi," *DSp*, II, 1520).

[77] See above, pp. 238-239. Cf. David of Augsburg, *De ext. et int. hom. compositione*, I, 84-85 and II, 5-7.

does not mention the act of faith or the vision of God.[78] All he discusses there is the spiritual knowledge required to combat sin and to cultivate virtue, as well as the means by which this knowledge may be obtained. As always, then, Zerbolt is interested primarily in the ascetical phase of the spiritual life and in everything that has a bearing on that part of man's spiritual ascent.

There are two ways, Zerbolt writes, by means of which the believer can acquire knowledge regarding the elimination of vice and the cultivation of virtue, namely by means of experience and instruction. It is with experience as a means to reform the intellect that he deals first, and he does so because he would appear to have been of the opinion that in spiritual matters understanding is determined by one's range of experience and the extent of one's moral reformation. For experience, he writes, is the best teacher in most spiritual matters, and, as vices are extirpated, many things in the Scriptures which were previously obscure will become intelligible.[79] Consequently, Zerbolt warns the reader not to expend all his energy on reading the Scriptures, but advises him to concentrate his attention in the first place on cleansing his heart of all vices. And *when* the Scriptures are being read, he adds, it must be treated not as a pastime, but it must serve as an inducement to purify the heart through the eradication of the vices. Zerbolt's attitude towards learning is clearly, then, a utilitarian one, and in his implied condemnation of study for its own sake he helped to give the Devotionalist movement its considerably anti-intellectual *cachet*.[80]

It has been demonstrated, Zerbolt begins his observations regarding the practical method to reform the intellect, that the struggle against vices and passions is extremely useful in arriving at an understanding of oneself. In much the same way, he continues, spiritual exercises, regardless of their nature, contribute to one's knowledge and enlightenment regarding piety and its subject matter. Those who exercise themselves in virtue, for example, will acquire insight into the nature of virtue and will learn to recognize its various degrees. And Zerbolt clearly regarded such knowledge derived from practical experience as essential

---

[78] *Ref.*, chs. 13-17 (pp. 241H-243A). The discussion of the reformation of the intellect which follows will be based primarily on these chapters.

[79] Cf. W. Lourdaux, "Gérard Zerbolt de Zutphen," *DSp*, VI, 285.

St. Bernard had written much the same thing in one of his *Sermons on the Song of Songs*, one of Zerbolt's major sources. In spiritual matters, he asserted, understanding can follow only where experience leads (St. Bernard, *Sermones in Cantica Canticorum*, XXII, 2; cf. McGiffert, *A History of Christian Thought*, II, 227).

[80] Cf. A. Gruijs, ed., "Jean de Schoonhoven, *De Contemptu Huius Mundi*," *Archivum Latinitatis Medii Aevi*, XXXIII (1963), 95-97, where the anti-intellectualism of the Devotionalists is discussed.

because, as will be seen in more detail below, he understood the development of each of the separate virtues to progress through three consecutive
stages.

While practical experience plays an important role in acquiring
knowledge and insight into the ascetical life, it must be accompanied and
supplemented by the theoretical instruction which Zerbolt divides, on the
authority of Anselm,[81] into two kinds, namely spiritual reading and
spiritual conversation. Since the first of these two will be discussed below
in connection with meditation and prayer, the vehicles of the spiritual ascent, only the latter will be dealt with here. By the conversations which
contribute to man's understanding of the ascetical life Zerbolt
understands in the first place those held with one's spiritual adviser. He
writes that it is important to submit to him for approval one's plan and
exercises for the ascetical life, and to follow his recommendations and
suggestions. Without him, his guidance, learning, admonishments and
insight into the spiritual life, one will not be able to advance in the
ascetical life. For his ideas regarding the spiritual adviser, and the role
played by him in the life of the religious,[82] Zerbolt would appear to be indebted to Cassian in particular, and perhaps to a lesser extent to William
of St. Thierry.[83] Zerbolt also mentions spiritual conversation with one's
confrères as a means to gain insight into the spiritual life.[84] Particularly
useful in this connection, he writes, is the discussion of one's vices and
sinful desires. It will help one not only to understand such matters, which
is a requirement if one is going to combat them, but it will at the same
time serve as a lay confession.[85] It is patently obvious, then, that in the
reformation of the intellect Zerbolt concentrates on the knowledge required to ascend in the spiritual life, and particularly on the knowledge
needed to overcome sin and to progress in virtue.

The reformation of the memory. Zerbolt writes that there are two distinct
bodies of information which must be absorbed by the memory—the
memory viewed as storehouse of both sensible and intellective impressions—for its reformation. There are, in the first place, those subjects
which, depending on their nature, will instil either compunction of fear

---

[81] Zerbold does not identify his source any further.

[82] The function of the spiritual adviser receives a good deal of attention from Zerbolt in
ch. 51 of *De Ascensionibus* (see footnote 78 above).

In *Omnes, inquit, artes* Radewijns quotes word for word about three-fourths of ch. 51 of
De Ascensionibus (*Omnes, Inquit, Artes*, II, 45). Radewijns, who names virtually all his
sources for *Omnes, inquit, artes*, opens this long passage from *De Ascensionibus* with: "Unde
quidam dicit; ..." (see above, p. 31, footnote 109).

[83] Cassian, *Conferences*, No. II, chs. 11-15; and *The Golden Epistle of Abbot William of St.
Thierry*, 48-49. Cf. Goossens, *Meditatie*, 129; and Radewijns, *Tractatulus Devotus*, 248.

[84] Cf. *Asc.*, 286A.

[85] See above, pp. 190-192.

or compunction of hope and love when the believer meditates on them.[86] Compunction of fear cleanses the heart of sin, while compunction of hope and love draws the believer to God.[87] The second body of information with which the memory must be reformed is, according to Zerbolt, knowledge of Christ's exemplary life and passion.[88] Imitation of Christ, we have seen earlier, plays an important role in Zerbolt's thought. Imitation is induced by meditating on Christ's exemplary conduct, and it is to make such meditation possible that Zerbolt includes an account of Christ's life and death in his discussion of the reformation of the memory. For unless the memory is supplied with information about Christ's exemplary life and death meditation on these matters will not be possible. However, in view of the fact that Christ's exemplary life, which when imitated aids the believer in his spiritual quest and in the eradication of vice in particular, has been discussed in detail in an earlier chapter, only compunction, its development and contribution to man's spiritual growth, will be dealt with here.

In the *Institutes* and *Conferences*, both of which influenced Western spirituality not a little and were among the most widely read works by the Devotionalists, Cassian speaks of compunction.[89] However, it was Gregory the Great's doctrine of compunction in particular that had a considerable impact on the spirituality of the middle ages, including that of the Modern Devotion.[90] In addition to Cassian and Gregory most of Zerbolt's favourite authors speak of compunction, and those matters conducive to the development of compunction, to a greater or lesser degree. Climacus stresses in particular the importance of sorrow, grief and pain experienced at the remembrance of sins committed, death, divine justice and the eternal punishment suffered by the unrepentant.[91] Compunction

---

[86] *Ref.*, 243D-E: Scire etiam...inveniantur ingrati. Zerbolt discusses the reformation of the memory in chs. 18-35 (pp. 243A-250C) of *De Reformatione*. For Zerbolt's understanding of the memory as storehouse of sensible and intellective impressions see above, pp. 60-62.
   Cf. D. of Augsburg, *De ext. et int. hom. compositione*, II, 7.
[87] Cf. *Asc.*, chs. 16-17 (p. 264B-F) and 22-23 (p. 266C-H).
   In *De Reformatione* Zerbolt does not really explain why the memory must be reformed with subjects conducive to the development of compunction of fear and compunction of hope and love. However, in *De Ascensionibus* he explains in some detail why the memory must be reformed in this fashion.
[88] *Ref.*, 245H: Nihil apparet utilius quo salubrius occupes memoriam tuam, quam mysterium incarnationis Iesu Christi.
[89] Cassian, *Institutes*, Bk. IV, ch. 3; and *idem*, *Conferences*, No. IX, ch. 29.
[90] De Guibert, "La Componction du Coeur," 226-234; P. Régamey, "La componction du coeur," *VSp*, XLIV (1935), Supplément, 65-82; and Leclercq, *The Love of Learning and the Desire for God*, 37-41 and cf. 65-86. Cf. P. Tihon, "Fin Dernières (Méditation Des)," *DSp*, V, 355-382.
[91] St. John Climacus, *The Ladder of Divine Ascent*, 110-124.

of fear is decidedly more prominent in Climacus' *Scala Paradisi* than is compunction of hope and love. In the *Meditationes piisimae de cognitione humanae conditionis*, a work which was very popular with the Devotionalists, the anonymous author does not mention compunction as such. However, he devotes a number of chapters to such topics as death, the final judgement and the joys of heaven which were held to be useful for the development of compunction of fear and compunction of hope and love respectively.[92] In the *Speculum Monachorum* Arnulf de Boeriis voices the opinion that unceasing meditation on death is the supreme wisdom.[93] David of Augsburg lists seven types of compunctions or devotions in the third book of *De exterioris et interioris hominis compositione*.[94] Compunction, he writes, may arise from fear, sorrow, desire, love, compassion, joy and the rapture of admiration. He then describes briefly how each one of these arises at the remembrance of this or that verity. Thus the remembrance of sin and divine justice, for example, will instil compunction of fear; and the remembrance of having offended God and having lost his grace will instil sorrow.[95] However, it is in Bonaventure's ascetical writings in particular, and more specifically in *De Triplici Via* and the *Soliloquium*, that compunction plays an important role. In the first mentioned work Bonaventure describes how remembrance of, and meditation on, sin, the hour of death and the final judgement will result in compunction of fear which will then be instrumental in purging the heart of sin, evil desires and inordinate concupiscence.[96] Zerbolt, it will be seen, adopts much the same approach in his writings for the purpose of cleansing the heart of sin. The *Soliloquium* is devoted almost entirely to those topics which had traditionally been considered effective for the development of compunction of fear and compunction of hope and love: the futility of this life, death, the final judgement, the pains of hell, and the joys of heaven.[97] It is quite obvious, then, that compunction, and how it

---

[92] *PL*, CLXXXIV, 487-489, 492-493 and 505-506.

[93] *PL*, CLXXXIV, 1178.

Compunction, and compunction of fear in particular, receives some attention as well in *De Spiritu et Anima* (*PL*, XL, 816).

[94] Compunction and devotion are closely related concepts, as will be seen below.

[95] D. of Augsburg, *De ext. et int. hom. compositione*, II, 183-187. Cf. J. Pegon, "Componction," *DSp*, II, 1316.

[96] Bonaventure, *De Triplici Via*, ch. 1, par. 1 (*Works*, I, 64-68).

[97] Bonaventure, *Soliloquium*, chs. 2-4 (*Works*, III, 77-129). As Goossens writes, the *Soliloquium* is a work on compunction (*Meditatie*, 135).

The *Cordiale de Quatuor Novissimus* must be mentioned as well. Written by Gerard van Vliederhoven, a member of the Teutonic Order, sometime between 1380 and 1396, it deals with the four last things, namely death, judgement, heaven and hell. Two of its most important sources are the pseudo-Bernardine *Meditationes piisimae* and the writings of Gregory the Great. Whether Zerbolt was familiar with this work cannot be readily determined, and he may not have been, since it may not have been completed until 1396, two

may be acquired and developed, was an important theme in many of the writings in vogue among the Devotionalists. Jean Leclercq, in his study on monastic culture, concludes that "medieval monastic literature is, in large part, a literature of compunction."[98]

Goossens is of the opinion that Zerbolt does not really define compunction,[99] but in chapter eleven of *De Reformatione* Zerbolt gives a description of this sentiment which may be taken to be its definition. Compunction, he writes, is a holy and salutary sorrow, a sweet pain, and an agreeable longing which causes the spirit to be depressed. On the other hand, he continues, it does not make the heart obdurate nor bitter, but rather humble, manageable and desirous of spiritual improvement and progress. Compunction understood as sorrow and pain springs, in very general terms, from the consideration of one's imperfect state and from the realization of being still far removed from the state of perfection. Compunction understood as longing or desire arises, in very broad terms once more, from the desire for a perfect life, spiritual perfection, a pure heart and *apatheia*.[100] Influenced by Gregory the Great, Zerbolt continues that all forms of compunction are motivated either by fear or by love. Compunction which is experienced as sorrow and regret for one's imperfect state and sinfulness is motivated by fear of the punishment which God metes out to sinful man. On the other hand, compunction which is experienced as a longing and desire for a pure heart, *apatheia* and spiritual perfection is motivated by the hope of eternal reward and love for the divine benefits.[101]

Following the definition of compunction, and the division of compunction into two main types, Zerbolt describes in detail the subject matter

---

years before his death. However, it was a favourite work with the later Devotionalists. See M. Dusch, ed., *De Veer Utersten. Das Cordiale de quatuor novissimus von Gerhard von Vliederhoven in mittelniederdeutscher Überlieferung* (Cologne-Vienna, 1975), 1*-39*.

Cf. C. M. Vos, *De leer der vier uitersten* (Amsterdam, 1866).

[98] Leclercq, *The Love of Learning and the Desire for God*, 83.

[99] Goossens, *Meditatie*, 137.

[100] *Ref.*, 241C-D: Ecce unde... desiderio proficiendi. Cf. above, pp. 177-180.

The affinity between compunction and contrition is clearly evident, for, as Zerbolt writes, compunction heals the present wounds of the soul, deletes those of the past, and prevents future ones. Furthermore, it appeases God and makes the believer pleasing to men and angels (*Ref.*, 241D: Hoc est... amabilis efficitur).

[101] *Ref.*, 241F: Potes autem haec et si qua alia genera compunctionis ad duo rducere; quia omnis compunctio, vel ex amore surgit vel ex timore. This passage in *De Reformatione* is based on Gregory's *Dialogues*, Bk. III, ch. 34 (*PL*, LXXVII, 300-301). The same passage may be found in Gregory's letter to Theoctista (*PL*, LXXVII, 779-780).

Gregory's doctrine that all compunction is motivated either by fear or by hope and love is a symbolical exposition of Joshua 15, 19. (Cf. de Guibert, "La Componction du Coeur," 229; P. Régamey, "La componction du coeur," *VSp*, XLIV [1935], Supplément, 67-70; and Goossens, *Meditatie*, 42 and 139.) In imitation of Gregory, Zerbolt offers the same symbolical interpretation of Joshua 15, 19. (*Ref.*, 241F: Et hoc...patre suo.)

which, when meditated on, will instil either compunction of fear or compunction of hope and love.[102] He begins with the observation that although everything in the Scriptures and creation speak of God and instruct man regarding him, not all things found in them are equally suitable for fruitful meditation. Consequently, he continues, the believer must select those topics for the reformation of his memory which are conducive to the development of compunction of fear and compunction of love.[103] Influenced to a large degree by Gregory the Great, Zerbolt enumerates four subjects which, when meditated on, will instil compunction of fear, and two topics which will implant compunction of hope and love.[104] In the first place he mentions the consideration of one's own sinfulness as a source of compunction of fear. For reflection on the depravity thus uncovered will result in fear of God's punishment of sin. He asserts, in fact, that the four examinations of conscience and the struggle against sin by means of which man's sinfulness is laid bare are the best sources for compunction of fear.[105] In addition to the consideration of one's sins as a means to promote compunction of fear Zerbolt mentions meditation on death, the last judgement and the horrors of hell. He devotes a chapter to each one of these three topics with which the memory must be reformed,[106] and these chapters are based on three similar chapters in Radewijns' *Tractatulus Devotus*,[107] although Zerbolt does not acknowledge any indebtedness to his *confrère*. Goossens, who has edited the *Tractatulus Devotus* and has made an attempt to establish its sources, writes that the three chapters in the *Tractatulus Devotus* which deal with the shortness of life, the last judgement and the pains of hell are reminiscent of Grote's letter to Johannes ten Water, Peter Damian's *Institutio Monialis*, Suso's *Horologium Sapientiae*, Bonaventure's *Soliloquium*, Ruusbroec's *Vanden Kerstenen Ghelove* and the *Legenda Aurea* of Jacobus de Voragine.[108] While

---

[102] See footnote 86 above.

[103] *Ref.*, 243D: Scire etiam debes, quod quamvis omnia quae in divina scriptura reperiuntur, imo coelum et terra, et omni quae in eis sunt, de Deo loquantur et instruant, non tamen omnia aeque conveniunt ad utiliter meditandum. Sed ea debes potius ad meditandum assumere, unde amplius timore concuteris, vel accenderis ad amorem.

[104] *Ref.*, 241D-F: Quamvis autem...suo loco. See footnote 86 above as well.

[105] *Ref.*, 241C: Ex hac...non proficis. *Ref.*, 241D-E: Quamvis autem... compunctionibus fructuosior:... *Ref.*, 241E: Videlicet ex...memoria peccatorum. *Ref.*, 241F: Aut cum...ex dictis.

The self-examinations Zerbolt refers to are the three which are peculiar to the spiritual life and the one which is required for the sacrament of penance.

[106] *Ref.*, chs. 21-23 (pp. 244A-245A).

[107] Radewijns, *Tractatulus Devotus*, 225-228. Cf. Radewijns, *Omnes, Inquit, Artes*, II, 124-126 and 156-157; and Goossens, *Meditatie*, 181-185.

[108] Radewijns, *Tractatulus Devotus*, footnotes on pp. 226-228 (the footnotes are not numbered).

Grote advised that Suso's *Horologium Sapientiae* and Ruusbroec's *Vanden Kerstenen Ghelove* be read for the purpose of generating compunction of fear, and compunction of hope and love (de Beer, *Spiritualiteit*, 83).

Zerbolt's most important source for the three chapters devoted to death, the final judgement and the horrors of hell was Radewijns' *Tractatulus Devotus*, it would appear that in a few instances he went directly to Bonaventure's *Soliloquium* itself. Finally, the meditations on the last things, which play an important role in Zerbolt's doctrine of compunction, lend his spirituality a gloomy quality, and in that respect too Zerbolt's spirituality helped set the tone for that of the Devotionalists following him.[109]

De Reformatione contains two chapters the purpose of which is to instil compunction of hope and love in the believer, and they, like the chapters devised to promote compunction of fear, must contribute to the reformation of the memory. The first chapter is a meditation on the joys of heaven and the second chapter a meditation on the benefits bestowed by God on the believer.[110] Furthermore, the former is based on a similar meditation in Radewijns' *Tractatulus Devotus*, and the latter on a chapter in Radewijns' *Omnes, inquit, artes*.[111] According to Goossens the meditation on the joys of heaven in the *Tractatulus Devotus* calls to mind, once again, Grote's letter to Johannes ten Water, Bonaventure's *Soliloquium* and Ruusbroec's *Vanden Kerstenen Ghelove*.[112] For the meditation in *Omnes, inquit, artes* on the divine benefits Radewijns is indebted to Bonaventure's *De Triplici Via* and David of Augsburg's *De exterioris et interioris hominis compositione*.[113]

The chapter entitled *De materiis meditandi* in the constitutions of the Brethren of the Common Life prescribes as suitable topics for meditation or rumination the sins committed, death, the final judgement, the pains of hell, the glories of heaven, the divine benefits bestowed on man, and the life and passion of Christ.[114] This list of topics for meditation, in-

---

[109] Cf. Acquoy, *Windesheim*, I, 176-177 and Th. a Kempis, *De Imitatione Christi*, Bk. I, chs. 22, 23 and 24.

[110] *Ref.*, chs. 24 and 25 (p. 245B-H). Cf. Goossens, *Meditatie*, 185-187.
Zerbolt includes the life of Christ in the section dealing with the reformation of the memory for the reasons given some paragraphs back. However, meditation on the fact that God gave his own Son for the salvation of man, and meditation on all that Christ did for man's salvation, can serve to stimulate compunction of hope and love, as well as thankfulness (*Ref.*, 243E).

[111] Radewijns, *Tractatulus Devotus*, 228-229; and *idem, Omnes, Inquit, Artes*, II, 158-162. Cf. Goossens, *Meditatie*, 185-187.

[112] Radewijns, *Tractatulus Devotus*, footnotes on pp. 228-229.
Zerbolt's description of the "heavenly country" itself cannot be found in Radewijns' *Tractatulus Devotus*, and it would appear that it was influenced by Suso's *Horologium Sapientiae*, either directly or by way of Radewijns' *Omnes, inquit, artes* (Suso, *Horologium Sapientiae*, ch. 11; and Radewijns, *Omnes, Inquit, Artes*, II, 146-150).

[113] Bonaventure, *De Triplici Via*, ch. 1, par. 2 (*Works*, I, 68-70); and D. of Augsburg, *De ext. et int. hom. compositione*, II, 143-152. Cf. Goossens, *Meditatie*, 186-187.

[114] "The Original Constitution of the Brethren of the Common Life at Deventer," ed. by Hyma, *The Christian Renaissance*, 442; and "*Consuetudines domus nostre* (= Brethren

cluding their sequence, is altogether identical to the catalogue of topics for meditation found in *De Reformatione*.[115] It is these topics which must dominate the thinking of the Devotionalists at all times.[116] Furthermore, the constitutions of the Brethren of the Common Life add, as is done by Zerbolt, that meditation on these topics must inculcate either compunction of fear or compunction of love. Thus the similarity and relationship between the works of Radewijns, Zerbolt and the constitutions, to which attention has been drawn before, is further demonstrated.[117]

Zerbolt concludes that the reformation of the memory, as described in the foregoing pages, must take place in three consecutive steps. In the first place the believer must strive to prevent the mind from wandering hither and thither, and if necessary he must keep it forcibly occupied with those topics which promote the growth of compunction. In the second ascent the believer must progress to the point where the mind willingly occupies itself with those topics which induce compunction. And finally, in the third ascent, the believer must be so absorbed in God as to be free from all obstreperous thoughts, imaginings and fantasies.[118] For this description of the reformation of the memory in three consecutive stages Zerbolt is indebted to David of Augsburg,[119] and the portrayal of the third ascent is more than merely reminiscent of the intellectual mysticism of the pseudo-Dionysian tradition.[120] However, the context in which the passage in question occurs makes it highly unlikely that Zerbolt actually has in mind the intellectual vision of God as it was commonly understood. What he almost certainly means is that in the third ascent the memory must be reformed to the point where the mind is capable of concentrating solely on those subjects which induce compunction, without the intrusion of idle thoughts, imaginings and fantasies.[121]

Second reformation of the will. In what Zerbolt calls the second reformation of the will the goal is essentially the same as it was in the reformation of

---

House at Zwolle)," in: Jacobus de Voecht, *Narratio*, ed. by Schoengen, 241. Cf. Goossens, *Meditatie*, 181.

[115] *Ref.*, 243D-E: Sunt autem...inveniantur ingrati.

[116] Goossens, *Meditatie*, 182.

[117] Cf. *ibid.*, 181-182; and van der Wansem, *Het Ontstaan en de Geschiedenis der Broederschap van het Gemene Leven tot 1400*, 25-47.

[118] *Ref.*, ch. 18 (p. 243A-B).

[119] D. of Augsburg, *De ext. et int. hom. compositione*, I, 86.

[120] Cf. T. Corbishley, "Mysticism," *NCE*, X, 175-178; E. E. Larkin, "Ways, The Three Spiritual," *NCE*, XIV, 835-836; and Knowles, *The English Mystical Tradition*, 21-38.

[121] One cannot, therefore, agree with Goossens who believes that in the passage in question Zerbolt has in mind the mystical contemplation of God (Goossens, *Meditatie*, 150).

the intellect and the memory, as well as in the first reformation of the will, namely purity of heart. In the second reformation of the will the soul is purified through an eradication of the capital sins which requires a reformation, or re-direction, of the will.[122] For sins, vices and sinful concupiscences establish themselves in the soul as a result of the will succumbing to rebellious concupiscence, and it is only the will, a faculty which suffered relatively little in the fall,[123] which can evict vices and keep them at arms length.[124] As the vices are extirpated the will itself is reformed. For as the will successfully eradicates established vices and resists rebellious concupiscence, the will itself is strengthened in its natural inclination towards the good.[125] In the reformation of the memory, then, the objective is to eradicate sinful concupiscence and inordinate love for created things in general, while in the second reformation of the will the aim is to eliminate the capital sins in particular. The extirpation of the capital sins is an integral part of the spiritual life and belongs to its ascetical phase.

Evagrius Ponticus was the first to draw up a list of what he called the eight temptations, which later became known as the capital or deadly sins. These temptations, as enumerated by him, were gluttony, luxury or lust, avarice, melancholy, anger, accidie, vainglory and pride. John Cassian, a disciple of Evagrius, introduced this classification of sins into the Latin Church, and he referred to them as the *"octo principalia vitia."* Evagrius' classification of sins was soon overshadowed, although not totally replaced, by that of Gregory the Great who counted seven capital sins. He arrived at this number by making pride the source of the seven principal sins without, however, counting pride as one of them as Cassian had done. Furthermore, Gregory combined melancholy with accidie, creating a single vice which he named accidie. He also added envy to the list of principal sins and rearranged their order. Consequently his

---

[122] *Ref.*, 250D: Secunda, qua pronitas voluntatis et inclinatio appetituum refrenetur. *Ibid.*, 250G: De secunda autem reformatione, qua inclinatio voluntatis ac pronitas appetituum per devota et sancta exercitia sub freno rationis moderatur. *Ibid.*, 251C: Secunda voluntatis reformatio, de qua diximus, per expurgationem vitiorum acquiritur. Nam extinctis nocivis desideriis quibus trahitur, voluntas erit ordinata et reformata. *Ibid.*, 252B: Accedentes autem vicinius ad extirpationem vitiorum et concupiscentiarum, qua ipsa voluntas reformatur. Cf. D. of Augsburg, *De ext. et int. hom. compositione*, I, 85; and P. Bourguignon and Fr. Wenner, "Combat Spirituel," *DSp*, II, 1135-1142. The *"combat spirituel"* is the fight against the vices, and the authors of this article in the *DSp* refer a number of times to Zerbolt as an important writer on the *"combat spirituel."*

[123] See above, pp. 84-86.

[124] Zerbolt points out a few times that sin must also be brought under the control of reason, and what he probably has in mind is right reason (*Ref.*, 252E-F and 255B; cf. *Asc.*, 279C and 280E). For sin is a violation of right reason (see above, pp. 75-77).

[125] See footnote 122 above.

list of capital sins reads as follows: vainglory, envy, anger, accidie, avarice, greed or gluttony, and luxury or lust.[126] Gregory's reasons for changing the sequence of the cardinal sins, and the reasons why Gregory's list of capital sins won out in popularity over the Cassianic sequence, are explored by M. W. Bloomfield in his historical study of the cardinal sins.[127] Finally, although they could not agree on the number and sequence of the cardinal sins, Cassian and Gregory both subscribed to the idea that the capital sins proceed from one another. Cassian wrote that, beginning with gluttony, the capital sins are "linked together in a chain, so that any excess of the one forms a starting point for the next."[128] Gregory borrowed this theory of concatenation from Cassian, but the first link in his chain of capital sins was vainglory, rather than gluttony.[129]

The patristic theory regarding the origin of the capital sins remained in vogue until the thirteenth century when many of the schoolmen rejected it. They preferred, instead, to see the capital sins as the result of a misdirected or disordered will, and among those to do so were Albert the Great, Bonaventure, Aquinas and Hugh Ripelin of Strasbourg.[130] Like these theologians, Zerbolt obviously regarded the vices as fruits of a disordered will, for we saw a moment ago that, according to him, the reformation of the will is a question of eradicating the capital sins. As the principal sins, which are a consequence of a disordered will, are uprooted, the will is regenerated. However, alongside this scholastic theory regarding the origin of the capital sins, Zerbolt also continued to entertain, as will become evident shortly, the patristic teaching concerning their cause.

As with the question regarding the source of the principal sins, Zerbolt takes an eclectic approach with respect to the number of capital sins and their arrangement. Acknowledging his indebtedness to Gregory the Great, Zerbolt writes in his introduction to the discussion of the capital

---

[126] Cassian, *Institutes*, Bks. V-XII; *idem*, *Conferences*, No. V, chs. 16-19; P. Resch, *La Doctrine Ascétique des Premiers Maitres Egyptiens du Quatrième Siècle* (Paris, 1931), 125-127; W. Völker, *Scala Paradisi: Eine Studie zu Johannes Climacus und zugleich eine Vorstudie zu Symeon dem neuen Theologen* (Wiesbaden, 1968), 69-70; Chadwick, *John Cassian*, 89-95; Cristiani, *Jean Cassien*, II, 57-65; Dudden, *Gregory the Great*, II, 386-388; A. Cabassut, "Défauts," *DSp*, III, 72-73; M. W. Bloomfield, *The Seven Deadly Sins. An Introduction to the History of a Religious Concept* (Michigan State University Press, 1967), 43-104; and S. Wenzel, "The Seven Deadly Sins: Some Problems of Research," *Speculum*, XLIII (1968), 1-22.

[127] Bloomfield, *The Seven Deadly Sins. An Introduction to the History of a Religious Concept*, 74-75.

[128] Cassian, *Conferences*, No. V, ch. 10.

[129] Wenzel, "The Seven Deadly Sins: Some Problems of Research," 4; and Bloomfield, *The Seven Deadly Sins. An Introduction to the History of a Religious Concept*, 73.

[130] Wenzel, *op. cit.*, 6.

sins that pride, the beginning—and that he uses the word beginning here points, perhaps, to the theory of concatenation regarding the origin of the principal sins—and queen of all sins, has under its command seven chief sins, and that together they constitute the eight capital sins.[131] He then enumerates the capital sins in the order first proposed by Gregory: pride, vainglory, envy, anger, accidie, avarice, gluttony and lust.[132] However, when Zerbolt deals with the capital sins separately, and in detail, he reverts to the sequence found in the writings of Evagrius and Cassian: gluttony, luxury, avarice, anger, envy, accidie, melancholy, vainglory and pride,[133] a sequence which, according to Bloomfield, was seldom used after the twelfth century.[134]

Zerbolt explains that these principal sins are commonly referred to as ''capital'' in view of the fact that others proceed from them as their head.[135] At other times, he continues, they are called the chief, or leading sins, because they are the leaders whom other sins follow. The latter are, therefore, known as the daughters and offspring of the capital or chief sins.[136] The reasons given by Zerbolt why the cardinal sins are commonly referred to as capital or chief sins reveal a patristic conception of the principal sins as proceeding the one from the other and not as misdirections of the will, the scholastic explanation for the existence of the cardinal sins. It is not altogether certain that we are dealing here with an inconsistency in Zerbolt's thought, because the two theories regarding the cause of the principal sins are not, from a logical point of view at least, necessarily contradictory.[136*] Lastly, Zerbolt draws attention to the fact that a third

---

[131] *Ref.*, ch. 43 (p. 253C-D). Cf. *Asc.*, ch. 52 (pp. 279H-280A); and *Asc.*, 278D.

[132] This sequence is found in the introduction to the vices in both *De Reformatione* and *De Ascensionibus*.

[133] Cf. Chadwick, *John Cassian*, 95.
This list is not exactly the same as that given by Cassian, for Cassian's list did not include envy, but it included melancholy instead, which Gregory the Great later combined with accidie. In devoting separate chapters in *De Reformatione* to accidie and melancholy, Zerbolt followed the example of Evagrius and Cassian who treated accidie and melancholy as separate sins. Furthermore, because Zerbolt sets apart separate chapters for *acedia* and *tristitia*, and discusses envy as well, he ends up discussing nine distinct vices in *De Reformatione*.

[134] Bloomfield, *The Seven Deadly Sins. An Introduction to the History of a Religious Concept*, 74.

[135] *Ibid.*, 144.

[136] *Ref.*, ch. 43 (p. 253C-D). Cf. *Asc.*, ch. 52 (pp. 279H-280A); and *Asc.*, 278D.

[136*] In *De Ascensionibus* Zerbolt offers what would appear to be a third explanation for the existence of the vices. He writes there that different individuals have different moral dispositions and inclinations which govern their entire behaviour. To explain why this is so he asserts that just as the different physical constitutions that men have are the result of the four humours being present in different proportions, so the different moral dispositions and inclinations are the result of the vices and virtuous affections being present in different proportions. (*Asc.*, 280C-D: Scire etiam...etiam virtuosae.) Consequently, each individual has a particular inclination or disposition, and Zerbolt is clearly of the opinion

name sometimes given to the cardinal sins is "mortal," and that they are so called because man can fall from the state of grace and be separated from God on account of them.[137] They are not, then, necessarily mortal, he points out, nor are they so by nature.[138] However, in regarding the capital sins as being at least potentially mortal, Zerbolt exemplifies the confusion that had grown up between the capital and mortal sins. This confusion first arose when the capital sins were adapted to penitential use in the seventh and eighth centuries, although Bloomfield doubts that the label "deadly" was ever attached to the cardinal sins before the fourteenth century.[139]

Zerbolt also divides the capital sins into two categories as had always been done: i.e., into carnal and spiritual. In harmony with tradition he calls gluttony and lust carnal sins, and the remaining capital sins he considers to be spiritual. In the battle against the cardinal sins the carnal vices must be attacked differently than the spiritual vices. The carnal vices, Zerbolt explains, are most effectively subdued by avoiding those things which may result in the commission of carnal sins, while spiritual sins are best overcome by practicing the opposite virtues.[140] Finally, Zerbolt concludes, the carnal vices must be subdued before the spiritual ones, and of all the sins gluttony must first be suppressed. For unless gluttony is first uprooted, the struggle against the spiritual vices will be in vain, and no solid progress in the spiritual life will be possible. Gluttony, being a carnal vice, lies near the surface and is on that account relatively easily subdued. If gluttony cannot be overcome, he asks, how will one be able to extirpate the spiritual vices which are not only less evident than

---

that this inclination is more often than not a sinful one, which is then the source of all the other vices. He adds that it may not be unfitting to call this inclination or disposition man's moral *complexio*. (*Ibid.*)

The theory of the four body humours is one which originated during the height of the Greek classical period, and was to hold sway until modern times. The humours were held to determine not only man's physical structure, but, because of the interdependence of mind and body, his psychological make-up as well. See R. Klibansky, E. Panofsky and F. Saxl, *Saturn and Melancholy: Studies in the History of Natural Philosophy, Religion and Art* (London, 1964), 3-15 ("The Doctrine of the Four Humours"); A. Cabassut, "Défauts," *DSp*, III, 81; and J. L. McIntyre, "Temperament," *Encyclopedia of Religion and Ethics*, ed. by Hastings, XII, 233-235.

[137] See footnote 131 above. Cf. Cristiani, *Jean Cassien*, II, 63-65; A. Cabassut, "Défauts," *DSp*, III, 73; and D. of Augsburg, *De ext. et int. hom. compositione*, I, 99.

[138] Cf. D. of Augsburg, *De ext. et int. hom. compositione*, I, 99.

[139] Bloomfield, *The Seven Deadly Sins. An Introduction to the History of a Religious Concept*, 43-44, 57, 73-74 and 97.

[140] *Ref.*, ch. 38 (p. 251C-D); and *Ref.*, 253D-E and 253F. See also *Asc.*, ch. 54 (p. 280F-H); and *Asc.*, 281B and 281H. Cf. Cassian, *Conferences*, No. V, chs. 3 and 4; and Dudden, *Gregory the Great*, II, 387.

the carnal ones, but also more tenacious.[141] For the reasons given by Zerbolt to begin the struggle against the capital sins with gluttony he is, once again, indebted to Cassian,[142] although he calls on the support of Gregory the Great as well.[143]

The theory of concatenation regarding the origin of the cardinal sins seems to underlie Zerbolt's insistence on the need to attack gluttony first. Gluttony is the first link in the Cassianic chain of cardinal sins, and hence it must be subdued first if the other sins are to be overcome. However, in his insistence on the need to begin the battle against the capital sins with gluttony, Zerbolt contradicts what he wrote in connection with the particular examination of conscience. There he maintained that, in the extirpation of the capital sins, one must begin with the most virulent one, and the purpose of the particular examination of conscience is to establish which of the vices deserves that questionable distinction. For both theories Zerbolt is, peculiarly enough, indebted to Cassian,[144] and in the latter's thought it represents a genuine contradiction; or must we see it as a development in his thinking?

It is to come to the aid of the believer in his struggle against the capital sins, Zerbolt explains, that he outlines in detail how to overcome each one of them individually. In fact, he devotes a chapter or two to the eradication of each one of the capital sins.[145] The discussion of each of the capital sins is fairly consistent. For, generally speaking at least, he begins in each instance with a definition of the vice. He then enumerates the offspring of the vice in question, for as a capital sin it has its own progeny. Following that Zerbolt suggests the remedies effective in healing that particular vice, and finally he discusses the promotion of its corresponding virtue. The eradication of a particular vice, or the development of its opposite virtue, is in most instances portrayed as a progressive development consisting of three consecutive steps.[146] Altogether typical of the Devotionalists' rigoristic approach to the spiritual life is the fact that Zerbolt generally pays more attention to the elimination of the vices than to the

---

[141] *Ref.*, 253D-E. Cf. *Asc.*, 281A-B.

In his discussion of gluttony Zerbolt writes that there are three forces that move one corporally: the natural force, the vital force and the mental force. He explains the operation of each of these three forces in some detail, and the entire passage is obviously inspired by *De Spiritu et Anima*, chs. 20-22 (*PL*, XL, 794-795).

[142] Cassian, *Institutes*, Bk. V, chs. 13, 16 and 17.

[143] See footnote 141.

[144] Cassian, *Institutes*, Bk. V, chs. 13, 16 and 17, and *idem*, *Conferences*, No. V, chs. 14 and 27 respectively.

[145] *Ref.*, chs. 44-58 (pp. 253D-257G). Cf. *Asc.*, chs. 56-63 (pp. 281A-285A).

[146] The exceptions are envy and vainglory. The battle against the former he divides into four stages, and the struggle against the latter into two.

See Appendix.

cultivation of the corresponding virtues.[147] Having said that, it may come as somewhat of a surprise that bodily mortification plays, on the whole, a relatively minor role in Zerbolt's instructions for the eradication of vice and the purification of the heart. He relies, instead, primarily on spiritual exercises to cleanse the heart of sin. Meditation on those topics which instil compunction of fear serves to eradicate most of the vices, and the two carnal sins, gluttony and lust, in particular. By contrast, the best remedy against pride, the queen of all vices,[148] is to meditate on the verity that all one's virtues and good works are defective and imperfect, and that such good qualities as they do possess are gifts of the merciful God.[149] Lastly, for his views regarding the capital sins and the way in which they may be overcome Zerbolt was indebted, in addition to Cassian and Gregory, to John Climacus and David of Augsburg.[150] However, it is more than likely that the teachings of these four authors regarding the capital sins were transmitted to Zerbolt by Radewijns' writings. For in both the *Tractatulus Devotus* and *Omnes, inquit, artes* Radewijns deals with the capital sins in detail,[151] but virtually everything he writes concerning them is taken word for word from Cassian's *Institutes* and *Conferences*, Gregory the Great's *Moralia in Job*, Climacus' *Scala Paradisi*, and David of Augsburg's *De exterioris et interioris hominis compositione*. It would appear that here, as in so many other instances, Radewijns' works served Zerbolt as his prime source books, and that Radewijns served as the intermediary between Zerbolt and the great masters of the spiritual life of earlier centuries.

In the discussion of the incarnation and its purpose it was concluded that, according to Zerbolt, Christ became man primarily to serve as the way to the knowledge and love of God. The most important aspect of his subjective work of atonement was, in turn, his role as *speculum vitae*. Consequently, one might have expected that in his discussion of the capital sins, their eradication and the acquisition of the corresponding virtues, Zerbolt would have made considerable use of Christ as the supreme example of all virtues who shows man the way in the fight against sin and vice. The truth is, however, that in his discussion of the capital sins, and

---

[147] Cf. Post, *The Modern Devotion*, 327.

[148] Cf. Bloomfield, *The Seven Deadly Sins. An Introduction to the History of a Religious Concept*, 69-71 and 95.

[149] See above, pp. 195-198.

[150] For his views on the capital sins Zerbolt is particularly indebted to the following: Cassian, *Institutes*, Bks. V-XII; *idem*, *Conferences*, No. V; Gregory the Great, *Moralia in Job*, Bk. XXXI; St. John Climacus, *The Ladder of Divine Ascent*, 138-168, 173-183 and 190-201; and David of Augsburg, *De ext. et int. hom. compositione*, I, 97-150 and II, 54-127. Cf. Wenzel, "The Seven Deadly Sins: Some Problems of Research," 1-22.

[151] Radewijns, *Tractatulus Devotus*, 234-235, 238-241 and 242-244; and *idem*, *Omnes, Inquit, Artes*, II, 11-34.

how they may be overcome, Zerbolt does not once mention Christ as the example to be followed. The necessity of imitating Christ in the quest for sanctity follows from Zerbolt's soteriology and his teaching that Christ is the supreme example of all virtues. However, Zerbolt never spells out how Christ serves as the example and may be imitated in a specific situation or in the eradication of a particular vice.[152] The necessity to follow Christ and to imitate him in the fight against temptations and in concrete situations is implied, but receives very little, or no, explicit emphasis. In spite of its title, the same holds true for Thomas a Kempis' *Imitation of Christ*. The necessity to follow and to imitate Christ in all of one's actions is an idea which underlies this entire work, but it is virtually never said in so many words.[153] Grote, for example, is much more explicit in his teaching on the imitation of Christ than are Zerbolt and Thomas a Kempis.[154]

Obviously influenced by David of Augsburg, Zerbolt writes that what counts in the struggle against the capital sins is not, in the first place, the eradication of those vices, but the intention and willingness to combat them. An unceasing battle against the capital vices, Zerbolt asserts, will be counted as a victory even if the vices are not actually extirpated. Consequently, those who have done their utmost to combat sin at all times will greatly increase their merits because of their readiness, intention and efforts to uproot the vices. The readiness, intention and effort will be counted as actual achievements.[155] Brinckerinck, also one of the first Devotionalists and *confrère* of Zerbolt, held much the same view. According to him reward and punishment after death will not be based on practical success or failure in the struggle against vice, but on the basis of man's willingness, or lack of it, to fight against sin and vice; God will accept man's inclination, desire and intention in place of his work.[156] In the writings of Zerbolt and Brinckerinck, then, as well as in those of David of

---

[152] Zerbolt does not, in spite of Lourdaux's assertion, portray the exercise of virtues as an imitation of Christ (W. Lourdaux, "Gérard Zerbolt de Zutphen," *DSp*, VI, 285).

[153] Vandenbroucke, "Le divorce entre théologie et mystique. Ses origines," 387.

[154] Cf. Mak, "Christus bij de Moderne Devoten," 117-122; Epiney-Burgard, *Grote*, 248-258; de Beer, *Spiritualiteit*, 84-88; Gall, "De Christus-gedachte bij Geert Grote," 229-240.
Cf. N. Lohkamp, "Imitation in Sanctification," *NCE*, VII, 375.

[155] *Ref.*, 253B: Cogita si non proficis vitium extinguendo, proficis tamen cumulando meritum laboribus tuis,...Cogita quod semper pugnare vicisse reputabitur, vere si ita fueris virilis in aggrediendo, et strenuus in sustinendo, non poteris non proficere. Si enim non proficis vitium extinguendo forsitan amplius non proficiendo proficis, id est, propter multos tuos labores inde amplius promerebis. Cf. D. of Augsburg, *De ext. et int. hom. compositione*, II, 64.

[156] Brinckerinck, "Collatiën," 151, 156 and 157.

Augsburg, we find evidence of the spiritualization of the religious life about which more will be said in the conclusion to this chapter.

ii. *De Ascensionibus*

Structure of De Ascensionibus. J. Mahieu writes that Psalm 83 provided Zerbolt with both the *incipit* and the underlying theme for *De Ascensionibus*.[157] The structure of *De Ascensionibus*, on the other hand, is determined by the concept of a threefold descent into sin discussed by Zerbolt in the opening chapters of that work. For over against this threefold descent into sin Zerbolt sets a threefold ascent by means of which the heart is cleansed of all sins which prevent the growth of charity.[158] These three ascents constitute the subject matter of *De Ascensionibus*, and they also give this work its name. Whether, and if so to what extent, Zerbolt is indebted to other works for the structure of *De Ascensionibus* is not altogether clear. Goossens expresses the view that the plan of *De Ascensionibus* is based to a considerable extent on John Climacus' *Scala Paradisi*.[159] Unfortunately Goossens does not describe the similarity between the structure of *De Ascensionibus* and that of the *Scala Paradisi*; but what he probably has in mind is that in *De Ascensionibus* Zerbolt compares the successive phases of the spiritual life to the rungs of a ladder as is done by Climacus in the *Scala Paradisi*.[160] However, it may be argued that the structure of *De Ascensionibus* reveals a greater resemblance to Bonaventure's *De Triplici Via* than to Climacus' *Scala Paradisi*. For *De Triplici Via* consists of three distinct 'ways', and each of these three 'ways' is subdivided into three progressions as are the three ascents in *De Ascensionibus*. Finally, it is not out of the question that the plan for *De Ascensionibus* may have been suggested to Zerbolt by chapter fifty-two of *De Spiritu et Anima* in which man's progress to the knowledge and love of God is outlined in three consecutive ascents.[161]

The first ascent reverses man's third descent, namely that into mortal sin, and this is achieved by means of the sacrament of penance. This sacrament deletes mortal sin, and as a result man is reconciled to God. Since the first ascent is not part of the ascetical phase of the spiritual life as it is commonly defined, it receives relatively little attention from Zerbolt. It is to the second and the third ascents, which reverse the second and first descents respectively, that *De Ascensionibus* is primarily devoted.

---

[157] Mahieu, ed., *De spiritualibus ascensionibus/Van geestelijke opklimmingen*, XVI—XVII.
[158] *Asc.*, ch. 11 (p. 262G-H). Cf. above, pp. 171-172; and Goossens, *Meditatie*, 68.
[159] Goossens, *Meditatie*, 68.
[160] *Asc.*, 259A and 262C.
[161] *De Spiritu et Anima*, ch. 52 (*PL*, XL, 817-818). For a schema of the structure of *De Ascensionibus* see van Rooy, *Zerbolt*, 124-127.

The second and third ascents are a continuation of the process of purgation begun in the first ascent, which is clear from the very fact that their
purpose is to annul the second and first descents respectively. Their purpose, then, is to purify the heart further following man's return to the
state of grace, and consequently they must be labelled ascetical. The
moral virtues are not totally neglected in the second and third ascents,
but, as in *De Reformatione*, Zerbolt places considerably more emphasis on
the eradication of sins and vices than on the cultivation of moral virtues.

Regarding the order in which the ascents are made it would appear
that Zerbolt adopts, as with the reformation of the faculties in *De Reformatione*, two different positions. On the one hand he makes the first ascent a
prerequisite for the ascetical life he describes in the second and third
ascents. For, unless man is first reconciled to God, he cannot progress in
the spiritual life. On the other hand, however, Zerbolt writes in *De Ascensionibus* that the third ascent is collateral with the first two ascents, and
that the third ascent in fact helps to make the first two possible.[162] If the
three ascents can be either consecutive or collateral developments that
reflects, as in *De Reformatione*, the two dissimilar ways of looking at man's
spiritual growth in circulation in the last quarter of the fourteenth century.

Each of the three ascents is divided into three stages which Zerbolt
clearly regards as consecutive developments. The first ascent is divided
into the three steps of contrition, confession and satisfaction. The second
ascent consists of compunction of fear on the one hand, and compunction
of hope and love on the other, followed by charity. The third ascent is a
question of the eradication of the capital sins, and Zerbolt divides the extirpation of each of them into three consecutive steps.

Self-examination and self-knowledge. In *De Ascensionibus*, as in *De Reformatione*,
Zerbolt discusses three types of self-examination typical of the spiritual
life: the general, the daily and the particular examinations of
conscience.[163] These self-examinations, except for the last one, follow immediately after Zerbolt's inquiry into the fall and just before he embarks
upon the discussion of the three ascents which reverse the three descents
into sin. Only through self-examination can the believer become familiar
with his descents into sin, and unless he is first confronted with his sin-

---

[162] *Asc.*, 278E: Et ita tertia ascensio cuius gradus nunc disponimus, quodammodo or-
dinatur contra primum descendum in Adam. Non est autem ista ascensio supra
praemissas ascensiones alterior, sed collateralis, vel certe una et eadem est ascensio cum
praemissis, diversis respectibus, et modis variis exercitandi. Ipsa est autem priores ascensiones promovens et adiuvans, rectificans et praeparans, sine qua nullus potest in
praemissis ascensionibus ambulare.

[163] *Asc.*, chs. 7, 8 and 53 (pp. 261C-262A and 280B-F).

fulness he will do nothing to ascend spiritually. The general, daily and particular examinations of conscience do not, however, correspond to what Zerbolt calls the three examinations of conscience in *De Ascensionibus*, which in turn correspond to the three descents and ascents around which this work is constructed. For what Zerbolt terms the first self-examination in *De Ascensionibus* corresponds to man's third fall,[164] namely that into mortal sin. Consequently it is carried out in connection with the sacrament of penance, and it is not peculiar to the spiritual life as are the general, the daily and the particular examinations of conscience. That which Zerbolt calls the second examination of conscience in *De Ascensionibus*,[165] the examination aimed at uncovering the effects of man's first descent: i.e., the descent into original sin, is the equivalent of the general examination of conscience.[166] What he designates the third examination of conscience in *De Ascensionibus*,[167] the purpose of which is to uncover the effects of man's second fall: i.e., the descent into sinful concupiscence in general, corresponds to the daily examination of conscience.[168] The particular examination of conscience, the object of which is to uncover the dominant vice which must then be extirpated, does not correspond to any descent or ascent in *De Ascensionibus*, and it is not discussed by Zerbolt until chapter fifty-three of that work. He discusses it there in preparation for the third ascent which deals with the extirpation of the seven capital sins in the order of their potency and influence. Finally, Zerbolt mentions, as in *De Reformatione*, the testimony of others, as well as the struggle against sin, as avenues to self-knowledge.[169] It is only when one attempts to extirpate one's vices, inordinate affections and sinful concupiscences that one becomes fully cognizant of one's sinful condition and of the fact that sin has become part of one's very nature.

The second ascent. Even though the removal of mortal sin through the sacrament of penance reconciles man to God, there remains much impurity in his heart on account of which he can still not be accepted into

---

[164] *Asc.*, ch. 6 (pp. 260F-261C). See above, p. 173.

[165] *Asc.*, ch. 7 (p. 261C-F).

[166] Even in *De Ascensionibus* Zerbolt divides the general examination of conscience into an examination of intellect, memory and will. However, it is most unusual for Zerbolt to divide the faculties along these lines in *De Ascensionibus* (see above, pp. 67-69).

[167] *Asc.*, ch. 8 (pp. 261F-262A).

[168] The sequences of the three descents into sin, the three self-examinations, and the three ascents in *De Ascensionibus* do not correspond. The first examination corresponds to the third fall, the second examination to the first fall, and the third examination to the second fall. The first ascent corresponds to the first examination and the third fall; the second ascent corresponds to the third examination and the second fall; and the third ascent corresponds to the second examination and the first fall.

[169] *Asc.*, ch. 8, second half (pp. 261G-262A).

God's friendship and be united with him in perfect charity.[170] Zerbolt calls this general state of impurity and sinful concupiscence, which is the consequence of original sin, man's second descent into sin;[171] and the second ascent is designed to overcome this generally impure and sinful condition in order that man may be united with God in charity. However, in this second ascent Zerbolt does not give us one, but two, presumably complementary, routes to charity and the vision of God. In the first of these two 'ways' he outlines how the believer may, following his reconciliation with God, ascend to charity, and perhaps even to the vision of God, by means of compunction. In the second of the two 'ways' he describes how in three steps the believer may ascend to union with God by means of Christ, the God-man. However, since the second 'way' to union with God described in the second ascent has been examined in the discussion of the doctrine of subjective atonement, we will concentrate our attention at this point on the 'way' to God by means of compunction.

Zerbolt divides the way to union with God by means of compunction into three consecutive steps.[172] In the first ascent the heart is cleansed of sin, inordinate concupiscence and love for things of this earth, both material and non-material, through meditation on death, the last judgement and the pains of hell.[173] For meditation on these matters instils compunction of fear which drives out sin, vice and inordinate desire for created things. Zerbolt also mentions the consideration of one's sins as a means to compunction of fear. Here he has in mind the sins uncovered in the various self-examinations: the self-examinations necessary for the sacrament of penance as well as those which are peculiar to the spiritual

---

[170] See footnote 2 of this chapter.

[171] See above, pp. 91-94.

[172] Zerbolt's basic reasoning is found in ch. 15 (pp. 263F-264A) of *De Ascensionibus*, a general introduction to what he calls the second ascent in *De Ascensionibus* which reverses the second descent. In ch. 16 (p. 264B-C) of *De Ascensionibus*, as well as in ch. 18 (p. 264F-G), Zerbolt elaborates the argument that compunction of fear purges the soul of inordinate concupiscence, but those chapters do not really add anything to what he has said in ch. 15. Furthermore, in chs. 15, 16 and 18 Zerbolt does not quote any sources, and they are, it would appear, fairly original. In chs. 22 and 23 (p. 266C-H) of *De Ascensionibus* Zerbolt explains further how compunction of hope and love draw man to God, and so prepare him for charity. Again, they do not add anything substantial to the argument put forth in ch. 15. Like chs. 15, 16 and 18, chs. 22 and 23 would appear to owe relatively little to other authors.
Cf. Goossens, *Meditatie*, 45, 155-157.

[173] For these three meditations see *De Ascensionibus*, chs. 19, 20 and 21 (pp. 264G-266C) respectively. Cf. Goossens, *Meditatie*, 184.
The meditations on death, the last judgement and the horrors of hell which purify the heart are identical to those discussed by Zerbolt in *De Reformatione* in connection with the reformation of the memory, and consequently require no further comment here.

life.[174] After the heart has been cleansed of all sins by means of compunction of fear, the believer must be drawn to God by means of compunction
of hope and love, the second ascent. Compunction of hope and love is instilled in man by confronting him with the joys of heaven and the benefits
bestowed on him in this life.[175] However, the compunction of love which
is generated as a consequence of meditating on God's goodness to man
and the joys of heaven is still a selfish love and falls short of charity.
Nonetheless, having reached the stage of self-centered love for God, man
is ready to proceed to charity, the third ascent, and from there to the vision of God.[176]

It is of some considerable importance to Zerbolt that, as they develop,
compunction of fear should precede compunction of hope and love. The
Holy Spirit, he writes, begins by planting unrest and fear in the heart of
the believer, and only then does he follow it up with the confidence which
stems from hope. Satan (the *dyabolicus spiritus*), on the other hand, takes
the opposite approach, beginning with hope and confidence and ending
with fear and despair.[177] If compunction of fear ought to precede compunction of hope and love, Zerbolt poses the question whether those who
have progressed from the first to the second ought to put behind
themselves all meditations on death, judgement and hell which are conducive to instilling compunction of fear. He answers this question in the
negative. Having achieved compunction of love, he elaborates, it is
necessary to descend once more and to meditate even more earnestly
than before on the vanity of worldly things, the shortness of life, and the
horrors of hell. Thus, he explains, one will at one and the same time be
drawn onward by hope and goaded forward by fear. Hope will prevent
the believer from being overcome with debilitating fear, and fear will prevent him from falling into a state of false security and presumption.
Quoting Gregory the Great he concludes that nothing is safer for man
than constant fear tempered by hope.[178]

---

[174] *Asc.*, ch. 17 (p. 264D-F).

[175] *Asc.*, chs. 24 and 25 (p. 267A-H).

The meditations in *De Ascensionibus*, as well as those in *De Reformatione*, were apparently
sufficiently popular that they circulated independently. Cf. van Rooy, *Zerbolt*, 308-309,
334-335 and 380; Goossens, *Meditatie*, 172 and 199; and above, pp. 30-31.

[176] *Asc.*, ch. 26 (p. 268A-F). The ascent to charity and the vision of God was, of course,
discussed earlier in this chapter.

[177] *Scriptum Pro Quodam*, 212: Nam spiritus divinus facit hominem intus humilem, flex-
ibilem, spiritus dyabolicus presumptuosum, pertinacem. Nam hee [sic] sunt vie Dyaboli
secundum Bernardum super "Qui habitat." Item ordo movendi spiritus sanctus est,
quod loquitur primo in turbine, id est, quod facit hominem pavidum, timoratum et percussum et propriam fragilitatem cognoscere et postea erigit in spem. Contra autem
dyabolicus spiritus.

[178] *Asc.*, 285D-F: Non ita,...de donis ruat.

In a later chapter near the end of *De Ascensionibus* Zerbolt returns to the question of compunction of hope and love which he then equates with *devotio*.[179] For, according to Zerbolt, devotion is nothing else but compunction of desire and love which is enkindled as the believer meditates on God's goodness to man and the joys of heaven. However, he continues that there are two types of devotion, and that both of them arise from a consideration of God's gifts to man, the joys of heaven and similar matters. Meditation on these topics, he explains, can shake the mind of the believer, and arouse in him a strong feeling or emotion. In many cases, however, it turns out to be unauthentic, and consequently short-lived. What Zerbolt apparently has in mind here is a sentimentality which has nothing to do with true devotion, and against which Brinckerinck also warned his audience.[180] This spurious type of devotion or compunction of love has, according to Zerbolt, affinity with the sensitive appetite, while true devotion is a quality of the will: i.e., it resides in the will.[181] True devotion or compunction of love, he continues, must be accompanied by a struggle against the capital vices, for one's devotion grows in proportion to the eradication of vice and the acquisition of virtue. The struggle against, and eradication of, vice constitutes not only the basis for true devotion, but for a lasting devotion as well. Zerbolt does not totally deny the usefulness of the spurious type of devotion, for he believes that it can lead man to true devotion or compunction of hope and love.[182]

In dividing man's ascent to God by means of compunction into three consecutive ascents consisting of fear, hope-love and charity, Zerbolt would appear to have been following in the footsteps of John Cassian and Bernard of Clairvaux.[183] However, he may also have been influenced by the triad of theological virtues, namely faith, hope and charity. For in his discussion of the development of compunction of fear Zerbolt writes that it is the first effect of faith.[184] The consecutive ascents of fear, hope-love and charity could perhaps also be compared to the three spiritual ways of purgation, illumination and union.[185] However, Zerbolt does not really

---

[179] *Asc.*, 49 (pp. 278F-279C). Cf. *Asc.*, chs. 24 and 25 (p. 267A-H).

[180] Brinckerinck, "Collatiën," 164.

[181] In the previous century Aquinas cautioned that feeling or emotion must not be mistaken for devotion on the ground that while devotion is an act of the will, feelings or emotions are activities of the sense appetite (J. W. Curran, "Devotion," *NCE*, IV, 832).

[182] Cf. Goossens, *Meditatie*, 109.

[183] Cassian, *Institutes*, Bk. IV, chs. 39 and 43; Goossens, *Meditatie*, 51-52; W. Yeomans, "St. Bernard of Clairvaux," in: Walsh, ed., *Spirituality Through the Centuries*, 117; T. A. Porter, "Spiritual Theology," *NCE*, XIII, 588; and E. E. Larkin, "Ways, The Three Spiritual," *NCE*, XIV, 836.

[184] *Asc.*, 266C. See above, pp. 167-168.

[185] E. E. Larkin, "Ways, The Three Spiritual," *NCE*, XIV, 834-836.

divide the spiritual life into three stages, but into two, as was established
earlier in this chapter: i.e., into an active (ascetical) phase and a contemplative (mystical) phase. The compunction of fear and the compunction of hope and love, which respectively cleanse the heart of sin and
draw man to God, both belong to the active phase of the spiritual life
from which man may ascend to the contemplative experience of God,
whether it be charity or the vision of God. Furthermore, as is typical of
Zerbolt, he devotes much more space to compunction which makes charity and the vision of God possible, than to charity and the vision of God
themselves.[186] As always, Zerbolt is concerned first and foremost with the
ascesis.

In the second 'way' of the second ascent Zerbolt describes how the
believer may ascend to charity and the vision of God through Christ in
three consecutive steps. It is through imitation of Christ in his humanity
that the believer achieves purity of heart, cultivates moral virtues, and is
united to Christ the man. From there he must proceed to a union with
Christ as God and man, and in the third ascent he must continue to the
love of the Godhead and to charity, the last ascent before he goes up to
the vision of God.[187] Imitation of Christ in his humanity as the means to
achieve a pure heart and to cultivate moral virtues belongs to the ascetical
phase of the religious life, and in neither *De Reformatione* nor *De Ascensionibus* does Zerbolt really move beyond imitation of Christ the man and
the unity thus established with him. It is with the cleansing of the heart
through the imitation of Christ in his humanity: i.e., with the active life,
that both *De Reformatione* and *De Ascensionibus* stop.[188] Apart from a brief
indication that Christ is also the way to charity and the vision of God, the
higher levels of the spiritual life, and the role played by Christ in achieving those spiritual heights, do not receive further attention in either *De
Reformatione* or *De Ascensionibus*.[189] It needs to be added that, although
Zerbolt attaches a great deal of importance to imitation of Christ as the
means to purify the heart and to cultivate moral virtues, he does not spell
out how imitation of Christ contributes to man's moral reformation. For
when we examine the third ascent in which Zerbolt describes in detail
how the seven capital sins must be eradicated and the corresponding virtues cultivated, it will be seen that there is very little explicit mention of

---

[186] In *De Ascensionibus* ten chs. (16-25) are set aside for compunction and its development, and one ch. (26) for charity and the vision of God.

[187] *Asc.*, ch. 27 (pp. 268F-269F). Man's ascent to God by way of Christ was discussed
in connection with Zerbolt's doctrine of subjective atonement.

[188] Cf. Post, *The Modern Devotion*, 327.

[189] Cf. Mak, "Christus bij de Moderne Devoten," 166; P. Debongnie, "Dévotion
Moderne," *DSp*, III, 731; and Goossens, *Meditatie*, 27-28.

the imitation of Christ, although its necessity in this connection is undoubtedly implied.[190]

The imitation of Christ in his humanity, and the union thus established with him, has been termed Christ mysticism, and it has been called practical mysticism as well.[191] However, from what has been said it is quite obvious that Zerbolt understood the imitation of Christ in his humanity, the means by which the heart is cleansed of sins, to be part of the active life which makes charity and the vision of God possible. Consequently it would appear erroneous and misleading to call Zerbolt's imitation of Christ in his humanity Christ mysticism,[192] and to call it practical mysticism would appear to be wrong for much the same reason. Zerbolt did not regard imitation of Christ's virtuous behaviour preceding the ascent to charity as being part of the contemplative life of the soul. Zerbolt did not consider his imitation of Christ to progress beyond the ascesis, nor did he claim that it did so. His asceticism, which was Christ-centered by implication rather than being so explicitly, could, of course, lead the believer to charity and the mystical vision of God; but Zerbolt did not, apart from indicating this possibility, describe the mystical contemplation of God itself.[193]

Since man may ascend to charity and the vision of God by means of Christ the God-man, Zerbolt includes an account of Christ's life in the second ascent of *De Ascensionibus*. In the final chapter of this account, which is based on a similar chapter in Bonaventure's *De Triplici Via*, Zerbolt describes how seven things hitherto hidden to man were revealed in the passion.[194] He asserts that meditation on these revelations will implant in the believer either compunction of fear or compunction of hope and love depending on the nature of each one of them. Consequently these revelations, when meditated on, will, like the earlier meditations on death, the last judgement, etc., lead the believer by way of compunction

---

[190] In making Christ, and the imitation of him, the way to the vision of God, Zerbolt pretty much repeated what Grote had written on this subject, for Grote divided the spiritual life into two major phases: the imitation of the humanity of Christ through which purity of heart is attained; and the union with God in love and the vision of him for which purity of heart is the prerequisite (de Beer, *Spiritualiteit*, 188, 191, 290-291 and 295; and Goossens, *Meditatie*, 144). Furthermore, as Zerbolt was to do later, Grote regarded the vision of God as the crown on the spiritual life, but on the other hand he held the development of virtues in imitation of Christ to be more beneficial than to be caught up, like St. Paul, to the third heaven (1 Cor. 13, 1).

[191] Van Rooy, *Zerbolt*, 269; Mak, "Christus bij de Moderne Devoten," 165-166; and Axters, *Vroomheid*, III, 26.

[192] Cf. Oberman, *Biel*, 351-352.

[193] Zerbolt writes that it is necessary to suffer with Christ (see above, pp. 151-152), but the so-called "passion mysticism" cannot be found in Zerbolt's writings (cf. B. Spaapen, "Middeleeuwse Passiemystiek, I," *OGE*, XXXV [1961], 261-268).

[194] *Asc.*, ch. 38 (274E-275B). See above, p. 151.

272   SPIRITUAL THEOLOGY AND LIFE

of fear and love to charity and the vision of God. In this way Zerbolt ties together the two distinct routes to charity and the vision of God outlined by him in the second ascent of *De Ascensionibus*.

The third ascent. The third ascent corresponds to the first fall,[195] namely the loss of that immunity from natural, rebellious concupiscence which Zerbolt equated with original justice. The purpose of the third ascent is not, however, to wipe out rebellious concupiscence, for that would be impossible since it is man's natural condition. However, as a consequence of rebellious concupiscence and the will's surrender to it, the soul has been defiled with sinful concupiscence and inordinate love for worldly things: i.e., with capital sins or vices. Unlike rebellious concupiscence, the capital sins can be eradicated, and it is on their extirpation that Zerbolt concentrates his attention in the third ascent.[196] For although the will has been weakened as a result of the fall, it is not 'bound' by evil and still possesses the capacity to withstand rebellious concupiscence and to eradicate established vices. As in the first and second ascents, Zerbolt's primary concern in the third ascent is purity of heart.

What Zerbolt writes in *De Ascensionibus* concerning the capital sins and their extirpation is essentially a repetition of everything he has said in *De Reformatione* concerning these same matters. The differences between his handling of the capital sins in *De Reformatione* and *De Ascensionibus* are, on the whole, minor and of no consequence.[197] One of the relatively significant differences is that in *De Ascensionibus* Zerbolt assigns a more prominent role to compunction in the eradication of the vices than he does in *De Reformatione*. In one of the introductory chapters to the third ascent he writes that all the capital vices must be overcome in three consecutive ascents. In the first ascent, that of the beginners, the heart is partially cleansed of the vice under attack through compunction of fear. In the second ascent, that of the proficient, the heart is further cleansed of the same vice by means of compunction of hope. Finally, in the third ascent, that of the perfect, the believer goes forward to a perfect eradication of that vice and so towards purity.[198] Those who divided the spiritual life

---

[195] The third ascent is discussed in chs. 47-63 (pp. 278A-285A) of *De Ascensionibus*.

[196] *Asc.*, 278E: Itaque sicut...continue praeliari. *Asc.*, 278F: ..., seroque sunt experti quod non est tutum cohabitare serpentibus concupiscentiarum, et motibus habituatis vitiorum. Cf. footnote 122 above.

[197] In *De Reformatione*, for example, Zerbolt devotes separate chapters to accidie and melancholy, but in *De Ascensionibus* he combines the discussion of these two vices in one chapter entitled: *Ascensus et expurgationes contra acediam*.

[198] *Asc.*, ch. 55 (p. 280H): *Quod tres sunt ascensus contra unumquodque vitium, id est, tres profectus ad oppositam virtutem. Asc.*, 280H-281A: Igitur contra quodlibet vitium tres potes distinguere gradus, quorum primus est incipientium, et pertinet ad primum gradum ascensionis ad cordis puritatem, qui est in timore. Secundus est proficientium, et pertinet

into three stages, instead of into two stages as was done by Zerbolt, attached the labels *incipientes*, *proficientes* and *perfecti* to those who were in the purgative, illuminative and unitive stages of the spiritual life respectively.[199] Zerbolt does not, however, employ the terms incipient, proficient and perfect to designate the three stages of the spiritual life, but he uses them simply to describe three successive stages of development within the limits of the active phase of the spiritual life.

Zerbolt's handling of the individual vices follows, as in *De Reformatione*, a consistent pattern.[200] First he defines the vice; secondly he enumerates its progeny; thirdly he suggests remedies in addition to compunction of fear and hope; and fourthly he discusses its corresponding virtue. The definitions of the vices given, the off-spring enumerated, the remedies offered, and the corresponding virtues named are all identical to those found in *De Reformatione*, the major difference being that in *De Ascensionibus* Zerbolt tends to elaborate on what he has written in *De Reformatione*. The eradication of a vice and the development of its corresponding virtue always takes place in three consecutive steps, and, as in *De Reformatione*, Zerbolt always pays more attention to the extirpation of the vice than to the cultivation of the opposite virtue. And, as in *De Reformatione* once again, Zerbolt never mentions imitation of Christ as a means to eliminate a particular vice or to acquire its opposite virtue.

C) *The Vehicles of The Spiritual Ascent*

Zerbolt writes that the believer can make progress in the spiritual life only when sustained by spiritual reading, meditation and prayer.[201] Manual labour belongs to the same category as do spiritual reading, meditation and prayer. Together they may be termed the vehicles of the spiritual ascent, for they are the means by which the spiritual ascent is

---

ad secundum gradum secundae ascensionis, qui in spe agitur. Tertius gradus est perfectorum, et pertinet ad ultimum gradum ascensionis ad puritatem. Cf. T. A. Porter, "Spiritual Theology," *NCE*, XIII, 588; E. E. Larkin, "Ways, The Three Spiritual," *NCE*, XIV, 836; and J. E. Wrigley, "Perfection, Spiritual," *NCE*, XI, 126-127.

[199] E. E. Larkin, "Ways, The Three Spiritual," *NCE*, XIV, 835-836.

[200] The eight capital sins are discussed in chs. 56-63 (pp. 281A-285A) of *De Ascensionibus*. Chs. 47-55 (pp. 278A-281A) are an introduction to the discussion of the capital sins.

[201] *Asc.*, ch. 43 (p. 275H): *De tribus, quibus sustentatur et promovetur spiritualis ascensio, scilicet lectione, meditatione, et oratione.* ...: Ita iam erecta scala ascensionum tria assignemus sustentamenta, in quibus requiescere valeas fatigatus, quibus possis te reficere deficientem in via.

The subject matter of meditation has, of course, been outlined by Zerbolt in detail in the reformation of the memory and the second ascent. Here he deals with the technical aspect of meditation.

maintained and moved forward.[202] Goossens has investigated in some detail what the earliest Devotionalists, including Zerbolt, wrote regarding manual labour and the practices of spiritual reading, meditation and prayer. Consequently we will not analyze Zerbolt's views on these matters in any great detail, but a brief review of them will round off the discussion of Zerbolt's teachings on spiritual theology and life.

i. *Manual Work*

What Zerbolt writes regarding manual labour is consistent with traditional thinking on this topic.[203] He bases his views on the writings of Jerome, Cassian, Augustine and William of St. Thierry,[204] to name but a few. However, in this instance, as in so many others, the teachings of the great masters of the spiritual life may have been transmitted to Zerbolt by the writings of Radewijns.[205]

In both *De Reformatione* and *De Ascensionibus* Zerbolt divides the chapter on manual work into three parts. In the first part, the longest in both instances, he explains the importance of manual work to the religious life. In the second part he discusses the kind of work that is suitable for the religious, and concludes that copying of books is the most appropriate. And in the final part he looks into the nature of the spiritual exercises in which the religious must be engaged while copying books.

Zerbolt gives a number of reasons why manual labour is necessary. Among the most important is that as long as man is weighed down by the body and is not a spirit as are the angels, he cannot be continually engaged in spiritual exercises. To be exclusively occupied with things spiritual would result in weariness and an aversion to the spiritual life. Man consists of body and spirit, and hence he is compelled on account of his very nature to engage in both bodily and spiritual work even if he has

---

[202] The Brethren's constitutions contain directives for manual labour, spiritual reading, meditation and prayer; and so the essential similarity between the contents and purpose of the Brethren's constitutions and Zerbolt's manuals is once again illustrated ("The Original Constitution of the Brethren of the Common Life at Deventer," ed. by Hyma, *The Christian Renaissance*, 442-443, 444-445, 445-446 and 470-471; and "*Consuetudines domus nostre* [= Brethren House at Zwolle]," in: Jacobus de Voecht, *Narratio*, ed. by Schoengen, 241-242, 243, 244-245 and 270-271). Cf. Persoons, "Het Intellectuele Leven in het Klooster Bethlehem in de 15de Eeuw," 47-48.

[203] For Zerbolt's view on manual labour see *Ref.*, ch. 39 (pp. 251E-252A) and *Asc.*, ch. 67 (p. 286B-H).

[204] *The Golden Epistle of Abbot William of St. Thierry*, 41-42; and cf. Radewijns, *Tractatulus Devotus*, 230-232; idem, *Omnes, Inquit, Artes*, II, 52-54; and Goossens, *Meditatie*, 115-118.

[205] See footnote 204.

adopted the religious life which aims at spiritual perfection. To persist in the religious life is extremely difficult unless one joins manual work to spiritual exercises. Furthermore, manual labour is an effective remedy for lust and sinful concupiscence, as well as an effective weapon against temptations, for while those who are occupied are besieged by only one temptation, the idle are beleaguered by countless temptations. Finally, a very important reason for manual labour is that it frees the community from being dependent on others for its livelihood,[206] while at the same time work enables it to aid the poor and needy. Zerbolt concludes with the observation that according to the desert fathers one's spiritual progress: i.e., purity of heart, charity and spiritual perfection, is in proportion to the faithfulness with which one carries out the assigned manual labour.

One must do such manual work as has the greatest resemblance to spiritual exercises, Zerbolt asserts, and he believes that the copying of holy books comes the closest to fulfilling this requirement. For the copying of such books is less of an impediment to spiritual progress than is any other type of manual labour. Furthermore, it is meritorious work in that it increases the number of spiritual writings available. Zerbolt then mentions a number of people who figure prominently in the history of monasticism who also copied books or advised that this be done as an occupation.[207]

Zerbolt concludes that as one is busy copying books, the mind must not be idle. One must meditate for the purpose of instilling compunction, pray, or perhaps ruminate on that which one is copying. Consequently, it is necessary to maintain silence while working, for otherwise these spiritual exercises are not possible. Furthermore, one must carry out one's work diligently and with care, but one must at the same time not be too intent on one's work or be too absorbed by it for that could impede meditation and prayer.

---

[206] Cf. A. de Vogüé, "Monachisme et Eglise dans la Pensée de Cassien," in: *Théologie*, 226.

Cassian points to the example set by St. Paul who earned his own livelihood.

[207] From the very outset the Brethren communities supported themselves by copying books. Thus in his advocacy of book production as the most suitable form of manual labour Zerbolt was, in a sense, merely endorsing an existing situation. However, his works, as well as those of Radewijns, must have contributed to the entrenchment of this occupation among the Brethren of the Common Life. The importance of book production in the Brethren Houses is perhaps most clearly reflected in some of their constitutions. The Brethren constitution published by Hyma contains a chapter entitled *De cura scribendorum* ("The Original Constitution of the Brethren of the Common Life at Deventer," ed. by Hyma, *The Christian Renaissance*, 454).

ii. *Lectio*, *Meditatio* and *Oratio*[208]

Zerbolt borrowed his views on spiritual reading, meditation and prayer from the familiar sources, namely from the writings of Cassian, Gregory the Great, St. Bernard, William of St. Thierry, David of Augsburg and Bonaventure. Other sources upon which he drew in this connection were the writings of Jerome, Benedict of Nursia and Hugh of St. Victor.[209] However, here, as in so many other instances, Radewijns' *Tractatulus Devotus* and *Omnes, inquit, artes* constituted Zerbolt's immediate sources, especially with respect to what he writes regarding spiritual reading and prayer. The chapters in both *De Reformatione* and *De Ascensionibus* devoted to spiritual reading and prayer are based on similar chapters in Radewijns' *Tractatulus Devotus* and *Omnes, inquit, artes*.[210] Meditation, its practice and purpose, are not discussed by Radewijns. Consequently, for his views on meditation Zerbolt could not draw on the writings of his *confrère*, and it would appear that he borrowed them directly from the works of Jerome, Cassian, Benedict of Nursia and William of St. Thierry.

Unless the believer intersperses spiritual exercises with manual labour he will not be able to ascend spiritually, Zerbolt wrote. However, spiritual reading, meditation and prayer are activities peculiar to the spiritual life. They are spiritual activities, and are particularly effective in promoting spiritual growth. They constitute, according to Zerbolt, the spiritual nourishment which sustains the believer in his spiritual ascent,[211] and it would appear that in making these three the prime pillars of the spiritual life he was following in the footsteps of Hugh of St. Victor in particular. Spiritual reading, meditation and prayer all play a role in every part of man's spiritual ascent, but not to the same degree. According to Hugh of St. Victor, Zerbolt explains, spiritual reading is particularly appropriate for the beginners in the spiritual life, meditation for those who have already made some progress, and prayer for those who have begun to cleave to God in charity.[212]

---

[208] For *lectio, meditatio* and *oratio* see *Ref.*, chs. 15 (p. 242C-F), 19 (p. 243B-F) and 35 (pp. 249H-250C); *Asc.*, chs. 43-46 (pp. 275H-278A); *De libris teutonicalibus*, 45-70; and *Super modo vivendi*, 59-71.

[209] See above, pp. 18-26. Cf. *De Spiritu et Anima*, ch. 50 (*PL*, XL, 816), as well.

[210] Radewijns, *Tractatulus Devotus*, 218-222; *idem, Omnes, Inquit, Artes*, II, 46-50.

[211] See footnote 201 above. Cf. Goossens, *Meditatie*, 98-99.

[212] *Asc.*, 276A: Lectio autem magis pertinet ad primum ascensionis gradum, qui in timore perficitur. Nam lectio secundum Hugonem ad incipientes pertinet, qui utique in primo gradu ab timore concipiunt, et parturiunt spiritum salutis. Meditatio magis spectat ad secundum gradum, id est, proficientes, qui iam lectionibus instructi sciunt secum in corde suo deambulare. Oratio vero quamvis ad omnes spectet ascensus, praecipue tamen et proprie ipsis congruit, qui in tertio ascensionis gradu incipiunt Deo adhaerere. Hugh of St. Victor, *Eruditio didascalia*, *PL*, CLXXVI, 797. Cf. Oberman, *Biel*, 347; and Goossens, *Meditatie*, 96 and 98-99.

Spiritual reading must serve man's spiritual progress. The believer must, therefore, select those writings which instil compunction of fear and hope,[213] for without this twofold compunction the believer cannot ascend to charity and union with God. When one reads, tears of compunction, rather than knowledge of words, are the goal, as Zerbolt quotes from Gregory the Great's *Dialogues*.[214] Furthermore, the believer must also select for his spiritual reading those works which instruct him how to eradicate the capital sins and to acquire the corresponding virtues as described by Zerbolt himself in *De Reformatione* and *De Ascensionibus*. The believer must, in other words, select for spiritual reading the *libri morales et devoti*.[215] Furthermore, spiritual reading must be carried out methodically and not haphazardly. Also, one must set aside a fixed hour of the day for spiritual reading, and not leave it to chance.

Lectio and *meditatio* are distinct activities, but they are, nonetheless, closely related. Spiritual reading provides the memory with those materials which, when meditated on, instil either compunction of fear or compunction of hope and love depending on their nature.[216] It is by means of spiritual reading, then, that the memory is reformed; and reformation of the memory is of the utmost importance because, as Zerbolt quotes from Cassian's *Conferences*, the soul is like a mill which grinds whatever is put into it.[217] Therefore, unless the memory is reformed by means of spiritual reading and provides the soul with spiritually beneficial subjects for meditation and reflection, the soul will be governed by a multitude of ideas and external impressions detrimental to one's spiritual well-being. A reformed memory, on the other hand, will enable the believer to meditate profitably, even when he is not engaged in spiritual reading, on those topics which induce compunction of fear and hope.[218]

---

[213] Persoons, "Het Intellectuele Leven in het Klooster Bethlehem in de 15de Eeuw," 57 and 59-60.

[214] Gregory the Great, *Dialogues*, Bk. IV (Zerbolt does not identify his source any further). Cf. W. Lourdaux, "Dévotion Moderne et Humanisme Chrétien," in: G. Verbeke and J. IJsewijn, eds., *The Later Middle Ages and the Dawn of Humanism Outside Italy* (Louvain and The Hague, 1972), 57-66.

Grote's attitude towards study was as utilitarian as was Zerbolt's. Grote wrote in this connection: Item bonus homo in studio vel lectione non debet querere scienciam, sed saporem et devotionem, quia melius est modicum spiritus quam multa litera vel scientia. Item. Inicium [sic] omnis studij debet esse timor sive amor dei (*Aliqua verba notabilia domini Florentii et magistri Gherardi magni*, ed. by J. F. Vregt, "Eenige ascetische tractaten afkomstig van de Deventerse Broederschap van het Gemene Leven in verband gebracht met de *Imitatio* van Th. a Kempis," *AGAU*, X [1882], 455).

[215] Cf. Goossens, *Meditatie*, 103.

[216] *Ibid.*, 97-99.

[217] Cassian, *Conferences*, No. 1, ch. 18.

[218] Zerbolt very conventionally defines meditation in terms of *ruminare* and *pertractare*

Zerbolt further deals with such questions as the times of day to be set aside for meditation, and the specific topics to be meditated on at such times.[219] He advises that meditation, as well as spiritual reading, be carried out mornings and evenings, which further illustrates the close relationship which existed between these two activities. Together they constituted the *studium spirituale*.[220] The evening meditation, he ends, may be carried out in connection with the daily examination of conscience.

Although certain hours of the day were set aside for meditation on certain prescribed topics,[221] that did not mean that for the remainder of the day one could dispense with meditation. According to Zerbolt it is necessary to meditate every hour of the day,[222] and this was facilitated by the type of manual labour engaged in by the Brethren of the Common Life.[223]

Zerbolt defines prayer as an affection of the believer who cleaves to God, and as a familiar and loving converse with him.[224] This definition of prayer Zerbolt derived directly from William of St. Thierry's *Golden Epistle*, for it cannot be found in Radewijns' *Tractatulus Devotus* or *Omnes, inquit, artes*.[225] In defining prayer in these terms Zerbolt makes affection the essence of prayer, and in doing so also makes prayer an act of the will.[226]

(*Asc.*, 276G). Cf. M. Goossens, "Méditation (dans la "Devotio Moderna")," *DSp*, X, 916.

Zerbolt adds that the topics which instil compunction have been discussed in earlier chapters.

[219] For the suggestions he offers in this connection he is indebted to Jerome, St. Benedict and William of St. Thierry (cf. Goossens, *Meditatie*, 99-102).

[220] Cf. Goossens, *Meditatie*, 97, 99-100 and 103-104.

[221] Cf. de Bruin, ed., *Epistola de vita et passione domini nostri Iesu Christi*, 11-18.

[222] *Ref.*, 245H.

[223] Earlier in this century H. Watrigant asserted that the early Devotionalists, of whom Zerbolt was one, already practised a methodical form of meditation like that found in some late fifteenth-century works such as the *Scala Meditatoria* of Wessel Gansfort and the *Rosetum exercitiorum spiritualum et sacrarum meditationum* of John Mombaer. Van Rooy repeated what Watrigant had written with regard to this question, and he asserted that Zerbolt's great contribution lay in popularizing a formal method of meditation through his two manuals: *De Reformatione* and *De Ascensionibus*. However, Goossens has shown quite conclusively that the first Devotionalists did not contribute anything to the development of a formal method of meditation. Their method of meditation was traditional. Goossens concludes that their contribution lies in the care with which they ordered and arranged the materials for meditation, in the care they took to have material for meditation at hand at all times, and in the great emphasis placed by them on the need to meditate at all times, even while working (Watrigant, "La méditation méthodique et l'école des Fréres de la vie commune," 134-155; Van Rooy, *Zerbolt*, 265; Goossens, *Meditatie*, 95-115 and 203-205; and Post, *The Modern Devotion*, 323-325, 328-330 and 542-549).

[224] *Asc.*, 276A: Est enim oratio hominis Deo adhaerentis affectio, et familiaris quaedam et pia allocutio.

[225] Cf. Goossens, *Meditatie*, 106-107.

[226] *Ibid.*, 107.

The source of *affectio* which constitutes the essence of prayer is meditation: i.e., meditation on one's sinfulness, the four last things and God's
goodness to man. Consequently *affectio* is a complex sentiment. It can be
compunction of fear, or compunction of hope and love. One must,
therefore, prepare oneself for prayer by meditating on one's sinfulness,
the four last things, etc. in order that one may come to prayer with an affection of repentance, grief, fear, hope, love or thankfulness.[227] The
strength and virtue of prayer arises from the affection of him that prays,
for God hears the desire of the heart rather than the sound of the lips,
Zerbolt explains. Thus *lectio*, *meditatio* and *oratio* constitute an organic
unit. Reading provides the material for meditation, meditation moulds
the affection, and it is out of an affection of fear, hope, love or
thankfulness that prayer arises.[228] For this relationship between *lectio*,
meditatio and *oratio* Zerbolt, like Radewijns, is indebted to Hugh of St.
Victor, directly as well as by way of David of Augsburg.[229]

D) *Spiritual Perfection Impossible in This Life*

Zerbolt wrote *De Reformatione* and *De Ascensionibus* to assist the religious
in their quest for spiritual perfection. However, he ends with the observation that, in this life at least, spiritual perfection lies beyond man's
reach.[230] As a result of the fall man lost his gratuitous immunity from
natural, rebellious concupiscence, and as a result of the fall the will's inclination towards the good was weakened as well. As a consequence of
these two developments man is forever lured into committing sins,[231] and
therefore a total purge of sins, vices, lusts and inordinate love for created
things is virtually impossible in this life. The result is that perfect charity,
namely the love of God above all in all things and the basis for the vision

---

[227] Cf. *De Spiritu et Anima*, *PL*, XL, 816; and P. Régamey, "La componction du
coeur," *VSp*, XLV (1935), Supplément, 15.

[228] Cf. Goossens, *Meditatie*, 110-111.

[229] Hugh of St. Victor, *De Modo Orandi*, *PL*, CLXXVI, 977, 978-979 and 985; D. of
Augsburg, *De ext. et int. hom. compositione*, II, 156-160. Cf. Goossens, *Meditatie*, 111 and
118-120; Persoons, "Het Intellectuele Leven in het Klooster Bethlehem in de 15de
Eeuw," 67-69; and H. J. Sieben, "Lectio Divina et Lecture Spirituelle, II: De la Lectio
Divina à la Lecture Spirituelle," *DSp*, IX, 490.

[230] Zerbolt deals with this question in ch. 42 (p. 275F-G) of *De Ascensionibus*, and the title of this chapter reads: *Quod perfecte in hac vita nullum de praemissis tribus gradibus possumus
consummare.*

[231] *Asc.*, 275G: Nec tamen putes quod aliquem istorum graduum usque ad summum
vel perfectum in hac vita possumus ascendere. Nec enim in hac vita possumus omnes con-
cupiscentias expurgare,... *Ref.*, 252F-G: Credite mihi,...severitate succidere. *Asc.*, 280E:
Cum autem...denuo excitanter. For the last two passages Zerbolt is indebted to one of St.
Bernard's *Sermons on the Song of Songs*, as Zerbolt himself indicates. Cf. Cassian, *Institutes*,
Bk. V, ch. 19.

of God, can never be anything more than a temporary and fleeting experience.

Rebellious concupiscence, which impedes the quest for a pure heart, is, of course, a natural consequence of the fact that man possesses a body, senses and sensible appetites. Therefore, as long as he is in the body it will be extremely difficult for man to love God perfectly, and he will virtually always remain alienated from God to a degree. While on earth man's affections will be divided; some will be directed towards God, others toward things of this earth, both material and non-material. The body with the sensible appetites weighs down the soul and prevents it from ascending to God, its proper end. The bodily senses and appetites draw man's soul towards many and varied creaturely things, and prevent its flight to God.[232] Zerbolt concludes with the admonition that the believer, even though he cannot achieve a state of spiritual perfection in this life, must, nonetheless, make a valiant effort in that direction. He must do his utmost to ascend as far as he can.[233]

Such contributions as man makes to his own spiritual improvement and ascent are not made naturally: i.e., without the aid of grace. Man cannot ascend by his own virtue, Zerbolt writes, but continually needs help from on high, for without the aid of grace man's diligence is in vain.[234] Like David of Augsburg, Zerbolt believes that in all one's virtues, spiritual progress and good works it is God's grace which arouses the will to act, and God's grace which enables man actually to fight vice, to progress in virtue and to do good works.[235] Man must reach up his

---

[232] *Asc.*, 275G: Sed nec quam diu vivimus possumus omnes affectiones sursum levare, quin aliquid remaneat in terra. Corpus quod corrumpitur aggravat animam, et deprimit terrena inhabitatio sensum multa cogitantem. Sed multo minus possumus tam parati et idonei fieri, ut possimus iugiter Deo adhaerere. Quoniam quamdiu sumus in corpore, peregrinamur ab Deo. Cf. W. Yeomans, "St. Bernard of Clairvaux," in Walsh, ed., *Spirituality Through the Centuries*, 117-119.

[233] *Asc.*, 275G: Sed isti sunt gradus et profectus, quibus nostra fragilitas ascensiones debet disponere, et successive quantum poterit proficere ascendendo.

[234] *Asc.*, 258H: Verum quia ascensus iste non est in currente vel ascendente, sed ex dono Dei miserentis, ideo quarto tibi consulitur ab Domino adiutorium et auxilium postulandum, quia nulla est industria tua, nisi te in omnibus divina gratia comitetur. Cf. van Rooy, *Zerbolt*, 252-253 and 254-255. *Asc.*, 282C: Sed super hunc est adhuc alterior et tertius gradus, cum videlicet per longa exercitia et multos labores, divina adiuvante gratia, ita concupiscentias carnis edomuisti, quod vix rarissime et tenuissime sentiatur, ... Cf. van Rooy, *Zerbolt*, 252-253 and 254-255.

[235] *Ref.*, 257D: Qui autem huius nequissimi spiritus laqueos vult evadere, debet in singulis virtutibus, in quibus se senserit profecisse dicere ex sententia: Gratia Dei sum id quod sum, et cogitare Deum esse qui operatur in nobis velle et perficere, pro bona voluntate. *Asc.*, 284G: Sed ut etiam hunc tumorem interdum deprimas et ad praefatum humilitatis gradum ascendas, debes in omnibus virtutibus in omni profectu, in omnibus bonis operibus, ex toto corde, et ex sententia dicere et sentire: Non ego, sed gratia Dei mecum, et gratia Dei sum id quod sum, et Deus est qui operatur velle et perficere pro bona voluntate. *Asc.*, 277G: ...: multo amplius et saepius debemus orare pro divina

hand to God who awaits him at the top of the ladder of the spiritual ascent, and beseech God to draw him unto Himself.[236]

E) *Assessment*

In the first pages of this chapter it was observed that for Zerbolt the end of the spiritual life is purity of heart, charity and the vision of God. There is little doubt that he understood the state of charity to be a contemplative one as he did the vision of God. Purity of heart is the indispensable precondition for charity as well as for the vision of God. However, while man, aided by divine grace, can, and must, contribute to purity of heart and charity, the vision of God remains a totally gratuitous gift. The believer can prepare himself for the vision of God by means of purity of heart and charity, but he himself cannot directly effect the vision of God as he can purity of heart and charity. Consequently Zerbolt concentrates his attention on achieving charity and its prerequisite, namely purity of heart. However, in the final analysis purity of heart rather than charity is his first concern.

By a pure heart Zerbolt understands the absence of sinful concupiscence, evil passions, sinful desires and vices. However, if all of these irregularities are present in the believer it is because the will is deformed, or is wrongly directed. The passions and vices result when the will succumbs to natural, rebellious concupiscence. Consequently, if the heart is to be cleansed the will must be reformed in order that it may be able to do battle with rebellious concupiscence which entices man into sin, and the established vices and passions must be extirpated. It is with the reformation of the will, and the eradication of the vices which are the result of rebellious concupiscence and a wrongly directed will, that both *De Reformatione* and *De Ascensionibus* are primarily concerned. Throughout both works, then, Zerbolt does not lose sight of his goal: purity of heart, which is the prerequisite for charity and the vision of God.

That it is necessary to cleanse one's soul of all vices and passions as a preparation for contemplation is a teaching which goes back to Origen at least, and it was passed on to Evagrius Ponticus who was John Cassian's

---

gratia, pro remissione peccatorum, pro adeptione regni coelorum, pro expurgatione vitiorum et acquisitione virtutum. *Asc.*, 279C: Quantum vitia extinguis, quantum in virtutibus proficis, tantum in hac devotione, nisi ab Deo tibi dispensatorie subtrahatur. Cf. *Ref.*, 238F-G; and D. of Augsburg, *De ext. et int. hom. compositione*, I, 110-111.

[236] *Asc.*, 259A-B: Sed adhuc in pede vel ascensu scalae positus in te deficiens et altitudinem eius prospiciens, debes sursum manus extendere ad Dominum, qui est innixus supremae parti scalae, et clamare: Trahe me post te, et ita beatus eris, et sempiterna beatitudine perfrueris. Sed de his omnibus in sequentibus dicetur clarius singulatim.

"*Trahe me post te,*" is from the Song of Songs 1, 4. It would appear to have been a favourite text with the Devotionalists.

teacher in the spiritual life.[237] Zerbolt borrowed his ideas about the purpose of the spiritual life from Cassian's *Conferences*. It was to combat vices and passions, to cleanse the heart of all sins, to achieve *apatheia*, that thousands, including Cassian, headed for the Egyptian desert in the fourth and fifth centuries.[238] *De Reformatione* and *De Ascensionibus* were primarily written to guide the religious in his search for *apatheia*, the prerequisite for charity and the vision of God. With respect to the goals of the religious life, then, Zerbolt followed in the footsteps of the entire monastic tradition.

For Zerbolt compunction more than anything else contributes to purity of heart. It will be recalled that *compunctio ex timore* and *compunctio ex amore* play an all important role in Zerbolt's doctrine of justification. They help to make contrition possible without which man cannot be justified.[239] Furthermore, we have observed that, after he has been justified through the sacrament of penance, man ascends to charity by way of compunction of fear followed by compunction of hope and love. Compunction of fear is necessary for the extirpation of sinful concupiscence and cupidity in general, while compunction of hope and love draw one to God and to charity.[240] Finally, compunction of fear and compunction of hope and love contribute to the eradication of the capital sins and the cultivation of the corresponding virtues in particular.[241] It may be concluded, then, that compunction plays a central role in Zerbolt's entire spiritual program in which purity of heart is the first objective.[242]

Since compunction was, in Zerbolt's opinion, the best way to achieve the end of the spiritual life, uninterrupted meditation also came to play an important part in Zerbolt's spirituality. For compunction is cultivated by means of meditation. This, of course, lent Zerbolt's spirituality a high degree of inwardness.[243]

It is in his reliance on compunction, an activity of the mind, as the way to purity of heart that Zerbolt differs from those belonging to the earlier monastic tradition. The latter, in contrast to Zerbolt, put much greater emphasis on bodily mortification as the method to eradicate sinful concupiscence, passions and vices.[244] In transferring the struggle for a pure heart from the body to the soul, or the mind, Zerbolt spiritualized an im-

---

[237] Mohler, *The Heresy of Monasticism*, 41.

[238] Cf. A. de Vogüé, "Monachisme et Eglise dans la Pensée de Cassien," in: *Théologie*, 230-231.

[239] *De Reformatione*: first reformation of the will; *De Ascensionibus*: first ascent.

[240] *De Reformatione*: reformation of the memory; *De Ascensionibus*: second ascent.

[241] *De Reformatione*: second reformation of the will; *De Ascensionibus*: third ascent.

[242] Cf. Goossens, *Meditatie*, 27 and 136-137.

[243] Cf. Richard, *The Spirituality of John Calvin*, 33.

[244] Cf. Mohler, *The Heresy of Monasticism*, throughout.

portant aspect of the religious life.[245] However, in doing so he was merely continuing a trend which was more than a century old when he was writing. In the thirteenth century, or even earlier, according to P. Salmon, there began a trend to spiritualize Christian asceticism, and it gained momentum in the following centuries.[246] David of Augsburg and Bonaventure, both of whom had a considerable impact on Zerbolt, were among the first important representatives of this new trend. Both of them stressed the importance of inner, spiritual exercises as the way to purity of heart and the contemplation of God. They did so at the expense of the traditional monastic practices which aimed at mortification of the body, although that was not their intention. The ascetical practices which had always been the essence of the religious life, because they constituted the means by which the religious achieved purity of heart and charity, now became, in a sense, irrelevant. Together they now constituted merely the external framework within which the religious strove for *apatheia* through internal, spiritual exercises. For Bonaventure, as was to be the case for Zerbolt, meditation was the most important spiritual exercise as a means to achieve the goal of the religious life.[247]

Salmon is of the opinion that the Devotionalists completed the process by which the traditional monastic practices were gradually spiritualized.[248] That is, perhaps, an overstatement, because Zerbolt, as well as the Devotionalists following him, did not deny the validity, and usefulness, of the traditional monastic practices and exercises in the struggle against the vices and for a pure heart. In fact, the Devotionalists were in the forefront of the observance movement which aimed at enforcing the traditional monastic vows of poverty, chastity and obedience, as well as all the other customary rules and practices.[249] We have noted that Zerbolt also attributed considerable importance to these practices in the fight against the capital sins. Nonetheless, on balance he regards compunction arising from meditation, a mental activity, to be the best method of cleansing the heart of concupiscence, vice and passion. In thus spiritualizing an important aspect of the religious life, Zerbolt made this mode of life accessible to a greater number of people than had been the case before, and in that sense he democratized it.[250] For meditation, the source of compunction which cleanses the heart of sin and draws man to God, can, of course, be carried out in a non-monastic setting.

---

[245] Cf. Klinkenberg, "Die Devotio Moderna unter dem Thema 'Antiqui-Moderni' Betrachtet," 416.

[246] Salmon, "L'ascèse monastique et la spiritualité," 238.

[247] *Ibid.*, 214-220; and Phillips, "The Way to Religious Perfection According to St. Bonaventure's *De Triplici Via*," 57-58.

[248] Salmon, "L'ascèse monastique et la spiritualité," 238.

[249] Post, *The Modern Devotion*, 310-313; idem, *Kerkgeschiedenis*, I, 325-361 and II, 97-175.

[250] Cf. Richard, *The Spirituality of John Calvin*, 33.

CONCLUSION

It has been asserted in the past that the unity between dogmatic theology and spirituality, typical of the church fathers as well as of later writers like the Victorines and Bonaventure, was totally absent from the thought of the Devotionalists.[1] This thesis clearly does not apply to Zerbolt. For his two manuals for the spiritual life, *De Reformatione* and *De Ascensionibus*, contain a considerable body of doctrines which are commonly classified as dogmatic theology, and Zerbolt's spiritual theology is based firmly on a foundation of dogmatic thought. For example, Zerbolt displays a considerable interest in Christ's two natures, and he does so because Christ's divinity and humanity can, when meditated on, contribute to the growth of compunction of fear and compunction of hope and love respectively.

Briefly recapitulating the major themes of Zerbolt's theological thought we may begin with his view that man can contribute to his own spiritual progress before and after his reconciliation with God in the sacrament of penance. Man can do so, because the fall has not totally destroyed his capacity to choose, and to do, the good. The will in particular is capable of promoting man's spiritual progress, and this reliance on the will, rather than on the intellect, in the quest for spiritual improvement may have been the consequence of an influence brought to bear on Zerbolt by the *moderni*.[2] Augustine's view that man is 'bound' by evil is rejected or, better, evaded. However, divine grace is far from superfluous. Without grace, faith and contrition are impossible, and thereby Zerbolt rejects the opposite extreme, namely that of a semi-Pelagian like Gabriel Biel. Grace is needed as well for man's further spiritual ascent following his justification, and for the good works performed in the state of grace. On balance, Zerbolt's views regarding the relative importance of grace and nature would appear to be moderate, and it would perhaps not be incorrect to label them Thomistic. Nonetheless, on occasion Zerbolt so emphasizes the primacy of grace, especially in connection with good works performed in the state of grace, that the otherwise prevalent 'balance' between grace and nature is lost. However, Zerbolt's strong emphasis on the need of grace to perform good works is motivated primarily by his concern to keep pride, the destroyer of all virtues, at bay.

---

[1] P. Debongnie, "Dévotion Moderne," *DSp*, III, 744.

[2] De Beer, *Spiritualiteit*, 284; and C. C. de Bruin, *Handboek der Kerkgeschiedenis*, Vol. II: *De Middeleeuwen* (Leeuwarden, 1980), 228.

The ultimate objectives of the spiritual life, which can be achieved only through Christ, are the affective contemplation and intellectual vision of God, although the latter remains, in the final analysis, a totally gratuitous gift for which the believer can prepare himself, but which he himself cannot effect. However, the immediate goal of the spiritual life is a pure and passionless heart: *apatheia*. For only someone who is free from all inordinate desire and love for created things can love God for his own sake, and it is on the means to cleanse the soul of sin and vice that Zerbolt concentrates his attention. *De Reformatione* and *De Ascensionibus*, both of them manuals for the spiritual life, serve in the first place as guides for those in search of *apatheia*.

The soul may be cleansed of sinful concupiscence and vices in two ways. In the first place they may be eradicated through imitation of Christ in his humanity, for Christ is the supreme example of virtue whose every action was carried out for man's instruction. Consequently, Zerbolt is interested primarily in Christ's exemplary work of atonement, and to a much lesser degree in his vicariously redemptive life and death. The second method to cleanse the soul of all inordinate desires and vices is not by means of an active imitation of Christ in one's daily life and conduct, but by means of meditation, an activity of the mind. Meditation on God's punishment of sin in the hereafter will instil compunction of fear, and it in turn will drive out sin. Meditation on the benefits bestowed by God on man, among which must be counted the incarnation of his own Son, will implant compunction of hope and love in the believer, and so draw man to God. For that reason Zerbolt's interest in God is restricted primarily to God's attitude *vis-à-vis* fallen man, which is one of wrath tempered by mercy. It is also for the purpose of instilling compunction that Zerbolt dwells at some length on Christ's dual nature. For meditation on Christ's divinity and role as judge stimulates the growth of compunction of fear, while meditation on his humanity and redemptive work fosters compunction of hope and love. In this instance Zerbolt's use of dogmatic theology in support of his spiritual theology is very clearly illustrated.

Taking everything into account, it would appear that, as a means of cleansing the soul of sin, Zerbolt regards meditation on those topics which instil compunction as being more effective than imitation of Christ in his humanity. Even practical imitation of Christ, then, is of secondary importance in Zerbolt's spirituality in comparison with meditation which is a mental activity. In thus replacing mortification of the body with meditation as the best means to achieve purity of heart, Zerbolt spiritualized an important aspect of the religious life. Spiritualization of the religious life in this fashion was particularly typical of the Franciscans.³ Mortification of the body played a central role in the spiritual theology of John Cassian and John Climacus. However, in the spiritual theology of the Franciscans, and in that of Bonaventure in particular, bodily mortification was replaced by spiritual exercises like meditation as the most effective means to cleanse the heart of sin. Consequently, if one must give Zerbolt's spirituality a name, the epithet Franciscan would best describe it,⁴ and in fact Franciscan spirituality dominated the spirituality of the later middle ages.⁵ However, the influence of Cassian, Climacus, Bernard of Clairvaux and William of St. Thierry, all of whom left their mark on the Franciscans as well, must not be overlooked.

Even though the label "Franciscan" may be a useful one to describe Zerbolt's spirituality, that does not mean that it lacked all idiosyncratic characteristics or traits. What sets Zerbolt's spirituality apart from that of Bernard of Clairvaux and Bonaventure is its almost exclusive preoccupation with the ascetical life, for Bernard and Bonaventure were very much interested in the mystical aspect of the religious life. Consistent with this rather limited interest, Zerbolt read primarily those works which assisted him in his quest for *apatheia*.⁶ Furthermore, Zerbolt's overriding concern with the ascetical phase of the spiritual life, in which the emphasis falls on the eradication of sinful concupiscence and vice, lends his spirituality a generally somber tone.⁷ Finally, the practical, concrete, anti-speculative and non-contemplative nature of Zerbolt's spirituality would appear to indicate a mentality profoundly influenced by the *via moderna* notwithstanding the fact that Zerbolt's thought also contains elements characteristic of the *via antiqua*, such as his epistemological views, for example.⁸

The analysis of Zerbolt's thought clearly reveals that he cannot be called a great theologian or an original thinker. However, the popularity of his writings in the fifteenth and sixteenth centuries suggests that he contributed not insignificantly to the spiritual development of northwestern Europe during this period. For it is commonly recognized now

---

³ Salmon, "L'ascèse monastique et la spiritualité," 195-240; and Phillips, "The Way to Religious Perfection According to St. Bonaventure's *De Triplici Via*," 47 and 57-58.

⁴ Cf. Post, *De Moderne Devotie*, 138-141.

⁵ Oberman, "The Shape of Late Medieval Thought: The Birthpangs of the Modern Era," 7.

⁶ Cf. Post, *De Moderne Devotie*, 138-142; and Richard, *The Spirituality of John Calvin*, 32-33.

⁷ Cf. W. Lourdaux, "Gérard Zerbolt de Zutphen," *DSp*, VI, 287-288; and Goossens, *Meditatie*, 26-27.

⁸ Cf. van Rooy, *Zerbolt*, 274-276; de Beer, *Spiritualiteit*, 283-285; Goossens, *Meditatie*, 31; de Bruin, *Handboek der Kerkgeschiedenis*, Vol. II: *De Middeleeuwen*, 228; and P. Mestwerdt, *Die Anfänge des Erasmus: Humanismus und "Devotio Moderna"* (Leipzig, 1917), 99-112.

that writings like those of Zerbolt, and especially when they circulated widely as did *De Reformatione* and *De Ascensionibus*, were as important in shaping the theological and spiritual thought of the later middle ages as were the works of greater, and more original, thinkers than the subject of this study.[9] Therefore, if one is to understand the general religious climate of north-western Europe in the later middle ages, Zerbolt's writings deserve as much attention as do those of more prominent writers. This fact alone would have justified an examination of Zerbolt's theological thought.

The widespread demand for Zerbolt's two manuals for the spiritual life throughout north-western Europe would appear to have had a number of reasons. In the first place they were doctrinally acceptable. There was nothing objectionable about Zerbolt's dogmatic theology which has, on the whole, an Augustinian-Thomistic flavour. Furthermore, Zerbolt's spiritual theology was in tune with the times in its tendency to spiritualize the ascetical life. However, perhaps the biggest reason why *De Reformatione* and *De Ascensionibus* enjoyed the popularity they did is Zerbolt's lucid and systematic presentation of the active phase of the spiritual life. It was this quality in particular which would appear to have generated such a great demand for Zerbolt's two manuals in the fifteenth century and the early part of the sixteenth.

If the influence of Zerbolt's writings on the general spiritual climate of north-western Europe during the later middle ages calls for an examination of their contents, an even more cogent reason for studying Zerbolt's thought is the fact that he, one of the first members of the Modern Devotion, contributed a great deal to determining the thought of the newly established movement and to giving direction to its spirituality in particular.[10] In addition to systematizing and giving form to the thought of Grote and Radewijns, the principal founders of the Modern Devotion, Zerbolt himself contributed a great deal to the form and content of Devotionalist thought and practice. What remains to be done, then, is to relate Zerbolt's theological thought, both dogmatic and spiritual, to that of the Modern Devotion. We are, however, somewhat hampered in doing so by the absence of a comprehensive, in-depth study of the thought of the

---

[9] Cf. H. A. Oberman, "Fourteenth-Century Religious Thought: A Premature Profile," *Speculum*, LIII (1978), 93.

[10] The relative importance of Zerbolt and other early Devotionalists in shaping the spirituality of the *Devotio Moderna* is, considering the present state of scholarship, difficult to establish with any degree of accuracy. A. Gruijs' argument, which is based on relevant extant manuscripts, that Jan van Schoonhoven (1356-1432) was the theorist *par excellence* of the Devotionalist movement is highly debatable (Jean de Schoonhoven, *De Contemptu Huius Mundi*, ed. by A. Gruijs, 97).

Modern Devotion.[11] In relating Zerbolt's dogmatic theological thought to that of the Modern Devotion we are forced to rely primarily on studies of individual Devotionalists, and on inquiries into certain aspects of Devotionalist thought such as Mak's study of the Devotionalists' understanding of Christ, his person and his work. Axters' study of the spirituality of the Devotionalists is useful for our purpose, in spite of the fact that it cannot be called an exhaustive and definitive inquiry into Devotionalist spirituality.[12]

With his relatively positive view of fallen man Zerbolt provided the Devotionalists with an anthropology which allowed them to stress the believer's ability to contribute to his own salvation prior to his justification through the sacrament of penance, as well as afterwards. Zerbolt did not, however, neglect the role played by grace in man's spiritual ascent. Every step of the way the believer needs aid from on high. That man cannot make a beginning with his salvation, or make any kind of spiritual progress whatsoever, without the aid of grace was generally acknowledged by the Devotionalists, and Thomas a Kempis, for example, emphasizes the indispensability of divine grace time and again.[13] However, the nature and operation of grace do not receive much attention from the Devotionalists, the result, no doubt, of their little interest in dogmatic

---

[11] A comprehensive, in-depth study of the thought of the *Devotio Moderna* has never been attempted, which is perhaps surprising in view of the fact that this aspect of the movement constitutes its soul (cf. Alberts, "Zur Historiographie der *Devotio Moderna* und Ihrer Erforschung," 15). However, apart from the fact that it is much easier to describe the institutional side of the *Devotio Moderna* than its thought, a detailed investigation of the latter soon reveals that with regard to thought the *Devotio Moderna* was not a monolithic movement (cf. Oberman, *Biel*, 351, footnote 87). That, of course, makes a comprehensive and detailed study of this aspect of the movement extremely difficult. As a movement for practical spiritual reform and improvement the *Devotio Moderna* advocated a distinct approach to the spiritual life to which its members generally subscribed, and in that sense one can speak of the *Devotio Moderna* as constituting a unique 'school' of spiritual thought and practice. However, apart from the generally accepted theories and views with regard to spiritual improvement and reform there is little unanimity among the Devotionalists. Once one goes beyond the commonly-held views on the spiritual life dissimilar and conflicting theological and philosophical opinions, to the extent that they are found in the writings of the Devotionalists, become evident. This perhaps stems from the fact that the Devotionalists lacked formal theological training and that they did not subscribe to the views of any particular theologian in contrast with most of the religious orders (cf. Mestwerdt, *Die Anfänge des Erasmus: Humanismus und "Devotio Moderna,"* 117). This philosophical and theological individualism of the Devotionalists was similar to that of the Carthusians (cf. B. du Moustier, "Carthusian Spirituality," *NCE*, III, 161; and van Zijl, *Groote*, 104-105 and 112-116), and the Devotionalists may have been influenced by the Carthusians in this matter.

[12] Axters, *Vroomheid*, III, 27-198.

[13] Th. a Kempis, *De Imitatione Christi*, Bk. I, chs. 7, 11, 12, 14 and 15; Bk. II, chs. 8, 9, 10, and 12; and Bk. III, chs. 9, 40, 54, 55 and 56.

theology.[14] Consequently the Devotionalists tend to leave the impression of depreciating the significance of grace for man's spiritual ascent.

A positive view of fallen man, a prerequisite for the belief that the believer can contribute to his own salvation, is a prominent feature in the works of Dirc van Herxen, after Zerbolt the most important writer to emerge from the Brotherhood. It is particularly in his four pedagogical tracts that van Herxen's anthropological views are found. He does not, of course, deny that man's predilection for the good has suffered as a result of the fall. From his birth onward, van Herxen writes, man is naturally inclined towards evil. However, he is of the opinion that the predilection for evil is relatively weak in children and adolescents. For that reason he regards it as highly important that adolescents be converted—and for him this means entry into a religious institution—before the considerable connatural inclination towards the good which remained after the fall is totally suffocated by the world.[15] It was for the purpose of inculcating a desire for the religious vocation in boys that the Brethren established *bursae* in such cities as Deventer and Zwolle where there were large Latin schools.

For Gerard Grote, Christ was in the first place *dux* who leads man to God and salvation by means of his exemplary life. Christ's vicariously redemptive work plays a smaller role in Grote's thought than does Christ's exemplary work of atonement.[16] For Johannes Brinckerinck, Grote's close associate, Christ was almost exclusively example and guide in the quest for spiritual perfection.[17] In his writings Zerbolt considerably reinforces this trend to stress Christ's exemplary work of atonement at the expense of his vicariously redemptive work. It is perhaps not surprising, then, that an important element in, and characteristic of, Devotionalist thought is a preoccupation with Christ's work of subjective atonement, and a considerable neglect of Christ's work of objective atonement.[18] This peculiarity of Devotionalist thought is very much in evidence in *De Imitatione Christi*. For in this work there are only a few vague references to Christ's redemptive death on the cross, all of them in the fourth book which is devoted to the eucharist. Christ's didactic and exemplary work receives, in comparison with Christ's vicariously redemptive work, considerable attention from Thomas a Kempis.[19] For

---

[14] Goossens, *Meditatie*, 30.

[15] Knierim, *Dirc van Herxen (1385-1457), rector van het Zwolse fraterhuis*, 107-109.

[16] Mak, "Christus bij de Moderne Devoten," 118, 125 and 135-136.

[17] *Ibid.*, 119.

[18] *Ibid.*, 105-166; and R. Steensma, *Het Klooster Thabor bij Sneek en zijn nagelaten geschriften* (Leeuwarden, 1970), 210.

[19] Th. a Kempis, *De Imitatione Christi*, Bk. I, ch. 25; Bk. III, chs. 18 and 43; and Bk. IV, chs. 4, 7 and 8.

him the cross represents in the first place the sum of all virtues,[20] rather than vicarious atonement for man's sins.

The Devotionalists were, on the whole, more interested in Christ the man than in Christ the God, a logical consequence of their soteriology.[21] For only Christ the man can serve as a guide and example in man's quest for spiritual perfection. Some Devotionalists were, in fact, so preoccupied with Christ's humanity, and his exemplary work of atonement, that they had difficulty in accepting the true divinity of Christ.[22] In its overriding preoccupation with Christ's humanity the Devotionalist movement differed from Zerbolt. For, even though Zerbolt stressed Christ's work of subjective atonement at the expense of his work of objective atonement, he did not neglect Christ's divinity. Zerbolt emphasizes the importance of reflecting and meditating on Christ's divinity to the same degree that one meditates on Christ's humanity which the believer can, and must, imitate.

Zerbolt's considerable efforts to strike a balance between Christ's divinity and humanity were determined and motivated by his views regarding compunction. He expressed the view that nothing is safer for man than to be suspended between compunction of fear and reverence on the one hand, and compunction of hope and love on the other. Fear drives out sin, as well as complacency, while hope and love prevent the development of despair and draw man to God. Meditation on Christ's divinity stimulates the growth of fear, while meditation on Christ's humanity contributes to the development of hope and love. Meditation on a variety of topics as a means to instil compunction played an important role in the Devotionalists' spirituality, but it does not appear that they were in the habit of meditating on Christ's dual nature as a way to cultivate compunction of fear and hope.[23]

Of the seven sacraments, only penance and the eucharist receive considerable attention from Zerbolt. He makes the sacrament of penance, by means of which the believer is reconciled to God, the basis of the spiritual life and progress. The eucharist, because it contains Christ himself, is of all the sacraments the most important vehicle of grace. Purity of conscience, one of the prerequisites for a valid and fruitful communion, can be achieved only by means of the sacrament of penance. And so Zerbolt establishes a close relationship between these two sacraments in *De Reformatione* and *De Ascensionibus*.

---

[20] *Ibid.*, Bk. II, ch. 12.

[21] Cf. Goossens, *Meditatie*, 30; and Steensma, *Het Klooster Thabor bij Sneek en zijn nagelaten geschriften*, 210.

[22] Mak, "Christus bij de Moderne Devoten," 112-113 and 127-128.

[23] Cf. Axters, *Vroomheid*, III, 27-198.

In view of the fact that Zerbolt, who played such a leading role in shaping the thought and practice of the Devotionalists, was particularly interested in the sacraments of penance and the eucharist, it comes as no surprise that these same two sacraments played an important role in the thought and lives of the Devotionalists.[24] Goossens' assertion that the Devotionalists were little interested in the sacraments is not borne out by the sources.[25] We have seen that the Devotionalists communed more frequently than their predecessors and contemporaries, and indications are that Zerbolt was at least partly responsible for the practice of frequent communion among the Devotionalists. Furthermore, because Zerbolt stressed the importance of confession as an indispensable prerequisite for fruitful communion, it would appear that he also helped to bring about the practice of frequent confession among the Devotionalists. The constitutions of the Augustinian Canons and Canonesses Regular of the Congregation of Windesheim prescribed communion, preceded by confession, once every two weeks.[26] The Brethren and Sisters of the Common Life did not communicate nearly as often as did the Augustinian Canons and Canonesses Regular, but communion presumably had, as with the latter, to be preceded by confession.[27] The importance which the Brethren attributed to confession is evident from their so-called 'confession books' in which they recorded all their misdemeanors, either real or imagined.[28]

In the past the Devotionalists have, on occasion, been accused of holding, and propagating, views detrimental to the hierarchy and the church.[29] However, most of these allegations lack credibility in the light of the importance attached by the Devotionalists to the sacraments of penance and the eucharist. The only point on which the Devotionalists could realistically be charged with undermining the church is that of spiritual communion. Brinckerinck, a contemporary of Zerbolt, already made a great deal of spiritual communion. He, in fact, went so far as to assert that the believer would not suffer should he never again attend church and commune sacramentally, provided he communed spiritually on a daily basis.[30] And a tendency, suggestive of a nominalistic influence,

---

[24] Cf. Axters, *Vroomheid*, III, 73-74, 163-164; G. J. M. Kuiper, *Huis en Klooster St. Antonius te Albergen* (n. pl., n. d.), 106.

[25] Goossens, *Meditatie*, 30.

[26] Axters, *Vroomheid*, III, 163; Acquoy, *Windesheim*, I, 154; and Post, *Kerkelijke Verhoudingen in Nederland voor de Reformatie*, 408.

[27] Hyma, *The Christian Renaissance*, 471-472; Jacobus de Voecht, *Narratio*, 272; and Alberts and Ditsche, eds., *Fontes Historiam Domus Fratrum Embricensis Aperientes*, 91.

[28] Axters, *Vroomheid*, III, 74.

[29] Cf. Post, *The Modern Devotion*, 17-49.

[30] Brinckerinck, "Collatiën," 146.

to stress the efficacy of spiritual communion to the detriment of sacramental communion was to be a characteristic of Devotionalist thought.[31] Zerbolt, however, does not mention spiritual communion even once, and the absence in his writings of all references to spiritual communion reinforces one's conception of him as a faithful son of the church. Of all of Zerbolt's views only those on lay confession can be construed as being detrimental to the authority and position of the church and the hierarchy.

Another point of dogmatic theology in Zerbolt's writings which can be easily related to Devotionalist thought in general is that regarding good works performed in the state of grace. Zerbolt places considerable emphasis on the imperfect nature of good works performed in the state of grace, and he implies thereby that they are, as a consequence, insufficient. Furthermore, such goodness and meritoriousness as man's works do possess are not the result of man's own efforts, but of grace. The imperfection and insufficiency of human works performed in the state of grace, as well as their dependence on grace, were to remain prominent themes in Devotionalist thought. They can be found in the writings of Dirc van Herxen, a Brother of the Common Life, in the sermons of the Augustinian Canon Regular Bernard Arbostier, and in *De Imitatione Christi* of Thomas a Kempis, likewise an Augustinian Canon Regular. Van Herxen stresses the insufficiency of good works for man's salvation,[32] while both Bernard Arbostier and Thomas a Kempis emphasize that man cannot perform good, and meritorious, works without the aid of grace.[33] Like Zerbolt, Thomas a Kempis asserts that the realization that good works are possible only with the aid of divine grace is an effective weapon to combat pride and vainglory.[34] Arbostier adds that when God rewards man for his good works he is under no obligation to do so. When God rewards good works performed by man in the state of grace, he is moved solely by his goodness and mercy.[35] The Devotionalists did not, however, stand alone in their views on good works. The view that good works performed in the state of grace are imperfect, and therefore insufficient for man's salvation, was widely held in the later middle ages.[36]

---

[31] Cf. Steensma, *Het Klooster Thabor bij Sneek en zijn nagelaten geschriften*, 214.

[32] Knierim, *Dirc van Herxen (1385-1457), rector van het Zwolse fraterhuis*, 127.

[33] Steensma, *Het Klooster Thabor bij Sneek en zijn nagelaten geschriften*, 213-214; and Th. a Kempis, *De Imitatione Christi*, Bk. I, chs. 12 and 14, Bk. II, chs. 8, 10 and 12, and Bk. III, chs. 9, 40 and 55.

[34] Th. a Kempis, *De Imitatione Christi*, Bk. III, ch. 9.

[35] Steensma, *Het Klooster Thabor bij Sneek en zijn nagelaten geschriften*, 213-214.

[36] Zumkeller, "Das Ungenügen der menschlichen Werke bei den deutschen Predigern des Spätmittelalters," 265-305.

Zerbolt's understanding of predestination is essentially Augustinian-Thomistic. He held that God chose a certain number of individuals to be saved from eternal damnation *ante praevisa merita*. However, he viewed predestination as part and parcel of divine providence in general. God directs everything in the universe in such a way that those elected to eternal life *ante praevisa merita* will reach their preordained goal of salvation. Thomas a Kempis' understanding of predestination would appear to have been very similar to that of Zerbolt. For he writes that God has preordained everything in the universe to serve the salvation of the elect.[37]

Zerbolt held that man can never be certain whether he belongs to the predestined, because it is impossible for him to know whether his repentance is motivated by fear only, or whether he possesses contrition, the condition for justification, through the grace that is infused into him. Furthermore, the believer does not see himself as he is seen by God. He does not know what lies concealed in his own soul, but which is not hidden from God and might be displeasing to him. Finally, God's judgements are inscrutable. Thomas a Kempis advances some of the same reasons why man cannot know with certainty whether or not he belongs to the elect. Man may believe that his good works will earn him his salvation, but God judges by standards which are different from those employed by man.[38] Besides, God sees the heart of the believer, and he may find iniquities there unknown to the believer himself.[39] Lastly, Thomas a Kempis, like Zerbolt, holds certainty with regard to salvation to be extremely dangerous. Such certainty, he writes, would lead to complacency and pride.[40] Bernard Arbostier too expresses the view that man can never be certain whether he belongs to the predestined. However, he believes that there are at least twenty signs which may indicate that one belongs to those predestined to eternal life. Some of these signs are repentance for one's sins and a decline in inordinate concupiscent desires.[41]

These are, then, some of the similarities between Zerbolt's dogmatic views and the dogmatic opinions which would appear to have been in vogue among the Devotionalists. A more detailed comparison between Zerbolt's dogmatic theology and that of the Devotionalist movement is not possible because we do not have a comprehensive study of Devotionalist dogmatics. While there is no doubt that Zerbolt, whose writings were widely read by the Devotionalists, played a role in shaping such dogmatic views as were held by the Devotionalists, it is difficult to

---

[37] Th. a Kempis, *De Imitatione Christi*, Bk. I, ch. 13. Cf. Bk. I, ch. 11.
[38] *Ibid.*, Bk. I, ch. 7.
[39] *Ibid.*, Bk. III, ch. 46.
[40] *Ibid.*, Bk. I, ch. 25. Cf. Bk. I, ch. 20.
[41] Steensma, *Het Klooster Thabor bij Sneek en zijn nagelaten geschriften*, 213.

establish a positive relationship of cause and effect. One of the difficulties
in this respect is that the Devotionalists had, generally speaking, little
training in dogmatic theology, and judging by most of their writings they
would appear to have been little interested in it. In comparison with the
bulk of Devotionalist writings *De Reformatione* and *De Ascensionibus* contain
a considerable amount of dogmatic theology. Since Zerbolt's writings
played an important role in shaping Devotionalist thought, one can
perhaps safely turn to them for the purpose of gaining some insight into
Devotionalist dogmatics. That one is indeed justified in doing so is evident from those instances in which later Devotionalist writers express
their views on dogmatic issues. For such dogmatic views as they do express virtually always agree with those of Zerbolt. Finally, it has been
said of Devotionalist spirituality that it lacked a dogmatic basis.
However, if Zerbolt's writings are used as a criterion, then one must conclude that Devotionalist spirituality possessed an adequate, although far
from elaborate, foundation of dogmatic theology.

This brings us to the question of the relationship and similarity between Zerbolt's spirituality and that of the Devotionalist movement.
Among the most striking features of Zerbolt's spirituality is the virtually
exclusive concern with the ascetical phase of the spiritual life. Although
Zerbolt writes that the mystical experience of God is the ultimate aim of
the religious life, he stops, for all practical purposes, with purity of heart
which is achieved through mortification of the body, but above all
through meditation on those topics which instil compunction. Preoccupation with the ascetical phase of the spiritual life and the resulting neglect
of its mystical aspect were to be the characteristic features of the collective
spirituality of the Devotionalists.[42] Zerbolt almost certainly had a hand in
the direction taken by Devotionalist spirituality. It would appear that he
helped to give Devotionalist spirituality its ascetical bent not only
through his two manuals for the spiritual life, but also through the constitutions in use by the Brethren Houses. The constitutions of the various
Brethren Houses show some variations, but indications are that they are
all based on the original rule drawn up for the first Brethren House,
namely the one at Deventer, and that Zerbolt had a hand in drawing up
this first code.[43] The constitutions state that the rationale underlying the
founding of the Brethren Houses is purity of heart, without which there

---

[42] Axters, *Vroomheid*, III, 68, 103, 109-110, 128-130 and 158-160; Goossens, *Meditatie*,
24-30; and Post, *De Moderne Devotie*, 138-146. Cf. Richard, *The Spirituality of John Calvin*,
32-33; and F. Oakley, *The Western Church in the Later Middle Ages* (Ithaca and London,
1979), 105.

[43] Goossens, *Meditatie*, 24-25 and 63-64.

can be no perfection which consists in perfect love.[44] In view of the fact
that the constitutions which guided the Brethren's daily life and conduct
so plainly make purity of heart the primary aim of the spiritual life, it is
perhaps not surprising that among the Brethren of the Common life so
few, if any, appear to have progressed beyond the ascetical phase of the
spiritual life. The constitutions of the Augustinian Canons and
Canonesses Regular of the Congregation of Windesheim did not set purity of heart, the special province of the ascetical life, as the primary goal of
the spiritual life. Nonetheless, their spirituality, like that of the Brethren
and Sisters of the Common Life, leaned towards the ascetical, although
not to the same extreme degree as did the spirituality of the latter. Among
the Augustinian Canons and Canonesses Regular there was a better balance
between the ascetical and mystical aspects of the spiritual life than there
was among the Brethren and Sisters.[45] The works of some of the greatest
writers among the Canons and Canonesses betray a considerable
mystical bent. In this connection we may name Gerlach Peters (d. 1411),
Hendrik Mande (d. 1431), Alijt Bake (d. 1455) and Thomas a Kempis.
In addition to the authors named whose writings reveal a familiarity with
the mystical experience of God, there were other Augustinian Canons
and Canonesses who achieved contemplative heights.[46] The Devotionalists' preoccupation with the extirpation of vices and the cultivation
of the corresponding moral virtues made their spirituality a very practical, non-speculative one. This concern with vices and moral virtues also
lent their spirituality a somber air. It was a spirituality in a minor key,
and it was aptly described by the Devotionalists themselves as a "dying
life."[47]

Zerbolt, we have seen, outlines two methods by means of which the
soul may be cleansed of all sins and be purified. The first method is that
of bodily mortification in which imitation of Christ plays an important
role. The second method Zerbolt employs to purify the soul is meditation, a mental activity. Of the two, Zerbolt would appear to regard
meditation as a more effective method to cleanse the soul of sins than
mortification of the body through imitation of Christ. Understandably,
then, meditation, which serves to cleanse the soul of sins, plays a large

---

[44] "The Original Constitution of the Brethren of the Common Life at Deventer," ed.
by Hyma, *The Christian Renaissance*, 442; and "*Consuetudines domus nostre* (= Brethren
House at Zwolle)," in: Jacobus de Voecht, *Narratio*, ed. by Schoengen, 240-241. Cf.
Goossens, *Meditatie*, 24-25.

[45] Axters, *Vroomheid*, III, 128-130.

[46] Axters, *Vroomheid*, III, 136-137 and 164-165; and Steensma, *Het Klooster Thabor bij
Sneek en zijn nagelaten geschriften*, 211-212.

[47] De Man, ed., *Hier beginnen sommige stichtige punten van onsen oelden zusteren*, 39 and 141;
and Th. a Kempis, *De Imitatione Christi*, Bk. II, ch. 12.

role in Zerbolt's essentially ascetical spirituality. In relying on meditation, an activity of the mind, as the best way to purify the soul Zerbolt
considerably spiritualized an important aspect of the religious life.

Meditation played an important role in the Devotionalists'
spirituality.[48] For not only was meditation the source of compunction
which purged sins and purified the soul, but imitation of Christ, by
means of which the body was mortified, had to be accompanied by
meditation. Meditation on Christ's life and suffering served to instil in
the Devotionalists the desire to follow in his footsteps. Grote had written
that the goal underlying meditation, whether it be on the passion of
Christ or any other subject, must be the eradication of vices and the
cultivation of virtues.[49] According to Goossens all the early Devotionalists, of whom Zerbolt was one, espoused this view of meditation, its
purpose and significance.[50] The importance attributed by the Devotionalists to meditation as a means to cultivate compunction and a desire
to imitate Christ is evident from other sources as well. The constitutions
of the Brethren of the Common Life prescribe topics for meditation for
each day of the week. Each day of the week the Brethren had to meditate
on a topic which instilled either compunction of fear or compunction of
hope and love, as well as on some aspect of Christ's life and passion
which would induce in them the desire to imitate Christ.[51] The
anonymous *Epistola de Vita et Passione Domini Nostri Jesu Christi*, which was
read by all Devotionalists, names three topics for meditation for everyday
of the week.[52] The *Epistola* prescribes, in contrast with the constitutions of
the Brethren of the Common Life, topics drawn primarily from the life
and passion of Christ.

It is somewhat difficult to establish whether as a body the Devotionalists, whose spirituality was, like that of Zerbolt, essentially
ascetical, regarded mortification of the body through imitation of Christ,
or meditation which leads to compunction, as the best method to purge
the soul of sins and to purify the heart. The evidence suggests that with
respect to this particular question it is hazardous to generalize. It would
appear that some individuals and groups saw the compunction which
arises from meditation on death, heaven, hell, etc. as the most effective

---

[48] Cf. Axters, *Vroomheid*, III, 70-72, 131-132 and 160-161.

[49] Goossens, *Meditatie*, 154-158.

[50] *Ibid.*

[51] "The Original Constitution of the Brethren of the Common Life at Deventer," ed.
by Hyma, *The Christian Renaissance*, 442-443; and "*Consuetudines domus nostre* (= Brethren
House at Zwolle)," in: Jacobus de Voecht, *Narratio*, ed. by Schoengen, 241-242. Cf. Axters, *Vroomheid*, III, 70-72.

[52] Hedlund, ed., *Epistola de Vita et Passione Domini Nostri*, 91-100. Cf. Axters, *Vroomheid*,
III, 131.

means to eradicate sin and to promote the growth of virtue. Others, however, would seem to have relied in the first place on imitation of Christ as a way to achieve their primary goal, namely purity of heart. The Brethren constitutions, the original of which Zerbolt may have helped to draw up, place at least as much emphasis on compunction, the fruit of meditation, as a means to achieve a pure heart as they do on imitation of Christ which is also preceded by meditation.[53] The anonymous author of the *Epistola de Vita et Passione Domini Nostri Jesu Christi*, on the other hand, clearly regards imitation of Christ, which is based on meditation, as the most effective method to achieve the Devotionalists' goal of a pure heart.[54] From Axters' study of the Devotionalists' spirituality one gets the impression that in the fight for a pure heart the Brethren of the Common Life and the Augustinian Canons Regular assigned, on the whole, a greater role to compunction than did the Sisters of the Common Life and the Augustinian Canonesses Regular.[55] In *De Imitatione Christi* of Thomas a Kempis, the Augustinian Canon Regular, compunction plays, in spite of the book's title, a more prominent role in the quest for a pure heart than does practical imitation of Christ.[56] In the spirituality of the Sisters of the Common Life and the Canonesses Regular devotion to Christ and imitation of him were very prominent features, more conspicuous it would seem than meditation which leads to compunction of fear, hope and love.[57] Furthermore, the Sisters' and Canonesses' devotion to Christ was not at all times totally free from erotic elements, it would appear.[58] In his spiritualization of the ascetical phase of the spiritual life, a practice in which he followed the lead of the Franciscans, Zerbolt was not, then, followed by all Devotionalists to the same extent. Among the female Devotionalists in particular practical, concrete imitation of Christ would appear to have remained a very important, and perhaps the most important, way to purge the soul of sins and to cultivate the moral virtues. Nonetheless, it was the kind of spiritualization of the ascetical phase of the spiritual life so typical of Zerbolt's spirituality which made it possible for the Canoness Alijt Bake to assert that poverty must, in the first place, be understood in a spiritual, rather than in a literal, sense.[59]

---

[53] See the references given in footnote 51 above.

[54] Hedlund, ed., *Epistola de Vita et Passione Domini Nostri*, 91-100.

[55] Axters, *Vroomheid*, III, 67-79, 103-111, 126-137 and 158-165.

[56] A. Rayez, "Humanité du Christ," *DSp*, VII, 1095; and Axters, *La Spiritualité des Pays-Bas*, 107.

[57] See the references given in footnote 55 above.

[58] Axters, *Vroomheid*, III, 162. Cf. A. M. Baaij, ed., *Jhesus Collacien: Een Laatmiddeleeuwse Preekbundel uit de Kringen der Tertiarissen* (Zwolle, 1962); and R. W. Southern, *Western Society and the Church in the Middle Ages* (The Pelican History of the Church, Vol. II; London, 1970), 326.

[59] Axters, *Vroomheid*, III, 159 and 168.

Goossens' assertion that for the Devotionalist compunction was the footing on which he placed the ladder of spiritual ascent needs some qualification.[60] For it is evident from the foregoing that certainly not all Devotionalists saw the compunction which arises from meditation on the four last things as the best way to achieve purity of heart. However, that does not exclude the possibility that the majority of them did so as a consequence of the influence exerted on them not only by Zerbolt's writings, but also by those of Grote and Radewijns who,[61] together with Zerbolt, were primarily responsible for moulding the spirituality of the *Devotio Moderna*. On account of the pivotal role of compunction in Devotionalist spirituality and the Devotionalists' impact on the spirituality of the Low Countries, Axters expresses the view that *"dans les dernières années du quatorzième siecle, la componction a, pour ce qui concerne la spiritualité des Pays-Bas, supplanté la métaphysique."*[62] He does not develop this thought any further. However, the idea he apparently wishes to convey here is that, in the Low Countries at least, the Devotionalists were instrumental in increasing the experiential element in the realm of religion at the expense of the theoretical. Thomas a Kempis illustrates this trend very nicely when he writes that he would rather experience compunction than know its definition.[63] Thus the Devotionalists' emphasis on compunction was part of the broader late-medieval trend towards increased subjectivity in religion.

It was the Devotionalists then who gave the doctrine of compunction, which was essentially Gregory the Great's, a considerable impetus in the late middle ages. Gabriel Biel and John Geiler, two late medieval preachers influenced by the *Devotio Moderna*,[64] stressed time and again the necessity of a salutary balance between compunction of fear and compunction of hope and love, the result of God's justice and mercy respectively. Fear was held to be necessary to prevent complacency, presumptuousness, and too much reliance on God's mercy and the meritoriousness of one's own works. Hope, on the other hand, was held to be a necessary antidote to fear. It had to draw the believer onward and prevent fear from gaining a debilitating hold on him.[65] However, what

---

[60] Goossens, *Meditatie*, 27.

[61] De Beer, *Spiritualiteit*, 76-83; and Goossens, *Meditatie*, 132-142 and 176-187.

[62] Axters, *La Spiritualité des Pays-Bas*, 100. Cf. Goossens, *Meditatie*, 134.

[63] Th. a Kempis, *De Imitatione Christi*, Bk. I, ch. 1. Cf. P. Régamey, "La componction du coeur," *VSp*, XLIX (1936), Supplément, 313.

[64] Gabriel Biel was himself a member of the Brethren of the Common Life although he was not a typical Devotionalist (see Post, *The Modern Devotion*, 486-490 and Oberman, *Biel*, 12-16).

Geiler, it has been noted, borrowed from Zerbolt's *De Reformatione* for at least one of his works.

[65] Oberman, *Biel*, 222-224; and Dempsey-Douglass, *Geiler*, 162-176.

had always been regarded as a salutary balance between fear and hope was experienced by Luther as an unbearable clash of religious emotions. Traditionally the balance between fear and hope had been kept intact by maintaining a rigid division between God's justice and mercy. By ending this divorce between God's justice and mercy Luther was able to overcome the dilemma facing him.

A question that remains to be answered is whether, and to what extent, Devotionalist spirituality, in the formation of which Zerbolt played a prominent role, can be called *sui generis*. Dom J. Huijben, one of the first to ask this question, answered it in the negative.[66] Following him Axters, Post and Goossens have argued that Devotionalist spirituality is certainly unique and that it must be regarded, and treated, as a distinct school of spirituality.[67] All of the features of Devotionalist spirituality which they regard as unique, and which, in their view, make Devotionalist spirituality *sui generis*, can be found in Zerbolt's spirituality as well. In the first place there is the Devotionalists' almost exclusive concern with the ascetical phase of the spiritual life: the purgation of sins and the development of moral virtues. Although Devotionalist spirituality owes much to Bernardine and Franciscan spirituality, it lacks the mystical bent of the two older schools. Devotionalist spirituality was active and practical, rather than contemplative and speculative. Consistent with their limited, ascetical interests, the Devotionalists read only those works which could assist them in their efforts to acquire a pure heart: *apatheia*. Consequently they were dependent on a specific genre of religious literature, rather than on particular authors. Typical of the Devotionalists as well was their uninterrupted reflection and meditation on those topics which instil compunction, as well as meditation on Christ's life and death followed by imitation of him. The purpose of both compunction and imitation of Christ was to purify the heart. In order to make uninterrupted meditation possible the Devotionalists carefully ordered and arranged the material for meditation, and they took great care to have subject matter for meditation at hand at all times, even while occupied with manual tasks. They read for the purpose of absorbing suitable material for meditation, and every Devotionalist was urged to compile his or her own *rapiarium* for meditational purposes.[68] The ripest fruit of the Devotionalists' concern with meditation is the *Rosetum exercitiorum spiritualum et sacrarum meditationum* in which the author, Johannes Mombaer (d. 1501), outlines a

---

[66] Huijben, "Y a-t-il une spiritualité Flamande?" 129-147.

[67] Axters, *La Spiritualité des Pays-Bas*, 120-134; Post, *De Moderne Devotie*, 137-144; and Goossens, *Meditatie*, 30-34.

[68] Goossens, *Meditatie*, 32-33 and 203-204; Axters, *Vroomheid*, III, 138-139; and Post, *De Moderne Devotie*, 142.

highly methodical and technical form of meditation, the foundations of which were laid by the early Devotionalists.[69]

To indicate the reform movement founded by Grote, the designation *Devotio Moderna* was first used some decades after Zerbolt's death, namely by Henry Pomerius who, in his *vita* of Ruusbroec written between 1417 and 1421, refers to Grote as *"fons et origo modernae devotionis in Bassa Almania..."*[70] M. Ditsche, who has studied the origin and meaning of the concept *Devotio Moderna*, found that the term *devotio* could have as many as three distinct meanings for the Devotionalists, but that they most frequently equated *devotio* with *affectio*.[71] Zerbolt, we have seen, did not altogether equate *devotio* with *affectio*, for he saw *devotio* as consisting in compunction of hope and love only, while he held that *affectio* can consist in either compunction of fear or compunction of hope and love.[72] Radewijns' understanding of the term *devotio* was similar to that of Zerbolt, for he wrote that *"devotio non est nisi desiderium anime ad deum."*[73] *Devotio*, as defined by Zerbolt and Radewijns, became such a prominent feature of the new movement's spirituality that it became part of its name.[74] Finally, the adoption of the term *devotio* to describe the new movement also implies a reaction against an excess of speculation in the spiritual life and the restoration of *affectio* to the spiritual life.[75] And what definitely characterized the movement as a whole was an anti-intellectual, or at least an anti-speculative, mentality.[76]

In describing their *devotio* as being *moderna*, its adherents wanted to convey the idea that it did not stand in opposition to the *devotio* of Christian antiquity, but that it was a renewal of the *devotio* first practised by the

---

[69] Goossens, *Meditatie*, 203-204; Post, *De Moderne Devotie*, 142; and *idem*, *The Modern Devotion*, 323-325, 328-330 and 542-549.

[70] H. Pomerius, *Vita B. Joannis Ruesbrochi*, ch. VIII, publ. in *Analecta Bollandiana*, IV (1885), 228.

[71] Ditsche, "Zur Herkunft und Bedeutung des Begriffes *devotio moderna*," 137-145. Cf. Richard, *The Spirituality of John Calvin*, 32.

In Middle-Dutch writings the term *devotio* was commonly translated as *innicheit* (Ditsche, *op. cit.*, 125), although the word *devocie* was used as well, and the two were clearly regarded as being synonymous (cf. "Wat ijnicheit is," in Ms. 101 E 13, Athenaeum Library, Deventer, folios unnumbered).

[72] See above, pp. 269 and 278-279.

[73] J. F. Vregt, ed., "Aliqua verba notabilia domini Florentii et magistri Gherardi Magni," *AGAU*, X (1882), 458.

[74] Cf. Ditsche, "Zur Herkunft und Bedeutung des Begriffes *devotio moderna*," 139-141 and 143-144.

[75] Cf. Richard, *The Spirituality of John Calvin*, 32.

[76] Cf. Jean de Schoonhoven, *De Contemptu Huius Mundi*, ed. by A. Gruijs, 95-97; Oberman, "Fourteenth-Century Religious Thought: A Premature Profile," 92; H. A. Oberman, *Werden und Wertung der Reformation* (Tübingen, 1979), 59; and Oakley, *The Western Church in the Later Middle Ages*, 104.

church fathers.[77] Like all ecclesiastical reform movements, that of the *Devotio Moderna* aimed at returning to the conditions as they had existed in the early church. However, in the *Epistola de prima institutione monasterii in Windesem* William Vornken interestingly enough placed the *devotio antiqua*, which the *Devotio Moderna* tried to imitate, not in the late classical period, but in the Low Countries of the late seventh and early eighth centuries when Willibrord and his companions first Christianized large parts of the Low Countries.[78]

---

[77] Cf. Ditsche, "Zur Herkunft und Bedeutung des Begriffes *devotio moderna*,"; and Klinkenberg, "Die *Devotio Moderna* unter dem Thema *'antiqui-moderni'* betrachtet," 394-419.

[78] Wilhelmus Vornken, "Epistola de prima institutione monasterii in Windesem," ed. by Acquoy, *Windesheim*, III, 237-238.

APPENDIX

The Capital Sins, the Cardinal Virtues and the Evangelical Counsels

Gluttony: Zerbolt's description of gluttony (see *De Reformatione*, chs. 44-46 and *De Ascensionibus*, ch. 56) is based for the most part on the definitions of Cassian and David of Augsburg (Cassian, *Conferences*, V, 11 and D. of Augsburg, *De ext. et int. hom. compositione*, I, 132). Being a capital vice, gluttony is the head of an entire family of vices. However, Zerbolt lists two different groups of "daughters"—a term used by Climacus as well—which descend from gluttony. For the one classification of progeny he is indebted to Gregory the Great, and for the other to Climacus (Gregory the Great, *Moralia in Job*, XXXI, 45 [*PL*, LXXVI, 621] and Climacus, *Scala Paradisi*, 145). Obviously influenced by Cassian (Cassian, *Institutes*, V, 14), Zerbolt writes that one of the best weapons against gluttony is to be inwardly occupied with spiritually beneficial matters. Spiritual idleness is the major cause of carnal vices. For if the powers of the soul are not inwardly occupied with matters of benefit to one's spiritual development they will invariably "wander abroad," occupy themselves with worldly, non-spiritual matters, and lead man into temptation and carnal sins. Consequently, among the best remedies for carnal sins, gluttony as well as lust, is meditation on the four last things, for compunction will cleanse the heart of sin and draw man to God. In addition to meditation as a weapon against gluttony Zerbolt mentions fasting and spiritual reading as well, but meditation on the four last things receives by far the most attention.

To sobriety, the virtue which stands opposed to gluttony, and its development Zerbolt does not devote as much space as to the extirpation of gluttony. For his description of sobriety he is largely indebted to Cassian, and the three-stage development of sobriety outlined by him in *De Reformatione* he copied word for word from David of Augsburg's *De exterioris et interioris hominis compositione* (Cassian, *Institutes*, V, 5, 8 and 9 and D. of Augsburg, *De ext. et int. hom. compositione*, II, 113-116). Like Cassian, Zerbolt advises moderation. Reasonable meals enjoyed daily, he quotes from the *Institutes*, are preferable to severe and prolonged fasting followed by excessive eating. Furthermore, Cassian observes that excessive fasting can undermine the constancy of the mind, and the Brethren of the Common Life were conscious likewise of the fact that excessive fasting can induce hallucinations and even result in incurable mental illness.

Luxury (Lust): Echoing Gregory the Great as well as Climacus, Zerbolt calls lust the daughter of gluttony (*De Reformatione*, chs. 47-48 and *De Ascensionibus*, ch. 57; Gregory the Great, *Moralia in Job*, XXXI, 45 [*PL*, LXXVI, 621]; and Climacus, *Scala Paradisi*, 140 and 146). Furthermore, being a carnal sin like gluttony, Zerbolt handles the topic lust in much the same way as he handled gluttony. Like gluttony, lust has its own offspring, and Zerbolt ascribes to lust those "daughters" first attributed to it by Gregory the Great. Like gluttony, lust resides in the concupiscent power, and it is the will which must fight lust as well as gluttony. Lust, he continues, has a twofold nature, bodily and mental, and each requires its own peculiar remedies. When it is of a bodily nature the best remedy is fasting, although manual labour and toil are useful as well. When it is of a mental nature: i.e., when it is a question of the imagination, the best remedies are contrition and compunction cultivated through meditation on the four last things and the like, and prayer. For lust, Zerbolt repeats after Chrysostom, is the passion of an empty mind. Furthermore, in order to combat lust, whether it be of a bodily or mental nature, it is necessary as well to guard the senses, to avoid contact with the opposite sex, and to control the thoughts, which can best be done through meditation on spiritual matters. All these remedies suggested by Zerbolt for the purpose of curing lust are found in Cassian's *Institutes* and David of Augsburg's *De exterioris et interioris hominis compositione* (Cassian, *Institutes*, VI and D. of Augsburg, *De ext. et int. hom. compositione*, I, 143-150).

Zerbolt places considerable emphasis on the need for humility and grace in the fight against lust, and he ties the two together, because where there is no humility God does not grant his grace. The believer must humbly admit that in the struggle against lust he is helpless without the aid of divine grace. Zerbolt concludes by very briefly outlining the three stages of chastity, the opposite of lust, and he refers to chastity as the daughter of sobriety. For the three stages of chastity, Zerbolt is indebted to David of Augsburg (*De ext. et int. hom. compositione*, II, 122-127).

Avarice: In both *De Reformatione* and *De Ascensionibus* Zerbolt sets apart a short chapter for the vice of avarice (*De Reformatione*, ch. 49 and *De Ascensionibus*, ch. 58), and they are based almost entirely on David of Augsburg's *De exterioris et interioris hominis compositione* (I, 129-132 and II, 107-110). About the nature of avarice he writes virtually nothing, and he concentrates his attention on the remedies for this vice. In order to overcome avarice, he explains, one must generally be disdainful and contemptuous of worldly things, and he divides the actual struggle against avarice into three consecutive ascents. The first step is not to desire anything that is unjustly gained; the second ascent is to be content not only with what is justly one's own, but to be satisfied with the bare necessities of life; and the third ascent is to possess nothing whatsoever. This third step, he continues, is the most effective remedy against avarice: i.e., to leave all for Christ's sake, to spend one's life under the charge and oversight of another, and not to claim ownership in anything even to the least degree. Manual labour, Zerbolt concludes, serves as a useful remedy against avarice as well. As the progeny of avarice he lists those vices enumerated by Gregory the Great (*Moralia in Job*, XXXI, 45 [*PL*, LXXVI, 621]).

Poverty, then, as well as chastity, both of them evangelical counsels, are discussed by Zerbolt in connection with the seven capital sins, but they do not receive any additional, or special, attention from him. This may have been a result of the fact that Zerbolt, like most of his contemporaries, spiritualized the ascetical life as we have seen above.

Anger: While gluttony, lust and avarice reside in the concupiscent power, anger resides in the irascible power, Zerbolt writes (anger is discussed in *De Reformatione*, ch. 50 and in *De Ascensionibus*, ch. 69). According to Jerome, he goes on, wrath is almost always the result of pride (Jerome, *Commentary on Ecclesiastes*; cf. Kelly, *Jerome: His Life Writings and Controversies*, 145 and 150-152), while wrath itself is the source of a number of other vices (Gregory the Great, *Moralia in Job*, XXXI, 45 [*PL*, LXXVI, 621]). A good remedy against anger is compunction, Zerbolt asserts, an idea for which he is indebted to Climacus (*Scala Paradisi*, 124). However the most effective weapon against anger, he continues on the basis of David of Augsburg's *De exterioris et interioris hominis compositione*, is to check one's speech and to repress one's impulses. The summit of patience is the ability to endure hardships with equanimity and even with rejoicing. Together these consecutive developments constitute the three stages into which Zerbolt, in imitation of David of Augsburg, divides the virtue of gentleness or patience (*De ext. et int. hom. compositione*, I, 123-126 and II, 93-96). Independent of David of Augsburg, Zerbolt observes that reason is an important tool in checking one's words and impulses (cf. de Beer, *Spiritualiteit*, 145-146).

Envy: Zerbolt begins his discussion of envy with the observation that while Gregory the Great counted envy among the capital sins, Cassian and Isidor of Seville did not (envy and its remedies are discussed in *De Reformatione*, chs. 51-53 and *De Ascensionibus*, ch. 60). He presumes that Cassian and Isidor did not do so on the basis that they understood envy to stem from some other capital sin and not to be itself the source of more sins. Cassian, in fact, did understand envy to be an outgrowth of pride

(*Conferences*, V, 16). Gregory added envy to the capital sins, Zerbolt explains, because he understood this vice to be the source of others, and as the "daughters" of envy Zerbolt lists those enumerated by Gregory (*Moralia in Job*, XXXI, 45 [*PL*, LXXVI, 621]).

Zerbolt's description of the threefold nature of envy and its characteristics is based on that of David of Augsburg (*De ext. et int. hom. compositione*, I, 119), and perhaps on Gregory the Great's definition of this particular vice. For the remedies for the vice of envy Zerbolt is largely dependent upon David of Augsburg and Cassian (D. of Augsburg, *De ext. et int. hom. compositione*, I, 120-121 and II, 77-80; and Cassian, *Conferences*, XVI, 5-6 and 8-9). The object in the fight against envy is love of one's neighbour and charity, and as always Zerbolt outlines a threefold ascent which takes the believer to the predestined goal. Charity is, of course, the fulfilment of the law, as Zerbolt points out, and he has in mind above all the maintenance of peace, concord and charity in the Brethren House for which he was writing in particular (cf. the ch. entitled *De caritate* in the constitution of the Brethren of the Common Life at Deventer, ed. by Hyma, *The Christian Renaissance*, 466). An indispensable part of friendship and charity, he adds, is the desire to promote the spiritual well-being of one's *confrères* in every way possible, and to display an interest in their spiritual state. In this connection he quotes from Hugo of St. Victor's *De Amore*.

Accidie and Melancholy: Cassian discussed melancholy and accidie separately, but Gregory the Great combined the two and spoke of only one vice, namely accidie (Cassian, *Conferences*, V, 18; and Dudden *Gregory the Great: His Place in History and Thought*, II, 386-388). In *De Reformatione* Zerbolt devotes a separate chapter to both accidie and melancholy (*tristitia*), but in *De Ascensionibus* he discusses both vices in one chapter (*De Reformatione*, chs. 54 and 55 and *De Ascensionibus*, ch. 61). However, in *De Reformatione*, as well as in *De Ascensionibus*, Zerbolt asserts that melancholy must be regarded as constituting one facet of accidie. Furthermore, he writes that the same remedies are effective to heal both accidie and melancholy.

For a definition of accidie Zerbolt goes to Cassian's *Institutes* (X, 2, 5 and 6), and he writes that this vice consists of essentially two elements: frequent changing of place of residence as well as of spiritual exercises, or the desire to do so. Both were considered to be highly detrimental to the spiritual life. As the daughters of accidie Zerbolt enumerates those cited by Gregory the Great (*Moralia in Job*, XXXI, 45 [*PL*, LXXVI, 621]).

For the remedies against accidie and melancholy Zerbolt goes to Climacus (*Scala Paradisi*, 139), William of St. Thierry (*The Golden Epistle of Abbot William of St. Thierry*, 46) and David of Augsburg (*De ext. et int.*

hom. compositione, I, 127-128 and II, 66-70). Just as love for one's
neighbour casts out envy, he asserts, so love of God overcomes accidie
and melancholy. This love of God, or charity, Zerbolt divides into three
degrees for which he is indebted to David of Augsburg (*De ext. et int. hom.
compositione*, II, 66-70). It must be pointed out, however, that David did
not use the three degrees of charity as remedies for accidie, and it would
appear that Zerbolt stands alone in applying charity in this fashion. Ad-
dressing himself specifically to the question of accidie understood as in-
stability, Zerbolt quotes St. Bernard (in reality William of St. Thierry) to
the effect that the mind will not be stable unless the body remains in one
place. In addition to charity and constancy Zerbolt mentions a number of
other remedies for accidie such as meditation which engenders compunction, prayer, spiritual conversation and the like. However, charity is for
him the most effective weapon against spiritual sloth and melancholy. He
concludes with the warning not to confuse melancholy and sadness with
compunction of fear.

Vainglory: David of Augsburg does not mention vainglory in his manual
for the spiritual life, and Zerbolt derives virtually everything he writes
regarding this vice from Cassian's *Institutes* and Climacus' *Scala Paradisi*
(*De Reformatione*, ch. 56 and *De Ascensionibus*, ch. 62; Cassian, *Institutes*,
XI, 1, 4-6, 9, 14 and 19; and Climacus, *Scala Paradisi*, 173-179).
However, for the description of vainglory, as well as for the remedies proposed, Zerbolt is indebted primarily to Cassian and to a much lesser extent to Climacus. There is no virtue opposite of vainglory, because this
vice is itself the fruit of virtue, Zerbolt explains. The virtuous and
righteous are always faced with the temptation to exult in their own virtuousness and righteousness. Another aspect of vainglory, according to
Zerbolt, is the desire to take holy orders for the purpose of winning over
many people for Christ (see above, pp. 188-190). As the progeny of vainglory he names those vices cited by Gregory the Great (*Moralia in Job*,
XXXI, 45 [*PL*, LXXVI, 621]).

Although there is no virtue which corresponds to vainglory as such,
Zerbolt does, nonetheless, maintain that it must be replaced by humility.
Exultation in one's own virtuousness and righteousness, even if it is in-
voluntary, can be overcome only if one accepts in humility that all virtues
are the consequence of divine grace. Furthermore, vainglory and pride
were commonly understood to be closely related (see Climacus, *Scala
Paradisi*, 173-179, for example), and humility was, of course, held to be
the virtue that corresponds to pride.

Pride: For his description of pride (*De Reformatione*, chs. 57 and 58 and *De
Ascensionibus*, ch. 63), the queen of the vices, Zerbolt is indebted to Cas-

sian (*Institutes*, XII, 2, 3, 24 and 29), and, like him, he distinguishes between carnal and spiritual pride. Pride is particularly dangerous to one's spiritual well-being, because it prevents one from truly knowing oneself and one's own worthlessness, and it is more destructive of righteousness and sanctity than any other vice. The remedies suggested by Zerbolt for the vice of pride are drawn almost entirely from David of Augsburg's *De exterioris et interioris hominis compositione* (I, 117-118 and II, 84-87). Another work he draws on as well in this connection is Cassian's *Institutes* (XII, 9). Influenced by David of Augsburg, Zerbolt asserts that the best remedy against pride is the realization that all one's virtues and good works are defective and imperfect, and that such good qualities as they do possess are gifts of the merciful God (see above, pp. 195-198).

For the three degrees of humility Zerbolt is indebted to David of Augsburg as well. These three degrees are: a) that man accepts himself to be weak, sinful, and incapable of doing any good; b) that he allows others to see him as he really is; and c) that he attributes whatever good there may be in him to God and his gratuitous mercy. If according to Zerbolt nothing so destroys virtue, righteousness and sanctity as does pride, then it follows that there is nothing more beneficial to righteousness and virtue than the opposite of pride, namely humility. He does not further elucidate the importance of humility in the spiritual life, but it had always been regarded as being of prime importance for those who wish to progress spiritually (cf. the ch. entitled *De humilitate* in the constitution of the Brethren of the Common Life at Deventer, ed. by Hyma, *The Christian Renaissance*, 466).

Obedience: Zerbolt does not treat of obedience in connection with the reformation of the will, although it would have been logical to do so, for obedience is an act of the will. Furthermore, obedience had always been coupled to pride and humility, both of which reside in the will and are discussed by Zerbolt in connection with the reformation of the will. Just as disobedience was held to be the first effect of pride, so obedience was thought to be the first degree of humility and a fundamental remedy for pride (cf. Resch, *La Doctrine Ascétique des Premiers Maitres Egyptiens de Quatrième Siècle*, 231-243). Also, with poverty and chastity, discussed in connection with avarice and lust respectively, obedience was, of course, one of the three evangelical counsels observed by the religious in particular. It is, therefore, not inappropriate to consider Zerbolt's views on obedience in connection with his discussion of pride and humility, although he himself deals with obedience in a somewhat different context.

Zerbolt discusses the question of obedience in connection with the *hēsychia*, the state of inner stillness, quiet, silence, peace and contemplation which the ascetics, or religious, had been pursuing since the birth of monasticism (see *De Reformatione*, ch. 37 and *De Ascensionibus*, ch. 68). Activities, and worldly activities in particular, were destructive of the desired inner tranquillity, stillness and peace, and even made them impossible. It was the desire and search for the *hēsychia* which populated the Egyptian desert in the fourth and fifth centuries and underlies monastic theology and life. Consistent with this traditional line of thought Zerbolt writes that the religious must aim for stillness and quiet (Zerbolt uses the term *"vacare"* [*Ref.*, 250G and *Asc.*, 287A]). He must flee the tumult of the world, and shun all "external occupations" (i.e., beyond the confines of the community) and positions of responsibility. He must imitate Mary, the symbol of inner quiet and stillness, and the model for all contemplatives. However, when the superior, who is Christ's vicar, calls to carry out a task, to assume a position of responsibility, or to take holy orders, then the religious must not tarry but yield immediately to the wishes of the superior. 'Mary' must descend and become 'Martha'. (Zerbolt uses the symbolism of Martha and Mary in a fairly conventional way.) For, as Zerbolt explains, a religious vocation, and the degree of spiritual perfection accompanying it, is no better than the devout fulfilment of the law of obedience. The "Holy Fathers," he continues, readily put off their spiritual exercises in order to preserve obedience inviolate, for they thought that to follow not their own, but another's, will came before all else. For the sake of obedience, then, one must relinquish one's inner tranquillity, stillness and quiet, and carry out some task, assume holy orders or some other position of responsibility. By the same token, Zerbolt observes, those who desire to assume holy orders or a position of responsibility of their own free will betray an aversion to things spiritual, and to inner stillness and quiet in particular (cf. the ch. entitled *De obedientia* in the constitution of the Brethren of the Common Life at Deventer, ed. by Hyma, *The Christian Renaissance*, 467).

BIBLIOGRAPHY

Sources

i. *Works of Gerard Zerbolt of Zutphen*

De Reformatione Interiori seu Virium Animae. Published by M. de la Bigne in *Maxima Biblio-theca Veterum Patrum et Antiquorum Scriptorum Ecclesiasticorum.* 27 vols. 8th ed. Lyon, 1677 (Vol. XXVI, pp. 234-258).

Over de Hervorming van de Krachten der Ziel, van Gerard Zerbolt van Zutphen. Introduced and translated by S. van der Woude. Klassieken der Kerk, Tweede Reeks: De Kerk der Middeleeuwen, Deel 3. Amsterdam, 1951.

De Spiritualibus Ascensionibus. Published by M. de la Bigne in *Maxima Bibliotheca Veterum Patrum et Antiquorum Scriptorum Ecclesiasticorum.* 27 vols. 8th ed. Lyon, 1677 (Vol. XXVI, pp. 258-289).

De spiritualibus ascensionibus/Van geestelijke opklimmingen. Edited by J. Mahieu. Brussels, 1936 and Bruges, 1941.

De Libris Teutonicalibus. Edited by A. Hyma. *NAKG,* N.S., XVII (1924), 42-70.

"De Dietse tekst van het traktaat *De libris teutonicalibus,* mogelijk van Gerard Zerbolt van Zutphen." Edited by C. G. N. de Vooys. *NAKG,* N.S., IV (1907), 113-134.

The tract published by de Vooys is not a Middle-Dutch translation of *De Libris Teutonicalibus,* but a Middle-Dutch translation of *Super Modo Vivendi,* ch. 7, which is quite similar to *De Libris Teutonicalibus* (see van Rooy, *Zerbolt,* 83, footnote 1).

Super Modo Vivendi Devotorum Hominum Simul Commorantium. Edited by A. Hyma. *AGAU,* LII (1926), 1-100.

Scriptum Pro Quodam Inordinate Gradus Ecclesiasticos et Praedicationis Officium Affectante. Edited by A. Hyma. *NAKG,* N.S., XX (1927), 179-232.

Het Tractaat "De Vestibus Pretiosis." Edited by D. J. M. Wüstenhoff. Ghent-The Hague, 1890.

Epistolae. We have nine letters written by Zerbolt, eight of which were published by G. Dumbar in *Reipublicae Daventriensi ab Actis Analecta, seu vetera aliquot scripta inedita.* 3 vols. Deventer, 1719-1725 (Vol. I, pp. 88-113). A ninth letter was published anonymously by V. Becker, "Onuitgegeven brief van Gerard Zerbolt, bijgenaamt van Zutphen." *De Katholiek,* XLI (1862), 120-121.

ii. *Devotionalist Sources other than the Works of Gerard Zerbolt*

1. Works of Anonymous Authors

Annalen und Akten der Brüder des gemeinsamen Lebens im Lüchtenhove zu Hildesheim. Band IX, Quellen und Darstellungen der Geschichte Niedersachsens. Edited by R. Doebner. Hannover-Leipzig, 1903.

Consuetudines domus nostre (Constitution of the Brethren House at Zwolle). Published by M. Schoengen in Jacobus Traiecti alias de Voecht, *Narratio de Inchoatione Domus Clericorum in Zwollis,* met Akten en Bescheiden Betreffende dit Fraterhuis. Werken uitgegeven door het Historisch Genootschap te Utrecht, 3rd Series, No. 13. Amsterdam, 1908 (pp. 239-273).

"De Dietse oertekst van de anonieme 'Epistola de vita et passione domini nostri Jesu Christi et aliis devotis exerciciis'." Edited by C. C. de Bruin. *NAKG,* N.S., XXXIV (1944-1945), 1-23.

Epistola de Vita et Passione Domini Nostri. Edited by M. Hedlund. Kerkhistorische Bijdra-gen, Vol. V. Leiden, 1975.

Fontes Historiam Domus Fratrum Embricensis Aperientes. Edited by W. J. Alberts and M. Ditsche. Teksten en Documenten, Vol. III, uitgegeven door het Instituut voor Middeleeuwse Geschiedenis, Rijksuniversiteit te Utrecht. Groningen, 1969.

Het Frensweger Handschrift Betreffende de Geschiedenis van de Moderne Devotie. Edited by W. J. Alberts and A. L. Hulshof. Werken uitgegeven door het Historisch Genootschap te Utrecht, 3rd Series, No. 82. Groningen, 1958.

Generalis modus formandi meditationes de regno coelorum ad habendam compunctionem et desiderium ad ipsum obtinendum. Edited by V. Becker, "Eenige meditaties uit den Windesheimer kring." *De Katholiek,* LXXXV (1884), 29-47 and 101-116.

"Gerard Zerbolt van Zutphen ("Biographieën van beroemde Mannen uit den Deventer Kring")." Edited by D. A. Brinkerink. *AGAU,* XXVIII (1902), 335-339.

Hier beginnen sommige stichtige punten van onsen oelden zusteren. Edited by D. de Man. The Hague, 1899.

Necrologie, Kroniek en Cartularium C.A. van het Fraterhuis te Doesburg (1432-1559). Edited by A. G. Weiler. Kerkhistorische Bijdragen, Vol. IV. Leiden, 1974.

The Original Constitution of the Brethren of the Common Life at Deventer. Published by A. Hyma in *The Christian Renaissance: A History of the "Devotio Moderna."* 2d ed. Hamden, Connecticut, 1965 (pp. 440-474).

"Parvum et Simplex Exercitium ex Consuetudine Humilis Patris Domini Florencii et Aliorum Devotorum. Item Excerpta ex Libello 'Beatus Vir'." Edited by D. J. M. Wüstenhoff. *Archief voor Nederlandsche Kerkgeschiedenis,* V (1895), 89-105.

"Sommige Vermaninge tot Eenen Doechliken Leven ("Eenige ascetische tractaten afkomstig van de Deventerse Broederschap van het Gemeene Leven, in verband gebracht met de *Imitatio* van Thomas a Kempis")." Edited by J. F. Vregt and F. J. van Vree. *AGAU,* X (1882), 342-368 (321-498).

2. Works of Known Authors

Claus van Euskerken. "Dit sijn goede punten vergadert uytten collatiën ons eersamen paters here Claus van Euskerken." Edited by D. A. Brinkerink. *NAKG,* N.S., III (1905), 225-264 and 353-395.

Florens Radewijns. *Omnes, inquit, artes.* Published by M. Th. P. van Woerkum in *Het Libellus "Omnes, Inquit, Artes," Een Rapiarium van Florentius Radewijns.* 3 vols. Mimeographed doctoral dissertation, Theological Faculty of the Society of Jesus, Louvain. Limited circulation. Nijmegen, 1950 (Vols. II and III).

———. *Tractatulus Devotus.* Published by L. A. M. Goossens in *De Meditatie in de Eerste Tijd van de Moderne Devotie.* Haarlem, 1952 (pp. 209-254).

———. *Aliqua verba notabilia domini Florentii et magistri Gherardi Magni.* Edited by J. F. Vregt, "Eenige ascetische tractaten afkomstig van de Deventerse Broederschap van het Gemeene Leven, in verband gebracht met de *Imitatio* van Thomas a Kempis." *AGAU,* X (1882), 427-472.

Gabriel Biel. *De communi vita.* Edited by Wm. Landeen, "Appendix. Biel's Tractate on the Common Life." *Research Studies, Washington State University,* XXVIII (1960), 79-95.

Gerard Grote. *Gerardi Magni Epistolae.* Edited by W. Mulder. Tekstuitgaven van *OGE,* Vol. III. Antwerp, 1933.

———. *Het Getijdenboek van Geert Groote naar het Haagse Handschrift 133 E 21.* Edited by N. van Wijk. Leiden, 1940.

———. "Het 'Tractatus de quatuor generibus meditationum sive contemplationum' of 'Sermo de nativitate Domini'." Edited by A. Hyma. *AGAU,* XLIX (1924), 296-326.

Gerlach Peters. *De Dietse Vertaling van Gerlach Peters' "Soliloquium."* Edited by J. J. Mak. Asten, 1936.

Jacobus Traiecti alias de Voecht. *Narratio de Inchoatione Domus Clericorum in Zwollis,* met Akten en Bescheiden Betreffende dit Fraterhuis. Edited by M. Schoengen. Werken uitgegeven door het Historisch Genootschap te Utrecht, 3rd Series, No. 13. Amsterdam, 1908.

Jean de Schoonhoven. *De Contemptu Huius Mundi.* Critical edition with doctrinal analysis by A. Gruijs. *Bulletin Du Cange Archivum latinitatis medii aevi*, XXXIII (1963), 35-97.

Johannes Brinckerinck. "Acht collatiën van Johannes Brinckerinck, een bijdrage tot de kennis van den kanselarbeid der Broeders van het Gemene Leven, uit handschriften der 15de en 16de eeuw." Edited by W. Moll. *Kerkhistorisch Archief*, IV (1866), 97-167.

Johannes Busch. *Des Augustinerpropstes Johannes Busch Chronicon Windeshemense und Liber de reformatione monasteriorum.* Edited by K. Grube. Geschichtsquellen der Provinz Sachsen und angrenzender Gebiete, Vol. XIX. Halle, 1886.

Peter Horn. *Vita magistri Gerardi Magni.* Edited by W. J. Kühler, "De 'Vita magistri Gerardi Magni' van Petrus Horn." *NAKG*, N.S., VI (1909), 325-370.

Rudolph Dier de Muden. *Scriptum de Magistro Gerardo Grote, Domino Florencio et aliis devotis Fratribus.* Published by G. Dumbar in *Reipublicae Daventriensis ab Actis Analecta, seu vetera aliquot scripta inedita.* 3 vols. Deventer, 1719-1725 (Vol. I, pp. 1-87).

Thomas Hemerken a Kempis. *Opera Omnia.* Edited by M. J. Pohl. 7 vols. Freiburg im Breisgau, 1910-1922. Particularly *De Vera Compunctione Cordis, De Imitatione Christi* and *De domino Gerardo Zutphaniae*, found in Vols. I, II and VII respectively.

Willem Vornken. *Epistola de prima institutione monasterii in Windesem.* Edited by J. G. R. Acquoy. *Windesheim*, III, 235-255 (= Appendix I).

iii. *Sources—General*

Arnulf de Boeriis. *Speculum Monachorum. PL*, CLXXXIV, 1175-1178.

Augustine. *On Christian Doctrine.* Translated by J. F. Shaw. *Nicene and Post-Nicene Fathers*, 1st Series, Vol. II. Buffalo, 1887 (pp. 513-597).

——. *The Confessions.* Translated by J. G. Pilkington. *Nicene and Post-Nicene Fathers*, 1st Series, Vol. I. Buffalo, 1886 (pp. 27-207).

——. *The Enchiridion on Faith, Hope and Love.* Translated by J. F. Shaw. *Nicene and Post-Nicene Fathers*, 1st Series, Vol. III. Buffalo, 1887 (pp. 229-276).

——. *The City of God.* Translated by M. Dods. *Nicene and Post-Nicene Fathers*, 1st Series, Vol. II. Buffalo, 1887 (pp. 1-511).

Pseudo-Augustine. *De Spiritu et Anima. PL*, XL, 779-832.

Bernard of Clairvaux. *Sermones in Cantica Canticorum. PL*, CLXXXIII, 785-1198.

——. *Sermones de Tempore, de Sanctis, de Diversia. PL*, CLXXXIII, 35-748.

——. *Five Books on Consideration. Advice to a Pope.* Translated by J. D. Anderson and E. T. Kennan. Cistercian Fathers Series, No. 37. Kalamazoo, 1976.

Pseudo-Bernard of Clairvaux. *Meditationes Piissimae de Cognitione Humanae Conditionis. PL*, CLXXXIV, 485-508.

Bonaventure. *The Triple Way (De Triplici Via). Works*, I, 59-94.

——. *The Tree of Life (Lignum Vitae). Works*, I, 95-144.

——. *Breviloquium. Works*, II.

——. *Soliloquy on the Four Spiritual Exercises (Soliloquium de quatuor mentalibus exercitiis). Works*, III, 33-129.

——. *Treatise on How to Prepare for the Celebration of Mass (Tractatus de praeparatione ad missam). Works*, III, 215-238.

——. *Opera Omnia.* Ad Claras Aquas: Quaracchi, 1882-1902.

Chadwick, O., ed. *Western Asceticism.* Library of Christian Classics, Vol. XII. Philadelphia, 1958.

David of Augsburg. *Spiritual Progress and Life.* A translation of *De Exterioris et Interioris Hominis Compositione* by Dominic Devas. 2 vols. London, 1937.

Gerard van Vliederhoven. *De Veer Utersten. Das Cordiale de quatuor novissimis von Gerhard von Vliederhoven in mittelniederdeutscher Überlieferung.* Edited by M.-L. Dusch. Niederdeutsche Studien, No. 20. Cologne-Vienna, 1975.

Gregory the Great. *Moralium Libri, sive Expositio in Librum B. Job. PL*, LXXV, 509-LXXVI, 782.

——. *Dialogorum Libri IV. PL*, LXXVII, 149-430.

Henry Suso. *Oerloy der Ewigher Wijsheit* (*Horologium Sapientiae*). Edited by Hildegarde van
de Wijnpersse. Groningen-Batavia, 1938.
——. "Suso's Honderd Artikelen in Nederland." Edited by H. U. Meyboom. *Archief
voor Nederlandsche Kerkgeschiedenis*, I (1885), 173-207.
Hugh of St. Victor. *Eruditio Didascalia*. *PL*, CLXXVI, 739-838.
——. *De Modo Orandi*. *PL*, CLXXVI, 977-988.
——. *De Amore Sponsi ad Sponsam*. *PL*, CLXXVI, 987-994.
Hugh Ripelin of Strasbourg. *Compendium Theologicae Veritatis*. In B. Alberti Magni, *Opera
Omnia*, edited by S. C. A. Borgnet, Vol. XXXIV. Paris, 1895.
John Cassian. *The Institutes of the Coenobia*. Translated by E. C. S. Gibson. *Nicene and
Post-Nicene Fathers*, 2d Series, Vol. XI. New York-Oxford-London, 1894 (pp.
201-290).
——. *The Conferences*. Translated by E. C. S. Gibson. *Nicene and Post-Nicene Fathers*, 2d
Series, Vol. XI. New York-Oxford-London, 1894 (pp. 295-545).
John Climacus. *The Ladder of Divine Ascent*. Translated by L. Moore. London, 1959.
McGinn, Bernard, ed. *Three Treatises on Man. A Cistercian Anthropology*. Cistercian Fathers
Series, No 24. Kalamazoo, Michigan, 1977.
Petry, R. C., ed. *Late Medieval Mysticism*. Library of Christian Classics, Vol. XIII. Phila-
delphia, 1957.
The Teaching of the Catholic Church. Compiled by J. Neuner and H. Roos, edited by K.
Rahner and translated by G. Stevens. Staten Island, New York, 1967.
Thomas Aquinas. *Summa Theologiae*. The Blackfriars' Latin-English edition. 60 vols. New
York-London, 1964-.
——. *Summa Contra Gentiles: On the Truth of the Catholic Faith*. Translated by A. G. Pegis,
F. Anderson, V. J. Bourke and C. J. O'Neill. Published in 5 parts. Garden City,
New York: Image Books, 1955-1957.
William of St. Thierry. *The Golden Epistle of Abbot William of St. Thierry*. Translated by W.
Shewring. London, 1973.

Literature

i. *Monographs*

Aalders, C. *Spiritualiteit. Geestelijk Leven Vroeger en Nu*. The Hague, 1969.
Acquoy, J. G. R. *Het Klooster te Windesheim en Zijn Invloed*. 3 vols. Utrecht, 1875-1880.
Alberts W. J. *Moderne Devotie*. Fibulareeks, No. 48. Bussum, 1969.
Aulén, G. *Christus Victor. An Historical Study of the Three Main Types of the Idea of the Atonement*.
London: S. P. C. K. Paperback, 1970.
Axters, S. *Geschiedenis van de Vroomheid in de Nederlanden*. Vol. III: *De Moderne Devotie*. Ant-
werp, 1956.
——. *La Spiritualité des Pays-Bas*. Louvain-Paris, 1948.
Beer, K. C. L. M. de. *Studie Over de Spiritualiteit van Geert Groote*. Brussels-Nijmegen, 1938.
Benrath, G. A., ed. *Wegbereiter der Reformation*. Bremen, 1967.
Bloomfield, M. W. *The Seven Deadly Sins. An Introduction to the History of a Religious Concept*.
Michigan State Universtity Press, 1967.
Bosch, P. van den. *Studiën Over de Observantie der Kruisbroeders in de Vijftiende Eeuw*. Diest,
1968.
Bouyer, L. *The Cistercian Heritage*. Translated by E. Livingstone. London, 1958.
——. *The Spirituality of The New Testament and the Fathers* (*A History of Christian Spirituality*,
Vol. I). Translated by M. P. Ryan. London, 1963.
Butler, C. *Western Mysticism. The Teaching of Augustine, Gregory and Bernard on Contemplation
and the Contemplative Life*. New York: Harper Torchbooks, 1966.
Chadwick, H. *The Early Church*. The Pelican History of the Church, Vol. I.
Harmondsworth, 1967.
Chadwick, O. *John Cassian*. 2d ed. Cambridge, 1968.
Clamens, G. *La Dévotion à l'Humanité du Christ dans la Spiritualité de Thomas a Kempis*. Lyon,
1931.

Copleston, F. *A History of Philosophy*. 8 vols. Garden City, New York: Image Books, 1962-1967.
——. *Aquinas*. Harmondsworth, Middlesex: Penguin Books, 1955.
Cristiani, L. *Jean Cassien*. 2 vols. Abbaye S. Wandrille, 1946.
Daniëls, F. A. M. *Meester Dirc van Delf, Zijn Persoon en Zijn Werk*. Nijmegen-Utrecht, 1932.
Davis, K. R. *Anabaptism and Asceticism. A Study in Intellectual Origins*. Scottdale-Kitchener, 1974.
Debongnie, P. *Jean Mombaer de Bruxelles, Abbé de Livry. Ses Ecrits et ses Réformes*. Louvain-Toulouse, 1927.
Dempsey Douglass, E. J. *Justification in Late Medieval Preaching. A Study of John Geiler of Keisersberg*. Studies in Medieval and Reformation Thought, Vol. I. Leiden, 1966.
Dols, J. M. E. *Bibliografie der Moderne Devotie*. Nijmegen, 1941.
Dudden, F. H. *Gregory the Great. His Place in History and Thought*. 2 vols. London, 1905.
Elder, E. R. ed. *The Spirituality of Western Christendom*. Cistercian Studies Series, No. 30. Kalamazoo, 1976.
Epiney-Burgard, G. *Gérard Grote (1340-1384), et les Débuts de la Dévotion Moderne*. Wiesbaden, 1970.
Fleming, J. V. *An Introduction to the Franciscan Literature of the Middle Ages*. Chicago, 1977.
Geesink, G. H. *Gerard Zerbolt van Zutphen*. Amsterdam, 1879.
Gerretsen, J. H. *Florentius Radewijns*. Nijmegen, 1891.
Gilson, E. *History of Christian Philosophy in the Middle Ages*. New York, 1955.
——. *Théologie et Histoire de la Spiritualité*. Etudes de Théologie et d'Histoire de la Spiritualité, Vol. I. Paris, 1943.
Goossens, L. A. M. *De Meditatie in de Eerste Tijd van de Moderne Devotie*. Haarlem, 1952.
Grabmann, M. *Die Geschichte der katholischen Theologie seit dem Ausgang der Väterzeit*. Freiburg im Breisgau, 1933.
——. *Mittelalterliches Geistesleben*. 3 vols. Munich, 1926.
Greitemann, N. Th. J. *De Studiis Exegeticis Devotionis Modernae*. Warmond, 1935.
Gross, J. *Geschichte des Erbsündendogmas*. Vol. III: *Entwicklungsgeschichte des Erbsündendogmas im Zeitalter der Scholastik*. Munich-Basel, 1971.
Hallier, A. *The Monastic Theology of Aelred of Rievaulx*. Cistercian Studies Series, No. 2. Shannon, 1969.
Hamell, P. J. *Handbook of Patrology*. Staten Island, New York, 1968.
Harnack, A. *History of Dogma*. Translated from the 3rd German edition by N. Buchanan. 7 vols. London-Edinburgh-Oxford, 1897-1899.
Hausherr, I. *Penthos. La Doctrine de la Componction dans l'Orient Chrétien*. Rome, 1944.
Hombergh, F. A. H. van den. *Leven en Werk van Jan Brugman O. F. M. (c. 1400-1473), met een Uitgave van Twee van Zijn Tractaten*. Groningen, 1967.
Huijben, J., and Debongnie, P. *L'Auteur ou les Auteurs de l'Imitation*. Louvain, 1957.
Hyma, A. *The Christian Renaissance: A History of the "Devotio Moderna."* 2d ed. Hamden, Connecticut, 1965.
——. *The Brethren of the Common Life*. Grand Rapids, 1950.
——. *Renaissance to Reformation: A Critical Review of the Spiritual and Temporal Influence on Medieval Europe*. Grand Rapids, 1951.
Kelly, J. N. D. *Early Christian Doctrines*. 4th ed. London, 1968.
——. *Early Christian Creeds*. 3rd ed. London, 1972.
——. *Jerome. His Life, Writings and Controversies*. London, 1975.
Knappert, L. *Het Ontstaan en de Vestiging van het Protestantisme in de Nederlanden*. Utrecht, 1924.
Knierim, P. H. J. *Dirc van Herxen (1385-1457), rector van het Zwolse fraterhuis*. Leiden, 1926.
Knowles, D. *The Evolution of Medieval Thought*. New York: Vintage Books, 1964.
——. *The English Mystical Tradition*. New York-Evanston: Harper Torchbooks, 1965.
Kohls, E.-W. *Die Theologie des Erasmus*. *Theologische Zeitschrift*, Special Issue, Vol. I, Pts. 1 and 2. Basel, 1966.
Koning, W. A. *Gerardi Zutphaniensis, vita, scriptis et meritis*. Utrecht, 1858.

Kuiper, G. J. M. *Huis en Klooster St. Antonius te Albergen.* N.pl., n.d.

Leclercq, J. *The Love of Learning and the Desire for God.* Translated by C. Misrahi. New York, 1961.

——., Vandenbroucke, Fr., and Bouyer, L. *The Spirituality of the Middle Ages (A History of Christian Spirituality,* Vol. II). Translated by the Benedictines of Holme Eden Abbey, Carlisle. London, 1968.

Lievens, R. *Jordanus van Quedlinburg in de Nederlanden. Een Onderzoek van de Handschriften.* Koninklijke Vlaamse Academie voor Taal- en Letterkunde, Series 6, No 82. Ghent, 1958.

Lovatt, R. W. "The Influence of the Religious Literature of Germany and the Low Countries on English Spirituality, c. 1350-1475." Unpublished D. Phil. dissertation, Oxford, 1965-1966.

Lücker, M. A. *Meister Eckhart und die Devotio Moderna.* Leiden, 1950.

McGiffert, A. C. *A History of Christian Thought.* 2 vols. New York-London, 1932-1933.

McGinn, B. *The Golden Chain. A Study of the Theological Anthropology of Isaac of Stella.* Cistercian Studies Series, No. 15. Washington, 1972.

Meinsma, K. O. *Middeleeuwse Bibliotheken.* Zutphen, 1903.

Mestwerdt, P. *Die Anfänge des Erasmus. Humanismus und Devotio Moderna.* Leipzig, 1917.

Mohler, J. A. *The Heresy of Monasticism. The Christian Monks: Types and Anti-types.* Staten Island, New York, 1971.

Moll, W. *Kerkgeschiedenis van Nederland voor de Hervorming.* 2 vols. Utrecht, 1864-1871.

Obbema, P. F. J. *Een Deventer Bibliotheekcatalogus van het Einde der Vijftiende Eeuw.* Archives et Bibliothèques de Belgique, Special Issue, No. 8. 2 vols. Brussels, 1973.

Oberman, H. A. *The Harvest of Medieval Theology. Gabriel Biel and Late Medieval Nominalism.* 2d ed. Grand Rapids, 1967.

——. *Werden und Wertung der Reformation. Vom Wegestreit zum Glaubenskampf.* 2d ed. Tübingen, 1979.

Pelikan, J. *The Christian Tradition. A History of the Development of Doctrine,* Vol. I: *The Emergence of the Catholic Tradition (100-600).* Chicago-London, 1971.

Persoons, E. *Recente Publicaties over de Moderne Devotie: 1959-1972.* Stencilled publication of the Institute for Medieval Studies, University of Louvain. Louvain, 1972.

Poschmann, B. *Penance and the Anointing of the Sick.* Translated by F. Courtney. New York, 1964.

Post, R. R. *De Moderne Devotie. Geert Groote en Zijn Stichtingen.* 2d ed. Amsterdam, 1950.

——. *The Modern Devotion. Confrontation with Reformation and Humanism.* Studies in Medieval and Reformation Thought, Vol. III. Leiden, 1968.

——. *Kerkgeschiedenis van Nederland in de Middeleeuwen.* 2 vols. Utrecht-Antwerp, 1957.

——. *Kerkelijke Verhoudingen in Nederland voor de Reformatie.* Utrecht-Antwerp, 1954.

——. *Scholen en Onderwijs in Nederland Gedurende de Middeleeuwen.* Utrecht-Antwerp, 1954.

Pourrat, P. *La Spiritualité Chrétienne.* Revised edition. 4 vols. Paris, 1947-1951.

Prestige, G. L. *God in Patristic Thought.* London: S.P.C.K. Paperback, 1964.

Puyol, P. E. *La Doctrine du Livre de Imitatione Christi.* 2d ed. Paris, 1898.

Renaudet, A. *Préreforme et Humanisme à Paris Pendant les Premières Guerres d'Italie.* 2d ed. Paris, 1953.

Resch, P. *La Doctrine Ascétique des Premiers Maitres Egyptiens du Quatrième Siècle.* Paris, 1931.

Revius, J. *Daventria illustrata sive historia urbis Daventriensis libri sex.* Leiden, 1651.

Richard, L. J. *The Spirituality of John Calvin.* Atlanta, Georgia, 1974.

Roelink, J. *De Moderne Devotie.* Dichterbij Series. Kampen, n.d.

Rooy, J. van. *Gerard Zerbolt van Zutphen,* Vol. I: *Leven en Geschriften.* Nijmegen, 1936.

Ruh, K. *Bonaventura Deutsch. Ein Beitrag zur deutschen Franziskanermystik und -scholastik.* Bern, 1956.

Salley, C. L. "The Ideals of the Devotio Moderna as Reflected in the Life and Writings of Jacques Lefèvre d'Etaples." Unpublished Ph.D. dissertation, University of Michigan, Ann Arbor, 1953.

Sassen, F. *De Wijsbegeerte der Middeleeuwen in de Nederlanden.* Lochem, 1944.

Savary, L. M. *Psychological Themes in the Golden Epistle of William of Saint-Thierry to the Carthusians of Mont-Dieu.* Analecta Cartusiana, No. 8. Salzburg, 1973.

Seeberg, R. *Text-Book of the History of Doctrines.* Translated by C. E. Hay. 2 vols. Philadelphia. 1905.

Slotemaker de Bruine, M. C. *Het Ideaal der Navolging van Christus ten Tijde van Bernard van Clairvaux.* Wageningen, 1926.

Southern, R. W. *Western Society and the Church in the Middle Ages.* The Pelican History of the Church, Vol. II. London-Toronto, 1970.

Spoelhof, W. "Concepts of Religious Nonconformity and Religious Toleration as Developed by the Brethren of the Common Life in the Netherlands, 1374-1489." Unpublished Ph.D. dissertation, University of Michigan, Ann Arbor, 1946.

Steensma, R. *Het Klooster Thabor by Sneek en Zijn Nagelaten Geschriften.* Varia Vrisica. Leeuwarden, 1970.

Steer, Georg. *Hugo Ripelin von Strassburg. Zur Rezeptions-und Wirkungsgeschichte des "Compendium theologicae veritatis" im deutschen Spätmittelalter.* Würzburger Forschungen: Texte und Textgeschichte, 2. Tübingen, 1981.

Steinmetz, D. C. *Misericordia Dei. The Theology of Johannes von Staupitz in its Late Medieval Setting.* Studies in Medieval and Reformation Thought, Vol. IV. Leiden, 1968.

Störig, H. J. *Geschiedenis van de Filosofie.* Translated by P. Brommer. 2 vols. Utrecht-Antwerp: Prisma Boeken, 1972.

Strijd, Krijn. *Structuur en Inhoud van Anselmus' "Cur Deus Homo."* Assen, 1958.

Sudbrack, J. *Die Geistliche Theologie des Johannes von Kastl.* Beiträge zur Geschichte des alten Mönchtums und des Benediktinerordens, No. 27. 2 vols. Münster, 1967.

Tanquery, A. *The Spiritual Life. A Treatise on Ascetical and Mystical Theology.* Translated by H. Branderis. 2d ed. Tournai-Paris-Rome-New York, 1930.

Tentler, Thomas N. *Sin and Confession on the Eve of the Reformation.* Princeton, New Jersey, 1977.

Théologie de la Vie Monastique. Etudes sur la tradition patristique. Etudes publiées sous la direction de la Faculté de Théologie S. J. de Lyon-Fourvière, No 49. Lyon-Fourvière, 1961.

Trithemius, Johannes. *De Scriptoribus Ecclesiasticis.* Cologne, 1546.

Ullmann, C. *Reformers before the Reformation, principally in Germany and The Netherlands.* Translated by R. Menzies. 2 vols. Edinburgh, 1885.

Völker, W. *Scala Paradisi. Eine Studie zu Johannes Climacus and zugleich eine Vorstudie zu Symeon dem neuen Theologen.* Wiesbaden, 1968.

Walsh, J., ed. *Spirituality Through the Centuries. Ascetics and Mystics of the Western Church.* London, n.d.

Wansem, C. van der. *Het Ontstaan en de Geschiedenis der Broederschap van het Gemene Leven tot 1400.* Louvain, 1958.

Watrigant, H. *Quelques Promoteurs de la Méditation Méthodique au XVe Siècle.* Paris, 1919.

——. *De Examine Conscientiae juxta Ecclesiae Patres, sanctum Thomam et Fratres Vitae Communis.* Enghien, 1909.

Webb, C. C. J. *Studies in the History of Natural Theology.* Oxford, 1915.

Weiler, A. G., et al. *Geschiedenis van de Kerk in Nederland.* Utrecht: Aula Boeken, No. 100, 1963.

Wentzlaff-Eggebert, Fr.-W. *Deutsche Mystik zwischen Mittelalter und Neuzeit.* Berlin, 1969.

Wilmart, A. *Auteurs Spirituels et Texts Dévots de Moyen Age Latin.* 2d ed. Paris, 1971.

Woerkum, M. Th. P. van. *Het Libellus "Omnes, Inquit, Artes," Een Rapiarium van Florentius Radewijns.* 3 vols. Mimeographed doctoral dissertation, Theological Faculty of the Society of Jesus, Louvain. Limited circulation. Nijmegen, 1950.

Workman, H. *The Evolution of the Monastic Ideal.* Boston: Beacon Paperback, 1962.

Zieleman, G. C. *Middelnederlandse Epistel-en Evangeliepreken.* Kerkhistorische Bijdragen, Vol. VIII. Leiden, 1978.

Zijl, T. P. van. *Gerard Groote, Ascetic and Reformer.* Washington, 1963.

ii. *Articles*

Alberts, W. J. "Zur Historiographie der Devotio Moderna und Ihrer Erforschung." *Westfälische Forschungen*, XI (1958), 51-67. This article can also be found in F. Petri and W. J. Alberts, *Gemeinsame Probleme Deutsch-Niederländischer Landes- und Volksforschung*. Bijdragen van het Instituut voor Middeleeuwse Geschiedenis der Rijksuniversiteit te Utrecht, Vol. XXXII. Groningen, 1962 (pp. 144-171).

Axters, S. "Inleiding tot een Geschiedenis van de Mystiek in de Nederlanden." *Verslagen en Mededeelingen van de Koninklijke Vlaamse Academie voor Taal- en Letterkunde*, 1967, pp. 165-306.

Bartoš, F. M. "Hus, Lollardism and Devotio Moderna in the Fight for a National Bible." *Communio Viatorum*, III (1960), 247-254.

Bosch, P. van den. "De Bibliotheken van de Kruisherenkloosters in de Nederlanden voor 1550." In *Contributions à l'Histoire des Bibliothèques et de la Lecture aux Pays-Bas avant 1600/ Studies over het Boekenbezit en Boekengebruik in de Nederlanden voor 1600*. Archives et Bibliothèques de Belgique, Special Issue, No. 11. Brussels, 1974 (pp. 563-636).

Bruin, C. C. de. "Opmerkingen Over de Inspiratiebronnen van de Moderne Devotie." In *Het Land van Cuijk, Kerkelijk en Politiek Verleden*. Verslagboek Historisch Congres Cuijk, 1971. No place, no date (pp. 68-91).

———. "Het Bonaventura-Ludolphiaanse Leven van Jezus." In *Dr. L. Reypens-Album*, edited by A. Ampe. Studiën en Tekstuitgaven van *OGE*, Vol. XVI. Antwerp, 1964 (pp. 115-130).

De Blic, J. "Syndérèse ou Conscience?" *RAM*, XXV (1949), 146-157.

Debongnie, P. "Les Thèmes de l'Imitation." *Revue d'Histoire Ecclésiastique*, XXXVI (1940), 289-344.

De Guibert, J. "La Componction de Coeur." *RAM*, XV (1934), 225-240.

Deschamps, J. "Middelnederlandse vertalingen van *Super modo vivendi* (7e hoofdstuk) en *De libris teutonicalibus* van Gerard Zerbolt van Zutphen." *Handelingen van de Koninklijke Zuidnederlandse Maatschappij voor Taal-en Letterkunde en Geschiedenis*, XIV (1960-1961), 67-108 and XV (1961-1962), 175-220.

Ditsche, M. "Zur Herkunft und Bedeutung des Begriffes *devotio moderna*." *Historisches Jahrbuch der Görres-Gesellschaft*, LXXIX (1960), 124-145.

Eis, G. "Fasciculus Myrrhae." *Leuvense Bijdragen*, XLIX (1960), 90-96.

Elder, R. "William of St. Thierry: The Monastic Vocation as an Imitation of Christ." *Citeaux*, XXV (1975), 9-30.

Gall, H. "De Christus-gedachte bij Geert Grote." *Ons Geestelijk Leven*, XX (1941), 220-240.

Gemelli, A. "The Ascetical Doctrine of St. Bonaventure." *The Cord, A Franciscan Spiritual Review*, VII (1957), 339-348 and 372-379.

Ginneken, J. van. "Trois textes pré-Kempistes du premier livre de l'Imitation." *Verhandelingen der Koninklijke Nederlandse Akademie van Wetenschappen*, Afdeling Letterkunde, N.S., XLIV (1940), 5-12.

Gleumes, H. "Der hl. Bonaventure und die Imitatio Christi." *Franziskanische Studien*, XV (1928), 294-315.

———. "Gerhard Groot und die Windesheimer als Verehrer des hl. Bernhard von Clairvaux." *Zeitschrift für Aszese und Mystik*, X (1935), 90-112.

Gosmann, E. "Devotio Moderna als Selbstbezeichnung einer geistlichen Erneuerungsbewegung." In *Antiqui und Moderni im Mittelalter. Eine geschichtliche Standortbestimmung*. Munich-Paderborn-Vienna, 1974 (pp. 117-125).

Grabmann, M. "Der Einfluss des hl. Bonaventura auf die Theologie und Frömmigkeit des deutschen Mittelalters." *Zeitschrift für Aszese und Mystik*, XIX (1944), 19-27.

Huijben, J. "Y a-t-il une spiritualité flamande?" *VSp*, L (1937), Supplément, 129-147.

———. "De Verspreiding der Nederlandsche Spiritualiteit in het Buitenland in de XIVe en XVe Eeuw." *OGE*, IV (1930), 168-182.

———. "Le *De Adhaerendo Deo*." *VSp*, VII (1922), Supplément, 89-93.

———., and Debongnie, P. "Geert Groote's Brief Over de Navolging van Christus." *OGE*, XXV (1951), 269-278.

Hyma, A. "Is Gerard Zerbolt of Zutphen the author of the 'Super modo vivendi'?" *NAKG*, N.S., XVI (1921), 107-128.

——. "The Original Version of 'De Imitatione Christi' by Gerard Zerbolt of Zutphen." *AGAU*, LXIX (1950), 1-42.

Jolliffe, P. S. "Middle English Translations of *De Exterioris et Interioris Hominis Compositione.*" *Medieval Studies*, XXVI (1974), 259-277.

Jong, J. de. "Karakter en Invloed der Moderne Devotie." *Historisch Tijdschrift*, IV (1925), 26-58.

——. "Een Nederlandse Godsdienstige Beweging: de Moderne Devotie." *Nederlandsche Katholieke Stemmen*, XXVIII (1928), 99-109.

Jostes, Fr. "Die Schriften des Gerhard Zerbolt van Zutphen. De libris teutonicalibus." *Historisches Jahrbuch der Görres-Gesellschaft*, XI (1890), 1-22 and 709-717.

Klinkenberg, H. M. "Die Devotio Moderna unter dem Thema 'Antiqui-Moderni' Betrachtet." In *Antiqui und Moderni. Traditionsbewusstsein und Fortschrittsbewusstsein im späten Mittelalter*, edited by A. Zimmermann. Miscellanea Medievalia, Vol. IX. Berlin, 1974 (pp. 394-419).

Kronenberg, M. E., and Hulshof, A. "De Bibliotheek van het Heer-Florenshuis te Deventer." *NAKG*, N.S., IX (1912), 150-164, 252-300 and 313-322.

Kruitwagen, B. "De Karthuizer Martinus van Schiedam en zijn ondergeschoven werkje 'De spiritualibus ascensionibus'." *Tijdschrift voor Boek- en Bibliotheekwezen*, VI (1908), 276-286.

Kurzinger, J. "Zur Deutung der Johannestaufe in den mittelalterlichen Theologie." In *Aus der Geisteswelt des Mittelalters*, Festschrift für Martin Grabmann. Münster, 1935 (pp. 954-973).

Longpré, E. "La Théologie Mystique de St. Bonaventure." *Archivum Franciscanum Historicum*, XIV (1921), 36-108.

Lourdaux, W. "De Broeders van het Gemene Leven." *Bijdragen. Tijdschrift voor Filosofie en Theologie*, XXXIII (1972), 372-416.

——. "Het Boekenbezit en het Boekengebruik bij de Moderne Devoten." In *Contributions à l'Histoire des Bibliothèques et de la Lecture aux Pays-Bas avant 1600/Studies over het Boekenbezit en Boekengebruik in de Nederlanden voor 1600*. Archives et Bibliothèques de Belgique, Special Issue, No. 11. Brussels, 1974 (pp. 247-325).

——. "Gérard Zerbolt de Zutphen." *DSp*, VI, 284-289.

——. "Dévotion Moderne et Humanisme Chrétien." In *The Late Middle Ages and the Dawn of Humanism Outside Italy*, edited by G. Verbeke and J. IJsewijn. Louvain-The Hague, 1972 (pp. 57-77).

Lovatt, R. "The Imitation of Christ in Late Medieval England." *Transactions of the Royal Historical Society*, 5th Series, XVIII (1968), 97-121.

Mak, J. J. "Christus bij de Moderne Devoten." *OGE*, IX (1935), 105-166.

Man, D. de. "Heinrich Suso en de Moderne Devoten." *NAKG*, N.S., XIX (1926), 279-283.

Mierlo, J. van. "Over het Ontstaan der Germaansche Mystiek." *OGE*, I (1927), 11-37.

Miert, L. van. "Een Bijdrage tot de Geschiedenis der Eucharistie in de Nederlanden." *Tijdschrift voor Liturgie*, III (1921-1922), 112-124 and 179-193.

Mikkers, E. "Sint Bernardus en de Moderne Devotie." *Citeaux in de Nederlanden*, IV (1953), 149-186.

Möllerfeld, J. "Die Schönheit des Menschen nach Dionys dem Kartäuser." In *Dr. L. Reypens-Album*, edited by A. Ampe. Studiën en Tekstuitgaven van *OGE*, Vol. XVI. Antwerp, 1964 (pp. 229-240).

Munz, P. "John Cassian." *JEH*, XI (1960), 1-22.

Oberman, H. A. "The Shape of Late Medieval Thought: The Birthpangs of the Modern Era." In *Pursuit of Holiness in Late Medieval and Renaissance Religion*, edited by C. Trinkaus and H. A. Oberman. Studies in Medieval and Reformation Thought, Vol. X. Leiden, 1974 (pp. 3-25).

——. "Some Notes on the Theology of Nominalism with Attention to its Relation to the Renaissance." *Harvard Theological Review*, LIII (1960), 47-76.

——. "'Iustitia Christi' and 'Iustitia Dei.' Luther and the Scholastic Doctrines of Justification." *Harvard Theological Review*, LIX (1966), 1-26.

——. "Fourteenth-Century Religious Thought: A Premature Profile." *Speculum*, LIII (1978), 80-93.

Persoons, E. "Het Intellectuele Leven in het Klooster Bethlehem in de 15de Eeuw." *Archief- en Bibliotheekwezen in België*, XLIII (1972), 47-84.

Phillips, D. "The Way to Religious Perfection According to St. Bonaventure's *De Triplici Via*." In *Essays in Medieval Life and Thought*, presented in honour of A. P. Evans, edited by J. H. Mundy, R. W. Emery and B. N. Nelson. New York, 1965 (pp. 31-58).

Preger, W. "Aus Gerhard Zerbolts von Zutphen Schutzschrift für die Brüder und Schwestern vom gemeinsamen Leben." *Abhandlungen der historischen Klasse der königlichen bayerischen Akademie der Wissenschaften*, Vol. XXI (1894), 54-61.

Rayez, A. "Gérard Zerbolt de Zutphen et Saint Bonaventure. Dépendances Littéraires." In *Dr. L. Reypens-Album*, edited by A. Ampe. Studiën en Tekstuitgaven van *OGE*, Vol. XVI. Antwerp, 1964 (pp. 323-356).

Régamey, P. "La 'componction du coeur'." *VSp*, XLIV (1935), Supplément, 1-16 and 65-84; XLV (1935), Supplément, 8-21 and 86-99; and XLIX (1936), Supplément, 179-186 and 302-315.

Reypens, L. "Le Sommet de la Contemplation Mystique." *RAM*, III (1922), 249-271; IV (1923), 256-271; and V (1924), 33-59.

Ruh, K. "Altniederländische Mystik in Deutschsprachiger Überlieferung." In *Dr. L. Reypens-Album*, edited by A. Ampe. Studiën en Tekstuitgaven van *OGE*, Vol. XVI. Antwerp, 1964 (pp. 357-382).

Salmon, P. "L'Ascèse Monastique et la Spiritualité." *VSp*, XXIX (1954), Supplément, 195-240.

Salley, C. L. "Jacques Lefèvre d'Etaples: Heir of the Dutch Reformers of the Fifteenth Century." In *The Dawn of Modern Civilization*, Studies in Renaissance, Reformation and Other Topics presented to honour Albert Hyma, edited by K. A. Strand. 2d ed. Ann Arbor, 1964 (pp. 75-124).

Sargent, M. G. "The Transmission by the English Carthusians of Some Late Medieval Writings." *JEH*, XXVII (1976), 225-240.

Saudreau, A. "La Doctrine de St. Jean Climaque." *VSp*, IX (1924), 353-370.

Schaepdrijver, E. de. "La Dévotion Moderne." *Nouvelle Revue Théologique*, LIV (1927), 742-772.

Slee, J. C. van. "Geschiedenis der Athenaeum Bibliotheek te Deventer." *Tijdschrift voor Boek- en Bibliotheekwezen*, V (1907), 145-170.

Smits, C. "David van Augsburg en de Invloed van Zijn *Profectus* op de Moderne Devotie." *Collectanea Franciscana*, I (1927), 171-203.

Smits van Waesberghe, M. "Iets Over Leer en Praktijk van de Geestelijke Communie in de Middeleeuwen, Voornamelijk in het Licht van de Vaderlandsche Devotie-Literatuur." *Studia Catholica*, XIX (1943), 129-140 and 172-187.

Spaapen, B. "Middeleeuwse Passiemystiek." *OGE*, XXX (1961), 167-185 and 252-299; XL (1966), 5-64; XLI (1967), 209-301 and 321-367; XLII (1968), 5-32, 225-261 and 374-421; and XLIII (1969), 270-304.

Stammler, W. "Studien zur Geschichte der Mystik in Norddeutschland." In *Altdeutsche und Altniederländische Mystik*, edited by K. Ruh. Darmstadt, 1964 (pp. 386-436).

Sudbrack, J. "Existentielles Christentum. Gedanken über die Frömmigkeit der 'Nachfolge Christi'." *Geist und Leben*, XXXVII (1964), 38-63.

Trapp, D. "Augustinian Theology of the 14th Century." *Augustiniana*, VI (1956), 146-274.

Vandenbroucke, Fr. "Le Divorce entre Théologie et Mystique. Ses Origines." *Nouvelle Revue Théologique*, LXXII (1950), 372-389.

Viller, M. "Le *Speculum Monachorum* et la 'Dévotion Moderne'." *RAM*, III (1922), 45-56.

——. "Le Praecordiale Sacerdotum de Jacques Philippi." *RAM*, XI (1930), 375-395.

Vos, C. M. "Gerard Zerbolt." *Kerkhistorisch Jaarboekje*, N.S., I (1864), 102-138.

Watrigant, H. "La Méditation Méthodique et l'Ecole des Frères de la Vie Commune." *RAM*, III (1922), 134-155.

Wenzel, Siegfried. "The Seven Deadly Sins: Some Problems of Research." *Speculum*, XLIII (1968), 1-22.

Woerkum, M. Th. P. van. "Florentius Radewijns: Leven, Geschriften, Persoonlijkheid en Ideeën." *OGE*, XXIV (1950), 337-364.

——. "Het Libellus '*Omnes, inquit, artes*,' Een Rapiarium van Florentius Radewijns." *OGE*, XXV (1951), 113-158 and 225-268.

Zumkeller, A. "Das Ungenügen der menschlichen Werken bei den deutschen Predigern des Spätmittelalters." *Zeitschrift für katholischen Theologie*, LXXXI (1959), 265-305.

——. "Die Augustinerschule des Mittelalters." *Analecta Augustiniana*, XXVII (1964), 167-260.

Encyclopedias, Dictionaries and Lexicons

Allgemeine Deutsche Biographie. 1857-1912.

Bouyer, L. *Dictionary of Theology.* Translated by C. U. Quinn. New York, 1965.

A Dictionary of Christian Theology. Edited by A. Richardson. London, 1969.

Dictionnaire de Spiritualité, Ascétique et Mystique. 1932-.

Encyclopedia of Religion and Ethics. Edited by J. Hastings. New York-Edinburgh, 1912-1927.

The Encyclopedia of Philosophy. Edited by Paul Edwards. New York and London, 1967.

Hoffmeister, J. H. *Wörterbuch der philosophischen Begriffe.* 2d ed. Hamburg, 1955.

Lexikon für Theologie und Kirche. 2d ed. 1957-1965.

New Catholic Encyclopedia. 1967.

The New Schaff-Herzog Encyclopedia of Religious Knowledge. 1908-1912.

The Oxford Dictionary of the Christian Church. Edited by F. L. Cross. 2d ed. London-New York-Toronto, 1974.

Die Religion in Geschichte und Gegenwart. 3rd ed. 1957-1965.

Rahner, J., and Vorgrimler, H. *Theological Dictionary.* Translated by R. Strachan. New York, 1965.

Sacramentum Mundi. An Encyclopedia of Theology. Edited by K. Rahner *et al.* Montreal, 1968-1970.

INDEX OF NAMES

Abelard, Peter, 130
Albert the Great, 258
Alexander of Hales, 64, 215
Ambrose, 20, 124, 129
Amoris, Helmicus, 32
Amoris, Johannes, 32
Anselm of Canterbury, 20, 50, 87, 129-130, 136, 138, 250
Anthony, Saint, 187
Aquinas, Thomas, 20, 22, 42, 43, 44, 45, 47, 55, 57, 58, 59, 61, 62, 63, 64, 65, 66, 67, 71, 73, 86, 87, 94, 108, 109, 119, 120, 121, 122, 123, 124, 125, 146, 167, 169, 183, 184, 185, 191, 199, 200, 204, 209, 215, 258
Arbostier, Bernard, 292, 293
Aristotle, 20, 43, 59, 61
Arnulf de Boeriis, 21-22, 24, 25, 244, 246, 252
Athanasius, Saint, 21, 73
Augustine, 19, 21, 42, 43, 44-45, 48, 52, 55, 57, 61, 63, 67, 68, 73, 75, 84, 90, 94, 110, 120, 129, 139, 143, 144, 146, 157, 161, 162, 165, 166, 196, 197, 198, 204, 217, 218, 222, 226, 232, 234, 274, 284
pseudo-Augustine, 21, 25
Aulén, G., 50, 129
Axters, S., 17, 288, 297, 298, 299

Badius Ascensius, Josse, 30
Bake, Alijt, 295, 297
Basil the Great, 20
Bede, 20, 190
Beer, K. C. L. M. de, 144
Benedict of Nursia, 20, 276
Bernard of Clairvaux, 19, 21, 24, 25, 57, 103, 104, 105, 110, 111, 139, 140, 143, 146, 156, 157, 178, 193, 196, 197, 223, 224, 235, 241, 247, 269, 276, 286, 306
pseudo-Bernard, 22, 24
Biel, Gabriel, 166, 202, 228, 284, 298
Bloomfield, M. W., 258, 259, 260
Bonaventure, 6, 16, 20, 22, 23, 24, 25, 41, 44, 63, 65, 68, 73, 87, 109, 110, 121, 122, 124, 125, 133, 151, 156, 157, 169, 203, 206, 215, 217, 219, 223, 235, 240, 241, 243, 244, 246, 252, 254, 255, 258, 264, 271, 276, 283, 284, 286
pseudo-Bonaventure, 22
Bosch, P. van den, 29

Bouyer, Louis, 75
Brinckerinck, Johannes, 63-64, 74, 157, 214, 224, 227-228, 229, 263, 269, 289, 291
Brugman, Jan, 34
Busch, Johannes, 1, 18, 30, 105

Calvin, John, 6, 36
Cassian, John, 15, 16, 19, 24, 30, 135, 157, 192, 240, 247, 250, 251, 257, 258, 259, 261, 262, 269, 274, 276, 277, 281-282, 286, 302-307
Chrysostom, John, 20, 100, 162, 303
Claus of Euskirchen, 158
Climacus, John, 15, 20, 24, 30, 157, 251-252, 262, 264, 286, 302-306

Damian, Peter, 254
David of Augsburg, 16, 22, 24, 26, 30, 48, 50, 55, 65, 66, 101, 156, 157, 206, 224, 226, 240, 242, 243, 246, 252, 255, 256, 262, 263, 276, 279, 280, 283, 302-307
Davis, K. R., 6-7, 88, 89-91, 229
Dieburg, Peter of, 229
Dier of Muden, Rudolph, 23
pseudo-Dionysius, 44, 236, 240, 256
Ditsche, M., 300

Epiney-Burgard, G., 53, 153
Evagrius Ponticus, 257, 259, 281

Francis, Saint, 103, 105, 111

Gansfort, Wessel, 89, 228, 229
Garcia-Villoslada, R., 106
Geesink, G. H., 5-6, 10, 17, 73
Geiler of Keisersberg, Johann, 34, 219, 298
Gerretsen, J. H., 49
Gerson, Jean, 219, 238
Goossens, L. A. M., 7-8, 23, 31, 244, 245, 253, 254, 255, 264, 274, 291, 296, 298, 299
Gregory the Great, 19, 25, 39, 136, 143, 157, 174, 177, 196, 198, 202, 207, 214, 218, 251, 253, 254, 257-258, 259, 261, 262, 268, 276, 277, 298, 302-306
Gregory of Nyssa, 129, 132, 133
Gronde, Jan van de, 184
Gross, Julius, 87

Grote, Gerard, 1, 2, 10, 12, 17, 24, 32, 36,
    49, 77, 88, 89, 105, 106, 142, 144, 145,
    150, 152, 153, 154, 157, 158, 160, 166,
    175, 183-184, 189, 197, 198, 227, 228,
    232, 236, 240, 254, 255, 263, 287, 289,
    296, 298, 300

Herp, Hendrik, 34
Herxen, Dirc van, 2, 13, 23, 101, 198,
    289, 292
Hilary of Poitiers, 129
Hugh of St. Victor, 20, 21, 276, 279, 305
Huyben, Dom J., 35, 299
Hyma, Albert, 6-7, 8, 9, 10, 18, 36, 82,
    88-91

Irenaeus, 74, 128-129, 132
Isidor of Seville, 20, 304

Jacobus de Voragine, 24, 254
Jerome, Saint, 19, 212, 274, 276, 304
John of Damascus, 129
Jong, Johannes de, 90

Kastl, Johannes von, 35
Kelly, J. N. D., 129
Kempis, Thomas a, 2, 10, 11, 18, 44, 64,
    84, 101, 207, 227, 228, 263, 288, 289-
    290, 292, 293, 295, 297, 298
Koning, W. A., 5, 10

Leclercq, Jean, 253
Lefèvre d'Etaples, Jacques, 36
Lombard, Peter, 183, 215
Lourdaux, W., 8
Loyola, Ignatius of, 36
Luther, Martin, 6, 36, 55, 88, 89, 90, 188,
    231, 299

Mahieu, J., 29, 264
Mak, J. J., 158, 288
Mande, Hendrik, 2, 198, 295
Mikkers, E., 153
Mombaer, Johannes, 2, 23, 228, 229, 299-
    300

Nicholas of Cusa, 44

Origen, 50, 281

Peters, Gerlach, 2, 101, 295
Philippi, Jacobus, 34
Plato, 42, 43, 44, 61
Plotinus, 45
Pomerius, Henry, 300
Post, R. R., 8-9, 11, 13, 17, 299
Prosper of Aquitaine, 21

Radewijns, Florens, 1-2, 6, 11, 12, 16-17,
    22, 23-24, 26, 56, 63, 66, 106, 146, 152,
    155, 157, 158, 200, 206, 237, 254, 255,
    256, 262, 274, 276, 278, 279, 287, 298,
    300
Rayez, A., 106
Ripelin, Hugh, 22-23, 258
Rooy, J. van, 7, 10, 17, 27-30, 150, 154,
    155
Ruh, Kurt, 34
Ruusbroec, Jan van, 254, 255, 300
Rijkel, Dionysius (the Carthusian) van,
    73, 87, 112

Salmon, P., 283
Savary, L., 57
Schoonhoven, Jan van, 2
Scotus, Duns, 73, 209
Seneca, 20
Spoelhof, William, 8-9
Srawley, J. H., 135
Standonck, Jan, 35, 36
Suso, Henry, 22, 24, 34, 254

Tauler, Johannes, 34

Ullmann, C., 5, 9

Vornken, William, 301
Vos, C. M., 5

Watrigant, H., 7-8, 244
William of Occam, 43
William of St. Thierry, 16, 21, 24, 57, 75,
    194, 240, 243, 244, 246, 250, 274, 276,
    278, 286, 305, 306
Willibrord, 301
Woerkum, M. Th. P. van, 18, 23, 26

Ximenes de Cisneros, Garcia, 36

INDEX OF SUBJECTS

A

Active Life, see Ascetical Life

Absolution, Priestly, 183; plays only a declaratory role, 183-184; in vain in absence of contrition, 183-184

Affectio: as essence of prayer, 279; source of, 279; description and definition of, 279, 300; and *devotio*, 300

Anabaptists: and Modern Devotion, 6-7, 89-91

Anthropology, General, 56-57; and spirituality, 57; Cistercian, Thomistic and Augustinian influences on Zerbolt's, 57, 94; Zerbolt's conventional, 90; that of the Devotionalists, 90-91

Anthropology, Philosophical, 58-68, 94

Anthropology, Theological, 57, 69-75; of the Devotionalists, 288, 289

Apologists, 128, 154

Apostolic Fathers, 128, 154

Appetite, Concupiscent, 67, 76, 81; consists of love and joy, 65; God as object of, 65, 81; effect of Fall on, 78, 81, 82, 85-86; natural inclination of towards things inferior, 81, cf. 76-77

Appetite, Intellective (or Rational): consists of will, 64, 65, 66, 69; God as object of, 66; as love, 66; rebellious concupiscence as going contrary to, 78; also see Will

Appetite, Irascible: consists of hope and courage, 65; function of, 65, 81-82; effect of Fall on, 78, 81-82, cf. 85

Appetite, Natural: and spiritual ascent, 231

Appetite, Rational, see Appetite, Intellective

Appetite, Sensitive (Sensible), 64-65, 86; consists of concupiscent and irascible appetites, 64-65; God as object of, 65; opposed to reason, 69; effect of Fall on, 78, 80-82, 86

Aristotelian/Aristotelianism, 42, 44, 57, 63, 67, 68, 90

Ascetical Life (also called Active), 241-273; eradiction of vice as most important goal of, 234, 242; as preparation for mystical life, 236, 239-240; reformation of will an important aspect of, 242; portrayed as consecutive or collateral

ascents, 264-265, cf. 243; greater emphasis on than on mystical life, 231-233, 286, 294-295; spiritualization of, 263-264, 282-283, 285-286; emphasis on typical of Devotionalists, 294-295, 299

Aseity, 99

Atonement: as redemption, 137-138

Atonement, Anselmian Doctrine of, 131, 134-139, 154

Atonement, Classic (or Dramatic) Doctrine of, 50, 129, 131-133, 137-138, 140, 146, 154, 155

Atonement, Subjective Doctrine of, 154-157, also see Soteriology

Attrition: rejection of implied, 180, 204; can be achieved without aid of grace, 204; not sufficient for valid communion, 215

Augustinian/Augustinianism, 26, 55, 57, 67, 68, 74, 84, 86, 90, 143, 166, 182, 198, 199, 287, 293

B

Baptism, 159, 169-171; removes guilt of original sin, not punishment of, 108, 159, 170; origin of, 169; and circumcision, 170; water as consecrated species for sacrament of, 169-170; through his Christ fulfilled all righteousness, 169-170; deletes actual sin, 170

Benedictines, 32-33

Bernardine, 102, 112, 143, 240, 299

C

Carthusians, 32-33

Charity: definition of, 234; as submission of will to divine will, 238; as goal of spiritual life, 56, 97, 139, 144, 233, 235, 236; as goal of second ascent in *De Ascensionibus*, 265; man can contribute to state of, 141, 236; eradication of vice as way to, 233; Christ as way to, 139-144, 153-154; compunction as way to, 265, 270; signs of success in quest for, 237-238; difficult to attain, 279-280; as a contemplative state, 234, 235-236, 238, 281; as a contemplative state acquired, not infused, 236, 238 (also see Contemplation)

Christ, Person of, 97-127; of one substance with Father and Holy Spirit, 98-99, cf. 99-101; as true God, 98-99, 103, 105-106; reason for emphasizing Christ's divinity, 106-107; as true man, 102-103, 105; reason for stressing Christ's humanity, 106-107; as God the Son (Logos) the *suppositum* (carrier) of both natures, 97, 103-104, cf. 113-115, 119; emphasis on oneness of person, 97, 103-104, 113-115, 119; no confusion of natures in, 97, 103-104, 105, 113, 115-117, 123, 125; emphasis on duality of natures in, 98, 103-104, 105-108, 113-119, 123-124, 125-126, 139, 141-142, 143, 154; reason for emphasizing duality of nature of, 106-107, 127, 154, 284, 285, 290; communication of divine and human attributes in, 113-119; beatific vision enjoyed by, 108, 109, 120, 123; sanctity of, 108-109, 126; as sum of all virtues, 109; humility of, 110-111; awareness of divine ego and Messianic mission, 109, 117-119; freedom of will, 119-120, 124-125; capacity for suffering and nature of, 120-125; physical appearance of, 112; and work of, 154

Christ, Work of: creator, 100; sustainer of universe, 100; performer of miracles, 100; fulfiller of all righteousness, 145-146, 169-170; in his infancy, 146-147; in his baptism, 145-146, 147; in his temptation by Satan, 146, 147; in his passion, 147-151; aim of salvific work, 131; salvific work in general, 127-158; salvific work as mediation, 139; salvific work as justification, 131; salvific work as glorification, 131; salvific work as instruction, illumination and enlightenment, 127, 128, 131, 139-141, 143, 144, 147, 148, 154, 155, 157-158; salvific work as exemplary, 110-111, 117-118, 127, 128, 129, 131, 139, 140, 143, 144-150, 152-153, 154-155, 155-158 (also see Imitation of Christ); salvific work as vicariously redemptive, 128, 129, 135, 136, 137, 139, 140, 146, 154, 155, 158; exemplary redemptive work most important, 289; passion central to salvific work, 154; death as expiatory sacrifice, 129-130, 137; death as propitiatory sacrifice, 129-130, 136; death as satisfying divine justice, 129-130, 134-137, 138, 139, 140, 155; vicarious death expiates original sin

only, 170, 207; sufficiency of vicarious death, 131, 137, 138; efficiency of vicarious death, 131, 138; benefits of vicarious death transmitted by sacraments, 159, 168-169; Christ's life as ransom for man's redemption, 133, 137-138; as way to God, 142, 143, 148; as means to charity, 139-141, 142, 143, 148; as means to vision of God, 139-141, cf. 148; as means to knowledge of God, 139-141, 143, 148, 154; as judge, 53, 100, 142, 153, 209, 216

Cistercians, 33, 56-57, 94

Cognitive Powers (of Soul), 60-64; exterior senses, 60-62; interior senses, 61-62; also see Intellect, Reason, *Synderesis*, and Law (Natural); impact of Fall on, 82-83, 86

Communion, Sacramental, see Eucharistic Communion

Communion, Spiritual, 227-229, 230; and Devotionalists, 227-229, 291-292; relative efficacy of sacramental communion and, 228-229

Compunction (of Fear and Hope): defined and described, 180-182, 253; devotion equated with compunction of hope and love, 269; belongs to active (ascetical) phase of the spiritual life, 270; means of generating, 39, 45-46, 48-49, 51, 52-53, 106-107, 150-151, 162, 164, 165, 173-174, 176, 180, 192, 202, 203, 205, 253-256, 265, 267-270, 271-272, 284, 290, cf. 177; of fear is first result of faith, 167-168; compunction of fear precedes compunction of love, 180; development of as second ascent in *De Ascensionibus*, 265, 267-270; role played by meditation in its generation, 282, 283; its relation to contrition, 177-181; purpose of, 267-270; indispensable to spiritual progress, 94, 167, 282; of fear as way to purity of heart, 167-168, 251, 282, 283, 285, 294, 295, 299; of fear prevents complacency, 298-299; of hope draws man to God, 251; of hope prevents despair, 298-299; more important than imitation of Christ in quest for purity of heart, 296-298; as way to charity, 265, 270; as condition for forgiveness of sins in sacrament of penance, 180-181; as preparation for eucharistic sacrament, 214; and reformation of memory, 250-251; of fear attainable without grace, 204; of hope unattainable without grace, 182, 204; doctrine of prominent in Zerbolt's sources, 251-253; doctrine of given impetus by Devotionalists, 298

Concupiscence, Rebellious or Negative, 69, 78, 79, 85, 86, 87-88; 91-93; definition of, 69, 78; resides in sensitive appetites, 79, 91; immunity from before Fall, 69, 72-73, 81, 88; assertion of after Fall, 78; aggravated in Fall, 81; loss of immunity from after Fall, 48, 51, 55; natural to man, 78, 79, 81, 88, 170-171, 280, cf. 91; immunity from not regained through Christ's death, 88, 131, 272; original sin constitutes and defined as, 86-87, 170; non-culpable for those in Christ, 170-171; guilt of removed through baptism, 88, 170-171 (cf. Baptism); resists intellect and will, 78, 91; prevents man from attaining spiritual goal, 280; subjection of as aim of spiritual life, 86; control established over as second reformation of will, 172; after conquest of, man governed by desire for good, 238; not sinful until after consent of will, 88; causes man to commit actual sins, 91-93, 159

Concupiscence, Sinful, 93; equals cupidity, 234; eradication of leads to purity of heart, 234; purged through reformation of powers of soul, 241-242; eradication of as aim of third ascent in De Ascensionibus, 272

Confession: as part of sacrament of penance, 177, 185-192; in vain without contrition, 184-185; importance of making a good confession, 185; importance of bearing of penitent at time of, 185-187; scrupulousness with respect to, 187-188; spiritual guidance received at time of, 188; as preparation for communion, 215; frequency of, 187, 291

Confession, Lay: defence of, 190-192, 292; benefits to be derived from, 191-192; as expiation of venial sins confessed, 191-192

Confessor: as one who has power of the keys, 188; importance of a prudent one, 188; not to be changed lightly, 188; canonical regulations with regard to, 188; difficulties encountered by scrupulous ones, 189

Conscience, Purity of: achieved through sacrament of penance, 290; a requirement for valid communion, 214-215, 290

Contemplation: as end of spiritual life, 233-241, 285; charity as affective contemplation, 234, 235-236, 238; as state of charity an acquired condition, 236; as intellectual intuition, or vision, of God, 236, 238, 239-241; as affective intuition, or vision, of God, 238, 240-241; as affective intuition, or vision, of God an acquired state, 238; intellectual contemplation an infused state, 236, 239, 240, 281; intellectual contemplation enjoyed by man before Fall, 239; affective contemplation precedes intellectual contemplation, 238, 240-241

Contrition: defined and described, 177-182; self-examination aimed at, 172-177; and compunction, 177-181; as condition for forgiveness of sins in sacrament of penance, 180, 181, 184, 204; as constituent part of sacrament of penance, 177; need of grace to achieve, 182-183; 204; its importance in relation to confession and satisfaction, 183-185, 204; forgiveness of sins in proportion to, 184, 185, 187, 204; as preparation for sacramental communion, 214-215, 219; no certainty that one has achieved state of, 200-202, 205

Conversio Mentis: as contrition, 177

Crosier Fathers, 32-33

Cupidity: definition of, 234; eradiction of leads to purity of heart, 234; purged through reformation of powers of soul, 241-242

Cura animarum: two kinds of, 189; priestly kind to be avoided, 189; non-priestly kind incumbent on all, 189-190

D

Desire, Natural: and spiritual ascent, 231

Depravity, Total, 54, 88-89, 90

Devotio Moderna, see Modern Devotion

Devotion: definition of, 300; to Christ, 140; and preparation for communion, 216-219, cf. 220 and 229-230; as fear of communicating unworthily, 216-217, 218-219, 230; as love and desire for union with Christ in communion, 216-219, 230; as fear and love, and their relative merits for communion, 218-219; as compunction of desire and love, 269; authentic and spurious types of, 269; and affectio, 300; as descriptive of spirituality of Modern Devotion, 300;

of movement founded by Grote as *moderna*, 300-201

Dona gratiae, 58-59, 69-75; effects of Fall on, 77-79, 86

Dona naturae, 58-59, 73-75; effects of Fall on, 51, 79-86

Donum superadditum, 58-59, 69-75; effects of Fall on, 77-79, 86

E

Epistemology, 40, 43, 44, 50, 55, 166; and the *fides quae creditur*, 160-161, 166

Epistola de Vita et Passione Domini Nostri Jesu Christi, 30, 34, 296, 297

Eucharist, 54, 206-230; and Sacrament of Penance, 206; power to consecrate elements of, 208-209, 217-218; real presence of Christ in, 127, 208-210, 212, 216, 230; and transubstantiation, 210; Christ in identical with historical Christ, 209-210, 216

Eucharistic Sacrifice, 206-209; and offering of oneself, 207; benefits of to living and dead, 207, 217; as expiatory sacrifice for sins, 135, 207; *ex opere operato* efficacy of, 207-208, 221-223, 228-229; derives its efficacy from Christ's death, 168-169

Eucharistic Sacrament, 206, 208-210, cf. 212-213; origin of, 208-209; most exalted of all sacraments, 210, 230; of all sacraments most important vehicle of grace, 290; effect of and communicant's disposition (*ex opere operantis* power of sacrament), 212-213, 221-223, 228-229, cf. 219-221; benefits derived from, 217-218, 223-225; and Devotionalists, 291

Eucharistic Commemoration, 207, 210-212; objective aspect of, 211, 212; subjective aspect of, 210-211

Eucharistic Communion: fast as preparation for, 213; requirements for valid and fruitful reception of, 212-219; Sacrament of Penance as preparation for and *facere quod in se est*, 220, 221; preparation for and grace, 220-221, 230; benefits derived from, 217-218, 223-225; frequency of, 218, 225-226, 227-228, 229, 291

Examination of Self, 172-177, 243-248, 265-266; that carried out to generate contrition (in preparation for sacrament of penance), 172-177; general, daily and particular examinations peculiar to spiritual life, 243-248, 265-266; as pre-

paration for sacramental communion, 214; leads to self-knowledge, 244-245; place of Modern Devotion in the history of, 244

Exemplars, Divine, 41-44

Ex opere operantis: and eucharistic sacrament, 212-213, 221-223, 228-229, cf. 219-221

Ex opere operato: and eucharistic sacrifice, 207-208, 221-223, 228-229

Exteriora interiora trahunt: principle of Devotionalist spirituality, 110, 187

F

Facere quod in se est: and preparation for communion, 220, 221; and eradication of capital sins, 263

Faith, 160-168; as *fides qua creditur (habitus fidei)*, 160, 166-168; as *fides quae creditur (articuli fidei)*, 160-166; as beginning of salvation, 167-168, 204; no Protestant elements in Zerbolt's understanding of, 168

Fall: effect of on various powers of soul, 58, 76-86, 161-162, 284; Hyma and Davis on Zerbolt's doctrine of the Fall, 88-91; not all effects of undone through Christ's death, 131; effects of partly undone through reformation of powers of soul, 172

Fides qua creditur (habitus fidei): an infused habit, 166, 204; as an act of will, 167

Fides quae creditur (articuli fidei): truth of proven through divine miracles, 160-161, 166; contents of, 161-165; as remedy for defective innate knowledge of natural law, 161-162

Fomes peccati, 79, 87, also see Concupiscence, Rebellious; resides in sensitive appetites, 79

Franciscan/Franciscans, 50, 55, 102, 105, 112, 155-156, 285-286, 297, 299

G

Generacy: as it relates to Christ, 99

God: nature of, 98-99; of one substance with Son and Holy Spirit, 98-99; impassibility of, 115-116, cf. 120; as creator, 41-42; as creator and *rationes seminales*, 44-45; as first cause, 42; as exemplary cause, 42-44, 55; as *Summum Bonum* (divine goodness), 48, 49-50, 55, 65, 66 (also see Good); as Truth, 160; power and wisdom of, 50, 55; providence of, 45-47, 49; and miracles, 47; will *versus* intellect in, 49, 52, 203; inscrutability of, 203-204; as love and mercy, 41, 48, 51, 53-54, 55, cf. 164, 165; justice of, 51-53, 55, 203, 204; as judge, 41, 52-53; relationship of his justice to his mercy, 54-55; his wrath and mercy as subject matter of Scriptures, 164, 165; salvific plan of, 46-47, 50, 51, 54; as object of concupiscent appetite, 65; as object of man's will, 66, 84; man's natural inclination towards, 66-67, 79-80, 232; affective and intellectual vision of, 70, 75, 238-241 (also see Contemplation and Charity); vision of as goal of spiritual life, 97, 232, 285; vision of as acquired or infused state, 236, 238, 239; vision of enjoyed by Adam before Fall, 239; Zerbolt mostly interested in his attitude towards man, 285

Good (God as *the*): natural inclination towards, 66-67; 79-80; effect of Fall on natural inclination towards, 79-80, 85-86, 89; spiritual ascent as restoration of natural affection for, 86, cf. 88; original sin defined as destruction of natural affection for, 86; destruction of natural affection for not healed by Christ's death, 88; natural inclination towards and rebellious concupiscence, 91, 92-93

Grace: will's need of to combat sin, 85, 89, 95, 167; necessary for all stages of spiritual ascent, 167, 176-177, 182-183, 280-281, 284, 288; need of to achieve contrition, 182-183; need of to achieve compunction of love, 182; need of to perform good works, 196-197, 204; need of to prepare for communion, 220-221, 230; merit possessed by good works result of, 292; Devotionalists' views on necessity of, 288-289; sacraments as vehicles of, 169; nature of, 183, 221-223, 228-229; and nature, 284

Grace, Justifying: not granted without contrition, 184

Grace, Sanctifying: as *donum superadditum*, 70-71, 73, 86; loss of in Fall, 77, 86; and original justice, 87; and original sin, 87

Grace, State of: a requirement for valid communion, 214

H

Heart, Purity of: defined and described, 237-238, 281; as foundation of spiritual life, 139; as basis for charity, 97, 167, 233, 281, and vision of God 97; first objective of the Devotionalists, 144, 237, 294-295; as (immediate) goal of the spiritual life, 233, 236, 237, 281, 285, 294; as aim of *De Reformatione* and *De Ascensionibus*, 241-242, 272, 281; concentration on in *De Reformatione* and *De Ascensionibus*, 285; acquired through compunction, 294, 299, mortification of body, 294, 295, imitation of Christ, 97, 140, 285, eradication of vices, 234, meditation on passion, 150 (cf. 151), meditation which instils compunction of fear, 285; criteria for success in struggle for, 237-238; man can contribute to, 281; Christ as example in quest for, 147, 151; compunction more effective than imitation of Christ in quest for, 285; meditation, leading to compunction, more important than mortification in quest for, 285-286

Heilsgeschichte, 46, 96

Holy Spirit, 54, 98-99; of one substance with Father and Son, 98-99

Humility: chief of all virtues, 110-111; as chief virtue of Christ, 110-111; Christ's as example for man, 144-145, 149; necessity of for penitent, 185-187; as first requirement in the spiritual life, 196; most effective means of generating, 196, 198; indispensable for fruitful communion, 219, 221, 230

Hypostatic Union, 97-98, 103-104, 108-109, 112, 113, 113-115, 122-123, 125-126; subsistence theory regarding, 103-104; dissolution of, 123-124, 125-126

I

Ideas, Divine, 41-44

Image and Likeness: man as ... of God and Trinity, 73-74; soul as ... of God seeks him, 231-232

Imitation of Christ, 97, 140, 151, 153-155, 157-158; made possible through reformation of memory, 251; generated through meditation on person and work of Christ, 106-107, 127, 296; fundamental to spiritual life, 111, 142, 155; role played by in Zerbolt's soteriology, 107, 111, 127; and eradication of capital sins, 262-263, cf. 273; as way to purity of heart, to cultivation of virtues, to charity, to God, to salvation, 140, 142, 143, 147-148, 149-150, 153-154, 157-158, 270-271, 285, 289,

295, 299, cf. 151-152; imitation of Christ's suffering, 148, 151-152, 154, 158; union with Christ which results not Christ mysticism or practical mysticism, 271; as means to purity of heart less important than compunction, 295; importance of to Devotionalists in relation to compunction, 296-298

De Imitatione Christi, 155, 289 (also see Thomas a Kempis)

Incarnation: purpose of, 83, 157-158; as act of humility, 110

Ingenium, 62

Integrity, Gift of, 69-73, 80-81; defined as original justice, 73; effects of Fall on, 77-78, 80-81; cannot be regained in this life, 88; practical consequences of its loss, 91-93; lost in the Fall, 170-171 and 279

Intellect (also called *mens*), 62-64, 67-68, 71-72, 82-83; active and passive 63; passive also called possible intellect, 63; impact of Fall on, 83-86; resisted by rebellious concupiscence, 91; reformation of, 243, 248-250; in reformation of emphasis on acquisition of knowledge required to combat sin and to cultivate virtue, 249-250

Internalization, see Spiritualization

J

Judgement, Final, 53; and good works, 197

Justice, Divine, 51-53, 55, 136; fulfilled by Christ in his baptism, 169-170; satisfied through acts of penance, 193-194; demands that man bear part of penalty for sins, 193, 204

Justice, Original, 73, 75, 77, 77-78; equals gift of integrity, 73, 78; as *donum superadditum*, 73; a preternatural gift, 73, 88; its substance is immunity from rebellious concupiscence, 73; deprived of in Fall, 77-78, 86; consequence of loss for natural inclination towards the good, 79-80, 86; cannot be regained in this life, 78, 86, 88, 131; absence of not included in definition of original sin, 87; effects of loss of in Fall, 91-93

Justification, 54, 159; acquired through sacraments of baptism and penance, 159, 177, 193; as first of three spiritual ascents in *De Ascensionibus* 183; short of charity and perfection, 195; as basis for charity, 195; no certainty with regard

to, 200-204, 205; certainty of dangerous to salvation, 202, 205; uncertainty with regard to will foster compunction, 202, 205; and predestination, 199; sanctification does not accompany, 231

K

Keys, Power of, 184, 185, 187, 188, 190-191, 192, 193, 204

Knowledge of Self, 243-248, 265-266; is beginning of salvation, 177, 244; and self-examination, 243-248, 265-266, cf. 172-177; acquired through self-examination, 244-245; acquired through testimony of others, 247-248, 266; acquired through struggle against sins, 248; serves as incentive to reform faculties of soul, 245

Knowledge, Supernatural: before the Fall, 70, 72; impact of Fall on, 77

L

Last Supper, 146, 149

Lectio, 276-279; indispensable to spiritual progress, 276-279; and *meditatio* and *oratio*, 276-279; appropriate for beginners, 276; reforms the memory, 277

Law, Natural: *synderesis* equated with or grounded in, 63-64; right reason (natural reason) equated with or grounded in, 63-64; and Scriptures complement one another, 161-162

M

Man: natural gifts (*dona naturae*), 58-59; preternatural gifts (*dona gratiae*), 58-59, 69-73; supernatural gifts (*dona gratiae*), 58-59, 69-73; as God's image and likeness, 73-74; as image and likeness of Trinity, 73-74

Mary, Virgin: immaculate conception of, 94; freedom from original sin, 94; as mother of Christ as man, 115; as mother of Christ as God, 115

Meditation, 276-279; its development by Modern Devotion, 7-8; definition of, 61; made possible by means of a reformed memory, 277; as means to generate devotion to Christ, 140, 147-148, 151-152; as foundation of imitation of Christ, 97, 296; its role in generating compunction of fear and hope, 39, 173, 282, 290, 296; if it leads to compunction most effective way to purity of heart, 293; its importance in Zerbolt's thought because it generates compunction, 295-296; indispensable to spiritual progress, 276-279, 299; its importance in Devotionalist spirituality, 296; role played by in spiritualization of ascetical life, 283; and *lectio* and *oratio*, 276-279; appropriate for those who have made progress, 276; role of *rapiaria* in, 299

Memory: as storehouse of sensory and intellectual impressions, 61, cf. 250; and passive (possible) intellect, 63; Augustinian understanding of, 67-68; reformation of, 97, 173, 243, 250-256; reformed through absorbtion of materials which instil compunction, 250-251, cf. 253-256, through information necessary for imitation of Christ, 251, through spiritual reading, 277; reformation of makes meditation possible, 277

Miracles: as proof of truth of revelation, 160-161, 166, 167

Modern Devotion: historiography of, 4, 6; its spirituality influenced by Bernardine and Franciscan traditions, 102, by Grote, 143-144; its thought and spirituality shaped by Zerbolt, 17-18, 24, 286-287; not monolithic in its thought, 4; as a school of spirituality, 2, 18, 299-300; practical, ascetical, active, concrete nature of its spirituality, 143-144, 299, cf. 53; spirituality of not mystical and contemplative, 299; spirituality of reliant on specific *genre* of literature, 26, 30-31, 299; as first religious movement native to Low Countries, 2; authors spawned by, 1-2, 13; and development of methodical meditation, 7-8; its impact on other religious literature, 33-34; and Protestant Reformation, 4-7, 9, 88-89, 90; and Anabaptists, 6-7, 89-91

Moderni: and *ex opere operato* efficacy of the eucharistic sacrament, 222

Mortification of Body: plays secondary role in eradicating vices, 282, 285-286, 293; role played by imitation of Christ in, 295

Mystical Life: union created with Christ through imitation not mystical, 271; neglect of by Zerbolt, 286, 294-295; neglect of typical of Devotionalists, 294-295, 299

N

New Testament: forms unity with Old Testament, 165-166

Nonconformity, Religious: and Brethren of the Common Life, 8-9

O

Obedience, 307-308

Old Testament: forms unity with New Testament, 165-166

Oratio, 276-279; indispensable to spiritual progress, 276-279; and *lectio* and *meditatio*, 276-279; definition of, 278; appropriate for the spiritually advanced, 276; *affectio* as essence of, 278-279

Orthodoxy: of Zerbolt's writings made them widely acceptable, 287

P

Passion: central to Christ's salvific work, 154

Penance, Acts of: required to satisfy divine justice, 193-194; those prescribed by confessor most efficacious, 193; emphasis placed on their importance, 194

Penance, Sacrament of, 159, 171-195; as means of recovering justifying grace, 159, 177, 194-195, cf. 264; after faith, first step in man's spiritual ascent, 171, 204; self-examination carried out in preparation for, 175, 244; consists of contrition, confession and satisfaction, 177; priestly absolution constitutes form of, 183; basis for spiritual life and ascent, 231, 241, 243, 290, cf. 265; as means to purity of conscience, 290; importance of among Devotionalists, 291

Platonic/Platonism, 43, 90

Prayer, see *Oratio*

Predestination, 198-200; 205, 293; *ante praevisa merita*, 198-200, 205; based on foreknowledge, 198-199; as part of divine providence, 198-200, 205, 293; and justification, 199; and free will, 200

Pride: as cause of sin, 76, 110; as essence of sin, 76; as queen of vices, 92; remedy against, 196; also see Sins, Capital

Protestant Reformation: and Modern Devotion, 4-7, 9, 88-89, 90; and Zerbolt, 4-7, 9

Providence, Divine: and predestination, 199-200

R

Rapiaria: served meditational purposes, 299

Real Presence, 208-210, 212

Reason, Deliberating, 62, 63, 69, 82-83; impact of Fall on, 83, 86; will acting contrary to after Fall, 78; rebellious concupiscence must be subjected to, 86; original sin inclining man contrary to dictates of, 86

Reason, Natural or Right: sin contrary to, 76; rebellious concupiscence as going contrary to, 78; will acting contrary to after Fall, 78; effect of Fall on, 83-84; rebellious concupiscence must be subjected to, 86; original sin inclining man to act contrary to dictates of, 86; also see *Synderesis*

Recapitulation (Soteriological Theory of), 128, 132-133

Redemption (Christ's Work of): equated with Christ's atoning death only, 137-138; achieved through Christ's life paid as a ransom, 137-138; from sin, powers of darkness, death, etc., 138

Repentance: as reformation of the will, 172; as preparation for communion, 214-215, 219; as an offering of oneself, 214

Revelation: natural, 39, 41; biblical, 39, 41; truth of authenticated by miracles, 160-161

Righteousness: fulfilled by Christ in his baptism, 169-170

S

Sacraments, 168-195; benefits of Christ's death transmitted by way of, 159, 168-169; number of, 168-169; origins of, 169; as vehicles of grace, 169; reason for their efficacy, 168-169

Saints: as teachers, 150; as examples, 150; attitude of Devotionalists towards, 150

Salvation: divine plan of, 50, 51, 53-54; man can contribute to, 284, 288, 289; uncertainty of, 293; uncertainty of salutary for believer, 293

Sanctification, 54; not simultaneous with justification, 231

Satisfaction (Made for Sins): demanded by God, 51, 52-53; as part of sacrament of penance, 177, 188, 193; as expiation, 192, 194; as therapy, 192, 194; as satisfying divine justice, 193-194; necessity of for salvation, 193, 204; importance of emphasized by Zerbolt, 194

Scintilla conscientiae: equated with *synderesis*, 64

Scriptures: as Zerbolt's source, 18-19; contents of, 39, 51, 55, cf. 164, 165; purpose of, 39, 51, 55, 83-84, cf. 161-164; remedy defective knowledge of natural law, 161-164; and natural law complement one another, 161-162; confrontation with reveals man's condemned state, 162-164; need to be read by laymen, 162-164; God's wrath and mercy as subject-matter of, 164, 165; man's salvation as subject-matter of, 164, 165; total contents of serve aim of spiritual life, 165

Seminal Reasons/*Seminales Rationes*, 87

Sin: contrary to natural or right reason, 76; pride as cause and essence of, 76; despoiled of grace on account of, 93-94; as outrage against divine justice and sanctity, 134, 136; divine justice demands that satisfaction be made for, 134, 136, 174; result of weak and wrongly directed will, 281; seriousness of attested to by Scriptures, 173-174

Sin, Mortal, 75, 93-94; self-examination into to generate compunction and contrition, 173; sinner insensible to, 173; Devotionalists' failure to distinguish it from venial sin, 175, cf. 173-174

Sin, Original, 75, 86-88; definition of, 86-87; a consequence of Adam's fall, 87, 132; transmission of, 87-88; guilt attached to removed through Christ's death, 88, 134-135, 136, 138, 170; guilt attached to removed through baptism, 88; remains as punishment at all times, 88; cause of personal sins, 91-94; 172; powers of soul deformed as result of, 172; Hyma's and Davis' interpretations of Devotionalists' view of, 88-91

Sin, Venial, 75, 93-94; Devotionalists fail to distinguish between it and mortal sin, 175

Sins, Capital: development of doctrine of, 257-258; Zerbolt's definition and description of, 258-263, 272-273, 302-308; source of Zerbolt's doctrine of, 302-308; how to eradicate, 258-263, 302-308; imitation of Christ not important in eradication of, 262-263; tendency to spiritualize eradication of, 263-264; eradication of as third ascent in *De Ascensionibus*, 265, 272-273; virtues opposite of, 302-208

Soteriology, 50, 96, 128-158; subjective type, 128, 130, 131, 139, 143, 154-157; objective type, 128, 131-139

Soul, Powers of: for appetitive powers see Appetites; for cognitive powers see Cognitive Powers; deformation of as a cause of personal sins, 172; reformation of as either successive or collateral developments, 243, cf. 264-265; self-examination a requirement for reformation of, 244-245; goal of reformation of is purity and charity, 241-242

De Spiritu et Anima, 21, 25, 57, 264

Spiritual Life: and anthropology, 56-57; goal of defined and described, 56, 86, 88, 97, 111, 139, 140-141, 147-148, 231-232, 241-242, 272, 285, 294; goal of consistent with monastic tradition, 281-282; divided into ascetical (active) and mystical (contemplative) phases, 234; emphasis on ascetical phase of at expense of mystical phase of, 231-233, 286, 294-295, 299, cf. 281; tendency to internalize, 263-264, 282-283; man's ability to contribute to objective of, 284, 288, 289; need of grace in, 167; goal of not attainable in this life, 171, 279-281

Spiritual Reading, see Lectio

Spiritualization: of ascetical life, 263-264, 282-283, 285-286, 296-297

De statu naturalis: man's condition before Fall as, 74-75

Studium spirituale: consists of lectio and meditatio, 278 (see Lectio and Meditatio)

Suppositum: the Logos as ... of both the divine and human natures, 103-104

Synderesis, 62, 64, 69, 83-84; and natural law, 63-64; sin contrary to, 76; will acting contrary to after Fall, 78; effect of Fall on, 83-84, 174 (also see Reason, Natural)

T

Theology, Ascetical: receives more attention than mystical theology, 232; Zerbolt's emphasis on imitates Grote's, 232; Zerbolt's emphasis on shapes Modern Devotion as an ascetical movement, 232, 237; also see Ascetical Life

Theology, Mystical: receives less attention than ascetical theology, 231-232; also see Contemplation

Theology, Natural, 39, 44, 50-51, 55, 167

Theology, Spiritual: subject matter of, 232; divides into ascetical and mystical theology, 232; aim of in general, 231-232, in De Reformatione, 241-242, and in De Ascensionibus, 272; Zerbolt's based on dogmatic theology, 284, 285

Thomistic/Thomism, 26, 44, 49, 63, 67, 68, 90, 177, 182, 199, 284, 287, 293

Toleration, Religious: and Brethren of the Common Life, 8-9

Transubstantiation, 210

Trinity, 98-101; man created in image and likeness of, 73-74; revealed at Jesus' baptism, 98; oneness of essence, 98-100; indivisible, 98-99, 100; continued distinction of persons of, 99; possesses one will and operation, 100; source of all good an holiness, 109; as essence of all beauty, 112

U

Universals, 41-44

V

Vernacular Languages: advocacy of their use for religious literature, 3, 4-5, 8-9, 55

Via antiqua: its position on natural law in relation to Scriptures, 162; its influence on Zerbolt, 286

Via moderna: 55, 94; its position on natural law and Scriptures, 162; rejects faith as an infused habit, 166; holds that contrition can be achieved ex puris naturalibus, 204; its influence on Zerbolt, 286; influence of on Devotionalists, 291-292

Vices: eradicated through imitation of Christ, 140; elimination of as most important aspect of spiritual life, 234; more emphasis on elimination of than on cultivation of virtues, 265, 273; elimination of main concern in Zerbolt's spiritual theology, 281

Vires Apprehensivae, 59-60

Virtues: definition of, 110; Christ sum and example of all, 109-110; acquired through imitation of Christ, 140; less emphasis on acquisition of than on eradication of vices, 265, 273

Virtues, Cardinal, 302-308; how they are cultivated, 302-308

Vis aestimativa, 61-62

Vision of God: as aim of spiritual life, 139, 140, 141; Christ as way to, 139-144; a gratuitous gift, 141

W

Will: defined as Intellective or Rational Appetite, 65, 66; Augustinian understanding of, 67-68, 74; God as object of, 66, 84; informed by reason, 69; freedom of before Fall, 76; impact of Fall on, 78, 82, 84-85, 279, cf. 88-91; freedom of after Fall, 78, 84, 85, 95, cf. 88-91; remains positive element in man after Fall, 84-85, 272, 284; spiritual ascent as an act of, 167; must be informed by grace, 167; charity as submission of to divine will, 238

Will, Reformations of, 242, 243; repentance constitutes first reformation, 172; first reformation achieved through sacrament of penance, 242; first reformation as basis for spiritual life, 242; second reformation an eradication of capital sins, 256-264; second reformation as struggle against rebellious concupiscence, 172, 242, 281; second reformation results in new nature, 237-238; central to Zerbolt's thought, 281

Work, Manual, 274-275; indispensable to spiritual ascent, 274-275; copying books most desirable type of, 275

Works, Good, 195-198; not altogether good, 195-196, 292; lacking in merit, 195-196; man incapable of, 195; good in man and his works result of grace, 196, 204, 292; insufficiency of, 292